Série Humanitas Supplementum
Estudos Monográficos

Pólis/Cosmópolis
Identidades Globais & Locais

Carmen Soares, Maria do Céu Fialho &
Thomas Figueira (coords.)
Universidade de Coimbra e Rutgers, The State University of New Jersey

IMPRENSA DA UNIVERSIDADE DE COIMBRA
COIMBRA UNIVERSITY PRESS

ANNABLUME

Série Humanitas Supplementum
Estudos Monográficos

Título Title
Pólis/Cosmópolis: Identidades Globais & Locais
Polis/Cosmopolis: Global & Local Identities

Coords. Eds.
Carmen Soares, Maria do Céu Fialho & Thomas Figueira

Editores Publishers
Imprensa da Universidade de Coimbra
Coimbra University Press

www.uc.pt/imprensa_uc

Contacto Contact
imprensa@uc.pt

Vendas online Online Sales
http://livrariadaimprensa.uc.pt

Coordenação Editorial Editorial Coordination
Imprensa da Universidade de Coimbra

Conceção Gráfica Graphics
Rodolfo Lopes, Nelson Ferreira

Infografia Infographics
Nelson Ferreira

Impressão e Acabamento Printed by
CreateSpace

ISSN
2182-8814

ISBN
978-989-26-1279-9

ISBN Digital
978-989-26-1280-5

DOI
https://doi.org/10.14195/978-989-26-1280-5

Depósito Legal Legal Deposit
427341/17

Annablume Editora * Comunicação

www.annablume.com.br

Contato Contact
@annablume.com.br

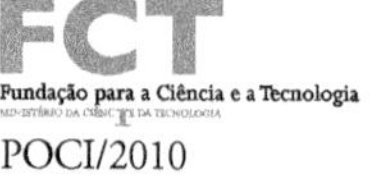 

POCI/2010

Projeto UID/ELT/00196/2013 -
Centro de Estudos Clássicos e Humanísticos da Universidade
de Coimbra

© Dezembro 2016
Annablume Editora * São Paulo
Imprensa da Universidade de Coimbra
Classica Digitalia Vniversitatis Conimbrigensis
http://classicadigitalia.uc.pt
Centro de Estudos Clássicos e Humanísticos
da Universidade de Coimbra

A ortografia dos textos é da inteira responsabilidade dos autores.

Pólis/Cosmópolis: Identidades Globais & Locais

Polis/Cosmopolis: Global & Local Identities

Coords. Eds.
Carmen Soares, Maria do Céu Fialho & Thomas Figueira

Filiação Affiliation
Universidade de Coimbra e Rutgers, The State University of New Jersey

Resumo – O livro *Polis/Cosmópolis* publica os resultados da investigação, feita a partir de perspectivas diversas, do modo como coexistiam, em tensão ou harmonia, no Mundo Greco-romano, na Idade Média e no Renascimento, identidades regionais e globais, minorias e maiorias, como se formaram e transformaram, desde o sistema da *pólis*, do fenómeno da colonização, das ligas hegemónicas, da imagiologia de uma Atenas ideal à de uma Atenas instável e de valores perdidos, retratada através das suas figuras públicas, do olhar sobre o Outro e sobre a variedade de regimes políticos do Outro, aos Reinos Helenísticos, enfatizando Alexandria. Segue-se o percurso que leva de Roma a uma *Romanitas* linguística e da Europa ao Novo Mundo. Mantiveram-se, no entanto, coexistentes, por muito tempo, as línguas locais e a língua do Império, como afirmação de identidade regional e de pertença global. Foi o caso dos Reinos Alexandrinos, mas também, como se verá, o caso da Hispânia.

Este percurso leva a que se atente ao modo como padrões estéticos evoluíram, de uma sociedade oral para uma sociedade do livro e da leitura, tendo como suporte o mito, na sua inesgotável variedade, que vai da Índia Antiga e do seu interagir com o universo greco-romano ao Mundo Novo, através da recepção dos Clássicos, estudada e exemplificada no contexto da Lusofonia, através de uma reflexão, feita a partir desse Novo Mundo, sobre o papel dos Clássicos na educação em espaços diversos.

Palavras-chave
Polis, Cosmopolis, Identidades Regionais, Identidades Globais, Minorias, Maiorias, Mundo Greco-romano, Idade Média, Renascimento.

Abstract
Polis/Cosmopolis publishes the results of research, arising from diverse perspectives, into the coexistence, in tension or in harmony, of regional and global identities, minorities, and majorities in the Graeco-Roman world, in the Middle Ages, and in the Renaissance. This work will explore the ways in which these cultural modalities were shaped, and transformed themselves, involving the *polis* system, the phenomenon of colonization, the hegemonic leagues, and Athens, both ideally imagined and historically beset with instability and lost values (as attested by its leading men). Our investigations also envision the Other, and consider the variety of political dispensations for the Other down to the Hellenistic kingdoms with, naturally, Alexandria first and foremost. There then follows the evolution that leads from Rome to a linguistic *Romanitas* and from Europe to the New World. Indeed, for a long time, local languages and the language of imperium coexisted as affirmations of regional identity and global integration, as was the case in the Hellenistic East as well as, in fact, in Hispania.

Keywords
Polis, Cosmopolis, Regional Identities, Global Identities, Minorities, Majorities, Graeco-Roman World, Middle Ages, Renaissance.

Coordenadores

Carmen Soares é Professora Associada da Faculdade de Letras da Universidade de Coimbra e membro do Centro de Estudos Clássicos e Humanísticos da mesma universidade. Os seus estudos e traduções desenvolvem-se na área científica de Estudos Clássicos, focando-se nos seguintes domínios específicos: historiografia (Heródoto), filosofia (Platão), tragédia (Eurípides), família, dieta e alimentação. Na qualidade de tradutora e comentadora de textos clássicos é co-autora dos livros V e VIII das *Histórias* e autora do *Ciclope* de Eurípides, do *Político* de Platão e de *Sobre o afecto aos Filhos* de Plutarco.
CV completo: www.degois.pt/visualizador/curriculum.jsp?key=7724126685525965

Maria do Céu Grácio Zambujo Fialho é Professora Catedrática da Faculdade de Letras da Universidade de Coimbra desde 1998 e coordenadora da Área de Estudos Gregos do Centro de Estudos Clássicos e Humanísticos da mesma universidade. Foi Coordenadora Científica do mesmo Centro entre 2000 e 2014. Actividades de ensino, interesses e publicações: Línguas e Literaturas Clássicas, Teatro Grego e Recepção, Poética e Ética (Platão e Aristóteles), Plutarco, épica alexandrina, novela grega. É autora de vários livros e artigos e tradutora para português de *Traquínias, Rei Édipo, Electra, Édipo em Colono*, de Sófocles, e também de Plutarco (*Vidas de Teseu* e de *Alcibíades*).

Thomas Figueira é "Distinguished Professor" de Estudos Clássicos e História Antiga na Universidade Rutgers, Universidade do Estado de New Jersey, onde leciona nos departamentos de Estudos Clássicos e História (tendo pontualmente ensinado no Departmento de Estudos sobre as Mulheres e de Género, bem como em "Honors Program" da Faculdade de Letras e Ciências). Deu aulas de História da Antiguidade Clássica, de Línguas e Literaturas Clássicas e de Humanidades Clássicas em tradução, a todos os níveis de ensino superior. Entre as suas mais de 120 publicações, destacam-se *Aegina: Economy and Society* (1981); *Athens and Aigina in the Age of Imperial Colonization* (1991); *Excursions in Epichoric History* (1993); *The Power of Money: Coinage and Politics in the Athenian Empire* (1998); refiram-se igualmente as seguintes obras publicadas em co-autoria (com T.C. Brennan & R.H. Sternberg) *Wisdom from the Ancients: Enduring Business Lessons from Alexander the Great, Julius Caesar, and The Illustrious Leaders of Ancient Greece and Rome* (2001), em co-edição (com G. Nagy) *Theognis of Megara: Poetry and the Polis* (1985) e como coordenador *Spartan Society* (2004).
CV completo: http://classics.rutgers.edu/docman list all/people docman category/7 figueira cv/file

Editors

Carmen Soares is Associate Professor of the University of Coimbra (Faculty of Letters) and member of the Centre of Classics and Humanistic Studies of the same university. Teaching activities, research interests and publications: Classics, Ancient Greek History and Food History. Author of several books and papers and translator into Portuguese of Herodotus' *Histories* (books V and VIII), Euripides (*Cyclops*), Plato (*Statesman*) and Plutarch (*On Affection for Offspring*).
Complete CV: www.degois.pt/visualizador/curriculum.jsp?key=7724126685525965

Maria do Céu Grácio Zambujo Fialho is Full Professor of Classics at the University of Coimbra since 1998 and coordinator of the Area Greek Studies of the Centre of Classics and Humanistic Studies of the same university. She was Scientific Coordinator of the same Center between 2000 and 2014. Teaching activities, research interests and publications: Classics, Greek Theatre and its Reception, Poetics and Ethics (Plato and Aristotle), Plutarch, Alexandrian Epic and Greek novel. Author of several books and papers and translator into Portuguese of Sophocles' *Trachiniae, Oedipus the King, Electra, Oedipus at Colonus,* and also of Plutarch (*Theseus'* and *Alcibiades' Lives*).

Thomas Figueira is "Distinguished Professor" of Classics and of Ancient History at Rutgers, The State University of New Jersey, where he teaches in the departments of Classics and History (with occasional teaching in the Department of Women and Gender Studies and the Honors program of the Faculty of Arts and Sciences). He has offered instruction in classical history, the Greek and Latin languages and literatures, and classical humanities in translation at all levels up to and including graduate studies. Among his over one hundred-twenty publications, he is the author of *Aegina: Economy and Society* (1981); *Athens and Aigina in the Age of Imperial Colonization* (1991); *Excursions in Epichoric History* (1993); *The Power of Money: Coinage and Politics in the Athenian Empire* (1998); (with T.C. Brennan & R.H. Sternberg) *Wisdom from the Ancients: Enduring Business Lessons from Alexander the Great, Julius Caesar, and The Illustrious Leaders of Ancient Greece and Rome* (2001), and has edited or co-edited (with G. Nagy) *Theognis of Megara: Poetry and the Polis* (1985) and *Spartan Society* (2004).
Complete CV: http://classics.rutgers.edu/docman-list-all/people-docman-category/7-figueira-cv/file

SUMÁRIO

Prefácio

É objectivo deste livro – *Pólis/Cosmópolis* – publicar os resultados da investigação, feita a partir de perspectivas diversas, do modo como coexistiam, em tensão ou harmonia, no Mundo Greco-romano, na Idade Média e no Renascimento, identidades regionais e globais, minorias e maiorias, como se formaram e transformaram, desde o sistema da *pólis*, do fenómeno da colonização, das ligas hegemónicas, da imagiologia de uma Atenas ideal à de uma Atenas instável e de valores perdidos, retratada através das suas figuras públicas, do olhar sobre o Outro e sobre a variedade de regimes políticos do Outro, aos Reinos Helenísticos, enfatizando Alexandria. Segue-se o percurso que leva de Roma a uma *Romanitas* linguística e da Europa ao Novo Mundo. Mantiveram-se, no entanto, coexistentes, por muito tempo, as línguas locais e a língua do Império, como afirmação de identidade regional e de pertença global. Foi o caso dos Reinos Alexandrinos, mas também, como se verá, o caso da Hispânia.

Este percurso leva a que se atente ao modo como padrões estéticos evoluíram, de uma sociedade oral para uma sociedade do livro e da leitura, tendo como suporte o mito, na sua inesgotável variedade, que vai da Índia Antiga e do seu interagir com o universo greco-romano ao Mundo Novo, através da recepção dos Clássicos, estudada e exemplificada no contexto da Lusofonia, através de uma reflexão, feita a partir desse Novo Mundo, sobre o papel dos Clássicos na educação em espaços diversos.

Todas estas transformações implicam incentivos de mobilidade e encontro em grandes espaços multiculturais, de intercâmbio de bens, de notícias, de novas produções culturais. O admirável sistema viário construído por Roma foi uma das infra-estruturas que permitiram tal mobilidade. Os mercados incentivaram-na. O culto imperial atesta essa síntese multicultural, decorrente da interacção religiosa com o Oriente, assim como a expansão e enraizamento do Cristianismo no Império levará, na dinastia constantiniana, ao conflito de religiões em tempo de paz. E este conflito inspirará Agostinho de Hipona a conceber, com marcas do pensamento platónico trabalhado pelo Proto-neoplatonismo, uma cidade global, universal, num universo ideal, no plano celeste, que é a Cidade de Deus, matriz inspiradora das futuras utopias do Renascimento.

Já no contexto do Cristianismo medieval, as ordens religiosas – toma-se como caso em estudo a dos monges de Cister – constituem um fulcro de convergência multicultural, pelos mercados à volta dos conventos, mas também pelo intercâmbio de conhecimentos do modo de trabalhar a terra e do cultivo de produtos tradicionais e novos, para além da preservação do *corpus* cultural transmitido das culturas antigas.

Com o advento das universidades, a mobilidade entre ordens, depois entre centros universitários, já em tempo de transição para o Renascimento, contribui para um diálogo cultural entre os homens de letras, para uma relação entre os pólos de cultura, que, ao mesmo tempo que se projetam com o enriquecimento cultural dos seus membros, afirmam o seu perfil específico de competências e a sua fama. Uma nova época se anuncia.

Viajar e descrever constituem uma actividade recorrente, desde a Antiguidade, impulsionada pelo incontido interesse em conhecer o Outro e confrontá-lo com a cultura própria, para perceber ambos, ou percorrer o espaço de pertença, descrito e detalhado, para memória dos vindouros. Entre o global e o local se situa este interesse dos viajantes e o atestam civilizações diversas.

No contexto do Renascimento, tais mobilidades criaram, por vezes, complexas teias relacionais com o poder, no contexto das universidades, das competências e do ideário dos Humanistas.

Finalmente, o estudo iconográfico transporta-nos para a modernidade, com a permanência de 'sinais', na própria publicidade, e recurso do marketing globalizado ao imaginário do Mundo Greco-romano.

Este estudo conjunto, constituído por vinte e três contributos de especialistas de áreas diversas e de centros de cultura diversos, atesta a actualidade e necessidade da convergência *cosmopolitana* de saberes, à volta de um projecto desenvolvido na Universidade de Coimbra. Possa ele inspirar e servir de base para alimentar um diálogo crítico e produtivo, para a cidadania contemporânea, com a modernidade.

Carmen Soares
Maria do Céu Fialho
Thomas Figueira

Foreword

It is the aim of this book – *Polis/Cosmopolis* - to publish the results of research, arising from diverse perspectives, into the coexistence, in tension or in harmony, of regional and global identities, minorities, and majorities in the Graeco-Roman world, in the Middle Ages, and in the Renaissance. This work will explore the ways in which these cultural modalities were shaped, and transformed themselves, involving the *polis* system, the phenomenon of colonisation, the hegemonic leagues, and Athens, both ideally imagined and historically beset with instability and lost values (as attested by its leading men). Our investigations also envision the Other, and consider the variety of political dispensations for the Other down to the Hellenistic kingdoms with, naturally, Alexandria first and foremost. There then follows the evolution that leads from Rome to a linguistic *Romanitas* and from Europe to the New World. Indeed, for a long time, local languages and the language of *imperium* coexisted as affirmations of regional identity and global integration, as was the case in the Hellenistic East as well as, in fact, in Hispania.

We shall also examine how aesthetic patterns evolved from an oral culture to one of the book and reading, a process drawing on ancient myth in its inexhaustible variety, which also reveals tokens of its interaction with other sources, as disparate as Ancient India and the intersection of Classical myth with the New World. Such reception may be studied and exemplified in the Lusophone context, which manifests the pedagogic potential of Classics for education in diverse settings.

All these transformations imply the existence both of incentives for cultural mobility – played out in great multicultural spaces – and of the interchange of goods, of news, and of new cultural productions. The admirable road system built by Rome was one of the infrastructures that enabled this mobility, and it was promoted by markets. The imperial cult attests this multicultural synthesis, which emerged through religious interaction with the East as well from the expansion and rooting of Christianity in the Empire that led, in the dynasty of Constantine, to religious conflict during a peaceful era. This conflict inspired Augustine of Hippo to conceive a global, universal city, with the marks of Platonic thought tinged by Proto-Neoplatonism, in an ideal world in a celestial realm, that is, a City of God, a "matrix" inspiring the later utopias of the Renaissance.

Already in the context of medieval Christianity, the religious orders constituted a fulcrum of multicultural convergence for markets around the monasteries - the Cistercian monks may be taken as a case study. The monasteries also promoted the exchange of knowledge regarding skills for working the land and cultivation of products, both traditional and new, in addition to preserving the cultural *corpus* transmitted from ancient cultures.

With the advent of universities, the mobility between religious orders and thence between centers of university teaching, especially during the transition to the Renaissance, contributed to the cultural dialogue among men of letters and to such a growth of connections between the nodes of cultural life that, at the same time as they manifested a cultural enrichment for their participants, they established a particular profile of intellectual competencies and earned their fame. A new epoch had announced itself.

Hence, traveling and reporting have been regular activities since Classical Antiquity, driven by an irrepressible impulse to know the Other and to confront him in his own culture, as a means to understand both traditions, or to move amid the spaces of identity, however described and detailed, in service of memory for future generations. Between the global and the local stand the preoccupations of the travelers, as various civilizations attest. In the context of the Renaissance, the mobilities interesting us create complex webs of power relations with the universities regarding their skills and Humanistic ideals. Finally, iconographic research can take us to modernity, with the persistence of the 'signs' of the Greek and Roman conceptual universe, where advertising, for example, has recourse to the ancient world as a globalized marketing resource.

The present collaboration, with twenty-three contributions from experts in various fields and from institutions in diverse cultures, speaks to the timeliness of and necessity for a cosmopolitan convergence of scholarly specialties, deriving from a project developed at the University of Coimbra. It is our hope that this research may inspire and serve as a basis to sustain a critical and productive dialogue about modernity for contemporary civic life.

Carmen Soares
Maria do Céu Fialho
Thomas Figueira

Defense and deterrence in the context of the foundation of the Delian League

Thomas J. Figueira (figueira@rci.rutgers.edu)
Rutgers University (New Brunswick, New Jersey)

ABSTRACT – This contribution examines the plans of the Athenians and their allies at the foundation of the Delian League in 478 by exploring conjectural force structures. Likely Persian forces of c. 600 triremes could be anticipated. Persia had also demonstrated noteworthy capacity to mount closely successive expeditions and to recover from losses. Therefore, the Delian League was severely challenged to match ship for ship and to find the requisite manpower. Various methodologies yield both total and practicable allied fleets of different sizes (with total hulls touching 600 at highest estimate). Financial administration and tactical deployment discouraged small ship contingents for the allies in favor both of levying monetary tribute which funded the Athenian fleet and of manning its ships with personnel from smaller maritime allies. Hypotheses on the costs of allied forces can be proposed in order to understand the high initial Aristeidian assessment of the allies. Eurymedon represents a turning point, demonstrating how early preemptive deployment and confrontation far eastward from the Aegean by the Delian League compensated for superior Persian resources.

KEYWORDS: Athens, Delian League, Eurymedon, Greek navies, Persians, tribute and assessment

The bibliography on the foundation of the Delian League is voluminous, as scholars have grappled with controversies as varied as the league's purpose, organization, classification of allies, and the nature and scale of tribute in the early alliance.[1] The primary text is Thucydides (1.96.1-97.1).[2] I intend to take a different approach through a consideration of the parameters of the military mission that was undertaken by the Greeks who united in confederation with Athens in the early 470s.[3] Let us start on the issue of force structure by considering the

---

[1] Main alternatives to the hypothesis on the tribute system offered below: 1) the assessment covered ship-contributing allies: e.g., *ATL* 3.234-7; 2) Cyprus was assessed: e.g., Meiggs 1972: 56-8; 3) the *phoros* constituted non-monetary services/payments in kind: e.g., Eddy 1968: 184-6; 4) the *aparkhai* lists do not reflect all the tribute collected: e.g., *HCT* 1.275-8; French 1972, 71-3; Unz 1985.

[2] Thuc. 1.96.1-2: [the Athenians] ἔταξαν ἅς τε ἔδει παρέχειν τῶν πόλεων χρήματα πρὸς τὸν βάρβαρον καὶ ἃς ναῦς· πρόσχημα γὰρ ἦν ἀμύνεσθαι ὧν ἔπαθον δῃοῦντας τὴν βασιλέως χώραν. καὶ Ἑλληνοταμίαι τότε πρῶτον Ἀθηναίοις κατέστη ἀρχή, οἳ ἐδέχοντο τὸν φόρον· οὕτω γὰρ ὠνομάσθη τῶν χρημάτων ἡ φορά. ἦν δ' ὁ πρῶτος φόρος ταχθεὶς τετρακόσια τάλαντα καὶ ἑξήκοντα. ταμιεῖόν τε Δῆλος ἦν αὐτοῖς, καὶ αἱ ξύνοδοι ἐς τὸ ἱερὸν ἐγίγνοντο.

[3] I am drawing on a research project on the finances of 5th-century Athens, following up on Figueira 1998. See also Figueira 2003; 2005; 2006; forthcoming[b]; forthcoming[c].

adversary forces that Athens and its allies reasonably expected to face. Table I outlines the evidence for Persian expeditionary forces against the Greeks during our period. Traditionally, analysis of these mobilizations has focused on whether the data, much of which was transmitted through Herodotus and Ephorus, are correct. Going back to the 19th century, a lineage of formidable scholars has expressed substantial doubts over the factuality of such mobilizations, with particular suspicion falling on details of Xerxes' expedition in 480.[4] Considerable ingenuity has been applied, for instance, in calculating whether hydrologic resources along his line of march would have provided sufficient fresh water for his vast host.[5] Secondarily, some doubts have also attached to the received figures for the invasion force of Datis that was eventually checked by Athens at the Battle of Marathon in 490.[6]

In thinking about the scale of the Persian threat in Greek eyes, however, our concern is not primarily the truth of such reports. Whether accurate or not, the received estimates shaped planning at the foundation of the Delian League regarding contingencies in defending Aegean Greece from Persian aggression.[7] This point is especially probative, since there is no evidence that popular and expert opinion diverged significantly in this matter. Herodotus and Aeschylus reflect popular opinion, but both also had access to elite informants aware about military planning at higher levels of decision-making. In any event, Thucydides, who had held the office of *stratēgos*, was manifestly conversant with privileged military thinking at Athens. Yet he makes no effort to correct Herodotus about the scale of Xerxes' forces, and, in fact, has an Athenian speaker at Sparta (1.73.4-74.2), just before the outbreak of the Peloponnesian War, provide an estimate of the Attic contribution at Salamis that seems even higher than Herodotus (1.74.1). Moreover, critiquing any individual figure in our evidence, albeit seemingly inadequate, is less important than allowing the general magnitudes of these forces to impart a quantitative sense of the Greek intentions when forming the Delian League.

It is worth noting at the start that deployed forces, whether Greek or non-Greek, were always less than the "administrative" forces conceived in the minds of leaders (which have sometimes perhaps been transmitted in later historiography). This is particularly valid for Herodotus' likely use of renditions of Persian documents.[8] Furthermore, intelligence and surveillance directed toward

---

[4] E.g., Macan 1908: 150-67; Wells 1923: 145-50; Munro 1926: 271-3, Hignett 1963: 350-5; Young 1981: 221-3; Lazenby 1993: 90-2; Cawkwell 2005: 237-54; Flower 2007.

[5] Maurice 1930: esp. 221-4.

[6] E.g., Hignett 1963: 58-9.

[7] Cawkwell 2005 offers a recent overview of this struggle, with pp. 126-38 dealing with our period.

[8] See Briant 2002: 197-200; Cawkwell 2005: 239-43.

an enemy's preparations could only be rather primitive in a classical military environment. Direct observers of varying expertise, care, and objectivity provided input about forces at the actual time of deployment. In that context, over-counting and duplication would probably have been more prevalent than underestimation. It may well be that by the 450s or 440s the Athenians had achieved a more realistic appraisal of the likely enemy forces. If that is so, it appears that their understanding was reflected in actual military dispositions and not used to "correct" the historical record of the earlier 5th century. Thus, the traditions on 480 and earlier Persian campaigns help to illuminate thinking during the first period of the alliance. Nonetheless, I should emphasize that 5th-century military planning was never so much a matter of how many, but rather how many at which place, and at which time.

Even if one discounts Xerxes' great expedition as a special effort, impossible to duplicate, the Persians often deployed considerable naval assets.[9] An armada of 600 triremes seems to emerge as a realistic fleet for regular periodic deployment, although realizable force in battle may have fallen closer to 300 at mid-century. That total appears three times before the foundation of the Delian League. Indeed, Herodotus claims that Dareios' force of 600 ships against Thrace was enumerated on *stelae* erected at Byzantion that contained rosters in both Aramaic and Greek which were later available for inspection (4.87.2). In principle, then, this muster of forces could be verified. Subsequently, a complement of 600 ships was also a total associated by the Attic local historian Phanodemos with Persian strength at the battle of Eurymedon in the early 460s (*FGH* 325 F22). While it is doubtful that 600 Persian warships faced allied forces together there, 600 ships might signify a mobilization toward which the Persians were building. The aggregation of their forces then was clearly preempted by the intervention of the Delian League fleet.

We can alternatively approach the Athenian and allied appraisal of the opposing military strength by examining the possible constituents of a Persian fleet to be mobilized against Greece after 478. According to Herodotus, Xerxes had mustered 600 Phoenician, Egyptian, and Cilician ships (7.89.1-90). Another 300 ships were supposedly gathered from Cyprus, Pamphylia, Caria, and Lycia (7.90-93). In 478, the Athenians and their Ionian allies might suppose that a forceful, preemptive showing in resistance to a future invasion might cut deeply into this mobilization in Asia Minor and Cyprus. A forward strategy might exclude the launching of such ships. Local rivalries there could probably drain off men and resources too. The Cypriot Greeks could be expected to show a lack of enthusiasm for Persia if only in the interest of their own autonomy. Their

---

[9] The recent treatment of Cawkwell 2005: 254-73 explores underlying facts, not Greek perceptions.

resistance could tie down Phoenician Cypriots, otherwise prepared to support the Great King. In these eventualities, a Greek planner in 478 might be prepared to discount the contingents from Cyprus and southern Anatolia by 50%. Yet, even so, 150 ships might be a reasonable estimate for those available. That reduced levy would still add up to 750 vessels when combined with Phoenicians, Egyptians, and Cilicians. My point is not that this is perforce a realistic prediction for a modern scholar envisioning a expedition against Greece in the 470s or 460s. Rather, I emphasize that such a prediction was not an over-estimate of the enemy in terms of the data apparently available to an observer in 478. Therefore, when we imagine Greek planners in 478 formulating contingencies in terms of a Persian force of 600 triremes, their estimate of their adversary may already reflect a 20% offset from the 750 ships that their recent experience implied as a possible opposing force.

In our investigation of how the founders of the Delian League measured a potential enemy force, two more aspects of past Persian mobilizations are significant: 1) the ability of the Persians to recover from military adversity; and 2) the effect on Persian strength of distance linked with time. The pattern of military activity presented on Table I attributes to the Persians remarkable recuperative abilities. Evidently they were well able to withstand the incidental losses that modern scholars tend to ignore, that is, ongoing, but by no means negligible, losses of ships that occur during warfare through meteorological circumstances, accidents, mishandling, and low grade combat.[10] Beyond weathering such losses, the Persians were also able to remediate the effects of major combat, such as the defeat at Cyprus or the battle of Lade, and natural catastrophes like the great storm at Mt. Athos in 492. As shall be noted shortly, Greek *poleis* did not possess such recuperative powers.[11] Thus, the balance of power offered risks to the Greeks on two levels of attrition. It seems from Herodotus' account of the Artemision campaign that they were vulnerable to a contest with the Persians of attritional rates in which Greek ability to inflict higher losses did not offset superior Persian numbers (cf. 8.16.3, 18). Nevertheless, there was a second Greek vulnerability in attrition because Persia could mount large expeditions into the Aegean at short intervals. As proof, note that Herodotus reports Dareios preparing to attack Greece with a huge force in the fourth year after Marathon, only preempted by a revolt in Egypt (7.1.1-3). Men and ships amassed against Greece were probably used by Xerxes to pacify Egypt (a revolt in Babylonia appears less consequential). Moreover, although two years later c. 300 ships were lost at Mt. Athos (Hdt. 6.44.3), Datis supposedly sailed against the Cyclades and

---

[10] Isoc. 8.87 refers to ongoing incidental Attic losses in amounts of five or ten.

[11] Kimon's striking force at Eurymedon primarily comprised triremes built by Themistokles (Plut. *Cimon* 12.2), and hence of long service life.

mainland with 600 ships that had entered the Aegean as a single armada (Hdt. 6.95.1-2). Thus he embarked without drawing on levies from the east Greeks. Similarly, the Persians sent a fleet of 600 vessels against Ionia, the force that would prevail at Lade in 494, only a few years after the Ionian rebels had won a major victory at sea in the waters off Cyprus (Hdt. 5.112.1).

Naval warfare from the mid-19th century onward has been characterized by the application of mechanical energy, which allows a projection of power over long distances. Previously, expeditionary warfare worked under the serious limitation that a campaigner striking over distance could not easily be resupplied or reinforced. Naturally, this factor constrained Xerxes in 480; for one thing, once his fleet withdrew from homeland Greece after Salamis, he was compelled to withdraw a large portion of his land forces. However, the geography of the eastern Mediterranean disadvantaged Greek military prospects. Because of the political fragmentation of the Greeks and their littoral disposition, Persian advances into the Aegean tended to subtract rapidly from potential friendly forces and convert some (at least) of their ships into Persian assets. In the nightmare scenario of Xerxes' invasion, Herodotus reports 347 Greek ships from the Aegean and Propontis mobilized for the Persians. At the crucial moment of Salamis, the Aiginetans were withholding some ships in home defense (Hdt. 8.46.1). Under this perspective, estimates in 478 of the potential strength of the Persians ought to have been couched in terms of not only how many enemy ships might set sail, but also where they might be met. Thus, 350 Greek ships deployed against the Persians in Cyprus, Pamphylia, or Cilicia might have the same defensive capacity as 500-600 ships operating from the Peiraieus in the Saronic Gulf and western Cyclades.

By the same token, even a relatively modest separation had a disproportionate impact on military strength if that distance was in Greek home waters while facing a strong adversary. Observe the notable difference in ships between the initial Greek fleet at Artemision and the subsequent fleet there and then later at Salamis (Table II.2-3). Yet standing at Salamis gave a bare margin of victory, as any further retreat would have dissolved the Greek confederates into individual squadrons. These could have been easily mopped up by the Persians, as both Herodotus and Thucydides note (Hdt. 7.139.1-5; Thuc. 1.73.3-4).[12] Clearly, dozens of miles of distance along the southern coast of Anatolia could never have an impact anywhere approaching this crucial difference of a few miles in homeland Greece.

Such a calculation of military power focuses our attention on the related issue of time and force deployment. Ancient sources are often read to indicate that

---

[12] Even the anti-Athenian Corinthian speaker in Thuc. 1.69.5 observed that the Spartan reaction to the invasion was tardy and conceded how nearly run a matter victory was.

great numbers of ships from multiple origins converged precisely at rendezvous and then advanced *en masse* toward their military targets. This is hardly true in our age of radio communications, as the naval battles (like that of Leyte Gulf) in the Pacific theater during World War II demonstrated. In the 5th century, the coordination of hundreds of ships must have been a daunting proposition even for a steeply hierarchal, authoritarian state like Persia. Major battles took place toward the ends of campaigning seasons for the reason that it took spring and early summer to get forces into place. Deploying a hundred ships entailed the management of, at least, 20,000 men. Our source material on the Eurymedon campaign indicates how aggregation of squadrons in antiquity proceeded. A Persian fleet and land army had advanced to the Eurymedon River in Pamphylia (Table I.8). That both land and sea forces were together there suggests that the army did not intend to march toward Sardis in Lydia or toward the Helles-pont, since such a force might then have diverged northward in Cilicia. The likely Persian target was Caria and Doris in southwestern Asia Minor, perhaps especially Kaunos, Rhodes, and Knidos. They intended to seize a base from which to operate in east Greece, possibly the next year after wintering over.[13] The Persian commanders at Eurymedon were indeed awaiting concentration of other contingents with their main force. After Kimon's great victory on sea and land, he was able to surprise 80 Phoenician ships arriving as reinforcements at Cyprus (Plut. *Cimon* 12.4; 13.3). Moreover, no Egyptian ships are cited as present at Eurymedon, so that a squadron was likely expected from that satrapy as well. The account in Ctesias of the later Egyptian revolt of 459 seems to describe an initial Persian reaction by a sizable army, one unbelievably large, as so often in Ctesias, (*FGH* 688 F14[36]). Yet its accompanying naval contingent was 80 ships, which might actually have been a standing Persian naval force in Egypt. At that juncture, 50 of these were incapacitated, with 20 captured with crews and 30 destroyed.

In the Eurymedon campaign, the Persian rendezvous in Pamphylia may not yet have been the initial rallying point for this expedition. Xerxes' great armada had massed further east in Cilicia. Wallinga has offered an elaborate hypothesis in which Cilicia plays a special role in Persian naval affairs,[14] pointing to an oth-erwise disproportionately moderate Cilician tribute. He ought not to be followed in imagining that a Cilician base served as arsenal and storage for hundreds of triremes. Nevertheless, the existence in Cilicia of supply depots for fleets intended to project Persian power toward Greece may not be inconceivable.

For the Greeks, we perceive similar difficulties in concentrating naval squadrons. A Corcyrean flotilla of 60 ships was supposedly delayed by adverse

---

[13] [Plato] *Menex.* 241D describes Artaxerxes' intent as the conquest of Greece.
[14] Wallinga 2005: 13-15.

winds from rounding Cape Malea in time to participate at Salamis (Hdt. 7.168.1-4). A certain reluctance to commit wholeheartedly to the cause of the Hellenic League was suspected as their motivation. Nonetheless, a genuine delay through factors beyond their control must have been sufficiently plausible that it was worth the Corcyrean effort in excusing themselves. Consequently, just as we have seen that a contingent of ships further east was more valuable militarily to the Delian League than a similarly sized contingent to its west, a body of warships early in the campaigning season was worth more than the same force later in the year. The coordination of large confederate forces that we perceive the Athenians making at Eurymedon and onward reveals their mastering of this relevant skill set.

To recapitulate, we have learned that Greek planners in the early 470s expected to face at least 600 Persian triremes. On the basis of previous Persian achievements, the build-up of this force might be thought to require c. 2-5 years. The dispatch of such a force into the Aegean basin ought not then have taken as long as a decade. The actual battle at Eurymedon probably occurred not earlier than 469 nor later than 466. From the vantage point of a planner in 478, a hypothetical Persian attack on the scale of Eurymedon should have happened years earlier. In other words, Eurymedon was late. A hint that this conclusion is not speculative emerges from the actions of the Naxians. At some point between 472 and 469, Naxos had recklessly defected from the Delian League, only to suffer a siege leading to surrender on unfavorable terms (Thuc. 1.98.4). Naxian foolhardiness in challenging Attic hegemony makes better sense if the Athenian allies were aware of Persian preparations already underway

Let us turn now to the other side of the planning equation in 478. What would a prudent strategist have considered a feasible force structure for the Delian League? Did any complement of triremes stand a reasonable chance of blunting another Persian effort at subduing Greece? Table II collects data about Greek naval potentialities during the early 5th century. Before considering this matter, however, preliminary discussion is in order about the development of early trireme navies. Our chief source is Thucydides, who takes pains both to emphasize the early introduction at Corinth and adoption at Samos of the trireme and to stress the late development of large all-trireme navies.[15] His first large trireme navies belonged to the Sicilian tyrants and Corycreans, his unspecified criterion perhaps being 100 ships. Thucydides also mentions Ionian navies built up in confrontation with Persia, singling out Polykrates of Samos. According to Thucydides, the Aiginetan and Athenian navies were late developing. We can reconstruct the history of their naval competition. Aigina had an

---

[15] Thuc. 1.13.1-4, 6; 14.2-3. See Figueira forthcoming[a].

early advantage, possessing perhaps 50 triremes as early as 520. By the early 480s, both *poleis* had c. 70 triremes, supplemented by *pentekontors*.

Themistokles' naval law broke this equilibrium, with 100 triremes in its first phase and perhaps 200 overall, using resources from the silver mines at Laurion. These ships defeated the Persians and saved Greece, as Herodotus observes forcefully (7.144.2-3). Continuation of ship building also explains the existence of more than 200 ships in Attic possession in 480. Herodotus has Athenian ships at Salamis numbering 180 (8.44.1). There were also 20 Attic ships manned by their allies from Chalcis in Euboia (8.46.2). Their total number was perhaps higher: the "Themistokles Decree" preserves a provision for 200 ships companies (*SGHI* 23.12-14), and as a step taken early in the process of mobilization that probably represents a minimum, without supplemental crews like the Chalcidians. A speaker in Thucydides speaks of an Attic contribution of a little less than two-thirds of 400 ships (1.74.1).[16] Let us estimate this force in the range of 230 to 260 triremes.[17] The evidence on Attic ship-building programs is weak, but sources imply later additions to the fleet of 10-20 triremes annually.[18] Hence, unsurprisingly figures of 200 or 250 Athenian ships appear several times after the founding of the Delian League (Table II.6-8). Even this larger number implies a notable reserve at home, since the Peiraieus and Saronic Gulf could never be left entirely unguarded.

For comparison, Athens possessed 300 seaworthy warships in 431; the qualification πλωίμους 'seaworthy' in Thucydides implies others in construction, storage, or salvageable (2.13.8; cf. Arist. *Ach.* 544-5; Xen. *Anab.* 7.1.27). A distinction between deployable ships and every hull in Athenian possession is also illustrated by two references to resources during the Peace of Nikias, or 421 to 415. Both Andocides (3.9) and Aeschines (2.175) derive material from a common historical source (Hellanicus, an Atthidographer, or a pamphleteer). This authority enumerated two types of warships, of which 400 represented all the hulls under Attic control and 300 the total vessels available for immediate service. Thucydides specifies the height of Attic naval power during the Archidamian War in 430 or 428 (3.17.1-2).[19] Athens actually had 250 triremes manned in this campaigning season, a total not taking into account 100 best-sailing triremes, kept aside each year as an "iron" reserve (Thuc. 2.24.2: for use only if an enemy fleet was sailing against Attica itself). Counting every vessel in

---

[16] The phrasing is difficult in interpretation, cf. *HCT* 1.234-5; Walters 1981; Wankel 1983.

[17] Moreover, captures from the Persians may have more than offset losses (Table I.7).

[18] DS 11.43.3; *PStrasbourg* 84 = *ATL* 1, T9, 2, D 13 = *Anon. Argentinensis* 10-11. Andoc. 3.3-5 has perhaps 100 new ships in 5 years around mid-century. See Blackman 1969: 202-12.

[19] This passage has been questioned in authenticity and placement, but, while redating to 430 is an option, its character as Thucydidean may be accepted. See Gomme *HCT* 2.372-77; Hornblower *CT* 400-1.

any condition, the upper end of the Athenian fleet before the debacle at Syracuse seems to have hovered around 350-400 triremes. Note also the number of trierarchs appointed annually was 400 ([Xen.] *Ath. Pol.* 3.4). However, there was probably a point after which it was no longer productive to add further triremes without taking older ships out of circulation. The real limits on the size of the Delian League fleet were set by manpower and logistics. Even if the alliance could have procured 600 ships in the 470s to match the Persians trireme for trireme, they probably could not have manned them.

As for the allied force which the Athenians intended to fuse with their own navy, our judgment is difficult. Herodotus' force totals for Lade are our first valuable data (Table II.1). The newly liberated Ionians and Aiolians of 478 were probably no longer able to match their earlier commitments to the Ionian revolt in the 490s. However, they still held the survivors of their fleets of 480, whose ships had been supplied by the Great King (DS 11.3.7) in the sense that he had ordered their building out of the tribute ordinarily paid by the Ionians. Chios had suffered greatly at Lade and in its aftermath (Hdt. 6.15.1-27.3). It had been ravaged by Histiaios of Miletos, who had also attacked and seized Lesbos (6.26.1-2). Miletos had provided eighty ships at Lade. Moreover, it may be thought that the fifteen ships from Priene and Myous are to be considered part of the Milesian contribution, as these two cities are otherwise attested as dependencies of Miletos.[20] Thereafter, Miletos had been besieged and sacked, with much of its population dead or deported (6.18-21). Samos had been afflicted earlier (c. 520), especially in an *andrapodismos* at Persian hands c. 510 (Hdt. 3.149; cf. 6.25). It had suffered less at Lade, where most Samian ships had quickly fled (6.14.2-3). Thus, its contribution of sixty may not have experienced the same erosion as that of the Chians, Milesians, and perhaps the Lesbians. Unsurprisingly, Xerxes had only 100 Ionian triremes with him during the Salamis campaign (Table I.7), which reflects the falling off from the 283 Ionian ships at Lade. And there must have been significant losses among these Ionians at Salamis and Mykale. Xerxes had 100 Aiolian ships, which might show less reduction than the Ionian complement because there were 70 Lesbian ships at Lade. A portion of the 100 Aiolian ships with Xerxes were from Kyme and the towns of the Troad. The latter were probably not participants in the Delian League at its inception. One supposes that the majority of Xerxes' 30 Dorian ships were from Rhodes. Rhodians had not fought at Lade.

The major insular allied states of the east Greeks recovered their economic vitality and military power in the second half of the 5th century. During the

---

[20] The Milesian dispute with Samos over Priene seems to establish an earlier Milesian hegemony there (Thuc. 1.115.2). For Myous, note its Hellenistic (re)absorption by Miletos (cf. Rhodes/Osborne *GHI* 16). See Rubenstein 2004: 1092, 1089.

prosperous years of the *pentekontaeteia*, the levels of the early 490s were probably reached or exceeded, as scattered testimonia appear to indicate.[21] The Egyptian expedition, the Samian and Lesbian revolts, and the Syracusan campaign provide our evidence. Samos is the only ally for which conjecture is possible about its naval strength in the early Delian League. Two inscriptions found at Samos celebrate the Samian contribution to the early fighting of the Egyptian campaign c. 459 (*IG* XII.6 279, 468). A notable exploit is reported in which the Samian contingent of the Greek fleet captured 15 Phoenician triremes (*IG* XII.6 279.3-4). That suggests about 25 to 30 Samian ships as a part of the 200-ship Greek expedition. The Samians could still mobilize 70 ships in the first main battle of their revolt against Athens in 440/39, after some earlier mischances (Thuc. 1.116.1).

In the same revolt, Athens summoned aid from Chios and Lesbos and was quickly supported by 25 Chian and Lesbian triremes, an impressive mobilization on short notice for a campaign against another Greek city (1.116.2). Thirty Chian and Lesbian ships are later noted (1.117.2), and these would be further reinforcements. At the time of the revolt of Mytilene in 428, the Athenians interned 10 Mytilenaean triremes on first rumors of sedition (Thuc. 3.3.4). Mytilene was surprised by the leaking of its intentions to the Athenians and had not completed their preparations for revolt, including equipping additional ships. When Athens sent a force of 40 triremes in a surprise intervention (3.3.2-3), the Mytilenaeans sought a negotiated settlement (3.4.4-5). Notably, the Athenians were not confident that their 40 ships could prevail in an engagement. That suggests that they were outnumbered by the remaining Mytilenaean warships. Chios had many available ships during the Peloponnesian War. Fifty Chian and Lesbian ships participated in the expeditions both of Perikles and of Hagnon and Kleopompos of 430 (Thuc. 2.56.2, 6.31.2). Thirty-four allied ships went to Sicily in 416 (6.43), of which the majority was Chian (6.85.2; 7.57.4-5). And another five Chian ships later sailed in the second expedition with Demosthenes (7.20.2). Yet, at the time of its revolt (412), Chios still had at least 60 triremes (8.6.4), though those sent to Sicily had never returned.

Some states in the Hellespontine region, like Byzantion, probably stood aloof from the early alliance and there were relatively few ship contributors in the area. Xerxes' 100 triremes from the Hellespont thus seem exaggerated, or the complement was perhaps owed to Persian subsidy and construction efforts (Hdt. 7.95.2). Xerxes' contingent from the Greek islands was only 17, while the Hellenic League got the help of 23 ships, as augmented by defectors and including 5 *pentekontors* (7.95.1; Table II.3). Herodotus gives us no figure for the Persian demands made upon the Thracian Greeks, but the Delian League would

---

[21] Figueira 1998: 79, 481-2.

certainly have had expectations of help there, starting with Thasos. Kimon would later take 33 of their triremes in battle during the Thasian revolt (Plut. *Cimon* 14.2). Let us suggest a 40-warship levy for Thrace and 30 ships for each of the two other regions, the Hellespont and the islands.

Thus, one might expect that the Athenians planned for a naval force of 250 to 300 of their own triremes, with 350 vessels as an outside upper limit. This is a total force and not one for practical deployment anywhere *en masse*. There are two ways to consider the total allied contribution accommodating this Attic force structure. First, for the Herodotean ship total of 378 for Salamis, the Attic contribution would be c. 53%. If the Athenians intended to imitate this success-ful fleet, an allied force of 47% can then be supposed. For Attic fleets of 250, 300, and 350, allied forces of 222, 266, and 310 are created, and total Delian League fleets of 472, 566, and 660. Second, the Athenian speaker at Sparta in Thucydides, who might perhaps be thought to have reason to exaggerate, refers to an Attic force of a little less than two-thirds. Could he be speaking under the influence of Attic practice during the Delian League, when the two-thirds Attic to a one-third allied split had become conventional?[22] Thus, his anachronism actually helps our analysis. Therefore, for Attic fleets of 250, 300, and 350, this ratio would yield 125, 150, and 175 allied ships and total fleets of 375, 450, and 525. Or, alternatively, we could add to an Athenian fleet of whatever size ap-propriate the number of allied ships that our previous discussion has proposed. Forty Thasian and other Thracian ships, 30 from the Cyclades, 30 from the Hellespont, 30 Rhodian ships, and 150 ships from the Samians, Lesbians, and Chians. That suggests a non-Athenian allied fleet in the Delian League that numbered 280 hulls or a total force of 530 to 630.

Once we begin to speculate about the nature of the Delian League fleet, we unsurprisingly generate force structures that balance the 600-ship fleets that appear in our records for the Persians. However, several points are to be stressed: 1) it was inconceivable for the Greeks to match the total maritime resources of the Persians; 2) the Delian League fleet approximated an armada fighting in the Aegean, i.e., in home waters, but that was the very setting which the allies wanted to avoid; 3) small naval contributors were to be discouraged while personal service and ship contribution were changing to tribute; and 4) manning the Delian League fleet would be challenging. Fortunately, for the Athenians and their allies, a smaller force for fighting in Pamphylia, Cyprus, or Egypt was equivalent to 600 triremes in their own environs. Thus, Kimon left Attica with 200 ships, and by the time he united with allied flotillas, he had 300; and the

---

[22] Note how DS 11.60.3 explicitly reports the ratio of 100 allied ships for 200 Attic ships at Eurymedon. The disagreement of our sources over fleet sizes of 200 ships or 300 ships for the Egyptian campaign and Kimon's final Cypriot expedition (Table II.7-8) may derive from the misunderstanding of this same 1:2 ratio.

total for the campaign might have been 350 (Table II.6). Both Athens and allies had to retain ships for home defense, the need for which was made manifest after Eurymedon by a closely ensuing Persian strike against the Chersonese (Plut. *Cimon* 14.1)

Turning next to the subject of small allies and large allies, we must remember that the Athenians would not have sought to maximize the number of available ships from lesser naval powers. It was preferable that certain maritime communities provide funds instead. In this, the Hellenic League did not provide a model, but rather an approach to be rejected. As far as known from Hellenic League operations, its members were self-policing in ship provision. The Athenians and Aiginetans seem to have completely controlled their changing contributions at Artemision and Salamis, with the final Aiginetan reinforcements an unexpected benefit for the allies.[23] Moreover, operations under the Spartan navarch, Eurybiadas, were conducted by a council of war composed of all contingent commanders. If similar patterns had prevailed for the Delian League, one could envisage a fleet constituted from many differently scaled squadrons. Some of these would be in tiny units resembling the Ionian fleet at Lade (which had contributed to defeat) or at Artemision and Salamis. Such an approach manifestly leaves much to be desired in terms of military efficiency. The Delian League fleets were commanded by Athenian *stratēgoi*. A council of war, limited to squadron commanders actually present, may have been consulted, but the Athenian generals seem to have managed tactical deployments. During Kimon's final Cypriot campaign of 451/0, his fellow *stratēgoi* were able to keep his death a secret for a month (Plut. *Cimon* 19.2; Phanodemos *FGH* 325 F23). That is indicative of a very tight command circle.

Moreover, small states in all periods are always much less efficient in generating military power since the cost for the first units of any technology, be it tanks, jet fighters, frigates, or triremes, is so high. It is known from galley warfare in different periods that oared warships are optimally packaged in units from 40 to 55.[24] Therefore, squadrons of c. 50 triremes would have to be amassed from a group of smaller *poleis*, those supplying 10 ships or less. Yet, Herodotus' account of the battle of Salamis seems to show that almost all the damage done the enemy was meted out by the large Athenian and Aiginetan forces (Hdt. 8.86, 91-93.2). The Corinthian role in the battle was controversial. As the *polis* supplying the third largest detachment, their performance was significant. While Herodotus shares an Attic report of their withdrawal without

---

[23] See Figueira forthcoming[d].

[24] Guilmartin 2002, 119; 2003, 215-17. In the early Delian League, 5 entities (Athens, Chios, Lesbos, Samos, and Thasos) would have provided over 75% of the combatant vessels. In the fleet of 250-350 at Eurymedon, for example, one small unit might have accommodated all the smaller ship-contributors.

fighting (8.94.1-4), he also reports their denial of this (8.94.4). The author of *De malignitate Herodoti* reports heroic fighting (*Mor.* 870B-871C).

This background material helps us appreciate the monumental departure marked by the organization of the Delian League. From the start Athens possessed the sole right to decide which allies would contribute ships and which would pay *phoros* (Thuc. 1.96.1). During the whole history of the alliance, the Athenians also held exclusive authority for assessing tribute. It is unknown whether this function was first exercised by the *stratēgoi* or by boards of *taktai* 'assessors'. The tradition on the first assessment focuses solely on the justice of the Attic statesman Aristeides, but he can hardly have wielded such power without colleagues.[25] Thucydides states that the main cause of revolts and dissension in the early alliance was Athenian rigor in enforcing obligations for tribute or service with ships (1.99.1-3). Plutarch's *Cimon* confirms this, although approaching from an opposite tangent: Kimon was allegedly gentle with delinquent allies by accepting contributions and empty ships in lieu of service (11.1-3).[26] Giving Athens sole control of the largest transfer of revenue in Greek politics tilted the essence of the league radically toward Athenian hegemonism at its start. It is almost superfluous to note the adage that power to tax is power to destroy.[27] By giving Athens so much power at the start, the allies showed the intensity of their fear of the Persians.

Each trireme ideally requires 200 oarsmen and other personnel, if one opts for a modest contingent of 10 *epibatai* 'marines', i.e., the infantrymen who fight from the deck. A fleet of 250 ships needs 50,000 men; 300 ships, 60,000; 350 ships, 70,000. Alternatively, if one imagines a more realistic contingent of 30 *epibatai*, split between 20 hoplites and 10 light troops, archers or peltasts, every 100 ships requires another 2,000 infantry.[28] These numbers are remarkable, considering the actual manpower of Athens in 480. They were hard-pressed to fill their ships during Xerxes' invasion, so much so that they manned 20 triremes with Chalcidians and supplemented other crews with Plataians, who were available at Artemision but late arriving for Salamis. They also probably freed all able-bodied slaves. Moreover, the Themistokles Decree relates the forming of two hundred ships' complements under trierarchs but only assigns 100 men to each unit (*SGHI*

---

[25] [Andoc.] 4.11; Dem. 23.209; Aesch. 3.258; Nepos *Arist.* 3.1-3; DS 11.47.1-3; Plut. *Arist.* 24.1-7, cf. 26.3; Paus. 8.52.2; Ael. *VH* 11.9. Cf. Thuc. 1.96.1-2; *Ath. Pol.* 23.5; Aristod. *FGH* 104 F 7. See Figueira forthcoming[b].

[26] On Kimon's naval policies: Blackman 1969: 188-9; Boffo 1975; Steinbrecher 1985: 98-115.

[27] This idea was raised by Daniel Webster, arguing before the US Supreme Court in *McCulloch* v. *Maryland* (17 U.S. 327) in 1819, and given its classic formulation by Chief Justice John Marshall in his decision in the case.

[28] This complement compromises between the minimal complement of 10 hoplites and 4 archers of the "Themistokles Decree" (*SGHI* 23.23-6) or 14 hoplites and four archers (Plut. Them. 14.1) and the Chians at Lade with 40 *epibatai* (Hdt. 6.15.1), Persians at Artemision with 30 (Hdt. 7.184.2), and Corcyreans at Sybota (Thuc. 1.49.1). Even later 5th century troop-carrying triremes could carry complements like the 45 hoplites, 10 archers, and 10 peltasts of *IG* I³ 60.

23.31-5). This may have been a muster of thetes, the lowest census class, since 20,000 later seems to be a conventional number for them (e.g. Arist. *Wasps* 709-11). These complements of 100 were later augmented with hoplitic zeugitai, metics, younger and older males, freed slaves, and Plataians. The difficulties become apparent if we try a thought experiment. If each ship had 10 hoplite *epibatai*, as specified in the "Themistokles Decree", 200 ships require 2,000 *epibatai* (besides the 800 non-hoplite archers). There were c. 10,000 Attic hoplites at Marathon, so that 8,000 would be left to supplement ships' crews. Thus, each trireme would have its original allotment of 100 supplemented by only 40, and still be left 40 rowers short. That leaves another 8,000 to make up from other sources. At some point the Chalkidians took over 20 triremes allowing the Athenians to reassign 2000 original sailors. Yet the ships may still have been undermanned.

Furthermore, this Athenian manpower deficiency existed despite access to the whole community for conscription. The depth of Xerxes' penetration into Greece carried with it the seeds of his defeat because, by over-running Attica, he ensured that every Athenian male above the age of puberty was freed from all other activities. Except for any who chose simply to abscond, all were available to man ships. The founders of the Delian League naturally could not plan on total suspension of the Athenian economy as a regular feature of future resistance to Persia. True, they may well have expected to draw many away for other activities at times of intense operations, but some semblance of normal existence had to continue in Attica. In the moment of Salamis, Athens had achieved a rare existential state, total mobilization for survival of the *polis*, a *polis* that was a virtual city because actual Attica was occupied. That moment was essentially beyond duplication.

As already seen, distant deployments of a large numbers of warships took place during the league's anti-Persian campaigns. The Athenians had to evolve toward professionalization of military service as a solution to manpower problems. In this new order, naval service became a regular salaried career and a minimum level of activation was maintained annually, with preference for Athenian citizens in order to sustain a pool of qualified personnel. The *Athenaion Politeia* mentions 20 guard ships (24.3). Plutarch refers to a practice where 60 triremes were manned for eight months annually, with priority given to citizens (*Per.* 11.4). In the naval profession, metics and *xenoi* eventually served alongside citizens. This arrangement probably did not exist in the early alliance, which is another reason why the division of the allies into tribute payers and those serving in person was fundamental. The demobilized sailors and soldiers from the smaller allied cities thereby became available to row the triremes of Athens and the larger allied states. This is perhaps why we find several smaller cities from the Cyclades missing from the early tribute lists in the late 450s.[29] They were too small to provide ships usefully, but they could provide crews.

---

[29] Cf. *ATL* 3.250; Lewis 1984; Wallace & Figueira 2010: 65; Rutishauer 2012: 94.

The scale of the fleets and mobilizations of the early Delian League sheds light on the tribute requirements of the alliance. As a matter of logistics, sailors needed money in order to embark with a stock of food, money to leave behind with their families, and money to purchase more supplies as operations continued. Even later in the century, at a time of greater administrative sophistication, Attic forces still depended on groups of private vessels under the control of merchants which aided in supply.[30] No administrative apparatus was in place in 478 to handle the departure of a large fleet. The larger the mobilization the less possible it was for crews to live off their areas of operations or even to purchase supplies from cooperative towns. Therefore, even in the dire emergency of the evacuation of Attica in 480 and total Athenian mobilization, money had to be found to disburse to those sailing. Who found and conveyed these funds became controversial in later Attic historiography. Partisans claimed both for Themistokles and for the Areiopagos the credit for providing an 8-drachma stipend to embarking sailors (*Ath. Pol.* 23.1; Plut. *Them.* 10.6-7; Cleidemus *FGH* 323 F1).[31] Once *poleis* had to utilize for ships' crews persons poorer than persons of affluence or smallholders, the zeugitic or hoplitic class and above at Athens and its counterparts elsewhere, in other words persons who could subsidize (at least) modest, short-term service from their estates, subsistence support for military personnel was crucial.

Let us then consider what an 8-drachma *per* man launching cost implies about the finances of the Delian League. Table III organizes such costs for forces of various sizes at two modest rates of subsistence (an obol or 2 obols daily; cf. Plut. *Them.* 10.3). Observe that we assume that the 8-drachma launching payment sustains operations for the first month. For example, to launch a 300-trireme fleet costs 80T. If allied states faced the same constraints as Athens, a 200-trireme allied fleet to accompany the Athenians requires 53T, 2000 dr. These are colossal sums of money in the context of the early 470s. That the early campaigning of the Delian League could have been very expensive is demonstrated by the huge cost of the later effort (440-39) to suppress the Samians, which cost 1200T.[32] French argued that this constituted an 8-10 months deployment of 215 triremes (over two years) and supporting troops.[33] Admittedly these costs reflect some inflation and the professionalization of allied forces, and the calculations to reach them are somewhat speculative. Yet the Samian War does portray well the immense expense of two years of intense mobilization.

The express purpose of the Delian League was to retaliate against the Great King by raiding his territory (Thuc. 1.96.1), a rationale that militated in favor

---

[30] See Figueira 1998: 261-2.

[31] See Rhodes 1993: 288-90; Figueira 2011: 199-203.

[32] Isoc. 15.111; DS 12.28.3; Nepos *Timoth.* 1; comparing *IG* I³ 363.5, 12, 17, 19.

[33] French 1972: 56.

of costly annual campaigning during the early years of the league. Even if there had not been occasions to liberate Greek *poleis*, expel Persian garrisons, and uproot pro-Persian tyrants, annual campaigning suited disparately the interests of the Athenians, major allies, and tributaries. Thereby the Athenians instilled obedience to their officials; the stronger allies exerted control over former dependencies (especially mainland *peraiai*); and the tributary allies reinforced the premise that the alliance was committed to defend even lesser Greek communities. There was always the danger that the Athenians would become distracted by relations in homeland Greece, including regional feuds with enemies like Thebes, Aigina, and Megara. The goals and structure of the early alliance were promoted by the east Greeks, who took the initiative to keep the Athenians engaged in order to keep the Persians out (Thuc. 1.75.2; 95.1, 4; 96.1). Yearly campaigning brought to the foreground the aforesaid challenge of sustainability.

Hence, another strong motivation for the creation of the class of tributaries was to provide resources to sustain the manning, equipping, replenishing, and replacing of the forces of the league. That last factor must be remembered, because the allies had to anticipate replacing the losses of each campaign before the next. Naturally, the Athenians could not depend much on the mining revenues from Laureion for the near term. One also suspects that some Ionian triremes had been built in the years of their earlier revolt and might soon require replacement. Thus, the Athenians were authorized to assign allied states to the ranks of the tributaries. The alliance was not and could not be organized on the principle that all those willing to serve be permitted to serve regardless of their preparedness or suitability. Despite the professed autonomy of the original allies, which we know from Thucydides (1.97.1), some cities that probably would have chosen to contribute ships were not allowed to do so.

Thus, in this context, some mysteries of the first, Aristeidian, assessment receive clarification. Intense fear of Persian counterattack and the required magnitude of the naval mobilization, which has just been outlined, led to an assessment of 460T, a very high amount in its context. Later, the Battle of Eurymedon would be a vindication of the organization of the alliance. In its aftermath, a larger alliance after 454/3 faced a less acute threat, and its annual burden was lower, somewhat exceeding 400T. Aristeides' acclaim can thus be seen to have resided in his equity in undertaking a daunting, if not impossible mission, in trying to find resources for anticipated standing fleets of 500-600 triremes and expeditionary forces of 300-350 triremes. Though I cannot argue my case exhaustively, the *dasmos* of the hated Persians, a direct tax, is unlikely to have been taken over by Aristeides. Rather, Aristeides and his collaborators carefully reviewed and compared the revenues from the existing indirect taxes (like harbor duties) of the allied states and calculated assessments that seemed equitable in cross comparison, despite their total reaching a huge amount of silver. This exercise probably still fell short of matching the Persians, man for man, ship for ship, and perhaps even of reaching their planned mobilizations (described above). Concomitantly, it may well have seemed quite infeasible to allocate shares among the tributary states of an unreasonably large (and rather abstract) total amount of money and men. Moreover, such a painful obligation would hardly have been celebrated except for the fear and loathing that Persian domination inspired in those Greeks who had experienced it. Yet the first assessment sustained annual well-subsidized operations by Athens and its better qualified allies on expeditions that took proactive strategies. Forward action was itself the result of a "virtuous" cycle in which incrementally higher quality and better subsidized forces could afford to operate farther from Attica and with smaller numbers of warships. After Eurymedon, a more manageable need for military funds was folded into a calculation of τὸ ἱκνούμενον ἀνάλωμα 'the expense that was incumbent' on each ally (Thuc. 1.99.3).

In conclusion, let us consider which evolution of the *phoros* of the Delian League offers a suitable context for this vision of threat assessment in the early years of the alliance. Naturally, I shall limit myself to a statement of results from other research, some of it still in preparation. The alliance had c. 100 (or less) tributary members in the early 470s and c. 25 *poleis* contributed ships with personnel.[34] By the beginning of the tribute lists only the Lesbians in their five cities, the Chians, and the Samians remained non-tributary. Many later tributaries were dependencies of non-tributary states in the early alliance, and, therefore, also effectively non-tributary. The relative average burden on each tributary in the early alliance was approximately 200-250% as heavy as at mid-century. Assessments started high and moderated as the Persian threat receded after the battle of Eurymedon. My student Aaron Hershkowitz has created a data base that covers all attested tribute payments. This data base has significant value for modeling various scenarios for the evolution of the Attic alliance. It has already yielded an important paper by Hershkowitz that addresses changes in assessment.[35] He has confirmed the strong tendency of the assessment process toward reducing tribute from 454 to 431. In this period, the total assessment hovered around 400T. It appears that, as Athens added tributaries through the break-up of larger ship contributors, through new accessions to the alliance, and through commutations to tributary status, some existing assessments were more likely to be reduced in cases where it was worthwhile for tributary to mount a campaign for a reduction. The majority of smaller tributaries had stable assessments, while only a few large states were tempting targets for increases.

---

[34] Islands: Andros, Naxos, and Paros; Ionia: Chios, Erythrai, Kyme, Lesbos (Antissa, Eresos, Methymna, Mytilene, and Pyrrha), Miletos, and Samos; Hellespont: Khersonesitai, Lampsakos, and Perinthos; Thrace: Abdera, Ainos, Mende, Poteidaia, and Torone. Caria: Rhodes (Ialysos, Kameiros, and Lindos).

[35] See Hershkowitz forthcoming.

However, memory of the higher Aristeidian assessments was preserved in Athenian institutional memory. When the Peloponnesian War depleted the reserve fund and an intensified tempo of operations was thought necessary against the Spartans, the Athenians, through the decree of Thoudippos (*IG* I³ 71), appear to have returned to assessments in the spirit of the initial Aristeidian valuation (2-3 times higher). Thus, the tradition of higher assessments justified rigorous exploitation of the allies during the Archidamian War. And later again, when a compromise was needed to establish the Peace of Nikias, a reference to the 'Aristeidian *phoros*' was included in its provisions, as appears in a verbatim citation of Thucydides (5.18.5-6). The Athenians had wanted Sparta to surrender a small group of Thracian cities to restore the *status quo ante bellum*, but Sparta lacked the ability and the stomach to do so.[36] A deal was reached that these cities would be autonomous and immune from Athenian invasion if they paid Athens the 'Aristeidian *phoros*', although it is unlikely that some (or indeed any) of these states had even belonged to the alliance when Aristeides made his first assessment. This created an anomalous status between defection to Sparta and reincorporation among Athenian subject tributaries. Furthermore, the 'Aristeidian *phoros*' also connoted in contemporary polemics the current level of assessment which the Athenians held both necessary and fair. Thus, in its last years – the tribute system was superseded in 413 by the 5% import/export tax – the *phoros* of the Athenian allies came full circle from the existential threat of Persian domination to the peril of Spartan victory and an anti-democratic upheaval.

---

[36] See Figueira forthcoming[b]

TABLE I: PERSIAN MOBILIZATIONS OF THE FIFTH CENTURY

Date/Occasion	Force Size	Contingents	Outcome
1) c. 512: Dareios' Balkan Campaign	600 ships (Hdt. 4.87.1)	Assorted allies including Phoenicians and Eastern Greeks	Only attritional losses?
2) c. 499: Campaign against Naxos	200 ships (Hdt. 5.31.3-4, 32)	Ionian and Aiolian Greeks (cf. Hdt. 5.37.1-38.2)	
3) c. 496: Persian fleet to Cyprus	"a great army with ships" (Hdt. 5.108.1)	Phoenicians	Badly defeated by Ionians (Hdt. 5.112.1)
4) c. 494: Fleet facing the Ionian rebels at Lade	600 ships (Hdt. 6.9.1)	Phoenicians and other non-Greeks	The Chians τῶν πολεμίων ἑλόντες νέας συχνὰς (Hdt. 6.15.2)
5) c. 492: Mardonios operates in Thrace	300+ ships (Hdt. 6.44.3)	Phoenicians and other non-Greeks	c. 300 destroyed in storm at Athos (Hdt 6.44.3)
6) 490: Datis' Campaign against Naxos, Euboia, and Attica	600 ships (Hdt. 6.95.1-2)	Phoenicians and other non-Greeks	Seven ships at Marathon (Hdt. 6.115) and attritional losses

7) 480: Xerxes campaign against Greece	1000 triremes (Aes. *Persae* 341-43) 1207 triremes: (Hdt. 7.89.1, 184.1; cf. DS 11.3.7) 1000 ships (Ctesias *FGH* 688 F12[27])	300 Phoenician ships (Hdt. 7.89.1; cf. DS 11.3.7) 200 Egyptian ships (Hdt. 7.89.2; cf. DS 11.3.7) 100 Cilician ships (Hdt. (Hdt. 7.90) 80 Cilician ships (DS 11.3.7) 150 Cypriot ships (Hdt. 7.90; cf. DS 11.3.7) 30 Pamphylian ships (Hdt. 7.91) 40 Pamphylian ships (DS 11.3.7) 50 Lycian ships (Hdt. 7.92) 40 Lycian ships (DS 11.3.7) 70 Carian ships (Hdt. 7.93) 80 Carian ships (DS 11.3.7) 320 Greek warships (DS 11.3.7) 30 Dorian ships (Hdt. 7.93) 40 Dorian ships (DS 11.3.8) 100 Ionian ships (Hdt. 7.94) 17 *nēsiotic* ships (Hdt. 7.95.1) 50 *nēsiotic* ships (DS 11.3.8) 100 Aiolian ships (Hdt. 7.95.1) 40 Aiolian ships (DS 11.3.8) 100 Hellespontine Greek ships (Hdt. 7.95.2) 80 Hellespontine & Pontic ships (DS 11.3.8)	400 ships lost to storm at Magnesia (Hdt. 7.188.1-190) 200 ships lost to storm at Hollows of Euboia (Hdt. 8.7.12; 131.4.2) 15 ships seized before the battle of Artemision (Hdt. 7.194.1-3) Many ships (including 30 taken the 1st day) lost at Artemision (Hdt. 8.11.2, 14.2, 16.3) Many ships destroyed at Salamis (Hdt. 8.86, 89.2; cf. 84-93.2) 100 ships destroyed (Dem. 14.29) Most of the remainder burnt at Mykale after withdrawal of the Phoenicians (Hdt. 9.106.1) 500 ships destroyed (Ctesias *FGH* 688 F12[30])

8) c. 468-66: Eurymedon Campaign	340 ships (Ephorus *FGH* 70 F 191, fr. 9-10, 192; DS 11.60.67; Plut. *Cimon* 12.5 [350 Ships]) + 80-ship Phoenician reinforcement from Cyprus (Plut. *Cimon* 12.4, 13.3) 600 ships (Phanodemos *FGH* 325 F 22 [Plut. *Cimon* 12.5])	80-ship Phoenician reinforcement from Cyprus (Plut. *Cimon* 12.4, 13.3)	200 ships taken or destroyed (Thuc. 1.100.1) 100 ships captured (Lyc. 1.72; Aristod. *FGH* 104 F11.2;) 200 ships taken and the 80 reinforcements (Plut. *Cimon* 12.6; Nepos *Cimon* 2.2) Many ships lost; 100+ with their crews; others empty (*FGH* 70 F 191, fr. 9-10; DS 11.60.67 340 ships taken: DS 11.62.1
9) c. 454: Suppression of the Egyptian revolt	300 ships: Ktesias *Persica FGH*, F14[37]; DS 11.77.1		Only attritional losses?
10) c. 451: Kimon's Last Cypriot Campaign	300 ships: DS 12.3.2		100 ships captured with their men and many others sunk (DS 12.3.3-4)

TABLE II: NOTABLE GREEK MOBILIZATIONS OF THE FIFTH CENTURY

Date/ Occasion	Force Size	Contingents	Outcome
1) c. 494: Fleet facing the Persians at Lade	353: Hdt. 6.8.1-2	Miletos: 80 ships Priene: 12 ships Myous: 3 ships Teos: 17 ships Chios: 100 ships Erythrai: 8 ships Phokaia: 3 ships Lesbos: 70 ships Samos: 60 ships (Hdt. 6.8.1-3)	Most of the 11 Samian ships that fought (Hdt. 6.14.2-3) Many of the 100 Chian ships (Hdt. 6.15.2-16.2)
2) 480: Greek fleet at Artemision	272 triremes: Hdt. 8.2.1 + 53 additional Attic ships after the initial fighting (Hdt. 8.14.1)	Athens: 127 triremes Corinth: 40 triremes Megara: 20 triremes Khalkis: 20 triremes Aigina: 18 triremes Sikyon: 12 triremes Sparta: 10 triremes Epidauros: 8 triremes Eretria: 7 triremes Troizen: 5 triremes Styra: 2 triremes Keos: 2 triremes, 2 pentekontors Opuntian Lokris: 7 pentekontors (Hdt. 8.1.1-2.1) 53 additional Attic ships after the initial fighting (Hdt. 8.14.1)	Many Greek ships destroyed in the third day of fighting (Hdt. 8.16.3), including 5 Greeks ships taken by the Egyptians (8.17) One half the Athenian ships s damaged on the 3rd day (Hdt. 8.18)

3) 480: Greek fleet at Salamis	310 ships (Aes. *Pers.* 338-40) 378 triremes (Hdt. 8.48) 400 ships (Thuc. 1.74.1) 200 triremes (Dem. 14.29 300 triremes: Dem. 18.238 700 ships (Ctesias *FGH* 688 F12[30])	Sparta: 16 triremes Corinth: 40 triremes Sikyon: 15 triremes Epidauros: 10 triremes Troizen: 5 triremes Hermione: 3 triremes Athens: 180 triremes Megara: 20 triremes Amprakia: 7 triremes Leukas: 3 triremes Aigina: 30+ triremes Khalkis: 20 triremes Eretria: 7 triremes Keos: 2 triremes, 2 pentekontors Naxos: 4 triremes Styra: 2 triremes Kythnos: 1 trireme 1 pentekontor Kroton: 1 trireme Melos: 2 pentekontors Siphnos: 1 pentekontor Seriphos: 1 pentekontor (all Hdt. 8.43.1-47) Athens: a little less than two-thirds of 400 (Thuc. 1.74.1) Athens: 200 (Dem. 8.238); 100 (Dem. 14.29) Cf. Athenians more than the rest (Lys. 2.42; Isoc. 4.98, 12.50)	Ionians capture many Greek ships (Hdt. 8.85.2)
4) 479: Greek fleet at Mykale	110 ships to Aigina + Aiginetans and islanders? (Hdt. 8.131.1)		Only attritional losses?

5) 478: Pausanias Campaign against Byzantion & Cyprus	?	20 ships from Peloponnesus 30 Attic ships A mass of other allies Thuc. 1.94.1) 50 triremes from Peloponnesus 30 Attic ships (DS 11.44.2)	Only attritional losses?
6) c. 468-66: Greek Fleet at Eurymedon	250 ships (Ephorus *FGH* 70 F 191, fr. 9-10; DS 11.60.6) 300 ships (Plut. *Cimon* 12.2; DS 11.60.3)	200 Athenian ships 100 allied ships (DS 11.60.3)	Only attritional losses?
7) c. 459: Egyptian Campaign	200 ships (Thuc. 1.104.2; Isoc. 8.86; Aristod. *FGH* 104 F11.3; Ael. *VH* 5.10 300 ships: DS 11.71.5	40 Athenian ships (Ktesias *FHG* 4, fr. 32)	Almost 250? (Thuc. 1.110.1-5; DS 12.3.1) 200 ships (Isoc. 8.86; Ael. *VH* 5.10)
8) c. 451: Cypriot Campaign of Kimon	200 ships (Thuc. 1.112.2; Plut. *Per.* 10.4; DS 12.3.1; Nepos *Cimon* 3.4) 300 triremes: Plut. *Cimon* 18.1		150 ships (Isoc. 8.86; Ael. *VH* 5.10)

TABLE III: ESTIMATED EXPEDITION COSTS IN THE *PENTEKONTAETEIA*

Expedition Size	Launching Fee = 8 dr. (covers one month's subsidy?)	+ an additional month at one obol@day/two obols@day	+ two additional months at one obol@day/two obols@day	+ three additional months at one obol@day/two obols@day
200 triremes	53T, 2000 dr.	87T, 2000 dr. / 120T	120T/ 193T	153T, 2000 dr./ 253T, 2000 dr.
250 triremes	66T, 4000 dr.	108T, 4000 dr./ 150T	150T/ 233T, 2000 dr.	191T, 4000 dr./ 316T, 4000 dr.
300 triremes	80T	130T/ 180T	180T/ 280T	230T/ 380T
400 triremes	106T, 4000 dr.	174T, 4000 dr./ 240T	240T/ 386T	306T, 4000 dr./ 506T, 4000 dr.
500 triremes	133T, 2000 dr.	217T, 2000 dr./ 300T	300T/ 466T, 4000 dr.	383T, 2000 dr./ 633T, 2000 dr.
600 triremes	160T	260T/360T	360T/ 560T	460T/760T

Regimes políticos nas *Histórias* de Heródoto. O "Diálogo dos Persas" (3. 80-82)
(Constitutions in Herodotus's *Histories*: The "Persian Dialogue" (3. 80-82))

Carmen Soares (cilsoares@gmail.com)
Universidade de Coimbra

Resumo – O propósito deste estudo é demonstrar que os capítulos 80-82 do livro III das *Histórias* de Heródoto apresentam não o retrato de três regimes e respectivos governates, o tradicional tríptico monarquia-oligarquia-democracia, mas permitem a subdivisão destas formas arquetípicas de governação em seis: três em que reina a excelência e outras tantas degeneradas.

Palavras-chave: Heródoto, teorização política, tirania, monarquia, democracia, oligarquia, regimes políticos de excelência, regimes políticos degenerados.

Abstract – The main goal of this analysis of Hdt 3. 80-82 is to demonstrate that the historian does not propose a political theory based on three different constitutions: monarchy, oligarchy, and democracy. On the contrary, it is clear that by applying the qualifiers *aristos* and *kakos* to these forms of government, he offers a more complex arrangement of six constitutional archetypes, subdivided into triads of good and degenerate examples.

Keywords: Herodotus, political theory, tyranny, monarchy, democracy, oligarchy, "good" constitutions, "degenerate" constitutions.

A pertinência da reflexão sobre o tema da "teorização política" decorre, antes de tudo o mais, da necessidade de procurar e na possibilidade de encontrar, para o assunto em apreço, em textos da época (e estou a reportar-me ao séc. V a. C), a fundamentação epistemológica caracterizadora do trabalho científico. Isto é, o estudo da *praxis* política é inseparável da reflexão sobre os princípios teóricos ou doutrinais que a enformam. Confirmando, neste domínio como em muitos outros, merecer o reconhecimento por parte dos estudiosos contemporâneos de ser voz fundadora da investigação histórica, Heródoto apresenta na sua obra uma análise pragmático-filosófica da *politeia*.

Nas *Histórias* vão sendo sucessivamente retratados monarcas bárbaros e tiranos gregos. Assim, quando, no livro III (caps. 80-82)[1], o leitor-ouvinte depara com o famosíssimo "Diálogo dos Persas" a sensação que tem é de que Heródoto, também em matéria de reflexão política, tem o cuidado de produzir um discurso científico, em conferir credibilidade ao seu *logos* (termo aqui aplicado no duplo

---

[1] Bibliografia principal sobre o episódio: Romilly 1959, Lasserre 1976, Evans 1981, Lateiner 1984, Rocha Pereira 1981 e 1990, Soares 2014.

sentido de 'raciocínio, argumentação'). Ou seja, sente a urgência de produzir uma discussão dos fundamentos dos regimes de que apresentou (e continuará a apresentar) realizações concretas. A este propósito, devo desde já esclarecer que, para mim, a questão (insolúvel) da historicidade do diálogo assume uma importância marginal, quando comparada com o seu significado *logikos*. Mais do que saber se um grupo de nobres persas, em 522/1 a. C., discutiu realmente entre si a possibilidade de o reino passar de uma monarquia a uma oligarquia ou democracia, ou se Heródoto apenas está a colocar na boca de Bárbaros os argumentos que contemporanamente animavam as discussões pelo menos de algumas elites gregas, importa entender o episódio como a confirmação da racionalidade herodotiana[2].

Isto é, o que verificamos é que o historiador não se limita a apresentar, de forma detalhada e em extensão diversa, retratos de monarcas orientais e tiranos gregos, cuja leitura nos permite tirar ilações sobre a caracterização dos respectivos regimes. Não! Ele próprio tem o cuidado (científico) de sustentar teoricamente essa pragmática política. Podemos, então, defender que os caps. 80-82 do livro III fornecem ao público uma "ficha de leitura" dos casos de governantes e governos já retratados e dos que as *Histórias* ainda lhe reservam.

É costume dizer-se, entre os comentadores do "Diálogo dos Persas", que aí encontramos a mais antiga fonte grega sobre a concepção de três regimes políticos distinguidos com base no critério numérico, a saber: o governo de um só (monarquia), o governo de poucos (oligarquia) e o governo de muitos (democracia). Pessoalmente não me revejo nesta interpretação, que considero redutora e, como tal, defensável apenas a um nível de leitura imediata. Entendo que o texto permite individualizar um maior número de *politeiai*, perfazendo um total de seis regimes distintos. Se não identifico já os respectivos nomes de cada um deles é porque sigo o método de investigação platónico[3] segundo o qual não se deve partir de um nome para conhecer uma realidade, uma vez que só podemos saber o nome certo a dar-lhe depois de a conhecermos.

Outra ideia generalizada, esta de validade incontestável, é a de que o móbil da discussão reside na busca da melhor forma de governo, noção particularmente enfatizada na fala do último dos intervenientes no diálogo, Dario. Deste passo cito um pequeno excerto, no qual se encontra a chave para entendermos o princípio da aceitação de dois grupos distintos de regimes: os "melhores" (a que vem aplicado no texto o adjectivo *aristos*) e os "piores" (assim designados por mim, com base na caracterização negativa de que são alvo, como passarei a esclarecer).

---

[2] Sobre a historicidade ou não do diálogo, leia-se Pelling 2002 ('History').
[3] Cf. *O Político* 261 e (trad. Soares 2008).

> Dos três regimes que temos à nossa disposição, afirmo que – apesar de todos
> eles serem os melhores (é o melhor o governo do povo, a oligarquia e a mo-
> narquia) – este último é de longe superior aos outros. De facto nada se revela
> melhor do que um só homem dotado de excelência! (3. 82. 1-2)

Na verdade, o futuro monarca persa nomeia apenas três formas de constituição. O que nos ajuda a compreender a tendência dos estudiosos para,
seguindo de perto esta afirmação, proporem que Heródoto identifica apenas
três *politeiai*[4]. Mas atentemos na contextualização das palavras de Dario. À
testa da sua intervenção o que ele declara é que existem três formas exemplares
de governar. No entanto, nas anteriores falas de Otanes e Megabizo, bem
como no decurso desta, admitem-se tipos de governação que não se exercem
sob o signo da excelência. Só num dos casos, no entanto, essa distinção entre
a forma perfeita e a degenerada –chamemos-lhe assim – está na origem de
nomenclatura distinta. Refiro-me, respectivamente, aos termos 'monarquia' e
'tirania'.

Assim, em vez de três *politeiai*, temos já quatro. Além disso, não é porque
não se atribuem designações autónomas às formas piores do governo das massas
e da oligarquia que devemos pensar que Heródoto não admita a individualização
de mais duas formas de governo. Aliás, que essa poderia ser uma prática comum
pelo menos às elites pensantes mais ou menos contemporâneas, é uma tese que
colhe apoio em Platão. Quando, n' *O Político*, o filósofo procede à divisão em
dois do governo de um só, do governo de poucos e do governo do povo, no caso
do último afirma:

> No respeitante à democracia, quer as massas exerçam o poder sobre os deten-
> tores da riqueza pela força ou livremente, quer respeitem escrupulosamente ou
> não as leis, não há, em absoluto, o hábito de lhe mudar o nome.(292 a)

O que verdadeiramente permite distinguir os regimes não são, pois, os
nomes que lhes damos, mas a ética dos seus governantes e alguns mecanismos
de governação, como passarei de seguida a analisar.

Comecemos pelo 'governo de um só', ao qual Heródoto reserva papel de
destaque, conforme se depreende até pelo facto de abrir e fechar o episódio com
considerações sobre ele. Embora Otanes e Dario usem os mesmos nomes para
falar dessa *politeia* e respectivo governante (*mounarchie, mounarchos*), pois são
aqueles que literalmente significam 'governo de um só' e 'governante único',
estão a reportar-se a realidades distintas.

---

[4] Repare-se que o autor nunca aplica este substantivo, mas sim *pragmata* (ou no singular
pragma), com o sentido de 'feitos, negócios' (públicos, por oposição a privados), a saber
'governação'. Sobre esta interpretação, vd. Cartledge 2009: 4.

O primeiro emprega a palavra monarquia ao exercício despótico do poder, da responsabilidade de um tirano, termo entendido no sentido pejorativo que ainda hoje lhe damos. Para que não haja dúvidas de que é esse o entendimento em causa, basta lembrar que o próprio Otanes usa como sinónimo do seu *mounarchos* a expressão 'homem tirânico' (*aner mounarchos:* 3. 80. 4). Concepção de que partilha Megabizo, que emprega não só o título *tyrannos* ao governante único (3. 81. 1), mas denomina de *tyrannis* o regime em que ele governa (3. 81. 2)[5]. Mais importante que os nomes, já o referi, é a caracterização dos regimes e respectivos governantes. Atentemos, então, neste aspecto.

Sobre a *politeia* de um só *stricto sensu*, apresentada por Otanes, retiramos um retrato do que ela não é: nem 'agradável' (*hedy*), nem 'boa' (*agathon*). Fica, assim,

---

[5] Em suma, o termo monarchos tem o sentido neutro de 'governante (único)', donde a sua utilização como sinónimo de *tyrannos*. Este, por sua vez, implica, no *Diálogo dos Persas*, o sentido de 'governante (único) despótico'. Este assunto foi já tratado de forma bem documentada por Ferril 1978. No entanto, ao contrário de Rosivach 1988, não considero que, pelo menos no que toca a Heródoto, possamos defender que *tyrannos* e *monarchos*, assim como *tyrannis* e *monarchia*, sejam apenas sinónimos. O que a análise do texto herodotiano atesta, como passarei a demonstrar, é que o desenho do retrato do tirano se faz por antítese com o do bom monarca (tratamento que, diversamente do que defende o estudioso na p. 56, não é apenas característico de Xenofonte e Aristóteles). Um outro estudo a ter em conta sobre o sentido do termo *tyrannos* é o de Parker 1988. Não obstante a validade do levantamento e estudo analítico das ocorrências do termo, as conclusões retiradas merecem-me algumas reservas, sobretudo quanto à interpretação apresentada para o texto das *Histórias*. Mas, mesmo fora do testemunho do autor agora em apreço, é possível encontrar contradicções no seio da argumentação de Parker. Refiram-se algumas das mais evidentes: a tese de que *tyrannos* se distingue de *basileus* porque este designa "a good or legitimate absolute monarch" e aquele "an in some way wicked or illegitimate absolute monarch" (p. 145) não se coaduna com a observação que faz a propósito da leitura da *Política* de Aristóteles, quando afirma que o Estagirita, ao denominar de 'tiranos' indivíduos que herdaram o poder, "simply neglects the hereditary characyer of tiranny" (p. 167). Ou seja, a legitimidade de um tirano subir ao poder baseia-se, pelo menos em parte, num critério que assiste também ao rei (a hereditariedade), logo tirania e realeza não se distinguem com base no argumento da legitimação do poder, porque nem sempre o tirano sobe ao poder ilegalmente. Particularmente forçada parece-me a argumentação de que só no dialecto ático há uma distinção clara entre *tyrannos* e *basileus* e que nos restantes contextos linguísticos funcionavam como sinónimos. Para não me alongar demasiado nesta questão, bastará lembrar que o próprio Parker abona a sua tese com testemunhos que a contradizem. Por um lado afirma (p. 169) que a comédia ática tanto usa o termo com o sentido positivo que se encontra na lírica, como com o valor de poder tomado pela força (logo ilegal). Tal não devia suceder se a distinção entre bom governo (monarquia) e mau governo (tirania) fosse uma marca linguística! Dizer que Heródoto, porque escreveu em iónico, não fez distinção entre tiranos e reis (p. 171), causa igual perplexidade. A verdade é que no seu texto, em particular no que agora estamos a analisar, essa distinção de valores é bem nítida. Se o historiador em determinados passos emprega *tyrannos* com sentido neutro (i. e., sinónima de *basileus* e *monarchos*) tal facto decorre, quanto a mim, da simples razão de ao seu tempo essa ser uma prática linguística corrente, que não é imcompatível com a clara consciência, já existente (e que não será, por conseguinte, uma inovação tucididiana, como defende o comentador, cf. pp. 170 sq.), entre monarquia, entendida como boa forma de governação de um só, e tirania, a realização negativa do exercício monocrático.

automaticamente excluída do grupo das melhores formas de governação. Como procedimentos emblemáticos do sistema identifica a ausência de mecanismos de controlo das finanças públicas e da actuação do governante. Ou seja, como diz o Persa, aquele não tem que prestar contas e faz o que lhe apetece (3. 80. 3). Se ao governante único é conferida, como estamos a ver, uma liberdade total de movimentos, é evidente que se está a transferir a responsabilidade da boa ou má governação para o seu carácter. Esta ingerência determinante da moral na política constitui no texto herodotiano, como terei o cuidado de sublinhar várias vezes no decurso desta reflexão, um elemento comum ao perfil de todas as *politeiai*.

O que nos diz Otanes sobre a alma do monarca tirano? Para responder a esta interrogação, terei que começar por apresentar duas ideias que, sendo prévias, no texto, a essa caracterização, são de todo indispensáveis ao seu cabal entendimento: o poder absoluto corrompe a alma, mesmo a de um indivíduo que mereça a distinção de ser tido na conta de 'o melhor de todos os homens' (*ton ariston andron panton*, ibidem); a alma humana possui um defeito inato, a inveja (*phthonos*, ibidem). Se adicionarmos a esta propensão natural para o vício da inveja uma vida próspera, estão reunidas as condições que explicam o aparecimento da 'insolência' (*hybris*), a segunda das características que autorizam Otanes a denominar de 'absoluta vilania' (*pasa kakotes*) e de 'todo o tipo de destemperos' (*polla kai atasthala*) a actuação do tirano.

A propósito da noção de que é a abundância de bens que estimula a faceta invejosa do tirano a cometer abusos de poder, a personagem tem o cuidado de sugerir que essa é uma das incompreensões (diríamos nós) da psicologia do governante único. A inveja, apesar de inata, deixa de ser moralmente justificável quando o sujeito vive desafogadamente, pelo que, ao contrário do que sucede, o tirano devesse ser 'não-invejoso' (*aphthonos:* 3. 80. 4). A segunda das perplexidades ético-comportamentais suscitadas pelo retrato do tirano consiste no que entendo designar por baixo nível de auto-estima. A falta de confiança no mérito pessoal e na aceitação social das suas acções levam o tirano a hostilizar os seus pares ou indivíduos moralmente superiores (ideias contidas no uso do adjectivo *aristos*, cf. ibidem) e a rodear-se de cidadãos de baixa extracção, social e/ou ética (os *kakistoi*, cf. ibidem). Uns – é fácil deduzi-lo – representam a ameaça de potenciais rivais; outros afiguram-se uma base de apoio manipulável e obediente. A mesma insegurança explica o entusiasmo com que o tirano acolhe as calúnias e a insatisfação permanente que nele causam os elogios de terceiros, ora tidos por desconsideração (quando moderados), ora encarados como actos de bajulação (quando mais profusos) (3. 80. 5).

Em jeito de corolário do retrato do monarca tirânico, Otanes enuncia três comportamentos por si qualificados de 'os mais graves' (*ta megista*, ibidem): alterar os costumes pátrios, exercer violência sobre as mulheres e condenar à morte sem julgamento. Ao ser apresentada nestes termos, a tirania, produto da actuação do tirano, significa o ruir de alicerces fundamentais da *pólis* grega: as normas, a moderação e a justiça.

Bem diversa deste governo despótico de um só é a monarquia retratada por Dario. O primeiro contraste evidente encontramo-la na relação entre *ethos* e política. Enquanto Otanes admite que o exercício do poder influencia o carácter do governante, corrompendo-o, Dario tem uma posição absolutamente contrária. Conforme vimos *supra* (a propósito da citação de 3. 82. 2), a preferência pela melhor forma de monarquia fá-la com base na ética. É porque a governa 'um único homem dotado de excelência' que o regime de um só é o preferido de Dario. O carácter do governante é que lhe confere a competência para ser o 'intendente' das massas.

O regime, mesmo quando governado por um monarca perfeito, continua, no entanto, a estar sujeito à ruína, como se depreende da condição identificada por Dario para que se mantenham as suas virtudes. O requisito em questão é, uma vez mais, de natureza moral, a saber: o monarca não pode revelar as suas decisões a 'indivíduos mal formados' (*dysmeneas andras*, 3. 82. 2). Ou seja, na monarquia os perigos de degeneração do regime não derivam do carácter do governante, como sucedia na tirania, mas da imoralidade de terceiros.

Esta ideia de que as formas de constituição podem degenerar constitui, aliás, um motivo central para percebermos a razão de Dario fazer a apologia da monarquia como o melhor dos melhores *pragmata*. Como vimos, a degeneração da monarquia, a acontecer, nunca derivará do governante, mas dos governados. Já no que se refere à oligarquia e ao governo do povo, são os próprios governantes os responsáveis pela sua ruína (manifestada em perturbações sociais sangrentas, próprias da *stasis*). Ou seja, porque a monarquia é, na essência (i.e., no que concerna o governante), sempre 'o melhor' (*to ariston*), cabe-lhe o papel de "constituição regeneradora". Como esclarece o texto, quando o regime de poucos e o da multidão colapsam, a monarquia é sempre a resposta para a salvação da *polis*. E este é o argumento político mais claro da primazia conferida pelo nobre persa à monarquia.

As duas formas de governo de um só, monarquia e tirania, são aquelas que mais extensamente vêm caracterizadas no texto. Esse relevo reflecte, quanto a mim, as posições extremas que parecem ocupar no quadro da teorização política herodotiana. A primeira, acabámos de ver, afigura-se a melhor das melhores (3. 82. 2), a segunda colhe, da parte dos dois intervenientes que a consideram, apenas críticas violentas. Por ser esta a única *politeia* a não merecer qualquer caracterização positiva, julgo legítimo propor para ela o título de "pior regime" de todos. Falta-nos considerar as formas de governo oligárquico e democrático, ambas alvo tanto de elogios como de críticas.

Embora conhecesse e usasse o nome *demokratie* (cf. 6. 43. 3 e 131. 1) e o verbo *demokrateomai* (cf. 4.137. 2, 6. 43. 3), Heródoto não aplica nenhum deles no único passo da sua obra em que faz a discussão teórica das diferentes *politeiai*.

Prefere falar de 'governo/poder (*arche/kratos*) das massas/povo (*plethos/demos*)', sinónimos de *isonomie* (3. 80. 6). Podemos ler, nestas escolhas de terminologia, um indicador de que, à volta do último quartel do séc. V a. C., i. e., volvido quase um século sobre o nascimento da democracia (se tivermos em conta o caso ateniense, que não foi o primeiro[6]), o regime é vulgarmente identificado através das suas duas características mais genuínas: ser um governo em que a maioria dos governantes (a 'multidão', como indica o termo grego *plethos*) é de origem social humilde (o *demos*); os governantes possuirem uma parte (*nomos*) igual (*isos*) no governo da polis.

A propósito da interpertação que estou a propor para *isonomia* ('ter uma parte igual de'), impõe-se esclarecer que é o texto herodotiano que sugere esta leitura abrangente. Ou seja, a declaração de Otanes de que *o governo do povo tem o mais belo dos nomes: isonomia*[7] vem seguida da descrição detalhada do *modus faciendi* político que justifica a atribuição dessa titulatura. É porque os cidadãos acedem aos cargos por tiragem à sorte, porque são obrigados a prestar contas do uso de fundos públicos e porque tomam as decisões em comum, é graças a estas três formas de funcionamento que se pode falar de 'governação partilhada' ou, se preferirmos o termo grego, de *isonomia*[8].

Não podemos, no entanto, descontextualizar a reflexão acabada de fazer. Assim, ao mesmo tempo que servem de emblemas do governo do povo, os mecanismos de gestão do poder enunciados desempenham, no âmbito da fala de Otanes, o papel de reversos positivos de defeitos concretos por ele apontados à tirania (poder discricionário e autocrático e impunidade de que goza o governante). Em suma, como sugere a atribuição do superlativo *kalliston* ao nome *isonomia*, estamos perante a versão perfeita da democracia ou, como escreve Heródoto na fala de Dario, perante 'o povo no seu melhor' (*demou te aristou*, 3. 82. 1).

Ao futuro rei da Pérsia e a Megabizo atribui o nosso Autor a descrição da versão negativa da democracia. Os dois apresentam-na como um 'mau' regime. O primeiro aplica-lhe o adjectivo neutro substantivado 'vil' (*kakon:* 3. 81. 3). O segundo reduz todas as suas acções a 'vilania' (*kakotes*), chama os governantes

---

[6] As instituições democráticas teriam surgido por volta de inícios ou meados do séc. VI a. C. em *poleis* como Mileto, Mégara, Samos e Quios (Ferreira 1990, *A democracia*: 11).

[7] *Isonomia* é a forma ática correspondente ao iónico que o texto apresenta: *isonomie*.

[8] Como facilmente se depreende, considero que Heródoto não usa o nome no sentido restrito de 'igualdade perante a lei'. Contudo, essa noção não fica excluída, se aceitarmos que se aplica a todas as decisões que o povo é levado a tomar no âmbito do governo das diversas instituições democráticas (grupo em que incluímos, além da Assembleia, o órgão deliberativo por excelência, os Tribunais do Povo). Também Rosivach (1988: 47-48 e nn. 11 e 14) defende esta interpretação etimológica, cuja validade vê confirmada na oposição que desde cedo (na canção de mesa de Harmódio e no frag. 4 Diels de Alcméon) se estabelece entre *isonomia* e poder de um só.

'vilões' (*kakoi*) e denomina o modo de agir destes pelo verbo da mesma família semântica (*kakeo:* 3. 82. 4). Verificamos, uma vez mais, que o carácter dos governantes (i. e., a ética) molda o regime (i. e., a *politeia*).

Os governantes *kakoi* são pessoas que carecem de virtudes morais e de instrução, de acordo com a caracterização que Megabizo faz das massas. O defeito da insolência, também apontado ao tirano, é uma das duas maiores pechas da gestão popular (veja-se o uso da forma superlativa 'o mais insolente', *hybristeteron*: 3. 81. 1). O outro é a estupidez ('o mais estúpido', *axynetoteron*, novo uso de superlativo), que, mais do que o resultado de um QI baixo (hipótese sem apoio no texto), deve derivar da falta de educação. É o que sugere Megabizo ao afirmar que, ao contrário do tirano, que, quando comete actos de *hybris*, sabe o que está fazer, o povo não possui conhecimento, pois como se lê em 3. 81. 2:

> Como poderia, pois, ter conhecimento quem não foi ensinado, não sabe o que é belo, nem sabe nada por si próprio e, sem pensar, se atira à governação, semelhante a um rio de torrentes invernosas?

Na verdade, o povo, por falta de recursos, não teria o mesmo acesso à formação que as elites (aristocráticas e/ou endinheiradas), paradigma de educação tradicionalmente referenciado pela expressão completa 'o belo e o bom'. Mais ainda: esse é um saber e uma formação moral que não se compadecem com autodidactismos – como acabámos de ouvir dizer a Megabizo. Convém lembrar que a denúncia da falta de competência (leia-se formação) do povo vem posta na boca de um legítimo porta-voz da classe privilegiado dos nobres. À falta de instrução parece também ligar-se a tomada de decisões irreflectidas, outra atitude censurável própria das massas.

Deixámos para o fim ponderar a atribuição do adjectivo 'incontrolável' (*akolastos*, 3. 81. 2) ao povo, uma vez que, ao implicar a noção de desordem, nos remete para o início da fala de Otanes. Aí, ao afirmar-se o que a monarquia tirânica não é, subentendem-se os princípios norteadores da boa governação. Esta deve buscar não só 'o que é agradável e belo' (3. 80. 2), como já referi, mas também 'a organização do estado' (*chrema katertemenon*, 3. 80. 3). Fica, deste modo, mais evidente que a governação democrática, concebida nos termos enunciados por Megabizo, não pode, de forma alguma, corresponder ao perfil da sua versão *aristos*, anteriormente desenhada por Otanes.

Mas voltemos à fala de Megabizo. Chegados a este ponto da análise, pensamos poder compreender melhor o porquê de chamar à 'multidão' uma 'mole incompetente' (*homilou gar achriou*). Se a ignorância, a insolência, a indisciplina e a irreflexão são defeitos dos indivíduos da classe popular, a consequência natural desses defeitos só pode ser um 'corpo governativo' (*homilos*) 'sem qualquer utilidade' (*a-chreios*). Também os governantes do regime oligárquico vêm designados por um substantivo da família de *homilos*, que, como acabámos de notar, Megabizo aplica ao povo: *homilia*. Ou seja, o contraste imediato entre monarquia e tirania, por um lado, e democracia e oligarquia, pelo outro, consiste em que, nas primeiras, o exercício do poder é exclusivo de um governante, nas segundas é partilhado por uma 'assembleia' de indivíduos (*homilos* ou *homilia*).

Para Megabizo a diferença entre o *homilos* popular e a *homilia* nobre reside na formação ética dos seus membros, o que tem consequências políticas directas, pois, como podemos ler no texto, é natural as melhores *decisões surgirem dos melhores homens* (3. 81. 3).

Na fala de Dario encontramos um critério novo para avaliar a boa governação: o serviço público ou, como se diz em grego, o serviço prestado ao 'interesse comum' (*to koinon*). Além de insistir na distinção social e ética entre oligarcas (possuidores da *arete*) e povo (os *kakoi*), a personagem põe em evidência a política contrastante que as duas formas de governo têm naquela matéria. Ou seja (3. 82. 3-4):

> 3. Na oligarquia é costume surgirem, entre o grande número de indivíduos que coloca o seu mérito ao serviço do interesse comum, poderosas rivalidades pessoais: de facto cada um deles, movido pelo desejo de liderar e de fazer vencer as suas propostas, leva a que apareçam, entre si e os outros, rivalidades insanáveis, das quais nascem dissensões, das dissensões homicídios e dos homicídios desemboca-se numa monarquia, e, com isto, torna-se evidente o quanto este é o melhor regime.
> 4. Quando o povo governa, é inevitável o aparecimento da vilania! E quando a vilania se orienta para o interesse comum, o que surge entre os vilões não são rivalidades, mas sim poderosas alianças! A verdade é que os que cometem actos de vilania contra o interesse comum se encobrem mutuamente.

Enquanto, no primeiro caso, a 'coisa pública' serve de palco à tradicional competição dos aristocratas pelo protagonismo (leia-se *arete*); no segundo estimula a união entre os mais humildes, pois só assim conseguem o mútuo encobrimento da responsabilidade de todos numa governação ruinosa.

Em conclusão, o "Diálogo dos Persas" revela a pluralidade de regimes conhecidos no séc. V. a. C. A partir de três *politeiai* nucleares – distinguidas com base no critério do número de governantes – as personagens herodotianas caracterizam seis regimes distintos: três "perfeitos" (ou, como se diz em grego, *aristoi*) e três "degenerados" (que no texto vêm associados à ideia de *kakotes*). Embora tenhamos de aguardar por Platão para encontrar uma reflexão teórica mais apurada desta distinção, a verdade é que as *Histórias* permitem individualizar claramente: monarquia, tirania, oligarquia "melhor", oligarquia "pior", democracia "melhor" e democracia "pior".

Este é o espectro conceptual que Heródoto conhece e apresenta. Apenas isso! Considero, portanto, despropositado questionar se se pode identificar alguma das posições dos três intervenientes no diálogo como sendo a do Autor. No domínio da teorização política, como noutros, o historiador mantém-se imparcial, pelo que, neste passo, apresenta todos os modelos de governação e respectivos governantes sem deixar transparecer qualquer juízo pessoal sobre a matéria.

Atenas, perfil de uma cidade modelo
(Athens Portrayed as a Model-City)

Maria de Fátima Silva (fanp13@gmail.com)
Universidade de Coimbra

Resumo – Produzida por poetas atenienses, para públicos atenienses, a expensas do governo de Atenas, não surpreende que a tragédia grega insista, em diversos tons, no elogio da cidade que lhe serve de moldura. Aliás a sua missão era 'política' em sentido etimológico, dirigida à *polis*, porque inspirada nas suas vivências e porque consciente de um papel didáctico, que a tornava 'conselheira' dos cidadãos. Assim, a par de uma análise sempre crítica de cada etapa da vida da cidade ao longo do séc. V a. C. – um período de grande agitação política e de permanente fluidez intelectual -, a tragédia adoptou também um tom de elogio, adequado a uma Atenas que procurava impor, no mundo grego, uma imagem de superioridade.

Palavras-chave: Eurípides, *Heraclidas, Hércules Furioso, Suplicantes, Ion,* Sófocles, *Édipo em Colono*

Abstract – As it was produced by Athenian poets for Athenian audiences, and subsidized by the Athenian government, it is not surprising that Greek tragedy contains, in diverse voices, an encomium of the city that provides its context. Its role was indeed political in an etymological sense, because it is inspired by the city's experiences and conscious of its own didactic role as counsellor of the citizens. This is why Greek tragedy, besides its always critical attention toward the city's life throughout the 5th century BC – a period both of substantial political turmoil and of intellectual change - adopted an encomiastic style as well, adjusting to an Athens which sought to impose upon the Greek world an image of superiority.

Keywords: Euripides, *Heraclidae, Hercules Furens, Suppliants, Ion,* Sophocles, *Oedipus Coloneus.*

Produzida por poetas atenienses, para públicos atenienses, a expensas do governo de Atenas, não surpreende que a tragédia grega insista, em diversos tons, no elogio da cidade que lhe serve de moldura. Aliás a sua missão era 'política' em sentido etimológico, dirigida à *polis*, porque inspirada nas suas vivências e porque consciente de um papel didáctico, que a tornava 'conselheira' dos cidadãos. Assim, a par de uma análise sempre crítica de cada etapa da vida da cidade ao longo do séc. V a. C. – um período de grande agitação política e de permanente fluidez intelectual -, a tragédia adoptou também um tom de elogio, adequado a uma Atenas que procurava impor, no mundo grego, uma imagem de superioridade.

No início do século, ao tempo das Guerras Pérsicas, Ésquilo, nos *Persas* (472 a. C., a tragédia que dedicou à batalha de Salamina, uma etapa decisiva no

https://doi.org/10.14195/978-989-26-1280-5_3

desfecho deste conflito), preocupava-se em estabelecer a supremacia da Grécia perante uma outra mentalidade, a oriental. E para cumprir esse objectivo dava a Atenas, no processo de resistência de uma aliança de cidades gregas, um ascendente incontroverso; esta era, para o velho poeta, a cidade que representava 'o espírito grego', nos seus ideais de coragem, patriotismo e, sobretudo, de liberdade e igualdade democrática. Com este retrato, Ésquilo explicava aos espectadores atenienses os motivos para um resultado tão imprevisto na batalha naval de Salamina; lá, onde os deuses estiveram, atentos a uma regulação equilibrada e justa do universo, um grande império, chefiado por um senhor monocrático, Xerxes, e assente na força e no número incontável dos seus efectivos, não teve capacidade para fazer frente a um país pequeno, pobre de recursos, mas animado de um ideal. E à frente desse país brilhava, com luz maior, o espírito ateniense.

Quando esta mesma Atenas, no fecho das Guerras Pérsicas, reconhecida por todos os Gregos como a protagonista do sucesso alcançado, se tornou uma ameaça temível por essa mesma vantagem, os poetas reorientaram o elogio de Atenas em novas perspectivas. O contraste estabelecia-se agora dentro do mundo grego, onde duas ligas, uma com Atenas, outra com Esparta diante, se disputavam. Em vez da reacção em nome da liberdade ameaçada por um invasor estrangeiro, discutia-se agora, dentro de fronteiras, o ascendente de uma ideologia política. Perante as outras cidades gregas, Atenas queria impor uma imagem de *arete*, afirmar os seus valores, fazer ver as vantagens das suas opções de cidade democrática; e, por todos esses méritos, ser aceite como cabeça de um império helénico. Vão neste sentido os múltiplos elogios que desta vez Sófocles e Eurípides lhe dedicaram, por vezes relativizados pela distância que separa um modelo ideal de uma realidade bem longe da perfeição.

'Única' entre todas as cidades da Grécia é um qualificativo que lhe cabe com uma insistência flagrante (E. *Heracl.* 151, *Supp.* 27-28, 188-189; S. *OC* 261-262, 1125-1126; Thuc. 2. 40. 4-5, 2. 41. 3). Neste 'única' vai contida a alusão a todas as virtudes de Atenas, quer as que provêm de uma origem superior, quer todas aquelas que, por mérito próprio, foi conquistando. Esse carácter de excepção ganha maior relevo por oposição ao anonimato das restantes ou sobretudo aos comportamentos de impiedade (E. *HF* 1285-1286), insolência (E. *Heracl.* 142-143, *Supp.* 384) ou cobardia (E. *Heracl.* 23-25, 144-146, 193-196, *Supp.* 188), que Argos, Tebas ou Esparta vão sucessivamente encarnando.

Na tragédia, a presença de Atenas materializa-se nos seus soberanos, figuras míticas que são a expressão da ancestralidade e símbolos de uma tradição coerente, que perpassou sucessivas gerações e constitui a sua marca identificativa. O *Íon* de Eurípides é a tragédia que melhor assinala a autoctonia como a primeira prerrogativa de Atenas[1] ('o povo autóctone da gloriosa Atenas', *Íon*

---

[1] *Vide* Rosivach 1977: 284-294.

29-30, 589-590, 735-737; cf. E. *Heracl.* 69, 826-827). Habitar a mesma terra desde tempos imemoriais estabelece entre os homens e a natureza que os cerca um vínculo profundo, que o mito exprimiu em termos ainda mais expressivos: autóctones são não só os que, desde sempre, habitaram o mesmo solo, mas aqueles que nasceram do próprio solo que habitam. O nascimento de Erictónio, antepassado mítico da casa real ateniense, marca uma etapa simbólica neste processo. Oriundo do solo (γηγενοῦς, *Ion* 20-21, 267-275, 999-1000), como legítimo 'filho da Terra', foi salvo do abandono dos pais pela deusa Atena, que o confiou, oculto num cesto, à primogénita de Cécrops, o soberano mítico do lugar (21-26). A curiosidade da princesa, que a levou, contra a determinação da deusa, a abrir o cesto e a espreitar-lhe o conteúdo, condenou à morte a culpada. Mas a partir deste episódio, para assinalar o vínculo das mães de Atenas com a sua deusa, salvadora de Erictónio e garantia de um continuador, originou-se o hábito de oferecer aos recém-nascidos uma serpente de ouro, como marca de origem, legitimidade e vínculo com a *polis*.

Deste mito fundador, Atenas manteve uma tradição que, ao tempo em que Eurípides compunha o *Íon* (c. 413-411 a. C.), gozava de grande simbolismo. Ser autóctone acumulava o mérito da antiguidade e o crédito de um passado que proporciona civilização e progresso. Enquanto povos migrantes procuravam ainda um rumo e um lugar onde estabelecer-se, já os autóctones perseguiam uma trajectória de desenvolvimento. Esta tradição - já referida em *Il.* 2. 547-548, que considera também Erecteu nascido do solo ático -, encontrou eco em autores contemporâneos de um tempo de afirmação de Atenas no mundo grego. Também Sófocles, *OC* 728, põe na boca do tebano Creonte, de visita à cidade, uma saudação aos 'nobres habitantes desta terra'; e Tucídides (2. 36. 1), no discurso, proferido por Péricles, de elogio aos caídos em combate no primeiro ano da Guerra do Peloponeso, não deixa de valorizar a mesma tradição. O reconhecimento dessa nobreza de raça, que se foi transmitindo como uma herança na casa real ateniense (cf. *Ion* 262-263, 1060, 1073, 1562), foi-se celebrizando, não só pela voz incansável dos poetas, mas em representações gráficas (*Ion* 271,1163-1165), em pintura e nos motivos de um tecido.

Teseu é, com certeza, a figura que melhor representa a excelência de uma cultura, depois de cumpridas todas as etapas, geracionais e civilizacionais, desde dias remotos[2]. Mas por detrás dele está seu pai, Egeu, 'filho do sábio Pandíon' (παῖς σοφοῦ Πανδίονος, *Med.* 665; cf. *Supp.* 6-7; S. *OC* 69, 549-550, 607), onde σοφός regista uma qualidade congénita nos soberanos de Atenas. As virtudes que Teseu encarna não são apenas resultado do espírito superior de que era dotado, mas também uma herança de tão ilustres progenitores a que não faltou sentido de justiça (*Supp.* 574-575) e amor à liberdade (Thuc. 2. 36. 2). Dos mesmos

---

[2] *Vide* Davie 1982: 25-34.

valores se fez transmissor aos seus dois descendentes, Demofonte e Acamante (*Heracl.* 34-38, 115, 320-326). Por isso, quando a tragédia traz a cena qualquer uma destas gerações 'gloriosas' (κλεινός, *Heracl.* 38, *Supp.* 656, *Ion* 1038, 1106), são iguais os valores que lhes estão atribuídos, pelo menos num plano ideal, como logótipo de identidade. Teseu, mesmo assim, é aquele que melhor se ajusta a esses ideais, uma espécie de dual contínuo com a cidade (*Supp.* 3-4, 27-28, 114, 382, 576, 1168, 1181, 1187; S. *OC* 558, 1519).

Mas quais são, em concreto, os comportamentos que fazem de Atenas uma cidade notável, e digna de todos os reconhecimentos e homenagens (*Supp.* 779-781, *Ion* 8), um paradigma para toda a Grécia (Thuc. 2. 41. 1)? Talvez a síntese de requisitos da *arete* enumerados por H. C. Avery[3] lhe possam assentar na perfeição: 'Importante para os homens era a obediência à vontade dos deuses, uma aceitação pronta dos fardos que lhes são impostos pelas fraquezas e temores dos companheiros, e pela disponibilidade para assumir riscos pessoais e políticos ou mesmo para aceitar sacrifícios em nome de ideais, crenças e responsabilidades'.

Pode a cidade orgulhar-se de gozar do patrocínio divino e da presença tutelar dos deuses, rendidos à sedução de um lugar paradisíaco, de que fizeram morada de eleição. Talvez Sófocles (*OC* 668-719) tenha sido o autor do maior elogio do que julgou 'o mais belo lugar da terra' (τὰ κράτιστα γᾶς ἔπαυλα, *OC* 669). Não lhe faltam os cantos harmoniosos dos rouxinóis, a verdura fresca e perene dos bosques, o colorido dos narcisos, o viço eterno da hera e da oliveira, o vigor dos cavalos, o rumorejar dos rios, o movimento ondulante do mar. Na perfeição idílica da sua paisagem, tomaram assento as Graças, as Musas e Afrodite (cf. *Heracl.* 379-380). Tocou-a Zeus de benesses, mas, sobre todos os deuses, protegeu-a Atena de olhos garços. Na deusa, o coro de *Heraclidas* reconhece 'a mãe, a senhora, a guardiã' do território e da cidade (770-772), a quem são devidas festas e celebrações, que animam, nas Panateneias, 'a colina batida pelos ventos' (777-783). O envolvimento da cidade com a sua padroeira espelha-se no nome, que uma recebeu da outra (E. *Ion* 9; S. *OC* 107-108); mas é também a excelência dos valores por que Atenas se rege o que deve garantir-lhe a benevolência divina e, com ela, a segurança e o respeito geral (*Heracl.* 901-903).

A piedade é, portanto, a primeira virtude da cidade de Palas e dos seus senhores (τὰ οἰκτρά, *Supp.* 190-191, σεβίζειν, S. *OC* 260-261, 1006-1007, 1125-1127). Implica o apelo, a prece, que traduz respeito e confiança, o reconhecimento, por parte dos homens, da superior vontade divina (*Supp.* 594-597): 'Tudo de que preciso' – afirma Teseu – 'é de ter os deuses do meu lado, os que patrocinam a vitória. É a aliança do seu socorro o que nos faz triunfar. A excelência de nada vale para os homens, se lhes faltar o apoio divino'. Como imagem da sua cidade, Etra, mãe de Teseu (*Supp.* 1 sqq.), dirige a Deméter,

---

[3] Avery 1971: 540.

a deusa de Elêusis, uma oração fervorosa, pedindo para a família real e para a cidade a bênção da deusa. Mas mais do que um apelo passivo, a piedade é um valor activo, que implica deveres e o cumprimento de regras; o acolhimento de perseguidos ou suplicantes a quem os deuses sempre dispensam protecção tem, entre esses deveres, prioridade[4]. E essa é uma regra de que Atenas, por tradição, mais do que nenhuma outra cidade grega, se mostrou cumpridora; pode afirmá--lo, sem hesitação, o coro nos *Heraclidas* (329-330): 'Desde sempre esta terra entendeu prestar aos aflitos o socorro a que têm direito' (cf. *Supp.* 32-36). Por isso, a protecção que Atenas recebe dos deuses é sobretudo a contrapartida da piedade que sabe dispensar aos que a suplicam (*Heracl.* 763-769).

Este é um valor que, nas *Suplicantes*, Teseu, ainda um jovem em formação[5] – ou, segundo outras interpretações, o modelo do político pragmático da nova Atenas[6] - apesar da responsabilidade que sobre ele impende, recebe da mãe, Etra, uma mulher carregada de experiência e uma espécie de elo transmissor, ao jovem monarca, da tradição ateniense e de um padrão heróico de existência. Conscientes da autoridade da rainha, é a ela que Adrasto e as mulheres argivas, mães dos heróis caídos às portas de Tebas – na campanha que Polinices desencadeou contra a cidade mãe para fazer valer os seus direitos ao trono -, dirigem os seus apelos: reclamam o direito de recuperar, para os sepultar condignamente, os cadáveres dos filhos (*Supp.* 24-26)[7]. O que está em causa, neste exemplo mítico, é a diplomacia de guerra, bem conhecida por uma sociedade sob pressão de um longo conflito. Aos suplicantes assiste um direito, o do sepultamento dos mortos em combate; a Etra cabe apelar ao sentido de dever, junto de um jovem superior (εὐτεκνία), apesar de ainda pouco amadurecido, ou, por força das circunstâncias, esquecido das implicações dos seus deveres (*Supp.* 65-70). Teseu merece, daqueles que o suplicam, o reconhecimento de provas inequívocas de *arete*; 'triunfante, senhor de muitas vitórias' (καλλίνικος, *Supp.* 113), 'o mais valente dos Gregos' (καθ᾽ Ἑλλάδ᾽ ἀλκιμώτατον κάρα, *Supp.* 163), 'homem ilustre entre todos na Grécia' (δοκιμώτατος, *Supp.* 277), são qualificativos que

---

[4] A justiça e a piedade estão subjacentes a este dever. Do mesmo modo, em *Heracl.* 101-104, o coro aconselha, em nome da justiça, o arauto argivo a não desrespeitar os direitos dos suplicantes; e logo a seguir pode condenar como ímpia (ἄθεον, 107-108) a cidade que se mostra surda às súplicas que lhe são dirigidas.

[5] Michelini 1994: *passim* salienta também a idade e o peso que ela tem na peça, para valorizar a imponderação e a ambição dos mais jovens, como um elemento perturbador de um político ideal.

[6] *Vide* Jiménez 1995: 150, estudo que sublinha as múltiplas e controversas interpretações a que esta peça foi sujeita.

[7] O tema do sepultamento dos caídos em combate é de enorme relevância numa sociedade sob a pressão de um longo conflito militar. Michelini 1994: 219 sublinha a relação que este tema tem com as orações fúnebres, um género muito em voga dentro do contexto de guerra. Daí resulta um compromisso claro entre a peça e outras formas de expressão do mesmo momento político.

abonam do sucesso militar e político de que o senhor de Atenas já deu provas. Falta-lhe, porém, associar ao rol de *aretai* a excelência moral, que a piedade e a filantropia exprimem[8]. Esse é um dos princípios que Etra faz valer junto de Teseu (*Supp.* 301-306) envolto em leves palavras de censura: 'É somente neste aspecto que a tua decisão, em tudo o mais tão sensata, falha'. É de diversos níveis a expectativa que Etra alimenta, quanto ao comportamento do filho: que actue como campeão das leis comuns aos gregos – neste caso a de sepultar os mortos (524-527, 531-538)[9] – e enfrente aqueles que ousam desrespeitá-la (307-313). Assim, além de satisfazer uma exigência sagrada, Teseu respeita a lei humana, condição para 'a salvação de uma cidade'. No plano pessoal, tem oportunidade de mostrar valentia, a qualidade de quem se dispõe a correr riscos pela defesa dos valores em que acredita (314-319), ao mesmo tempo que enobrece o nome que usa, o de 'filho de Etra' (320). Diante de Teseu – e do público de Eurípides – Etra hierarquiza uma escala de deveres: depois de honrar os deuses, há que defender o direito aceite por todos os Gregos, antes de se ter em conta o mérito pessoal e a dignidade da família de que se é herdeiro. Neste apelo da rainha, segundo vários comentadores, os valores firmes e heróicos, a carácter com a antiguidade do mito, associam-se com um sentido de ambição e de promoção social, que faz parte da mentalidade da Atenas da segunda metade do século; deste paradoxo de argumentos parece resultar um conflito entre a Atenas ideal, bastião da pureza de valores, e a real, a dos oportunismos políticos.

Consciente do alcance das recomendações maternas, Teseu desencadeia as diligências, políticas e militares, que lhe são exigidas[10]. Atento aos seus

---

[8] Fitton 1961: 430-431 colhe da actuação de Teseu a imagem 'de um político cauteloso mais do que a de um herói nacional'.

[9] Para alguns comentadores (*apud* Shaw 1982: 3) este é o grande tema da primeira parte da peça, a importância da lei e da sua defesa como um elemento de sobrevivência para uma cidade regulada.

[10] A complexidade da figura de Teseu está relacionada com a própria controvérsia na interpretação da peça. Depois de criticar Adrasto por, em nome de motivos nobres, cometer a insensatez de provocar uma guerra, Teseu resiste a acudir aos suplicantes, em conformidade com essa mesma posição; mas é evidente que, a essa coerência, corresponde a *apragmosyne*, ou seja, uma apatia que não responde à acção que um código heróico imporia; por outro lado, a decisão de intervir em nome dos suplicantes – e também do êxito pessoal, da valentia e da glória - arrasta-o para uma guerra, em contradição com a atitude pacifista que tinha defendido, levando-o de certa forma a repetir a insensatez que censurava em Adrasto. Como tanta vez acontece em Eurípides, em tempo de crise os melhores princípios parecem estranhamente contribuir para o mal e para a inconsequência. Fitton, 1961: 434-435, por seu lado, entrevê nesta decisão de guerra uma crítica à facilidade, bem conhecida da Atenas do tempo de Eurípides, com que os chefes políticos arrastavam a cidade para a guerra. Do seu ponto de vista, Teseu, inicialmente 'frio e prático', transforma-se 'num jovem tomado de zelo excessivo'. Sem dúvida o poeta pretendia espelhar os paradoxos com que anos de guerra confrontaram a cidade democrática, e avaliar o cromatismo plural de motivos que justificam cada decisão, mesmo as que se inspiram em ideais. Acaba discutindo o conceito de 'guerra justa', que para outros comentadores fundamenta a decisão do rei de Atenas.

movimentos, o coro de mães argivas reconhece nele (366-367, 558-563) a atitude de um homem piedoso e temente aos deuses (esta é uma característica consensualmente atribuída ao rei de Atenas; cf. E. *HF* 1236; S. *OC* 556). Vemo-lo capaz de enfrentar todos os riscos, para si mesmo e para a cidade, que o cumprimento de um dever – e talvez também alguma ambição – acarreta; é esse o sentido da proclamação que dirigiu aos seus homens na hora do combate (*Supp.* 670-672): 'Nós vimos resgatar os mortos para lhes dar sepultura. Defendemos um direito universal entre os Gregos. Não é a carnificina o que pretendemos'. Teseu parece aceitar a violência como uma necessidade, quando está em causa um bem maior. Cumprido o seu dever de recuperar os cadáveres, o monarca, agora amadurecido e mais sensível ao valor da piedade, leva mais longe o humanismo; por suas próprias mãos ocupa-se do enterramento dos cadáveres (763-766), para poupar as mães enlutadas à dor de verem, maltratado pela guerra, o que resta dos filhos (944, 946). A uma palavra de incentivo, Teseu crescia aos olhos de todos como um exemplo de piedade, ao mesmo tempo que descobria a acção como requisito, talvez egoísta, para conquistar glória e mérito social. É, neste contexto, a rainha quem valoriza a natureza superior do povo ateniense – mesmo se, por vezes, acusado de alguma fraqueza – e a importância de dispor de um chefe à altura que o conduza (321-323): 'Não vês como o teu povo, embora censurado por falta de determinação (ἄβουλος), é capaz de erguer a cabeça e lançar aos inimigos um olhar feroz? É no perigo que ele cresce'[11].

Dois valores afins da piedade, porque também eles focados na assistência e apoio a vítimas de perseguição e de perigos, são a *xenia*, 'hospitalidade', e a *philia*, 'amizade e solidariedade'. Sem deixarem de merecer a exigência e o apreço divinos, *xenia* e *philia* são também princípios com uma enorme carga social, num colectivo onde a protecção de cada indivíduo não encontra ainda uma resposta institucionalizada. Ambos assentam no dever de prestar, sem condições, socorro a quem se encontra em dificuldade; um simples 'estranho', no caso da *xenia*, alguém com vínculos de parentesco, amizade ou proximidade, no da *philia*. Assiste-lhes um alcance, antes do afectivo, pragmático. É sua regra elementar a reciprocidade, o dever de retribuir, em qualquer momento e com generosidade, os favores recebidos. Obedecem a uma tradição profunda na cultura grega, a avaliar pelo testemunho homérico. Quem os não cumpre, ainda na Grécia clássica, assemelha-se a um bárbaro, incivilizado e selvagem (*Heracl.* 130-131); portanto *xenia* e *philia* são marcas de identidade helénica. A observância, e o mérito que dela resulta, são reclamados por uma Atenas que se quer paradigma; afirmar-se hospitaleira e solidária faz parte da sua publicidade

---

[11] Michelini 1994: 231, interpreta estas palavras de Etra como o reflexo de uma polémica que dividia facções em Atenas nesta altura: entre os pacifistas de um lado, e aqueles que defendiam a guerra como um terreno onde se expõe brios e se repudia cobardias.

cívica, de cidade cosmopolita e aberta a todos. E, no entanto, em tempos de conflito, Atenas afirma-se, com algum exagero, como excepção, quando o egoísmo e os interesses políticos campeiam. Os filhos de Hércules, a mãe, Alcmena, e o velho companheiro, Iolau, um grupo indefeso depois da morte do herói, nos *Heraclidas*, afirmam esse sinal de decadência civilizacional como generalizado; vêm cumprindo um longo itinerário, foragidos de cidade em cidade (15-16), expulsos de toda a Grécia (31), face ao temor que se instalou perante as ameaças do perseguidor, o argivo Euristeu (19-20). Em último recurso, é de Atenas que esperam refúgio e protecção (305-306, 320-328). Por toda a Grécia soa a fama de uma Atenas hospitaleira, que nos chega, entre outras vozes, pela das mães argivas que, em *Suplicantes*, acorrem a Atenas (377-381): 'Acode a uma mãe, acode, cidade de Palas, não desprezes as leis humanas. Tu veneras a justiça, a injustiça reprova-la; tu és sempre, para todos os aflitos, a salvação'. É ainda com igual expectativa que o velho Édipo, depois de percorridos os penosos caminhos do exílio, se abeira de Atenas, a que é em uníssono louvada como a cidade entre todas piedosa e salvadora (S. *OC* 260-262, 2282-2283).

Alguns quadros dramáticos exploram a projecção e as nuances destes valores, sempre com Atenas como protagonista. É célebre o caso de Medeia, expulsa de Corinto e condenada ao exílio depois que Jasão, o marido traidor, a abandonou. Ao seu desespero vem responder Egeu, o rei de Atenas, de passagem pela cidade no regresso de Delfos, no preciso momento em que o coro da peça assinalava o terror supremo de quem não tem pátria a que se acolha (ἄπολις, *Med.* 644-651, 655), nem amigos em quem se apoie. Esta é a condição que Jasão e a cidade de Corinto têm para oferecer a Medeia. Perante o ateniense apiedado do seu olhar sombrio, Medeia assume uma atitude suplicante (709-711) e implora acolhimento numa cidade que sabe generosa. Esta é uma súplica a que Egeu responde, hierarquizando os motivos que o demovem: antes de quaisquer outros, o respeito pelos deuses (720); tal significa, em cumprimento de um dever, acolhê-la como sua hóspede (προσξενεῖν, 723-725, 730) e preservá-la de qualquer perseguição.

Deste episódio breve – e, para alguns comentadores, até dispensável – não faz parte a exploração do perigo a que, em geral, se expõe quem acolhe. Só ao de leve, o motivo é aludido por Egeu; não quer ser ele mesmo a levar Medeia para Atenas, para evitar a ruptura diplomática com Corinto; mas acrescenta (727-738), que se ela tomar a iniciativa de lá se dirigir pelos seus próprios meios, 'ficará inviolável, sem perigo de ser entregue seja a quem for'. J. R. Dunkle[12] assinala que, apesar desta promessa, a intervenção de Egeu não tem o brilho habitual nestas cenas do 'rei salvador'; há dois factores de egoísmo que lhe empalidecem a actuação: o interesse, de ganhar, com a ajuda que presta a Medeia, a

---

[12] Dunkle 1969: 106.

promessa de que ela o ajudará a combater a esterilidade; e o egoísmo, que o leva a respeitar um dever, procurando não incorrer em qualquer perigo. Mesmo assim, ainda que de forma condicionada, a cena de Egeu na *Medeia* de Eurípides põe em evidência o valor da *xenia* e o respeito que merece aos Atenienses.

Mais tenso, e mais rico de análise e de significado, é o uso de motivo equivalente em *Heraclidas*. Ameaçados são, nesse caso, os filhos de Hércules, com Alcmena e Iolau. O perseguidor, Euristeu, reclama que todas as portas se fechem aos fugitivos, com o argumento do poder de Argos, a cidade que dirige. Pelo seu poder, a simpatia ou antipatia de Argos não são despiciendas para aliados e amigos. O argumento político, muito discreto no caso de *Medeia*, ganha aqui uma força nova. A cidade de Euristeu é mais do que um exemplo de cobardia; exibe arrogância e crueldade para com os fracos. Perante o argumento do poder do mais forte, as diversas *poleis* a que os perseguidos se dirigem colocam mal a sua piedade; veneram não os deuses, mas o mais forte (τοὺς κρείσσονας σέβοντες, 23-25; cf. 109-110). Da vantagem desta atitude amoral fala um arauto, o representante, diante da autoridade ateniense, de uma política pragmática de alianças que Argos pratica. Acima da ética, há que pesar o lucro e os interesses; valerá a pena correr riscos por um velho e umas crianças indefesas (*Heracl.* 165-168; cf. *Supp.* 474-475), sem qualquer benefício palpável? Ao passo que a neutralidade, ou mesmo a aliança, com quem detém a força traz vantagens e poder (153-157, 176-178). Atenas coloca-se – única excepção – incondicionalmente do lado da justiça; o medo, o maior condicionador das decisões políticas na Grécia do momento (191-192)[13], não entra nas opções que se vê obrigada a tomar. A avaliação da *xenia*, abrangente nos *Heraclidas*, ganha também uma conotação política de grande importância, nas relações entre cidades, e dá a Atenas um lugar único na teia helénica de relações.

Havendo um parentesco entre Demofonte[14], aqui o rei de Atenas, e os Heraclidas (συγγενεῖς, 223-224), a questão do acolhimento reveste um outro nível de solidariedade, o familiar. À *xenia*, a hospitalidade devida a estranhos, vem juntar-se a *philia*, o apoio devido a amigos e parentes. Na ponderação que Demofonte faz dos seus deveres está patente, uma vez mais, uma ordem de prioridades (238-242); obriga-o, em primeiro lugar, Zeus, o protector dos suplicantes; depois o parentesco que tem com eles[15]; junta-se-lhe *charis*, 'a gratidão', que une a casa de Atenas a Hércules, outrora salvador de Teseu, quando prisioneiro de

---

[13] Esta perspectiva do medo como elemento central numa política de conflitos e alianças tem, na *História da Guerra do Peloponeso* de Tucídides, um relevo evidente.

[14] Demofonte não é personagem em nenhuma outra tragédia conhecida; são-lhe feitas apenas alusões; E. *Hec.* 123, *Tr.* 31; S. *Ph.* 562. Para Avery 1971: 546-547, esta preferência de Eurípides obtém o efeito de aproximar, em geração, o filho de Teseu dos filhos de Hércules.

[15] Em E. *HF* 207-212, Eurípides retoma este elemento da tradição, esclarecendo a genealogia que faz de Hércules e Teseu primos, parentesco de que estão conscientes as novas gerações de ambos os heróis, que agora se encontram frente a frente.

Hades (cf. *HF* 214-219); por fim, pesa nele um sentido de honra, que tem por contrapartida o temor da reprovação geral. O Demofonte que assim raciocina é o soberano consciente dos seus deveres e de cada uma das componentes que os definem[16].

Idêntica *philia* serve de suporte ao quadro que aproxima os dois heróis do passado, Hércules e Teseu, no *Hércules Furioso* de Eurípides. A hora é, para o grande herói da Grécia, o filho de Zeus e de Alcmena, depois de cumpridas com sucesso todas as suas façanhas, de enorme sofrimento. Vítima do ciúme de Hera, a esposa ofendida pelas infidelidades conjugais do divino marido, Hércules comete, sob o efeito de uma loucura passageira mas tempestuosa, a pior das chacinas: mata Mégara, a mulher, e os filhos, a quem o herói protector dos fracos devia, antes de mais, proteger. Devolvido à lucidez, para constatar – crueldade suprema da deusa ofendida – o resultado da perturbação que fez dele um homicida, Hércules, em desespero, pondera o próprio suicídio. Hera reduziu o inimigo, apesar de inocente, a um farrapo humano. É então que chega o salvador, Teseu, para, em nome de *charis*, a gratidão devida ao salvador de outrora, acorrer em seu socorro. Mas acima da retribuição face a uma dívida em aberto, o Teseu desta peça é sobretudo um paradigma de *philia*, de uma solidariedade não só activa, mas também emocional e afectiva.

A saudação com que um Hércules desesperado anuncia a vinda de Teseu – 'meu parente e meu amigo' (συγγενὴς φίλος τ' ἐμός, *HF* 1154) – define o nível de uma expectativa. E porque a amizade é, para os Gregos, um bem activo e útil, Teseu vem revestido de armas, porque não é só a palavra de consolo que traz, mas um socorro efectivo, se necessário (1163-1165). Neste caso, a *philia*, empolada como um valor, além de prático, emotivo, dispensa a componente política e situa-se principalmente no plano pessoal. Com o arredar do véu que cobre o rosto e a vergonha do homicida (1214-1215), Teseu penetra na intimidade do amigo, para lhe declarar o conteúdo da *philia* tal como a entende (1223-1225): 'Detesto os amigos para quem a gratidão envelhece, dispostos a partilharem os bons momentos, mas abandonando o barco quando chega a hora da desgraça' (cf. 1338-1339). Mais do que palavras de consolação, Teseu oferece ao amigo a hospitalidade de Atenas (1324-1333), asilo, purificação, presentes e um culto que lhe imortalize a memória. Ao mesmo tempo que homenageia um grande homem – apesar da sua experiência profundamente dolorosa -, o rei colhe para Atenas as homenagens de toda uma Grécia que saiba reconhecer o valor da solidariedade (1334-1335).

A defesa dos valores ganha uma qualidade suprema quando, para satisfazer imposições da consciência moral, inclui risco para quem a concede. Respeitar a

---

[16] Demofonte não sente necessidade de consultar o povo, a sua decisão é firme e imediata, de tal forma são claras as obrigações que a situação exige.

piedade, solidariedade ou o acolhimento põe à prova a responsabilidade de um soberano, repartido entre o dever de prestar assistência e o risco a que expõe a própria vida e a dos seus. Há, portanto, na decisão que lhe é exigida, um dilema, em cuja solução os cidadãos têm uma palavra a dizer. Dentro de um quadro de vida democrática, ainda que no respeito pelas figuras simbólicas do mito e pela sua individualidade, rei e povo funcionam como uma única voz. A autoridade popular é uma presença incorporada na própria personalidade do rei. É em uníssono que Atenas pode afirmar a sua independência, posta em contraste com as opções politicas das cidades adversárias[17].

Argos é, em *Heraclidas*, como Tebas em *Suplicantes*, um desses contrapontos. Ἐλευθέρα, 'livre', é um qualificativo aplicado a Atenas com insistência evidente (*Heracl.* 61-62, 111-113, 197-198, 244-245, 285-287, 957). 'Livre' significa capaz de uma afirmação corajosa, de uma confrontação determinada, perante todos os que, com ameaças, pretendem exigir-lhe uma decisão que afecta os seus princípios. Assim nos *Heraclidas*, diante do arauto argivo – um motivo que, nas suas linhas gerais, se repete em *Suplicantes* – que persegue os parentes de Hércules, Iolau afirma a liberdade de Atenas, um valor que lhe permite proteger os mais fracos contra a arrogância dos mais fortes (61-62; cf. *Supp.* 518-521). Esta é uma tradição sem a qual Atenas se descaracteriza (*Heracl.* 197-198); faz parte da sua natureza perseverar no bem, 'preferir morrer, porque, aos olhos da gente de bem, a honra conta mais do que a vida' (200-201). Esta, que é a imagem que a cidade projecta para o exterior, está bem entranhada na consciência dos Atenienses, a crer no eco que encontra no próprio soberano, Demofonte (*Heracl.* 243-246): ceder é trair os suplicantes, mas sobretudo abdicar do bem maior da liberdade. Pelo seu comportamento ético e generoso, Atenas ganha 'amizades' e cobra reconhecimentos, criando em volta de si mesma uma teia de alianças promissoras para a sua segurança e ascendente (*Heracl.* 309-318, *Supp.* 373-374, 1169-1181, 1187-1188, 1191-1195; S. *OC* 629-630, 1496-1498, 1552-1555; cf. Thuc. 2. 40. 4). Percebe-se, por trás de uma política democrática, um objectivo imperialista, potencialmente ameaçador da limpidez dos valores tradicionais, numa correlação com a vivência do séc. V a. C. ateniense.

Prezar a liberdade é também, no plano interno, conferir esse mesmo direito a cada um dos cidadãos, sem mesmo assim prescindir da valorização do mérito e do benefício da clarividência dos melhores (Thuc. 2. 37. 1-2). E os melhores são, nos exemplos trágicos que vimos a analisar, representados pelo rei da cidade. Todos eles são tidos como o fruto de uma educação ajustada, que a cidade aplica aos seus homens (*Supp.* 913-917)[18]: 'A coragem (εὐανδρία) é matéria que se ensina

---

[17] No *OC* 911-916, a ameaça vem de um indivíduo, Creonte, o representante de uma facção com interesses próprios; a atitude injusta que assume merece a discordância da cidade a que pertence (921-923).

[18] Tucídides 2. 39. 1 inclui também no elogio de Atenas o papel essencial da educação, que,

(διδακτός), se é certo que se ensina uma criança a falar, a ouvir, o que por si só ela não alcança. E o que se aprende em criança, o adulto conserva-o até à velhice. Por isso, eduquem bem os vossos filhos'. O conselho, escutado com respeito e atenção, acrescenta saber e apura as almas mais dotadas; esse é o papel que Etra, a velha rainha, desempenha junto de um Teseu mais jovem, em *Suplicantes*, de modo a enriquecer-lhe a capacidade pragmática de reinar com a responsabilidade humanística que um verdadeiro chefe não dispensa. A experiência pessoal do sofrimento é mais um contributo na formação de um adulto pleno. Perante Édipo, velho e destroçado por anos de exílio, no *Édipo em Colono*, Teseu, desta vez amadurecido também pelas penas do exílio, manifesta uma piedade assente na compreensão, de quem viveu o mesmo destino (562-568). A lição de vida que ambos receberam, como tantos outros homens poderosos, é idêntica: o que poderá reservar-lhes o dia seguinte, quando a fortuna humana é tão incerta? É sobre todos estes pressupostos que se construiu a figura de um Teseu, tal como a cidade que representa, um paradigma de virtudes ideais, mesmo se abaladas por uma realidade decadente.

No exercício do poder, do rei espera-se que projecte o resultado das suas qualidades pessoais, associadas à moldagem que família e sociedade nele imprimiram. Apesar de representante natural da cidade e interlocutor primeiro de todos os que a ela recorrem, no respeito pela democracia em que vive o soberano não decide sem consultar o voto colectivo; a audiência é, de facto, concedida aos suplicantes pela cidade (*Heracl.* 95-96). Quando a decisão é extrema – como aquela que os oráculos impuseram a Demofonte, nos *Heracl.* 411-413, de sacrificar a vida de uma jovem para garantir a vitória na guerra –, a sensatez do rei é posta à prova. Executor de uma autoridade comedida, Demofonte recusa-se a matar ou a obrigar alguém a fazê-lo contra sua vontade. Mesmo que fundamentada pela vontade divina, tal exigência produziria uma guerra civil, entre os que a aplaudissem e os que a censurassem (418-419). A moderação democrática não se compadece com excessos (423-424): 'É que eu não sou um tirano, como os há entre os bárbaros. Devo agir com justiça, para ser tratado com justiça'.

Sabe-o, em geral, o monarca de Atenas, exige-o, com força maior, Teseu, que se arroga o papel de criador da democracia, como algo que faz parte do 'espírito ateniense' desde os seus primórdios[19] (*Supp.* 349, 'quero que a cidade inteira me aprove'; 352-353, 'dei à cidade a liberdade e a igualdade de voto'). E apesar de saber que o povo o aprovará – partilhados que são, por um e outro, os mesmos princípios –, não prescinde de lhe dar a palavra, depois de o persuadir da importância dos seus deveres (350-351, 355-356)[20]. Esta conivência entre chefes

---

dispensando-se de severidades extremas, dá, mesmo assim, bons frutos.

[19] Tornou-se comum, no séc. V a. C., atribuir a Teseu a reforma da constituição monárquica; cf. Arist. *Ath.Pol.* 41. 2; Plu. *Th.* 25.

[20] Houve comentadores da peça (e. g., Fitton 1961: 433) que assinalaram o paradoxo entre

e povo merece a Eurípides, o contemporâneo dos demagogos, uma reflexão mais ampla. Convencido da necessidade de agir, o Teseu de *Suplicantes* desempenha o seu papel: faz valer, diante do povo, os seus deveres, mobiliza-lhe a vontade e prepara-se para enfrentar o inimigo (393-394). Este consenso entre o soberano e o povo vai ter o seu momento de afirmação e de comentário no diálogo que o rei trava com o arauto de Tebas, a voz em cena do inimigo, que é também um confronto entre dois modelos de poder, o democrático e o monárquico[21].

A explicação dada por Péricles, no discurso que Tucídides lhe atribui de elogio a Atenas (2. 37. 1), para o nome do regime que Atenas pratica – 'como tudo depende não de um pequeno número, mas da maioria, chama-se-lhe democracia' – torna central, no projecto como na denominação, a natureza do regulador. O chefe, promotor da organização e da iniciativa colectiva, é a mola essencial do modelo. Se um só ou múltiplo, nele reside a chave de todas as variantes[22].

A defesa do poder de um só, que é a posição do arauto tebano, assenta num pressuposto frágil: o da superior qualidade do chefe, que parece uma circunstância de excepção. Várias vozes se levantam para apontar os vícios de um chefe único (423-425), o que merece o título de *tyrannos*. A pergunta ingénua do arauto (399) – 'onde está o vosso tirano?' – recebe de Teseu uma rejeição enérgica (403-404), em nome da cidade onde o poder está entregue ao povo[23]. Na monarquia, acusa Teseu, falta a organização cívica e o escrutínio popular, algo como 'a prestação de contas' praticada pela democracia ateniense, no fim do exercício de um cargo pelos magistrados em rotação (406-407; cf. *Heracl.* 223). Ao poder absoluto associa-se inevitavelmente o orgulho, em resultado da prosperidade, e a inveja, que não devia existir em quem tudo tem; mas a verdade é que o tirano tende a competir com os melhores, os que lhe fazem sombra (445-446), e a aproximar-se dos súbditos invertebrados e bajuladores. O monarca evolui para o déspota e não hesita perante o crime; desrespeita as regras e os valores ancestrais, dá desafogo aos impulsos íntimos e à satisfação de prazeres reprováveis; mata sem critério, porque a lei é ele mesmo quem a faz (430-432).

---

a autoridade de que o povo goza em Atenas e a certeza que o rei pode ter da anuência colectiva à sua vontade. O comentário feito por Tucídides a propósito do governo de Atenas sob a superintendência de Péricles (2. 65. 9) – 'em teoria uma democracia, na prática um poder subordinado a um único homem' – vem naturalmente à nossa memória.

[21] Este debate, que implica uma ruptura cronológica com a Atenas mítica em que o Teseu tradicional se move, replica em cena uma discussão de grande interesse para a Atenas do séc. V.

[22] Dentro do mesmo ponto de vista, Romilly 1959: 81-99, defende que a subdivisão de formas de governo, de três – as que os testemunhos do séc. V a. C. consideravam – para seis – que encontramos nos filósofos do séc. IV, Platão e Aristóteles – depende exactamente deste factor: de uma estrutura baseada na atribuição do poder, partiu-se para a valorização da qualidade do seu agente; passou então a distinguir-se como determinante o funcionamento, bom ou mau, de cada um dos três modelos primitivos.

[23] No entanto, Teseu é o rei de Atenas, o que assinala a diferença entre as palavras 'tirano' e 'monarca', isto é, a forma má ou boa de realeza (cf. Arist. *Rh.* 1365b; X. *Mem.* 4. 6. 12).

A iniciativa individual que conduz ao progresso, prática dos melhores, é barrada pelo tirano; a própria concentração do poder desmoraliza a iniciativa: para quê produzir fortuna, se ela vai cair nas mãos do tirano (450-451)? Até mesmo o desrespeito social pelas filhas de família, que é marca de egoísmo, faz parte da forma como o tirano humilha os melhores (452-455).

Por contraposição, a democracia é referida como o modelo que mais elogios merece. Acima de qualquer outro princípio, a lei aparece como a condição essencial de uma sociedade equilibrada. Tucídides (2. 36. 4, 37. 1) especifica as condições a que a lei deve obedecer num regime de qualidade. Deve, antes de mais, ser adequada à índole de cada povo; a importação neste caso é nefasta: 'O nosso regime político' – diz Péricles no seu discurso – 'não se propõe usar as leis (νόμους) dos outros; somos mais autores do que imitadores'. Eurípides (*Supp.* 430-436) introduz novos factores numa lei sólida e fiável; a lei deve ser pensada no interesse de todos, e não propriedade arbitrária de quem governa. Assim entendida, elimina fracturas como a que a riqueza ou a classe social produzem. A objectividade que lhe é exigida é assegurada pela versão escrita dos fundamentos legais, como garantia de permanência e de imparcialidade. Se convencidos do rigor da lei, os cidadãos tendem a pôr de parte o recurso a uma justiça pessoal e popular. O proveito mais louvável de uma lei eficaz chama-se liberdade, um valor que interfere positivamente na vida individual e colectiva (Thuc. 2. 37. 2). Liberdade pressupõe, no funcionamento democrático, partilha de poder e intervenção individual nos destinos colectivos. A relação de quem governa com toda a comunidade é assegurada pelo maior instrumento da liberdade: o uso livre e igual da palavra – a *parrhesia* e a *isegoria* (*Heracl.* 181-183, *Ion* 671-672), que elimina prerrogativas de classe (435-441); 'o fraco pode responder ao insulto do forte, e o pequeno, se a razão lhe assiste, pode vencer o grande'. Mas o direito à palavra inclui também a protecção da diferença; nem todos, neste recurso, têm igual competência; logo a *isegoria* proporciona, aos que têm para isso capacidade, ensejo de pôr a sua prudência ao serviço do bem comum; mas o direito de brilhar não elimina a prerrogativa contrária, a de manter o silêncio. Em tal regime, a verdadeira *arete* não tem a ver com riqueza, numa arquitectura em que ricos e pobres são iguais (407-408; cf. Thuc. 2. 37. 1); não é por falta de meios que o indivíduo capaz se vê privado de colaborar no interesse comum.

A todas estas virtudes que rodeiam o modelo de uma cidade ideal acresce a valentia, o vigor bélico, que exige à *polis* o cumprimento de uma tradição épica. No campo de batalha, se necessário, Atenas põe à prova os seus valores. Antes de conseguida a vitória, um brado do rei para mobilização dos subordinados lembra ainda os ideais que lhes devem justificar cada golpe; são eles que consolidam, na hora do perigo, todas as vontades num só braço (*Heracl.* 825-827, 839-840, *Supp.* 710-712). Mas obtido o sucesso, ao soberano cabe ainda uma palavra de contenção, para evitar excessos ou saques ambiciosos, que poriam em causa o objectivo, apenas altruísta, da campanha (*Heracl.* 964-966, 1012-1013, *Supp.* 723-730).

O tempo, no entanto, permitiu constatar que, sob um traçado ideal, a democracia denunciava fraquezas. A realidade provou a modéstia daqueles que assumiram as rédeas do poder. Na prática, as questões económicas e o estatuto social estabeleceram diferenças; os pobres, os lavradores humildes, não têm capacidade de intervir (420-421). A honestidade não compensa, porque o êxito cabe aos oportunistas, gente anónima catapultada para o poder, cuja arma poderosa é o discurso (423-425). A oratória, em vez de servir à construção de decisões ponderadas, é usada demagogicamente, na compra de votos em favor de interesses ocultos (412-416). Por seu lado, a massa anónima é susceptível ao logro e atraída pelo vazio dos discursos (417-418). Falta-lhe cultura, educação e, por isso, competência. A chamada 'psicologia de massas' não é mais inócua do que a *hybris* do tirano; precipitação e excesso são as suas propensões naturais. Mas apesar dos seus defeitos, a Atenas democrática podia, mesmo assim, orgulhar-se do avanço que a sua experiência governativa representava, para o mundo grego e afinal para toda a Humanidade.

Alcibíades em Plutarco:
O espelho da Pólis ateniense em época de crise
(Alcibiades in Plutarch: the mirror of the Athens in a time of crisis)

Maria do Céu Fialho (mcfialhofluc@gmail.com)
CECH/Universidade de Coimbra

Resumo - O jovem Alcibíades tem todos os atributos para se vir a tornar num político brilhante e conduzir Atenas ao equilíbrio político e a uma posição forte na guerra. Sócrates percebe que Alcibíades contém o germe de qualidades que o podem levar à Filosofia e ao Bem. No entanto, à influência de Sócrates sobrepõe-se a influência dos aduladores que incentivam, em Alcibíades, a vaidade, a ambição, o gosto pelo protagonismo fácil. Os múltiplos escândalos em que se envolveu levam a que o povo o admire e o tema, a ponto de Alcibíades procurar refúgio em Esparta. Político volúvel, e depois de mais escândalos em Esparta, passará à Pérsia, será de novo recebido em Atenas e de novo expulso. O modo como Plutarco constrói a sua narrativa biográfica converte Alcibíades na imagem da sua cidade em tempo de crise.

Palavras-chave: Alcibíades, Atenas, Sócrates, vaidade, ambição, eros.

Abstract - The young Alcibiades has all attributes that allowed one to expect him to become a brillant politician and to lead Athens into political stability and to a strong position in the war. Socrates perceives in Alcibiades the seeds of qualities that can lead him to the Philosophy and to the Good. Nevertheless Socrates's influence on him is eroded by the influence of adulators who encouraged Alcibiades's vanity, ambition and inclination toward facile self-dramatization.. The numerous scandals to which he was connected provoked people's attraction and fear, so that Alcibiades fled to Sparta. As an inconstant politician, and after new scandals in Sparta, Alcibiades went to Persia and thereafter will be received back again at Athens and again expelled from Athens. The way that Plutarch conceives his biographical narrative converts Alcibiades into an image of his polis in time of crisis.

Key words: Alcibiades, Athens, Socrates, vanity, ambition, eros.

A figura de Alcibíades ficou, na memória histórica dos Gregos e para a posteridade, como a de um indivíduo bafejado pela fortuna e pela beleza, nascido de nobres famílias, invulgarmente inteligente e ambicioso mas, ao mesmo tempo, incapaz de dominar os seus impulsos ou de resistir em se fazer centro das atenções, quer por uma coragem notável, quer por gestos reprováveis.

As expectativas que este jovem, de ascendência aristocrática, faz criar na Atenas do tempo, agitada pela Guerra do Peloponeso, exposta às ameaças e até invasão da facção espartana, desgastada por campanhas de pesadas consequências, conhecendo, no palco de guerra, uma terceira presença com que ambas as facções vão cautelosamente jogando (os Persas), serão expectativas levadas a um

https://doi.org/10.14195/978-989-26-1280-5_4

ponto demasiado elevado, pelos seus talentos e pela sua pose, ou defraudadas e motor de ódio colectivo, como resposta à sua volubilidade.

Como é típico da escrita biográfica de Plutarco, a estrutura e configuração da *Vita* 'diz' o carácter do biografado.

Assim, não encontramos nesta biografia propriamente um prólogo, a determinar um ritmo de gradação e uma reflexão prévia até se entrar na matéria biográfica[1]. Plutarco entra, no caso de Alcibíades, directamente na matéria biográfica: Alcibíades descende de heróis da saga épica: Clínias, seu pai, pertencia à família dos Eupátridas, que se dizia descendente de Ájax, e alia-se, pelo casamento, a uma das famílias mais notáveis de Atenas, a dos Alcmeónidas, a que pertencera Clístenes. Sua mãe era filha de Mégacles, irmão de Péricles.

Seu pai combateu os Persas em Artemísio e os Beócios em Coroneia, onde morreu. A coragem do pai parece ser espelho dos futuros feitos militares do filho. Péricles e Arífron foram então seus tutores. Plutarco faz questão de informar o leitor de que Alcibíades teve uma mulher da Lacónia, como ama, de que nos dá o nome, Amicla, como que para deixar no ar essa ligação a Esparta, premonitória da que futuramente terá, a par da ascendência ateniense - e como pedagogo um homem chamado Zópiro, de quem mais nada se diz.

A referência à ama lacónia, a par da mais ilustre ascendência ateniense, insinua, como perceberá o leitor a posteriori, o próprio caos em que se tornará a carreira política de Alcibíades, general de Atenas, desertor em Esparta (depois na Pérsia), de novo herói em Atenas, que tinha, à partida, todas as condições para se tornar um político de carreira fulgurante. Assim o sublinha Plutarco ao notar (1.3, 3-7) que: "De Nícias, Demóstenes, Lâmaco, Fórmion, Trasibulo e Terâmenes, que foram homens ilustres e seus contemporâneos, não se sabe sequer o nome da mãe de um só deles, enquanto de Alcibíades conhecemos até o nome da ama..."

Plutarco antecipa também aqui, como uma espécie de determinante da futura sorte de Alcibíades, o papel da presença de Sócrates na sua vida: foi a *eunoia* e a *philanthropia* do filósofo que contribuiram substancialmente para a *doxa* de que o jovem viria a gozar (1.3.) (ainda que os seus defeitos não domados a tivessem gerido mal).

Da sua excepcional e incorruptível beleza física, de que outros autores dão também testemunho[2], Plutarco passa para a referência às inconsistências de carácter reveladas na idade adulta (2.1):

Τὸ δ'ἦθος αὐτοῦ πολλὰς μὲν ὕστερον, ὡς εἰκὸς ἐν πράγμασι μεγάλοις καὶ τύχαις πολυτρόποις, ἀνομοιότητας καὶ πρὸς αὐτὸ μεταβολὰς ἐπεδείξατο.

---

[1] Stadter (1988) 275-295 distingue duas espécies de prólogos, nas *Vitae* de Plutarco, e inclui o da presente *Vita* no grupo dos prólogos integrados.

[2] Xenofonte, *Mem.* 1.2,24. Veja-se, também, a abertura do *Protágoras* de Platão.

O seu carácter, numa fase posterior da sua vida, manifestou-se inconsequente e instável, como é natural, dadas as empresas em que esteve envolvido e as vicissitudes da sorte que o atingiu.

O autor sublinha, nestas considerações prolépticas, como se viria a reconhecer em Alcibíades um *philonikos* e *philoprotos*, para regressar à sua infância e juventude e ilustrar, com breves anedotas, o carácter que já se anunciava. A sua rebeldia para com os mestres denuncia até que ponto este jovem promissor é avesso à influência da educação e sabe desde cedo, por intuição, jogar com as circunstâncias e manipular, servindo-se dos seus dotes. Mostra Th. Duff[3] até que ponto esta ordenação aparentemente caótica dos capítulos iniciais da vida de Alcibíades contém uma semiótica própria. Plutarco joga com uma espécie de prefiguração do que será a própria anarquia da vida do biografado, embora os episódios relatados corroborem a sua extrema incrível capacidade de resposta rápida às situações e o seu arrojo. Uma leitura mais superficial deixaria o leitor criar expectativas de estar perante um indivíduo genial — que o era — de quem se poderia vir a esperar um brilhante futuro.

Não foi qualquer um que Sócrates vislumbrou como capaz, por natureza, de se dedicar à filosofia. Mas essa mesma *physis* envolvia o embrião da paixão pelo protagonismo e a irresistível vaidade de quem quer ser admirado por todos e centro de todas as atenções. Daí os vários episódios de escândalo ou exibicionismo em que se envolvia, como o do saque no banquete de Ânito (4.5-6), a agressão ao mestre que não possuia um exemplar de Homero, as suas aparições públicas com um longo manto de púrpura, para não falar na questão da mutilação dos hermes e na paródia dos Mistérios, uma vez que não é de arredar a hipótese de que esta tenha sido uma campanha orquestrada para ferir a sua credibilidade.

Plutarco apresenta a consolidação do *ethos* de Alcibíades como fruto de uma vitória desses atributos negativos sobre a influência de Sócrates – e essa vitória tem algo de dramático. Sempre que Sócrates tentava trazer Alcibíades à temperança e à filosofia, a força da *tyche*, como uma força adversa, fazia que entre os dois se interpusesse o círculo de aduladores de Alcibíades, que assim o arredava da influência do filósofo.

Esta espécie de tensão agonística entre as potencialidades do biografado (aqui vislumbradas por Sócrates) e o embrião de forças negativas, na sua *physis*, que agentes externos, estímulos e contingências fazem soltar para sufocar as primeiras, é recorrente, aliás, em outras biografias de Plutarco.

Neste contexto revela-se particularmente interessante o caso da *Vida de Alcibíades*. Sobre esta fascinante e polémica figura afirma Plutarco (4.2.)

---

[3] Duff (2003) 94 sqq.

— curiosamente no mesmo capítulo inicial em que refere, de forma enfática, a força positiva da presença de Sócrates:

Οὐδένα γὰρ ἡ τύχη περιέσχεν ἔξωθεν οὐδὲ περιέφραζε τοῖς λεγομένοις ἀγαθοῖς τοσοῦτον ὥστ'ἄτρωτον ὑπὸ φιλοσοφίας γενέσθαι...

É que não há outro homem a quem a fortuna tenha envolvido e rodeado de um tal conspecto de atributos, para o tornar invulnerável à filosofia...

O texto citado pertence ao conjunto de capítulos iniciais que se ocupam, de modo deliberadamente desordenado assim parece - da ascendência e de episódios da infância e adolescência desta figura. E a posterior referência a um dos seus admiradores, aliás por si humilhado na famosa cena do banquete – Ânito – mais insinua essa luta, na vida de Alcibíades, entre a influência do 'bom eros' de Sócrates, por um lado, e o eros dissoluto do grupo de aduladores que o envolviam: é que Ânito é, precisamente, um dos perseguidores e juíz no julgamento de Sócrates, que levará o filósofo à condenação à morte, como se sabe.

Para além dos dotes de inteligência, beleza, força e coragem, capacidade de sedução, Alcibíades distinguia-se pelos seus dotes oratórios (e.g.10.4) além de um sentido estratégico apurado e uma pronta capacidade de resposta às situações. Péricles era amigo dos mais notáveis sofistas, e deve ter dado ao seu sobrinho ensejo para educação retórica e treino oratório. Como nota Romilly[4], em Atenas, ao tempo, a democracia directa, em que a Assembleia tinha um papel determinante, permitia que qualquer cidadão tomasse a palavra. Era fácil e natural que um cidadão de famílias notáveis e de excepcionais dotes oratórios dominasse a Assembleia, como foi o caso de Alcibíades. Ele foi responsável pelas campanhas atenienses de maior êxito na Guerra do Peloponeso, mas igualmente responsável por reveses que a sua cidade pátria sofreu, responsável por se quebrar um acordo de paz (Paz de Nícias), pela sofreguidão de protagonismo e comando. É que aos dotes naturais correspondiam características que os moldavam e conduziam, muitas vezes, no sentido das piores condutas.

Alcibíades ficou conhecido como alguém de vaidade desmedida, de extrema ambição, a que se associava a procura incontida de notoriedade. Tais características são já palpáveis no primeiro episódio em que ele participa, no contexto da Guerra do Peloponeso, segundo Tucídides (50.5.43)[5]. A propensão para o excesso determinou a sua vida dissoluta, rodeado de amantes, entregue à bebida e à influência de aduladores. Estes traços negativos, potenciados por factores de ordem externa, levaram a que a influência filosófico-pedagógica de Sócrates[6], que,

---

[4] Romilly 1995: 60.
[5] Romilly 1995: 59.
[6] Becchi (1999) 25-43.

como se disse, nele soube vislumbrar o que havia de virtude e potencial congénito, se esbatesse e fosse anulada, como se a *Tyche*[7], como um vento, arredasse o filósofo e envolvesse o jovem por essa nuvem de agentes de dissolução. Não é alheio ao retrato desta relação o *Banquete* de Platão, bem como a abertura de *Protágoras* (309a 1-2)[8].

A sua existência agitada e instável é imagem da da própria pólis ateniense do tempo da sua maturidade, envolvida na Guerra do Peloponeso, onde se jogaram interesses, alianças, sedições e traições que levaram Atenas da hegemonia à queda e perda da democracia de que tanto se orgulhava. Se os cidadãos temiam os traços que, em Alcibíades, poderiam denunciar a sua propensão para a tirania, foi, contudo, sem Alcibíades, que sofreram a experiência tirânica imposta pelos inimigos, no final da guerra.

Não admira, pois, que a figura de Alcibíades tivesse atraído a inveja dos seus contemporâneos e que, mediante acusações de fundamento nebuloso, tivessem querido anular a sua preponderância para, depois, lamentarem o facto de, com isso, o terem empurrado para a facção inimiga. É o próprio Tucídides quem reconhece (6.15.4) que Atenas sofreu um grande prejuízo ao ter-se descartado de Alcibíades, para dar ouvidos a outros, ainda que o tivesse feito por temer eventuais intuitos escondidos, baseada no que conhecia da sua vida privada.

O fascínio que esta personagem exerceu na Antiguidade e continua a exercer até nós está comprovado pelo número de autores antigos, quer contemporâneos quer posteriores, que lhe devotaram atenção, na sua obra: Aristófanes, Tucídides, Xenofonte, Platão, Teofrasto, a filosofia de tradição platónica, estóicos como Zenão e Cleantes, oradores diversos, historiógrafos dos sécs. IV e III a. C., historiadores romanos, autores de literatura biográfica, de que distingo Cornélio Nepos, e, não esquecer, Plutarco.

Do mesmo modo, o fim da vida de Alcibíades condensa, numa espécie de simbologia, a síntese da sua própria existência: é um fim envolto em incerteza, polémico, escandaloso e ambíguo pela própria cosmética feminina com que aparece no seu sonho premonitório e pelas vestes de cortesã com que, por fim, Timandra o cobre.

O processo de condensação simbólica constitui um recurso de escrita do gosto de Plutarco, para tornar mais forte o poder de sugestão do quadro final sobre o percurso que a ele leva.

Outros desfechos de biografias o ilustram, como, por exemplo, o da de Teseu, de Catão de Útica ou de César. Esta última envolve na narrativa o fim do assassinado, do assassino e da república romana. Diga-se, de passagem, que se trata de um recurso próprio da narrativa poética e que provoca, por parte do

---

[7] Pérez Jiménez (1973) 103 sqq.
[8] Ramsey 2012: 63.

leitor, uma adesão ao texto que está para além da razão e que se prende com os efeitos de sugestão e representação próprios de uma escrita poética.

Por outro lado, o registo da beleza física antecede considerações sobre o *ethos* de alguém que parece preso não só das alterações da fortuna, mas da sua própria beleza que o condiciona a ser admirado e assediado sem ter estrutura ética para resistir à pressão desse assédio. Alcibíades apresenta-se, à partida, condicionado por essa beleza, pelo arrojo demonstrado, por um carácter fraco e volúvel e por uma inteligência brilhante a desempenhar um agitado protagonismo na vida de Atenas. Frequentemente utiliza Plutarco a conjugação *tolma kai synesis* para definir esses actos de arrojo que vão da infância ao fim da vida. Não é *andreia* o termo escolhido — mas este é o termo que Plutarco selecciona, em contrapartida, para designar a coragem de Coriolano e sublinha, na biografia correspondente, que este termo equivale ao que os Romanos designam por *arete*. Isto é, adivinhamos no grego do autor, o esforço de equiparação ao latim *uirtus*. Com ela se conjugam a temperança e o sentido de justiça (*enkrateia kai dikaiosyne*). O lado negativo do seu carácter reside na extrema arrogância e orgulho que o hão-de perder.

Por um lado, considere-se o conjunto daqueles que admiravam o corpo e manifestações físicas de Alcibíades – os aduladores, os jovens movidos pelo impulso de um *eros* físico, que nele exacerbavam o desejo de satisfazer o prazer imediato. A este estímulo facilmente se associa o prazer do vinho e a embriaguez, a imoderação nos banquetes e na vida pública, a procura da glória fácil, ainda que com o sacrifício da coerência, da correcção ética, do bem da cidade. O episódio relatado por Plutarco em 4.5 serve como de pórtico a um historial de atitudes de insolência e prepotência de Alcibíades, manifestadas no espaço de convívio social, como é o do banquete, provocadas pela imoderação na bebida e pela consciência de que as pessoas que humilha estão sob o império do fascínio que ele exerce, como é o acima mencionado caso de Ânito[9].

A intervenção de Alcibíades a meio do banquete do antagonista de Sócrates recorda um outro *Banquete*, o de Platão, onde a problemática de *eros* é discutida e em que Alcibíades, chegando também com atraso, manifesta não estar apto a passar além do plano da erótica do mundo sensível.

A corrupção de Alcibíades arrasta a corrupção de companheiros da sua geração. E se as adversidades da *Tyche* podem funcionar como uma espécie de teste de carácter, enfraquecê-lo mas também fortificá-lo, no caso de Alcibíades o factor *Tyche*, como se pode ver no passo acima referido (4.2), por lhe ter sido excepcionalmente favorável, não o pôs à prova e arredou-o da disposição de alma para reconhecer as limitações do humano e a necessidade de uma reflexão filosófica e da adesão a uma filosofia prática.

---

[9] Vide Cerezo Magán (1999) 171-180.

De facto, as alusões à presença de Sócrates estão contidas nesta primeira fase da vida do jovem e aparecem intencionalmente entremeadas com os desmandos do protagonista. A referência à relação erótica física com Ânito, fonte de arrogância e desequilíbrio para Alcibíades (4.5), aparece antecedida da referência ao *eros* de Sócrates por Alcibíades, ao qual se contrapõe (4.1). É que este representa o *eros* direccionado para as qualidades inatas, que se dedica a ajudar a desenvolver na alma do *eroumenos*. Numa espécie de vivência caótica Sócrates representa a voz da Filosofia, o apelo da ordem e à ordem da alma, pela *askesis* de uma filosofia prática que faz desenvolver no indivíduo o amor ao Belo e ao Bom, nunca separando eticamente aquele deste. E se se percebe uma relação recíproca de eros entre Alcibíades e Sócrates, eco da relação entre estas duas figuras nos diálogos de Platão, é bem visível essa demarcação platónica: o interesse do filósofo por Alcibíades é motivado por potencialidades éticas que permitiriam conduzi-lo à filosofia e, logo, ao bem e à moderação, e não se atém ao plano físico. Alcibíades é tocado por esse interesse e não é insensível aos parâmetros socráticos, mas o seu eros físico fala mais forte. Daí o desencontro entre ambos, já visível em *Banquete* e *Protágoras*[10].

Mas Sócrates constituia uma excepção. Apenas Sócrates, pela visão privilegiada de um *daimonios*[11] que depurou a capacidade de ver através do desprendimento do plano do material ao cultivar a verdadeira Filosofia como modo de vida verdadeiro, podia vislumbrar as qualidades, em estado seminal, que existiam na alma de Alcibíades e que era urgente fazer frutificar. Este constitui o segundo agente que luta por anular o primeiro de que se falou. No entanto, a estratégia das referências à acção e às intenções de Sócrates faz perceber que a sua acção se tornará ineficaz, sobre um jovem envolvido por um turbilhão de estímulos que apelam para o que de pior há em si, reforçados por uma *tyche* em aparência excepcionalmente favorável, como se vê em 4.1..

Segue-se a referência à *tyche* excepcional, que tornou o jovem "invulnerável à filosofia", como antecipação, entremeada no discurso sobre a influência de Sócrates na sua pessoa e a atracção por Sócrates, que o levava a ouvi-lo com encanto, com quem ouve um amante, e a tornar-se companheiro habitual do filósofo, desprezando "amantes ricos e famosos". Terá Alcibíades sido alguma vez verdadeiramente tocado pela sabedoria socrática? A planta frágil possuia qualidades para isso, mas o campo em que nasceu (antecipando a imagem da *Vita* de Coriolano) e todas as condições adversas ao seu crescimento tornaram vã a acção de Sócrates. É o que Plutarco pretende mostrar à partida com a organização do seu discurso. Mais tarde será mais explícito, ao referir

---

[10] Romilly 1995: 28 sqq.; Ramsey 2012:63 sqq.

[11] Sobre a tradição, na filosofia e literatura antigas, do Socrates *daimonios* vide Hershbell (1988) 365-382.

ten tes physeos anomalian deste homem (16.6). Nem o próprio Alcibíades se apercebeu, na fase de proximidade de Sócrates, que a acção benfazeja do génio filosófico não encontrava verdadeiramente condições para exercer a sua eficácia (4.3-4).

Segue-se de imediato o episódio da embriaguez e excessos no banquete de Ânito.

A partir daí o motivo da acção de Sócrates é tratado por Plutarco com uma hábil expressividade, de modo a deixar perceber que a influência do filósofo em Alcibíades se vai progressivamente perdendo, como se o crescimento desse rebento com potencialidades, na alma do jovem, fosse asfixiado por ervas daninhas (6.1).

Não é já a imagem do amor, segundo Platão, que Alcibíades sente que Sócrates nele consegue despertar, mas o medo e a reverência, de que tenta escapar, enquanto o filósofo tenta, já em vão, exercer o seu múnus nesta alma prestes a perder-se no turbilhão dos prazeres. A eficácia da influência de Sócrates é agora posta a par da dos aduladores, como seus rivais, não é já constante e não se impõe pela sedução natural. Expressiva é a imagem do escravo fugitivo.

O retrato de Sócrates, como um ser excepcional, assistido pelo *daimon* (17.4), como só o pode ser alguém que cultiva em tão alto grau a filosofia prática e a ela conduz os seus formandos, está em perfeita sintonia com a visão tida com respeito a Sócrates na época de Plutarco e com o próprio tratamento da figura em outras obras de Plutarco, sob influência do modelo dos diálogos platónicos. O seu *De genio Socratis*, em especial, é perceptível em vários passos das diferentes *Vitae*[12].

A última tentativa de Sócrates para fazer desabrochar o sentido dos valores, em Alcibíades, é já uma tentativa de recurso extremo, na sequência da batalha de Potideia, para que o mérito que verdeiramente cabia ao próprio Socrates, mais do que a Alcibíades, fosse reconhecido a este. Comenta Plutarco (7.5):

Ἐγίνετο μὲν οὖν τῶι δικαιωτάτωι λόγωι Σωκράτους τὸ ἀριστεῖον. ἐπεὶ δ'οἱ στρατηγοὶ διὰ ἀξίωμα τῶι Ἀλκιβιάδηι σπουδάζοντες ἐφαίνοντο περιθεῖναι τὴν δόξαν, ὁ Σωκράτης βουλόμενος αὔξεσθαι τὸ φιλότιμον ἐν τοῖς καλοῖς αὐτοῦ, πρῶτος ἐμαρτύρει καὶ παρεκάλει στεφανοῦν ἐκεῖνον καὶ διδόναι τὴν πανοπλίαν.

O prémio de mérito cabia, com toda a justiça, a Sócrates. No entanto, como os generais mostravam o desejo de distinguir Alcibíades com esta honra, em

---

virtude da sua alta posição, Sócrates, que pretendia estimular no jovem a ambição de praticar acções belas, foi o primeiro a testemunhar em seu favor...

Isto é, o filósofo faz um apelo desesperado a algo que é, em Plutarco, negativamente valorizado — a *philotimia* — e que constitui um traço de carácter acentuado em Alcibíades, para o direccionar para as boas acções e, assim, para o que é belo, sendo bom[13].

Na retirada dos Gregos em Délio, a retirada de Sócrates, embora protegida por Alcibíades, representa a saída do filósofo da vida deste homem.

Toda esta tensão de forças parece traduzir-se estilisticamente no jogo de palavras compostas, no grego, com o radical *phil-*: à *philanthropia* de Sócrates (1.2) ficou a dever um contributo fundamental para a sua fama (*doxa*), mas o facto de se manifestar, desde cedo, *philoneikos* e *philoprotos* (2.1), fizeram-lhe alcançar fama fácil e protagonismo sem virtude, de modo a se tornar impenetrável à *philosophia* do mestre (4.2). Sócrates diagnostica nele uma *philotimia* que tenta encaminhar para o eticamente correcto, mas em vão o faz. Essa *philotimia* desenvolver-se-á com a adulação, com a consciência dos seus dotes naturais, o pendor para o excesso e a prepotência, com a sua sorte favorável, a ponto de os cidadãos de boa reputação a encararem como um perigo, já que facilmente se poderia associar à tirania (16.1-2). No vulgo Alcibíades desperta sentimentos tão contraditórios quanto a sua própria natureza, já que é amado, odiado, e a sua presença desejada.

No contexto de uma Hélade em profunda crise, que se digladia e em que a sorte e o poder, na guerra, facilmente se alteram e favorecem uns ou outros, Alcibíades aprende, por essa mesma incontrolável ambição e sede de protagonismo, a mudar facilmente de lado e a facilmente persuadir os aliados de momento ou a trai-los, se oportuno, usando a sua *synesis kai tolme* ('inteligência e audácia', 35.2). Com igual facilidade assume, ou melhor, o comportamento honesto e o desonesto, a prática do excesso e os hábitos de pompa, entre os Persas, como os costumes mais sóbrios e severos, entre Espartanos. Tudo isto em função da ambição e do proveito. Para o vulgo esta volúvel e genial adaptação às circunstâncias despertará o sonho da tirania (35.1). Para Plutarco, esta aberração monstruosa de carácter, que se vai agravando com a própria crise da Hélade, assume características comparáveis às de um animal, rastejante — o camaleão (23.3).

Assim, este homem que teve a capacidade de dividir e desestabilizar todo o Peloponeso, que anulou o esforço pacificador de Nícias, sedento de novas empresas militares que lhe granjeassem prestígio e poder, converteu-se numa espécie de corporização da própria crise, de materialização do espírito do tempo. Se a ordem da cidade algum paralelismo tem com a ordem da alma, a anomalia de

---

[13] Sobre as acepções positivas ou negativas do termo, consoante os contextos vide Fialho (2008) 114, n. 11 e Frazier (1988) 109-127.

uma *physis* que Sócrates não conseguiu modelar está em consonância com uma Atenas ao sabor de maiorias movidas pela tiranização de impulsos – e que acabará por sacrificar Sócrates mediante um julgamento infame. É esse o contexto em que se multiplicam os demagogos e os chefes sem escrúpulos, os senhores da guerra, que dela tiram proveito.

A morte de Alcibíades é o quadro que melhor ilustra a sua vida: vítima dos temores da ameaça da tirania que representava e dos sentimentos contraditórios que a sua *doxa* despertava, vítima das intrigas que semeou, envolvido, ambiguamente, em roupas de cortesã, ou pura e simplesmente apanhado em fuga depois de saciar o seu *eros*, perseguido por Espartanos e Atenienses.

Em toda a sua vida, pelo seu carácter, qualidades indesmentíveis, conduta política ora brilhante, que levou Atenas a grandes vitórias, ora contraditória, inesperada e de traição (também por se sentir perseguido), Alcibíades consubstancia a própria ambição e espírito de imperialismo atenienses, a que Atenas, a pólis que alcançou as mais altas manifestações do espírito, não soube pôr freio.

Jacqueline de Romilly vai, com razão, mais longe[14]: "há na vida de Alcibíades uma espécie de valor paradigmático que a torna simbólica e inesquecível. Ela ganha um sentido em todas as épocas. E também para a nossa ela ganha sentido, talvez mais que para qualquer outra. Alcibíades, como imagem da ambição individualista numa democracia em crise, ilumina, com as suas seduções e os seus escândalos, as nossas próprias crises…"

---

[14] Romilly 1995: 32-33.

Relações diplomáticas na construção da "Paz de Filócrates"
(Diplomatic Relations in the "Peace of Philocrates")

Elisabete Cação (elisabetecacao@gmail.com)
Centro de Estudos Clássicos e Humanísticos da Universidade de Coimbra

Resumo – Este trabalho tem por objectivo estudar as relações diplomáticas da construção da Paz de Filócrates de 346, celebrada entre Atenas e Filipe II da Macedónia. Nele, analisamos a conjuntura político-militar que propiciou as negociações; trabalhamos a relação instável das *poleis* durante o processo da construção da paz, nomeadamente as *poleis* intervenientes na Terceira Guerra Sagrada (Fócida, Atenas e Esparta por um lado, e por outro a Liga Anfictiónica, Tebas, Tessália e a Macedónia). Analisando os discursos políticos de Demóstenes e Ésquines, sobre as embaixadas que se levaram a Pela durante o processo, concluímos a falibilidade do tratado, que estava votado a um fracasso iminente. A estratégia geo-política de Filipe II da Macedónia estava delineada há muito e os discursos dos embaixadores, acerca das *poleis* que deveriam figurar do tratado – sobretudo a Fócida –, constituíam um simples *pro forma*. A 'burocracia' ateniense previa o juramento do Tratado em Assembleia, e mesmo antes de a embaixada o fazer jurar por Filipe, ele teria já invadido a Fócida. Com um território invejável, desde a Trácia, passando pela Ilíria, até às Termópilas, e nomeado arconte na Tessália, acabaria por ganhar uma posição confortável dentro da Liga Anfictiónica, que lhe reconhecia a helenidade.

Palavras-chave: Paz de Filócrates, Atenas, Filipe II da Macedónia, diplomacia, política, Terceira Guerra Sagrada, aliança

Abstract – The aim of this work is to study the diplomatic relations regarding the creation of the Peace of Philocrates of 346, concluded between Athens and Philip II of Macedon. This paper analyzes the military and political situation that started the negotiations, as well as the unstable relations of the *poleis* during the process of peacebuilding, namely the states involved in the Third Sacred War (Phocis, Athens, and Sparta on the one hand; on the other hand, the Amphictyonic League, Thebes, Thessaly, and Macedon). We also examine the political speeches of Demosthenes and Aeschines concerning the embassies to Pella during the negotiating process, and we conclude that the peace was fragile, doomed to an imminent breakdown. The geopolitical strategy of Philip II of Macedon had been devised long before, and the speeches of the ambassadors about what the *poleis* should achieve in the treaty – especially Phocis – were simply *pro forma*. Athenian 'bureaucracy' required the taking of an oath on behalf of the peace in the Assembly. Yet before an embassy could do so on Philip's behalf, he invaded Phocis. Thus, with a desirable territory extending from Thrace, along Illyria, as far as Thermopylae, and after having been named archon of Thessaly, Philip succeeded in gaining a secure position in the Amphictyonic League, one that the Greek world recognized.

KEYWORDS: Peace of Philocrates, Athens, Philip II of Macedon, diplomacy, politics, Third Sacred War, alliance

Para a contextualização da Paz de Filócrates, devemos ter em conta, principalmente, os testemunhos de Demóstenes e Ésquines, oradores do século IV a.C., cujos discursos homónimos, *Sobre a Falsa Embaixada*[1], de ambos os oradores, são os mais significativos para a interpretação dos acontecimentos. Demóstenes e Ésquines participaram das embaixadas, constituídas por 10 enviados[2], que tinham por função levar as condições de paz dos Atenienses, receber as instruções e condições de Filipe II da Macedónia, e fazer jurar, de ambas as partes, os constituintes do contrato.

As fontes que nos acompanham sobre a construção da Paz de Filócrates, essencialmente Demóstenes e Ésquines, embora exagerando factos que cada um julga proveitoso para a sua causa, dão-nos conta do processo que levou à complexa Paz de Filócrates.[3]

Devemos, no entanto, enumerar as causas e analisar a conjuntura política e militar em que se celebraria o tratado de paz.

Primeiro, consideraremos a duração e o arrastamento de tempo da Terceira Guerra Sagrada (356-346) na qual Atenas participou imediatamente após o fim da Guerra Social (357-355). Seguidamente, no que toca aos beligerantes da Terceira Guerra Sagrada, Atenas, aliada da Fócida, viu-se impedida de estabelecer no tratado de paz alianças com povos inimigos da Macedónia, ainda que no momento fossem aliados de Atenas, o que, na realização clausular do tratado, nos leva a questionar a situação da Fócida, isto é, em que base se sustentaria o apoio de Atenas à Fócida pois que por um lado é sua aliada, mas ao mesmo tempo celebra um tratado de paz com o seu inimigo macedónio.[4] Mais premente ainda

---

[1] Περὶ τῆς παραπρεσβείας (*De falsa legatione*) é o título partilhado das obras de Demóstenes e Ésquines ambas apresentadas em 343 a.C, respectivamente.

[2] Vide Mosley 1965: 265-266 e Mosley 1972: 54-57. Analisando um elenco de embaixadas, constituídas por 3, 5 ou 10 homens, apresentadas por Mosley (1972) aceitamos a opinião do autor quando este nos explica que a constituição das embaixadas atenienses com determinado número não tem que ver com a importância da situação para a qual a embaixada é constituída, comparando a sua justificação com o exemplo da constituição das embaixadas espartanas no seu artigo de 1965. Contudo, não devemos descartar a relevância do facto de que, geralmente, eram enviadas para negociações de paz ou observância da paz embaixadas "com plenos poderes", constituídas por 10 homens.

[3] D. 19.1-2; Aeschin. 2.3. Os primeiros parágrafos dos discursos de cada orador fazem prever o ataque de um ao outro.

[4] Ainda que Atenas e Macedónia não fossem os primeiros intervenientes nesta Guerra, de facto, eram as cidades mais influentes neste período que apoiavam por um lado a Fócida, e por outro a Liga Anfictiónica, respectivamente. Sobre este assunto, vide Rhodes 2006: 302 e sqq.

é a reacção focídia, ao não ceder território perto das Termópilas aos Atenienses[5], admitindo assim a recusa de auxílio ateniense, o que, por parte deste último, é motivo para acelerar e aceitar as negociações e condições de paz com Filipe II da Macedónia. Por fim, aceita-se ainda também o motivo que devido a uma rusga em tempo de paz[6], durante o mês de tréguas em 348 para os Jogos Olímpicos, se estabeleceram contactos mais activos entre Filipe e Atenas.

Para a celebração do contrato, na Assembleia, um decreto de Filócrates[7] permitia a recepção de embaixadores da Macedónia e o envio dos de Atenas, com o propósito de discutir os termos da paz.

A primeira embaixada enviada a Filipe, em 346, era constituída por 10 homens. Diz-nos Edward Harris[8] que esta constituição dever-se-á ao facto de reunir opiniões diferentes na mesma embaixada, e facilmente inferimos se são 'partidários' de Demóstenes ou de Ésquines, consoante a política defendida por cada um: Demóstenes, por um lado, pretendia a realização imediata da paz por razões anteriormente explicadas, e Ésquines, por outro, pretendia a união de todos os Gregos para uma luta conjunta contra Filipe ou para a formação de uma aliança com outros Gregos que fosse prevista no futuro tratado de paz.

Já em Pela, discursaram os oradores atenienses, por ordem de idade, sendo Demóstenes o último, que, com ou sem surpresa, não concluiu o discurso pela gravidade do assunto e por estar diante de figura tão detestada, quanto imponente. Na sequência dos discursos, Filipe responde a todos os oradores, excepto a Demóstenes, e termina com o desejo de paz e, sobretudo, de aliança com Atenas.

A embaixada regressa a Atenas, cerca de um mês depois, e apresenta os seus relatórios à Assembleia[9]. Os termos de Filipe impunham uma decisão difícil a Atenas quanto à fixação dos seus aliados para a constituição da paz, nomeadamente, o caso mais gritante, a Fócida. A Fócida era, na Terceira Guerra Sagrada, aliada de Atenas e inimiga dos Tebanos e Tessálios que eram apoiados por Filipe II da Macedónia. Ou seja, a consciência de que a Fócida não poderia fazer parte do tratado implicava uma restruturação nas cláusulas da paz, o que, por vontade

---

[5] Admitimos que a conjuntura militar da Fócida estava a tornar-se demasiado pesada de suportar, mesmo com Atenas por aliada, e a intenção seria conceder e celebrar uma paz com a Macedónia, rejeitando o apoio ateniense.

[6] Vide Lewis 1994: 750. Frínon reclamava ter sido capturado por piratas da Macedónia.

[7] Vide Rhodes 2006: 306-307. Filócrates foi acusado por ter apresentado este decreto à Assembleia numa *graphe paranomon*, pela qual foi defendido por Demóstenes e absolvido. A partir desta data, Demóstenes mostra-se favorável à realização da paz, não tanto por considerar esse caminho viável, mas, sobretudo, com o fim de mostrar que os seus avisos, convicto de que Filipe atacaria os Atenienses, eram justificáveis.

[8] Harris 1995: 55-56.

[9] Os dois discursos *Sobre a Embaixada* de Demóstenes e Ésquines são contraditórios e acusatórios de acção de um e de outro. Vide capítulo um "Whom to Believe" de Harris 1995: 7-16.

de Filipe, era impraticável[10]. A Assembleia decide concordar com a paz, sem fazer qualquer menção à aliança que Filipe II da Macedónia propunha: que, em três meses, os aliados de Atenas deveriam estar especificados para constarem do tratado. Esta especificação contornaria o caso da Fócida e permitia que esta fizesse, em devido tempo, parte do tratado.

A realização de paz e aliança neste período para Atenas actuava como um impedimento, pois o apoio à Fócida na Terceira Guerra Sagrada seria travado pela aliança com o seu inimigo, a Macedónia, que agora celebrava. No entanto, visto por outra perspectiva, a própria Macedónia ficava impedida de atacar a Fócida, enquanto aliada de Atenas. Adensa-se, no entanto, a 'guerra fria' entre as duas potências já que ambas sabiam da falibilidade de um tratado que estava votado ao fracasso imediato.

A possibilidade de se estabelecer uma aliança que fosse mais além do que a simples paz – condição única de Filipe não passível de alteração – implicaria que a Fócida não pudesse constar do tratado como aliado de Atenas. Por este motivo, prossegue-se com a proposta de Filócrates – um tratado que excluísse a Fócida nominalmente – mas com nova atribuição: a paz seria para "Atenas e os seus aliados" (Ἀθηναίους καὶ τοὺς Ἀθηναίων συμμάχους[11]), subentendendo quaisquer que eles fossem no momento, expressão que Atenas poderia explorar melhor quando lhe conviesse, incluindo, desta forma, a Fócida.

Para validar este tratado, ambos as partes teriam de o jurar. Os Atenienses deverão tê-lo feito passado pouco mais de um mês. No que respeita a Filipe, constituiu-se segunda embaixada, provavelmente com os mesmos elementos que integraram a primeira, e que se dirigiu novamente a Pela.

Demóstenes estaria interessado na concretização rápida da paz, mais precisamente na ratificação por parte de Filipe, pois desta forma impor-se-iam limites nas suas restantes intenções de conquistas – o que, por esta altura, traduzia a possibilidade de atacar território ático, mais a sul das Termópilas até onde já teria chegado –, mas sobretudo porque possibilitaria a inclusão da Fócida no tratado como "aliada" de Atenas e o cessar imediato das hostilidades na Terceira Guerra Sagrada. No entanto, acreditamos que Demóstenes estaria já a prever que o Macedónio quebraria o tratado de paz rapidamente e que, com este incumprimento, Atenas poderia declarar-lhe uma guerra aberta e directa.

A segunda embaixada, para ratificação do tratado de Paz na Macedónia, embora tivesse partido em Abril, só regressaria a Atenas em Julho. A razão da demora da embaixada prende-se, primeiro, com as campanhas de Filipe na Trácia e no Quersoneso (a este da Macedónia) e, segundo, com a própria demora da embaixada de Atenas: encaminhou-se lentamente para Pela, por terra, e aí

---

[10] Aeschin. 3.71-72. Rhodes 2006: 310.
[11] D. 19.159.

esperou cerca de um mês pelo retorno de Filipe. Em Pela, além da embaixada de Atenas, aguardavam a chegada de Filipe outros enviados de toda a parte da Grécia: Espartanos, Eubeus, Tebanos, inclusive Focídios que desejavam terminar, definitivamente, as hostilidades com Filipe na Terceira Guerra Sagrada e, de alguma maneira, concluir uma eventual paz por todo o território grego.

Com a chegada de Filipe à capital da Macedónia, Pela, procederam-se aos discursos dos vários representantes das várias partes da Hélade. Maliciosamente, o rei da Macedónia não se declara nem a favor de uns, nem de outros; pelo contrário, faz promessas paradoxais, de modo a agradar cada ouvinte[12], claramente uma estratégia diplomática para obter a melhor resolução para os seus interesses. Mas enquanto decorriam os discursos, Filipe estaria já, contudo, em preparações para marchar para sul, em direcção à Fócida, com a intenção de capturá-la finalmente. Cremos, sobretudo, que as promessas paradoxais de Filipe são o meio de não se comprometer belicamente, contra Atenas ou até mesmo contra os seus aliados tebanos, para que, enfim, tivesse caminho livre para satisfazer aquilo a que se propunha há muito. É que uma derradeira vitória sobre a Fócida apenas lhe traria vantagens. Ficaria com território invejável, que se estendia desde a Ilíria, a norte da Macedónia, à costa este da Trácia, controlando também território a sul, a Tessália e a passagem das Termópilas. Com a interferência nos assuntos da Tessália, já conquistada anteriormente (crê-se que terá sido nomeado arconte), ganharia uma posição confortável dentro da Liga Anfictiónica, que lhe reconhecia a helenidade. E teria, por fim, uma imagem de um homem inflexível em assuntos religiosos gregos, ao lutar contra os sacrílegos causadores da Terceira Guerra Sagrada, nomeadamente a Fócida.

A segunda embaixada chega a Atenas, com os juramentos de Filipe, no 13º dia do mês de Scirophorion (em Julho), quando o rei da Macedónia teria já chegado à Fócida. Três dias depois, Demóstenes teria apelado à Assembleia por um auxílio expresso e expedito[13], mas a sua proposta não teria sido levado em conta, pois os atenienses sabiam já que seria tarde demais para ajudar os Focídios contra Filipe.

---

[12] Carlier 1990: 159 explica muito claramente que "Aux Thébains qui sont ses alliés depuis 353 et qui ont imploré son aide en 347, Philippe promet de containdre les Phocidiens à la capitulation, de démanteler toutes leurs forteresses, et de laisser la décision sur le sort des Phocidiens à l'amphictionie restaurée – qui ne manquera pas de les traiter très durement; le Macédonien, d'autre part, s'engage à laisser les Thébains rétablir leur autorité sur toute la Béotie. Aux envoyés Athéniens qui sont ses nouveux alliés, quoique lui-même n'ait pas encore prété serment, Philippe assure qu'il ne châtiera que les responsables des pires sacrilèges, mais qu'il traitera avec douceur le reste des Phocidiens. Dès qu'il aura franchi les Thermopyles, declare-t-il aux ambassadeurs athéniens, son souci principal sera de reduire «l'insolence thébaine»; il restaurera l'indépendance des cités béotiennes et fera reconstruire Platées et Thespies: si les Athéniens engagent leurs forces à ses côtés, Philippe leur fera restituer Orôpos et les aidera à rétablir leur autorité sur l'Eubée." De facto, Demóstenes refere este assunto na *Segunda Filípica*, 30.

[13] D.19.44.

No entanto, isso não foi obstáculo a uma nova moção de Filócrates, propondo o alargamento da paz para os descendentes de Atenas e dos seus aliados. Nem tão pouco foi obstáculo a constituição de nova embaixada a Filipe para reportar estes novos assuntos.

Em resoluções-relâmpago (em menos de uma semana), a embaixada parte, apenas para regressar de imediato a Atenas ao saber da capitulação dos Focídos no 23º dia desse mês. A capitulação dos Focídios foi a justificação psicológica para o alvoroço ateniense. De nada lhes serviria enviar auxílio, nem nada poderiam fazer "legalmente" uma vez que a Atenas, ao ter jurado o tratado de paz e ao submeter-se à vontade de Filipe, tornava-se aliada da Macedónia e inimiga da Fócida.

Por conseguinte, ultrapassada a barreira das Termópilas e esta recente rendição final dos Focídios actuavam como passos definitivos para um ataque iminente em pleno território ático. Tal não sucedeu e prosseguiram-se negociações, pois Filipe convocara uma reunião da Liga Anfictiónica para que se determinasse as sanções a aplicar à Fócida. Os Atenienses fizeram-se representar, mas terminaram as efémeras boas relações com Filipe traduzidas na ausência da participação ateniense nos Jogos Píticos, aos quais Filipe presidia.

A acção passiva dos atenienses leva-nos a crer que a urgência do estado de guerra nunca foi verdadeiramente interiorizada, nem Atenas sentiu necessidade, como dizia anteriormente, de utilizar a expressão "paz para Atenas e os seus aliados" no apoio aos aliados que agora sucumbiam ante Filipe.

A degradação da paz era cada vez mais uma realidade e o estabelecimento de novos contactos uma necessidade[14]. No entanto, esta nova situação reporta-se a necessidades diplomáticas posteriores e consequentes da degeneração da Paz de Filócrates.

---

[14] Demóstenes dá-nos conta de uma viagem que teria feito e encena até um diálogo na cidade dos Messénios, na *Segunda Filípica*, parágrafos 19-23.

Conflitualidade religiosa em tempo de Paz. Religião e política na dinastia constantiniana
(Religious Conflicts in a Time of Peace. Religion and Politics in Constantinian Dynasty)

Paula Barata Dias (pabadias@hotmail.com)
Universidade de Coimbra

«Não penseis que vim trazer paz à terra; não vim trazer paz, mas espada. Pois vim causar divisão entre o filho e seu pai, entre a filha e sua mãe e entre a nora e sua sogra, assim os inimigos do homem serão os da sua própria casa." (Mt 10, 34)

Resumo – Entre o séc. IV e V o cristianismo evoluiu de religião marginalizada a religião dominante e a única a gozar de legalidade para o império romano. A cumplicidade dos imperadores contribuiu para esta progressiva homogenia e identificação entre o império como estrutura política e um outro poder, espiritual e institucional, que foi a Igreja pós-constantiniana. É nossa intenção analisar a história do cristianismo após a sua legitimação no espaço público e observar o papel que o contexto político da dinastia constantiniana exerceu na conquista da exclusividade para uma única religião, em detrimento da diversidade religiosa do mundo antigo e da modesta importância que, até então, Roma atribuíra à unidade de profissão religiosa enquanto condicionante política. Esta comunhão uniforme de interesses entre Estado e Igreja foi reciprocamente benéfica, ao reforçar o centralismo, a autoridade e os mecanismos de repressão contra a divergência religiosa, percebido pelas autoridades como métodos legítimos para combater a desintegração do império.

Palavras-chave: Constantino, cristianismo, Antoguidade Tardia, Igreja, Édito de Milão, legislação imperial, concílios ecuménicos

Abstract – Between the 4th and the 5th century, Christianity evolved from a marginalized religion to a religion of dominant status, uniquely recognized as legal by the political authorities of the Roman Empire. The sympathy and complicity of Roman emperors after Constantine contributed to a progressive homogeneity and mutual identification between the Empire, as a political structure, and the post-Constantine church, a different kind of power, both spiritual and institutional. My goal is to analyze the history of Christianity immediately after the legalization of the church, and to consider the consequences of political action by the Constantinian dynasty leading to religious uniformity and exclusivity under the Christian church. By associating their interests, the Constantinian state and church helped each other to reinforce not only unity of faith, but also centralism, authority, and political repression over religious matters as acceptable ways to avoid disintegration of the Empire.

Keywords: Constantine, Christianity, Late Antiquity, Church, Edict of Milan, imperial legislation, ecumenical councils.

https://doi.org/10.14195/978-989-26-1280-5_6

O tema deste trabalho teve duas principais motivações. Em primeiro lugar, celebrou-se em 2013 um milénio e sete séculos sobre o Édito de Milão, ou seja, da concessão da liberdade para o cristianismo no Império Romano. Com ele, Constantino e Licínio garantiram, para uma religião cujos fundamentos radicam numa mentalidade e civilização diferentes da grega e romana, a sua acomodação no espaço público da Antiguidade Tardia, na Europa e na cultura ocidental, no que estas têm de legatárias do mundo greco-romano.

À parte a circunstância da efeméride, em segundo lugar, portanto, entram pelas nossas casas adentro, todos os dias, as notícias que revelam serem ainda as mesmas margens do Mediterrâneo que se veem abaladas pelas divisões étnicas, políticas, económicas, sociais, em que a religião, não tendo um impacto substantivo, é evocada como bandeira identitária pelas partes desavindas e reivindicada como pretexto para os conflitos: Cairo, Damasco, Antioquia, Alepo, Istambul, a antiga Bizâncio, nunca deixaram de ser, ao longo dos séculos que separam a Antiguidade Tardia dos dias de hoje, lugares de fronteira e de confronto para a diversidade humana historicamente constituída ao longo dos tempos nestas turbulentas margens do Mediterrâneo, com quem nós, habitantes da aparentemente tranquila e tolerante Europa, partilhámos um *continuum* político. A verdade é que são hoje nítidos os sinais da permanência do mesmo tipo de respostas das autoridades políticas e religiosas face à diversidade, percebida não tanto como uma riqueza, mas como uma ameaça para a ordem da *kosmopolis*, seja esta o Império Romano dos sécs. I-V ou o arco mediterrânico de hoje.[1]

A natureza conflitual da religião, a dificuldade em conviver com a diferença, a reivindicação, por parte de um poder político, de um unanimismo religioso de recíproca legitimação, foram questões a que a História nos habituou, em particular até à Época moderna, com os movimentos laicistas e as progressivas reivindicações de separação da Igreja do Estado. Mesmo neste domínio, formalmente a Europa vive uma situação ambígua: no Reino Unido, nos países nórdicos e na Grécia encontramos formas nacionalizadas de religião, historicamente consagradas. Não podemos, no entanto, dizer que hoje a religião professada gera, no espaço europeu, circunstâncias de divisão entre os seus cidadãos, embora pontilhem, aqui e ali, sinais de perturbação desta neutralidade do fator religioso.

No Sul e no Leste do mediterrâneo, contudo, as linhas de fronteira são visíveis entre as diferentes versões do islão, tendo ao seu lado, como comunidades minoritárias, os outros monoteísmos mediterrânicos nascidos no mundo antigo, eles próprios mais antigos e outrora dominantes num espaço islamizado, a saber, o judaísmo e o cristianismo.[2]

---

[1] N. do A.: Este texto foi escrito em 2013, no pico dos conflitos civis que eclodiram em alguns países de África e do Médio-Oriente após a chamada Primavera Árabe.

[2] Demos o exemplo do Egipto atual, em que o conflito se faz entre comunidades que defendem a refundação do Estado pós-Mubarak à luz do fundamentalismo islâmico e os que

Partamos, por isso, de uma análise muito sumária da linguagem para verificarmos que o tempo não desfez a constância da degradação da diversidade, uma vez desencadeada uma linguagem de força a partir de uma posição de poder. A intolerância religiosa face ao diferente com que o homem europeu conviveu durante séculos marcou o nosso quotidiano, despontando na linguagem contemporânea como peças arqueológicas num presente mais diverso e multicultural: cristãos ortodoxos foram todos os que emergiram do Concílio de Niceia e de Calcedónia (325-451), quando se decretou a humanidade e divindade dual de Cristo e a igualdade das Pessoas da Trindade. Ou seja, durante alguns séculos, o cristianismo latino também foi "ortodoxo", em contraponto aos heterodoxos, ou heréticos (*haeresis*- "os que dividem"), que defendiam a natureza una de Cristo (monofisitas), entre outros. No entanto, novos cismas se produziram durante a Idade Média, e, à luz dos Patriarcados da Igreja ortodoxa de Constantinopla, Alexandria, Antioquia, Jerusalém e Moscovo, os católicos são "heterodoxos". Mas nenhum católico, no Ocidente, dirá de si próprio que é um heterodoxo, o que se torna um contrassenso, porque se reserva pacificamente para os irmãos do Oriente o apodo de "Ortodoxo" que lhes coube desde Calcedónia.

Uma divergência religiosa não nasce do nada. Surge como "seita" "*secta*", de *sectum* "divisão, corte" produzido numa linguagem religiosa maioritária, num momento de crise suscitada no espaço extrarreligioso. O cristianismo surge como uma *secta* para o judaísmo no séc. I d.C., pois leva consigo muito da fonte, pontilhado com a Revelação de Cristo e um relacionamento mais aberto com o mundo não judaico. Hoje, nem judeus nem cristãos se pensam desta maneira, tendo o processo histórico encarregado de exprimir, com a força dos números, a transformação das posições de poder. *Superstitio praua*, eram termos empregues nos relatos que os autores romanos fizeram no seu primeiro contacto com as práticas cristãs (Suetónio, Tácito, Plínio o Jovem). Para os que estavam ao lado do poder e da verdadeira religião, o cristianismo surgia como uma perigosa expressão religiosa que, ao contrário das outras religiões estrangeiras de fundo monoteísta acolhidas pela tolerância romana (Ísis, Mitra, Cíbele), tinha de ser reprimida.

A principal diferença entre estes monoteísmos anteriores ou contemporâneos ao cristianismo decorre da sua atitude quanto às outras expressões religiosas: o mundo antigo, mesmo quando envereda por cultos monoteístas, não exige exclusividade, numa prática secular de diversidade religiosa. Assim,

reivindicam a democracia laica, de créditos e virtudes mal compreendidas, porque laico era o Estado militarizado de Mubarak. A democratizada Turquia defende um frágil equilíbrio entre a liberdade de escolha e de expressão religiosa, com pequenas cedências a um movimento de islamização do Estado e das leis, consciente de que a realpolitik força a autoridade do Estado a considerar os grupos que divergem parceiros credíveis para um diálogo e uma presença no espaço público de consequências imprevisíveis.

entre os fatores que conduziram à hostilização do cristianismo pelas autoridades romanas nos primeiros séculos está a perceção da perigosidade de uma *secta* que, não se limitando a existir, defendia propósitos incompatíveis com o dever do cidadão romano, o de prestar culto ao imperador e aos deuses protetores de Roma, contrato em que assentava o bem-estar público e a preservação da ordem. A maioria não cristã do séc. II, verdadeira praticante de *religio* (entregue à uma multiplicidade de cultos igualmente lícitos), concordaria com as vozes críticas do cristianismo que o classificaram como uma *superstitio*.

Esta situação inverteu-se quando, ao tornar-se dominante, o cristianismo se afirmou como religião universal (*catholica*), e os cultos não cristãos, politeístas e henoteístas foram considerados manifestações religiosas restritas, superstições rústicas, das pessoas pouco instruídas que eram os' habitantes do *pagus*, os *pagani*. Neste processo, o cristianismo construiu a sua posição de força religiosa, material e política no centro da sociedade romana, uma vez cristianizadas as elites urbanas. Assim, inverte-se a linguagem: as *superstitiones* passaram a ser as crenças vagas e pouco estruturadas dos habitantes remetidos para a periferia do sistema económico e social do mundo romano.

O biógrafo Eusébio de Cesareia e o polemista e orador Lactâncio contribuíram para deixar da época constantiniana – caracterizada pela afirmação militar e política de Constantino sobre os outros tetrarcas, e que corresponde sensivelmente ao primeiro terço do séc. IV – uma imagem de restauração da autoridade imperial, associada à Paz entre o Estado romano e os cristãos. Chegado ao poder unitário, após um desgastante período de Guerra civil, Constantino pacificou o império nas duas frentes, militar e religiosa. Tornou-se senhor absoluto no Ocidente, ao derrotar o rival Maxêncio em 212, após a Batalha da Ponte Mílvia. Logo em 313, Constantino e Licínio, o Augusto do Oriente, proclamam o Édito de Liberdade para os cristãos, no qual se consagra o estatuto de *religio licita* para o cristianismo[3].

Política e religião, reciprocamente legitimadas, unidas na pessoa do imperador, serão as traves que hão-de sustentar a génese estruturante das nações pós-romanas. Ressalta deste Imperador a determinação de colocar as instituições e a política a dialogar com a Igreja, sob a legitimação de uma religiosidade homogénea, una e *catholica*[4].

O primeiro imperador a assumir-se cristão permaneceu na história da Europa cristã como modelo e fundamento das relações patrimoniais e diplomáticas entre uma religião e o Estado. A construção da imagem de Constantino conforma-se, contudo, a uma interpretação da sua biografia, quando, logo em

---

[3] Ver a tradução comentada do édito de Galério (311) e do Édito de Constantino (313) nas in Dias 2012: 43-47.

[4] Dias 2013: 455-464.

313, trouxe a Igreja até ao estatuto jurídico de *persona christianorum*[5], o que lhe conferiu a visibilidade institucional e legitimidade patrimonial decorrente da sua integração na *romanitas*. Deixou de ser, portanto, um assunto da justiça e da sanção penal pela ilicitude e pelo *crimen*, para ser alvo da regulamentação do direito comum: pode ser interpelada ou ela própria interpelar em sede de justiça, deter património e agir sobre ele. Este acesso legal ao espaço público, na verdade algo com origem relativamente neutra, pois tratou-se de atribuir à cristandade prerrogativas que outros colégios e associações beneficiavam dentro da liberalidade romana, constituiu o primeiro de muitos atos de aproximação e de influência recíprocas entre o Estado romano e a Igreja durante a dinastia constantiniana, após os quais a projeção da Igreja no século estaria consolidada[6].

Para este processo contribuiu o facto de a época de Constantino ter sido percecionada pelos seus contemporâneos como um retorno à Paz e de o reinado de seu filho se ter erigido como o tempo da "reparação dos anos felizes". Com eles, a propaganda fez vingar a ideologia do retorno à estabilidade imperial, proporcionada pela ausência de *intestina bella*, ou seja, de conflitos dentro do império, que haviam sido tenebrosamente despertados com a queda de Diocleciano, trazendo à memória de muitos os anos em que Roma quase desapareceu, os da instabilidade do séc. III[7]. A perceção da Paz teve efeitos reforçados sobre um particular tipo de súbditos imperiais, os cristãos, que viram terminado o período de perseguição.

Paralelamente, assistimos à deslocação progressiva dos interesses estratégicos do imperador para a parte grega do império, concluída com a deslocação da sede imperial para a nova Constantinopla[8]. Mas a presença no espaço público e a

---

[5] Dias 2012: 47.

[6] Conjugam-se circunstâncias favoráveis, em muitos aspetos fortuitas: Constantino manteve o poder, partilhado ou em exercício solitário, trinta e dois anos. Silvestre I, papa praticamente seu contemporâneo (314-335), foi o primeiro papa a ser canonizado sem ter sofrido martírio. Constantino teve uma família numerosa, gerindo com dureza a sua sucessão, e tornou-a cooperante com o exercício de um poder unificado. Constâncio II (338-361) deu continuidade à transformação iniciada pelo seu Pai, como diria um insuspeito César Juliano em 356, numa das suas *Orationes* (1, 9) "é como se o teu pai ainda governasse", num panegírico politicamente correto. Petri 1989: 113-178.

[7] A estabilização imperial, de cunho centralizador, apoiada na lealdade do exército, sendo uma caraterística do modelo monocrático de Constantino não põe em causa a fórmula política da tetrarquia, uma vez que designava figuras de poder intermédio, embora as relações familiares, naturais e em resultado de casamentos diplomáticos se constituíssem penhor e não garantia de lealdade. Ruggini 1989: 179-243. Cf. o prólogo de Lactâncio, *De Mortibus Persecutorum* 1, 1-3. (nossa trad.) "O Senhor ouviu as tuas preces, caríssimo Donato [...] vê que todos os nossos adversários foram aniquilados, e que a paz foi devolvida a toda a terra, a Igreja, dantes abatida, hoje se ergue (...) é que Deus fez surgir príncipes que destruíram o governo cruel e criminoso dos tiranos e forneceram o maior bem aos homens, dissipando a nuvem de uma época triste, outorgando a todos os corações a alegria e a doçura de uma paz serena..."

[8] A razão parece-nos suficientemente lógica: o maior número de cristãos estava na parte oriental do império, e eram já uma importante percentagem da demografia das grandes cidades helenófonas (Alexandria, Antioquia, Nicomédia, Constantinopla, todas sedes provinciais;

progressiva identificação com o poder político tornam visíveis a natureza diversa e ainda problemática do cristianismo. A diversidade de expressões do cristianismo, associada à sua transversalidade social e presença disseminada, refletiu, não um, mas muitos cristianismos. Este desenvolvera-se de modo fulgurante a partir de pequenos núcleos semeados pela atividade proselítica dos apóstolos e seus sucessores, inicialmente em torno de casas privadas, depois, enfrentando as perseguições esporádicas e assistemáticas, em torno dos bispos e das cidades imperiais, num regime de grande descontinuidade temporal e espacial.

Apontemos, portanto, as principais causas para esta diversidade de "cristianismos" na alvorada da *Pax* Constantiniana:

Em primeiro lugar, muitas comunidades de cristãos viram, com frequência, uma geração dos seus membros ser perturbada pelas perseguições intermitentes. A perturbação sobre as comunidades prolongava-se para além da perda de vidas humanas como consequência dos martírios. O alcance particular de algumas medidas revelavam-se danosas para a estabilidade, continuidade de cultura e robustez do próprio núcleo teológico: os bispos, presbíteros e batizados eram, por esta ordem, os principais visados nas perseguições. Os bens eram-lhe confiscados, os livros sagrados, as relíquias e as alfaias litúrgicas, encerrados ou destruídos os lugares de culto. Afetando a face visível da Igreja, a ação persecutória do Estado romano não teve sucesso, não só pela ausência de um esforço contínuo e concertado nesse sentido, mas também porque não afetava o espaço íntimo da igreja militante, a que garantia, pela missionação de proximidade, a difusão da fé.

Esta continuava assente no ambiente doméstico, entregue aos seus mais caraterísticos habitantes, mulheres, servos, jovens, partilhado em cumplicidade e segredo entre os aderentes. Periodicamente, portanto, as Igrejas recolhiam ao seu ponto de partida, o da segurança do espaço interno do lar, de hierarquia difusa, mas essencialmente horizontal, entre os seus membros, vivendo entre si a experiência religiosa, sem grandes comunicações com comunidades análogas.

Em segundo lugar, o princípio da autonomia apostólica era ainda dominante. Apesar de a cátedra de Pedro em Roma ser reconhecida como o lugar de martírio de Pedro e de Paulo, esta preeminência teve, ao princípio, uma incidência mais espiritual do que temporal ou administrativa. Esteve claramente ameaçada pela progressiva perda de importância da capital do império face às novas capitais, em particular as que aliavam a legitimidade de lugar apostólico (lugar de primeira pregação dos apóstolos, ou do seu martírio), com uma importância económica e política (Antioquia, Jerusalém, Alexandria, Éfeso, Corinto).

---

mas também Cesareia, Jerusalém, Éfeso, Constantinopla). Além do efeito da quantidade, a Igreja a Oriente apresentava um maior grau de organização hierárquica e uma mais elevada presença nos meios intelectuais. Marrou 1963: 26-35.

Em terceiro lugar, destaque-se aquilo a que se pode chamar de "incompletude" da mensagem evangélica, sendo esta característica essencial para a identidade do cristianismo enquanto religião revelada, dotada de um texto que é, ele próprio, o relato da Revelação (o Evangelho). O cristianismo resulta da Revelação contida nos evangelhos e da interpretação que dela foi feita pelos homens. Este discurso não cobria todos os aspetos da vida, deixando margem para a continuidade do trabalho e da construção dos homens nas coisas de Deus. Para o cristianismo, em particular o católico romano, essa é a missão da Igreja, e a Revelação, pela ação do Espírito Santo, continua a operar-se ainda hoje. Como se o livro não estivesse fechado, portanto. E a margem da interpretação humana sobre todos os documentos ligados à génese do cristianismo e considerados inspirados é enorme, como o prova o trabalho dos Padres da Igreja na Antiguidade Tardia. Portanto, o cristianismo é, sobretudo interpretação sobre a experiência da vida e feitos de Jesus, relatada por terceiros, nos Evangelhos.

Em quarto lugar, temos como fator adjuvante da diversidade dentro do cristianismo o substrato social, filosófico e religioso de acolhimento do cristianismo. Este não se desenvolveu no vazio, antes conquistou e ocupou um espaço público modelado por outras vivências religiosas. A conversão de cada consciência, de cada espaço mental fazia-se sobretudo em acomodação do novo credo dentro da matriz cultural, as memórias, a formação, a mentalidade prévias de cada um, de que ninguém se desfazia *ex abrupto*.

S. Paulo foi exemplo do pragmatismo no espalhar do Evangelho fazendo uso das expetativas do seu destinatário, adaptando assim no método a ser usado, que era o de persuasão, diante de um destinatário novo. No discurso do Areópago, em Atenas (Act. 17, 22-23), o Apóstolo mostra-se capaz de transmitir o cristianismo aproveitando as fissuras do que poderia ser percebido como menos consequente para as estruturas mentais do mundo antigo: começa por elogiar a *eusebeia* dos Atenienses, até lhes apresentar Cristo como o Deus que desconheciam, mas a quem até já haviam, como era próprio da sua natureza sensata e expectante, erigido um altar. Mesmo como os efeitos deste discurso denotam, o risco de se ser rejeitado era considerável.

Também Pedro, ao sair do cenáculo, após a descida do Espírito Santo no Pentecostes (Act. 2, 1-4), fala uma língua que cada um que o ouve entende como sendo a sua língua materna, numa espécie de "tradução automática miraculosa". A glossolalia é bem o símbolo da capacidade e também da vontade de acomodação da revelação cristã à especificidade cultural de cada um. Reside nesta adaptabilidade o sucesso do proselitismo cristão, ou seja, em que a mesma mensagem chega a cada um de modo plástico, de modo a adaptar-se às expectativas e à realidade de base.

Será pois compreensível o retrato, ou melhor, os retratos, desta Igreja descentralizada em núcleos que reproduziam, *grosso modo*, a administração provincial de Diocleciano, com as dioceses a constituírem as sedes episcopais, resultando os seus líderes das escolhas a partir das comunidades de base. Verdade é que a *Pax* entre a Igreja e o Século trazida pela liberdade constantiniana foi, no interior das comunidades religiosas, um período de agitação também porque, pela primeira vez, as igrejas enquanto instituições e comunidades hierarquizadas, puderam conhecer-se reciprocamente, relacionando-se entre si e buscando um modo de relacionamento com as outras estruturas sociais licitamente estabelecidas.

Com largos efeitos sobre a diversidade da expressão dogmática, litúrgica, artística e literária, o cristianismo dos três primeiros séculos trouxera consigo uma explosão de criatividade que, no novo contexto de cumplicidade e aliança com um poder imperial ideologicamente centralizador, era urgente ordenar. A época constantiniana constitui para a Igreja um período de "ordenação da casa" porque, compreensivelmente, esta beneficia da tranquilidade que lhe permitiu observar-se a si própria, e, uma vez resolvida a questão da sobrevivência, dominante nos três primeiros séculos, urgia unificar o corpo dogmático do cristianismo, os princípios da catequese, a liturgia, o calendário cristão, o cânone de textos sagrados, os lugares de culto, a disciplina hierárquica.

O processo de fixação do cânone dos textos sagrados para os cristãos tornou-se um bom exemplo da lenta sedimentação de uma ortodoxia, ou de uma voz dominante. Os autores que se pronunciam pela canonicidade ou não de determinados textos raciocinaram sobre uma realidade de facto: quais eram os livros maioritários? Que textos as comunidades elegeram para sua orientação? Ireneu de Lião, Tertuliano, Tatiano, Marcião (séc. II-III), cristãos que se pronunciaram, em algum momento, sobre a canonicidade dos textos bíblicos, criticaram textos em uso a que tiveram acesso, e não textos que pudessem vir a usar, que não conheciam. A primeira condição para um juízo crítico era ser atestado o seu uso nas comunidades cristãs. Os menos lidos, os menos consensuais (e, neste domínio, como se sabe, funcionou o princípio do *consensus*, isto é, são mais credíveis os textos que se apresentam conformes com uma maioria), migraram para a periferia do sistema literário do cristianismo, fixaram-se em determinadas comunidades mais isoladas, em línguas de estatuto regional, como o Siríaco, o Copta e o Arménio. O estágio dos textos entre comunidades, ao longo de gerações, contribuiu para a sua aceitabilidade quando, tempos após, sobre eles pendeu um juízo hermenêutico[9].

---

[9] Segundo o Biógrafo Eusébio de Cesareia (VC 4, 36). Data do período constantiniano a fixação do cânone de textos sagrados, em particular o NT (veja-se o cânone revelado por L. Muratori a partir de um ms. do séc. II, apresentou já lista de textos canónicos para o NT estável, e semelhante à atual). Atanásio de Alexandria, (Ep. 36), em 367, enumerava já a lista atual, que é, segundo as suas palavras "*kanonizomena*", isto é "modelo aceite como norma". A avaliação do Patriarca Alexandrino é testemunho da dominância do princípio da consensualidade: a questão estabilizara como uma realidade de facto, porque era aceite por todos. S. Dâmaso e S. Jerónimo, no final do séc. IV, apresentam já uma ordem diferente de preocupações para além da discussão da canonicidade, percebida como resolvida: tratava-se agora de garantir fiabilidade interna aos textos canónicos através de um exercício de revisão das fontes, análise das traduções e crítica textual. Fixar o texto numa versão oficial representa também recusar, ou remeter para o silêncio, o que se classifica como heterodoxo.

Não se pretende branquear quaisquer exercícios de censura sobre versões divergentes da Revelação num período de busca de unanimidade, mas antes atenuar as consequências de eventuais atos deliberados. A avaliação de certos textos como periféricos também se desenvolveu nas próprias comunidades cristãs primitivas que, ao apoiarem a circulação de uns e ao colocarem de lado outros, condenaram os últimos a uma menor difusão, logo, à sua segregação. Este exercício chegou, em grande parte, concluído ao séc. IV, cabendo ao imperador, com a sua ascendência, dar voz a um modelo já aceite: assim, sabe-se, pela *Vida de Constantino*, que ele autorizou a reprodução de cinquenta exemplares da Bíblia, em 331, para serem distribuídos pelas Igrejas da sua nova capital. Ou seja, depreendemos que, nas proximidades do Imperador, um novo cristão e da sua nova cidade, havia uma Bíblia percebida como consensual, com suficiente mérito para servir de modelo à cópias legadas às Igrejas da nova capital.

Em meados do séc. V, contudo, toda esta predisposição para a diversidade havia sido neutralizada, ficando a imagem oficial do cristianismo clara e homogénea: tinha, portanto, nascido o catolicismo.

No entanto, o processo de sedimentação textual, disciplinar e dogmática da Igreja dentro de uma ortodoxia, apresentado segundo esta lógica racional, não faz justiça a uma circunstância que conduziu este processo de construção da ortodoxia, que foi o do envolvimento empenhado da dinastia imperial na pessoa dos seus príncipes[10].

Recupere-se a feliz expressão de H. Marrou, que, ao comentar a harmonização entre a gestão dos problemas religiosos e os problemas políticos no quotidiano institucional do período constantiniano, pautando-se pelo propósito da união de interesses (op. cit., 28) *"il y a compénétration intime entre les deux"*,. O imperador converte-se no *episcopos ton ektos* – "o bispo das coisas externas da Igreja". Esta ascendência política deve, portanto, ser sempre tida em conta quando se fala da fixação da identidade e do dogma cristão que ocupou estes dois séculos pós-constantinianos. Ou seja, a versão do cristianismo que emergiu, não só nos aspetos institucionais[11], mas

---

[10] Constantino estava profundamente lúcido quanto ao lugar de vigilante que lhe cabia. Eusébio de Cesareia, *Vita Constantini* 4, 24 narra que o próprio, num banquete cerimonial oferecido aos Bispos, afirmaria: "que também ele era um bispo", dirigindo-se a eles com as palavras que testemunhei – se vós sois bispos dos assuntos internos da Igreja, eu, é como se fosse. E na verdade as suas palavras eram exatas, pois vigiou todos os assuntos com um zelo episcopal, e exortava-o, tanto quanto podia, a conduzirem uma vida prudente (*eusebe bion metadiokein*)" (nossa tradução).

[11] Gaudemet 1947: 25-61, p. 27 ss: as dezoito constituições (entre 313 e 335) legislam sobre as três religiões, cristianismo (as várias correntes, data de 313 a primeira intervenção imperial sobre questões internas da Igreja, e é sobre o Donatismo), judaísmo e, indistintamente consideradas, as religiões tradicionais. Aos bispos é reconhecido poder de julgar, e os cristãos podem optar pela apresentação das suas causas à autoridade religiosa (CTH 1, 16, 2, 5). Com

também ideológicos e teológicos, encontra-se fortemente implicada com a supervisão imperial.

O envolvimento político nas questões internas da Igreja fundamentava-se numa conceção ideológica de Estado absoluto próprio do império: o bom governo e a preservação do império implicavam garantir o apoio das forças religiosas protetoras de Roma. Com a cristianização promovida por Constantino, a nova religião deveria, como as outras, e a partir da escolha afetiva do imperador, mais do que as outras, zelar pela continuidade de Roma. Por isso, para o Imperador, participar e ser protagonista do processo de sedimentação do dogma e da organização da Igreja em curso é uma extensão do seu *imperium*. Deste modo, não se alhear do "problema religioso" cristão, participar, influenciar e, através da iniciativa legislativa, formular medidas de enquadramento da Igreja e seus agentes no Século, fizeram parte da estratégia de construir a unanimidade e união entre os súbditos, eliminando ou neutralizando os focos de cisão percebidos como ameaçadores para a preservação de Roma assente num ideário de *Pax* e da *reparatio* da propaganda imperial.

Além da ideologia de princípio, o período conturbado da história da Igreja no séc. IV constituiu uma circunstância agravante para a necessidade de o poder político intervir de vários modos nas questões religiosas, em particular nas que tivessem incidência sobre a organização social, o acesso e a intervenção no espaço público[12].

Paralelamente, a construção e a imposição aos súbditos desta unanimidade, em condições sociais e económicas bastante degradadas como foram as do último século da Roma do Ocidente, converteram-se num agravamento da

---

ganhos evidentes para a estabilização do património eclesiástico; em 320, são abolidas as penalizações patrimoniais quanto ao celibato e viuvez que datavam da legislação augustana; em 321, o direito de *manumissio* atribuído às igrejas (CTh1. 4, 7, 1); o direito a testamentar em benefício da Igreja (CTh 1. 16, 2, 4); o repouso generalizado do *Dies Solis* (CTh 1. 2, 8, 1), são exemplos de disposições que, ordenando um modo *sub lege* na relação entre o Estado e a Igreja, com ganhos para a paz pública, dentro e fora da Igreja, representam, progressivamente, uma alienação das responsabilidades jurídicas do estado, que delega, numa instituição que considera credível e honorável, *funções extra-religiosas*.

[12] Elliott, Th. 1990: 349-353 deixa claro que não há alterações significativas de referentes e de retórica entre os panegíricos imperiais e as inscrições em honra dos imperadores préconstantinianos e pós constantinianos. O próprio Eusébio de Cesareia nos dá conta desta linguagem de poder que associa o Imperador à vontade da divindade (o *instintu diuinitatis* inscrito no Arco de Constantino), em que se salvaguarda a pose sacerdotal do Imperador, mas sem os sinais específicos da sua identificação com o Deus cristão, em particular com a figura de Cristo. Cf. também o *Laus Constantini* (V, 1-5) composto por Eusébio de Cesareia (Martin 2005: 125-126, nossa tradução), em que se define a função imperial como uma epistasia (vigilância): «...corajoso graças às suas ligações com a potência do alto (*anotato metaschon dunameos andreios*). É com justiça que ele carrega o título de imperador, ele, cujas qualidades de espírito conformaram as virtudes imperiais como uma prefiguração do reino do universo (...) considera o governo dos humanos como um ministério de vigilância (*epistasian ousa*) e de ajuda ao desenrolar de uma vida breve e passageira...».

intolerância face à divergência, identificada como uma ameaça à *oikonomia*. A linguagem unanimista e o reforço da propaganda da paz e da concórdia nacionais formularam-se em coerência com a modelação de um cristianismo oficial pouco disponível para a diversidade religiosa, viesse ela do paganismo sobrevivente, ou da heterodoxia cristã de cuja génese falámos anteriormente.

É neste sentido que nos parece dever ser enquadrado o protagonismo dos imperadores no período de discussão dogmática que se situa entre a celebração dos quatro concílios ecuménicos do séc. IV-V, Concílio de Niceia de 325 d.C.; Constantinopla de 380; Éfeso I, 431 e Éfeso II em 449; e o Concílio da Calcedónia de 451 d.C.: após este período, resulta uma imagem mais depurada, mais definida da Igreja, que é, no núcleo das verdades fundamentais da fé, a mesma de hoje. A fórmula da fé (o Credo) em debate em todos os concílios mencionados estabilizou no modelo de Calcedónia, mas cada palavra foi pensada, pesada, disputada entre partes desavindas, adotando o imperador a função de presidente moderador, árbitro, e instância de apelo.

A unidade interna da fé constituiu um trabalho de desbaste da divergência, um exercício de purificação e de restrição face à liberdade especulativa e exuberância de inspiração e de práticas que o cristianismo até então gozara, animado pelo vigoroso motor da vivência religiosa a partir das bases. Neste domínio, o abraço e a vigilância imperial convergiram com um propósito unificador e condicionaram as partes desavindas em função de um programa político, para quem era reconfortante um modelo monolítico de cristianismo, porque se conformava com uma ordem cósmica e política em harmonia de formulação antiga: uma visão uniforme da fé, uma hierarquia eclesiástica, humana e territorialmente decalcada da administração civil, dócil e reconhecedora da ascendência do imperador sobre a Igreja, em sintonia com o esforço de unidade em torno do imperador e do frágil ideal de império apesar de todas as forças desintegradoras do mesmo se encontrarem já em marcha, é o retrato da Igreja desejada por Constantino, alcançada pela dinastia Constantiniana, por Teodósio I e II, os Imperadores vigentes e interventores nos concílios ecuménicos[13].

---

[13] A este propósito, destaque-se que, mesmo Galério, o imperador que suspendeu a perseguição dos cristãos em 311, dá sinal, no seu Édito, de que os cristãos "nem o próprio Deus dos Cristãos respeitam" (nossa tradução de Lactâncio 2013, *De Mortibus Persecutorum*, 34-35, in Dias 2012: 44) no que consideramos ser uma alusão à carga conflitual já exibida pelo cristianismo antes de Constantino. O Édito de Galério, aliás, adota o tom condescendente de quem considera que, ao conferir legalidade ao cristianismo, está a por em prática uma estratégia de contenção de males. Os primeiros cismas na Igreja a merecerem a atenção imperial ocorreram no Ocidente, e em causa estavam questões de interpretação pastoral ou divergências do calendário litúrgico. Na África do norte, primeiro o Novacianismo, depois o Donatismo traziam à discussão o delicado assunto dos *lapsi*, ou seja, qual o estatuto dos cristãos que, diante da perseguição, apostasiavam. Em 314, um ano após proclamar a liberdade da Igreja, Constantino convoca um sínodo em Arles para confirmar as decisões da Igreja provincial de Cartago anteriormente tomadas. Minerath 1996. Também Eusébio

Portanto, parece-nos fundamental destacar que, da parte dos imperadores da dinastia constantiniana, a aproximação, adesão e o favorecimento do cristianismo devem ser percebidos dentro de um propósito estratégico e político, por muito cativante ou interessante que seja observar os relatos das conversões dos imperadores e a intervenção de fatores transcendentais nas mesmas. Não discutimos o crédito ou o interesse na análise das mesmas. Mas, como motivação principal, parece-nos restritivo aceitar a motivação transcendental, em termos de racionalidade histórica.

Esta pode ser discutida ao nível da ficção alegórica do poder e explorada enquanto discurso literário, mas não pode integrar a procura mais objetiva dos processos históricos. Assim, estamos em crer que a emotiva conversão de Constantino ao cristianismo após a visão da Batalha da Ponte Mílvia convive mal com o calculismo da sua ação, que, sendo favorável aos cristãos, se revela gradual, feita de progressivas concessões, visando a gestão de um frágil equilíbrio perante as crises de unidade da Igreja e os problemas do império. A vitória de Constantino sobre os seus rivais, só concluída uma década após a vitória sobre Maxêncio, acordou um império exangue, dilacerado por toda a espécie de conflitos.

Já no édito de Tolerância de Galério, de 311, é possível constatar que o cristianismo se revela, na linguagem jurídica do documento imperial, como uma questão a ser regulamentada, não porque seja um bem, mas porque é preferível para a ordem do Estado que as questões a ele associadas decorram *in lege*. No essencial, este modo de agir, mesmo com imperadores solidários ou eles próprios cristãos, não se alterou com Constantino e seus sucessores. A salvaguarda e a preeminência da função imperial, que havia sofrido uma clara erosão durante o séc. III, necessitavam de ser aceites e reconhecidas pelo importante grupo de pressão que era a comunidade de cristãos, em particular pelas suas elites urbanas, líderes de opinião dentro das suas fações, e frequentemente associadas ao ministério episcopal[14]. De certo modo, o estado romano tardo-antigo cristianizado serve-se da bem organizada e sedutora máquina de envolvimento das consciências proporcionada pela Igreja, com uma notável capacidade de gerar paixões e de galvanizar multidões, como veículo para comunicar e manter reconhecível o estatuto sagrado do imperador e o zelo pela continuidade de Roma,

---

de Cesareia (Eusébio, HE 10, 5) dá conta de que Constantino e Licínio aprovaram, com o Édito de Milão, a liberdade de culto para os "judeus, samaritanos, marcionitias, montanistas, novacianos, sabelianos", o que indicia uma diversidade dos monoteísmos judeo-cristãos no séc. IV e um retrato muito complexo da paisagem religiosa.

[14] Millar 2006: 131: "the bishops came, as is well known, both to play a large part in the managements and physical development of cities, and to speak for them to officials in the imperial service". No domínio religioso, a popularidade e a adesão ao cristianismo das massas urbanas das cidades orientais trouxeram à visibilidade grupos turbulentos, empenhados em refletir no Século as suas conceções religiosas.

posto que esta fora escolhida pela providência divina como legatária do tempo imperfeito e provisório de passagem dos homens na terra.

Constantino tomou medidas favoráveis aos cristãos, começando justamente pela estabilização material da Igreja, o que prova a sua atitude empenhada numa Igreja institucionalmente forte. Ela tornou-se herdeira dos mártires que pereceram nas Perseguições e pôde ser constituída sujeito de doações feitas livremente. Proibiu que os cristãos fossem escravizados por alguém não cristão. Foi generoso com as igrejas e santuários, contribuindo para restaurar o que havia sido destruído ou patrocinando novos espaços[15]. As leis acompanharam a transformação social, aceleraram-na, e transmitiram a aspiração de um Estado ideal para quem legisla. Não há, no império, zonas cinzentas à presença do imperador. E quando uma parte significativa dos seus súbditos professam o cristianismo, religião até então fora da ordem pública, então é bom que o imperador se torne presente, integre, exerça autoridade e legisle sobre esta realidade que se afirmava com tanto vigor. Manifesta-se portanto uma simbiose de interesses entre o poder político e o poder religioso.

Além disso, o exercício de cargos eclesiásticos, nomeadamente o do episcopado, tornou-se um lugar de poder cada vez mais importante e acessível aos membros das famílias tradicionais do império. Graças à legislação de Constantino, estes postos concentravam recursos materiais próprios disponíveis para a assistência e o serviço público. Estes cristãos, entre consagrados e leigos, foram chamados a constituir a corte régia, por vontade imperial substituindo o aparato pagão, o que é sinal da nobilitação e de reconhecimento público inerentes ao estatuto cristão, operado sob a continuidade da simbologia do poder em Roma entre o período pré-cristão e a época constantiniana[16].

---

[15] Eusébio de Cesareia, *VC*, II.36.1. III, 27, 1III, 28, 1.

[16] A *VC* (1, 16, 2; 32, 3; 42, 1) menciona que Constantino reformou a sua corte, integrando nela homens da Igreja. As inovações jurídicas de Constantino contribuíram para a integração na vida pública dos titulares de cargos religiosos. Algumas destas iniciativas nasceram, na governação constantiniana, enquanto formas de estender os direitos dos sacerdotes das religiões pagãs e dos *collegia* tradicionais aos *clerici* e às *ecclesiae*: os membros da cúria que fossem clérigos beneficiavam de isenções fiscais (CTh. 16.2.1-2); o direito à constituição de tribunais próprios para julgamento de assuntos internos (CTh. 16.8.2-16.8.4). Outras, embora sejam apresentadas com motivações pragmáticas, resultam num claro benefício da Igreja, pois atribuíam aos bispos competências que os equiparavam ou os colocavam como substitutos dos executores da administração imperial civil e militar: é o caso da licença para usar o *cursus publicus*, o correio e os entrepostos imperiais exclusivos para os funcionários imperiais, por ocasião da celebração do Concílio ecuménico de Niceia de 325, convocado pelo imperador. Tal como está redigida, tratou-se de uma medida conjuntural, destinada a facilitar a deslocação dos delegados ao concílio. Mas não foi revogada (também porque as discussões conciliares provinciais se tornaram frequentes). Em 382, este privilégio passou a ter uma formulação definitiva (CTh. 12.12.9). Os bispos passaram também a exercer a *manumissio in ecclesia*, isto é, o direito de manumissão dos escravos pelos cristãos na Igreja tinha a mesma validade legal que pelos meios tradicionais (CTh. 1.13.1); os membros do clero podiam libertar os seus

Um aspeto nos parece relevante para explicar as motivações do Imperador: envolver-se e interferir nas questões da Igreja são tarefas inerentes ao propósito de garantir a estabilidade e a paz públicas, uma vez que a Igreja se havia tornado um espaço de conflito interno, por interpretações teológicas divergentes que serviam de pretexto para a reivindicação de causas particulares, como foram a rivalidade estratégica das cidades orientais como Alexandria e Antioquia face ao abraço apertado da hegemonista Constantinopla.

Um exemplo paradigmático deste delicado esforço de retirar benefícios políticos de legitimação da ordem e do poder instituído, fosse ele civil ou religioso, constitui o modo ambíguo como poder e Igreja secular lidaram com o monaquismo. Detendo este as suas origens na espiritualidade ascética dos primórdios do cristianismo, onde se manteve como força ativa na modelação da Igreja, eclodiu, a partir deste século IV, como um movimento de contestação ao acordo entre a Igreja e o poder político centralizado, e de crítica aos benefícios que estas duas estruturas de poder se vão, mutuamente, concedendo (isto é, a Igreja legitima e integra o imperador na ordem sacerdotal e este promove a sua integração no século).

Os primeiros testemunhos de disposições jurídicas conciliares ou imperiais dirigidos aos monges dão conta da reserva que estes inspiravam aos detentores do poder político e eclesiástico, pela sua mobilização, espírito contestatário e perturbação da ordem pública, fosse em atos violentos de destruição dos lugares pagãos, fosse na volatilidade com que se reviam na causa da sua ortodoxia, que consideravam lícito defender pela violência. Esta forma de cristianismo sofreu também um processo de conformação ao século, e disso dá-nos conta toda a determinação imperial e episcopal em garantir que os monges não deambulassem (a estabilidade passa a ser uma virtude), sobretudo pelas cidades, adotassem formas comunitárias de vida *sub regula uel sub abbate,* por fim, que estas comunidades, ainda que internamente autónomas, não existissem à revelia do Bispo da diocese em que se instalam[17].

Em conclusão:

As intervenções imperiais em prol da unidade religiosa, qualquer que fosse a linha teológica desta unidade, como se pode verificar pela oscilação imperial

---

servos por testamento ou por uma simples declaração, sem necessidade de testemunhas (CTh. 4.7.1). Em 321, a situação inverteu-se, quando os bispos absorveram a prerrogativa de *notatio manumissionis,* isto é, de serem eles a confirmar, por documento, a libertação de escravos ("affranchissement" DACL 1 (1924): 554-76). A prática veio a mostrar que muitos senhores cristãos libertavam os seus escravos por ocasião do baptismo, do diaconato, da ordenação ou da recepção do hábito monástico. Em 412, os bispos passaram a ser também os *notatores* das crianças órfãs (CTh. 5.9). Nestas circunstâncias, a aprovação destas leis pode resultar de um hábil reconhecimento dos factos: a Igreja lidaria com um maior volume de manumissões e, uma vez diminuídas as práticas sociais o aborto e a exposição de crianças, também era ela quem acolhia as crianças não desejadas.

[17] Dias 2011: 1-34.

entre o apoio ao arianismo e a linha ortodoxa, decorria, em primeiro lugar, da própria função imperial em garantir que as forças ativas do império se empenhavam na preservação de Roma. Em segundo lugar, tratava-se de uma estratégia pragmática de afirmação do poder do Estado, mantendo este a sua *auctoritas* e identificação com os interesses da sociedade pelo seu envolvimento e incorporação dos grupos com crescente influência e demograficamente significativos.

Em terceiro lugar, a aproximação do Imperador às questões internas da Igreja decorreu, também, do contexto "aberto" em que emergiu o cristianismo após a sua legalização. Como pudemos explicar, muito havia que fazer pela Igreja no sentido de definir o seu lugar no século e mesmo a substância doutrinal que sustentava a sua identidade. Quando o Imperador Constantino recebeu o assunto da Igreja, esta encontrava-se suficientemente fluída no plano institucional e organizativo, o que lhe permitiu condicionar a sua inserção em sociedades milenares, hostis ou neutras à novidade cristã, necessariamente desformatadas para acolher institucionalmente e legalmente o cristianismo.

Acresce a este cenário a própria circunstância histórica de crise e fragmentação do Estado romano, tendência com altos e baixos mas consistente movimento de fundo desde o séc. III. Mesmo as intervenções legislativas dos imperadores que versam questões religiosas constituem, frequentemente, *rescriptiones*, ou seja, respostas diante de um relatório ou de uma exposição; ou *petitiones*, apresentadas pelos delegados municipais, mostrando portanto que a autoridade imperial perdera o comando dos acontecimentos, restando-lhe reagir face ao curso imparável da história. Cada vez mais os interlocutores locais da autoridade imperial eram bispos, a quem foi sendo delegado o exercício do poder temporal sobre os cristãos.

Esta medida, que nascera com a finalidade de garantir aos cristãos a gestão dos seus assuntos segundo os seus valores e critérios, na época ainda plural do período constantiniano, teria um efeito gigantesco, numa sociedade que caminhava, progressivamente, para o domínio dos cristãos sobre o espaço público urbano. Se todos são cristãos, então os bispos legitimam-se como novos agentes da coisa pública e novos funcionários numa época de progressivo abandono do estado das suas funções administrativas e militares, tornando-se, com frequência, as únicas autoridades consistentes, os únicos mediadores legitimados para dialogar com o Imperador ou com os invasores, que ameaçavam a segurança urbana.

Desta forma se dissolveu a fronteira entre o religioso e o não religioso. Assim, com a Antiguidade Tardia cristã, nascera esta forma particular de instabilidade social, e política associada a controvérsias de identidade religiosa[18].

---

[18] Rapp 2005: 236; s.v. "Access to the Emperor: *Parrhesia* of Bishops and Holy men": 260-262, sobre a permissão concedida aos bispos de realizar atos jurídicos até então pertencentes ao estado, como a transmissão da propriedade, a aplicação da justiça.

Assim, os imperadores foram instados pelos líderes religiosos locais a intervirem como moderadores e decisores na controvérsia donatista no Norte de África; no cisma meleciano no Egipto; na longa crise arianista das províncias orientais que se estenderia até ao Ocidente. E isto sucede não só porque ele é um legítimo interventor nas questões teológicas da Igreja, mas sobretudo porque estas controvérsias assumiram contornos de perturbação e de instabilidade sobre a ordem pública do império.

O envolvimento imperial nas questões internas da Igreja não nasceu de modo potencial ou preventivo, tal como as crises de heterodoxia tornadas públicas a partir do séc. IV não constituíram exercícios especulativos e teóricos sobre o modelo de cristianismo a seguir. Império e Igreja responderam a crises declaradas, sentidas sinceramente como ameaças à unidade e à autoridade. Tanto o Imperador como as autoridades eclesiásticas agiram, pela elaboração de leis, pela fixação de dogmas conciliares e controlo da ordem pública, sobre uma realidade em mutação efervescente, pondo em risco a unidade espiritual do Império, e com ela a concórdia e a unanimidade em torno da preservação de Roma.

Até ao período constantiniano, a unanimidade de fé religiosa nunca tinha sido, ao longo da sua história, um desiderato, ou uma condição para a estabilidade de Roma. O princípio da liberdade e da não exclusividade religiosa da Roma pré-cristã, tolerante face aos cultos estrangeiros, traduzia-se no pequeno impacto que o sagrado, sobretudo a fé individual de cada um, exercia sobre a condução do Estado. Bastava que as mais variadas expressões, não exclusivas entre si, aceitassem conviver com as exigências dos cultos cívicos ao imperador, família imperial e à deusa Roma.

Todo este equilíbrio se rompeu com a progressiva elevação do cristianismo a religião dominante, alçada a religião exclusiva e de propósitos ecuménicos, universalistas, militantemente contra a diversidade religiosa no espaço público e na esfera privada. Esta impossibilidade intrínseca em o cristianismo antigo incorporar a diferença e diversidade religiosas contribuiu para que todas as ameaças a este unanimismo, viessem elas da fricção entre os cultos tradicionais do velho paganismo com a nova ordem cristã, viessem da heterodoxia interna ao próprio cristianismo, se tornassem um problema grave de unidade social e política, de consequências gravíssimas para a concórdia da pátria.

A Cidade de Deus e a Cidade dos Homens:
génese de um paradigma
(The City of God and the City of Men: Genesis of a Paradigm)

Marleine Paula M. e F. de Toledo (marleinepaula@hotmail.com)
Universidade de São Paulo

Resumo – Este ensaio faz um estudo comparativo entre duas obras que tratam de *poleis* e cosmópoles: *A cidade de Deus*, de Santo Agostinho, e *Pauliceia dilacerada* , de Mário Chamie. *Polis* é a cidade. *Kosmos* é o mundo. Cosmópolis pode ser entendida como uma grande cidade, cidade mundial, que abriga gente numerosa e diferenciada. Em sua obra *De civitate Dei*, Santo Agostinho propõe a gênese de um paradigma para todas as cidades do mundo, *poleis* e cosmópoles: à cidade concreta –*polis* ou *urbs* - sobrepõem-se duas *civitates*, isto é, sociedades humanas. A primeira é a *civitas hominum*, cidade dos homens. É constituída pelos homens que vivem segundo sua própria vontade e, por isso, comporta divisões, uma vez que cada indivíduo ou facção coloca o bem supremo em "lugar" diferente. Seu fim é a morte. A segunda, *civitas Dei*, cidade de Deus, é constituída pelos homens que vivem segundo a vontade de Deus. Por essa razão, é unívoca a respeito do bem supremo, não abriga divisões internas, uma vez que a vontade de Deus é uma só e é boa. Seu fim é o céu. No livro *Pauliceia dilacerada*, o poeta brasileiro e paulista Mário Chamie "finge" um monólogo póstumo "dialogado" do também poeta e também paulista (aliás, paulistano) Mário de Andrade, em que o referente é a cidade de São Paulo. Nesse monólogo poético a quatro mãos, podem ser identificadas as duas cidades do paradigma agostiniano: a cidade dos homens, na Pauliceia real, dilacerada; a cidade de Deus, na Pauliceia possível, anseio dos dois Mários.

Palavras-chave: *urbs*, *civitas*, *polis*, cosmópole, cidade de Deus, cidade dos homens, sumo bem, morte, céu.

Abstract – This essay makes a comparative study of two works that treat *poleis* and *kosmopoleis*: *The City of God* by Saint Augustine, and *Pauliceia dilacerada* by Mario Chamie. *Polis* is the city; *kosmos* is the world. *Kosmopolis* may be understood as a big city, a global city, one that receives numerous and different people. In *De civitate Dei*, Augustine proposes the genesis of a paradigm for all the cities of the world, the *poleis* and *kosmopoleis:* the actual city, *polis* or *urbs*, contains two *civitates*, that is, two human societies. One is *civitas hominum*, the city of the men. It comprises men who live according to their own will; therefore it involves divisions, because each man or faction puts the highest good in a different "place". Its end is death. Another is the *civitas Dei*, the city of God, which comprises the men who live according the will of God. Therefore it is univocal about the highest good and does not encompass divisions, because the will of God is only single and good. Its end is heaven. In the book *Pauliceia dilacerada*, the Brazilian and *Paulista* (i.e., from São Paulo) poet Mário Chamie "fictionalizes" a posthumous monologue reimagined as dialogue of a poet Mario de Andrade, likewise a Paulista, in which the point of reference is the city of

https://doi.org/10.14195/978-989-26-1280-5_7

São Paulo. In this four-handed poetic monologue, the two cities of the paradigm of Augustine are identified: the city of the men, in the real and lacerated Pauline city, and the city of God, in the potential Pauline city, the aspiration of the two Marios.

Keywords: *urbs, civitas, polis, kosmopolis,* city of God, city of the men, highest good, dead, heaven

1. A Cidade de Deus e a Pauliceia dilacerada

De civitate Dei, A cidade de Deus, é a obra mais importante de Santo Agostinho. Vinte e dois livros, dois alentados volumes, somando mais de mil páginas, traduzidas para o português, na edição aqui utilizada, por Oscar Paes Leme. Santo Agostinho escreveu-a entre 413 e 426, para retratar, no que fosse possível, a "gloriosa Cidade de Deus", que "prossegue em seu peregrinar através da impiedade e dos tempos, vivendo pela fé, e com paciência", à espera da mansão eterna[1]

Sua intenção era apologética. Pretendia defender essa santa cidade contra os homens que "a seu divino fundador preferem as divindades" do paganismo[2]. Daí o subtítulo: "Contra os pagãos".

As circunstâncias históricas eram as seguintes: em 410, as hostes do godo Alarico conquistaram Roma, com o séquito de calamidades que acompanham toda vitória militar. Era o prenúncio da queda, embora o domínio de Alarico tenha sido breve, porque a falta de provisões o obrigou a retirar-se para o sul[3].

Os romanos acusaram a Deus e aos cristãos por esse desastre. O edito de Constantino, de 313, institucionalizara o Cristianismo como religião oficial do Império, de sorte que ficava proscrito o culto aos antigos deuses. Realmente, "a vitória do cristianismo assinala o fim da sociedade antiga"[4]. Julgaram, então, os romanos que seus antigos deuses, outrora cultuados e agora não, negaram-lhes a proteção e assim Roma fora vencida.

Santo Agostinho insurge-se contra essa acusação e prova que, em nenhum momento da história romana, os deuses foram os responsáveis por vitórias ou derrotas. Por exemplo, durante a República, houve inúmeras e sangrentas sedições. Então,

"onde estavam esses deuses que julgam se lhes deva culto, por causa da mesquinha e enganadora felicidade deste mundo, quando os romanos, a quem com diabólica astúcia se entregavam para que lhes rendessem culto, se viram atormentados por tantas calamidades?"[5].

---

[1] Santo Agostinho 2009, v. I: 27.
[2] Santo Agostinho 2009, v. I: 27.
[3]. Mattoso 1935: 490.
[4] Coulanges 1971:470
[5] Santo Agostinho 2009, v. I: 127.

O verdadeiro Deus, pelo contrário, favorecera cristãos e não cristãos no desastre então causado por Alarico, pois comovera o coração desse chefe, que permitiu que cristãos e não cristãos se abrigassem nas basílicas cristãs. Muitos, assim, foram poupados da morte: "Detinha-se, nos santuários, a ferocidade que faz vítimas, embotava-se a cupidez que quer cativos"[6].

Tal fato é inaudito em toda a história romana. Os deuses proscritos pelo cristianismo nunca permitiram que seus fiéis se abrigassem dentro de seus templos para se defenderem nas batalhas. Quando, por exemplo, Troia foi tomada pelos gregos, os deuses não se manifestaram:

> "Troia, como afirmei, Troia, mãe do povo romano, não pôde, nos templos das divindades, defender seus próprios cidadãos contra as chamas inimigas, contra o gládio dos gregos adoradores dos mesmos deuses" [7]

A Pauliceia dilacerada é a cidade brasileira de São Paulo, na visão do poeta paulista Mário Chamie. Em um monólogo póstumo, ficcional, mas baseado em documentos, Chamie veste a pele de seu "xará", Mário de Andrade, também poeta e também paulista, aliás paulistano, e derrama-se sobre a grande cidade.

Em que pese à distância no tempo, é possível estabelecer um paralelo entre a cidade de Santo Agostinho e a dos Mários. Santo Agostinho fala de duas cidades, a de Deus e a dos homens. Os Mários, de certa forma, também.

2. *POLIS* E COSMÓPOLIS

Para designar cidade, o grego usa a palavra *polis,* cujo primeiro significado é o de cidade com seu território concreto onde vivem as pessoas. Em especial, chegou a designar a cidade de Troia, em Homero, e de Atenas, entre os áticos. Mas designa também a reunião dos cidadãos, a sociedade, o estado[8]. Com esse último significado é que passou ao português pólis: "um estado ou sociedade, especialmente quando caracterizado por um senso de comunidade"[9].

Contudo, o grego *polis* manteve em português a referência territorial no radical pospositivo - polis, formador de toponímicos (Petrópolis, Florianópolis), bem como no composto cosmópole. A cosmópole, ou o erudito cosmópolis, é uma categoria especial de *polis*, que se caracteriza "pela vultosa dimensão e pelo grande número de habitantes, frequentemente originários dos mais diversos pontos do país ou também de outros países"[10]. Nova Iorque, São Paulo são cosmópoles.

---

[6] Santo Agostinho 2009, v. I: 28
[7] Santo Agostinho 2009, v.. I: 31
[8] Bailly 1963: polis
[9] Houaiss 2001: "polis"
[10] Houaiss 2001: "cosmópole".

Por outro lado, levando-se em conta o primeiro radical de cosmópolis (*kosmos*, mundo), pode-se estabelecer um confronto entre *polis* e cosmópolis: a primeira diz respeito à individualidade local de uma cidade; a segunda, a uma hipotética cidade global, em que todas e cada uma das cidades concretas se vejam representadas. *Polis* pode ser a cidade, cosmópolis pode ser o mundo.

3. *URBS E CIVITAS*

O latim tem duas palavras para traduzir o grego *polis*: *urbs* e *civitas*. *Urbs* é a cidade concreta[11], aquela de quem diz Santo Agostinho: "Depois da cidade ou da urbe vem o orbe da terra, terceiro grau da sociedade humana, que percorre os seguintes estágios: casa, urbe, orbe"[12]. O poeta Mário Chamie, tantos anos depois, parece ter tido a mesma inspiração: "Primeiro esbocei o povoado. Depois, a vila. Em seguida, a urbe, antecipando a cidade"[13].

Civitas designa o conjunto de cidadãos que constituem uma cidade, um estado[14]. A *civitas* inclui a *urbs*, porém ultrapassa-a.

Para Santo Agostinho, a cidade verbalizada por *civitas* é a *societas*, a sociedade, humana quando se trata da *civitas hominum*, divina quando se trata da *civitas Dei*. Tanto uma quanto outra constituem uma *polis* (comunidade) ideal e exemplar, potencialmente presente em todas as *poleis* e cosmópoles concretas.

4. GÊNESE DE UM PARADIGMA

Quando Santo Agostinho escreveu *De civitate Dei*, estava propondo a gênese de um paradigma. Com a denominação *civitas*, para ele existem duas espécies de cidades, que abarcam as *urbes* de todo o orbe, todas as *poleis* e cosmópoles: a cidade de Deus e a cidade dos homens.

Afirma, no Livro Décimo Quarto, que os povos disseminados por toda a terra formam duas sociedades: a dos que querem viver segundo a carne e a dos que querem viver segundo o espírito.

Viver segundo a carne não significa seguir o ideal epicurista, que considera o prazer do corpo o supremo bem para o homem. Viver segundo o espírito não significa, por sua vez, seguir os estoicos, que colocam esse sumo bem no espírito. Ambos esses modos de viver são carnais, porque a carne designa o homem.

Viver segundo a carne significa viver o homem segundo o próprio homem, sendo seu próprio princípio; é viver na mentira, porque Deus é a verdade e criou

---

[11] Gaffiot: *urbs*
[12] Santo Agostinho 2009, v. I: 389.
[13] Chamie 2009: 97
[14] Gaffiot: *civitas*

o homem para viver não "segundo ele mesmo, mas segundo quem o fez, isto é, para fazer a vontade de Deus e não a sua"[15]. Viver segundo o espírito é viver o homem segundo Deus, fazendo a vontade de Deus.

Do fato de viverem uns segundo a carne e outros segundo o espírito originaram-se duas cidades diferentes e contrárias entre si: a cidade dos homens e a cidade de Deus, as quais "neste mundo andam ambas misturadas e confundidas uma com a outra"[16]. Isso porque a cidade celeste, enquanto é peregrina, vive nas cidades terrenas e adota os costumes do lugar onde vive, contanto que não vão de encontro aos preceitos divinos.

O paradigma agostiniano é, pois, o seguinte: todas as *urbes, poleis* ou cosmópoles podem abrigar, misturadas, duas *civitates*, a dos homens e a de Deus. A dos homens tem seu fim em si mesma, não tem dimensão escatológica nem transcendental. A de Deus é peregrina aqui na terra; possui dimensão escatológica e transcendental; começa aqui na terra e consuma-se gloriosamente no céu.

5. Urbes

A *urbs* de Santo Agostinho é representada por Roma, em todas as suas fases, até a pós-invasão de Alarico, em 410:

"Após a destruição de Troia, Eneias arribou à Itália com vinte navios, portadores dos despojos troianos. Então Latino reinava na Itália ... Morto Latino, Eneias reinou por três anos...[17]. Para abreviar o mais possível, direi que Roma foi fundada como outra Babilônia, como filha da primeira, e que aprouve a Deus servir-se dela para humilhar o universo todo e pacificá-lo, reduzindo-o à unidade da mesma república com as mesmas leis" [18]

Em sua trajetória, Roma passou pelos reis, pela República, pelos imperadores, com todas as suas sedições. Conheceu a grandeza e a decadência. A grandeza, paradoxalmente, foi-lhe a decadência, corrompidos os costumes pelo fausto oriental. Segundo Salústio, citado por Santo Agostinho, entre a segunda e a terceira guerra púnica, os romanos "viveram em ótimos costumes e máxima concórdia" (id. ibid. V. I: 135). Santo Agostinho concorda com Cipião, que, contra a opinião de Catão, julgava que era preciso vencer a inimiga Cartago, mas não destruí-la:

"Receava outro inimigo das almas fracas, a segurança, e não queria do necessário tutor, o medo, emancipar a pupila romana. Os acontecimentos

---

[15] Santo Agostinho 2009, v.. II: 131.
[16] Santo Agostinho 2009, v.. II: 17.
[17] Santo Agostinho 2009, v. II: 328
[18] Santo Agostinho 2009, v. II: 331

justificam-lhe a previsão. Destruída Cartago, sufocado e sepulto em suas ruínas o eterno terror de Roma, então é que o destino engendra lamentável série de calamidades. O jugo da concórdia quebra-se, ... sedições, ... guerras civis ... ; os romanos que, quando virtuosos, nada receavam senão dos inimigos, agora, decaídos dos costumes hereditários, tudo têm a sofrer dos concidadãos"[19]

A Roma de Agostinho é uma cosmópole, pela dimensão e diversidade populacional: ali viviam, misturados aos autóctones, estrangeiros vindos de todas as colônias.

A *urbs* de Mário Chamie é um misto da São Paulo dos anos 20 e 30, época de Mário de Andrade, e a sua São Paulo cosmopolitana do século 21.

Essa Pauliceia concreta já foi cabana, vila, e é hoje urbe e cidade. Cidade amada pelos Mários: "As ruas de São Paulo transformaram-se em minhas veias e artérias. As praças de São Paulo instalaram-se nas ramificações do meu fígado, do meu coração"[20]. "Eu era São Paulo, São Paulo me era", diz o Mário mais velho pela boca do mais novo[21]. Cidade que, à semelhança da Roma de Santo Agostinho, corrompida pelo fausto e dividida pelas sedições, depois se dilacerou com o progresso desumanizador do "São Paulo não pode parar":

"... no ritmo evolutivo da Paulistânia, cujos marcos assinalados têm nome e visibilidade histórica, a saber: da casa de pau-a-pique, a Paulistânia evoluiu para a casa de taipa; da casa de taipa para a casa de tijolo; da casa de tijolo para a alvenaria marmórea do sobrado; da alvenaria do sobrado para as argamassas refinadas dos palacetes; dos palacetes para os edifícios de concreto; e destes para os arranha-céus de metal e vidro" [22].

6. *Civitas hominum* e *civitas Dei*

Nos limites da *urbs* de Santo Agostinho desenvolveram-se duas *civitates*, que se distinguem pelo bem absoluto que procuram:

"A cidade terrena, que não vive da fé, apetece também a paz terrena; porém, firma a concórdia entre os cidadãos que mandam e os que obedecem, para haver, quanto aos interesses da vida mortal, certo concerto das vontades humanas. Mas a cidade celeste, ou melhor, a parte que peregrina neste vale e vive da fé usa dessa paz por necessidade, até passar a mortalidade, que precisa de tal paz"[23].

Assim, a cidade terrena, a sociedade dos homens, tal como existe alojada em todas as cidades do mundo, anseia pela paz terrena e, para tanto, governantes e

---

19 Santo Agostinho 2009, v. I: 60
20 Chamie 2009: 5.
21 Chamie 2009: 92.
22 Chamie 2009: 60.
23 Santo Agostinho 2009, v. II: 402.

governados tentam um acordo de concórdia, nos limites humanos da vida mortal. A cidade celeste e espiritual, não alojada, mas peregrina nas mesmas cidades do mundo, busca também a paz, mas aquela que ultrapassa a mortalidade e alcança o plano das eternas essências; não tem a paz terrena como finalidade, mas como instrumento para conseguir a eterna e essencial.

O discurso de Mário Chamie, embora não seja teológico como o de Santo Agostinho, segue as mesmas trilhas ao tratar da cosmópole de São Paulo, Pauliceia dilacerada.

Os Mários, simbolizando toda a paulistaneidade, buscaram a paz terrena em sua *urbs*, como em sua *civitas hominum*. Buscaram-na como um acordo interior consigo mesmos, feito por meio da vivência de momentos gratos da vida paulistana. Não parecem, à primeira vista, ter buscado a paz essencial e transcendental. Mas só à primeira vista, como se verá.

7. *Civitas hominum* na Pauliceia dilacerada

Os Mários identificam a paz terrena que caracteriza a *civitas hominum* com uma tranquila felicidade vivida no passado, o supremo bem que *florebat olim* e não mais voltará. Persistiria, se São Paulo evoluísse para o futuro sem desfigurar o passado: "eu, o que mais queria era o equilíbrio polifônico das cumulações de uma São Paulo híbrida , aberta à presença de um passado ativo nas entranhas de um seu futuro virtualizado"[24].

O supremo bem era a São Paulo antiga, provinciana, religiosa, que já não existe:

> "Vocês sabem, as cidades brasileiras nasceram e cresceram em torno de uma igreja, de uma pracinha matriz. As casas enfileiradas em quarteirões, ao redor, voltavam as suas fachadas para a igreja também matriz, em estado de devoção à cruz de Cristo, a Deus. Eu sei e vocês sabem: matriz é mãe, é mulher. Nossas cidades, por isso, sempre nasceram teocêntricas, com Deus no centro do mundo, no centro das casas e das nossas vontades"[25].

Poderia ter sido também a Biblioteca Mário de Andrade, que o primeiro Mário começou com os livros que tinha espalhados pelo chão, em sua casa da Rua Lopes Chaves. Mas não foi, porque ela não teve a continuidade que ele desejava, como lamenta, pela boca de seu homônimo:

> "Hoje me infecta o ânimo ver como os meus sucessores emperraram o movimento interno de seus espaços, auditórios e salas. A biblioteca que imaginei

---

24 Chamie 2009: 20.
25 Chamie 2009: 67.

era para que o frequentador, que lá chegasse e sentasse, tivesse, de imediato, sobre sua mesa, o livro que procurou. Mas qual o quê! O cidadão chega, e logo na portaria tem que deixar carteira de identidade, CIC, RG, e não sei que mais outros adereços seus de suposta identificação pessoal"[26].

Ou a Villa Kyrial (cujo nome cabalisticamente deriva de *kyrios*, Senhor). Assim se chamava a chácara da Rua Domingos de Morais, 34, na Vila Mariana. Pertencia ao senador e mecenas José de Freitas Valle, que ali promovia saraus, almoços e outros eventos para a intelectualidade paulistana. Apesar de suntuosa, era um recanto acolhedor.

Ali acorriam personalidades como Olívia Guedes Penteado, Mário de Andrade, Oswald de Andrade, Lasar Segall, Anita Malfatti, Victor Brecheret, Francisco Mignone, Heitor Villa-Lobos, Washington Luís, Osvaldo Aranha, o tenor italiano Enrico Caruso, Sarah Bernhardt, Blaise Cendrars, Coelho Neto e Olavo Bilac.

Freitas Valle faleceu em 1958. Dois anos depois, a Villa Kyrial foi vendida, e, em 1961, foi demolida[27].

A Villa Kyrial, "tragada pela varredura predatória que se abateu sobre São Paulo"[28], abrigava, em consonância, o velho e o novo, consórcio caro a Mário de Andrade. Está no paraíso de suas lembranças perdidas, retomadas pelo xará Chamie:

> "...a Villa Kyrial era a imagem, era a síntese e era o emblema polido dessas mansões e palacetes. ... A demolição, portanto, da casa de Freitas Valle valeu por uma sentença de morte, decretada contra uma Paulistânia que, já plena metrópole, havia encontrado a plenitude de sua cara no esplendor *belle époque* de seus edifícios, habitações, parques, jardins, praças e viadutos, tudo formando um ambiente de convívio aberto à cordialidade interpessoal dos nossos cidadãos.[29]

Nos saraus da Villa nasceu muita inspiração para a Semana de Arte Moderna, momento grato às lembranças do primeiro Mário, revividas pelo segundo:

> "... dos saraus da Villa transportei para o Teatro Municipal os suportes e apoios que tornaram viável a realização da Semana de 22. Realizada a Semana, retornei, dois dias após, à casa de Kyrial, numa homenagem aos nossos elos acumulados, ao longo de nossas mudanças convergentes"[30]

---

[26] Chamie 2009: 82.

[27] Camargos: 2001. (Cf. http://flanelapaulistana.com/2007/07/vila-kyrial/, acessado em 10/02/2011. Cf. também: Camargos 2001).

[28] Chamie 2009: 62.

[29] Chamie 2009: 62.

[30] Chamie 2009: 20.

Precedeu a Semana e, de certa forma, influenciou-a o Armory Show, ou *a International Exhibition of Modern Art,* mostra itinerante de artes plásticas, inaugurada em Nova York, em 1913, com obras desde Goya, Delacroix, Ingres, Daumier, Corot, Courbet, passando por Manet, Van Gogh, Cézanne, Munch, até Matisse, Picasso, Braque, Picabia e Duchamp[31]. Seus idealizadores, embora soubessem do "conteúdo revolucionário do que estavam apresentando ao público, pareciam ter a intenção de convencê-lo 'pacificamente' de sua relevância cultural, o que, obviamente, não conseguiram"[32]. Não era o caso dos modernistas brasileiros, à frente o primeiro Mário, que pretendiam mesmo *épater.*

Ao supremo bem passado pertencem também os palacetes, que tiveram o mesmo destino da Villa: "...o lema "São Paulo não pode parar"condenou os palacetes, as mansões e os arranha-céus da Paulistânia à destruição e ao arraso intempestivo e inescapável"[33].

De sorte que essa paz terrena só subsistiu sugestivamente nos artísticos cemitérios. Quer dizer que o paraíso era e definitivamente se foi. Do fundo de seu jazigo, no cemitério da Consolação, um dos Mários, o de Andrade, desabafa:

> "Melhores do que todos, os mausoléus da Consolação, meu lar e meu teto, autenticam o hálito da sobrevivência: eles preservam e revitalizam a imutabilidade perene dos restos íntegros e despertos de nossa memória morta e renascida"[34].

No entendimento dos Mários, a Paulistânia foi, por assim dizer, demitida. Como foi demitido um dos Mários, o de Andrade. Demitido do Departamento de Cultura da Prefeitura de São Paulo, onde queria pôr em prática muitos planos, ele nunca mais se recuperou. Foi uma expulsão do paraíso, que, como se sabe, não tem volta. Mudou-se para o Rio de Janeiro: "Quando o corpo do Departamento fragmentou-se e se expeliu explodido, eu catapultei-me em frangalhos, remetido rumo à Guanabara"[35]. Chegou a voltar a São Paulo, mas não chegou a recuperar-se do desgosto. Ele demitido e a Paulistânia desfigurada e dilacerada pelo progresso irreverente se contraponteiam:

> "O despejo do meu lugar de permanência fraturou os andaimes e os suportes de meu mirante. Pôs por terra a ponte que me levava à cidade e que da cidade me levava a mim.

---

[31] Bastos 1991: 104.
[32] Bastos 1991: 103.
[33] Chamie 2009: 61.
[34] Chamie 2009: 63.
[35] Chamie 2009: 41.

Do alto dessa ponte, eu, destroçado, divisei o início fatídico da demolição da metrópole[36]

Segundo os Mários, os prefeitos Prestes Maia, Abraão Ribeiro e Faria Lima foram os autores dessa demolição: atulharam a superfície de São Paulo de prédios, pontes e viadutos, esfacelando-a e entupindo-lhe o trânsito[37]. "A trinca não entendeu e nem se sintonizou com o leque alternativo das soluções subterrâneas" (isto é, o metrô), "que a cidade de São Paulo levava consigo, à margem de seus ímpetos de superfície e dos arrojos monumentais dos seus arranha-céus"[38]. Preferiram as vias de superfície, "destinadas ao seu próprio estrangulamento"[39].

Essa tríplice aliança não estrangulou apenas São Paulo; estrangulou também as veias do primeiro Mário, apressando-lhe a *angina pectoris,* [40] que o levou ao enfarte e à morte:

> "Mas, ao me eliminarem – diz o Mário mais velho – fizeram com que a profecia que carrego comigo florescesse na manifestação de minha última vontade: a vontade de ser esquartejado e de ver vísceras e estilhaços de mim espalharem-se como raízes camufladas no meu solo bandeirante" [41]

Uma vez morto, Mário de Andrade, que vivo era "trezentos e cinquenta"[42], quer que os pedaços de seu corpo sejam distribuídos pelos logradouros da Pauliceia: os pés na Rua Aurora, o sexo no Paiçandu, a cabeça na Rua Lopes Chaves, o coração no Pátio do Colégio, o ouvido direito no Correio, o esquerdo nos Telégrafos, o nariz nos rosais, a língua no alto do Ipiranga, os olhos no Jaraguá, o joelho na Universidade, as mãos por aí, as tripas ao diabo, o espírito a Deus[43].

Mário de Andrade dilacerado, Pauliceia dilacerada. Essa fragmentação e demolição, humanas e urbanas, em Santo Agostinho sinalizam fragmentação e demolição de outra espécie.

8. Divisão e concórdia

Para Santo Agostinho, a fragmentação é a marca da cidade dos homens, a qual se divide internamente, porque seus cidadãos não se põem de acordo acerca

---

[36] Chamie 2009: 97.

[37] Mais recentemente Paulo Maluf orientou parte da verticalização de São Paulo para a promoção humana e social, com o projeto Cingapura: prédios populares para abrigar as populações faveladas. Cf. Figueiredo, Lamounier 1996: 183 e segs.

[38] Figueiredo, Lamounier 1996: 185-186.

[39] Figueiredo, Lamounier 1996: 186.

[40] "... a minha *causa mortis* motivada pela *angina pectoris* que sofri, provocada pela violência demissionária com que me coroaram". Figueiredo, Lamounier 1996: 112.

[41] Figueiredo, Lamounier 1996: 186.

[42] Figueiredo, Lamounier 1996: 162.

[43] Cf. Andrade 1974: 300-301; cf. Chamie, op. cit: 186-187.

do bem supremo; dividem-se os cidadãos, divide-se a cidade:

> "Estendida pela terra toda e nos mais diversos lugares, ligada pela comunhão da mesma natureza, a sociedade dos mortais divide-se com frequência contra si mesma e a parte que domina oprime a outra[44]. Deve-se isso a que cada qual busca a própria utilidade e a própria cupidez e a que o bem que apetecem não é suficiente para ninguém nem para todos, por não ser o bem autêntico[45].

Nessa cidade terrena, "uns fazem consistir o supremo bem no corpo; outros na alma; outros, em ambos; outros a ambos acrescentam os bens extrínsecos"[46].

Não acontece o mesmo com a cidade de Deus, unívoca a respeito do sumo bem: nela é "a vida eterna o soberano bem, a morte eterna o soberano mal"[47].

9. A ORIGEM

Santo Agostinho vem de um referencial filosófico platônico, em parte superado em sua conversão ao cristianismo. Mas em seu pensamento persistem as categorias platônicas[48]. Faz radicar a origem mais remota das duas cidades no "princípio", quando Deus, o sumo bem, a partir do nada fez a criação e o tempo.

As primeiras criaturas da cidade santa foram os santos anjos, parte "não pequena de tal cidade e tanto mais feliz quanto jamais foi peregrina"[49]. Mas houve anjos que apostataram.

Quando os anjos apóstatas (o diabo e todos os demônios) se afastaram de Deus, continuaram a ser racionais e eternos, mas, por uma defecção da vontade, perderam a felicidade e a bondade.

Nas duas sociedades de anjos, os bons e os maus, encontra-se o princípio das duas cidades, a divina e a humana.

Santo Agostinho privou com a doutrina dualista dos maniqueus[50]. Diferentemente dos platônicos, esses pensadores foram definitivamente banidos de suas reflexões. Implicitamente refutando-os, afirma não existir criador que não

---

[44] Quanto ao domínio dos fortes sobre os fracos na cidade terrena, secunda-o mais tarde Maquiavel, para quem , numa dominação política, é preciso favorecer os mais fortes e esbulhar os mais fracos: aqueles serão mais fiéis e não desejarão ofender o conquistador, para não sofrer o mesmo que os esbulhados; as partes prejudicadas, por sua vez, "pobres e dispersas, não serão capazes de causar danos". Cf. Maquiavel 2010: 21.

[45] Santo Agostinho 2009, v. II: 311.

[46] Santo Agostinho 2009, v. II: 354.

[47] Santo Agostinho 2009, v. II: 381.

[48] "Platão é o teólogo do mundo clássico. Sem ele não existiria a teologia nem como realidade nem como nome." Cf. Jaeger, (s/d): 817. Cf. Altaner, Stuiber, 1972: 413.

[49] Santo Agostinho 2009, v. II: 25.

[50] Altaner, Stuiber 1972: 412.

seja o Deus único. Portanto não pode existir natureza má, contrária a Deus, que é o sumo bem. Os inimigos de Deus não o são por natureza, mas por vontade.

Quanto ao homem, diferentemente dos outros seres, Deus criou-o a sua imagem, dando-lhe alma dotada de razão e inteligência, que o torna superior aos restantes animais. Criou-o para que, se lhe obedecesse, passasse, sem morrer, a gozar junto aos anjos de imortalidade feliz. Se desobedecesse por soberba, seria sujeito à morte, "escravizado pela libido e destinado depois a suplício eterno"[51].

O homem pecou e, depois do pecado, suprema soberba: apresentação de escusas ("a serpente me seduziu"; "a mulher deu-me da árvore") e nenhum pedido de perdão, "nenhum recurso à compaixão do Médico".[52]

10. A MORTE

O castigo do pecado foi a morte. Santo Agostinho considera três tipos de morte. Existe uma morte da alma; esta, embora seja imortal porque nunca desaparece, experimenta certa morte que lhe é própria, quando Deus a abandona. Existem outras duas mortes do homem. Dá-se a primeira, quando a alma se separa do corpo. Antes disso, mesmo se a alma estiver morta pela separação de Deus, o homem vive. Ocorre a segunda morte, quando, estando morta a alma pela separação de Deus e o corpo pela separação da alma, o homem incorre na condenação eterna, em eternos suplícios. Por causa do pecado, Deus cominou ao homem todas as mortes: a separação da alma e do corpo, a morte da alma e a segunda morte, a eterna.

A morte é castigo do pecado original e o homem não a experimentaria, se não tivesse pecado. Toda a humanidade tem de passar por ela, porque todos os homens estavam em germe no primeiro. "A enormidade da culpa e a consequente condenação corromperam a natureza e veio a ser natural nos descendentes o que nos primeiros homens pecadores precedeu como castigo"[53].

Desde que se nasce já se começa a morrer; o tempo vivido é subtraído daquele que se deve viver[54] e a morte não é bem para pessoa alguma, é contrária à natureza: o homem de tal maneira quer "ser" e não quer deixar de "ser", que, mesmo velho, doente ou mutilado, prefere a vida diminuída à morte.

Por isso Deus veio em socorro do homem que pecara, enviando-lhe um salvador para tirá-lo do poder da morte: seu Filho, Jesus Cristo, Deus e homem, Mediador entre Deus e os homens. Sem ter pecado, assumiu a carne de pecado,

---

[51] Santo Agostinho 2009, v. II: 84.
[52] Santo Agostinho 2009, v. II: 149.
[53] Santo Agostinho 2009, v. II: 94-95.
[54] Cf. Santo Agostinho 2009, v. II: 100. O poeta brasileiro Cassiano Ricardo parece ter haurido nessa passagem de Santo Agostinho a inspiração para seus belos versos: "Desde o instante em que se nasce/já se começa a morrer".

pregando-a na cruz, pagando em si os pecados dos homens. Ao terceiro dia ressuscitou, em corpo e alma, para garantir que pela fé nele o homem pode também passar pela morte e ressuscitar, igualmente, em corpo e alma.

O Batismo é um banho de regeneração, de novo nascimento. O homem batizado participa sacramentalmente da morte e ressurreição de Jesus Cristo. Se persevera no seguimento de Cristo, sua alma é salva da morte. Torna-se cidadão da cidade de Deus.

Não é assim que os Mários entendem a morte. O primeiro Mário morto fala pela boca do segundo Mário vivo. Machado de Assis já utilizara esse recurso em suas *Memórias Póstumas de Brás Cubas*, porém com uma diferença, como se verá.

No pensamento de Santo Agostinho, a morte física é um átimo: antes dela não há morte, uma vez que se está vivo e "antes" da morte, e depois dela também não há, porque se está morto e "depois" da morte[55]. No pensamento dos Mários, estetizada, a morte tem duração, por ser a "barca de Caronte"[56], a "viagem para o insondável"[57], a "descida aos infernos"[58], e é uma presença, por ser a "indesejada das gentes" [59] a "finitude"[60].

No pensamento de Santo Agostinho, a vida não deixa de ter sentido por incluir a premissa da morte. Os Mários, secundando a aporia da máquina do mundo de Carlos Drummond de Andrade, não veem a vida como um *non sense*, mas renunciam "à revelação dos segredos do mundo e de sua oculta maquinaria"[61].

Para Santo Agostinho, depois da morte, a alma, aguardando a ressurreição do corpo, ou está na eterna bem-aventurança ou nos eternos suplícios. A alma do Mário morto está viva, mas sepultada no cemitério da Consolação, que parece ser sua morada eterna. É seu "exílio póstumo e postergado"[62], seu "retiro tumular de entristecidas recordações"[63]. Não experimenta nem alegria nem tristeza. Conquistou "a paz enfezada do Paraíso"[64]. O corpo, estetizado também, está espalhado pelos logradouros de São Paulo, como já se viu.

11. O FIM

Para Santo Agostinho, no primeiro homem, na presciência de Deus,

---

55 Santo Agostinho 2009, v. II: 99-100.
56 Chamie 2009: 29.
57 Chamie 2009: 149.
58 Chamie 2009: 148.
59 Chamie 2009: 29.
60 Chamie 2009: 149.
61 Chamie 2009: 149.
62 Chamie 2009: 29.
63 Chamie 2009: 37.
64 Chamie 2009: 187.

estavam prefiguradas "duas sociedades de homens ou duas espécies de cidades"[65]. Dele procederiam os que seriam, por oculto mas justo desígnio de Deus, companheiros de suplícios dos anjos maus, e os que, salvos por Cristo, associar-se-iam à felicidade eterna dos anjos bons. Nesta vida terrena, ambas as sociedades caminham juntas e misturadas, como o joio ao trigo. Na vida eterna se separarão.

A cidade de Deus prosseguiu no povo judeu, escolhido por Deus, depositário da Lei divina contida nas Sagradas Escrituras, e do qual Cristo descende segundo a carne. Apesar da evidência das profecias, não creu no messianismo de Cristo e, por isso, a cidade de Deus mudou-se para a sociedade dos cristãos, a Igreja.

A cidade dos homens teve continuidade nos outros povos.

Contudo, antes do cristianismo e fora do judaísmo, houve certamente homens de bem no mundo, verdadeiros cidadãos da Cidade de Deus. Por outro lado, dentro da própria Igreja, convivem bons e maus, os quais serão separados apenas no fim.

No fim dos tempos se consumarão definitivamente as duas cidades, por um juízo definitivo de Deus sobre os homens, o juízo final:

> "Eis as coisas que sucederão no juízo ou até esse tempo: a vinda de Elias Tesbita, a conversão dos judeus, a perseguição do anticristo, a vinda de Cristo para julgar, a ressurreição dos mortos, a separação entre os bons e os maus, a conflagração do mundo e sua renovação"[66].

Nesta vida terrena, bons e maus passam igualmente por bens e males, para que os bons não absolutizem os bens terrenos e coloquem sua esperança nos eternos. No dia do Juízo, haverá a justa retribuição e se entenderá que Deus tudo fez com justiça.

Os condenados e os anjos apóstatas sofrerão um suplício eterno, isto é, sem fim, que consiste no fogo que queima e causa as máximas dores no corpo e na alma.

Os santos, isto é, os homens que se acolhem à graça de Deus, serão concidadãos dos santos anjos na cidade celeste; hão de ter os mesmos corpos em que na terra se santificaram, mas renovados e incorruptíveis. Não pecarão nem morrerão nunca mais. Gozarão de eterna bem-aventurança.

12. Voltando aos Mários

À primeira vista, os Mários são avessos a toda metafísica. Confessam a Carlos Drummond, em seu "eu" simbiótico: "Despojado de transcendências e

---

[65] Santo Agostinho 2009, v. II: 89.
[66] Santo Agostinho 2009, v. II: 474-475.

metafísicas, na minha finitude certa e estrita, eu, amigo Carlos, não marcho mais rumo a portos e fronteiras"[67]. Aqui se vive, aqui se morre.

Entretanto, Santo Agostinho propõe um *paradigma*, que, por ser paradigma, *a fortiori* tem de aplicar-se a todas as cidades, inclusive à cosmópole da Pauliceia dilacerada: se ela abriga a cidade dos homens, deve abrigar também a cidade de Deus.

Deus está na origem da cidade de São Paulo que os Mários recordam. São Paulo, como todas as cidades coevas, nasceu em torno de uma cruz alçada: "Nossas cidades, por isso, sempre nasceram teocêntricas, com Deus no centro do mundo, no centro das casas e das nossas vontades"[68].

Em contrapartida, Brasília transformou a cruz em avião, deitou por terra a cruz, que nem por isso deixou de ser cruz:

> "Niemeyer e Lúcio Costa bagunçaram o coreto: arrancaram a cruz, lá do alto, e a deitaram no chão, em forma de plano-piloto, em forma de avião desenhado sobre a terra. ... Mas eu sei que avião é outra cruz deitada, e a cidade de Brasília perdeu o centro; nela ninguém mais tem sua matriz, cada um que descubra e invente a sua cruz"[69].

Muito sugestivo que Brasília tenha perdido o centro por ter deitado por terra sua cruz. Não há necessidade de muita explicação. O fato é que o discurso dos Mários, aí, sabe a transcendências.

O recurso ao narrador defunto é machadiano, mas não é. O defunto autor Brás Cubas é corrosivo; de sua morada tumular vê o mundo com pessimismo, ironia e complacência; não tem nada que reclamar, nem nada que esperar. É isto mesmo: não teve filhos, não transmitiu a ninguém o legado de nossa miséria, e acabou-se. Morto, ele está em seu túmulo, à espera do primeiro verme que lhe roerá a carne.

Não é essa a postura do defunto Mário, falando pela boca de seu vivo xará Chamie. Deixa escapar que, embora carnalmente esteja no cemitério da Consolação, encontra-se num "desterro sobrenatural"[70], que também sabe à transcendência, à eternidade da alma, por enquanto "desterrada" do corpo. Não se esqueça de que o corpo é terra.

Diferentemente de Brás Cubas, nos Mários não existe nem ironia, nem apatia, nem abulia. Há um inconformismo que esconde reivindicação: tudo o que foi poderia ter sido melhor. O progresso de São Paulo, o traçado viário de São Paulo, as ruas de São Paulo, os prédios de São Paulo, a vida cultural de São

---

[67] Chamie 2009: 180.
[68] Chamie 2009: 67.
[69] Chamie 2009: 67.
[70] Chamie 2009: 37.

Paulo, os prefeitos de São Paulo. Ora, raciocinando *a contrario sensu* (herança de Santo Agostinho), se os Mários lamentam amargamente e esperneiam pela realidade que viveram, é porque conhecem (ou vislumbram) uma realidade melhor, ideal, absoluta, e anseiam por ela. Só se pode lamentar quando é possível comparar. Não estão longe da santa cidade do platônico Santo Agostinho.

Para Santo Agostinho, a cidadania celeste não é um fundamentalismo, nem exclusividade de judeus e cristãos. Fora de Israel, diz ele "não ser incongruência acreditar que em outras nações existiram homens a quem se revelou tal mistério" e que "também entre as demais nações existiram homens que viveram segundo Deus, agradaram-lhe e são membros da Jerusalém espiritual"[71].

Tais homens receberam de outra forma a revelação de Jesus Cristo, porque em toda sociedade existe o que Eusébio de Cesareia chamou de *preparatio evangelica*[72].

Onde houver questionamentos, há abertura para a transcendência, mesmo que se recuse a percorrer o caminho. Quando se julga que algo é inapreensível, pressupõe-se que esse algo exista:

> "... a grandeza da pequenez humana consiste em ela manter-se incessante, na procura da explicação da natureza das coisas que, presentes em nossas gastas retinas, continuarão sempre esquivas e secretas. ... Deus e o mundo permanecerão inapreensíveis, a fim de que as nossas perguntas sobre eles continuem alertas e, explicavelmente, perturbadoras"[73].

13. *Ergo...*

A Paulicéia dilacerada também abriga a cidade de Deus.

Santo Agostinho propôs um paradigma para todas as cidades do orbe: todas as *urbes* abrigam duas *civitates*, a *civitas hominum* e a *civitas Dei*.

Seu ponto de partida local foi a cidade (*polis, urbs*) concreta de Roma. Roma já era uma cosmópole, pela extensão territorial e por abrigar muitos estrangeiros provindos de suas colônias, inclusive judeus e gregos. A essa Roma concreta, viu-se, aplica-se o paradigma agostiniano: nela estiveram misturadas as duas cidades, porque ali coexistiram e conviveram cristãos e detratores de cristãos.

A cidade (*polis, urbs*) de São Paulo, ponto de partida local de Mário Chamie, secundando Mário de Andrade, é também uma cosmópole: muito chão, muita gente, muitas nacionalidades, muitas raças, muitas cores. Na visão dos Mários, São Paulo realiza igualmente este paradigma: tem o bem e o mal misturados, é cidade dos homens por realidade e de Deus por possibilidade.

---

[71] Santo Agostinho 2009, v. II: 362.
[72] Altaner e Stuiber 1972: 226.
[73] Chamie, 2009: 180.

Por indução, o paradigma agostiniano aplica-se a todas as cidades do mundo. Associando-se *polis* ao local e cosmópolis ao global, como propõe este congresso: a primeira é toda cidade concreta; a segunda é o mundo, grande cidade virtual e projetada, em que todas as cidades concretas se reconhecem, nas misérias de sua carnalidade e em seus anseios de eternidade.

Resumindo:

A cidade dos homens é instalada na urbe; não leva em conta a transcendência nem a escatologia, embora no fim haja de submeter-se a elas. Procura a paz terrena, imperfeita e efêmera. Divide-se contra si mesma, porque seus cidadãos colocam o bem supremo em diferentes lugares. Não conhece o resgate do pecado e da morte pela mediação de Jesus Cristo. Seu fim é a morte.

A cidade de Deus é peregrina em todas as urbes e só se consumará na eternidade, em que coloca seu verdadeiro e sumo bem. É unívoca quanto a esse bem, por isso não abriga divisões. Conheceu Jesus Cristo e por Ele foi libertada do pecado e da morte. Seu fim é o céu.

Lenguas e identidades: el caso de Hispania
(Languages and Identity: the Case of Hispania)

Francisco Beltrán Lloris (fbeltran@unizar.es)
Universidad de Zaragoza

Resumo – En este trabajo se analiza a una serie de casos que ilustran cómo lengua e identidad no parecen relacionarse de una manera unívoca ni mecánica en el occidente romano. Los nexos entre lengua e identidad requieren ser examinados y precisados en cada ocasión en función de factores que no siempre resultan transparentes más allá de líneas de fuerza evidentes como la vinculación del latín con la identidad cívica romana o con la comunicación epigráfica, sobre todo a partir de Augusto. En particular se analizan diversos casos como las inscripciones lusitanas, en las que el uso de la lengua vernácula parece obedecer a razones de eficacia en la comunicación con los dioses tradicionales; el epitafio celtibérico de Ibiza, que pretende afirmar la pertenencia de un individuo a una determinada comunidad; o bien las leyendas monetales de la Hispania Ulterior, que renuncian al empleo de las lenguas vernáculas en beneficio de idiomas vehiculares como el latín o el púnico, al contrario de lo que ocurre en la Citerior, en la que predomina el uso de las lenguas locales. La confrontación de las lenguas vernáculas hiapanas, dotadas de una mínima tradición literaria, con un idioma dominante como el latín que, además de lengua del poder, de la cultura y la ciencia, y de la comunicación general y escrita, se manifiesta ante todo como un símbolo cívico imperial compatible con otras identidades locales, étnicas o culturales fue sin duda un factor que inhibió el valor simbólico de las lenguas vernáculas en estos terrenos, en abierto contraste con la sobrevaloración del idioma como elemento identitario que defiende la moderna tradición occidental de raíces nacionalistas.

Palavras-chave: Lengua, identidad, latín, Hispania, inscripciones lusitanas, leyendas monetales.

Abstract – Language and identity do not seem to relate in a uniform or mechanical way in the Roman West. The links between language and identity need to be examined and defined in each case depending on factors that are not always transparent beyond obvious bonds such as those which link the Latin language with Roman civic identity or with epigraphic communication, especially from Augustus on.

This paper deals with a series of illustrative cases: Lusitanian inscriptions, in which the use of the vernacular seems to be owed to reasons of efficiency in communicating with traditional gods; a Celtiberian epitaph from Ibiza, which aims to affirm the membership of an individual in a particular community; and the coin legends from Hispania Ulterior, which renounce the usage of vernaculars in favour of vehicular languages such as Latin and Punic, contrary to what happens in Hispania Citerior where the norm is the use of local languages. In the confrontation of the vernacular languages of Hispania, furnished with a minimal literary tradition, with Latin, the language of power, culture, and learning that prevailed in general and written communication, there was a crucial factor: Latin acted primarily as an imperial civic symbol, but one compatible with local, ethnic or cultural identities. This fact inhibited the symbolic value of vernacular languages in these areas, in stark contrast to the overvaluation of language as an identifying element that upholds the modern Western nationalist tradition

KEYWORDS: Language, identity, Latin, Hispania, Lusitanian inscriptions, coin legends.

1. La diversidad cultural era uno de los rasgos más característicos de Hispania cuando, a fines del siglo III a. E., Roma inició su expansión por la península Ibérica. Este hecho se aprecia con particular nitidez en el terreno lingüístico gracias a la generalización de la escritura, limitada con anterioridad al litoral meridional y oriental, pero difundida a partir del siglo II a. E. por amplias regiones del interior como queda de manifiesto en la proliferación de emisiones monetales con leyendas en diferentes lenguas y escrituras e, incluso, de una incipiente cultura epigráfica en el nordeste ibérico, de manera que, salvo para el cuadrante noroccidental de la península, contamos con un registro bastante satisfactorio para identificar las lenguas que se utilizaban, al menos por escrito, en dos terceras partes de Hispania. Entre ellas pueden mencionarse, tres que cabría calificar de coloniales, el fenicio, el griego y el latín, aunque algunas de ellas contaran con muchos siglos de arraigo en Hispania,[1] y otras tres vernáculas documentadas epigráficamente, el ibérico, el celtibérico y el lusitano,[2] sin contar con los vestigios onomásticos de al menos otras dos, el turdetano o tartesio – cuyos testimonios epigráficos cesan hacia el siglo IV a. E. – y el vascónico.[3] A partir de Augusto, sin embargo, si exceptuamos los testimonios epigráficos en griego, que se utilizó en todo el Mediterráneo romano como lengua de cultura, el latín se convirtió en el único idioma escrito del que tenemos constancia en la península Ibérica con muy pocas salvedades como las monedas bilingües de *Abdera*

---

[1] Los testimonios epigráficos de estas tres lenguas están recogidos respectivamente en Fuentes 1986, de Hoz 1997 y Díaz 2008.

[2] El *corpus* de referencia de la epigrafía paleohispánica es *MLH* con las periódicas actualizaciones publicadas en las crónicas de *Palaeohispanica y las secciones abiertas del banco de datos Hesperia* (http://hesperia.ucm.es/)". La datación de las escasas inscripciones lusitanas conocidas hasta la fecha es incierta: la de Arronches (Carneiro, d'Encarnação, de Oliveira y Teixeira 2008: 167-178) ofrece rasgos paleográficos como la *P* abierta que inducen a datarla hacia fines del siglo I a. E.; a cambio, otras, como la de Lamas de Moledo (*MLH* IV, L.2.1), con abundantes nexos en el encabezamiento latino y *P* cerrada, parecen responder mejor a una cronología más avanzada, de época ya imperial. Para las leyendas monetales, además de *MLH* I, *DCPH sub uoce* y el banco de datos Hesperia

[3] Sobre el tartesio o turdetano ver ahora de Hoz 2010: 217 ss. La propuesta de entender la lengua de las inscripciones tartesias o del sudoeste (*MLH* IV, J) como céltica, sugerida por J. Koch 2009 y 2009a ha sido recibida con un cierto escepticismo. Sobre los testimonios vascónicos, Gorrochategui 1987 y, recientemente, Velaza 2009.

(Adra) y *Ebusus,* con leyendas en latín y fenicio de la primera mitad del siglo I d. E.,[4] y seguramente varias de las inscripciones en lengua lusitana, sobre las que volveremos después, dos de ellas al menos con encabezamientos latinos,[5] aparte de otros ejemplos más inseguros o menos relevantes.[6] Ello, desde luego, no obsta para que las lenguas vernáculas se siguieran empleando en la comunicación oral como, por ejemplo, se documenta en el conocido caso del celtíbero de Termes, acusado en 25 d. E. de asesinar al legado jurídico de la Hispania Citerior,[7] que al ser interrogado se obstinó en responder *sermone patrio.*[8] Sin embargo el cese del empleo por escrito de los idiomas indígenas, más allá del abrumador peso de la cultura epigráfica latina desde época augústea,[9] parece demostrado por la ausencia casi absoluta de epígrafes paleohispánicos durante el Principado, en particular de grafitos sobre cerámica, tan frecuentes, por el contrario, durante las centurias previas en algunas regiones.

De esta manera, finalizaba de manera abrupta una tradición que en la costa mediterránea ibérica, por ejemplo, contaba con no menos de cinco siglos de antigüedad. Esta rápida desaparición de las lenguas vernáculas peninsulares contrasta vivamente con la situación imperante en otros lugares del occidente romano. Así, en las Galias no faltan inscripciones célticas durante el Principado, caso de los grafitos de los alfareros de La Graufesenque en el siglo I d. E. o más tardías aún como el calendario de Coligny, datado a fines del II d. E., ni referencias literarias al uso del galo que llegan hasta el siglo V d. E.;[10] y en el norte de África persistieron durante todo el Imperio tanto el púnico,[11] empleado durante

---

[4] *DCPH* II, 18, con *Ti. Caesar diui Aug. f. Augustus* y *'bdrt* en el anverso y *Abdera* en el reverso, y 119, para *Ebusus,* donde alternan las leyendas con el nombre del emperador e *Ins(ula) Aug(usta)* e *'ybsm* en época de Tiberio, Calígula y Claudio; véase p. 154, para la emisión de *Gades,* de autenticidad discutida, con la poco esperable leyenda para un municipio *Col(onia) A(ugusta) Gad(es),* y *'gdr,* en época de Tiberio.

[5] *MLH* IV, L.1.1 y L.2.1. En lusitano y latín parece estar redactada un ara procedente de Viseu datable en la segunda mitad del I d. E., Fernandes, Carvalho y Figueira 2009; véase también *HEp* 7, 1214; Búa 1997: 59-60.

[6] Caso del grafito **kabani**, en una lengua indeterminada, editado por Gómara 2007: 263-268, grabado sobre una jarrita de época julio-claudia. De fecha augústea podría ser el epígrafe sobre mármol de Montaña Frontera (Sagunto), *MLH* III, F.11.30 y más tardío aún, de hacia 100 d. E., el discutido grafito sobre una estela latina de Requena (Corell 1989: 278; Martínez 1993: 247-251) que de Hoz 2001: 61, prudentemente, prefiere tomar con toda cautela.

[7] Se trata de Lucio Calpurnio Pisón, Alföldy 1969: 67.

[8] Tac. *ann.* IV 45, 2, Beltrán 2011: 19-23; ésta sería la noticia más tardía sobre el empleo del celtibérico junto con los grafitos rupestres de Peñalba de Villastar (Teruel), *MLH* IV, K.3 y Beltrán, Jordán y Marco 2005, y las *trullae* de Tiermes (K.11.1-2). Sobre el latín en Hispania véase la síntesis de Beltrán 2004.

[9] Al respecto, véase Alföldy 1991 y, para occidente, los trabajos recogidos en Beltrán (ed.) 1995.

[10] Lambert 1994: 10, 109, 129, 177, *passim.* Para las inscripciones galas, *RIG* espec. II.2, 83 ss. (Graufesenque) y III, 35-36 (Coligny).

[11] Röllig 1980; Millar 1968: hay testimonios del uso literario del púnico hasta la

el siglo I d. E. en inscripciones públicas de ciudades como *Leptis Magna*,[12] cuanto el líbico, del que se conserva un relevante conjunto de inscripciones bilingües y que fue hablado sin solución de continuidad hasta desembocar en el bereber actual.[13] Incluso en Italia, pese al contacto más estrecho y dilatado con Roma, hay testimonios del empleo epigráfico de otras lenguas paleoitálicas a comienzos del Principado como el osco en Pompeya.[14]

Este diferente comportamiento de las lenguas paleohispánicas requiere una explicación que puede abordarse desde varias perspectivas, entre las que me interesa ahora insistir en la identitaria, habida cuenta de que la lengua suele ser considerada, entre los lingüistas desde luego, pero también entre los historiadores, incluidos los de la Antigüedad, como un elemento fundamental en la construcción de las identidades según puede ilustrarlo la conocida afirmación, múltiples veces invocada, de David Crystal: "Language is the primary index, or symbol, or register of identity".[15]

Evidentemente, determinar los elementos sobre los que se fundamenta una identidad colectiva en un momento preciso y valorar, en concreto, el papel que la lengua desempeña en ella son operaciones que exigen disponer de testimonios escritos que los expliciten de una manera discursiva,[16] pues de lo contrario estas construcciones sociales continuamente reelaboradas y subjetivamente percibidas resultan muy difíciles de definir.[17] En lo que a la Antigüedad se refiere, esto resulta posible tan sólo en el caso de aquellas culturas como la griega o la romana de las que conservamos una nutrida tradición literaria, mientras que se hace mucho más difícil, a cambio, en aquellas sociedades periféricas como las hispanas, para las que no contamos con otros testimonios escritos que las inscripciones, documentos que, en estas circunstancias, se convierten en el único instrumento a través del cual la cuestión resulta abordable, por más que sea de una manera marginal y profundamente mediatizada por las dificultades de comprensión de estas lenguas y por los condicionamientos peculiares que impone la lógica de la

---

Antigüedad Tardía, entre los que sobresalen los de Agustín de Hipona; en las monedas persiste hasta mediados del I d. E., y en las inscripciones públicas hasta comienzos del III, aunque se enrarezcan notablemente en el II; en *Leptis Magna* no parecen ser posteriores a época de Domiciano.

[12] *IRT*, y la reedición electrónica de G. Bodard y Ch. Roueché (http://irt.kcl.ac.uk); sobre las inscripciones bilingües, Adams 2003: 213 ss.

[13] Rössler 1980; Adams 2003: 245-247; Millar 1968; Marcy 1936; Rebuffat 2007.

[14] Cooley 2002.

[15] Crystal 2000: 40; remiten a ella, por ejemplo, Adams 2003: 751 ss. o Mullen 2007: 35.

[16] En este sentido Hall 1997: 182 ss.

[17] A este respecto, Beltrán 2004a: 87-145; paradigmática resulta, por ejemplo, la comparación entre los elementos identificadores de la helenidad que suministran Heródoto (VIII 144: raza, lengua, santuarios, costumbres) y, poco tiempo después, Isócrates (*paneg.* 50: educación, cultura).

cultura epigráfica, tan distinta del resto de la cultura escrita[18] y, por supuesto, de la comunicación oral. Ello no significa que carezcamos de ejemplos significativos para analizar la cuestión en el seno del Imperio Romano, como queda de manifiesto en los tres siguientes ejemplos.

2. Empecemos con un epitafio procedente de la frontera septentrional del Imperio, concretamente de la localidad portuaria de *Arbeia,* la actual South Shields, situada en el norte de Inglaterra, junto al muro de Adriano. En este epígrafe, datado en un momento avanzado del Principado (II-III d. E.), un palmireno llamado *Barates* honra la memoria de su esposa y liberta, Regina, natural de Britania, muerta a los treinta años.[19] Esta conocida inscripción debe su notoriedad al hecho de que el epígrafe no sólo está redactado en latín, la lengua habitual de la cultura epigráfica romana occidental,[20] sino que incluye una frase en palmireno que resume el contenido del texto latino y constituye el testimonio de este idioma más alejado de la ciudad siria conocido hasta la fecha. Además, según la bien recibida sugerencia de Adams, el hecho de que el nombre de Regina pudiera estar declinado, erróneamente, en acusativo, revelaría la familiaridad del redactor del epitafio, seguramente el propio Barates, con el griego, lengua en la que dicho caso es el normal para las personas honradas en las inscripciones honoríficas.[21] Este documento ilustra, aunque de manera quizás extrema, el multilingüismo imperante en el seno del Imperio Romano durante el Principado, incluso en este lugar fronterizo y remoto, a través de un documento redactado en latín – con interferencias del griego – y palmireno, sin contar con la posibilidad de que Regina, pese a su nombre latino, hablara la lengua céltica local, al tiempo que pone de manifiesto la profunda afección identitaria de Barates por su lengua, que no duda en emplear en un lugar en el que tales idioma y escritura difícilmente contarían con muchos lectores.[22]

Varios siglos antes, a fines del período republicano, en una época en la que la movilidad geográfica aún no había alcanzado la intensidad que fomentó la *pax Romana* del Principado, ilustran una situación similar ocho hitos terminales, alzados en fecha imprecisa, quizá hacia el I a. E., en la región de Zaghouan (Túnez), en el interior del África Proconsular, el viejo territorio de Cartago

---

[18] Sobre esta cuestión en la Hispania preaugústea, Beltrán 2005.

[19] *RIB* 1065 = *AE* 2000, 804: *D(is) M(anibus) Regina(m) liberta(m) et coniuge(m)* (!) / *Barates Palmyrenus natione / Catuallauna an(norum) XXX. / rgyn' bt hry br't' hbl.*

[20] Es bien sabido que la lengua céltica local de Britania, de la que hay testimonios onomásticos en esta misma región (por ejemplo, *RIB* 1053; sobre los nombres célticos en Bath, Mullen 2007), no fue utilizada por escrito (Jackson 1953: 99-100), sino excepcionalmente: por ejemplo en la *defixio* de Bath, Tomlin 1987; Lambert 1994: 174.

[21] Adams 2003: 253-255; Mednikarova 2003: 117.

[22] Otro palmireno, vexilario, llamado también *[Ba]rathes,* que no debe excluirse que fuera la misma persona, está atestiguado en Corbridge, unos 40 km al oeste de South Shields (*RIB* 1171).

convertido en provincia romana apenas cincuenta años antes, donde las lenguas predominantes eran el púnico y el líbico.[23] El texto, redactado en escritura y lengua etruscas, parece interpretable como "Marce Unata Zutas dedica a Tinia (Júpiter) los confines de los Dardanios. 1000",[24] en el que el término *tartanium* – según Heurgon, con diacrítico en las dentales para expresar su valor sonoro, es decir *Dardanium* – parece un préstamo latino en genitivo de plural que indicaría una interferencia de esta lengua. Los cipos han sido atribuidos a colonos de época silana procedentes, a juzgar por la escritura, del norte de Etruria, quizá de *Clusium*, en donde el nombre *unata* está bien atestiguado, o de *Cortona*, ciudad en la que, según Colonna, se habría forjado la leyenda de que sus habitantes descendían de Dárdano y, de esta manera, se convertían en ancestros de los romanos, progenie a su vez de Eneas.

Para terminar, en fechas no muy alejadas de éstas, hacia el año 100 a. E., un natural de *Beligio* (por Azuara, Zaragoza), en el interior de la Hispania Citerior, fallecido en la isla púnica de Ibiza, fue enterrado en la necrópolis local de Puig des Molins bajo un epitafio redactado en lengua celtibérica y en la variante de la escritura paleohispánica propia de su región de origen: "Dirtano, de (la familia) de los Abúlocos, hijo de Letondo, beligiense".[25] Lengua y escritura contrastan vivamente con el predominio de los rótulos púnicos en la isla, y más aún con la ausencia casi completa de epigrafía monumental funeraria en Ibiza[26] – y en el resto de la Hispania púnica – [27]: además, el epitafio de Dirtano corresponde a un tipo de inscripción apenas utilizado en el interior celtibérico, donde sólo se conoce una decena de epitafios,[28] y muestra más puntos de contacto con la epigrafía ibérica funeraria del litoral mediterráneo,[29] fuertemente influida por los modelos

---

[23] Sobre las lenguas del norte de África, Rössler 1980: 267-299.

[24] *ET Af* 8.1-8: *M. Unata Zutas tul Dardanium tins f*; Heurgon 1969 y 1969a; Colonna 1980; Bonfante y Bonfante 2002; Martínez-Pinna 2002: 139-140.

[25] *MLH* IV, K.16: **tirtanos / abulokum / letontun/os ke(ntis) beli/kios**; Beltrán 2004b: 50-51; 2004a: 122-123; 2006: 238-239. Esta inscripción ofrece el único ejemplo celtibérico – y quizá paleohispánico – de mención de la *origo*, al respecto, Beltrán 2004b y 2011a; el único posible caso de mención de *origo* en la epigrafía ibérica es el ampuritano señalado por Velaza 2003: 184.

[26] Fuentes 1986: 07.1-21, recoge una veintena de epígrafes en Ibiza, de los que sólo uno, votivo, fue grabado sobre una estela (07.14), probablemente en el siglo IV a. E., cronología similar a la de un grafito realizado sobre un *askos*, quizá de carácter funerario (07.10)

[27] Sobre la falta de proclividad de los fenicios hispanos hacia la epigrafía pública, Beltrán 2005: 32-33, 36; sobre la epigrafía feno-púnica en la Península Ibérica, Zamora 2005; Belmonte 2010.

[28] *MLH* IV, K.4.1. (El Pedregal, de carácter discutido); 8.1 (Torrellas); 10.1 (Trébago); 12.1 (Langa de Duero); 13.2-3 (Clunia); 23.2 (*Vxama*), además de la de *Iuliobriga*, en alfabeto latino (26.1). Sobre las inscripciones celtibéricas sobre piedra ver ahora Simón 2013: 88-93 y P-121-131, espec. P-131.

[29] Beltrán 2005: 36-37; 2004b: 50-51; 2004a: 122-123; 2006: 238-240.

romanos.[30] Como en los otros dos ejemplos aducidos, el uso de una lengua y una escritura desconocidos en la ciudad en la que se erigieron estos epígrafes, pone de manifiesto cómo estas personas, sobre todo en el caso de las inscripciones monolingües, dieron preferencia a la expresión de su identidad a través del empleo de sus propias lenguas y escrituras en detrimento de la comprensibilidad del mensaje, que resultaría opaco para la mayor parte de la población local.

Aunque podrían señalarse otros ejemplos semejantes, estos epígrafes no dejan de ser casos extraordinariamente atípicos en el mundo romano. El comportamiento lingüístico de los palmirenos, como es bien sabido, resulta excepcional no sólo por el abundante empleo de su lengua,[31] junto al griego y el latín, en Palmira misma, que les distingue del resto de las comunidades de la región,[32] sino porque no dudaron en utilizarla fuera de su ciudad y no sólo en localidades vecinas como Dura Europos, Palestina o el desierto sirio, sino también en lugares muy alejados de ella como Egipto, Numidia, Mesia, Dacia, Roma o en el oasis de Marw, en el Turkmenistán.[33] Igualmente excepcional es el caso de los hitos terminales etruscos de Zaghouan, pues, pese a la abundante presencia durante el período republicano de tropas auxiliares así como de emigrantes y mercaderes itálicos en occidente, la sola lengua utilizada por las gentes de procedencia italiana de la que tenemos constancia en los epígrafes provinciales es el latín.[34] Por último, el epitafio de Ibiza es uno de los rarísimos documentos paleohispánicos hallado fuera de su región lingüística.[35]

---

[30] Beltrán 2012.

[31] La lengua local tradicional podría no ser el palmireno, un dialecto arameo occidental, sino el árabe safaítico como atestiguaría una serie de inscripciones de los alrededores y de la propia ciudad, hasta el punto de que se llegó a poner en duda si el palmireno era la lengua hablada localmente (Rosenthal 1936: 105), como parece ser la opinión actualmente predominante, o sólo un idioma escrito (Cantineau 1935: 6).

[32] En Siria la lengua de las inscripciones públicas por antonomasia es el griego, empleado también en los documentos escritos sobre papiro o pergamino, entre los que las lenguas semíticas tienen un uso minoritario pese a dominar la comunicación oral; además de las inscripciones públicas palmirenas, el ejemplo más llamativo lo suministran las decenas de miles de grafitos safaíticos procedentes de las zonas desérticas del sur de Siria y el nordeste de Jordania; un panorama de la cuestión en Butcher 2003: 283-289.

[33] Schmidt 1980: 203; Adams 2003: 248-260.

[34] En Hispania, por ejemplo, en donde contamos con cerca de dos centenares de inscripciones de época republicana (Díaz 2008), ninguna de ellas está redactada con seguridad en otra lengua itálica que no sea el latín: sobre el polémico grafito sobre campaniense de Tarragona con el texto *Vrnii* (?), considerado por algunos como etrusco (Asensi y Musso 1990: 5-11), Mayer 1995: 98; Díaz 2008: C64.

[35] Si se excluyen algunos plomos ibéricos que, por su presumible carácter epistolar o documental, es normal que aparezcan fuera de contexto, aunque siempre en áreas lingüísticamente ibéricas, al menos en lo que al registro epigráfico se refiere, y, naturalmente, la debatida columnita, también ibérica, del Museo de Cagliari (*MLH* III, X.0.1), sobre la que no existen noticias relativas a sus condiciones de hallazgo, una circunstancia que aconseja cautela a la hora de interpretarla, Pallottino 1952, 153-154.

3. Pero, además de la excepcionalidad de estos testimonios, conviene subrayar que en los tres casos propuestos el empleo de la lengua y la escritura vernáculas fuera de su contexto no se vinculan a la afirmación de una identidad étnica o cultural, sino que, por el contrario y sin valorar ahora factores individuales – como la condición peregrina de los comitentes – , se inscriben dentro del marco cívico, explícitamente en el caso del palmireno de Britania y del beligiense de Ibiza, y de manera implícita en los hitos terminales africanos que remitirían a Cortona si se acepta la hipótesis de Colonna. Ésta es una observación relevante a la hora de valorar la vinculación entre lengua e identidades colectivas en el mundo romano, habida cuenta del estrecho nexo que, un tanto mecánicamente, se suele presuponer entre lengua y etnia – o nación – en los estudios lingüísticos modernos, fruto de la perspectiva esencialista impuesta en la Europa de los últimos siglos por los nacionalismos, que tan bien expresan estas palabras de Hoffmann: "In the history of nations, especially in Europe, the survival of a nation's language has frequently been equated with the continued existence of the nation itself".[36] La vinculación entre lengua y etnia o nación, sin embargo, no es un hecho cultural que se imponga por sí mismo como defienden los substancialistas, sino un factor construido socialmente como queda de manifiesto, por ejemplo, en el caso de la Francia moderna, en donde hasta la Primera Guerra Mundial la lengua francesa – tenida por elemento central de la identidad nacional – no se hizo mayoritaria.[37] Por lo tanto el nexo identitario entre lengua y etnicidad no debe darse por presupuesto, sino examinarse en cada caso de manera específica.

Por otro lado, la valoración identitaria de las lenguas vernáculas hispanas resulta imposible sin establecer primero cuál era el valor que en este terreno los romanos atribuían a su propio idioma, el latín – una cuestión sobre la que, además, estamos mejor informados – , pues la construcción de una identidad, más allá del sujeto y del objeto de la misma, se encuentra en íntima relación con el otro – o los otros – frente al cual esa identidad se define[38] y esta alteridad, obviamente, fue ante todo la romana para unas comunidades como las hispanas, que, en el curso de dos siglos, hubieron de hacer frente a la conquista militar, primero, a la incorporación en el Imperio como comunidades subalternas peregrinas, después, y a la integración como miembros de la comunidad cívica romana, por último.

---

[36] Hoffmann 1991: 199.

[37] Kozakai 2000: 75: según el nada sospechoso *Atlas de la langue française* de la Ed. Bordas (Rossillon (ed.) 1995), antes de la revolución de 1789 más de la mitad de los habitantes del entonces territorio de Francia no hablaban francés, sin contar con que una buena parte del resto no lo manejaba bien; en 1914, se utilizaban, además, alemán, alsaciano, bretón, vasco, occitano, catalán y corso. Como lo subraya Seignobos 1969: 15, las fronteras francesas siempre han sido geográficas o políticas: "l'unité nationale n'a pu se faire par aucune communauté naturelle ni d'origine, ni de coutumes, ni de langue".

[38] Kozakai 2000: 84-85.

Aunque el latín pudiera tener inicialmente connotaciones étnicas, su estrecha vinculación con la ciudadanía, a la que se fueron incorporando progresivamente amplias masas de población de diferentes orígenes étnicos primero en Italia, tras la Guerra de los Aliados, y después en la provincias, sobre todo occidentales, a partir de César y Augusto, terminó por vaciar a este idioma de referentes étnicos para ligarlo a una noción de ciudadanía que adquiría rápidamente tintes de universalidad y resultaba compatible con las identidades locales o étnicas, además, obviamente, de su importante papel como idioma vehicular.[39] Las autoridades romanas manifestaron un evidente desdén por las restantes lenguas del Imperio,[40] con excepción del griego por el que los romanos albergaban sentimientos ambiguos, entre el respeto y la desconfianza,[41] y se dirigieron sistemáticamente a las poblaciones peregrinas en latín,[42] pero no hicieron, salvo en ocasiones excepcionales, ningún esfuerzo por facilitar el aprendizaje de su lengua y mucho menos por imponerla,[43] con una actitud, por lo tanto, muy diferente a la de los modernos imperios coloniales, independientemente de que el latín fuera la lengua propia del ciudadano, del ejército o del derecho y, en occidente, del comercio o de la comunicación epigráfica: probablemente esta actitud romana poco apreciativa de las lenguas ajenas influyera negativamente en la propia consideración de los hablantes sobre sus idiomas vernáculos, sobre todo cuando no contaban con una tradición literaria relevante.

Por otra parte, aunque el manejo del latín se presupusiera en el ciudadano romano, sobre todo como lengua hablada,[44] es cierto que, técnicamente, resultaba posible disfrutar de esta condición e ignorar la lengua latina como lo pone de manifiesto la famosa anécdota de época de Claudio relativa a un griego a quien se privó de la ciudadanía por no conocer el idioma,[45] siglo y medio antes de que la *constitutio Antoniniana* de 212 d. E. incorporara a la comunidad cívica romana a millones de habitantes del Imperio que, sobre todo en oriente, ignoraban el latín. Sin embargo el nexo existente, al menos durante el Principado, entre la

---

[39] Sobre el latín y la identidad romana es fundamental Adams 2003a: 184-205.

[40] Hay desde luego excepciones: según Plutarco (*Sert.* 3), Sertorio aprendió el galo durante la campaña contra cimbrios y teutones para infiltrarse en sus líneas.

[41] Kaimio 1979; Dubuisson1981.

[42] Val. Max. II 2.2, a propósito del griego, aunque en realidad ésta fue la única lengua, aparte del latín, en la que, en oriente, se expresaron las autoridades romanas. Significativo es el empleo del latín por los gobernadores en los documentos públicos oficiales, aunque resultara ininteligible para los provinciales como es evidente, por ejemplo, en el caso del decreto de Emilio Paulo hallado en Alcalá de los Gazules, redactado muy poco tiempo después – hacia 189 a. E. – de la conquista de la región (*CIL* I2 614 = *CIL* II 5041), Beltrán 2009: 33-34.

[43] Dubuisson 1982: 197-210. El fomento del latín entre los hijos de los nobles britanos atribuida a Agrícola (Tac., *Agr.* 21) o la 'escuela' establecida por Sertorio en *Osca* para los hijos de los nobles hispanos (Plut., *Sert.* 14), son conocidas excepciones.

[44] Como ha puesto de manifiesto Woolf 2002: 182.

[45] Suet. *Claud.* 16, 2.

extensión de la ciudadanía y la difusión del latín parece incuestionable, pues fueron las provincias más intensamente afectadas por la política de colonización y municipalización inauguradas por César y Augusto – Hispania, Narbonense, África Proconsular, Dalmacia – [46] las que más profunda y tempranamente se latinizaron. A este factor fundamental de tipo político deben agregarse otros dos que contribuyen a explicar tanto el diferente comportamiento del oriente y occidente del Imperio Romano en este terreno cuanto el hecho de que en determinadas áreas las lenguas locales persistieran varios siglos, como en las Galias o el norte de África, mientras que en otras desaparecieron rápidamente, como ocurrió en Hispania: se trata, por un lado, de la existencia o no de otras lenguas vehiculares prestigiosas, caso del griego en oriente – y Sicilia – [47], y de la valoración de su propia lengua por parte de los hablantes,[48] dependiente también de la existencia o no de una previa tradición literaria y de la percepción de la utilidad social de dicho idioma.

En lo que afecta a Hispania, la rapidez tanto en la difusión del latín cuanto en la desaparición de las lenguas vernáculas se explica por varios factores: la amplitud de la integración política, muy superior a la de otras regiones, que, en tiempos de César y Augusto, afectó a una quinta parte de las comunidades municipales hispanas, según los datos de Plinio el Viejo,[49] y a toda la península con la concesión del *ius Latii* por los príncipes flavios;[50] la inexistencia de una lengua vehicular previamente difundida, salvo el fenicio en sur peninsular; y la escasa tradición literaria de las lenguas vernáculas. A todo ello debe agregarse el hecho de que, frente a otras regiones como las Galias o el norte de África en las que la relativa homogeneidad lingüística, ya mencionada, pudo facilitar la persistencia del galo, el púnico o el bereber como lenguas de comunicación general, la fragmentación lingüística peninsular seguramente coadyuvó a que el latín terminara por desempeñar esta función.

En definitiva, la poderosa vinculación del latín con una identidad cívica de tendencias universalizantes y compatible con otras identidades locales o culturales,[51] el predominio de esta lengua en la comunicación epigráfica de occidente así como la diversidad de situaciones apreciable en el conjunto del Imperio Romano aconsejan desvincular el latín, sobre todo en su empleo por escrito, de

---

[46] Al respecto, puede verse la obra clásica de Vittinghoff 1951.

[47] Para Sicilia, Prag 2002.

[48] Un factor esencial en la pervivencia o desaparición de una lengua, al respecto Dixon 1997: 9 ss., 109 ss.

[49] Plin. *NH* III 7, 18 y 117.

[50] Plin. *NH* III 30; al respecto, Andreu 2004.

[51] En este sentido es ejemplar el caso del poeta Marcial que se consideraba, además de romano, hispano, celtíbero y bilbilitano, pese a que, según todos los indicios, no hablaba la lengua celtibérica; al respecto, Beltrán 2004a, 133-135.

la discusión acerca de las identidades culturales o étnicas,[52] sobre todo a partir del Principado cuando empezaron a operar las profundas transformaciones que desembocaron en la nueva sociedad imperial.[53]

Desde esta perspectiva, examinaré, para finalizar, algunos ejemplos hispanos previos a la afirmación de la sociedad del Principado que ilustran las posibles vinculaciones entre lengua e identidad.

4. La primera afecta al empleo de la lengua en las leyendas monetales de época republicana, un tipo de documentación particularmente sensible en la materia que estamos abordando por ser las monedas, en palabras de F. Millar, 'the most deliberate of all symbols of public identity'.[54] En Hispania, como se ha visto, el latín se convirtió en la única lengua empleada en las monedas a partir de Augusto – con la excepción ya señalada de las leyendas bilingües de *Abdera* y *Ebusus*, ambas significativamente fenicias – [55] como consecuencia de las nuevas condiciones culturales y políticas que impuso el Principado y, en especial, de la concentración de las cecas en colonias y municipios romanos,[56] que, tanto en occidente como en oriente, acuñaron sistemáticamente en latín,[57] en lo que constituye una palmaria ilustración de la dimensión más cívica que étnica de esta lengua, pues el empleo del latín – o del griego – en detrimento de una lengua vernácula no significa forzosamente la desaparición de una conciencia étnica o local diferenciada.[58]

Con anterioridad a Augusto, cabe señalar una marcada contraposición entre las cecas de la Hispania Citerior y las de la Ulterior. En la provincia septentrional la norma fue en principio la esperable, es decir que cada ceca acuñara en su propia lengua y escritura: tanto las coloniales – griego en *Emporion* y *Rhode*,[59]

---

[52] Woolf 2002: 187 aconseja "to move 'cultural identity' away from the centre of discussion of both cultural history and identity in antiquity (…). Perhaps we should not expend too much effort on establishing the links between writing Latin and Roman identity".

[53] Woolf 1996.

[54] Millar 1993: 230; 'The most explicit symbols of a city's identity and status were its coins' (257); al respecto, Howgego 2004: 1 ss. y 12-16.

[55] *DCPH*, 18 y 119, y 154 para la sospechosa emisión de *Gades*.

[56] Beltrán 2004c: 133 ss. Sobre las monedas y las identidades cívicas, Beltrán 2002; también, Ripollés 2004.

[57] Como ha subrayado Howgego 2004: 12, el latín fue empleado sistemáticamente en sus emisiones por las colonias romanas – incluso las meramente titulares – y los municipios romanos de oriente al menos hasta época de los Severos, momento a partir del cual, significativamente, una vez concedida la ciudadanía a todos los habitantes libres del Imperio, empezaron a utilizar el griego.

[58] Williamson 2004: 26: "Nevertheless the apparent disappearance of local languages such as Lycian did not mean the disappearance of those who called themselves Lycian. It is an elementary, but often ignored, point that acquisition of either of the two most widespread tongues, Latin or Greek, even as a mother tongue, did not inmediatly lead one to think of oneself as either a Roman or a Greek".

[59] *DCPH*, 127 ss., 318 ss.

fenicio en *Ebusus*,[60] latín en *Valentia*[61] – cuanto las indígenas ibéricas y célticas,[62] y también las vascónicas.[63] No se alejan de esta pauta una serie de cecas ibéricas que emplearon leyendas bilingües latinas en época cesariana como *usekerte, kelse, kili* o *saitabi*[64] y, antes aún, *arse / Saguntum,* cuya condición de colonia latina ha sido recientemente establecida.[65] Por el contrario, en lo que respecta al empleo de la iconografía se observa una sorprendente renuncia al empleo de símbolos locales en beneficio de tipos generales, la cabeza viril y el jinete, extraordinariamente homogéneos en toda la provincia.[66]

La situación en la Hispania Ulterior es, sin embargo, radicalmente distinta.[67] Aquí las lenguas vernáculas sólo fueron empleadas en áreas marginales: "*Salacia*", al oeste, en donde se utilizan un idioma y una escritura paleohispánicos discutidos; *tamusia*, al norte, con leyendas celtibéricas; y *kastilo, ipolka, abra* o *iliberri*, entre otras, al este, que acuñan en lengua ibérica y en la variante meridional de esta escritura,[68] algunas con emisiones bilingües o que alternan latín e ibérico.[69] Por el contrario, las restantes cecas, que conforman la inmensa mayoría – exceptuando las colonias latinas y fenicias que acuñan en sus propios idioma y escritura – , recurrieron a lenguas y alfabetos vehiculares: el latín o la variante de la escritura púnica denominada 'libio-fenice'.[70] A cambio, en lo que a la iconografía se refiere, las cecas de la Hispania Ulterior plasman en sus emisiones, como es habitual en la numismática antigua, símbolos locales diferenciados como divinidades tutelares de la comunidad u otros más difíciles de desentrañar.[71]

Esta contraposición entre ambas provincias[72] resulta particularmente paradójica teniendo en cuenta que la región meridional era la cuna del sistema

---

[60] *DCPH*, 117 ss., aunque la mayor parte de las emisiones son anepígrafas.

[61] *DCPH*, 401 ss.

[62] *DCPH, passim.*

[63] En el territorio de los Vascones, además del vascónico – que, como el aquitano, no se empleó nunca en la epigrafía monumental – están atestiguados epigráficamente el ibérico y el celtibérico: varias cecas vasconas emplean con seguridad el celtibérico, mientras que en otras la lengua no es determinable: no puede excluirse que en algunas de ellas se empleara el vascónico: Beltrán y Velaza 2009.

[64] Sobre las inscripciones bilingües hispanas, Beltrán y Estarán 2011. Significativamente las mencionadas cecas levantinas se encontraban próximas a la colonia latina de *Valentia* y las aragonesas, a la zona en donde César fundó la colonia *Celsa*; sobre las condiciones históricas y el ambiente cultural en esta comarca, Beltrán 2000: 46.

[65] Velaza 2003a, 141, y Ripollés y Velaza 2002; sobre las colonias latinas hispanas ver ahora, Beltrán 2011b. Sobre las razones del empleo del latín en las leyendas saguntinas, Beltrán 2011: 31-36.

[66] Beltrán 2004c: 130 ss.

[67] Beltrán 2004c: 127 ss.

[68] García-Bellido y Blázquez 2001: *s. u.*

[69] Beltrán y Estarán 2011.

[70] *DCPH* II, 317 y 373.

[71] Beltrán 2004c: 128 ss.

[72] Que afecta también a los tipos monetales, Beltrán 2004c: 127 ss., 130 ss.

de escritura paleohispánico y que los turdetanos, al decir de Estrabón, eran los únicos hispanos que contaban con una tradición literaria,[73] factores que, en principio, deberían traducirse en una más elevada valoración de la escritura y la lengua propias. Sin embargo las ciudades turdetanas no sólo optaron muy tempranamente por emplear el nuevo idioma vehicular en documentos oficiales como eran las monedas, privilegiando así el uso de una lengua de prestigio y de comunicación general sobre cualquier afirmación identitaria por vía lingüística, sino también en las inscripciones de los particulares[74] e, incluso, en la comunicación oral si damos crédito a Estrabón, según quien, en sus días, los turdetanos habían adoptado el latín hasta olvidar prácticamente su lengua materna.[75] Es muy probable que en la rápida adopción del latín pudiera influir la previa existencia de una lengua vehicular regional como el fenicio,[76] cuyo empleo se mantiene no sólo en los dos siglos previos a la Era, sino, como se ha dicho, durante los primeros años del Principado en los casos de *Abdera* y *Ebusus*. Y sin duda influyó también la acusada fragmentación lingüística de la Ulterior, en la que convivían céltico, turdetano, fenicio e ibérico en un espacio relativamente reducido en comparación con los más extensos y homogéneos territorios ibérico y céltico de la Citerior.

Estos hechos ponen de manifiesto el diferente comportamiento lingüístico de los pueblos hispanos de una y otra provincias ante estímulos similares, pues el grado de la presencia romana en el este de la Citerior no puede considerarse en nada inferior al de la Hispania meridional. Esta actitud diferenciada se observa también en lo que afecta a la propia cultura epigráfica, mucho más potente, por el contrario, en el litoral mediterráneo de la Citerior que en el sur, circunstancia que demuestra cómo en el período republicano ese conjunto de rasgos culturales que implica el llamado proceso de romanización, incluidas la lengua y la escritura en sus diversas manifestaciones, es seleccionado de manera diferente por las comunidades provinciales:[77] los turdetanos, pese a su empleo multisecular de la escritura paleohispánica, creada en esa misma región, y a la existencia, según Estrabón, de una cierta cultura literaria muestran una evidente falta de afección identitaria por su lengua vernácula y se inclinan por el uso del idioma de la potencia emergente, siglos antes de que la integración política de sus comunidades se pusiera en marcha, en abierto contraste con las ciudades fenicias que permanecieron apegadas a las suyas hasta comienzos del Principado y de las

---

[73] Strb. III 1, 6; sobre este pasaje ver ahora, de Hoz 2010: 481-484.

[74] En este mismo sentido apunta la escasez de inscripciones paleohispánicas sobre otros soportes en la Hispania meridional de los siglos II y I a. E., *MLH*, H; al respecto Beltrán 2005: 35 ss.

[75] Strb. III 2, 15.

[76] Como sugirieran *DCPH* I, 39; Beltrán 2004c, 127; 2005, 36.

[77] Beltrán 2005: 35 ss, 41 ss.

comunidades indígenas de la Citerior que optaron por expresarse en sus propios idiomas y escrituras, utilizados, además, con una cierta intensidad en la naciente cultura epigráfica, hasta fines del siglo I a. E.

5. Para concluir querría aducir, muy brevemente, un último ejemplo de particular interés, pues introduce un factor diferente en la discusión, el religioso, y constituye, probablemente, el episodio final del uso epigráfico de las lenguas vernáculas hispanas. Se trata de las inscripciones en lengua lusitana, varias de ellas mixtas con secciones del texto en latín.

Las inscripciones vernáculas bilingües son raras en el occidente romano,[78] si se excluyen las líbico-latinas del norte de África, de fecha más bien avanzada:[79] en las Galias, son excepcionales como la greco-gala de Genouilly,[80] mientras que en Hispania, al margen de las monetales ya comentadas, sólo cabe mencionar la greco-latina de Ampurias, datada hacia 100 a. E.,[81] y las latino-ibéricas de *Tarraco*,[82] *Saguntum*[83] y *Castulo*,[84] sobre piedra, además de los sellos sobre mortero hallados, por ejemplo, en Caminreal (Teruel),[85] en varios casos alusivas a libertos – *Saguntum, Castulo* – .[86] En estos casos el empleo del ibérico y el latín parece íntimamente vinculado al desarrollo de la cultura epigráfica en lengua vernácula, particularmente en ciertas ciudades en las que la presencia romana era, además, notable, un rasgo que, de cualquier modo, implica una valoración positiva de la lengua ibérica por sus hablantes, que, como se ha visto, con anterioridad a Augusto rara vez utilizan el latín en la expresión epigráfica a diferencia de lo que ocurría en el sur peninsular.

Diferente, sin embargo, es el caso de las inscripciones lusitanas, todas ellas de contenido religioso, con reiteradas menciones de dioses – *Trebaruna, Trebopala, Reve, Bandua,...* – y alusiones a sacrificios animales,[87] en dos de las cuales, mixtas y seguramente datables ya en el Principado, se introduce al comienzo una breve frase en latín que alude en ambos casos al autor material del epígrafe

---

[78] Sobre este tema está prevista la presentación, a comienzos de 2014, de la tesis de doctorado de M. J. Estarán en Zaragoza.

[79] Millar 1968; Rebuffat 2007.

[80] *RIG* II.1, L-4.

[81] Fabre, Mayer y Rodà 1991, núm. 15; Beltrán 2006, 224 ss.

[82] *MLH* III, C.18.5, 6 y 10.

[83] *MLH* III, F.11.8.

[84] *MLH* III, H.6.1.

[85] *MLH* III, E.7.3. Sobre las inscripciones bilingües y mixtas hispanas, Beltrán y Estarán 2011; sobre la estampillas ver en último lugar Estarán 2012.

[86] Sobre el papel de los libertos en el nacimiento de la cultura epigráfica hispana y su posible sensibilidad hacia las lenguas vernáculas, Beltrán 2004d, 171.

[87] Además de las tres recogidas por Unterman en *MLH* IV, L.1.1 (Arroyo de la Luz), con dos textos, L.2.1 (Lamas de Moledo) y L.3.1 (Cabeço das Fragoas), hay que añadir al menos otra más de Arroyo de la Luz (Villar y Pedrero 2001), la de Arronches (Carneiro, d'Encarnação, de Oliveira y Teixeira 2008) y probablemente el altar de Viseu (Fernandes, Carvalho y Figueira 2009).

o quizás al responsable de la puesta por escrito o, incluso, de la conducción de las ceremonias a las que los textos aluden, *Ambatus scripsi* (Arroyo de la Luz)[88] y *Rufinus et Tiro scripserunt* (Lamas de Moledo),[89] que preceden al desarrollo del epígrafe, en alfabeto latino y lengua lusitana, alusivo como se ha dicho a sacrificios y dioses. En estos casos parece evidente que, en un contexto de evidente latinización, visible en el predominio abrumador de las inscripciones latinas en esta parte de la antigua Lusitania tanto entre gentes de nombre romano como de onomástica indígena,[90] la elección de la lengua vernácula para estos textos religiosos, como se ha subrayado recientemente,[91] parece vinculada a la eficacia del ritual empleado, que los autores quizá temieran que se debilitara si no se realizaba en la lengua tradicional, en un contexto de conservadurismo religioso. Precisamente por ello, el empleo del lusitano sólo en estos casos, es decir exclusivamente vinculado a rituales religiosos,[92] más que afirmar la identidad a través de la lengua,[93] como el palmireno de South Shields, los etruscos de Zaghouan o el beligiense de Ibiza, remite a una esfera distinta, ligada a la eficacia de un ritual religioso, en un contexto en el que la población local no dudaba en utilizar el latín para todas las restantes manifestaciones epigráficas sin que ello parezca provocarles ningún conflicto identitario.

6. A lo largo de estas páginas se ha pasado revista a una serie de casos que ilustran cómo lengua e identidad no parecen relacionarse de una manera unívoca ni mecánica en el occidente romano. Los nexos entre lengua e identidad requieren, por el contrario, ser examinados y precisados en cada ocasión en función de factores que no siempre resultan transparentes más allá de líneas de fuerza evidentes como la vinculación del latín con la identidad cívica romana o con la comunicación epigráfica, sobre todo a partir de Augusto. Así, el uso de la lengua vernácula puede obedecer a razones de eficacia en la comunicación con los dioses tradicionales, como parece ser el caso de las inscripciones lusitanas, sin que en ello se manifieste necesariamente una manifestación de identidad étnica o cultural, habida cuenta del uso habitual del latín en las inscripciones coetáneas. En otras ocasiones, por el contrario, es el deseo de afirmar la pertenencia a una determinada comunidad, el que predomina por encima incluso de

---

[88] *MLH* IV L.1.1.

[89] *MLH* IV L.2.1.

[90] Salinas 1995: 281-291; Edmondson 2002: 51-52.

[91] En este sentido ya me pronuncié en Beltrán inédito; Alfayé y Marco 2008, 296-299; Beltrán 2011: 43-47.

[92] El altar de Viseu (Fernandes, Carvalho y Figueira 2009) tiene un claro final latino, pero un comienzo en lengua vernácula: *Deibabor / igo / Deibobor / Vissaieigo/bor / Albinus / Chaereae / f. / u. s. l. m.*; si debe darse la misma explicación al uso de la lengua vernácula en este epígrafe, habría que concluir que mientras el nombre del dedicante y la fórmula votiva se expresan en latín, por el contrario para la invocación de los dioses mismos se prefiere mantener la forma lusitana. Para otros casos, Gorrocahtegui y Vallejo 2010.

[93] Esta, sin embargo, parece la conclusión de Alfayé y Marco 2008, 300.

la inteligibilidad del mensaje que se desea transmitir, como ocurre en el epitafio de Ibiza, en el que el finado es explícitamente identificado como ciudadano de *Beligio*. Por otra parte, en las acuñaciones monetales de la Hispania Ulterior, pese a su larga tradición en el uso de la escritura paleohispánica y a la existencia de una cierta tradición literaria vernácula, se enfatizan los elementos locales distintivos en la iconografía, mientras que se renuncia al empleo de las lenguas vernáculas en beneficio de idiomas vehiculares como el latín o el púnico, al contrario de lo que ocurre en la Citerior, en donde las ciudades renuncian al empleo de tipos iconográficos propios en beneficio de emblemas que adquieren casi un significado provincial, pero utilizan sistemáticamente sus lenguas vernáculas.

La confrontación de las lenguas vernáculas occidentales, dotadas de una mínima tradición literaria, con un idioma dominante como el latín que, además de lengua del poder, de la cultura y la ciencia, y de la comunicación general y escrita, se manifiesta ante todo como un símbolo cívico imperial compatible con otras identidades locales, étnicas o culturales fue sin duda un factor que inhibió el valor simbólico de las lenguas vernáculas en estos terrenos, en abierto contraste con la sobrevaloración del idioma como elemento identitario que defiende la moderna tradición occidental de raíces nacionalistas.

Da pólis à cosmópolis: dos mosteiros cistercienses portugueses ao Capítulo geral de Cister[1]
(From "Polis" to "Cosmopolis": From Portuguese Cistercian Monasteries to the Cistercian General Chapter)

Maria Alegria Marques (alegriamarques@sapo.pt)
Universidade de Coimbra

Resumo – A partir da presença das referências aos mosteiros portugueses nas reuniões do capítulo geral de Cister, desde os finais do século XII ao século XIV, estudamos os problemas que eles aí suscitaram e as missões que foram cometidas aos seus representantes, relativamente à vivência das normas, à gestão dos mosteiros e às relações com a sociedade.

Palavras-chave: Ordem de Cister; capítulo geral; mosteiros cistercienses; Cister português.

Abstract – Utilizing the references to the representatives of Portuguese monasteries in the meetings of the General Chapter of Citeaux, from the late twelfth century to the fourteenth century, I examine the issues which they raised there and the missions with which they were charged, in areas such as standards of living, monastery management, and social relations.

Keywords: Cistercian Order, general chapter, Portuguese Cistercian monasteries.

1. Introdução

Na força do ideal ou na letra da norma, um mosteiro beneditino ou, posteriormente, cisterciense, deveria ser a imagem da cidade ideal, dotado de todos os requisitos necessários à vida da comunidade que o habitava. Segundo a regra que lhes servia de matriz, a beneditina, um mosteiro deveria "ser construído de forma a ter de portas a dentro tudo o necessário, a saber: água, moinho, horta, oficinas onde se exerçam os diversos ofícios, para que os monges não tenham necessidade de andar lá por fora, o que não é nada conveniente para as suas almas"[2] e situar-se longe do mundo e do convívio dos homens, como determinava a normativa de Cister, patente no *Exordium Cistercii*[3].

Daí, as determinações próprias para a construção dos parcos edifícios de morada dos monges, oratório, refeitório, casa para hóspedes e para o porteiro[4],

---

[1] Pelo que havemos de considerar acerca do capítulo geral de Cister e da sua importância, tendo em conta essencialmente a sua composição, entendemos que o tema teria lugar num Congresso subordinado ao tema *Pólis e Cosmopolis,* que o Centro de Estudos Clássicos da Universidade de Coimbra houve por bem realizar, e cujo convite de participação muito nos honrou e agradecemos.

[2] Regra do Patriarca S. Bento: 132.

[3] Cf. Nascimento, 1999: 57 e 81.

[4] Nascimento: 57.

https://doi.org/10.14195/978-989-26-1280-5_9

bem como a indicação daqueles que se podiam situar fora dos muros do mosteiro, entre os quais nenhum para habitação, apenas os destinados aos animais[5]. Tudo, de acordo com um desejo de fuga ao mundo e de mortificação do corpo, na busca de um ideal de purificação, de uma sede de além, de uma união a Cristo.

Se o tópico do deserto, do ermo, foi traço comum dos movimentos de reforma espiritual ao longo dos tempos (já assim o exprimiam as palavras de S. Jerónimo (345-420?), *nudos amat eremus*), e está bem presente nas diversas tentativas do séc. XI[6], foi a experiência cisterciense a sua expressão mais pura e duradoura. Ele dá o sentido profundo de reforma que animava os monges que, em 1198, retirando-se de Molesme, se estabeleceram em Cister. Mas a busca do deserto, do ermo, da solidão, era, ao mesmo tempo, simbólica e real. Era simbólica, enquanto sinal de ruptura total com o mundo e exigência de um sentimento de amor e caridade entre os homens, que os fazia comunicantes pela oração. Era real, quando exigia a busca do isolamento físico dos locais de fixação das comunidades que pretendiam dedicar-se à imitação de Cristo. Ambos se caldeavam com uma vertente mística, na transcendência da realidade e do quotidiano e tornavam-se sonho, volvendo-se em condição de ligação íntima do homem e da natureza, a exemplo de S. Bernardo, que aconselhava o seu amigo Henri Murdach, abade de Vauclair, a procurar, porque encontraria, "mais alguma coisa nas florestas que nos livros" e lhe garantia que "as árvores e os rochedos" lhe ensinariam o que ele "não poderia aprender com nenhum mestre"[7]. Solidão, vida eremítica, pobreza, em contraponto com a rotina diária, confortável, segura, da vivência dos monges das grandes abadias do séc. XI, particularmente das beneditinas, mas garantia de restauração do princípio da "cidade monástica autónoma"[8], na sua pureza, permitindo, ao monge, a possibilidade da simbiose perfeita da solidão, da pobreza e do trabalho manual[9].

2. Os princípios da organização cisterciense

Apresentado desta forma, o projecto revela-se sob uma egoísta, quiçá, perigosa independência. Mas assim não foi. Os fundadores da nova observância souberam dotar a sua obra de regras mínimas de organização e convivência, tendentes a fomentar um espírito de fraternidade e a manter uma união. Aliás, elas tornavam-se necessárias, tanto quanto os mosteiros cistercienses rapidamente

---

[5] Nascimento: 57.

[6] "El comúm denominador de todos los esfuerzos reformadores del siglo XI, fue el deseo de establecer una vida heroica de mortificaciones, vivida fuera de toda complicación mundana" (Lekai, 1987: 15).

[7] Pressouyre, 1990 : 30. Sobre o tema, ver também Nascimento, 1999: 7. Sobre a ligação do Santo à natureza, ver a sua *vida, em Voragine,* 2004: 100.

[8] Pressouyre, 1999: 39.

[9] Pressouyre, 1999: 37-47, sobre a organização espacial e funcional da abadia cisterciense.

cresceram em membros e em número, pois, como afirma o *Pequeno Exórdio*, no seu final, "Desde então instalaram abadias em diferentes dioceses. E elas foram crescendo dia a dia pelo efeito de um tão abundante e tão poderosa benção do Senhor que, [em] menos de oito anos, foram construídos doze mosteiros, uns saídos directamente de Cister e os outros provenientes da sua descendência"[10].

As primeiras normas nesse sentido, foram registadas, por escrito, em 1114 (data da fundação de Pontigny, a primeira das filhas de Cister), tendo-se multiplicado e enriquecido com novos elementos (documentos oficiais relativos aos primórdios da Ordem, estatutos complementares e ainda bulas papais de privilégio), durante a primeira metade do séc. XII[11].

O documento primitivo, de importância fundamental para a nova Ordem, nasceu ainda em tempo de Santo Estevão Harding, o segundo abade de Cister, e foi denominado, por ele próprio, por *Carta de caridade*. Nas palavras desse fundador, ele surgia para salvaguardar a "paz recíproca", "a fim de que não haja nenhuma discórdia nos nossos actos, mas que, numa só caridade, numa só regra, vivamos segundo costumes semelhantes"[12]. Verdadeiro instrumento jurídico da Ordem de Cister, procurava, como nele se afirma, "elucidar, estatuir e transmitir (…) um pacto de amizade, por qual modo de vida, ou antes por que tipo de caridade se deviam unir indissoluvelmente em espírito, os seus monges, corporalmente espalhados pelas abadias (…)"[13]. Por outras palavras, procurava regulamentar alguns aspectos práticos que poderiam concorrer para a concretização do preceito "Não tenhais para com ninguém nenhuma espécie de dívida a não ser a dívida do amor recíproco"[14].

No essencial, estatuíam-se os aspectos fundamentais da organização que haveriam de dar um aspecto uno e único à Ordem, no seu conjunto: obrigatoriedade de compreensão e observação da regra por todos, de uma única maneira; obrigatoriedade do uso dos mesmos livros litúrgicos e observância dos mesmos usos e costumes em todos os mosteiros. Esta proposta de observância de um mesmo modelo – concebido a partir das normas beneditinas – favorecia a coesão e estabelecia laços orgânicos entre os mosteiros aderentes, que eram todos os que se acolhiam à sombra da nova observância.

Ao mesmo tempo, e porque fundamental a uma Ordem que nasceu de uma cisão, estabeleciam-se minuciosamente as relações jurídicas entre os mosteiros que, entretanto, se fossem multiplicando no seu seio. Este é, na realidade, o verdadeiro elemento inovador na organização institucional cisterciense. Enquanto a regra de S. Bento se centrou na vida no seio do mosteiro, Cister havia de se

---

[10] Os cistercienses: 67.
[11] Pacaut, 1993: 38 e 64.
[12] Pacaut, 1993: 64.
[13] Os cistercienses: 73.
[14] Os cistercienses: 139.

preocupar com a definição das relações entre as casas que se acolhiam ao seu projecto.

O primeiro aspecto que se nos impõe é a própria nomenclatura das abadias, nas suas relações entre si: abadias-mãe e abadias-filha, conforme faziam surgir ou aceitavam na sua dependência e protecção outras abadias entretanto surgidas por crescimento e vontade das existentes ou por outras vias, desejosas de entrar na nova organização. Assim se criavam laços, se estimulavam elos, se pretendia afastar a discórdia, se ultrapassava a distância e a sujeição.

As normas que haviam de definir os aspectos jurídico-económicos e jurídico--administrativo da organização que se pretendia afirmar e salvaguardar estavam já inculcadas na *Carta de Caridade*. Quanto aos primeiros, o documento matricial declarava a plena independência material entre as casas da organização, ao estabelecer que nada se imporia sobre bens temporais que pudesse redundar em vantagem para uma e prejuízo para outra. Quanto ao segundo, a sua regulamentação constitui a grande preocupação e a grande aposta dos seus mentores e autores. Por isso, o documento estatuía o quadro de obrigações do abade-pai em relação às suas filhas. Entre elas, destacava-se a visita anual à abadia-filha, talvez a sua obrigação maior, pois que era o modo de assegurar a unanimidade da Ordem, sem intervir na gestão de cada casa em particular[15], com a necessária regulamentação (precedências, direitos e deveres de visitandos e visitados)[16]. Nas responsabilidades da abadia-mãe, caberia também, aos seus superiores, velar por qualquer abadia--filha em caso de ocorrência de uma qualquer vacância. Bem como lhe competia zelar pela qualidade do abade-filho, na correcção de faltas ou, no limite, na deposição dos incorrigíveis. No primeiro dos casos, cumpria ao abade-pai assumir a responsabilidade da administração da abadia-filha até à eleição de novo abade. Por isso, era também a ele que competia a convocação da eleição, com a chamada de outros abades oriundos da casa-mãe em questão. Todos eles - estes e os monges sem pastor - com o conselho e aprovação do seu abade-pai procediam, então, à eleição de novo abade. Ela tanto podia recair sobre um irmão do mosteiro em causa, como sobre um de qualquer outro mosteiro, mesmo da própria abadia-mãe. No caso, apenas se proibia a escolha de alguém estranho à Ordem[17]. Se a vacância de um mosteiro se anunciava, quando um abade pretendia renunciar ao seu cargo, também aí estava reservado um papel ao abade-pai: competia-lhe ser paciente e conselheiro, não dando facilmente o seu consentimento. Ele só viria depois de um conselho com outros abades da Ordem.

Papel importante lhe ficava ainda, quando, numa abadia-filha, surgia um abade pouco cumpridor, menos responsável. Então, cabia-lhe admoestá-lo ou,

---

[15] Era, digamos, o momento do jogo do equilíbrio de interesses e de objectivos.

[16] Na lógica do "amor recíproco", própria da tutela parental, igualmente se estabeleciam as regras a respeitar quando se verificasse a visita de um abade-filho a uma abadia-mãe.

[17] Igualmente se proibia a cedência de um irmão para responsável em qualquer outra Ordem.

em caso limite, suspendê-lo mesmo e, caso tivesse apoiantes no próprio mosteiro, lançar também a excomunhão sobre esses membros prevaricadores.

Ainda na busca da unidade se registava a obrigatoriedade da realização de um capítulo geral dos abades dos seus mosteiros[18], anualmente, em Cister, para "se verem pessoalmente, estreitarem os laços de disciplina da Ordem, reforçarem a paz e conservarem a caridade"[19]. Por isso, eram esse o momento e o local indicados para a "denúncia pública, mas com caridade", dos erros e desvios dos abades, das suas faltas e dos seus litígios. Igualmente, e porque "a caridade é a maior das virtudes"[20], era também o capítulo o local indicado para a informação sobre a incapacidade económica das abadias, cuja "pobreza intolerável" "todos os abades, inflamados pelo fogo ardente da caridade se apressarão a socorrer, cada um dentro das suas possibilidades"[21]. Na conjugação de ideal e pragmatismo, o capítulo geral concedia a cada abade um lugar de direito, igual para todos, refreando, assim tentações de ingerência de abades-pai.

São estes os principais princípios jurídicos da Ordem cisterciense. Definiam a sua constituição, regulamentavam a administração das casas, na sua gestão e continuidade, estatuíam as relações das diferentes casas entre si. Num grau superior, garantiam a unidade da Ordem[22]. E ainda que com algumas modificações mais ou menos pontuais, surgidas de novos tempos, as grandes linhas desta organização marcaram a vida da Ordem até ao séc. XVI[23].

Ao mesmo tempo, tais princípios tanto reflectem o mundo em que a reforma cisterciense nasceu, como ofereciam propostas válidas para a própria sociedade, quiçá, mesmo, protótipos para novos tempos. Assim, as relações jurídicas ofereciam um novo modelo, afastado já da hierárquica matriz cluniacense, de relações de subordinação entre vassalos e senhores; antes se pretendia que as suas casas vivessem em capacidade autonómica, embora em união espiritual às outras a que se ligavam por laços de fraternidade. A culminar o seu edifício jurídico-administrativo, a proposta de um capítulo geral, a sua continuidade e funções revelaram-se o elemento mais inovador da ordem de Cister[24]. Nascido de uma exigência da própria dinâmica e crescimento da Ordem – como poderia ser possível a visitação de tantas abadias, nascidas ou filiadas nas quatro casas

---

[18] Reconhecido explicitamente desde 1127 como o órgão supremo da Ordem, sob a autoridade do abade de Cister (Pacaut, 1993: 66).

[19] "Resumo da Carta de caridade", IV, 1, in Nascimento, 1999: 54.

[20] S. Paulo, *1.ª Carta aos Coríntios*, 13, 13.

[21] *Os cistercienses*: 89.

[22] Sobre todos estes aspectos dos tempos primitivos da ordem de Cister, ver Pacaut, 1993: 13-109.

[23] Sobre esses tempos de mudança, quando não crise, ver id., ibid.: 279-307.

[24] A existência do capítulo, nas ordens existentes, Cister incluída, tinha um carácter bem diferente; era o paradigma de uma participação dos membros de uma comunidade na questão colectiva e na verificação da adequação de comportamentos pessoais a normas institucionais.

primeiras, filhas mais velhas de Cister? –, o capítulo geral foi a grande revolução no campo das estruturas político-administrativas da Idade Média[25]. Quando as monarquias se debatiam com questões de poder, ameaçadas pelas pretensões pessoais e particulares de senhores feudais, o capítulo de Cister apresentava-se como uma verdadeira assembleia supra-nacional, experiência primordial de um regime parlamentar, a haver nos reinos em afirmação. Exigindo a participação dos abades de todas as casas cistercienses, tinha o direito de legislar, fosse na inovação de normas, fosse na sua modificação e interpretação. Detinha também poderes administrativos e judiciários, relativamente a qualquer questão e lugar, a qualquer norma e a qualquer membro. Assumiu-se simultaneamente como fonte de direito e instrumento da sua interpretação e aplicação, bem como foi o preventor do dirigismo e da anarquia. Como estrutura supra-nacional, relativamente aos particularismos locais da Europa medieval, ou como estrutura de cúpula da organização cisterciense, na aliança perseguida entre as duas vertentes, o capítulo de Cister tentou uma experiência federativa na Europa, mais ou menos bem sucedida. Além de que, sob a sua égide, em última instância se desenrolaram acções de expansão europeia que marcaram os tempos medievais[26]. Num plano mais comum, ele foi, sem dúvida, a oportunidade para muitos dos seus membros deixarem as suas terras, ultrapassarem fronteiras, conhecerem mundos e gentes, ou, na letra deste Congresso, passarem da *polis* à *cosmopolis*. Se mais não fosse, só por isso, a experiência de Cister e do seu capítulo geral, com alguma utopia que os animava, merecia bem um lugar de destaque também no campo das instituições de cultura.

Com alguma titubeação nos primeiros tempos, relativamente à data da sua realização, a sua reunião acabou por consagrar-se a 14 de Setembro, de cada ano, na casa-mãe de Cister. As suas actas chegaram até nós, permitindo um conhecimento apurado dos seus trabalhos, hesitações e determinações[27].

3. A PRESENÇA DOS MOSTEIROS PORTUGUESES

Ora, é a singularidade e o individualismo dos mosteiros e das questões portuguesas nesse excepcional fórum da Cristandade que pretendemos aqui

---

[25] Evidentemente que, ele próprio, haveria de ser vítima do crescimento da Ordem: o seu gigantismo foi factor do seu enfraquecimento e da sua desvalorização ao longo do tempo. Diga--se, a propósito, que entrados em certa decadência já a partir do séc. XIII, em 1514, apenas se lhe apresentaram 18 abades! Contudo, tenha-se em atenção que as casas femininas não participavam no capítulo, por decisão deste, do ano de 1237, pois que há indícios de, primitivamente, as abadessas aí terem tido participação. As suas decisões foram codificadas, em certos momentos; sobre elas, ver Lucet, 1997.

[26] Referimo-nos à actividade das ordens monástico-militares que militaram sob os "Usos de Cister", como o Templo, Calatrava, Alcântara, Avis, Cristo. Tudo isto, para nos cingirmos ao Ocidente, pois que houve também expansionismo europeu para Oriente sob a mesma tutela.

[27] Foram publicadas por Joseph-Marie Canivez, 1933-1941.

apresentar e que entendemos por matéria *local*. Em complemento, indicaremos outros elementos, relacionados com as visitações ordenadas pelo capítulo, os quais ajudam a compreender melhor a organização cisterciense, no que ela teve de urdidura de teias e relações entre os seus mosteiros, tornada, assim, obviamente, matéria *geral*, no entanto secundária, em vista das notícias registadas e, sobretudo, do conhecimento dos seus resultados.

Em vista das premissas enunciadas, seria de se esperar um conjunto de informações que ajudassem, até, a esclarecer alguns dos muitos problemas com que se debate a presença de Cister em Portugal, pelo menos no seu primeiro século de existência. Infelizmente, também não é por aqui que ficamos elucidados; bem ao contrário, nalguns dos seus registos são até maiores as interrogações que se suscitam que os problemas que se resolvem.

De qualquer modo, os registos das suas presenças são um dos sinais de como os mosteiros portugueses participaram do cosmopolitismo que foi apanágio da Ordem de Cister, em exemplo pioneiro da Idade Média.

3.1. A matéria local

Ilustremos, então, a presença de portugueses no capítulo geral de Cister. Tenhamos em conta que ia já adiantada a reforma cisterciense quando, em Portugal, algum mosteiro se lhe ligou[28]. Por outro lado, não esqueçamos que, sendo obrigação a presença dos abades, ela só se faria notada quando havia lugar a algo de excepcional, ou quando eles fossem comissionados para qualquer missão especial.

Limitamos a nossa pesquisa até ao ano de 1400, quando se anunciavam novas preocupações no capítulo geral e que se centravam na reforma da Ordem. No entanto, temos consciência de que será importante levar a pesquisa até aos meados do séc. XVI, quando se verificou a cisão entre as casas portuguesas e a grande organização, com a fundação da Congregação de Portugal.

Nos três séculos que nos propomos tratar, contam-se mais de seis dezenas de referências a portugueses, seja em assuntos relacionados com muitos dos seus mosteiros, seja com os seus membros, normalmente os abades. O séc. XIII é, de longe, o mais representado[29], com mais de meia centena de casos, distribuídos de forma muito irregular pelas suas décadas[30].

A primeira referência de um problema relacionado com um mosteiro português, levantado no capítulo geral de Cister, remonta a 1190, quando a Ordem já tinha cerca de meia dúzia de décadas de presença em Portugal. A última,

---

[28] Em nossa opinião, o primeiro terá sido S. Cristóvão de Lafões, filiado em Claraval. Ver Marques, 1998: 29-73.

[29] No séc. XII, apenas se colhem três referências e cinco no séc. XIV.

[30] Veja-se a distribuição: 1201-1210: 8; 1211-1220:7; 1221-1230: 9; 1231-1240: 4; 1241-1250: 3; 1251-1260: 4; 1261-1270: 6; 1271-1280: 8; 1281-1290: 2; 1291-1300: 3.

de 1400, liga-se à necessidade de visitação dos mosteiros portugueses, numa perspectiva mais lata, que englobava a orientação de vida das casas peninsulares de Portugal, Castela e Leão.

Ao longo do tempo considerado, foram muitas as razões da presença de nomes portugueses no registo do capítulo geral. Consideramo-las pelos temas a que se reportam.

3.1.1. A vivência das normas

Do que ficou dito, nos registos do capítulo geral percebe-se a vivência da norma, exactamente pela indicação da falta cometida. Sem dúvida, que a matéria que mereceu mais referências foi a ausência ao capítulo, alvo de observações de carácter censório. São nomeados e penalizados os abades portugueses faltosos ou negligentes, são censurados os responsáveis peninsulares ausentes, são justifica-dos os abades da Hispânia, ausentes em tempo de guerra[31]. Porém, os responsáveis e os capitulares eram homens do seu tempo e percebiam que quando a crise se anunciava, havia que procurar-se formas de conjugar a diminuição de despesas com as obrigações estatutárias, tanto mais necessário se as abadias eram muito afastadas de Cister (como as portuguesas), o que significava despesas acrescidas. Então, diminuíam-se obrigações e aplanavam-se as censuras.

Outras referências ligadas ao esquecimento das normas estatutárias de Cister dizem respeito à falta da visitação das abadias-filha, pelos responsáveis da abadia-mãe[32], aos problemas relacionados com o acesso[33] ou a renúncia a cargos[34], ao desrespeito pelo próprio capítulo e suas determinações[35].

---

[31] Em 1197, anotava-se que os abades da Hispânia estavam ausentes por causa da "incur-são dos pagãos" e em 1269 por causa dos prejuízos da guerra; Canivez (ed.), 1933: 216-217 e 1935: 70. A primeira referência evoca ainda os ecos da derrota dos cristãos, sobretudo do rei de Castela, face aos muçulmanos, em Alarcos; a segunda referir-se-á a uma década de confrontos entre cristãos e muçulmanos, sobretudo Castela e Leão, que haviam de culminar na conquista de Cádis (1265) e de Múrcia (1266).

[32] Caso do mosteiro de Tarouca (1198); Canivez (ed.), 1933: 228.

[33] Em 1208, percebe-se um problema na eleição do abade de Alcobaça, no qual haveria par-ticipação do abade de Bouro, que aspirava à abadia alcobacense. Já em 1237, era a determinação da inquirição sobre o abade de Maceira-Dão, que recebera a abadia de forma irregular, ao que parecia, com a conivência de um certo Fr. Estêvão, que o registo apelida de seu "sócio". Por sua vez, em 1243, era o caso do abade de Osseira, que recebera, indevidamente, a profissão do abade de Alcobaça; Canivez (ed.), 1933: 352 e 1934: 182-183, 265, respectivamente.

[34] O caso do abade de S. Pedro de Águias que renunciou e cuja renúncia foi indevidamente recebida pelo abade de Claraval; ambos foram castigados no capítulo de 1205; Canivez (ed.), 1933: 316.

[35] É o caso do abade de Moreruela, comissionado para tratar da causa do abade de Santa Maria de Aguiar, desobediente e contumaz (1212), o de Alcobaça, com igual incumbência sobre o de Seiça (1216), e o dos abades de Salzedas e de Alcobaça, que, em 1242, também não informaram o capítulo acerca das causas de que tinham sido comissionados anteriormente. O caso repete-se, em 1277, de uma forma mais genérica, envolvendo os abades da Hispânia que assim procederem. Esta censura deixa perceber o modo de funcionamento do capítulo: sendo-

Os aspectos comportamentais, no que tinham de desvio da norma, haviam de assumir um lugar especial nos capítulos. De comum, seriam casos mais ou menos chocantes, que convinha punir, morigerar, até pelo contágio do exemplo que poderiam representar. Cabem, neste ponto, o caso do abade de Aguiar, que "falou" desabridamente e de forma desumana contra o seu antecessor[36], a "experiência" do abade de Santa Maria de Aguiar, que, para se subtrair ao ofício, se fez monge, na mesa, e um seu monge, abade[37,] a falta do abade de Salzedas, ao ajustar um converso para coabitar com uma nobre mulher[38], a contumácia de um abade de Tarouca, expulso da sua casa e que vagueava pela Hispânia, com o hábito da Ordem e tendo um mulo, por propriedade[39], ou, genericamente, excessos de monges[40] ou abades[41].

Neste aspecto dos desvios comportamentais, assume particular interesse, pelo seu pitoresco, o acontecimento que envolveu os abades de Seiça e S. Pedro de Águias, em 1217. Hospedados na abadia de Marmoutier[42], a caminho do capítulo geral, não se contentaram com os alimentos que aí lhes foram oferecidos, cebolas, ovos e salmoura, tendo diligenciado por obter bom peixe no burgo. Com uma ração de pão e vinho, oferecida pelo mosteiro hospedeiro, comeram na vila, à porta, "onde nenhum monge costumava comer". Por qualquer razão, não indicada, os conversos que estavam com eles, foram a pé, à abadia de L'Aumône. Mais se disse que os conversos que estavam com eles cheiravam mal, apesar de não se escusarem a pedir água para lavar as mãos. Como resultado de tudo isto, o capítulo entendeu censurá-los e determinar, como castigo, que, todos, se abstivessem de peixe, por um ano, a não ser em caso de grande necessidade ou enfermidade.

O erro podia ir além da falta pessoal, para se achar presente nas relações entre mosteiros. Era a falha da caridade fraterna que deveria unir todos num só corpo, expressa em situações de abades que se digladiavam pela "pecunia" de membros

---

-lhe denunciado uma qualquer falta, discutia-se o caso e nomeava-se um ou mais abades para inquirirem e informarem o capítulo, posto o que este tomava as deliberações adequadas, segundo os "Usos da Ordem"; Canivez (ed.), 1933: 392, 454, 1934: 257-258 e 1935: 171.

[36] 1190; Canivez (ed.), 1933: 125. Terá de entender-se que se tratou de alguma veemente censura ou de algo que manchou a memória do anterior abade.

[37] 1206; Canivez (ed.), 1933: 330.

[38] 1221; Canivez (ed.), 1934: 4.

[39] 1221; Canivez (ed.), 1933: 6-7. Para ele, o capítulo mandava aos abades e priores da Ordem que lhe retirassem o hábito e o mulo e o considerassem como excomungado e ex-ordenado.

[40] Por regra, apontam-se os excessos, mas não se concretizam. Assim, o dos monges de Tarouca, em 1204, que chegaram a merecer a intervenção do rei de Portugal (D. Sancho I), que, por eles, escreveu ao abade de Claraval; Canivez (ed.), 1933: 299.

[41] Em 1279, referem-se os "excessos gravíssimos" do abade de Alcobaça, recomendando-se que o abade-pai, na sua visitação, inquirisse a verdade e punisse com a deposição ou outra pena que o caso merecesse; Canivez (ed.), 1935: 191.

[42] Abadia beneditina da diocese de Tours.

fugitivos de um mosteiro a outro[43], abades que não se entendiam por questões que nos escapam[44]; abade que denunciava abade por qualquer falta específica[45].

Numa prova de que o castigo era o sentido da correcção da falta, ou, dito de outra forma, de como o capítulo que castigava era o mesmo que usava de caridade para com os faltosos, em 1281, e a propósito do abade de Alcobaça, acusado de faltas gravíssimas e de dilapidação de bens da sua abadia, castigado no ano anterior, por se opor à visitação, a assembleia considerava que um abade deposto podia ser recuperado, com capacidade de elegibilidade, caso apresentasse méritos para isso[46].

Por último, numa das expressões maiores do poder do capítulo e de exigência de vivência da norma, assistimos à determinação de realização de visitações em Portugal (e noutros reinos peninsulares), em 1390, 1397 e 1400. Isto é, o capítulo tinha bem presente quer a norma da sua carta fundadora, a *charta charitatis*, quer a noção do valor que tributava a tal prática.

3.1.2. Os mosteiros portugueses e a sociedade do tempo

Mas outros assuntos portugueses foram levados ao capítulo geral de Cister, nestes três séculos que consideramos. São de sentido bem diverso dos anteriores e ajudam à leitura das relações dos mosteiros portugueses com a sociedade do tempo.

São de natureza diversa, desde as intenções de novas fundações em Portugal, fossem ligadas à família real[47] ou proviessem de iniciativa particular[48], a

---

[43] Caso de Maceira-Dão e Valbuena, registado em 1217 e 1218; Canivez (ed.), 1933: 477-478.

[44] Tarouca e Bouro, em 1228; Alcobaça e Carracedo, em 1230-1231; Alcobaça e Espina, em 1241; Estrela e Tarouca, e S. Paulo e Lorvão, em 1278; Bouro e Lorvão, em 1280; Valparaíso e Montederramo, Espina e Santa Maria de Aguiar, em 1291; Canivez (ed.), 1934: 69-70, 90, 238-239; 1935: 177, 181, 202, 256.

[45] Como o abade de Salzedas, castigado pelo capítulo, em 1241, por desenterrar um monge, porque ele tinha consigo uma amante e 60 soldos; Canivez (ed.), 1934: 244.

[46] Tratou-se de D. Pedro Nunes; cf. Gomes, 2000: 27-71.

[47] Em 1227, os abades de Tarouca e Alcobaça eram comissionados para o caso da construção de uma abadia da filha do rei de Portugal, do que deveriam dar informação ao capítulo no ano seguinte; ver Canivez, 1933: 62. Sobre este caso e os seguintes (notas 48 e 49), ver o nosso estudo, já citado supra, n. 28.

[48] Em 1220, o capítulo considerava o pedido do chantre de Lisboa para construir uma abadia, em herdade sua e que fosse filha de Alcobaça. O capítulo comissionava os abades de Osseira, Oya e Melón, para inspeccionarem o local e informarem o próximo capítulo; Canivez (ed.), 1933: 529-530. Tratava-se da fundação do mosteiro de S. Paulo de Almaziva, nos arredores de Coimbra; cf. Santos: 1998. Quatro décadas depois, era o tempo de o capítulo se debruçar sobre o andamento do pedido do chanceler do rei de Portugal, para a fundação de um mosteiro no lugar de Logo de Deus, já inspeccionado pelo abade de Alcobaça. Agora, o capítulo mandava que ele ordenasse o convento, verificasse a suficiência dos bens e a filiação em Alcobaça. Como já afirmámos noutro lugar, esta fundação nunca veria o seu dia. Desconhecendo-se, por completo, onde seria o lugar do seu estabelecimento, hoje, estamos em crer que o nome seria o da própria abadia a fundar e não o do de seu assentamento. Com este nome, havia casas em França e em Itália (Pacaut, 1993: 375). Por último, em 1278, o capítulo comissionava os abades de Maceira e Seiça para inspeccionarem o local onde a nobre senhora Domingas Soares pretendia fundar um

problemas de mudança do lugar de assentamento das abadias[49]. Igualmente estão presentes questões de dificuldades económicas, como são patentes os problemas com o poder régio. No primeiro caso, o mosteiro de S. Pedro de Águias passava pela "máxima pobreza", em 1216, a ponto de o capítulo entender por bem que o abade de Claraval dele dispusesse segundo a utilidade e a honestidade da Ordem e tentasse restabelecer a boa administração em tal casa.

Se no início do séc. XIII, o rei de Portugal se preocupava com os excessos dos monges de Tarouca, a ponto de ter escrito ao capítulo, em 1209 já as questões entre a Ordem e o rei de Portugal eram de outra natureza. Sem qualquer outra informação, apenas o registo do capítulo desse ano nos diz que tais problemas afligiam muito a Ordem, pelo que a magna reunião entendia por bem que o abade de Cister procurasse pessoa conveniente, do círculo do rei, que o levasse "ao amor e reverência da Ordem", e, se ele persistisse nas suas atitudes vexatórias, então, o abade deveria denunciá-lo, ao papa[50].

De bem maior alcance e futuro, foi a resposta do capítulo de 1320 ao pedido do rei de Portugal, de aceitar que a Ordem de Cristo se estabelecesse sob o poder do abade de Alcobaça, tanto mais quanto já se achava incorporada, na Ordem, pelo Sumo Pontífice.

Um outro tema que se nos afigura de interesse maior à ordem de Cister em Portugal, prende-se com o pedido régio registado no ano de 1294[51]. O rei desejava fazer um estudo para a Ordem, na diocese de Lisboa[52], para o qual já teria local escolhido. Na circunstância, o capítulo limitava-se a nomear os abades de Salzedas e S. João de Tarouca, para a respectiva inspecção e para considerarem a petição, se o achassem capaz.

3.1.3. Gestão corrente

Sob este título, englobamos um conjunto variado de assuntos, não específico da ordem de Cister, pois que percorrem todo o meio monástico ou até eclesial. Foram também apresentados ao capítulo geral, pois que importavam a casas da Ordem. Por isso lhe chamamos gestão corrente. Encontram-se pedidos

---

mosteiro para monjas; Canivez (ed.), 1935: 184.

[49] Em 1227, pelos abades de S. Pedro de Águias e de Alcobaça. No primeiro caso foram comissionados os abades de Tarouca (abadia-mãe) e Salzedas e, no segundo, os mesmos e o de S. Pedro de Águias; Canivez (ed.), 1934: 63-64.

[50] No fim da vida, D. Sancho I ainda sustentava questões com o clero do reino, particularmente com o bispo do Porto. Na documentação portuguesa, não se rastreia qualquer animosidade entre o rei e os mosteiros de Cister.

[51] Era abade D. Domingos II; cf. Gomes, 2000: 46.

[52] O documento deveria apresentar qualquer problema de conservação ou leitura, pois que a indicação do local se faz pela expressão "loci ....bonam", sinal de incompletude de leitura paleográfica; Canivez (ed.), 1935: 270.

de celebração de aniversários por benfeitores, da família real[53] ou particulares[54], ou de particular intenção do rei de Portugal[55]. Bem como nos deparamos com a licença para a instituição da festa de Santiago, com a sua história[56], e a da Santa Coroa, em Alcobaça, em 1263[57].

A existência do capítulo geral, se, por um lado, fazia acorrer, a Cister, os abades de todas as partes da Cristandade, pois que, por elas se espalhou a Ordem, por outro lado, colocava os seus membros sob a alçada dos mais variados riscos. Apesar do longo tempo que abraçamos na nossa análise e das muitas viagens que ele representa, apenas achamos notícia de um caso de violência que atingiu o abade de Salzeda e o de Moreruela, quando se dirigiam ao capítulo, em 1252. Foram roubados e atrozmente feridos, acabando presos, na passagem pela diocese de Blois. Do facto, apresentaram queixa à rainha de França[58], atitude que foi reiterada pelo capítulo, que a considerou excesso e injúria, bem como cometeu aos abades de Notre-Dame du Val (dioc. Versalhes) e Royaumond (dioc. Beauvais) a atribuição de ajuda nas despesas necessárias.

4. A MATÉRIA GERAL

Como anunciámos, sob este título importam aspectos registados nos capítulos sem uma identificação precisa, mas que envolviam casas portuguesas. Relacionam-se com a observância da norma cisterciense, no que dizia respeito

---

[53] Era o caso da infanta D. Mafalda, falecida em 1256, pedido pelo abade de Salzedas, em 1257, para a sua abadia e para mais duas, de monjas, de que não se menciona o nome, mas de que uma seria Arouca e a outra, talvez, Bouças. Em 1280, foi a hora do pedido de Alcobaça e de Salzedas, pela memória do rei D. Afonso III, falecido no ano anterior; Canivez (ed.), 1934: 431 e 1935: 201.

[54] Foi o caso do abade de Salzedas, que, em 1252, apresentou o pedido da instituição de um aniversário em memória de Miana Teresa, fundadora da abadia. Trata-se de D. Teresa Afonso, mulher de Egas Moniz. É muito curioso verificar este pedido tão tardio; de qualquer modo, ele representa a presença bem viva, da sua memória no mosteiro. Em 1294, foi a vez de o bispo de Lisboa, D. João Martins de Soalhães, apresentar, ao capítulo, o seu pedido de instituição de um aniversário no mosteiro de Alcobaça, obtida a concordância do convento; Canivez (ed.), 1934: 379 e 1935: 275, respectivamente.

[55] Assim entendemos o pedido apresentado em 1344, de duas missas, uma do Espírito Santo, outra da Virgem Santa, em cada uma das casas da Ordem. Talvez que o rei se encontrasse bastante doente, pois que viria a falecer em 28 de Maio de 1357; Canivez (ed.), 1935: 500.

[56] Canivez (ed.), 1935:13. Esta indicação leva-nos a aceitar a hipótese de estarmos perante qualquer representação teatral.

[57] Id., ibid.; esta festa liga-se ao culto das relíquias, tão em voga na Idade Média. Concretamente, trata-se das relíquias da Coroa de espinhos, compradas por S. Luís ao imperador Balduíno II de Constantinopla, por intermédio de um veneziano, em 1239, e para a qual mandou construir a Sainte Chapelle (1248); no intervalo, a relíquia ficou no palácio, no altar de S. Nicolau. (Muito penhorada, agradecemos esta informação ao Senhor Professor Doutor Aires Nascimento).

[58] Deve ser referência a Branca de Castela, mãe de Luís IX, que faleceria em 27 de Novembro de 1252, em Melun.

à importante prática da visitação e à participação em acções expressamente comissionadas pelo capítulo. Parecem-nos determinações importantes, pois que colocavam em acção e, sobretudo, em contacto, membros portugueses da Ordem com outras casas, noutras paragens, sobretudo em Leão e Castela, e permitiam a presença de membros estrangeiros, especialmente peninsulares, em Portugal.

Relativamente a abades, casas ou questões portuguesas, ao longo do tempo encontramos comissionados[59] os abades de Sacramenia (1), Huerta (2), La Espina (6), Osseira (5), Armenteira (1), Melón (3), Moreruela (3), Sobrado (1), Oia (2), Montederamo (1), Meira (1), Sandoval (1), Valbuena (1) e Valdeiglesias (1). Ao invés, apenas os responsáveis de Aguiar e de Fiães foram chamados a intervir em questões relacionadas com agentes ou instituições de além-fronteiras, mas sempre peninsulares[60]. Sem percebermos como se fazia a nomeação, mesmo assim arriscamos que haveria um qualquer factor pessoal, a interferir na escolha[61].

Estas intervenções revelam-se bem desiguais. Ora se tratava apenas de comunicar a resolução do capítulo acerca de certa questão ou situação, normalmente censuras por faltas cometidas, ora se tratava de tentar resolver qualquer conflito nascido entre dignitários ou instituições, por vezes de espaços políticos diferentes[62].

No primeiro século da existência de Cister, encontramos ainda o apelo a Cister e a Claraval, relativamente a questões portuguesas. Ou porque houvera resignação injustificada, ou porque o rei de Portugal se intrometia, indevidamente, nos assuntos das casas monásticas, ou porque algum mosteiro se achava em extrema pobreza, afinal questões de cumprimento das normas, exercício de política ou da caridade fraterna.

Decorrentes ainda dos capítulos, provinham as visitações, como afirmámos momentos excepcionais na vida dos mosteiros cistercienses, pelo que representavam de união entre si. De um modo geral, bem aceites, porque das normas da Ordem, não se acha qualquer acta para o tempo sobre o qual nos debruçamos[63], embora haja prova da sua realização[64].

---

[59] Entre ( ), indicamos as vezes que o foram.

[60] Ou relativos aos abades da Hispânia (1197) ou a Leão e Castela.

[61] É o que se nos sugere o caso do abade de Fiães, que, em 1242, é nomeado para três casos; Canivez (ed.), 1934: 257-258.

[62] Por exemplo, em 1217 e 1218, entre Maceira-Dão e Valbuena; em 1230, entre Alcobaça e Carracedo; em 1291, entre os abades de Valparaíso, Montederramo e Santa Maria de Aguiar; cfr. supra, notas 44 e 45.

[63] Sobre este tema, ver Gomes, 1998.

[64] Em Marques, 1998: 73-88, publicamos um documento de 13 de Dezembro de 1381, no mosteiro de Salzeda, pelo qual o abade do mosteiro de S. Pedro das Águias, comissionado para a causa da eleição de Fr. João Dornelas como abade de Alcobaça, por comissão de Fr. João de Chassagnollis, mandatário do abade de Claraval para a visitação aos mosteiros cistercienses nos

5. Conclusão

Nos cerca de três séculos de existência de Cister em Portugal, que agora percorremos, foram estes os aspectos salientes que os representantes portugueses de Cister levaram às reuniões do capítulo geral da sua Ordem ou aí viram propostos, para discussão e determinação. Na sua essência, não diferiam dos que outros mosteiros, de outras partes da Cristandade, viram tratados nesse areópago da Ordem. Nas suas misérias e nas suas grandezas, todos se irmanavam no espírito e nas práticas da Ordem.

A comunhão dos representantes das casas portuguesas, nas suas faltas e petições, com os de outras casas da Ordem, dos locais mais próximos, Galiza ou Leão e Castela, ou aos mais longínquos, fazia-os participar de um espírito e de uma visão cosmopolista que só a Ordem de Cister soube imprimir à sua organização. É certo que não sabemos até que ponto chegou essa comunhão. Mas estamos em crer que muito da cultura que se bebeu nos mosteiros portugueses, Alcobaça à sua cabeça, teve a sua origem ou, pelo menos, o seu anúncio em muitos desses encontros, como momentos privilegiados de troca de experiências, de recepção de novidades do tempo e aquisição de repertórios culturais[65].

Quanto à documentação percorrida, fica demonstrado que, embora não dê muitas das respostas desejáveis e necessárias à elucidação de problemas da Ordem de Cister em Portugal, ela não pode e não deve ser descurada em estudos sobre as instituições cistercienses portuguesas; se questiona, também pode ajudar a esclarecer e, sobretudo, a complementar, a que perdurou em Portugal.

E esta nota é tanto mais de realçar, quanto o grande movimento monástico precedente, o cluniacense, apesar da sua grande influência cultural inicial em Portugal, a exemplo da Península, não proporcionou assinalável influxo por parte da própria congregação de Cluny[66].

---

reinos da Península, entre os quais Portugal, dá conta de todo o processo. Por documento incluso no mesmo, de 9 de Junho desse mesmo ano, em Guimarães, Fr. João de Chassignollis fez saber que visitou os mosteiros portugueses sujeitos a Claraval, como lhe fora ordenado, e que delegava os seus poderes de visitador, na sua ausência, nos abades de S. Pedro das Águias e de Torre de Aguiar.

[65] Sobre esta matéria, ver a muita bibliografia de Aires Nascimento. Entretanto, o caso fica bem ilustrado com o que acima se diz acerca da festa da Santa Coroa.

[66] Na realidade, também não teria condições para tal, uma vez que só tinha vinculadas, a si, três casas portuguesas e sem grande expressão: os priorados de S. Pedro de Rates (1100), Santa Justa de Coimbra (1102), e de Vimieiro (1127), que haviam de fazer parte da "camararia" da Galiza.

Calímaco e a linguagem universal do mito
(Callimachus and the Universal Language of Myth)

Marta Várzeas (mvarzeas@letras.up.pt)
Universidade do Porto

Resumo – Um dos aspectos da história do mito na Grécia antiga é a sua gradual passagem a objecto de estudo. O interesse intelectual pela interpretação dessas narrativas, que passam a ser entendidas quer como alegorias quer como reminiscências históricas, começa relativamente cedo, mas é na Época Helenística que conhece os seus maiores desenvolvimentos. Contra tais formas racionalizantes de tratar as narrativas tradicionais se ergue a voz do poeta Calímaco. A ideia que preside à composição dos seus poemas é a de que só a arte dos poetas podia salvar o mito e resgatá-lo desse processo de esvaziamento operado pelas interpretações racionalistas que dele retiravam o encanto capaz de suscitar o prazer e o deleite.

Palavras-chave: Calímaco, Mito, Poesia, Evémero.

Abstract – One aspect of the history of myth in ancient Greece is its gradual transformation into an object of study. Intellectual interest in the interpretation of these narratives – which became understood as allegories or historical recollections – began in quite early times, but it is the Hellenistic period that saw the most intense development. The poet Callimachus reacts against these rationalizing ways of reading the traditional narratives. The idea behind the composition of his poems is that only the art of poets could save myth from the process of draining through rationalistic interpretation that deprived it of the enchantment capable of arousing pleasure and delight.

Keywords: Callimachus, Myth, Poetry, Euhemerus

Um dos aspectos da história do mito na Grécia antiga é a sua progressiva transformação em mitologia, isto é, a sua gradual passagem a objecto de estudo. Apesar de a constituição da mitologia como "ciência dos mitos" ser um fenómeno relativamente recente, a verdade é que a questionação acerca do mito começa muito cedo na Antiguidade. São do final do século VI a.C. os escritos dos primeiros historiógrafos, como Hecateu de Mileto que, em defesa da verdade, rejeita aquilo a que chama as 'histórias dos Gregos';[1] ou as primeiras explicações alegoristas de um Teágenes de Régio, de quem se sabe ter visto na *theomachia* da

___

[1] Cf. frg 1a Jacoby. A tradução é de Rocha Pereira 2003: 157. Curiosamente é a palavra λόγος e não μῦθος que Hecateu usa para se referir a essas histórias contrárias à verdade, o que é bem sintomático da inexistência de uma clara distinção semântica entre os vocábulos. Para a dilucidação dos conceitos de μῦθος e de λόγος e da sua evolução semântica, vide Rocha Pereira 2012: 254-260; 296-297.

https://doi.org/10.14195/978-989-26-1280-5_10

Ilíada a alegoria da luta entre os elementos[2]. Mas aquilo a que Walter Burkert chama a "crise do mito" começa talvez com Heraclito e Xenófanes e, embora ela não tenha impedido, como afirma o mesmo helenista, o surgimento da sua "mais poderosa forma poética: a tragédia ática", certo é que deixou irremediavelmente aberto o caminho para a desconfiança em relação a essa forma de dizer o mundo[3].

Sem nunca abandonar o universo da poesia, o mito passa, por conseguinte, a concitar o interesse de filósofos e pensadores – que procuram interpretá-lo de forma racional – e de mitógrafos – que se ocupam da recolha e do registo, sob forma de catálogo ou outras, dessas histórias ancestrais que representavam o património da pólis arcaica e clássica[4]. Mas, quer as tentativas de interpretação, quer essa actividade de recolha e de registo implicaram um processo de distinção entre os dados das histórias e o seu tratamento poético, uma espécie de processo de decomposição, digamos assim, de elementos que passaram a ser entendidos como distintos. E isso transformou completamente as atitudes dos Gregos, pelo menos dos mais cultos, em relação às narrativas que, durante séculos, haviam sido transmitidas pelos poetas e, transformadas em poesia, constituíam um poderoso veículo de educação e de afirmação dos valores da comunidade. Com a distinção destes dois universos, e de novo cito Walter Burkert, "começa-se a separar mais claramente do que antes mitologia dos heróis e mitologia dos seus deuses. Os mitos dos deuses nunca mais puderam salvar-se com seriedade..."[5].

O interesse intelectual pela interpretação dos mitos, que passam a ser entendidos quer como alegorias quer como reminiscências históricas, continuará a fazer o seu caminho e consigo arrastará, embora com novos contornos, aquele antigo debate entre poesia e filosofia de que Platão falava na República (607b).

Quase dois séculos depois de Hecateu e de Teágenes, um dos nomes que se distingue neste percurso racionalizante é o de Paléfato que, segundo os testemunhos da Suda, teria sido contemporâneo de Aristóteles e originário do Egipto ou do Helesponto[6]. Ao que sabemos, na obra Περὶ ἀπίστων, Paléfato enveredou pela

---

[2] As principais fontes para o conhecimento de Teágenes de Régio são a enciclopédia bizantina Suda e os testemunhos de Porfírio nas *Quaestiones Homericae. Cf.* Sodano 1970. De acordo com Tate 1927, apesar de Porfírio se referir a Teágenes como "o primeiro que escreveu sobre Homero", é em Ferecides de Siro que se deve encontrar, ainda que de forma embrionária, a prática da interpretação alegórica da epopeia homérica. Outros nomes de alegoristas do século seguinte são Metrodoro de Lâmpsaco, discípulo de Anaxágoras, e Estesímbroto de Tasos, citados por Platão no *Íon* 530d como comentadores de Homero.

[3] Sobre as críticas de Heraclito e de Xenófanes ao antropomorfismo dos deuses homéricos e hesiódicos, vide frg 42 Diels-Kranz para o primeiro e frg. 11 Diels-Kranz para o segundo. Cf. Burkert 1991: 59-63.

[4] De uma maneira geral o objectivo dos mitógrafos era apenas o de coligir essas histórias, sem quaisquer pretensões literárias, em compêndios que depois poderiam ser consultados por todos aqueles que as quisessem conhecer e trabalhar. Sobre este assunto, vide Higbie 2007.

[5] Burkert 1991: 60.

[6] Sobre os dados biográficos relativos a Paléfato, vide Stern 1996: 1-4.

via de racionalização das histórias do passado, despindo-as dos elementos mais fabulosos e inverosímeis, num esforço de as tornar mais críveis de acordo com um padrão de verdade factual e histórica. O princípio era, para este autor, o de que as narrativas míticas possuíam uma base real que era necessário descobrir debaixo do véu da fantasia. Por essa razão, como o próprio afirma logo no início do seu livro, não alinha nem com os que, alheios à filosofia e à ciência, acreditavam nas histórias tradicionais, nem com aqueles que as rejeitavam completamente como falsas[7]. Lembrarei apenas o primeiro exemplo que aparece na obra remanescente de Paléfato – o dos Centauros – por ser muito elucidativo do seu tipo de análise.

Primeiramente apresenta uma solução para o problema da incoerência entre o nome – cujo elemento *taurus* é inequívoco – e a forma daquelas estranhas figuras, com corpo de cavalo e cabeça de homem. A discrepância é explicada com a história, para si verdadeira, segundo a qual, alguns jovens da cidade de Néfele, respondendo à promessa de uma rica recompensa oferecida por Ixião, rei da Tessália, montaram em cavalos – actividade até então desconhecida – e mataram, com os seus dardos, os touros selvagens que arrasavam as plantações e os rebanhos. O nome Centauro não era, pois, descritivo da forma ou dos atributos dos nomeados, mas derivava das suas acções: Centauros eram os que "haviam espetado os touros". Trata-se de uma história claramente sugerida por um raciocínio etimológico[8]. Quanto à forma tradicional dos Centauros, Paléfato explica-a como a interpretação errada de uma visão enganadora. Conta ele que os Centauros se tornaram insolentes a ponto de raptarem as esposas dos Lápitas que os haviam convidado para um festim. Declarada a guerra entre ambas as partes, sempre que os Centauros eram vistos em fuga a imagem perceptível era apenas a de corpos e pernas de cavalos sem cabeça e no cimo cabeças de homens sem corpo ou pernas.

Desta maneira tentava o autor ultrapassar o problema da falsidade dos mitos que, assim, passavam a ser entendidos como deturpações involuntárias de acontecimentos reais ocorridos num passado muito distante.

Mas é a Época Helenística, logo nos seus alvores, que vê surgir um dos maiores expoentes desta interpretação dos mitos como reminiscências históricas – Evémero de Messene. Aquilo que conhecemos de Evémero parece ser inversamente proporcional à importância e à fortuna que as suas ideias tiveram na Antiguidade e depois dela. Com efeito, apenas o testemunho indirecto de autores como Diodoro Sículo ou Lactâncio[9] nos permite saber alguma coisa

---

[7] Daí a afirmação de Stern 1999: 215: "Palaephatus is a corrector not a rejecter of the myths he inherits".

[8] Como observa Stern 1996: 31 em nota à tradução deste passo, Paléfato vê no primeiro elemento da palavra Centauro, a raiz *kent* que traduz a ideia de 'espetar', 'picar'.

[9] Estes e outros testemunhos e fragmentos, incluindo os que restam da *Sacra Historia* de Énio, encontram-se em Jacoby, FGrH.63. Um resumo pode encontrar-se em Brown 1946: 259-261 e ainda em Pinheiro Futre 2006.

acerca das suas ideias, enquanto na Antiguidade, apesar de o próprio ter sido alvo de críticas de ateísmo, elas colheram a adesão de Gregos, de Romanos (o poeta Énio traduziu para latim a sua obra) e até, mais tarde, de autores cristãos[10].

A tese, se assim lhe podemos chamar, defendida por Evémero, era a de que os deuses do panteão grego teriam sido num passado longínquo homens poderosos, cujos súbditos, num acto de gratidão e de reconhecimento pela sua acção benéfica, os teriam erguido à condição divina. Este conhecimento tê-lo-ia adquirido o autor numa das viagens que fizera ao serviço de Cassandro, rei da Macedónia. De acordo com Diodoro Sículo, Evémero contava que no decurso dessa viagem chegara a uma ilha no Oceano Índico, chamada Pancaia, cujo povo, composto de autóctones – os Panqueus – e de elementos vindos de fora – Oceanitas, Indos, Citas e Cretenses – prestava honras aos deuses. Nessa ilha teria o narrador visitado um templo dedicado a Zeus, em que estavam inscritas as datas do nascimento e da morte dessas divindades, outrora simples mortais. Esta era a narrativa que ilustrava a sua interpretação do politeísmo grego[11].

É muito curioso e sobretudo revelador do espírito universalizante característico da Época Helenística que esta ilha, decerto imaginária[12], fosse composta por um povo multirracial que parece ser o símbolo dessa ideal união entre Ocidente e Oriente que constituía o projecto de Alexandre. O denominador comum a todas estas gentes e o sinal da sabedoria por todos partilhada e sobre a qual, quiçá, se basearia a sua coexistência, estava na forma como concebiam os deuses. Mas não menos curioso e significativo é também o facto de os elementos helénicos dessa população serem os Cretenses, para lá levados no passado por Zeus, um soberano mortal. Como sabemos, Creta é, na mitologia grega, e a par de Tebas ou de Micenas, um local de referência para toda a Hélade, berço de figuras míticas tão importantes como Minos ou Radamanto e palco de várias histórias que faziam parte do imaginário helénico. Creta era, além disso, nada menos do que o local onde o próprio Zeus passara a sua infância. E, segundo tradições locais, lá também ocorrera a sua morte, havendo mesmo um túmulo do

---

[10] Sobre a fortuna da obra de Evémero vide Winiarczyk 2013: 123-258.

[11] Ao defender a diferença de objectivos entre a abordagem de Paléfato e a de Evémero afirma STERN 1999: 219: "The Euhemeristic tradition is essentially atheistic and aims to create disbelief. Palaephatus, on the other hand, ignores the gods and concentrates instead on reinforcing belief – belief, however, not in the existence of the gods, but rather in the historicity of the heroes of old." Todavia, o testemunho de Diodoro Sículo (FGrH 63 F3) parece indicar que Evémero fazia uma distinção entre os deuses olímpicos da tradição grega e aqueles que designaria como οὐράνιοι θεοί aos quais Urano teria sido o primeiro a prestar honras. É, pois, provável que a narrativa de Evémero se destinasse mais a explicar o antropomorfismo dos deuses olímpicos do que a negar a existência de divindades. Esta é também a opinião de Winiarczyk 2013: 99-100.

[12] Já Plutarco dizia que nenhum Grego ou Bárbaro alguma vez tinha visto tal lugar. Cf. *FGrH* 63 T4e.

deus que era destino de peregrinação[13]. Não admira, pois, que, entre os Helenos, Evémero escolhesse os Cretenses para fazerem parte da sua utopia[14].

Contra tal diluição dos Gregos no meio dos outros povos e contra a uniformização implícita neste microcosmo imaginário parece erguer-se a voz poética de Calímaco. A julgar pela sua actividade de estudioso e erudito na Biblioteca de Alexandria e pelo seu próprio trabalho poético, para Calímaco o lugar dos Gregos no novo mundo em formação era justamente o contrário: era o da afirmação da sua identidade, à qual haviam dado forma as narrativas míticas. De resto, uma proposta como a de Evémero ou mesmo a de Paléfato, levada às últimas consequências, faria ruir por completo os alicerces em que assentava a mundividência e o modo de vida dos Gregos. Ora, é disto que Calímaco parece ter consciência, ao desprezar as ideias de Evémero.

No primeiro dos seus iambos, faz vir do Hades o velho poeta Hipónax. O iambo está muito fragmentado, mas nele surge uma referência a Evémero, bem sintomática da polémica que o poeta terá mantido com as ideias deste pensador[15]. Calímaco, pela boca de Hipónax, refere-se-lhe muito negativamente, chamando aos seus escritos ἄδικα βιβλία, isto é, livros ou escritos injustos, quer dizer, impróprios, no que parece ser uma réplica irónica à forma pela qual eles eram conhecidos – ἱερὰ ἀναγραφή, *escrito sagrado*[16].

Não obstante a brevidade da referência, ela é uma indicação muito clara de que a Calímaco não agradavam essas formas racionalizantes de tratar as narrativas tradicionais. E esta posição parece ser corroborada num poema em que celebra Zeus, o primeiro da sua colecção de *Hinos*, que faz eco, segundo creio, dessa polémica com Evémero[17].

Após os três versos de apresentação do tema do canto – *no momento das libações, que outro deus cantar senão Zeus, deus sempre grande, sempre rei* – continua, dizendo (4-9):

"Mas como o cantaremos? Como Dicteu ou Liceu?
O meu coração está dividido: grande é a disputa acerca do seu nascimento.
Ó Zeus, dizem uns que nasceste no monte Ida,
Outros, ó Zeus, que foi na Arcádia; quem mentiu, ó pai?

---

[13] Num escólio ao verso 8 do *Hino a Zeus de* Calímaco encontra-se a informação de que a crença na existência de um túmulo deste deus em Creta se devia a uma inscrição existente no túmulo de Minos, filho de Zeus – Μίνωος τοῦ Διὸς τάφος – da qual haviam desaparecido as duas palavras iniciais. Winiarczyk 2013: 40 crê que Evémero terá sido o primeiro autor a escrever sobre esse túmulo do deus olímpico.

[14] Sobre a obra de Evémero como "romance utópico", vide Winiarczyk 2013: 19-21. Cf. Pinheiro Futre 2006.

[15] Para uma análise dos fragmentos remanescentes do Iambo I vide Kerkhecker 1999: 11-48. A edição de referência da obra de Calímaco é a de Pfeiffer 1949-1951.

[16] Como observa Acosta-Hughes 2002: 46, é aos escritos e não ao seu autor que o poeta atribui o adjectivo ἄδικα, o que aponta para o alcance estético-literário da sua crítica a Evémero.

[17] Idêntica opinião encontra-se, por exemplo, em Spyridakis 1968: 340.

> Os Cretenses sempre foram mentirosos. Até um túmulo eles construíram
> Para ti, ó rei; mas tu não morres; tu existes sempre."

Ao rejeitar as mentiras dos Cretenses em favor de uma imagem mais orto-doxa dos deuses, o poeta aproveita para referir uma versão menos conhecida do nascimento de Zeus – a que o situava na Arcádia – fazendo gosto ao seu papel de erudito[18]. Mas a recusa da possibilidade da morte do deus supremo tem algo de programático neste que é o primeiro Hino do seu livro. Com ela o poeta parece afirmar o princípio geral que justifica toda a construção dos *Hinos*: as histórias acerca dos deuses gregos continuavam a fazer sentido e a ter valor universal num mundo que tinha visto abrirem-se as suas fronteiras às mais variadas gentes. Efectivamente, por si só, todo o conjunto dos *Hinos* é uma defesa da validade estética das narrativas tradicionais acerca das divindades. Não quero com isto enfileirar nas leituras da obra de Calímaco que a vêem como uma manifestação do princípio da "arte pela arte". Mas, a meu ver, a ideia que preside a estas composições é a de que só o trabalho dos poetas podia salvar o mito e resgatá-lo desse processo de esvaziamento operado pelas interpretações racionalistas que dele retiravam o encanto capaz de suscitar o prazer e o deleite. A Calímaco também não interessava certamente que as histórias permanecessem inertes nos escritos dos mitógrafos, catalogadas, mas sim mantê-las vivas através da poesia.

Vejamos como o poeta procede neste *Hino a Zeus*.

Assumindo o seu lugar na tradição, Calímaco condescende, num registo bem humorado, em adoptar a visão pueril, encantadora e leve do relato das origens e infância de Zeus – dados indispensáveis nas narrativas hímnicas tradicionais. Chega mesmo a cometer lapsos à maneira homérica e hesiódica, anacronismos propositados, como aquele em que, ao descrever a Arcádia *illo tempore*, no reinado de Cronos e antes do nascimento de Zeus, afirma que as águas ainda se encontra-vam nas entranhas da terra e os homens (v. 25 – a palavra ἀνήρ surge destacada no final do verso, numa piscadela de olho ao leitor) passavam a pé, a seco, por cima daqueles que haveriam de ser os leitos dos rios. Toda a narração dos pormenores do nascimento e infância de Zeus decorre no mesmo registo leve e sem preocu-pação de coerência. Depois de anteriormente ter afirmado a sempiterna grandeza e soberania do deus – *sempre grande, sempre rei* – conta como, afinal, Zeus foi um bebé e, como qualquer humano recém-nascido, teve de ser lavado da sujidade das entranhas maternas, deixou cair o cordão umbilical e esteve dependente dos cuidados de Amalteia e Panacris, uma cabra e uma abelha, respectivamente.

No entanto, é de novo a lógica do senso comum que ele invoca alguns versos depois, agora para rejeitar Homero em favor de Hesíodo[19]. Diz ele (60-67):

---

[18] Morrison 2007: 104 defende que a erudição é um dos aspectos do Calímaco biográfico que compõem a sua *persona* poética.
[19] Cf. Hutchinson 1988: 66.

"Os aedos antigos não diziam a verdade.
Contaram que os três filhos de Cronos tiraram à sorte as respectivas moradas.
Mas quem, se não um idiota, entregaria à sorte a escolha
entre o Olimpo e o Hades? Isso seria verosímil se estivessem em jogo
partes iguais…
Mentirei, se isso persuadir os ouvintes…
Não foi a sorte que fez de ti rei dos deuses, foram as obras das tuas mãos,
Foi a tua força e poder…"

Se rejeita as mentiras dos Cretenses, e agora a do próprio Homero, não é claramente por razões morais, pois admite a mentira desde que ela tenha força persuasiva sobre os ouvintes. A referência aos ouvintes e aos antigos aedos delimita o âmbito desta afirmação: é de poesia que se trata e em poesia – notem-se as ressonâncias aristotélicas – o que é falso é apenas o que não é verosímil, o que não persuade um ouvinte mais exigente. São claríssimos os ecos de Sólon na crítica aos aedos e de Píndaro na escolha da versão hesiódica de uma ascensão de Zeus baseada no poder e na justiça de que falará mais abaixo. E também isto mostra a sua homenagem à tradição poética que herdou.

Os versos que acabei de citar servem de transição para a segunda parte do Hino que é um verdadeiro louvor a Zeus. Há algo de desconcertante nesta divisão do poema, entre uma primeira parte em tom bem-humorado, de erudito espirituoso, e esta segunda cujo tom celebratório e reverente parece ser para levar a sério. E, no entanto, também neste aspecto existe algo de tradicional, pois essa sempre foi a maneira de os Gregos falarem acerca dos seus deuses: muito próxima, às vezes pueril, mas também elevada, séria e reverente.

Que esta segunda parte deve ser levada a sério, mostra-o a visão – que é, como sabemos, hesiódica, pindárica e esquiliana – de Zeus como garante da justiça e da ordem, como fundamento último do poder que, na terra, possuem os reis; mostra-o também a associação explícita que o poeta estabelece entre Zeus e o próprio Ptolomeu.

O alcance político deste *Hino* é inegável e ele só vem mostrar, como todos os outros, aliás, que, para Calímaco, *malgré* Evémero, para lá da verdade e da mentira, os mitos dos deuses continuavam a ter a capacidade de falar sobre aspectos importantes da vida dos homens, e que a sua preservação na linguagem universal da poesia era porventura a única forma de manter viva uma parte importante do passado, sem a qual, no espaço alargado deste novo e fascinante mundo, seria talvez mais fácil perder o rumo[20].

---

[20] Uma interessante reflexão sobre a valorização do passado mítico no mundo helenístico encontra-se em Scheer 2003: 216-231.

Troia egineta, ou a apropriação cosmopolita de um mito heroico
(Aeginetan Troy, or the cosmopolitan use of an heroic myth)

Carlos A. Martins de Jesus (carlosamjesus@gmail.com)
Centro de Estudos Clássicos e Humanísticos-Universidade de Coimbra

Resumo – O presente estudo debruça-se sobre as relações culturais, tanto poéticas como iconográficas, de Baquílides com a ilha de Egina. Partindo sobretudo da ode 13 do *corpus* de Baquílides, analisam-se as relações intersemióticas no tratamento do mito dos Eácidas que combateram em ambas as campanhas contra Troia, buscando compreender como poesia e artes plásticas, neste como noutros casos, mantinham uma relação de complementaridade essencial para o funcionamento do encómio do atleta e da sua pátria, no percurso simbólico da pólis à *cosmopolis*.

Palavras-chave: Baquílides, Egina, epinício, encómio, Templo de Afaia, Templo de Apolo, intersemiose.

Abstract – This paper focuses on the cultural relations, both poetic and iconographic, between Bacchylides and Aegina. Working mostly upon Bacchylides' thirteenth epinician ode, I analyse the intersemiotic treatment of the myth of the Aeacids that fought in both the Trojan campaigns, while trying to understand how poetry and the plastic arts retained a complementary relationship, necessary to achieve the encomium of the athlete and his homeland along the symbolic path from *polis* to *cosmopolis*.

Keywords: Bacchylides, Aegina, epinician, encomium, Temple of Aphaea, Temple of Apollo, intersemiotics.

Remontam ao início do século VI[1] as hostilidades entre Egina – essa pequena ilha rochosa de escassos 87 km², bem ao centro do Golfo Sarónico – e a mais importante pólis do mundo grego, ao que tudo indica pela supremacia marítima, na qual desde há muito a primeira ilha se destacava e se apresentava como perigosa ameaça à hegemonia ateniense. O conflito atingiu o seu expoente máximo com as guerras medo-persas, durante as quais Egina foi acusada pelos Atenienses de medismo (alinhamento na facção persa). São complexos – e desnecessário expô-los aqui ao pormenor[2] – os contornos destas rivalidades, multiplicando-se os episódios militares e políticos que contribuíram para o agudizar das divergências, narradas sobretudo por Heródoto. Mais importa, para já, conceber como nesses primeiros anos do século V Egina se via atacada e caluniada pela pólis dos

---

[1] Todas as indicações cronológicas, a menos que o contrário se diga, são anteriores a Cristo (a.C.).
[2] Entre os muitos títulos dedicados a este assunto, vd. o estudo sistemático de Podlecki 1976: 396-413.

https://doi.org/10.14195/978-989-26-1280-5_11

Atenienses, necessitando justificar o seu poderio e defender-se das acusações.

É comum que uma pólis busque, ao longo dos séculos, justificar etiologicamente o seu valor, fazendo a sua ancestralidade remontar a uma figura ou um grupo de figuras míticas de inegável valor. São conhecidas as apropriações atenienses dos dois maiores heróis, Héracles e Teseu, progressivamente – e em séculos consecutivos – transformados em heróis fundadores. Não poucas vezes, porém, é aos heróis que combateram em Troia, nesse passado mítico impossível de situar no tempo, mas que ocuparia, para os Gregos antigos, um lugar limítrofe entre a realidade histórica e o mito, que recorrem os agentes encarregues desta tarefa: poetas, pintores, escultores, logógrafos e historiadores. No caso de Egina, constitui a ode 13 de Baquílides o mais antigo testemunho de um processo poético de legitimação do passado mítico da ilha (vv. 91-99):

> e elas, coroadas de rubras
> flores e folhas de cana,
> enfeite da sua terra,
> essas donzelas cantam [o teu filho,
> ó soberana de terra a todos hospitaleira,
> e Endeide de róseos braços,
> a que gerou [Peleu, semelhante a um deus,
> e Télamon, o guerreiro do escudo,
> quando a Éaco se uniu no leito;

A ode, dedicada a Píteas de Egina, filho de Lâmpon (v. 68), pela vitória no pancrácio em Nemeia, cuja datação, insegura, deve rondar os anos de 487-480, celebra a mesma vitória que cantou Píndaro na *Nemeia* 5[3], e não mais constitui opinião geral que teria sido o poeta tebano o contratado para a celebração oficial, ao passo que Baquílides, ainda jovem, teria enviado o seu epinício de maneira voluntária. Com efeito, parece indicar que também a ode de Baquílides foi encomendada a proeminência que nela é dada a Lâmpon, pai do atleta, referido por duas vezes e alvo de especial atenção entre os versos 226-227[4]. Nos versos que transcrevemos, o poeta coloca-nos diante dos olhos uma realidade local, a celebração por meio de coros femininos do passado mítico da ilha, o que, em simultâneo, lhe permite a reconstrução da genealogia (vv. 95-99) que legitima os

---

[3] Apenas Mann 2001: 192-193 sugeriu que os epinícios celebrariam vitórias diferentes, atribuindo a *Nemeia 5* de Píndaro a um triunfo no pancrácio na categoria dos jovens, em 485, e a ode de Baquílides a outra vitória, conseguida na mesma modalidade e em categoria etária desconhecida, em 481. A hipótese de Mann foi discutida por Cairns 2010: 129-131, que dela discorda, considerando, em conclusão, que se de facto os epinícios correspondem a duas vitórias distintas, elas devem ter ocorrido com poucos anos de intervalo; mas que, em seu entender, "the most probable and economical explanation remains that the odes celebrate the same victory" (131).

[4] Vd. Maehler 1982: 290-291, ad vv. 226-227 e Fearn 2007: 115 e n. 78.

dois protagonistas da narrativa mítica central, resumível no seguinte esquema: Zeus uniu-se a Egina, uma das ninfas filhas do deus-rio Asopo, e gerou Éaco; este, unindo-se a Endeide, gerou Peleu e Télamon, de quem descendem Aquiles e Ájax, respectivamente. São eles os protagonistas da aristeia combinada que, com profundo sabor épico, é narrada entre os versos 100-167, a recriação lírica condensada do episódio amplamente descrito na *Ilíada* do recontro entre Gregos e Troianos junto das naus dos primeiros (*Il.* 15.415-746, 16.1-111, 114-123).

A genealogia seguida por Baquílides seria, ao tempo, assumida como verdadeira pelos Eginetas. Não obstante, a relação mítica entre os Eácidas que se evidenciaram em Troia e Egina é relativamente tardia. Na *Ilíada* (21. 187-189), o próprio Aquiles apenas diz ser filho de Peleu e neto de Éaco, este último filho de Zeus, não havendo qualquer menção à ninfa filha de Asopo como progenitora da sua raça; igualmente, Ájax é dito filho de Télamon (e.g. *Il.* 2. 768), mas não há qualquer referência à ascendência da ninfa. A situação poderá ter começado a mudar, contudo, ainda durante os séculos VII-VI, se levarmos em conta o escólio ao verso 21 da *Nemeia* 3 de Píndaro (datável de 475), que informa que, no *Catálogo das Mulheres* tradicionalmente atribuído a Hesíodo (= Hes. fr. 205 M-W)[5], a geração descendente de Éaco (os Mirmidões) habita numa ilha, que Tzetzes (*ad Lyc.* 176) confirma tratar-se de Egina[6]. Independentemente do risco desta interpretação – porquanto Tzetzes, o comentador, data apenas do século XII da nossa era –, parece haver dados que sustentam o desenvolvimento relativamente prematuro de um nacionalismo pró-egineta, o mesmo que estaria já perfeitamente consolidado na época de Píndaro e Baquílides.

É portanto credível que, quando os episódios da *Ilíada* se tornaram frequentes, as semelhanças entre a tradição dos Mirmidões da lenda tessálica e a dos homens--formiga de Egina tenham levado à fusão, intencional, de ambas as tradições. Os cantores locais passaram a identificar o seu fundador, Éaco, com o pai do Peleu homérico, por via da ninfa Egina, uma ligação que cedo terá sido aceite, de forma que, já nos finais do século VI, Éaco e os seus descendentes pertenceriam a Egina, pelo menos do ponto de vista dos Eginetas. Prova-o de forma segura a iconografia, sobretudo a estatuária local, que reproduz o episódio da perseguição de Egina por Zeus, em presença do pai, Asopo. Com efeito, a cena terá sido incorporada num dos pedimentos do templo de Apolo (cuja reconstrução estaria concluída por volta

---

[5] Assunto muito polémico tem sido a datação do *Catálogo*. Desde Janko 1982: 85-87, que entende, por questões linguísticas, que o poema pode ser contemporâneo de Hesíodo (c. 700); Schwartz, considera que terá atingido a sua forma final entre 506-476; e West 1985, talvez a opinião mais autorizada, situa-o algures entre 580 e 520. Um dado levado em conta tem sido a referência a Cirene (frs. 215, 216 M-W), cuja fundação data apenas de 630.

[6] O fragmento, que os editores não conseguiram inscrever em nenhuma obra em concreto, apenas refere como Egina deu à luz Éaco e como Zeus, para aplacar a solidão dessa ninfa, transformou todas as formigas da ilha em homens e mulheres. A interpretação de Tzetes, com efeito, pode proceder de outras fontes textuais às quais tivesse acesso, desde logo o próprio Píndaro.

de 510) e na primeira versão, perdida, de um dos pedimentos do templo de Afaia (c. 490), esculturas nas quais adiante nos deteremos.

A outro nível, o da geografia mítica, pode igualmente iluminar-se a assimilação da genealogia dos Eácidas a Egina. G. A. Privitera 1988: 63-70 demonstrou que os Eginetas, algures no século VI, terão construído um canal subterrâneo artificial que transportaria a água do Monte Panhelénio, situado no interior da ilha, directamente para uma fonte no centro da cidade, à qual se dava o nome de Asópis. Assim se criava uma relação topográfica assente nas lendas do principal rio do continente, o Asopo, além de que sabemos da relação do espaço dessa fonte com execuções corais. De resto, Pausânias (2.30.4) informa que Éaco era originalmente honrado por ter posto termo a uma grande seca na ilha, em consequência do que teria sido instituído o culto a Zeus Helânio[7]. O mito egineta dos Eácidas tem assim, ao que parece, uma forte relação com a topografia da ilha, pois é credível que a fonte Asópis se localizasse no mesmo local onde fora construído um santuário em homenagem a Éaco[8], o *Aiakeion*, o monumento que descreve Pausânias (2.29.6-7) e que se crê, hoje, que marcaria o local do túmulo do herói e ficaria bem ao centro da ilha[9].

Neste recinto os vencedores atléticos ofereciam as suas coroas à memória do herói fundador, como demonstra Píndaro (*N.* 5.53-54 + schol. Pind. *N.* 5.94e-f), e aí se realizava também um festival em sua homenagem, as *Aiakeia*, onde se pensa que Píndaro terá apresentado o Péan 15 e, provavelmente, o prosódion do Péan 6 (vv. 123-183), numa apresentação independente. Mais, um passo em concreto do poeta tebano (*Ol.* 13.109), com a sua alusão, num catálogo de vitórias de um atleta de Corinto, ao "túmulo de Éaco", sugere que as *Aiakeia* incluiriam também competições atléticas e que seriam jogos abertos a estrangeiros, o que ilustra a ânsia de pan-helenismo da ilha também ao nível desportivo. Quanto ao epinício de Baquílides, pese embora a ausência de referências concretas ao local e circuns-tâncias da sua apresentação, é plausível que também ele tenha sido executado no mesmo contexto, relacionando-se com a actividade cultual das *Aiakeia*.

Pelo que ficou dito, não estranha o leitor minimamente informado da poesia grega encontrar desenvolvido na ode 13 um segmento mítico que lida com um episódio em concreto dos Eácidas, neste caso a aristeia de Ájax e Aquiles perante o ataque dos troianos às naus gregas, em plena guerra de Troia (vv. 100-169). Com efeito, dos onze epinícios que Píndaro compôs para celebrar a vitória de atletas dessa ilha, datáveis entre 485 e 446, apenas a oitava *Pítica* não trata, no

---

[7] Éaco havia ficado conhecido como o herói que salvou a Grécia da carestia. Perante a cala-midade, embaixadas de vários pontos da Hélade teriam, a conselho do oráculo de Delfos, vindo à sua presença, solicitando-lhe que pedisse a seu pai por chuva (Isoc. 9.15; schol. Pind. *Pa.* 6.125).

[8] Para uma reconstrução topográfica da ilha de Egina ao tempo vd. Fearn 2007: 94-95.

[9] Sobre este recinto e a sua arqueologia vd. Walter 1993: 54-56.

mito central, de episódios protagonizados por descendentes de Éaco[10]. São estas composições mostra de um investimento no folclore e nas tradições locais vestido de ânsias de projecção pan-helénica, um esforço patrocinado de afirmação da legitimidade guerreira e política de Egina enquanto força pan-helénica digna de respeito e de temor, como respeito e temor inspiravam Ájax e Aquiles – ou Peleu e Télamon, na geração anterior – aos Troianos.

Se atentarmos na pouco extensa quantidade de cerâmica proveniente da ilha de Egina que conservamos[11], poucas conclusões se podem retirar quanto à utilização gráfica dos mitos dos Eácidas em Troia, como vimos os preferidos de Píndaro e Baquílides para a composição dos seus epinícios para atletas locais. Não obstante, algumas peças em particular atestam esse tratamento e corroboram a conclusão de que se trata de um segmento mítico caro aos Eginetas da segunda metade do século VI e dos inícios do século V[12].

Destacamos duas peças provenientes da ilha. A primeira, uma ânfora de colo ateniense de figuras negras, atribuída por Beazley ao Grupo das Três Linhas, datada de c. 550-500 (*ABV* 320.7, 290, 694 = *LIMC* 'Priamos' 88), exibe uma cena da destruição de Troia, desta feita a morte de Príamo num altar às mãos de

---

[10] Damos, por ordem cronológica dos poemas que integram, uma síntese dos episódios míticos tratados pelo poeta tebano: *N.* 7 [485?], para Sógenes de Egina, vencedor no pentatlo infantil: Ájax e o seu suicídio por humilhação; Neoptólemo, filho de Aquiles que, no regresso de Troia e depois de um breve reinado sobre os Molossos, encontrou a morte em Delfos às mãos de um sacerdote, na luta pelas carnes do sacrifício. *N.* 5 [487-480?], para Píteas de Egina, vencedor no pancrácio (a mesma vitória que celebra Baquílides): Peleu, a recusa do casamento com Hipólita e as bodas com Tétis; Télamon e Peleu (filhos da Endeide) e Foco (filho de Psamateia). *I.* 6 [480], para Filácidas de Egina, vencedor no pancrácio de jovens: Télamon parte com Héracles para a primeira Guerra de Troia; súplica de Héracles a Zeus para a descendência de Télamon; profecia acerca de Ájax. *I.* 8 [478], para Cleandro de Egina, vencedor no pancrácio infantil: bodas de Peleu e Tétis; profecia do futuro glorioso de Aquiles, filho de ambos. *I.* 5 [478?], para Filácidas de Egina, vencedor no pancrácio: Aquiles mata Cicno, Heitor e Mémnon. *N.* 3 [475], para Aristoclides de Egina, vencedor no pancrácio: feitos de Peleu (conquista de Iolcos), Télamon (com Iolau, matou Laomedonte – primeira Guerra de Troia – e lutou contra as Amazonas) e Aquiles (destruição de Troia); a educação do último com Quíron. *N.* 4 [473?], para Timasarco de Egina, vencedor na palestra: Télamon, Teucro, Aquiles, Neoptólemo, etc.; bodas de Peleu e Tétis. *N.* 6 [465], para Alcímidas de Egina, vencedor na luta infantil: morte de Mémnon às mãos de Aquiles. *O.* 8 [460], para Alcimedonte de Egina, vencedor na luta infantil: construção da muralha de Troia por Apolo, Poséidon e Éaco; Apolo interpreta um prodígio durante a construção como presságio das futuras conquistas de Egina, uma por Héracles, Télamon e Peleu, outra por Neoptólemo, filho de Aquiles. *N.* 8 [459], para Dínias, vencedor na corrida dupla: Ájax, filho de Télamon, ilustra as funestas consequências da inveja; alusão fugaz à campanha dos Sete contra Tebas. Não sendo este o momento para citar a extensa bibliografia, pontual para cada ode, que trata da ambiência cultural e mítica das odes pindáricas dedicadas a Eginetas, remetemos para o estudo introdutório de Burnett 2005: 13-44, que oferece uma notável visão de conjunto.

[11] A base de dados online que recebeu o nome de Beazley elenca 329 peças.

[12] De meados do século VI é datada uma banda de escudo (*LIMC* 'Achileus' 415) que parece apresentar, face a face, Aquiles e Ájax, o que os coloca já na posição de heróis míticos paradigmáticos.

Neoptólemo, sendo igualmente visíveis dois heróis troianos (Heitor e Astíanax? = **estampa 1**) e um grego, supostamente Aquiles. A segunda, um lécito ateniense de figuras negras de fundo branco, datado de c. 500-490 (= *LIMC* 'Achilleus' 361 = **estampa 2**), retrata a morte de Astíanax e às mãos de Aquiles, que segura a criança por uma perna. No que ao mito da descendência de Asopo diz respeito, mais concretamente ao rapto de Egina por Zeus – a origem das duas gerações de heróis que venceram Troia – não conservamos, estranhamente, qualquer vaso proveniente da ilha que o atualize, situação que contrasta com a de Atenas, onde esse mito, sobretudo nos inícios do século V, passa a ter uma representação considerável na cerâmica[13].

É porém na escultura local que vamos encontrar, para ambos os mitos, os exemplos mais flagrantes, em particular na escultura monumental de índole pública. Desta, centramo-nos nos dois pedimentos do Templo de Afaia[14], pese embora outros pudessem ser alvo de estudo[15]. O primeiro templo, construído durante o século VI, teria sido consumido pelas chamas nos últimos anos desse século, e a grande maioria dos críticos acredita que o novo Templo de Afaia teria ficado concluído na década de 90 do século V. Das esculturas que incluíam o primeiro edifício, não conservamos quaisquer informações. Quanto à segunda versão do templo, os dois pedimentos originais mostrariam a perseguição da ninfa Egina por Zeus e uma Amazonomaquia, mas cedo foram substituídos, não havendo qualquer prova de que tal tenha sido motivado por um desastre natural ou qualquer outro factor semelhante. Acredita-se, embora não de forma unânime, que primeiro foi substituído o pedimento ocidental, e só depois o oriental[16], sendo opinião global que, por volta de 480, as segundas versões de ambos os pedimentos estariam concluídas e colocadas *in situ*, costumando a conclusão do pedimento ocidental

---

[13] Heródoto (5.89) refere um oráculo recebido pelos Atenienses que os terá levado a construírem, nas imediações da Ágora, um santuário a Éaco, o que tem sido interpretado como forma de contra-propaganda ateniense no contexto das lutas entre Atenas e Egina. Com efeito, é neste sentido que deve entender-se também a pintura de vasos, que parece corroborar a apropriação política do mito do rapto de Egina por Zeus, que por este período (transição da primeira para a segunda década do século V) se torna mais evidente.

[14] Afaia, simultaneamente uma ninfa e uma náiade, representava a combinação entre a terra e o mar, as duas valências territoriais da ilha de Egina. Era patrona dos pescadores (Diod. Sic. 5.76; Ar. *V.* 369) e, pelos seus atributos, uma divindade próxima de Ártemis e Hécate. Estatuetas votivas suas provam a sua característica de *kourotrophos*, à semelhança de Ártemis. O seu nome explicar-se-ia pela capacidade de se tornar invisível e reaparecer noutro local (Paus. 2.30.3). Segundo uma versão tardia (Ant. Lib. 40) teria sido perseguida por uma criatura semi-monstruosa e aportado a Egina. A deusa seria também tutelar de rituais de iniciação, como prova a arqueologia do seu templo. Vd., a este respeito, Burnett 2005: 30-31.

[15] Walter 1993: 48, fig. 42, supõe que também no pedimento oriental do templo de Apolo em Egina a figura central seria a de Atena.

[16] Ohly 1976: 15 considera que o pedimento ocidental terá sido substituído por volta de 490 e o oriental entre 480-475; Martini 1990: 246 data ambas as substituições de c. 480; Stewart 1990: 183 considera a primeira substituição (ocidental) de 490 e a segunda (oriental) de 480.

ser datada de 490, o que permite concluir que Baquílides ou Píndaro, uma vez na ilha para a execução das odes que dedicaram aos atletas vencedores – todas elas por certo posteriores a essa data – possam ter contemplado essas esculturas. Não obstante a impossibilidade de confirmar esta coincidência, é inevitável não ler nestas esculturas a actualização iconográfica, a um nível público, dos mesmos temas míticos que também Baquílides e Píndaro utilizaram nos seus encómios a atletas da aristocracia local, com semelhantes propósitos políticos de afirmação pan-helénica. Com isto não estamos a defender qualquer dependência artística de um em relação a outro (poeta e artista plástico), apenas a partilha de um património de temas e motivos com significado especial no folclore local.

Estes segundos pedimentos, dos quais conservamos vestígios significativos que permitiram a D. Ohly o seu estudo e reconstrução (**estampa 3**)[17], incluindo-se no estilo arcaico-tardio, ilustram duas cenas das duas campanhas gregas contra Troia. No pedimento ocidental estão em destaque, ao lado de Atena, Ájax e Aquiles, os mesmos dois Eácidas cujas aristeias Baquílides contempla no epinício para Píteas, ilustrando-se o primeiro assalto da segunda campanha grega contra Troia. No pedimento oriental, recua-se no tempo do mito: a cena parece representar a guerra de Héracles contra Laomedonte (pai de Príamo), no contexto da primeira campanha grega contra Ílion. Sendo mais difícil de identificar as figuras, à direita da deusa está quase de certeza Peleu e, à esquerda, a penúltima figura (com elmo de leão) é Héracles, relegado para um plano menos evidente para dar realce aos verdadeiros heróis eácidas, provavelmente Peleu e Télamon (identificação não segura).

Fearn (2007: 98) acredita que a mudança das esculturas dos pedimentos – iniciada, ao que tudo indica, em 490 ou no ano anterior –, e a inclusão de Atena ao centro, poderá indicar uma intenção de neutralização política da rivalidade com Atenas ou mesmo a apropriação da divindade como pró-egineta, no contexto de um clima de orgulho nacionalista que se vivia na ilha[18]. Para o autor (pp. 99-100), os novos pedimentos teriam essencialmente dois significados: dar mostra da maior importância de Egina, face a Atenas, no contexto do passado

---

[17] O estudioso faleceu, no entanto, sem deixar a tarefa concluída.

[18] A substituição dos pedimentos terá acontecido logo após a batalha de Maratona (490) e diversos acontecimentos políticos nos anos circundantes a essa data parecem iluminar as motivações desse orgulho nacionalista que teria estado na base das esculturas. Em 491 a recepção em Egina de emissários persas levou a que o espartano Cleómenes se deslocasse à ilha para fazer reféns contra qualquer possível colaboração (Hdt. 6.50). Sob o comando de Crios, os oligarcas locais resistiram e, algum tempo depois, os principais aristocratas eginetas foram deportados para Atenas. Após a batalha de Maratona, tendo falhado uma tentativa para trazer os exilados de novo à ilha, os Eginetas capturaram um navio ateniense que transportava uma embaixada sagrada (Hdt. 6.87), ao que tudo indica na primavera de 489, ficando na posse de um grupo de reféns atenienses. Meses depois, assassinaram Nicódromo – um egineta que tentara o poder absoluto – e 7000 dos seus seguidores (Hdt. 6.89-91). Egina, nos meses que se seguem, repele a ofensiva marítima de Atenas e toma mais quatro navios seus (Hdt. 6.92-93).

mítico troiano e, a um nível muito mais concreto, argumentar que o passado mítico da ilha a tornava mais preparada para enfrentar os Persas, dessa forma respondendo inequivocamente à acusação ateniense de Medismo. E tal parece depreender-se sobretudo da presença de uma figura com trajes orientais no pedimento ocidental que tem sido identificada como Páris.

O que ambos os pedimentos querem proclamar publicamente, e com eles as odes de vitória para atletas eginetas que conservamos, é que por duas vezes essa ilha guiou, vitoriosos, os Gregos até Troia, o maior inimigo da Hélade (no plano do mito), um poder resultante da aliança entre os descendentes de Éaco, Héracles e Atena. E, como tal, perante um igualmente poderoso inimigo – os Medos – uma vez mais tem que caber a Egina um papel central na sua neutralização. No contexto das hostilidades com Atenas, tem afinal razão Williams (1987: 673) quando fala da "réplica à propaganda de guerra de Atenas", de uma ilha que, pela poesia e pelas artes plásticas – nenhuma delas, afinal, como Simónides consideraria, uma arte silenciosa – se apresenta ao mundo grego como a legítima pátria ancestral dos vencedores de Troia.

Estampa 1 - Ânfora de colo ateniense de figuras negras, atribuída por Beazley ao Grupo das Três Linhas, datada de c. 550-500 (*ABV* 320.7, 290, 694 = *LIMC* 'Priamos' 88).

Estampa 2 - Lécito ateniense de figuras negras de fundo branco, proveniente de Egina. C. 500-490 (Copenhaga, Nat. Mus. Chr. VIII. 383 = *LIMC* 'Achilleus' 361).

Estampa 3 - Reconstituição das esculturas da segunda versão dos pedimentos do Templo de Afaia em Egina. 3A) Pedimento ocidental do templo de Afaia em Egina. Segunda campanha troiana. i (Atena), ii (Aquiles), iii (Mémnon), iv (Teucro), v (companheiro de Teucro), vi e vii (2 troianos), viii (Ájax), ix (Heitor), x (Páris), xi (troiano), xii e xiii (2 gregos).

3B) – Pedimento oriental do templo de Afaia em Egina. Primeira campanha troiana. i (Atena), ii (?), iií (Télamon), iv (Iolau), v (Héracles), vi (soldado grego), vii (Peleu), viii, ix, x (?), xi (Laomedonte).

A Índia na mitologia grega
(India in Greek Mythology)

Nuno Simões Rodrigues (nonnius@letras.ulisboa.pt)
Universidade de Lisboa, CH-UL/CECH-UC

Resumo – Apesar de termos consciência da pertinência do tema Grécia/Índia no quadro da problemática indo-europeia, este estudo analisa sobretudo as referências à Índia que podemos encontrar na mitologia grega, tentando-se relacionar as mesmas com as datações dos vários textos que integram o *corpus* mitológico dos Gregos. Além do caso evidente de Nono de Panópolis, há vários outros episódios e referências mito-lógicas que aludem ao universo indiano, sugerindo que o conhecimento que os Gregos tinham da região e seus costumes não era etno-geograficamente o mais correcto, mas que também não era totalmente desprovido de sentido. A associação de Dioniso à esfera indiana é nesse sentido paradigmática.

Palavras-chave: Índia, Mitologia Grega, Nono de Panópolis, Ctésias, Dioniso.

Abstract – Despite being aware of the relevance of the theme Greece/India in the context of the Indo-European question, this study examines mainly the references to India which can be found in Greek mythology, trying to relate them to the dating of the various texts that comprise the *corpus* of Greek mythology. Besides the obvious case of the Nonnus of Panopolis, there are several other episodes and mythological references that allude to the Indian cultural context, which suggests that, although the knowledge that the Greeks had of the region and its customs was not ethnographically correct, it was not entirely deprived of meaning. The association of Dionysos with the Indian sphere is in this sense paradigmatic.

Key-Words: India, Greek Mythology, Nonnus of Panopolis, Ctesias, Dionysos.

É em Nono de Panópolis, autor talvez egípcio do século V d. C., e nas suas *Dionisíacas* que encontramos parte substancial das referências à Índia na mitologia grega. Significa isso que a maioria destas alusões é tardia. O que, por outro lado, não é nada de muito extraordinário se tivermos em conta que, por essa época, os contactos do Mediterrâneo com o Médio Oriente, designadamente a região da Ásia Central e do Vale do Indo, eram já uma realidade com provas dadas[1].

Com efeito, processos e momentos específicos como, e.g., as campanhas de Alexandre na região a que os Antigos chamavam Índia[2] ou os que marcaram

---

[1] Ver Rawlinson 1916.

[2] Na Antiguidade Clássica, por «Índia» entendia-se sobretudo a região do rio Indo e eventualmente a costa ocidental da Península Índica, sendo que os contactos entre esta área

https://doi.org/10.14195/978-989-26-1280-5_12

a manutenção de rotas comerciais regulares entre esses territórios e o Império Romano fazem com que as referências de Nono não constituam nada de muito significativo no seu contexto cultural[3].

Por outro lado, há que recordar que alguns pretendem que, séculos antes de Alexandre, os contactos entre a Grécia e a Índia seriam já uma realidade, que se teria reflectido na obra de Pitágoras, por exemplo, o qual teria sido influenciado por princípios da filosofia védica. De facto, há autores que têm salientado as coincidências que se verificam ao nível das doutrinas religiosas e dos princípios filosóficos das várias áreas do Mediterrâneo e da Ásia, entre os séculos VII e V a. C.[4]

Esta é, porém, matéria polémica que está longe de reunir consensos[5]. O facto é que apenas com Alexandre, e os seus historiadores, possuímos informação segura acerca desses contactos directos, não sendo todavia de excluir a possibilidade de à Grécia ter chegado algum conhecimento da Índia por via da Pérsia. Convém referir que Heródoto dá notícia dos contactos entre Persas e Indianos, notando a presença de mercenários indianos nos exércitos de Xerxes, mencionando o desejo de Dario descobrir o lugar onde o Indo desaguava no mar – anota, e.g., que o Indo seria o único rio do mundo que juntamente com o Nilo albergaria crocodilos – e referindo-se à multidão dos Indos como «de longe a maior, entre todos os povos conhecidos» (o contexto é o da descrição da administração persa)[6]. Séculos depois, na obra de Plutarco, por exemplo, o país vem já identificado como uma região da Ásia, sendo referido algumas vezes, ao longos de várias das *Vitae* escritas pelo autor[7]. Mas, tal como aconteceu com Nono, Plutarco escreve já depois das campanhas de Alexandre, sendo que esse foi o momento da viragem na história desta relação cultural. E ainda antes de Plutarco, a obra de Ctésias de Cnido continha também referências específicas ao território. Os *Indica* de Ctésias, aliás, centrar-se-iam exclusivamente nesse tema[8]. De igual modo, a vida de Apolónio de Tíana, atribuída a Filóstrato, incluía no século III, com remissão para o século I, uma viagem do filósofo à Índia, evocando essas *Bildungsreisen* que teriam sido essenciais para formar os vários pensadores gregos e romanos[9]. Neste sentido, a Índia parece reivindicar, ao lado do Egipto, uma posição de fonte de sabedoria.

---

e o Mediterrâneo se faziam sobretudo através do Mar Arábico, do Golfo Pérsico e do Mar Vermelho; ou através do planalto indiano, Pérsia e Mesopotâmia. Ver Conger 1952: 103-104. Assinale-se, porém, que as regiões da Bactriana e do Punjab (actuais Afeganistão e Paquistão) eram também associadas ao «universo indiano».

[3] Ver Rawlinson 1916.

[4] Conger 1952: 102-128.

[5] Stowe Mead 1901: 81

[6] Hdt. 3.38, 3.94, 3.98-106; 4.44, 7.64-68, 86, 8.113, 9.31.

[7] Plu. *Alex.* 13.4; 47.11; 55.9; 57.1; 59.1; 62.1, 4; 66.3-4; *Pau.* 12.11; *Ant.* 81.4; *Cra.* 16.2; *Eum.* 1.5; *Lic.* 4.8; *Dem.* 7.2; 32.7; *Pomp.* 70.4.

[8] Ureña Prieto 2001: 115.

[9] Philostr. *VA 2-3.*

Assim, apesar de não ser um tema abundante na literatura greco-romana, a Índia tem nela presença assegurada. Não é, contudo, nos textos acima referidos, escritos entre os séculos V a. C. e III d. C., que encontramos as referências de natureza mitológica. Essas estão presentes em outros autores, sobretudo em Nono de Panópolis.

As *Dionisíacas* de Nono são um poema épico de tipo «barroco»[10], dividido em 48 cantos e escrito c. 470 d. C., no qual se celebra uma expedição bélica de Dioniso à Índia. Enquanto os primeiros doze livros narram os mitos em torno da infância do deus da *mania*, os restantes 36 centram-se na aventura guerreira e no *nostos* do deus. Num quadro deste tipo, parece-nos evidente que as alusões à Índia e aos Indianos se tornem recorrentes e surjam «de forma natural», digamos assim[11].

Como notámos, porém, no *corpus* mitológico grego, as alusões à Índia não se limitam à obra de Nono de Panópolis, ainda que, frisamos, seja nela que encontramos as mais significativas. Apesar de não serem abundantes e de existirem mesmo problemas de natureza exegética que nos levam a colocar questões inevitáveis em torno dos conceitos de «Índia» e de «Indianos» no quadro cultural de cada texto em que surgem mencionados, o facto é que, em algumas narrativas mitológicas, essa categoria geográfica e étnica é mencionada algumas vezes. Comum mesmo é o facto de essas referências surgirem em contextos etno-geográficos, designadamente a associação de tipo etiológico para a nomeação de lugares. Trata-se de uma mitologia tópica, portanto, eventualmente tardia, na sequência de uma certa tradição metamórfica ovidiana e pausaniana, de gosto pelos mitos locais e pouco conhecidos, a que se associa a percepção relativamente tardia da Índia entre os Gregos[12].

Nesse contexto, são de salientar em particular as etiologias relacionadas com rios e montanhas. A título de exemplo, a etiologia que os Gregos ofereciam para o Monte Lileu, localizado perto de Taxila no actual Paquistão e que para os Antigos cabia no conceito de «Índia», por exemplo, fazia-se com recurso ao mito. Segundo essa tradição, algo bucólica, Lileu teria originalmente sido um pastor que apascentava os seus rebanhos junto ao Indo e que apenas reconhecia Selene como divindade. Enfurecidos, os restantes deuses teriam feito com que dois leões se atirassem ao pastor com o intuito de o devorar, acabando por despedaçá-lo. A Lua, porém, ter-se-ia apiedado do jovem e tê-lo-ia transformado na montanha que recebeu o seu nome[13]. Parece-nos evidente que neste mito narrado

---

[10] Ureña Prieto 2001: 314-315; Shorrock 2011.

[11] O tema das campanhas indianas de Dioniso aparece também em Ps.-Plu. *De Flu.* 16.3.

[12] Neste sentido, convém referir que em alguns casos os mitos gregos ou suas versões chegaram-nos por via da literatura latina.

[13] Ps.-Plu. *De Flu.* 25.4. Cf. *Fiumi e monti* apud Calderón Dorda, De Lazzer, Pellizer 2003: 30-44.

pelo pseudo-Plutarco, em *Acerca dos Rios*, texto que tem sido datado do século II d. C., há uma influência ovidiana, como mostra, por exemplo, uma comparação com os passos que o poeta latino dedica a Atlas e a Níobe[14].

O mesmo processo parece verificar-se em relação aos rios. Vejamos o caso do Indo. Segundo Nono, Indo seria um gigante de quem descenderiam os Indianos[15]. Esta deverá ser, todavia, uma tradição lendária formulada pelo próprio Nono de Panópolis, que, na sequência do que conhecemos em processos anteriores, terá sido contaminada por via de outras fontes mitológicas. Aliás, a Índia de Nono assenta fundamentalmente nesta percepção etiológica dos elementos naturais. O mesmo princípio de contaminação intertextual deverá presidir à história da filha de Oxialces, segundo a qual a jovem teria sido violada por um rapaz indiano de nome Indo, que, ao fugir de Oxialces, se teria lançado ao rio Mausolo. Doravante, este ter-se-ia passado a chamar precisamente Indo. Neste caso, a notícia dada por Nono aparecia no já citado texto do pseudo-Plutarco, em que o rio é localizado no espaço como correndo em direcção à terra dos Ictiófagos, i.e., «os comedores de peixe»[16]. O mais provável é que Nono a tenha retirado daí ou de uma fonte comum. Por outro lado, no universo mitológico, as histórias de violação com metamorfoses e suicídios associados são frequentes (e.g. Filomela e Procne[17]), pelo que é também possível estarmos perante uma adaptação temática proveniente de uma qualquer outra fonte[18].

Além do Indo, também a nomeação do Ganges, que no *corpus* mitológico grego é entendido como o deus homónimo do rio indiano – à boa maneira grega, o deus confunde-se com o próprio rio –, foi alvo de tratamento mítico-literário por parte dos Gregos. Estes tinham Ganges como um filho de Indo e da ninfa Caláuria, protagonista de uma história de incesto. Um dia, estando embriagado e por isso inconsciente, Ganges ter-se-ia unido à própria mãe. Quando tomou consciência de si, todavia, o jovem ficou horrorizado com o que tinha feito e lançou-se ao rio Clíaro, que a partir de então passou a chamar-se Ganges[19]. Tal como aconteceu com a de Indo, de que aliás parece repetir parte, a história de Ganges parece ter várias narrativas como pano de fundo, designadamente a de Egeu que, nas versões de Apolodoro, de Plutarco e sobretudo de Pausânias, por exemplo, morre lançando-se do alto de um penhasco, dando o seu nome ao mar em que cai[20]. De igual modo, reconhecem-se aqui outros aspectos tópicos, como a genealogia dos rios Indo e Ganges, aspectos esses igualmente presentes nos

---

[14] Ov. *Met.* 4.656-662. Podemos citar as várias metamorfoses em rochedo.

[15] Nonn. 18.268.

[16] Ps.-Plu. *De Flu.* 25.1; *Nonn.* 18.21.

[17] Ov. *Met.* 6.451-667.

[18] A versão inversa, em que o rio Indo passa a chamar-se Hidaspes pelo suicídio deste, na sequência da paixão incestuosa da filha, é igualmente narrada em Ps.-Plu. *De Flu.* 1.1.

[19] Ps.-Plu. *De Flu.* 4.1; Philostr. *VA* 3.6.

[20] Paus. 1.22.5; Apollod. *Epitome* 10; Plu. *Tes.* 22; ver ainda Hyg. *Fab.* 43; D.S. 4.61.6-7.

mitos de Egipto e Nilo[21]. Por outro lado, também o tema do incesto entre mãe e filho é frequente no *corpus* grego, como mostram os casos de Édipo, Hália e Cíniras por exemplo[22].

Também no âmbito desta mitologia-tópica, a nomeação do rio Orontes era associada por alguns mitógrafos gregos à Índia. Segundo uma tradição que remonta pelo menos a Pausânias, também este rio da Síria teria recebido o seu nome na sequência de um episódio em que um herói indiano, chamado precisamente Orontes, filho de Dídnaso, comandava um exército ao serviço do rei hindu Deríades, quando Dioniso fez a sua expedição contra os Indianos[23]. Quer em Pausânias quer em Nono, a descrição de Orontes corresponde à de um gigante guerreiro – Pausânias estabelece mesmo uma etiologia «racionalizante» para a personagem ao referir o aparecimento de um esqueleto no rio de tamanho desmesurado – com características que o aproximam do Golias bíblico. Segundo a epopeia de Nono, Orontes teria sido ferido por Dioniso e, depois disso, ter-se-ia suicidado e o corpo arrastado pelas águas do rio, que assim passou a chamar-se Orontes. Portanto, tendo em conta os mitos precedentes, do Indo ao Ganges, será caso para dizer: «Nada de novo, na frente ocidental...»

Neste episódio de Nono encontramos a aliança do primeiro «tema indiano» da mitologia grega com o «segundo». Esta é outra característica comum nestas referências. Parece-nos claro que, além da mitologia tópica, existe também o uso frequente de um contexto de «barbarismo exótico», também ao gosto grego, no qual têm particular relevância as questões da alteridade e uma certa noção de *limes* ou fronteira do território que definia o que pertencia ao universo helénico e o que estava para além do mesmo.

Assim, pertence a essa categoria de «exotismo» o mito dos Ciápodes, referidos por Filóstrato, segundo o qual estes eram um povo indiano, dotado de uns pés enormes (o nome significa literalmente «pés de sombra»), que lhes permitiam abrigar-se do Sol, com a sombra que obtinham quando se deitavam e erguiam as pernas[24]. De igual modo, o mito dos Grifos, seres híbridos com cabeça de águia e corpo de leão alado, cuja função era guardar o ouro, era também associado à Índia[25]. Ou ainda o dos Pigmeus, o povo de pequena estatura, já mencionado na *Ilíada* e que se supunha habitar o sul do Egipto ou a Índia. O facto de, na arte greco-romana, os Pigmeus serem associados ao nanismo e a uma certa desproporcionalidade física (designadamente ao nível da representação dos genitais) torna-os emblemas dessa «bizarria» que se define pela «anormalidade»

---

[21] Apollod. *Bibl.* 2.1.4; Hyg. *Fab.* 170; *Paus.* 7.21.6.

[22] Soph. *OT*; D.S. 5.55; Ov. *Met.* 10.298-502.

[23] Paus. 8.29.3-4; Nonn. 17.196-289, 314; 26.79; 34.179; 35.80; 44.251.

[24] Philostr. *VA* 3.47; Plin. *Nat.* 7.2.2.23.

[25] Eram também associados a outros povos como os Citas, os Hiperbóreos e os Etíopes; A. *Pr.* 803; Hdt. 3.102, 116; Ael. *NA* 4.27; Plin. *Nat.* 7.10; Ctes. *FGH* 688F 45e45h.

humana e que configura o exotismo de que falámos. Por conseguinte, enquanto representantes do espaço indiano, os Pigmeus – hoje entendidos como possíveis representações dos povos da África Central –¹são assim vinculados «além norma», própria dos espaços além fronteiras²⁶. Isto é, seja qual for o território a que estas criaturas são associadas, elas estão sempre nas franjas da Hélade «civilizada», ou até mesmo da *oikoumene/kosmopolis* helenística. Assim acontece com estes *exempla* indianos, confirmando o exotismo que se associa ao conceito.

A ideia de Índia como «país longínquo» reflecte-se também no mito de Hélio, segundo o qual, todas as manhãs, o deus, precedido pelo carro da deusa Eos/Aurora, encetava viagem na sua própria viatura, pelo firmamento, de modo a espalhar a luz e o calor solares. De acordo com esta mesma tradição, o carro de Hélio partia do país dos Indianos (do Oriente, portanto) e fazia o seu percurso através de um caminho estreito que atravessava o céu pelo meio. Também aqui, a Índia é o país do *horos* ou do *limes*.

Do mesmo modo, a lenda de Semíramis é em parte localizada na longínqua Bactriana, território da Ásia Central identificado com o sul do Afeganistão e o norte do Paquistão. Nela, Semíramis aparece como uma guerreira que chefia um contingente militar, alimentando a ideia de que um dia conquistará a Índia, tarefa para a qual faz demorados preparativos. Aliás, segundo a tradição, a rainha teria chegado a atravessar o Indo, mas teria sido forçada a recuar. Apesar de a rainha ser referida em Heródoto, porém, esta relação de Semíramis com a Índia aparece apenas em Diodoro Sículo, autor coevo de Augusto, o que contribui para retardar o aparecimento do tema indiano na cultura grega, de acordo com o que notámos e confirmando as nossas primeira impressões²⁷. Aqui, o exotismo parece vincular-se à caracterização de Semíramis como guerreira, na linha do que conhecemos acerca das Amazonas, entre os Gregos sempre associadas ao universo da *ataxia*, que se reflecte, por exemplo, nos traços persas que frequentemente exibem, como os trajes²⁸.

O mito de Téctafo é a excepção a essa regra binária, em que a Índia parece vir associada ora à necessidade de justificar topónimos e acidentes geográficos ora à ideia de exotismo *extra limites* – em qualquer dos casos, trata-se de um conceito de espaço alternativo/alteridade à Hélade.

A história é igualmente narrada por Nono. Segundo o autor de Panópolis, Téctafo seria um príncipe indiano que teria sido feito prisioneiro por Deríades, encerrado num subterrâneo, sem direito a luz ou ar, impedido de qualquer comunicação com o exterior e condenado a morrer de inanição. Téctafo, porém, tinha uma filha chamada Eéria, que acabara de ser mãe. A rapariga conseguiu

---

²⁶ Cf *Il.* 3.3ss.; Verg. *A.* 10.264ss; Hdt. 2.32; Plin. *Nat.* 7.26ss; Ov. *Met.* 6.90ss.
²⁷ Cf. Hdt. 1.184; 3.155; D.S. 2.4ss; 13ss.
²⁸ Rodrigues 2007.

autorização para visitar o pai, sendo a sua suposta intenção, contudo, levar ao progenitor «uma suprema consolação». Os guardas que controlavam o calabouço verificaram que Eéria nada transportava consigo que pudesse violar a ordem de Deríades, pelo que deram permissão à jovem para que entrasse na masmorra. Uma vez na prisão, porém, a filha alimentou o pai, dando-lhe leite do seu próprio peito. Ao tomar conhecimento deste acto de piedade filial, Deríades decidiu libertar o príncipe indiano[29].

Neste mito, as categorias de «Índia» e «Indianos» são meros pretextos para a apresentação de uma narrativa a que subjaze uma ética que vai além do interesse tópico ou etnográfico. Aliás, como argumento suplementar que comprova esta nossa ideia, podemos acrescentar que encontramos este mesmo mito em Valério Máximo, contado a propósito de um outro contexto, o da piedade filial, pelo que o mais provável é que Nono o tenha colhido no autor romano ou numa fonte comum e o tenha adoptado para a sua epopeia, como aliás parece ter feito noutras ocasiões. Em Valério Máximo, conta-se de forma ecfrástica a história de Péro, filha de Mícon, a quem ela teria alimentado através do próprio seio, como se o pai fosse seu filho, quando ele estava encarcerado[30]. Mas, há que referir que também a história que o autor romano transcreve sobre Péro e Mícon repete uma outra contada pelo mesmo autor em parágrafos anteriores e segundo a qual uma mulher teria sido condenada à morte e por isso entregue aos guardas prisionais para que a executassem na prisão. O chefe da guarda, porém, apiedando-se da mulher, decidiu não a executar de imediato, permitindo que, em vez disso, a filha da prisioneira a visitasse, tendo todavia o cuidado de a revistar de modo a que nada, inclusive nenhum alimento, entrasse no cárcere. Na verdade, o carcereiro mantinha a esperança de a mulher morrer de inanição, não sendo por conseguinte necessário ser ele a executá-la. Ao fim de algum tempo, porém, o guarda começou a perguntar-se por que razão a mulher não morria. Foi então que ele decidiu vigiar a visita da filha e descobriu que a jovem amamentava a própria mãe para a aliviar do seu sofrimento. A notícia espalhou-se e a mulher acabou por ser perdoada e libertada[31]. Apesar de neste episódio a pessoa alimentada ser a mãe e não o pai, o facto é que estamos perante exactamente a mesma história, que deverá ter influenciado Nono de Panópolis por alguma via. Aliás, esta narrativa, que aparece citada em alguns outros autores antigos, serviu também de mote aos alegoristas cristãos que passaram a utilizá-la para representar a Caridade[32].

---

[29] Nonn. 26.101ss.

[30] V. Max. 5.4.1; cf. Hyg. *Fab.* 254, que chama Xantipa à jovem. Naturalmente, esta narrativa remete para uma outra, eventualmente anterior, e que se referia ao momento em que Héracles era amamentado por Hera (num episódio etrusco) cf. Thomson de Grummond 2006: 83-84.

[31] V. Max. 5.4.7.

[32] Ver e.g. Plin. *Nat.* 7, Beagon 2005: 314; sobre a alegoria da Caridade, inspirada neste episódio, ver Levy 2010: 165-176.

Assim, o enquadramento indiano desta história extrapola a categoria «Índia», tratando-se essencialmente do aproveitamento de uma narrativa mais antiga, com uma função decerto mais alargada, com actualização na epopeia de Nono.

Em conclusão, apesar da presença da Índia e dos Indianos na mitologia grega, o facto é que esta parece estar limitada, ser pouco abundante e resumir--se a visões de um país e de um povo bárbaro longínquos, de onde provêm seres bizarros, híbridos, e em relação aos quais se sente a necessidade de explicar nomes, orografias e hidrografias. Aparentemente, pouco é dito acerca da religiosidade, costumes, tradições ou até mesmo vivências políticas dos Indianos, o que deverá traduzir sobretudo uma percepção superficial, que muitas vezes aparenta recorrer a processos de contaminação de outros textos, autores e tradições. Neste sentido, não hesitaríamos mesmo em falar de *interpretationes graecae* de histórias que são aplicadas ao universo indiano, sugerindo-se o total desconhecimento da realidade do outro lado. E porquê? Terá a Índia provocado pouco impacte entre os Gregos? Terá ela despertado pouco interesse mesmo após os contactos encetados no período de Alexandre? Esta é uma conclusão que nos permite colocar ainda questões complementares à problemática das origens de ambos os povos (questão indo-europeia) e da das eventuais mútuas influências literárias, que exigem outro espaço de análise, que poderá resumir-se numa pergunta: o que sabiam os Gregos de facto acerca da cultura da Índia clássica?

"Selecionando crepúsculos":
A função dos clássicos na concepção de cultura e civilização de Luis da Câmara Cascudo.
("Selecting Twilights": the Function of the Classics in Luis da Câmara Cascudo's Conception of Culture and Civilization)

Maria das Graças de Moraes Augusto (mgmaugusto@yahoo.com.br)
Universidade Federal do Rio de Janeiro

Resumo – Luis da Câmara Cascudo foi um dos intérpretes mais argutos dos diferentes níveis em que a "cultura" e a "civilização" se estabelecem no âmbito das "tradições brasileiras". Nesse sentido, estudou o folclore, a literatura oral, os gestos, as narrativas, a geografia dos mitos, os hábitos, os ritos e os cultos, os alimentos e as bebidas, e em todos esses estudos encontramos as marcas da tradição clássica tanto como ponto de partida ou mesmo como ponto de chegada de suas análises, pois, como sublinhou em diferentes ocasiões, "a literatura clássica me preservou da tirania das idéias".
Partindo da assertiva acima, o objetivo de nosso trabalho é mostrar como, na obra de Câmara Cascudo e em sua estrutura hermenêutica de nossas tradições, a cultura greco-romana é um dos elementos formadores para a compreensão da "cultura" e da "civilização" brasileiras.

Palavras-chave: Tradição Clássica no Brasil. Civilização e Cultura. Mito e folclore.

Abstract – Luis da Câmara Cascudo was one of the most astute interpreters of the different levels at which "culture" and "civilization" were organized within the scope of "Brazilian traditions". In this sense, he studied folklore, oral literature, gestures, narratives, the geography of myths, habits, rites and cults, and food and beverages. In all these studies, it is possible to find the marks of the classical tradition both as a starting point and as a culmination of this analysis, because, as he pointed out on several occasions, "classic literature protected me from the tyranny of ideas".
Starting from the above-mentioned statement, the aim of my paper is to show how, in the work of Câmara Cascudo and in the hermeneutic structure of our traditions, Greco-Roman culture is one of the formative elements required to understand Brazilian "culture" and "civilization".

Keywords: Classical Tradition, Brazil, Civilization, Culture, Myth, Folklore

"Já a leste uma levíssima névoa azulada crepusculizava as linhas distantes."
D. João de Castro, *Jornadas no Minho*, p. 268.

"No day of my life passes now to its sunset, without leaving me more doubtful of all our cherished contempts, and more earnest to discover what root there was for the stories of good men, which are now the mocker's treasure."
Ruskin, J. *St. Mark's rest. The shrine of the slaves*, p. 17.

https://doi.org/10.14195/978-989-26-1280-5_13

No conjunto das "cascudianas", pequenas histórias que evidenciam o "bom humor" de Luis da Câmara Cascudo, recolhidas por Diógenes da Cunha Lima, encontramos a reprodução de um diálogo entre ele e o então governador do Rio Grande do Norte, Sylvio Pedroza, que, acostumado a ir ter com ele ao final do expediente no Palácio Potengi, reclama por não mais encontrá-lo:

"- Que aconteceu, Cascudo? No fim do expediente não o encontro em casa. Não o vejo mais.
- Estou selecionando crepúsculos. Toda tarde, cinco e meia, saio de casa e vou ver o crepúsculo de um ângulo novo. Não é pra nada, só alegria íntima."[1]

Ora, se, tal como fazia o próprio Cascudo quando investigava ou citava a obra e as idéias de um pensador, começarmos pela identificação de sua data de nascimento e morte, verificaremos que Luis da Câmara Cascudo nasceu na cidade do Natal, em 30 de dezembro 1898 e aí faleceu em 30 de julho de 1986. Isto significa que sua vida transcorre entre o final do século XIX e o penúltimo decênio do século XX, portanto, um homem entre dois mundos, ou, talvez, um homem que viu esses dois mundos em sua dupla dimensão crepuscular, a matutina e a vespetina:

"Ôrai, Hora, Horae, Horas, as três estações gregas, vinte e quatro horas do dia e da noite, filhas de Cronus, o Tempo, sempre tiveram respeito para o espírito dos homens de outrora. Dividiam a luz e as trevas com as gradações de penumbra. Assistiam aos mistérios, aos encantamentos, ao nascer e morrer de todas as coisas deste mundo. Tudo em sua hora! ... Boa hora, má hora, são os quadros normais da atividade humana. Vinte séculos caíram sobre as devoções greco-romanas às Ôrai mas os vestígios resistiram e são reconhecíveis nos dias contemporâneos. (...)
O grego inventou o mito de Alectrion, o companheiro de Marte, encarregado de vigiar e guardar os seus encontros com a deusa Vênus. Alectrion descuidou-se e o Sol avistou os dois amantes, indo denunciá-los a Vulcano, marido enganado. Por isso o galo canta estridentemente durante a noite, anunciando a aproximação do Sol, lembrando do castigo e da perdida dignidade custodial. O canto do galo é a divisão mais universal. Dividia a noite grega e passou para Roma. Para os romanos *noctis septem tempora sunt*. Eram os *crepusculum, Fax*, quando as luzes se acendiam; *concubium*, hora de dormir, *quo nos quieti damus*, a noite alta, *nox intempesta*, seguindo-se o *gallicinium*, quando o galo canta, e *conticinium*, quando ele cessa o canto, finalmente *aurora, tempus quod ante solem est*. Literariamente dizem *antelecucem*, quando a manhã bruxuoleia, *ad*

---

meridiem, meridiem, perto do meio-dia e meio-dia etc. (...)

No tocante às supertições diz-se em Portugal *horas abertas*, horas sem defesas, tempo em que as forças do Mal estão livres de reação maior, aos quatro períodos do dia, Meio-Dia, Meia-Noite e os crepúsculos vespertino e matutino. Surgem nessas horas os fantasmas, animais encantados, pavores, formas assombrosas e vagas que o canto do galo dissipa. Nos crepúsculos portugueses passam a galinha com os pintos, a porca dos sete leitões, a ovelha, a moura, o tardo, o coisa-ruim, a zorra de Odeloca berrando. (...)

No sertão rezam as velhas senhoras pela madrugada, quando os galos amiúdam os cantos. Há horas melhores para Deus escutar o pedido. Antes do sol nascer, com sinais-de-dia no horizonte, as rezas são de efeito prodigioso. Mantém-se a tradição de orar com velas acesas, (...). A muita luz dispersa a atenção e a penumbra concentra o pensamento.

A Morte prefere visitar os doentes nessas horas abertas, especialmente nos dois crepúsculos. Quando o Sol nasce ou morre são as horas-da-Morte.[2]

A reflexão sobre as *Ôrai* no ensaio XVI, do famoso *Anúbis e outros ensaios*, no qual os temas de nossa "mitologia" são recenseados em seu passado mais remoto, onde a literatura clássica é fonte constante de informação e recurso hermenêutico para uma avaliação das matrizes temporais de nossas tradições, a explicitação da função crepuscular, os crepúsculos matutinos e vespertinos, já nos oferece um quadro valioso dos limites, dos temas e das ambições da investigação cascudiana: a "civilização" e a "cultura"; a morfologia das "coisas do povo" e das "coisas da ciência", expressas pela determinação das atividades humanas no intervalo crepuscular, tanto no nível das crenças quanto no nível do determinismo das "ciências iátricas".[3]

Por outro lado, a angulosidade nova de cada crepúsculo selecionado por Cascudo parece apontar não somente para a dupla formação intelectual de "nosso etnógrafo": a medicina, que estudou até o 4o. ano, primeiro na Faculdade de Medicina da Bahia, em 1918, e depois na Faculdade de Medicina Rio de Janeiro, de 1919 a 1922, e, o direito cursado na Escola do Recife de 1924 a 1928,[4] quando concluiu o bacharelado, mas, sobretudo, para a função que exerceu ao longa de toda a sua vida, a de professor.[5]

---

[2] Cascudo, 1983, 2a: 117-120.

[3] Ver também, Cascudo, 1983: 611: "Ainda o povo de Portugal e Brasil aceitará a presença tenebrosa das horas abertas, em que a moléstia é mais traiçoeira e a Morte câmais freqüente. Horas dos crepúsculos matutino e vespertino, hora em que se morre, coincidente com os abaixamentos de temperatura, descompressão, desequilíbrios climático. (...). O determinismo que as ciências iátricas pretendiam impor ao organismo humano é irmão da ditadura endocrínica ou do fatalismo biotipológico."

[4] Gico, 1998: 7-18.

[5] Luis da Câmara Cascudo foi professor da Escola Normal, do Colégio Atheneu Norte-
-Riograndense, dos Colégios Pedro II, Marista e N.ª S.ª das Neves, do Instituto de Música,

Foi como professor que Cascudo escreveu grande parte de sua obra e conduziu suas pesquisas "além das limitações dos currículos" tal como expõe na *Preliminar* de *Civilização e Cultura*,

> "Já as fogueiras de São João seis vezes foram acesas desde que comecei este livro. E seis vezes ouvi a missa-do- galo na noite de Natal. Trabalho em dezembro, quando os cursos estão encerrados e eu posso viajar na quarta dimensão das simpatias bibliográficas, *além das limitações dos currículos.*
> Naturalmente não compendiei a matéria de etnografia geral talqualmente exponho aos meus alunos da Faculdade de Filosofia, e sim reuni documentário sobre os vários ângulos de possível curiosidade, finalizando o programa total."[6]

Assim, acreditamos, será o valor reflexivo que a metáfora da seleção de crepúsculos indicar-nos-á na aparente 'brincadeira' bem humorada da história contada por Diógenes da Cunha Lima, o crepúsculo evoca vários níveis da investigação cascudiana, expressando a busca de algo cuja duração se repete na pluralidade das horas, mas que, para ser visto, exige acuidade de visão para valer-se, como método de trabalho, da penumbra propiciadora da concentração do pensamento, capaz de demarcar uma "ação criadora" que emerge dos inconciliáveis fim e começo, fluxo e refluxo, como uma "contemporaneidade do milênio, o presente da 'antiguidade', as formas vivas na diuturnidade do exemplo."[7] A busca das "constantes etnográficas" serão agenciadas a partir de uma rotina de trabalho que levou-o a ler a literatura grega e latina, pois, nelas, descobria, conforme contou a Zila Mamede, que "a farinha de peixe da Amazônia era conhecida dos babilônios; que o costume de estirar a língua já fora anotada em Tito Lívio, supertições ouvidas na cozinha doméstica estavam em Horácio, Tácito e Suetônio, em Aristótles e Xenofonte."[8]

Portanto, o que pretendo discutir aqui, nesse curto tempo confenrencial, são as grandes linhas interpretativas contidas na imensa obra de Luis da Câmara Cascudo, que nos remetem a uma hermenêutica original, mas não solitária, porque no mesmo lastro podemos divisar autores como João Guimarães Rosa, Manuel Bandeira, Gilberto Freyre e Sérgio Buarque de Hollanda, no contexto do pensamento brasileiro do século XX: uma leitura do Brasil à luz de uma certa concepção de 'civilização' e de 'cultura', na qual viajam os elementos mas não o

---

e, Professor Emérito da Universidade Federal do Rio Grande do Norte, da qual foi um dos fundadores, e onde ensinou Direito Internacional, na Faculdade de Direito e Etnografia, na Faculdade de Filosofia. Na UFRN, Cascudo foi diretor do Instituto de Antropologia, onde funciona, atualmente, o Museu Câmara Cascudo. Cf. Gico, op. cit., p.7 e a nota da Editora Itatiaia com os dados biográficos do autor, na edição de 1983, de *Cultura e Civilização*.

[6] Cascudo,1983: 15. Grifo nosso.

[7] Cascudo, 1983: 693.

[8] Mamede, 1970: 12, v.1.

corpo da civilização determinante.[9] Para tanto, vou dividir esta apresentação tomando por base duas obras de Câmara Cascudo: a basilar *Civilização e Cultura*, e o confessional *Prelúdio e fuga do real*, desconhecido, creio, de boa parte dos intérpretes do pensamento brasileiro do século passado.

1. CIVILIZAÇÃO E CULTURA: O PRESENTE DA "ANTIGUIDADE"

A publicação dos dois volumes de *Civilização e Cultura – Pesquisas e notas de Etnografia geral*, pela Livraria José Olympio Editora, em 1973, foi o fim de um conturbado percurso editorial. Segundo nos conta Cascudo, em "História de um livro perdido", separata dos Arquivos do Instituto de Antropologia da UFRN, publicada em junho de 1966,[10] durante dez anos ele trabalhou intensamente na elaboração da obra, e uma vez concluído o trabalho, o original foi entregue à Imprensa Estadual de Pernambuco, por convite de "afetuoso amigo". Com a demora na publicação do trabalho, Cascudo foi instado, em dezembro de 1964, por Zeferino Vaz, então reitor da Universidade de Brasília e pelos professores Onofre Lopes e José Tavares da Silva, da UFRN, a transferir a edição da obra para uma coleção brasileira de divulgação científica que Vaz pretendia inaugurar em Brasília. Foi quando, então, telegrafou a Recife solicitando a devolução dos originais, e, para sua indignada surpresa, descobriu que o livro, do qual não tinha cópia, havia desaparecido, restando apenas o "título melancólico de livro perdido"[11]. Dos originais desaparecidos apenas três capítulos já haviam sido publicados[12], e dada a impossibilidade de "reavivar o roteiro das pesquisas, análises e conclusões, nem sempre maquinais dos cursos na Etnografia Geral"[13], a divulgação do Índice geral e do Índice de assuntos, que com algumas notas esparsas, constituíam o saldo total do esforço de todos aqueles anos, visava resgistar e comprovar os temas estudados e investigados direta e indiretamente, em viagem e livro, em uma "simples indicação denominadora, desde que o texto não existe mais."[14]

Quatro anos depois os originais reapareceram e foram devolvidos "amarrotados como papel de embrulho, sujos, riscados, alguns capítulos incompletos, páginas e páginas inutilizadas por um delírio neurótico de riscos e interrogações! O livro perdido passara a Livro Morto. Guardei-o numa gaveta para todo o sempre."[15] Entretanto, com a intervenção de Daniel Pereira, diretor da José Olympio, "pretendendo reaver o defunto", e a ação efetiva de Onofre Lopes, em

---

[9] Cf. Cascudo, 1983: 17-21.
[10] Cascudo, 1966: 5-19.
[11] Cascudo, 1966: 5.
[12] Idem, ibidem.
[13] Idem, ibidem.
[14] Cascudo, 1966: 6.
[15] Cascudo, 1983: 23.

maio de 1971, desejando a publicação do livro tal como "estivesse no arquivo, sem prever prêmio ou recompensa, para documentar o labor desinteressado e tenaz, dos professores provincianos do Brasil Universitário", e uma vez que, em 1963, a Etnografia Geral havia sido suprimida do currículo da ex-Faculdade de Filosofia, o que equivalia, segundo Cascudo, a ensinar álgebra sem aritmética ou a "semear no mar", como suspirara Bolívar, ele decide por sua publicação, concluindo, assim, a "odisséia de sua tarefa" com o ressarcimento das "melancolias de onze anos angustiados."[16]

As 741 páginas que compõem o texto estão estruturadas em três eixos centrais: [i] a questão histórica, isto é, a apresentação das diversas tentativas de conceitualização da antropologia como disciplina e dos sentidos aí atribuídos à etnografia e à etnologia, desde a etimologia até ao contexto "evolutivo" de suas teorias e doutrinas; [ii] a determinação de uma teoria da cultura e da civilização que conforma a determinação dos "elementos da estabilidade humana"; e, [iii] a descrição de cada um desses elementos: a ecologia, o instinto aquisitivo, a conduta e a norma, o fogo, o abrigo, o agasalho, a ornamentação, as jóias, o cabelo, a barba, o bigode, o corpo humano como medida do mundo, as funções físicas e simbólicas, o senso de orientação, o primeiro lar, a propriedade, a caça, a pesca, a domesticação de animais, a agricultura, a alimentação, o comércio, os transportes, o solidarismo, a economia e as indústrias milenarias, a religião, a antropofagia, a arte, a lúdica, a dança, os instrumentos sonoros, o canto, a poesia, o teatro, os esportes, a medicina, a fala, a escrita e o poder do nome, a família, o governo, a lei, a delegação e o direito, e, a cultura popular; a partir de uma exaustiva exemplificação do que Cascudo chamará de "constantes etnográficas", obtidas pela confluência de dados e informações que atravessam distancias geográficas e culturais como uma "ação criadora".[17]

Avesso às questões de método, o que por mais de uma vez será sublinhado em *Civilização e cultura*,

> "Não me alistando sob qualquer bandeira doutrinária, e tendo para os mestres uma admiração fervorosa que não implica submissão deslumbrada nem preito de obediência, tive nessa etnografia geral a mesma curiosidade de percurso com que viajei pelo mundo, sem guias letrados e sem itinerários marcados pelo asterisco do Baedeker. Fui procurando com a simples alegria da identificação e a todos ouvindo sem a obrigatoriedade devocional.
> Não me arrependo da ausência de métodos e menos ainda de ter recorrido aos elementos que julgo úteis para um esclarecimento,"[18]

---

[16] Cascudo, 1983: 24.
[17] Cascudo, 1983: 17.
[18] Cascudo, 1983: 15.

e seguidor ativo da máxima machadiana de que a epígrafe "não é somente um meio de complementar as pessoas da narração com as idéias que deixarem, mas ainda um par de lunetas para que o leitor do livro penetre o que for menos claro ou totalmente escuro"[19], Cascudo aporá como epígrafe às 741 páginas de *Civilização e cultura*, a passagem dos *Atos dos Apóstolos*, IV, 20: "Não podemos, pois, deixar de falar das coisas que temos visto e ouvido", para marcar toda sua tarefa etnográfica, isto é, a exposição de motivos e argumentos sem o sentido da decisão doutrinária, de modo sempre provisório, atendo-se ao caminho como uma conseqüência natural da própria percepção do conjunto.[20]

É nesse 'caminho' que a Antiguidade Clássica parece subsidiar boa parte dos argumentos e dos motivos que irão possibilitando essa 'percepção do conjunto', e, é pois, buscando trilhar esse caminho que tentarei delinear os temas clássicos nos argumentos cascudianos.

---

[19] Machado de Assis, 1970: 966.
[20] Cascudo, 1983: 21.

1.1 *A parte é maior do que o todo?*

Ao afirmar, logo no começo de suas análises que o objeto de estudo da etnografia é a origem e estabelecimento, modificações e vitalidade das culturas humanas e que, por isso, tudo o que interessa ao homem no plano da temporalidade tem raiz etnográfica, constituindo uma "memória no tempo":

> "A simpatia natural pela etnografia é que ela evoca documentadamente a história de nossa grande família humana, evidenciando continuidades e seqüências que orgulham ou decepcionam. (...).
> E nota-se que o passado imemorial não desapareceu de todo, e deparamos as sombras milenárias nos gestos diários e às vezes no mecanismo do raciocínio, para a soma surpreendente de soluções psicológicas.
> Um ato comum e banal pode ter cinqüenta séculos (...). E tudo vive em nós, herdeiros de gerações incontáveis e sucessivas.
> Por isso a etnografia é sedutora. É a nossa memória no tempo! ..."[21] ,

Câmara Cascudo, ver-se-á frente à necessidade de diferenciar Civilização e cultura para que o objeto da etnografia possa ser corretamente delineado: "civilização é todo e cultura é parte".[22]

A civilização será, então, o conjunto das culturas, o elemento que lhe dá caráter, coloração, a peculiaridade do nacional; a cultura é a parte sem o espírito do todo no tempo e no espaço, e a cultura geral de um país é a sua civilização, é "um órgão indispensável no corpo mas não é o corpo e menos o espírito unificador e orgânico. Civilização não se exporta, arrenda, empresta, compra, imita. Essa é a característica das culturas. A cultura emigra e a civilização é sedentária, estática quanto à permanência no âmbito sócio-geográfico.

Por isso, dirá Cascudo,

> "a cultura é um exercício aplicado a um esforço para finalidade determinada e única. Nunca o geral, o conjunto, a totalidade. É um músculo, um órgão, um nervo. Jamais o organismo inteiro. Um rio, uma árvore, uma montanha. Não a paisagem completa",[23]

e será nesse sentido movente e perseverante do patrimônio tradicional de normas, doutrinas, hábitos, acúmulo do material herdado e acrescido pelas aportações inventivas de cada geração que ele sublinhará o "encanto heróico da etnografia" ao fazer findar "a imagem rutilante da civilização única que deve ser a mesma em todo o mundo e quem não lhe pertencer está condenado a selvageria. A lição,

---

[21] Cascudo, 1983: 27.
[22] Cascudo, 1983: 17.
[23] Cascudo, 1983: 39.

dirá ainda, nem por todos percebida, é que cada povo organizará a sua civilização e que as culturas constituintes devem ser livremente escolhidas, mantidas ou
criadas na mentalidade nacional reajustadora. Padronização! Voilà l'ennemi ...".[24]

Assim, a discussão das relações entre a parte e o todo, tomada como media-
dora da teoria e do ofício etnográficos, parece estar atrelada ao velho contexto
grego exposto, por exemplo, nos *Trabalhos e Dias* de Hesíodo, e feito método
e princípio nas doutrinas da medicina hipocrática, para falarmos em autores
clássicos citados e epigrafados por Cascudo em vários momentos da discussão
em *Civilização e cultura*, e que já estava perfeitamente delineada no texto de
abertura da obra intitulado "Preliminar" quando elenca os antigos clássicos no
contexto de sua investigação:

> "Não é novidade encontrarem-se em Terêncio, Virgílio, Horácio, Cícero,
> Aristófanes, Hesíodo, o infinito Homero, nos trágicos, epigramistas gregos,
> eróticos, votivos, funerários e descritivos, elementos elucidadores da vida
> cotidiana da Grécia e Roma não registados noutras paragens. Um pormenor
> que não está em Estrabão vive numa comédia de Plauto. Ausente em Diodoro
> da Sicília mas presente no Satyricon de Petrônio. Não consta em Denis de
> Halicarnasso mas Luciano de Samosata anotou. Para certos momentos da
> história social, da normalidade romana, são indispensáveis Juvenal, Ovídio,
> Marcial, Tíbulo, Propércio, Catulo, Lucrécio, Sêneca, Lucano. Por que
> não aproveita-los mesmo retirando-os do mostruário alheio? Aparecem
> comumente com notícias que eles viram e viveram.
> Um objeto prova sua existência surgindo num rol do linear B de Cnossos ou
> numa sátira de Pérsio."[25]

Nesse sentido, a cultura será a seguir estudada em todos os seus aspectos, das questões teóricas relativas a sua origem, sua conformação primeva,
os usos do ouro, prata, cobre, bronze e ferro, as relações entre pré-história e
proto-história e os processos de aculturação e miscigenização, para só, então,
introduzir a análise dos elementos da estabilidade humana. Em toda a discussão
acerca da formação da cultura a presença do "infinito Homero", de Hesíodo e
Heródoto, Virgílio, Ovídio e Tácito, serão exemplares no auxílio compreensivo
das questões mencionadas acima, cuja análise proponho deixarmos para uma
outra oportunidade, de modo a podermos passar para o segundo item de nossa
recensão temática, contido no contexto dos elementos da estabilidade humana
que serão denominadas por Camara Cascudo, na mesma obra, de "formas vivas
na diuturnidade do exemplo".

---

[24] Cascudo, 1983: 42.
[25] Cascudo, 1983: 20. Grifo nosso.

1.2 *Os elementos da estabilidade humana e as formas pretéritas vivas na diuturnidade do exemplo*

Os elementos da estabilidade humana serão definidos por Câmara Cascudo como provenientes do "instituto gregário" do homem e de sua disposição para uma "convergência fatal" de atração pelo semelhante, e são decorrentes da conquista de uma economia sucessiva e do uso consciente das primeiras técnicas aquisitivas ou simplificadoras da tarefa diária, indispensável, normal e regular.[26]

O primeiro desses elementos, a ecologia, será objeto da crítica de Cascudo de modo a mostrar que o cultural é mais definidor do homem do que o meio ambiente, que o fator humano é que é decisivo, e criticando Hipócrates pela defesa da "quase onipotência geográfica"[27], exemplificará sua tese com a história do ovo enviado de Natal, em 1933, para a Alemanha, e do qual nasceu um galo, alemão pelo *jus soli* e brasileiro pelo *jus sanguinis* , e que ao longo dos seus 5 anos de vida cantou unicamente no horário dos galos do Brasil que ele jamais ouvira: "não houve meio do galo potiguar assimilar o ritmo pregoeiro dos colegas renanos. Manteve a diferença das quatro horas distantes para as doze locais. Levara *ab ovo*, não apenas o canto mais também a regra imutável dos momentos em que devia cantar. Ecologia alemã inoperante."

O exemplo acima aponta para toda uma concepção da relatividade do tempo cultural que permite que o "antigo" seja presente e permeie o que Cascudo chamou de "contemporaneidade do milênio". Essa contemporaneidade será mostrada na análise de cada um dos elementos estudados, quase sempre com formas pretéritas da Antiguidade Clássica, e aqui vou retomar apenas uma dessas análises, a relativa à 'cultura popular' dada sua vitalidade e importância na inquietação investigativa de nosso autor.

O povo, dirá ele, tem uma cultura que recebeu dos antepassados através do exercício de atos práticos e audição de regras de conduta, religiosa e social, e faz parte de uma camada terciária anteposta aos conhecimentos escolares, transmitidos como ciência indispensável e geral pelo livro e pela voz do ensino magistral. Os dois extratos acompanham a vida normal do homem, existindo entre eles uma intercomunicação viva porque estão no mesmo organismo, tal como dois gêmeos divinos coexistindo na mentalidade humana, disputando o domínio soberano da decisão psicológica: os dióscuros serão, pois, o modelo de toda a concepção cascudiana de cultura popular: "Castor humano e Pólux imortal irmanizam-se na mesma constelação rutilante do conhecimento. Esses dióscuros são a Cultura Popular e a Cultura Letrada, ministrada sob os auspícios das normas oficiais, hierárquicas, rituais. *Non adversa, sed diversa.*"[28]

---

[26] Cascudo, 1983: 147.
[27] Cascudo, 1983: 153.
[28] Cascudo 1983: 680.

A análise pautada hermeneuticamente na história dos dióscuros trará
também outros elementos que denotam a vitalidade do pensamento antigo na
reflexão cascudiana: a função da memória como reminiscência, como fonte do
conhecimento:

> "A orelha era dedicada a MNEMOSINE, DEUSA DA MEMÓRIA, mãe
> das nove Musas. A Fé e a Ciência, no plano do Conhecimento, entravam pela
> audição. Os velhos Mestres puxavam o pavilhão auricular aos estudantes para
> que decorassem ou não esquecessem quanto aprendiam nas aulas. Processos de
> mnemotécnica. Valia castigo, excitando a retentiva dos alunos desatentos ou
> vadios. Quando alguém puxa a própria orelha, pune-se de não haver ouvido a
> voz da Razão em tempo oportuno. É o gesto simbólico do Arrependimento.
> Na *Romagem dos Agravados* de Gil Vicente (1533), a vendedora de peixe Maria
> do Prado, lastima-se: Se tu não deras à golhelha, / Nunca o nosso agravo fora,/
> Nem eu torcera a orelha.
> 'Dar a golhelha' era falar demasiado imprudentemente. Assim, puxar a ore-
> lha, significa "lembre-se". Torcê-la, vale confessar, "pequei"! Em Siracusa,
> Apolo Cintio belisca, *vellit*, de *vellicatio*, a orelha do pastor Titiro: (Virgílio,
> Égogla,VI-3)."[29]

e a eficácia da imitação, da *mímesis*, em detrimento da imaginação, na preservação da cultura:

> "Mas não existe Civilização original e isenta de interdependência, distantes
> ou próximas, e já constitui dogma etnográfico ensinar-se a pobreza e
> raridade da imaginação humana e a prestigiosa ascendência da Imitação
> como processo inevitável normal de ampliação técnica. A cultura é
> transmitida pelo replantio de galhos floridos e não pelas sementes unitárias.
> (...) Nesse rumo da Imitação estará a força radicular do instinto aquisitivo,
> de impressionante persitências."[30]

Assim, o valor da memória e da *mímesis* na mecânica aculturativa é uma forma de permanência das formas pretéritas que "vêm de longe e agitam as chamas
que não mudam de lugar":

> No *Fedro,* de Platão, conta Sócrates que o deus egípcio Toth encarece ao rei
> Thamus o uso da escrita e o soberano recusa porque a fixação do acontecimento
> dispensará no povo o exercício da memória. A sabedoria vive mais ardente na
> consciência e não nos registos que a sepultam para uma consulta, que é uma
> breve ressureição. (...) Entre o povo a inteligência aquisitiva e o conhecimento

---

[29] Cascudo 1987.
[30] Cascudo 1983: 682.

fazem um *en kai pan*, um todo, perpetuamente ao alcance de todos, à luz do sol e das estrelas. A mobilidade da comunicação oral que, aparentemente, seria um processo dispersivo e tumultuoso de esquecimento, é uma forma plástica mas indeformável de conservação e continuidade. A evaporação e perda de certos motivos residem na fraca densidade do interesse e seu desaparecimento não prejudica o restante conteúdo residual, parcialmente renovado na dinâmica dos elementos convergentes e assimilados."[31]

O que seriam essas formas pretéritas que vêm de longe mas não mudam de lugar? Uma variante das idéias platônicas no contexto da etnografia cascudiana?

Deixando a vocês a resposta e a discussão acerca da legitimidade da pergunta, vou passar agora para o segundo texto, *Prelúdio e fuga do Real*, onde os antigos refluem de sua função de fundamentação teórica e passam a ser personagens de um diálogo com o nosso "professor de província".

2. *A ALMA QUE PENSA: IMORTALIDADE E CONTEMPORANEIDADE*

Prelúdio e fuga do real é uma obra na qual a influência platônica parece decisiva, seja nos aspectos formais, seja na dimensão conteudística das conversas de Luis da Câmara Cascudo com 33 interlocutores, considerados por ele decisivos no âmbito da contemporaneidade do milênio, em um argumento exemplar: a imortalidade da alma.[32]

Como já vimos anteriormente, Câmara Cascudo foi leitor assíduo da literatura clássica, que, como gostava dizer, o tinha imunizado contra a tirania das idéias, e a presença dos diálogos platônicos pode ser vista desde suas citações nominais, mas, também, na menção indireta interlineada à exposição do argumento. No texto que nos detemos agora as menções explícitas são muitas, mas as interlineadas são essenciais para encontrarmos os parâmetros nos quais *República* e *Fédon* são modelo de reflexão.

O texto, configurado como um diálogo entre o velho professor e uma interlocutora anônima a quem ele expõe seus temas maiores, a contemporaneidade dos deuses e a imortalidade da alma, e valendo-se da *mímesis* compõe 34 diálogos com os homens que marcaram a vida intelectual da humanidade, em circunstancias geográficas, antropológicas e sociais distintas daquelas em que, historicamente, eles viveram.

Por outro lado, os dois termos que compõem o título, prelúdio e fuga do real, podem ser entendidos como variantes de dois grandes temas platônicos expostos na *República*, o proêmio, traduzido aqui por prelúdio, e a habilidade narrativa de fabricar, dialogicamente, com o *lógos*, uma *pólis* e uma *politeía* onde quase todos

---

[31] Cascudo 1983: 686.
[32] Cascudo 1974.

os "elementos da estabilidade humana" estão mimeticamente descritos através
da "fuga" para a pluralidade temporal e social.

Por sua vez, o título do prelúdio é já significativo anúncio do valor dialógico
da cultura: "Não abaneis a cabeça!", foi retirado do artigo de Machado de Assis,
publicado em *A Semana*, no Rio de Janeiro, em 22 de novembro de 1898, indicação crepuscular e referência dupla à ironia socrática e machadiana, e também, à
regra mais fundamental que norteia a vida intelectual de Câmara Cascudo.

Nesse sentido, o prelúdio será um decálogo de sua vida intelectual, expressando os grandes temas de sua obra:

[i] a contemporaneidade dos deuses,

> "Não, Madame, não creio que os deuses hajam morrido com a vitória do
> cristianismo, como a senhora leu em Flaubert. (...) Os deuses do Olimpo
> estão vivos, como Belzebu, Xangô, Iemanjá (...). Sim, Madame, também os
> de Nínive, Babilônia, mesmo aqueles que ignoramos, diluídos na solidão do
> Tempo. (...)
> Não madame, não me refiro às sobrevivências nas supertições e costumes dos
> nossos dias, mas a eles mesmos personalidades miríficas que estão representadas,
> morfologicamente, em restos de mármores, camafeus, moedas, ex-votos."[33]

[ii] a intuição como processo aquisitivo de conhecimento,

> "Tenho a intuição e madame sabe que a intuição é um processo aquisitivo do
> conhecimento, da vida eterna dos deuses, brancos, pretos, encarnados, verdes.
> Não, não vi ainda nenhum deles. A existência independe de comprovação."[34]

[iii] a imortalidade da alma, pois, se há uma alma para cada corpo, esta, no
nível eterno, manterá a figura material que a alojou na terra,

> "As almas não sucubem. São eternas desde a criação. (...) Quem tem alma
> viverá. Não estou enganado, Pilatos, sim."[35]

[iv] a duração da cultura brasileira pela via do colonizador português,

> "Nós do Brasil, Madame, possuímos o panteão português. ... Os deuses enco-
> bertos seriam os deuses da divulgação romana."[36]

---

[33] Cascudo 1974: 5.
[34] Cascudo 1974: 13.
[35] Cascudo 1974: 7.
[36] Cascudo 1974: 9.

[v] resistência ao padrão, a norma dominante, pois os deuses não podem se restrijir às irradiações mentais captadas misteriosamente, e diametralemente opostas ao nosso critério e norma de conduta.

[vi] o pensar está na alma, como o fundamento da lógica cascudiana, cada um de nós é soma de individualidades disputadora de poder executivo na intimidade da vontade, aparentemente una, indivisível. Sentimos as vozes diversas, nos timbres característicos: o legislativo discutindo, o judiciário aconselhando, o executivo agindo ...

Posto isto, chegamos ao final da conversa e o velho professor conclui com sua interlocutora:

> "Disse Platão no *Fédon*: 'As almas dos mortos, vivem!'
> As impressões vêm vindo, a idéia brusca, veemente e fortuita, de Montaigne, repetindo-se, atingindo o córtex cerebral, encontrando o vestígio das reações anteriores. Uma assustadora contemporaneidade de milênios ....
> A morte existe, os mortos, não!
> Madame, o jantar está servido! ..."

Città pubblicitarie
(Advertising Cities)

Delio De Martino (deliode@alice.it)
University of Bari

Resumo – Frammenti delle più importanti città del presente e del passato vengono smembrati e riassemblati all'interno del linguaggio pubblicitario. Come in un enorme gioco di specchi le città sono rivestite di segni di altre città che compaiono nei manifesti, negli spot, nel *packaging*, nel *merchandising* e nei loghi dei prodotti commerciali, in particolare delle automobili. Queste città pubblicitarie tendono a trasformare ogni *polis* in un'enorme *cosmopolis*, ovvero in una "città continua", come la definisce Calvino, una città senza confini e senza barriere, uniforme, che va coprendo il mondo intero. I frammentari pezzi di città pubblicitarie sono infine utilizzati dal consumatore per rivestirsi di narrazioni e costruire la propria identità.

Parole chiave: città, pubblicità, televisione, manifesti

Abstract – Fragments of the most important ancient and modern cities are dismembered and reassembled in the language of advertising. As in an enormous game of mirrors, cities are re-dressed with the signs of other cities that appear in advertising posters, in spots, in packaging, in merchandising, and in logos of commercials products, especially in the automotive industry. These cities of advertising tend to transform every *polis* in an enormous *cosmopolis*, that is a "continuous city", as Calvino defines it, a city without confines, barriers, and uniform, a city covering the entire world. The fragmentary pieces of advertising cities are ultimately used by the consumer to dress himself with narratives and to build his identity.

Keywords: cities, advertising, television, posters

Dalla città alla città-annuncio. La città è il luogo pubblico per eccellenza, lo spazio dove da millenni si sono esercitate le prime forme di pubblicità, inizialmente nella forma dell'architettura, simbolo di potere economico, divino e sociale. Ma è nell'800 che, con la rivoluzione industriale, le strade della città sono diventate il primo luogo di diffusione dei manifesti e delle *affiche*[1]. Lentamente gli annunci a stampa hanno conquistato sempre più spazio divenendo parte dell'estetica della città moderna e soprattutto postmoderna. Nei vari livelli, da quello dei marciapiedi, fino a quello dei grattacieli e delle loro cime, passando per i cartelloni, le città si sono lentamente ricoperte di pubblicità, che è diventata una seconda pelle urbana[2]. Una rappresentazione

---

[1] Menegazzi 1995.
[2] Solas 2008: 37-62, in part. 47.

artistica della città-annuncio è offerta dalla futuristica Los Angeles del film *Blade Runner* di Ridley Scott (1982) o dalla New York del 3000 della serie Tv *Futurama*[3] di Matt Groening. Ma anche una fotografia contemporanea di una piazza reale come Times Square di New York, tempio mondiale delle insegne commerciali, può dare l'idea di come l'*advertising* si sia ormai trasformato da superstrato ad elemento di identità.

D'altronde questo processo può risultare così invasivo da provocare forme di rigetto come è avvenuto a San Paolo in Brasile, dove nel 2005 con la Legge Cidade Limpa si decise di ripulire la città dalle affissioni commerciali che avevano stravolto l'estetica urbana.

Ad ogni modo la metamorfosi della pubblicità da guaina, pelle ad elemento identitario della città non è a senso unico.

Città o meglio per un processo sineddotico frammenti di città, come elementi di cultura e di identità, sono dispersi nella pubblicità e nei *brand*. Soprattutto da quando, in seguito alla saturazione del mercato di prodotti simili, la pubblicità si è focalizzata più sul fascino della marca che sul prodotto[4], frammenti di città vengono sfruttati per costruire l'immagine della marca o *brand image*.

Elementi culturali della città si ritrovano così nei diversi linguaggi della pubblicità. Partendo dal linguaggio verbale, per poi proseguire nei vari linguaggi più complessi, si osserva quanto la toponomastica abbia influito sul *naming* di marche e di prodotti.

Toponomastica. Iniziando dai marchi dalle case automobilistiche[5], sono vari gli esempi di *naming* derivato dalla toponomastica di origine classica. Il nome della casa automobilistica Albion (1899-1980), deriva dall'antico nome greco della Gran Bretagna: Ἀλβιών. Dal toponimo latino Florentia deriva una delle più antiche imprese automobilistiche toscane avviata nel 1903 ma fallita dopo appena sette anni. Ancora alla toponomastica latina deve il suo nome anche la Helvetia, società dedita ai kit e ai componenti aerodinamici per auto. Ma anche la Fiat cita, seppur in maniera non esplicita, la sua città d'origine essendo un acronimo di "Fabbrica Italiana Automobili Torino".

Anche i nomi dei modelli citano spesso città e molto spesso si creano vere e proprie isotopie toponomastiche all'interno della strategia di *naming*. La Seat per esempio per quasi l'intera sua storia ha utilizzato nomi di città (Arosa, Ibiza, León, Toledo, Altea) e una scelta simile seppur più snob ed elitaria ha fatto la Lancia scegliendo nomi di vie romane come l'Augusta (1933-1937), l'Aurelia (1950-1958), l'Appia (1953-1963), la Flaminia (1957-1970) e la Flavia

---

[3] Ivi, 49.

[4] Caro 2009: 109-114 e Caro 2010: 36.

[5] De Martino 2011 e De Martino 2010bis.

(1960-1971). Altre vetture mutuarono il nome da toponimi che richiamano la romanità della marca: la Artena (1934-1943) da un comune romano, la Astura (1931-1939) dall'omonimo fiume del Lazio, la Aprilia (1937-1949) dal sobborgo romano o dalla città della provincia di Latina, e l'Ardea, dal nome dell'antica capitale della popolazione preromana dei Rutuli. Ma forse l'esempio più suggestivo è la cinese Gonow Katay Troy, pick up *low cost* sbarcato anche in Europa. Un caso limite di citazione non del nome di una ma di due città è costituito dall'Alfa MiTo, acronimo di Milano-Torino.

Anche prodotti meno costosi dell'automobile utilizzano la toponomastica, come saponi di Marsiglia, l'acqua di Colonia, le gomme da masticare Brooklyn (dette anche "le gomme del ponte"), prodotti gastronomici, i limoni di Sorrento, gli agrumi di Ribera (Sicilia), il vino Porto o l'aglianico Castel del Monte, le lasagne alla Bolognese. Ma questa attenzione alla provenienza agroalimentare stava già nella tradizione mediterranea come mostrano Archestrato di Gela o Ateneo[6].

La località di provenienza è sempre stata importante ed è oggi divenuta tanto fondamentale nel settore agroalimentare da essere registrata con le sigle IGP (indicazione geografica protetta) e DOP (denominazione di origine protetta).

Pittogrammi. Passando alle iconografie commerciali dei loghi, ovvero i pittogrammi, è ancora più evidente il processo di frammentazione delle città. Generalmente si scelgono dettagli che riassumono l'intera cultura della città. Di questi le aziende si appropriano dopo un processo di traduzione grafico-commerciale spesso in continua fase di aggiornamento. Emblematico è il biscione dell'Alfa Romeo[7]. Il biscione con un uomo in bocca è infatti tratto dalla torre del Filarete di Milano. Simbolo araldico dei Visconti, il biscione è legato all'antica leggenda del drago Tarantasio o Tarànto. Si racconta che questo mostro sia nato dal cadavere del condottiero Ezzelino III da Romano, tiranno della Marca Trevigiana a cui fu dedicata la tragedia *Eccerinide* di Albertino Mussato e che è anche da Dante[8]. Il poeta lo inserisce infatti nel XII canto dell'*Inferno* nel girone dei violenti verso il prossimo (vv. 109-110 "e quella fronte c'ha 'l pel così nero, / è Azzolino... ") e lo cita successivamente nel IX canto del *Paradiso* in occasione dell'incontro con la sorella Cunizza da Romano (vv. 29-31). Diversamente da questa, Ezzelino fu scomunicato, morì suicida e fu sepolto a Soncino nel 1259. Dal suo sepolcro nacque Tarànto. Secondo la leggenda il drago viveva nel lago longobardo Gerundo, presente nella pianura padana fino al XIII secolo, divorava uomini e soprattutto bambini e produceva terribili esalazioni mefitiche.

---

[6] García Soler 2010: 345-366.

[7] Pellegrini 2003: 35.

[8] De Martino 2013: 22-23.

Proprio mentre divorava un bambino il mostro fu ucciso da Uberto Visconti, il cavaliere che originò la dinastia dei Visconti. La leggendaria morte del drago è in realtà legata alla bonifica dell'area dove il Gerundo provocava disagi e pestilenze. L'Alfa Romeo non è l'unica azienda ad essersi impossessata di questo simbolo. Dal drago Taranto deriva anche il logo del cane a sei zampe - quattro automobilistiche e due del conducente - dell'Agip, realizzato da Luigi Broggini per il concorso indetto da Enrico Mattei negli anni '50 per la creazione del logo aziendale. Ma anche il logo di Canale 5 nasce dall'evoluzione del biscione, nel corso degli anni sempre più stilizzato fino ad oggi quando l'elemento più identificativo è la rondella di fuoco del drago.

Un altro frammento di città si ritrova nel logo della Maserati. La casa del Tridente è infatti così denominata poiché si è appropriata, per volere dell'artista Mario Maserati, di un'iconografia mitica urbana: il tridente di Nettuno, dettaglio della fontana del Nettuno sita nella piazza centrale di Bologna e realizzata dal Giambologna, al centro della quale troneggia Nettuno con il tridente in mano.

Iconografia e toponimia si possono coniugare sui cofani automobilistici. Tra i loghi delle auto di lusso quello della Porsche si distingue poiché sopra il cavallino, simbolo araldico della città Stoccarda, è impresso anche il toponimo Stuttgart.

Ma anche altri elementi che circondano il marchio citano elementi della città che vengono decontestualizzati e reinterpretati in chiave commerciale. La calandra della Rolls Royce per esempio racchiude ancora oggi ricombinandole in una forma inedita le icone dei prodotti più alti della scultura e dell'architettura classica. Tutte le autovetture Rolls ostentano un'imponente griglia del radiatore cromata disegnata sul modello del colonnato del Partenone reinterpretato in chiave automobilistica.

Sul "timpano" della calandra è inserito il logotipo (le due R sovrapposte) mentre sulla sommità del "frontone", a mo' di acroterio, ove originariamente era posto il tappo del radiatore, è montata la mascotte del cosiddetto Spirit of Ecstasy (originariamente denominato Spirit of Speed), una prestigiosa statuetta realizzata sul modello della Nike di Samotracia, una scultura che ha già nel nome il suo legame con la città dove fu ritrovata. Della realizzazione della statuetta fu incaricato l'artista Charles Sykes. Questi integrò le forme della dea della Vittoria con le curve di Eleanor Thornton, segretaria di Lord Beaulieu e sua amante: l'opera guadagnò gli elementi mancanti dell'originale, testa e braccia, e assunse una postura maggiormente flessa verso la strada.

Le sole ali della Nike di Samotracia ristilizzate nel celebre baffo (*swoosh*) si sono trasformate nel logo di una delle aziende più note al mondo: la Nike.

Packaging e merchandising. Schegge di città si riscontrano anche nel *packaging*. Il confezionamento come elemento di identità sfrutta elementi urbani dal passato glorioso. Oltre a confezioni con stampe che ripropongono miti urbani - come l'imballaggio dello yogurt Greco di Danone con l'immagine del Partenone - a volte si creano confezioni dalle forme architettoniche. È il caso ad esempio di uno dei profumi italiani più famosi: Roma, lanciato nel 1988 da Laura Biagiotti. Il flacone del profumo presenta due *packaging* culturali: la versione da donna ha la forma di una colonna romana, mentre quella da uomo ha un *packaging* che cita le forme del monumento simbolo della città eterna: il Colosseo.

Simili per forme, anche i prodotti del *merchandising* possono essere attinti dall'architettura della città. In questo settore si ritrovano oggetti di varia natura e di varia qualità come le borracce a forma di colonne greche del Partenone o Ercolini con schiume da bagno vendute in occasione dell'uscita del cartone animato *Hercules* (1997) o, altre volte, la città diventa un marchio con cui si firmano magliette e riproduzioni di architetture urbane vendute come souvenir.

Città nelle pubblicità. Ma è soprattutto nella pubblicità a stampa e audiovisiva che città reali o letterarie si trasformano in icone commerciali. Sfruttate come scenografie di parodie o di "pubblicità mitiche", nobilitanti il prodotto, il loro ruolo è tanto strategico che spesso il toponimo diventa nome della campagna. La promozione *Opel Operazione Itaca*, per esempio, diede vita a una trilogia di spot ambientati nella patria di Ulisse ma dove Penelope invece di aspettare lo sposo corre in concessionaria[9]. Con anacronismi le vetture Opel circolano tra le colonne greche e finiscono in templi trasformati in concessionari. Città antiche e moderne si possono combinare con il filtro di altre opere letterarie che svolgono la funzione di ipertesti. Un capitolo della campagna del 2009 della Seat Exeo dal titolo *Itaca* cita versi dell'omonima poesia di Kavafis, mostra immagini di un'*Odissea* moderna che si svolge tra le strade di Lisbona. Per merito dell'auto le emozioni del viaggio di Ulisse, paragonato dal poeta al viaggio della vita, si possono rivivere nel breve tragitto cittadino effettuato a bordo di una Seat. Nello spot Poseidone e i Lestrigoni moderni si trasformano in statue ed elementi architettonici della capitale portoghese e il Ciclope in un suo cittadino. Il più noto antecedente nel quale Itaca si trasforma in una boutique cittadina è lo spot *Ulysses' return* della Renault Laguna del 2002.

Il nome di una città è il titolo anche della fortunata animazione pubblicitaria *Opel Troya* (2006, Produzione Como SL-Madrid). Qui la vicenda è riletta in tono ironico: la guerra di Troia non ha l'esito sperato cosicché i Greci provano a

---

[9] L'immagine di una Penelope di dubbia fedeltà risale a una tradizione già presente in epoca antica e che si è evoluta nella letteratura e nel teatro in particolare del XX secolo. Vd. García Romero 2002: 187-204.

posizionare davanti alle porte della città di Troia uno dopo l'altro diversi tipi di cavallo di Troia ma questi vengono puntualmente incendiati. Subiscono cioè per contrappasso la sorte di Troia. Infine decidono di posizionare una Opel Corsa. Lo stratagemma ha successo. I Troiani aprono finalmente le porte della città e accolgono l'auto. I Greci, nascosti nel bagagliaio, possono conquistare la città.

Non è un caso che i due modelli a cui *Opel Troya* si ispira siano ricchi di immagini di città: il film *Troy* di Petersen per la vicenda e la regia e il cartone Disney *Hercules* per lo stile del disegno e dell'animazione bidimensionale. Le scene sono infatti costruite dall'animazione di pitture vascolari a figure nere secondo un modello ampiamente utilizzato nel cartone disneyano. Gli unici colori del filmato sono infatti il rosso e il nero eccetto per l'auto bianca. Anche le citazioni di *Troy* sono evidenti: già dai primi secondi l'inquadratura di una nave greca in navigazione si allarga fino a mostrare un'enorme flotta greca, come in una nota scena del film di Petersen resa ancora più celebre dal trailer del film.

Una Troia ricostruita digitalmente è stata la location di due campagne pubblicitarie di assicurazioni: la RAS diffuse uno spot (2003, Produzione Movie Magic) dove Ulisse a causa della mancanza degli strumenti giusti, riesce a costruire non un cavallo ma una matrioska, Anche la Liberty mutual assicurazioni (anno 2009) creò un video ambientato come *Opel Troya* alle porte della città, dove però i Troiani furbescamente rifiutano il dono del cavallo di Troia sospettando che si tratti di un inganno. L'ingresso di Ilio è il cuore anche dello spot *Troy* della birra Amstel del 2006, dove il cavallo di Troia rimane bloccato a causa dell'eccessiva altezza nella porta della città.

Un esempio nobile di pubblicità d'autore è il fortunato spot *Il diesel si scatena* del 1982 (agenzia Publicis) girato da Sergio Leone con musiche di Morricone. Nel video una Renault 18, dotata di vita propria per una riuscita prosopopea, al centro dell'arena dell'anfiteatro di El Jem in Tunisia (chiamato Colosseo), "si scatena" per liberarsi delle catene della lentezza dei motori diesel. La stessa ambientazione è stata poi riproposta e parodiata anche nel film *Attila Flagello di Dio* di Diego Abatantuono. Una struttura simile a questo spot d'autore presentano altri video basati sul motivo del Colosseo trasformato in una sorta di autodromo: quelli della Honda Odyssey (2007), della New Beetle (anni '60 e 2005) e della Mazda 6 (2010).

Anche città degli dei fanno da sfondo scenografico a prodotti commerciali: l'Olimpo, abitato da Ercole, Giove, Eolo e altri dei per esempio si trasforma nella ironica *location* della saga pubblicitaria intitolata *Findus. I piatti che sono diventati un mito* (2001), nel regno delle praline Ferrero Rocher (2008), abitato da golosi dei e dorato come il *packaging*, o nel misterioso mondo che si cela dentro un asciugacapelli quando si utilizza lo shampoo Thermasilk (2000). Non si segnalano solo città celebrate dalla letteratura classica ma anche città citate nella letteratura più moderna: la cittadina inglese di York, da dove nel 1652 Robinson Crusoe si sta per imbarcare insieme ai suoi compagni di viaggio, appare nello spot dei surgelati *4 Salti in padella Findus*. Negli spot appaiono anche distopie, come la Londra governata dalla dittatura del Grande Fratello immaginata da George Orwell. La grigia capitale britannica, dove tutti sono privati di ogni libertà, omologati e sorvegliati da migliaia di teleschermi, è protagonista del celebre spot della Apple intitolato *1984* e girato da Ridley Scott un anno dopo aver terminato le riprese di *Blade Runner*.

Ma la città, oltre che sfondo suggestivo e struttura di base del prodotto, può essere anche direttamente l'oggetto da promuovere. Numerose sono le campagne dalle istituzioni politiche a favore del turismo. Anche nell'ambito di queste campagne la cultura della città si sposa spesso con la cultura letteraria. Come esempio si può citare lo spot italiano della Presidenza del Consiglio dei Ministri[10] del 2000 nel quale la voce fuori campo legge un passo dal *De vita duodecim Caesarum* di Svetonio (*Nero* 31), mentre scorrono le immagini della Domus aurea.

Città globali. Tutto questo complesso di segni popolano l'industria e, diffondendosi in un mercato globale e globalizzato, affollano con sempre maggiore densità le strade, gli edifici e le architetture e perfino lo *skyline* urbano. Il campo visivo del cittadino si riempie dunque di elementi di altre città creando delle prospettive di meta-luoghi globali. Schegge di città deformate contaminano altre città e nel loro insieme, come in un gioco di specchi in continua mutazione, creano uno scenario urbano in cui i frammenti di identità tendono a riflettersi, a mescolarsi e a confondersi rendendo incerti i confini delle città. Come racconta Calvino ne *Le città invisibili*, la megalopoli diventa «città continua, uniforme, che va a coprire il mondo intero»[11], un'unica città «che non comincia e non finisce, cambia solo il nome all'aeroporto»[12].

Cartelloni, statici o animati, spot, insegne luminose, ma anche loghi automobilistici, per loro natura in continuo movimento, trasformano la città in una sorta di Babele architettonico-culturale dove ognuno, per sentirsi integrato nella società, deve appropriarsi di simboli culturali e dove in definitiva tutto è ridotto a mercato.

---

[10] De Martino 2010: 126.

[11] Così spiega l'autore nella Presentazione, p. IX.

[12] Così è descritta la città "continua" di Trude.

Città visibili
(Visible Cities)

Francesco de Martino (frademartino@alice.it)
Università di Foggia

Resumo – Non solo le grandi metropoli, da Troia in poi, ma anche le "nano-città" (Itaca, Ascra, Delo, ecc.), nonostante i loro espliciti difetti, reclamano "visibilità". La visibilità delle città trova precocemente espressione nella personificazione al femminile testimoniata sia nella letteratura, come per Delo nell'inno omerico *Ad Apollo*, sia nell'arte, come è testimoniato per Nemea e per altre città, specialmente Tebe. La storia delle personificazioni femminili delle città a partire dalla Grecia arcaica precede quella più massiccia di Roma oltre che quelle moderne di città italiane e straniere.

Parole chiave: metropoli, nano-città, personificazioni, Grecia

Abstract – Not only large *metropoleis*, from Troy onward, but also the "nano-cities" (Ithaca, Ascra, Delos, etc.), despite their explicit defects in detail, claim "visibility". An early expression of such visibility is the female personification of cities that is witnessed in literature, such as that of Delos in the Homeric *Hymn to Apollo*, or in art, as attested for Nemea and for other cities, notably Thebes. The history of female personifications of cities in archaic Greece precedes the better known example of Rome and those of modern cities, both Italian and foreign.

Keywords: metropolis, "nano-cities", personifications, Greece

Città invisibili. Sono le 55 di Italo Calvino, descritte da Marco Polo al Gran Khan: «tutte città inventate […] chiamate ognuna con un nome di donna», di solito grecheggianti, per esempio Teodora, Berenice e Pentesilea. Città immaginarie, "mentali", di uno scrittore con la mania per le città ma incapace di «stabilire rapporti personali con i luoghi» e che diceva: «resto sempre un po' a mezz'aria, sto nelle città con un piede solo»[1].

Le città visibili sono invece quelle vere, quelle di Renzo Piano che in più di quarant'anni ha cercato di recuperare la tradizione umanistica della città europea o di Ippodamo di Mileto, il primo grande architetto occidentale, che ideò la pianta a griglia per città con 10.000 abitanti, meno che nel teatro di Atene e solo un terzo degli inquilini di tre grattacieli di New York[2], ma dieci

---

[1] Calvino 1996: V-VI, XXXV, 156-157, e 1996. Vd. anche Gómez García 2010 e Affatato 2010. Analoghe città sono quelle nell'isola dei Beati (Luc. *VH* 1. 12-16).

[2] L'attenzione alle città è testimoniata già prima anche dai vari componimenti sulle *ktiseis*: *Fondazione di Colofone e Deduzione di colonia a Elea* di Senofane, *Smirneide* di Mimnermo, *Fondazione di Chio* di Ione di Chio, ecc. Una bella riflessione sull'età di una città è in Plut., *de sera num. vind.* 15. 559a-b.

https://doi.org/10.14195/978-989-26-1280-5_15

volte di più dei 1000 abitanti dell'immaginaria Doulopolis, la città-ghetto degli schiavi[3]. La sua città campione era Turi – la nuova Sibari – fondata nel 443 a.C. per volere di Pericle, la cui architettura influenzò anche Rodi e Alessandria. Ancora più innovativa era la città a piazza centrale con vie a raggiera del famoso astronomo-geometra Metone descritta in Aristofane (*Av.* 1004-1009).

«Una città più grande di Alessandria non esiste»[4]. Alessandria, Olimpia, Rodi, Efeso e Alicarnasso erano invece le cinque città più belle della Grecia, secondo una graduatoria stilata nel III sec. a.C., cinque delle sette meraviglie del mondo[5], precedute solo da Giza, alla periferia del Cairo, con la piramide di Cheope (c. 2570 a.C.), e da Babilonia con le sue mura e i famosi giardini pensili, che già dai tempi di Erodoto (1. 178-200 e 2. 124-129) suscitavano meraviglia. Ciò che rendeva quelle città greche meraviglie del mondo erano i monumenti meravigliosi: lo Zeus di Fidia ad Olimpia, il Mausoleo ad Alicarnasso, il Colosso a Rodi, il Faro ad Alessandria. Ottava meraviglia antica è Roma[6] col Colosseo, l'unico pezzo antico nelle sette meraviglie moderne, proclamate a Lisbona il 7.7.2007.

Ma l'intera Grecia è una terra delle meraviglie, grazie a poeti – a partire da Omero –, scrittori e geografi (Eraclide Critico, Strabone, Pausania, ecc.). Dopo la vittoria di Pidna su Perseo re della Macedonia nel 168 a.C., Lucio Emilio Paolo volle fare un *tour* in Grecia: «stabilì di utilizzare la parte iniziale di quella stagione per un viaggio intorno alla Grecia e per la visita di quei centri che, magnificati dalla fama (*nobilitata fama*), la tradizione ha fatto più grandiosi di quanto riveli la vista (*maiora auribus sunt, quam oculis*)». Gli appunti di viaggio (Liv. *Hist.* 45. 27-28 = T 360 Gualandi) sono una piccola "guida" su famosi centri greci: Delfi, Lebadia, Aulide, Oropo, Atene e Pireo, Corinto, Sicione, Argo, Epidauro, Lacedemone, Megalopoli, Demetriade.

Il primo grande monumento ad una città è l'*Iliade*, il poema di Ilio. Troia è una «città grande» (*Il.* 17. 160 *astu mega*), omonima di due del Portogallo e di una in provincia di Foggia, una "città vasta", "ben costruita", "con belle torri", "con porte maestose", "con belle mura", con strade larghe, scoscesa, ventosa. Ma soprattutto, come ha notato Gérard Genette (1997: 215), è l'unica vera città.

---

[3] St. Byz., s.v. δούλων πόλις : "città della Libia [...] alcuni dicono che sta a Creta e che è di 1000 uomini (χιλίανδρος)"; cf. Cratin. fr. 223. 2 K.-A. e Anaxandr. fr. 4 K.-A. Mnasone, amico di Aristotele, fece scalpore per aver comprato un migliaio di schiavi (Timae. *FGrHist* 566 F 11 = Ath. 6. 264c-d). "Di mille uomini" è anche la città nella quale mettere a frutto la scienza politica (Plat. *Plt.* 292e). Una curiosa città tutta di auleti è ipotizzata da Platone (*Prot.* 327a-c): Se una città potesse esistere soltanto a condizione che tutti fossimo suonatori di aulo, ecc.

[4] Nel *Romanzo di Alessandro* (*Vita Alex.* 1. 31.10) le misure di Alessandria sono sedici stadi e trecentonovantacinque piedi.

[5] Vd. Clayton 1989, Gualandi 2001: 312-325 (TT 168-183), Eco 2013: 65-96.

[6] Un elogio di Roma e della nuova Roma, cioè Bisanzio, è in una lettera di Crisolora, cf. Maltese-Cortassa 2000.

"Nell'*Iliade*, come dopo tutto (prima di tutto) indica il titolo, l'unica città è Troia, mentre gli Achei hanno semplicemente un «campo»: tende e navi". Infatti "una città è in primo luogo e quanto meno il punto in cui i guerrieri, fra una battaglia e l'altra, ritrovano nelle loro case le mogli e i figli". La descrivono Christopher Morley all'inizio del romanzo *Il cavallo di Troia* del 1937, tradotto nel 1940 da Cesare Pavese[7] e Italo Calvino per bocca di Marco Polo in uno dei corsivi che aprono e chiudono i capitoli de *Le città invisibili*. Marco Polo la vede come la vecchia Costantinopoli e «dalla mescolanza di quelle due città ne risultava una terza, che potrebbe chiamarsi San Francisco e protendere ponti lunghissimi e leggeri sul Cancello d'Oro e sulla baia, e arrampicare tramvai a cremagliera per vie tutte in salita, e fiorire come capitale del Pacifico di lì a un millennio, dopo il lungo assedio di trecento anni che porterebbe le razze dei gialli e dei neri e dei rossi a fondersi insieme alla superstite progenie dei bianchi in un impero più vasto di quello del Gran Kan» (Calvino 1996: 139-140).

Città leggendaria, fino a quando nel 1872, Heinrich Schliemann annunciò la scoperta dei resti della città di Omero, la settima (1250-1200 a.C.) distrutta da un incendio, situata nella provincia Hisarlik, non distante da Canakkale sullo stretto dei Dardanelli. Metropoli orientale, ponte per l'Occidente, Troia diventa il paradigma della città in guerra, l'opposto dell'isola dei Feaci, la città neutrale. Nella *Mappa Mundi* di Hereford[8], la più grande mappa medievale della Terra (c. 1300), la città turrita presenta una sventolante bandiera bianca, tipica della resa, ed è accompagnata dalla didascalia: *Troia civitas bellicosa*[9].

Iconograficamente Troia diventa un fondale: mura, dalle quali esponenti della famiglia reale guardano cosa avviene fuori o dalle quali far entrare il cavallo di Troia, o città in fiamme. Il tema delle fiamme doveva essere sviluppato nella *Distruzione di Ilio* attribuita ad Arctino di Mileto. Ma delle fiamme di Troia si parla anche in *Od.* 22. 411: «Sembrava proprio che da cima a fondo / la dirupata Ilio fosse tutta in fiamme (*puri*)» (trad. G. Cerri). La scena tipica è con Troia in fiamme sullo sfondo e in primo piano Enea in fuga con i suoi familiari. In un olio su tavola di El Greco in primo piano c'è *Laocoonte* (c. 1610-1614), ma sullo sfondo al posto di Troia è raffigurata Toledo, la città nella quale il pittore cretese si era stabilito e dove morì.

Persino lo Scamandro, uno dei due fiumi di Troia col Simoenta (*Il.* 5. 774), va in fiamme, un tema sfruttato nella pittura pompeiana del 30 a.C. nella Casa

---

[7] "È la città più famosa della Terra, e appartiene quindi a tutti quanti, e a tutti i tempi. Dovete edificarvela da voi. Drizzatela su di un pendìo rupestre, sopra uno stretto di acqua verde e gorgogliante. Stendeteci sopra il vostro cielo favorito; fornitela degli uccelli e dei fiori, dei suoni e dei sentori, che vi sono più familiari. Per un istante, fermatevi alle cose essenziali: la vostra freschezza dell'aria aprica, l'alito del pino, della felce e del cedro, la smagliante distesa azzurra del mare lontano, la serpe sul sasso ancor tiepido nel crepuscolo".

[8] Cf. Zanichelli 2005: fig. 7.

[9] Cf. Westrem 2001: 132 e fig. 7.

del Criptoportico, in una statua del II sec. d.C. ed in una miniatura dell'*Iliade* Ambrosiana (V-VI d.C.)[10]. In Omero il fiume parla, «supplica il dio» (*Il.* 21. 357-360), un dettaglio ripreso in un'*ekphrasis* di Filostrato Maggiore (1. 1 *Scamandro* = T 217 Gualandi):

> *"Questa è la città alta e questa è la rocca di Ilio, questa è la vasta pianura capace di contenere l'Asia schierata contro l'Europa, questo è il fuoco che, sterminato, invade la pianura e in gran parte serpeggia attorno alle rive del fiume, al punto che non vi sono più alberi. E ormai il fuoco che Efesto porta con sé, scivola sull'acqua e il fiume ne soffre e supplica il dio. Il fiume, però, non è dipinto con le chiome, perché sono state bruciate, né Efesto è dipinto zoppicante, perché sta correndo e la fiamma del fuoco non è rosseggiante e non ha l'aspetto consueto, ma è dorata e solare."* (trad. G. Schilardi)

Itaca. Non meno "visibili" sono anche le città piccole e brutte, città-senza, piene di difetti, e tuttavia amate. L'esempio migliore è Itaca, una "nano-città" di periferia, piccola e rocciosa. Due volte è chiamata *astu* (*Od.* 18. 1-2, 22. 223), più spesso *demos* qualcosa come "pueblo" in spagnolo (13. 97, 14. 329, 15. 534, 16. 419, 19. 399, 22. 52). Ma, per quanto piccola, è di grandissimo valore, insostituibile. Elena, Odisseo, Telemaco e Atena non nascondono i difetti di Itaca, ma «non c'è nulla di più dolce» di essa. Come si dice in Italia, «casa mia, casa mia, per piccina che tu sia, tu mi sembri una badia». In *Od.* 9. 21 e 13. 234 Omero usa per Itaca l'aggettivo «visibile (*eudeielos*)», usato anche per Crisa (*h. Hom. Ap.* 438). Per una città come per un eroe o un poeta la questione è il "nome". Come dice Atena, quello di Itaca, «senza nome» ma non troppo, «è arrivato fino a Troia» (*Od.* 13. 239 e 248).

Il. 3. 200-201: Elena *cresciuto* (*sc.* Odisseo) *nel demo di Itaca, benché tutta rocciosa*.

Od. 1. 247: Telemaco *e quanti signoreggiano in Itaca rocciosa*; 4. 174-177: Menelao *E nell'Argolide gli avrei dato una città e costruito un palazzo / trasferendolo d'Itaca i suoi beni, col figlio, / con tutta la popolazione, svuotando una delle città / che abitano qui intorno, e che sono sotto la mia personale signoria*; 4. 605-608: Telemaco *Ad Itaca non ci sono strade larghe né prati: / terra da capre, ma più cara di terra da cavalli. / Nessun'isola è adatta a carri o ricca di prati / di quante stanno sul mare: Itaca meno di tutte*; 9. 21-28: Odisseo *Abito Itaca visibile: in essa c'è un monte, / il Nèrito frondoso, di spicco: intorno isole / molte ci stanno, vicine una all'altra, /*

---

[10] Cf. Schilardi 1997: 226-227. Eliano (*VH* 2. 33) fornisce una scheda sull'iconografia umana e bovina dei fiumi e delle sorgenti. Plinio ricorda il pittore Enico, forse di scuola neoattica, che dipinse un Oceano e il pittore Studius o Ludius di età augustea specializzato in paesaggi (*Nat.* 36. 33 e 35. 116). Vitruvio (7. 5) ricorda che si usava dipingere porti, promontori, rive, fiumi, sorgenti, stretti, santuari, boschi sacri, montagne.

Dulichìo, Same e Zacinto selvosa. / Ma bassa, estrema là, nel mare, / verso la notte: le altre più avanti verso aurora e sole. / Aspra, ma buona nutrice di giovani e io nulla / più dolce di quella terra riesco a vedere [11]. 13. 233-249: Odisseo: «[…] *Che terra? Che paese? Che uomini vivono qui? / È un'isola visibile (eudeielos) oppure una punta, / giace distesa nel mare, del continente dalle grosse zolle?».* / *Gli rispose la dea Atena glaucopide: / «Sei ingenuo, straniero, o vieni da lontano,/ se mi domandi di questa terra. Davvero non è / tanto sconosciuta* (νώνυμος), *ma la conoscono moltissimi, / sia quanti abitano verso l'aurora e il sole, / sia quanti vivono in fondo verso l'ombra nebbiosa. / È aspra e non adatta ai cavalli; / non è troppo spoglia, ma non è molto vasta. / C'è grano infinito, c'è vino / e sempre pioggia la bagna e umidità abbondante. / È buona nutrice di capre e di buoi: e una selva / c'è, d'ogni tipo di piante: pozzi perenni ci sono. / Sì, straniero, il nome* (ὄνυμ') *d'Itaca fino a Troia è arrivato, / che dicono è lontana dalla terra d'Acaia!».* 13. 344-351: Atena «*Su, ti mostrerò la terra di Itaca, perché tu mi creda. / Questo è il porto di Forchis, del Vecchio marino, / questo in cima al porto l'***olivo*** frondoso, / e qui vicino l'antro amabile oscuro / sacro alle Ninfe che si chiamano Naiadi; / questo è lo speco vasto coperto, dove tu spesso / facevi alle Ninfe perfette ecatombi. / E questo è il Nerito, il monte vestito di boschi*».

h. Hom. Ap. 428: «la montagna sublime di Itaca».

Ascra. Come Itaca (e come Tomi, Ovid. *Ep. ex Ponto* 4. 14) anzi proprio «brutta» è Ascra: *Ascra, brutta (kaken) d'inverno, difficile d'estate, mai splendida* (Hes. *Op.* 640). Al contrario di Ulisse, Esiodo si è allontanato da Ascra solo una volta per andare ad Aulide, il porto internazionale ma da cui parte per andare non a Troia ma a Calcide, a strappare il successo nella gara poetica per i funerali di Anfidamante[12]: *Aulide, dove una volta gli Achei / aspettando la fine della tempesta, una vasta armata raccolsero, / dall'Ellade sacra contro Troia dalle belle donne; / là io per le gare in onore del forte Anfidamante / per Calcide m'imbarcai* (*Op.* 651-655). Cf. Menand. I, 347. 27 Spengel.

---

[11] Su Itaca omerica e Itaca storica e sulle critiche di Strabo 10. 2.8-9, cf. Heubeck 1983: 182-183.

[12] Di Aulide abbiamo la descrizione liviana nel resoconto del viaggio di Lucio Emilio Paolo in Grecia: *Aulide, posta alla distanza di tre miglia, porto famoso per esservi un tempo rimasto alla fonda il migliaio di navi della flotta di Agamennone e visitò il tempio di Diana, dove quel famoso re dei re [chiese] per le sue navi la possibilità di veleggiare verso Troia, portando sull'altare come vittima la propria figlia* (Liv. *Hist.* 45. 27). Nel passo vengono anche descritte Atene, Lacedemone e Corinto: *Atene, città anch'essa piena di fama antica, ma che comunque possiede anche molti monumenti degni d'esser veduti, l'acropoli, i porti, le mura, effigi di dei e di uomini, notevoli per l'impiego di materiali d'ogni genere e delle tecniche più disparate* (45. 27; trad. Gualandi); *Lacedemone, città degna di memoria non tanto per la magnificenza delle opere d'arte, quanto per la ferrea disciplina delle sue istituzioni* (45. 28); *La città* (= Corinto) *era insigne allora, prima della distruzione; anche l'acropoli e l'Istmo gli offrirono un grande spettacolo: l'acropoli all'interno delle mura, che si eleva a notevole altezza, ricca di fonti; l'Istmo che divide due bracci di mare vicini [da] ovest e da est con una sottile lingua di terra* (45. 28; trad. I. Gualandi).

Delo. Come Itaca, e come Ascra, anche Delo è "invisibile", un luogo di nessun valore. Ma un avvenimento la rende visibile, la trasforma in un luogo famoso. Leto, in procinto di partorire il grande Apollo, propone un "affare" alla poverissima isola, che l'accetta ammettendo di essere una terra "senza" e esplicitando le varie cose che non ha:

> *h. Hom. Ap.* 50-72: Leto «*Delo, vorresti essere la dimora di mio figlio, / Febo Apollo, e accogliere in te un pingue tempio? / Nessun altro mai si occuperà di te, né ti onorerà; / e io credo che tu non sarai davvero ricca di armenti, né di greggi, / né porterai raccolti, né produrrai molti alberi. / Ma se tu ospiti un tempio di Apollo arciere, / tutti gli uomini ti porteranno ecatombi / qui riunendosi; e da te sempre un infinito aroma / di grasso si leverà, e tu potrai nutrire il tuo popolo / per mano di stranieri: perché non hai ricchezza nel tuo suolo.» / Così parlava; e Delo ne fu rallegrata, e rispondendo diceva: / Delo «[...] infatti, io sono eccessivamente oscura (dyseches) / fra gli uomini; così invece diventerei famosa (peritimeessa). [...] temo assai, nella mente e nel cuore, / che, quando egli vedrà per la prima volta la luce del sole, / dispregiando l'isola (neson atimesas) – poiché io sono invero una terra rocciosa –, / calcandomi coi piedi mi sprofondi nelle acque del mare*» (trad. F. Cassola).

Rispetto a semplici metafore che presuppongono personificazioni di città[13] o a mere ipotesi di prosopopee[14], Delo è nell'inno *persona loquens*[15]. Tra le parallele personificazioni nell'arte, le quali la più sicura – grazie all'iscrizione di identità – è quella su una *pyxis* attica a figure rosse, conservata a Ferrara, Museo Archeologico (inv. 20298) con Leto, Artemide e Delo (ΔΗΛΟΣ) con una fiale, seduta su un *omphalos*. La scena sembra testimoniare la stessa politica ateniese di avvicinamento tra Delo e Delfi, implicata dall'inno[16].

Permettendo a Leto di partorire Apollo, e ricevendo in cambio la fondazione del Santuario, Delo ormai città natale del dio diventa per questo il luogo

---

[13] Sulla *fictio personae*, cf. Lausberg 1990: 411-413. Degl'Innocenti Pierini 2012: 217-220 ricorda la personificazione di città dell'oratore greco Carisio, imitatore di Lisia (Rut. Lup. 2. 6), alcune espressioni omeriche (*Il.* 2. 117-118, 9. 24-25 «ha (sc. Zeus) spezzato la testa di molte città», 16. 100 «sciogliere il velo sacro di Troia», *Od.* 13. 388 sciogliemmo i ricchi veli di Troia, cf. Yatromanolakis 2005: 269ss.) che presuppongono la personificazione femminile di città, favorita dal fatto che *polis, patris, gaia* sono femminili, e la metafora biologica e organologica in riferimento a città (Solone, Teognide, Pindaro, Platone, Isocrate, Demostene, Dinarco, Iperide). Sulla personificazione in generale, cf. Shapiro 1993, Messerschmidt 2003, Stafford-Herrin 2005, Moretti 2007, Smyth 2011.

[14] Arist. *Rhet.* 3. 1411a la Grecia gridò, la Grecia si tagliasse i capelli, ecc., Ps.Demetr. περὶ Ἑρμ. 265 *Immaginate che i vostri antenati o l'Ellade o la vostra terra natale, assumendo la forma di una donna, così vi rispondesse e così vi rimproverasse* (citazione da autore ignoto). Altre ipotesi in Cic. *Catil.* 1. 27 e *Rhet. ad Her.* 4. 53. 66.

[15] Smyth 2011: 34-35. Per Delo in *AP* 9. 100, 408, 421, cf. Degl'Innocenti Pierini 2012: 235. Parlante è Roma in Luc. *Phar.* 1. 285ss.

[16] Vd. de Santerre 1976; contra Bruneau 1985, e *LIMC* III, 1 (1986): 368-369, s.v. *Delos* e II, 2: 270.

preferito da Apollo, che pure ne frequenta e ne ama molti. Dopo aver elencato le varie tappe, il Cinto, le isole, le cime, i fiumi, il poeta infatti dice:

> 140-150: *E tu, o signore dall'arco d'argento, che colpisci lontano, / ora ti recavi sull'impervio Cinto / ora vagavi per le isole e tra gli uomini; / molti templi ti appartengono, e boschi sacri folti di alberi, / e ti sono care tutte le cime, le alte vette / dei monti sublimi, e i fiumi che si versano in mare: / ma tu, o Febo, più che di ogni altro luogo, ti compiaci nel tuo cuore di Delo, / dove per te si adunano gli Ioni dalle lunghe tuniche / coi loro figli e con le nobili spose; / essi, col pugilato, la danza ed il canto, / ti allietano, ricordandosi di te, quando bandiscono l'agone.* (trad. F. Cassola)

Delo diventa una "nano-meraviglia", proprio grazie al santuario e al festival che ospita e al «grande *thauma*», cioè le Deliadi professioniste dell'imitazione (156-164).

Cartea a Ceo. Un'altra città brutta è Cartea a sud-est dell'isola di Ceo, una della tetrapoli o pentapoli dell'isola, come la più nota Iulide, patria di Simonide e di Bacchilide.

Cartea era sede di un tempio di Apollo (Ath. 10. 84). Pindaro (*Pae.* 4. 11-13, 21-34) la descrive come uno «scoglio», ma migliore di Babilonia:

> [...] *Delo famosa* [...] *piccolo petto della terra* [...] *non permuto con Babilonia* [...] *sebbene abiti uno scoglio, sono famosa fra gli Elleni per la bravura negli agoni, sono famosa anche perché offro materia di canto. Se anche sul suolo mi reca il dono di vita Dioniso che è sollievo all'indigenza, non posseggo cavalli e non sono adatta all'allevamento degli armenti* [...] *La città nativa e (il focolare) e la sua stirpe ami l'uomo, e ne sia pago: è da stolti (bramare) le cose lontante*[17] (trad. G. Bona).

Babilonia era una delle sette meraviglie del mondo antico. "Cartea e Babilonia sono come i due poli d'un'antitesi: piccola e cara la prima, ricca ma lontana la seconda: il vicino e familiare, per piccolo che sia, è sempre preferibile ad un lontano Eldorado" (Bona 1988: 77). La dichiarazione di amore per la patria è in un *Peana* posposto all'*Istmica* 1 per Erodoto di Tebe, suo concittadino, perché *cos'è più caro per i buoni dei diletti genitori?* (*Pae.* 4. 5)[18]. Come "pegno", Pindaro si impegna a concluderle insieme le due odi, unite anche dal riferimento al topos dell'amor di patria. Le città grandi sono città lontane, quelle piccole sono vicine, sono la patria.

La nozione di "permuta" della patria non era una stranezza in una società con frequenti fondazioni e rifondazioni. Nell'elegia *Salamina* Solone polemicamente

---

[17] Il topos è diffuso: Archiloco, fr. 19 West², Pi. *P.* 3. 20-22 e 4. 92, *N.* 2. 48. Vd. anche Thgn. 783-788.

[18] Per Artem. 4. 60 sognare la città natia significa sognare i genitori.

esprimeva un desiderio irrealizzabile: *magari fossi di Folegandro o di Sicino, cambiando patria* (fr. 2 Gentili-Prato² = fr. 2 West²). Saffo, quando dice di non voler cambiare la figlia con la Lidia intera, usa lo stesso topos, come se Cleide fosse la sua "patria" (fr. 132 Voigt).

Una permuta di città è ipotizzata per sé anche da Temistocle, in polemica con Timodemo, che gli rinfacciava di aver avuto onori dagli Spartani solo perché ateniese:

> Hdt. 8. 125.2: *Poiché Timodemo non smetteva di parlare così, Temistocle disse: «È proprio vero; se io fossi belbinite, non sarei tanto onorato dagli spartiati, né tu, amico, benché tu sia ateniese.»* (trad. A. Masaracchia)

In altre fonti Timodemo è di Serifo, isoletta delle Cicladi:

> Pl. *R.* 329e-330a: *E torna buona la frase di Temistocle rivolta a quel tale di Sèrifo che l'offendeva e gli diceva che a suo parere la fama di cui godeva gli veniva non dal merito personale, ma dalla città in cui era nato: gli rispose Temistocle che quanto a sé, se fosse stato di Sèrifo, non sarebbe, no, diventato famoso, ma non lo sarebbe diventato nemmeno quell'altro, anche se fosse stato di Atene.*

> Plu. *Them.* 18. 5: *E quando quel tale di Serifo gli disse che doveva la sua fama non a se stesso, ma alla sua città, replicò: «È vero; ma come io non sarei divenuto famoso se fossi stato di Serifo, così neppure tu se fossi stato di Atene».* (trad. C. Carena)

> Cic. *Sen.* 3. 8: Catone *«Eh sì, caro Lelio, questi privilegi valgono qualcosa, ma non sono certamente tutto. Per esempio, si racconta che Temistocle, in un litigio, abbia risposto a uno di Serifo che gli rimproverava di aver raggiunto lo splendore per gloria non sua, ma della patria: «Mai, perdio, disse, sarei diventato famoso se fossi di Serifo, ma nemmeno tu, se fossi di Atene»* (trad. P. Sanasi).

Tra le tante permute di città la più antica e la più bizzarra è quella immaginata da Menelao tra Itaca ed una città migliore vicina a Sparta dove trapiantarvi Odisseo (*Od.* 4. 174-177, cit. *supra*). Più semplicemente, nell'ambasceria suo fratello Agamennone offriva ad Achille in moglie una delle proprie figlie a scelta e sette città (*Il.* 9. 286-298).

Città pindariche. Cartea a Ceo è come Itaca e come Delo, un luogo minore che acquista visibilità grazie ad un evento. In *Pae.* 4 Ceo si descrive così: *sebbene abiti uno scoglio, sono famosa fra gli Elleni per la bravura negli agoni, sono famosa anche perché offro materia di canto* (4. 21). Pindaro promuove varie altre città: Agrigento è *bellissima (kallista) fra le città mortali* (*P.* 12. 1), Cirene è *bellissima (kallistan) e famosa per i giochi* (*P.* 9. 69-70). Abdera dice: *io sono città nuova (neopolis)* (*Pae.* 2. 28). Cf. *Pae.* 6. 1. 123-125 *o aurea Pito* [...] *Isola* (= Egina) *dal nome famoso che* *domini il mare dorico*; *P. 2. 1 O Siracusa grande città (megalopolies)*; *P. 7. 1-2 Bellissimo (kalliston) preludio la grande città di Atene (hai megalopolies)*; *I. 1. 1 Madre mia, Tebe, dall'aureo suolo, I. 7. 1 O Tebe, beata; I. 8. 15a-21 deve, chi a Tebe con sette porte è cresciuto, / offrire ad Egina il fior delle Cariti, / perché furono figlie / gemelle d'un padre, ultime / tra le figlie d'Asopo, e al re Zeus piacquero. / Egli pose l'una sulla bella / corrente di Dirce, qual regina / d'una città che ama i carri (philarmatou polios) / e si giacque con te, dopo averti portata / nell'isola Enopia* (trad. G.A. Privitera). Tebe ed Egina sono le due gemelle, ultime figlie di Asopo[19].

La *Pitica* 1 per Ierone di Siracusa vincitore a Delfi con le quadrighe (470 a.C.) è eseguita ad Etna per festeggiarne la recente fondazione della città, con gli ex coloni di Catania e altri coloni di stirpe dorica. Anche le *Etnee* di Eschilo erano un omaggio alla nuova città. Nell'*Olimpica* 5, per Psaumide di Camarina, vincitore col carro di mule (460 o 456 a.C.), Pindaro descrive nel dettaglio la struttura urbanistica della nuova città di Camarina, ricostruita nel 461/460 a.C.: il bosco, il lago, il fiume Ippari, i canali, i tetti: "Vivida è l'immagine della città e delle sue case alte a vedersi e folte come una selva (*halsos*) e del sacro, benefico fiume che la irriga a nord-ovest, l'Ippari, fertile di limo che feconda la terra circostante e serve anche a cementare come materiale coesivo la moltitudine delle nuove dimore (cfr. v. 8), che il poeta indica non a caso come talami, quasi anticipando l'augurio di prolificità rivolto poco dopo (v. 22 sg.) a Psaumide per aver contribuito con la sua vittoria alla rinascita di Camarina"[20].

Le città sono belle o brutte, come Ascra *kake*. Città femminili non meravigliano, dal momento che solitamente, anche se non sempre, hanno una ninfa o una naiade eponima. Le città sono donne ed è probabile che la *persona loquens* in Alc. fr. 10 Voigt sia Mitilene, non una donna vera[21].

Le tette della città. Come abbiamo visto, in un *Peana* (4. 14) Pindaro usa l'espressione *piccolo petto della terra*: "Il vocabolo in questo luogo pare indicare il breve altopiano su cui sorge Cartea, e non è da escludere una certa umanizzazione, non priva d'un contenuto affettivo, in questo parlare di 'petto' della terra"[22].

Allo stesso modo, nella *Pitica* 4 per la vittoria col carro di Arcesilao IV, re di Cirene a Delfi (462 a.C.), Pindaro definisce Cirene *città dai bei carri / sopra una candida mammella [enarginoenti masto(i)]* (v. 8). La stessa metafora torna secoli dopo in Nonno per descrivere il "paesaggio mammellonare"[23].

---

¹⁹ Privitera 1982: 231 (sugli epiteti di Tebe).

²⁰ Gentili 1995: LXV e n. 1.

²¹ De Martino-Vox 1996: 1334-1338 e Yatromanolakis 2005, Degl'Innocenti Pierini 2012: 219-220, per la quale i femminili *polis*, *patris* e *gaia* hanno favorito la personificazione femminile dei territori.

²² Bona 1988: 76.

²³ Elliger 1975, Waern 1951 e soprattutto Gigli 1985: 195-202. Per il paesaggio Nonno usa anche altre metafore corporali (schiena, unghie, piedi, caviglia, ecc.).

Città vestite. Se le città sono donne, esse non hanno solo le tette, ma anche abiti femminili. La metafora del mantello è già in *Od.* 13. 338 (cf. *h. Hom. Cer.* 151, Hdt. 7. 139). Le mura sono «il vestito della città» (Ath. 3. 99d) o un capo *di lino di Gaza* (Nonn. *D.* 26. 55-58) o *fila di torri dal mantello di lino* (Dyonis. *Bass.* fr. 4.1-2 Heitsch). Le mura di Atene vengono rivestite *come da un mantello* (Nonn. *D.* 32. 158), cioè fuori metafora dal tripudio delle mani e dei colori. Ma più spesso le mura sono la "corona" della città (*D.* 41. 268). La corona muraria caratterizzerà anche Roma e la Statua dell'Italia a Reggio Calabria e l'iconografia sui francobolli. Una delle prime rappresentazioni dell'Italia turrita si troverebbe nell'*Iconologia* di Cesare Ripa, un illustratore del Rinascimento esperto di allegorie: *Iconologia overo Descrittione Dell'imagini Universali cavate dall'Antichità et da altri luoghi*, (Heredi di Giovanni Gigliotti, Roma, 1593). In epoca più moderna venne realizzata, all'inizio del '900, dall'artista e disegnatore Daniele Fontana (Milano 1900-1984).

Vestire le città diventò una necessità concreta nel teatro comico[24]. Menandro Retore (2: 381. 13-15 Spengel) quando ipotizza *se fosse possibile dare voce alle città e assumere figure di donne come nei drammi…*, fa riferimento a città comiche[25]. Isole sono personificate in commedie (Epich. *Nasoi*, Ar. *Nesoi*, Plat. Com. *Hellas e Nesoi*) e *poleis* nelle quattro commedie intitolate *Città* (Eup.[26], Anaxandr., Phil. o Philuim., Eunic.). Nelle *Città* di Eupoli il coro della città della lega Delio-Attica doveva avere una maschera ed un vestito specifici.

Città monetali. Il fenomeno della personificazione delle città era presente anche nell'iconografia. La statua di Tyche/Fortuna di Antiochia è considerata modello dell'iconografia di Roma[27]. Ma il "più antico documento archeologico della presenza di Fortuna a Praeneste è fornito dai fregi delle sime fittili dei templi presso S. Rocco e S. Lucia databili già alla fine del VI sec. a.C., poco prima della comparsa delle divinità cittadine sui documenti monetali"[28].

Messana "auriga" femminile di una biga di mule (fine del V sec. a.C.); Kyme (lett. Gravida, cf. Parthenope "Vergine") campana; Hyele per Velia vicino Salerno, Terina nel Brutium, Aegeste per Segesta, Himera ("Desideria"), Camarina, esaltata da Pindaro (*O.* 5. 4). Anfione di Cnosso aveva inoltre realizzato ad Atene un monumento per Delfi nel decennio 430-420 a.C. Esso raffigurava Cirene che guidava la quadriga del re Batto incoronato da Libia. Cirene era la regina della Libia e la madre di Aristeo, concepito con Apollo (Paus. 10. 15.6).

---

[24] In A. *Pers.* Atossa sogna Europa ed Asia (vv. 181-195) ben vestite con pepli persiani e dorici.

[25] I comici amano descrivere città immaginarie. Negli *Uccelli* Aristofane mette al centro la costruzione di una città aerea, Nubicuculia.

[26] Storey 2003: 216-229. Le città certe erano: Tenos, Chio, Cizico e forse Amorgo. *Éupolis* è il nome di un'associazione italiana in difesa delle piccole città.

[27] Vd. Moretti 2007.

[28] Caccamo Caltabiano 2003: 141.

Pindaro dunque personificava città, già personificate sulle monete, quelle monete che tanto peso avevano nella committenza e negli appalti dei poeti di successo, come lui.

Demos. Nella storia delle personificazioni, Sparta tendeva a personificare piuttosto sentimenti e atteggiamenti, come la Paura o il Riso. Aristofane personificò invece Demos nei *Cavalieri* e lo stesso fecero ad Atene alcuni artisti famosi del IV sec. (Eufranore, Leocare, Lisone). Le fonti sono Plinio e Pausania.

> Pl. *Nat.* 35. 69 (= T 63 Gualandi): (*sc.* Parrasio, *fl.* IV sec.) *dipinse il* Popolo degli Ateniesi (*Demon Atheniensium*) *con una risorsa pittorica davvero ingegnosa* (*argumento ingenioso*). *Infatti lo mostrava di carattere variabile: iracondo, ingiusto, incostante, al tempo stesso placabile, clemente, misericordioso, vanitoso, sublime, umile, feroce, timido e tutto questo insieme* (trad. R. Mugellesi).

> Paus. 1. 1.3: *Dietro il lungo portico* (*sc.* del Pireo), *dove c'è il mercato per quelli che abitano sul mare* (*infatti coloro che abitano lontano dal porto dispongono di un altro mercato*), *dietro il portico sul mare, dunque si trovano le statue di Zeus e del Demos, opera di Leocare* (*fl.* 368 a.C.); 1. 3.5: *in questo edificio* (*sc.* il *bouleuterion*) *si conservano anche una statua lignea di Zeus, una statua di Apollo, opera di Pisia, e una del Demos, opera di Lisone*; 1. 33.3-4: *Dietro* (*sc.* al portico del re) *si erge un altro portico, dove sono dipinti i cosiddetti Dodici Dei; sul muro al di là sono dipinti Teseo, la Democrazia e il Demos».* (trad. D. Musti)

Nemea. Proprio di Atene è l'unico artista greco che personificò una città. L'unico dipinto da parete con una città personificata di cui abbiamo notizia è infatti quello di Nicia. La fonte è Plinio:

> 35. 27 *Augusto nella Curia, che egli inaugurava nel Comizio, murò due quadri nelle pareti:* Nemea, *seduta su di un leone e con una palma in mano presso un vecchio appoggiato al bastone; sul capo del vecchio pende un quadretto con una biga. Nicia dice, con un'iscrizione, di averla dipinta lui a encausto; adopera infatti questa parola greca.*
> 130 [...] *La sua* (*sc.* di Antidotos) *gloria maggiore è stata l'aver avuto come scolaro Nicia Ateniese, espertissimo pittore di donne.* 131. *Curò scrupolosamente il giuoco delle luci e delle ombre, e massimamente curò che la pittura avesse rilievo. Le opere di lui: la* Nemea, *portata d'Asia a Roma da Silano e posta nella Curia come dicemmo* [...] (Plin. *Nat.* 35. 27 e 130-131; trad. S. Ferri).

Il primato fra le città di quelle che erano sede di festival è confermato da Callimaco nel *Giambo* 6, dove descrive con pignoleria di architetto l'attrattiva di Olimpia, cioè lo Zeus di Fidia, una delle sette meraviglie del mondo.

Città personificate nell'arte. Altre personificazioni di qualche interesse sono quelle orientali. Antiochia sarà modello della Roma personificata[29] e persino "parlante" – come il fiume Scamandro – in Lucano. Ad essa si può aggiungere la personificazione di Edessa in un mosaico locale.

Alessandria è personificata nel mosaico centrale del pavimento (III-II a.C.), trovato nell'antica Thmuis[30], ora al Museo di Alessandria, con la firma «Sophilos faceva». Imponente e molto colorata, ha in testa una corona a forma di prua di nave da guerra[31], in quanto città marinara.

Una città piccola della Pentapoli era Olbia, in Libia, nota solo per la visita del vescovo Sinesio nel VI sec. Ma proprio nel VI sec., tra il 539 e il 540, il vescovo Makarios, commissionò un ciclo di mosaici, in occasione della "ri-fondazione" dell'antica città in una nuova città, chiamata Theodorias, in omaggio all'imperatrice Teodora, la moglie di Giustiniano. Ma la "targa" di Makarios è accompagnata da un'altra targa del vescovo Teodoro, che evidentemente subentrò al precedente. Il ciclo si apre con il Faro di Alessandria (= fig. 143 Guarducci), una delle sette meraviglie, costruito nell'isola di Faro di fronte al porto di Alessandria d'Egitto, nel III sec. a.C. (300-280 a.C.) dal mercante Sostrato di Cnido, all'inizio del regno di Tolomeo I Sotere e completato dal figlio Tolomeo II Filadelfo. Fu distrutto da due terremoti nel XIV sec.

Il Sole punta la spada sulla meridiana e indica l'itinerario. Seguono i fiumi personificati Geone (fig. 144 Guarducci) e Fisone (fig. 145 Guarducci), Tigri e Eufrate. Tra Geone e Fisone c'è la personificazione di Rinnovamento (Ananeosis) e tra Tigri ed Eufrate la ninfa Castalia. Segue l'ingresso di una città con torri, con una tenda sui cui bordi si legge da una parte *polis nea* e dall'altra *Theodorias*. Due pannelli laterali presentano due altre personificazioni: Fondazione (*Ktisis*), che offre una corona, e Toletta (*Kosmesis*) che sparge incenso. Teodoriade, la Città nuova, è la città di Teodora, ma è anche etimologicamente la città celeste "Dono di Dio"[32]. Interessante la personificazione di Toletta, in riferimento ad una città. Un'orazione di Dione Crisostomo (47: *Demegoria in patria*) ha come tema proprio la toletta di Prusa, la sua città natale, cioè l'abbellimento con nuovi monumenti e strutture[33].

Tebe e le sue porte sono descritte creativamente già nei *Sette a Tebe* di Eschilo. Nell'arte l'iconografia è più convenzionale. Su un'urna etrusca dell'inizio del I sec. a.C. (Perugia, Museo Nazionale 321, cf. *LIMC*, s.v. *Menoikeus*) sono

---

[29] Come suo modello è indicato anche il culto orientale di Demos o la Tyche di Antiochia di età ellenistica.

[30] Nel basso Egitto sul canale orientale del Nilo.

[31] Brown 1957: 67-68, 70-74 e tavv. 38, 40.

[32] Guarducci 1978: 476-481 e figg. 143-145.

[33] Cf. anche le orazioni 40 e 45. 12-14.

raffigurate le mura con i difensori[34]. Filostrato Maggiore (*Im.* 1. 4.1-2 = T 23 Gualandi) descrive un quadro con l'assedio di Tebe:

> *ecco infatti le mura con le sette porte e l'esercito di Polinice [...] Piacevole è l'artificio del pittore che, collocando sulle mura degli uomini armati, alcuni li fa vedere interi, altri coperti fino alle gambe, di altri si vede solo il petto, di altri solo la testa, poi gli elmi, infine le aste. Ragazzo mio, questa sì che è prospettiva: bisogna infatti ingannare con opportuni piani pittorici gli occhi che percorrono il quadro.* (trad. G. Schilardi)

Molto originale è una pittura murale scoperta nel 1933 ad Ermopoli in Egitto in una tomba datata alla tarda età di Adriano. È un tentativo di raccontare più momenti del mito, reinterpretando il mito come ricerca di se stesso. A destra Edipo uccide Laio. Entrambi sono identificati da un'iscrizione. A sinistra Edipo nudo e con un mantello allacciato alla spalla con il dito della mano destra puntato alla fronte. Di fronte la Sfinge su un basamento con cornici. Ai suoi piedi teschi. A destra Edipo uccide il padre Laio in ginocchio e di spalle, non come al solito sul carro. Al centro TEBE (con iscrizione di identità), riccioluta e rivolta a destra con espressione di spavento, non sappiamo se seduta perché manca la parte inferiore. Agnoia (Ignoranza) con tunica e manto, arrotolato sui fianchi, e annodato sul davanti, volge lo sguardo, spaventata, verso Laio ma ha le braccia e le mani verso destra. Zetema (Ricerca) con il volto tra le mani è stata interpretata come allegoria di Narciso, eroe beotico come Edipo, che scruta se stesso nella fonte, anche se non si capisce cosa veda, se se stesso o un teschio. Agnoia iconograficamente ricorda una figura femminile della Villa dei Misteri di Pompei, che ha la stessa posa e lo stesso movimento delle mani (Lehmann). Il dipinto pompeiano, grazie a questo affresco egizio, significherebbe che l'ignoranza si supera con l'iniziazione dionisiaca. Agnoia è personificata nel prologo della *Tosata* di Menandro. Nella *Calunnia* 5 di Luciano, Agnoia è dipinta vicino al giudice. Al plurale le Ignoranze si trovano nella *Tavola di Cebete* 23. 1[35].

La storia delle personificazioni femminili delle città nasce dunque in Grecia ed è l'archetipo delle personificazioni successive, da quella più massiccia di Roma a quelle moderne di città italiane e straniere. Tra di esse mi piace ricordare quelle pugliesi del pittore Mario Prayer (Torino, 1887- Roma, 1959), che studiò col fratello Guido nell'Accademia di Belle Arti di Venezia e nell'Accademia di Lione. Dal 1915 lavorò in varie città pugliesi (Bari, Foggia, Toritto, Ostuni ecc.) oltre che in Basilicata e a Roma. Un suo stupendo ciclo

---

[34] Schilardi 1997: 230 e Abbondanza 2008: 266-267.

[35] Gabba-Drioton 1954: 10 e tav. 15, Baldassarre 1979, Guarducci 1971: 435, Lehmann 1962, Ghedini 2000: 184-185.

di città personificate è nella splendida aula Magna dell'Ateneo di Bari[36]: tutte personificazioni femminili, tranne una, quella - eccezionalmente maschile - di Taranto.

[36] Semerari 2000. Una *Allegoria della Provincia di Brindisi* (1949) dello stesso Prayer è nel salone della provincia di Brindisi.

Pólis grega e colonização
(The Greek Polis and Colonization)

José Ribeiro Ferreira (jriparius@gmail.com)
Universidade de Coimbra

Resumo – Este trabalho tem como objectivo construir uma perspectiva global do processo de colonização na Grécia Antiga: como se iniciou, as suas diferentes fases, peculiaridades, de acordo com essas mesmas fases com as metrópoles de onde os colonizadores provinham. Os laços entre a metrópole e a nova pólis eram decisivos para a organização da colónia, as suas leis, os seus deuses, a sua expectativa de protecção por parte da cidade-mãe. O princípio da reciprocidade levou à criação de acordos com o objectivo de manter o domínio marítimo: o que teve consequências que a história viria a comprovar.

Palavras-chave: Colonização, *metropolis*, colónia, constituição, tratados.

Abstract – This paper aims to give a global perspective of the colonisation process in ancient Greece: how it began, its different phases, and its peculiarities, which accord with the phases of colonisation and with the 'metropoleis' from which colonisers came. The ties between the metropolis and the new polis were determinant for the organisation of the colony, its laws, its gods, and its expectation of protection by the mother-city. The principle of reciprocity led to the creation of alliances in order to maintain dominion over the sea, which had consequences that history came to demonstrate.

Keywords: Colonisation, *metropolis*, colony, constitution, treaties.

Falar da pólis grega, como acentua W. Jaeger, equivale a descrever a vida total dos Gregos. Significa que aqui apenas me poderei ater a alguns breves aspectos. Tenho pena todavia de não me poder demorar no seu desenvolvimento e solidificação, porque a pólis grega criou a estrutura institucional (regime republicano) que hoje vigora nos Estados modernos – a que Roma depois deu também poderoso contributo. É assim mais um dos aluviões do fecundo rio que é a cultura clássica: fruto, quer da estruturação e experiência da prática governativa na pólis, quer da reflexão teórica que, ao longo dos tempos, os seus dirigentes e pensadores produziram. Herança também, e inquestionável, o vocabulário da terminologia política hoje usado que, na sua grande maioria, deriva do grego ou do latim.

Nome genérico dos inumeráveis pequenos estados independentes em que a Hélade se encontrava dividida, alguns de muito reduzida dimensão quanto ao território e à população[1], a pólis era uma célula autosuficiente, quer no domínio político, quer no económico: concedia direitos a todos os seus cidadãos e deles exigiu também deveres. E o Grego queria exercitar pessoalmente esses seus

---

[1] Vide Ehrenberg 1976: 59-66; Ferreira 2004: 13-14.

https://doi.org/10.14195/978-989-26-1280-5_16

direitos: como observa Finley, os cidadãos, através do voto (como um todo ou, nas oligarquias, como um sector do todo) participavam directamente na condução dos destinos da pólis e não por representação como num parlamento moderno[2].

Traduzido o termo pólis, nas línguas modernas, por "cidade-estado" ou apenas "cidade" – embora, como veremos, nenhuma dessas designações corresponde exactamente ao conteúdo da palavra grega –, quando apareceu e como se foi formando este modelo de sistema político?

Se nos textos literários mais antigos que possuímos, os Poemas Homéricos *Ilíada* e *Odisseia*, a referência à pólis ainda não existe ou não aparece com clareza, ele já existe em Hesíodo – um poeta cuja datação oferece dificuldades, mas se tende a colocar nos finais do século VIII a.C. –, embora não esteja ainda totalmente definido (Ferreira 2004: 27-29).

Aos dados literários juntam-se os testemunhos arqueológicos. As escavações de algumas das cidades gregas revelam o aparecimento de um templo e de fortificações a defenderem as povoações, primeiro nas cidades da Ásia Menor e ilhas adjacentes, – as muralhas construídas na segunda metade do século IX e ao longo do VIII a. C. e o templo de data ligeiramente mais tardia. A. Snodgrass analisou as descobertas, em curto mas sugestivo estudo, e conclui que a existência de templo, pelo menos, ao reconhecer e eleger uma divindade políade protectora, será a garantia de se ter atingido uma pólis independente e uma prova física de que a emergência da pólis se verificou ou está em curso (1977: 24). Por outro lado, como veremos, a colonização grega – um fenómeno que se inicia ainda na primeira metade do século VIII a. C. – funda cidades que são quase todas póleis independentes.

Sem necessidade de recorrer às características físicas do solo grego, muito compartimentado por montanhas e vales e penetrado pelo mar em enseadas e golfos, parece-me evidente que o surgir do sistema de pólis se pode perfeitamente explicar por razões históricas, embora sem pôr totalmente de lado o concurso das condições geográficas do solo e de factores económicos[3]. Com o declínio micénico no século XII-XI a. C., verifica-se uma acentuada e longa movimentação populacional que provoca um grande fraccionamento e uma busca afanosa dos locais mais propícios e férteis – ou seja, mais adequados à defesa e à produção dos bens necessários à sobrevivência. As ameaças são constantes, as lutas intensas, e os habitantes, sem um poder centralizado forte que os protegesse, acolhem-se à protecção de antigas cidadelas micénicas ou refugiam-se em regiões menos acessíveis, tentando defender-se em pequenas comunidades, frequentemente no alto de colinas que rodeavam de muralhas – a acrópole.

A partir de determinada altura, para melhor resistirem aos ataques

---

[2] Finley: 7. Sobre o assunto vide também Ferreira 1990: 69-76.

[3] Para a discussão sobre a possível influência das circunstâncias geográficas vide o meu estudo, já citado (Ferreira 2004: 30).

constantes, essas pequenas comunidades agrupam-se em unidades mais amplas, através de sinecismo – uma outra via para a formação das póleis. E tais células políticas fecharam-se sempre num individualismo orgulhoso, sem nunca atingirem uma unidade política e mantiveram o sistema por vários séculos, até se diluir nos fins do séc. IV a. C.[4] – continuidade que se torna difícil de perceber sem o recurso ao entranhado particularismo dos Gregos.

As movimentações da Época Obscura são as chamadas Migrações (sécs. X-IX a. C.) – nome que é costume dar-lhes, e que prefiro. Durante elas, muitos grupos, quer de Iónios, quer de Eólios, quer de Dórios, sentiram a necessidade de abandonar os locais em que viviam, ou foram empurrados e forçados a isso, e partiram para as ilhas e a zona costeira da Ásia Menor, onde constituíram nesta última a Eólia (a norte), a Iónia (ao centro) e a Dória (a sul) e estabeleceram povos iónios e dórios, nas ilhas. Desse modo transformaram o Mar Egeu no centro do mundo grego arcaico.

As cidades gregas não apareceram todas na mesma altura nem com a mesma pujança económica e o mesmo poder político. As da zona costeira da Ásia Menor e as das ilhas foram as primeiras a surgirem, como vimos, e a desenvolverem-se. Na Eólia, sobressaíam Mitilene, na ilha de Lesbos, e Cime que dominava a baía do mesmo nome e parece ter estado na origem da fundação de muitas outras cidades eólias. No que respeita à Iónia, a mais importante das três partes da zona costeira da Ásia Menor, refere a tradição que, nos tempos históricos, havia doze principais cidades – a chamada dodecápole iónica –, embora se distingam e se imponham Foceia, Esmirna, Mileto, Éfeso, Priene, Cólofon, Samos e Quios (as duas últimas nas ilhas do mesmo nome). A Dória surge ao sul da Iónia quando os Dórios se estabelecem nas ilhas de Cós e de Rodes e depois passam à zona costeira fronteira onde fundam cidades importantes como Cnidos, Halicarnasso[5].

No espaço da Grécia propriamente dita, a primeira região a adquirir projeção económica, poder político e relevo cultural foi a ilha de Eubeia, onde sobressaem duas cidades, das primeiras a enveredaram pela empresa colonizadora, Cálcide e Erétria que ladeiam a planície de Lelanto, por cuja posse lutaram as duas nos finais do séc. VIII a.C., com vários aliados gregos a apoiarem uma e outra – a chamada Guerra Lelantina que conduz ao ermamento da referida planície. Depois outras póleis se foram impondo e destacando: Corinto – situada no istmo que une o continente grego à península do Peloponeso – desde cedo se desenvolve económica e politicamente, devido à sua localização, e entra nas primeiras empresas colonizadoras; chegou mesmo a construir um antecedente do canal, o *diolkos*, um caminho empedrado por onde os barcos eram transportados,

---

[4] Sobre a pólis e significado de tal sistema, vide Ehrenberg 1976 : 88-192; Ferreira 2004: 13-35.

[5] Para mais pormenores sobre as cidades da Eólia, da Iónia e da Dória vide, entre outros, Cook 1971.

em carretas, do Golfo Sarónico para o Golfo Coríntico, assim passando do Mar Egeu para o Mar Iónico, e vice-versa, sem necessidade de contornar o Peloponeso.

Mégara gozou de prosperidade na Época Arcaica e teve relevo cultural e político, mas sofreu as consequências da sua localização entre duas cidades poderosas, com as quais andou em constantes guerras, Corinto e Atenas.

Atenas ganha importância, a partir de Sólon, torna-se centro de uma simaquia depois das Guerras Medo-Persas (490 e 480-479 a.C.) e, senhora de uma frota poderosa que domina o Egeu.

Argos, situada na planície argiva, foi das cidades mais importantes no período arcaico, embora depois tenha perdido protagonismo por ter sido superada aos poucos por Esparta que, a partir de determinada altura se tornou o Estado mais poderoso do Peloponeso.

Egina, uma ilha localizada frente à Ática, teve importância comercial e cultural, e possuía uma frota que só foi superada por Atenas nos inícios do séc. V a.C.

A Élide, situada na parte ocidental do Peloponeso, impôs-se por conter a cidade de Olímpia, sede do santuário em que se realizavam os Jogos Olímpicos, as mais afamadas competições desportivas da antiga Grécia.

Delfos adquire renome sobretudo devido ao Santuário e Oráculo de Apolo Pítico que, sede de uma anfictionia de povos gregos, exerceu influência política, moral, religiosa e cultural sobre toda a Hélade e mesmo sobre Estados e povos não gregos.

Tebas, cidade da Beócia que tem o seu nome ligado a Cadmo, Édipo, Píndaro, gozou de importância económica, cultural e política na época arcaica e clássica gregas, mas sobretudo no século IV a.C., com os generais Pelópidas e Epaminondas, em que teve momentos de hegemonia na Grécia. Poderíamos referir aqui ainda muitas outras póleis gregas que, por uma razão ou por outra, se distinguiram ao longo da história da Grécia: por exemplo, Corcira, Iolcos, Naupacto, Plateias, Nemeia, Epidauro, Sícion, Potideia, Acanto, Olinto, Abdera e, entre as ilhas, Ceos, Paros, Naxos, Lemnos, Tasos. O tempo e o espaço requerem, no entanto, medida – a tão apregoada medida grega.

Apenas refiro que a pólis, ao longo da Época Arcaica, evoluiu e passou por um conjunto de inovações e fenómenos que muito a marcaram, como o aparecimento de uma nova táctica militar – a hoplitia, que substitui a cavalaria –, o desenvolvimento do comércio e o incremento da produção dos mais competitivos vinho e azeite, a introdução da moeda, a acção dos legisladores e o governo dos tiranos que imprimem à polis uma nova estrutura e feição[6]. E refiro ainda que, numa Grécia de solo parco, ossudo e pobre, muitas póleis se viram na contingência de enveredarem por empresas colonizadoras, em busca de terras mais férteis, e assim espalharam a Hélade pelas margens do mediterrâneo e do Mar Negro.

---

[6] Sobre esta evolução da pólis na época arcaica vide Ferreira 2004: 37-74.

Antes, porém, de abordar este fenómeno, solicito vénia para breve excurso sobre uma das várias tentativas dos Gregos em ultrapassarem o individualismo da pólis: a Simaquia do Peloponeso e a Simpolitia dos Beócios – nomes que prefiro ao generalizado Liga.

A simaquia resulta de uma aliança entre duas ou mais póleis que, pela troca de juramentos, se tornam aliados: *symmakoi* "que combatem juntos". São sobretudo acordos militares, como o seu nome indica, que os unem. De modo geral, ligam-se em volta de uma pólis hegemónica. Há uma dualidade de estrutura, onde coexistem a pólis hegemónica e os seus aliados. Não conhece a cidadania comum e não era uma entidade de direito público E entre os detentores da hegemonia e os aliados, entre a liberdade e autonomia de uns e outros, reinava uma inevitável tensão que leva as potências hegemónicas a usurparem o poder supremo da aliança e a restringirem progressivamente a autonomia dos aliados e por fim até a suprimirem-na.

A Simaquia do Peloponeso organizou-se em volta de Esparta, a grande opositora de Atenas (política, ideológica e militarmente), atinge projecção e torna-se uma potência de primeiro plano antes da sua rival. Já no século VI a. C. era uma máquina de guerra e cabeça de uma simaquia, que aparece ligada ao desenvolvimento da política espartana no Peloponeso, na segunda metade do século VI a. C., e nasceu de um conjunto de alianças bilaterais com cidades dessa península para formar uma rede hostil à volta de Argos. Esparta e o seu sistema político tornou-se o modelo para os oligarcas que recorriam à simaquia para pedir ajuda nas lutas internas das suas cidades. A influência foi grande na Grécia antiga e não mais deixou de se fazer sentir ao longo dos tempos. É um exemplo a atracção exercida sobre os Revolucionários franceses e sobre as ideologias nazis e fascistas[7].

Como meios para realizar essa aliança militar, Esparta possuía a solidez da constituição cuja elaboração se acaba cerca de meados do século VI a. C.; um exército que era dos mais poderosos – se não o mais poderoso – e o mais bem treinado da Grécia; certa preponderância sobre os Gregos.

A formação da simaquia aparece ligada ao desenvolvimento da política espartana no Peloponeso na segunda metade do século VI a. C., como política antitirânica e mudança da via de expansão territorial para a de alianças de carácter militar.

A simaquia do Peloponeso saiu de um tratado (c. 550 a. C.) entre Esparta e Tégea, em que esta era compelida a expulsar os Messénios e não podia fazer deles cidadãos. Cidade da Arcádia com grande importância estratégica devido à sua localização no caminho que ligava Esparta e o Istmo de Corinto, Tégea tornou-se pólis por meio de um sinecismo de nove povoações, que D. Asheri

---

⁷ Vide, para a Revolução Francesa, Ferreira 1988, Ferreira 1991:75-96; para as ideologias nazis e fascistas, Marrou 1965: 45-60, em especial 45-46 e 57-58.

atribui aos inícios do século VI a.C.[8] A guerra contra a Arcádia marca uma viragem na política expansionista de Esparta. Depois da conquista completa, com anexação da Messénia, a Lacedemónia vira-se para a Arcádia, e, a partir dela, contenta-se com uma política da alianças e de hegemonia que estará na base da Simaquia do Peloponeso.

Depois a simaquia desenvolveu-se, com a adesão de novas póleis. Era servida por um exército que assentava nas forças de Esparta, o núcleo das tropas federais, embora os outros membros fossem também obrigados a fornecer um contingente. E até Atenas o forneceu, em 400 a.C., depois da derrota na Guerra do Peloponeso (Xenofonte, *Helénicas* 3. 1. 4).

No que respeita a instituições a Simaquia do Peloponeso não tinha assembleia nem magistrados federais. Os delegados enviados pelos aliados formavam um congresso que só se reunia ocasionalmente. Embora pudesse fazê-lo a pedido de um dos aliados[9], por norma era convocado e presidido pelos Éforos e pronunciava-se antes da Apella, a assembleia de Esparta. As suas decisões, tomadas por maioria, eram válidas para toda a simaquia. Mas não prevaleciam contra os tratados anteriores nem contra os impedimentos religiosos. Teoricamente, era Esparta quem decidia, mas não podia ultrapassar o voto do Congresso dos aliados, em que não participava[10]. Por vezes a cidade lacónia não conseguia fazer que os outros aprovassem as decisões ou tratados que ela concluía sozinha. É um bom exemplo a Paz de Nícias que, em 421 a. C., estabeleceu com Atenas e depois tentou em vão que os aliados a aceitassem (Ehrenberg 1976: 190).

Os laços que uniam os membros da Simaquia a Esparta e entre si eram relativamente frouxos, laços defensivos. Além de não haver magistrados federais, como vimos, não passava de um agrupamento de cidades autónomas, sem organização estável e com ausência total de poder dirigente oficialmente reconhecido: cada uma por si tinha uma representação igual no congresso federal (cf. Tucídides 1. 125); um membro da simaquia podia fazer a guerra por sua conta e combater outro dos constituintes da organização, se ela não se encontrasse no momento em guerra (cf. Tucídides 1. 103 e 141; 4. 134). A decisão final acaba por pertencer às cidades interessadas e o cuidado em salvaguardar a autonomia das cidades transforma, como observa Mathieu, *Les idées*, p. 13, as reuniões em simples congressos diplomáticos. Daí as longas discussões, os protelamentos, as frequentes ameaças de secessão para forçar o vota da assembleia federal ou da espartana (Tucídides 1. 71. 4).

---

[8] In Erodoto 1988: 307. Moggi 1976 131-139 pende a colocá-lo entre 478 e 473.

[9] Por exemplo, Tucídides 1. 67 refere um caso em que o congresso dos delegados reúne a pedido dos Coríntios.

[10] Xenofonte·*Helénicas* 5. 2. 11-12 informa que era Esparta que tomava as decisões sozinha e que depois tentava que os aliados aceitassem.

Nos primeiros tempos, as relações entre Esparta e os aliados, que de início não pagavam tributos (Tucídides 1. 19), parecem ter sido de relativa autonomia entre estados. A posição inicial de Corinto e a influência que exerceu em 432 a. C. na política de Esparta é uma prova característica dessa independência, pelo menos de certos aliados. Aliás todas as precauções parecem ter sido tomadas para assegurar a autonomia. Mas nesse facto reside também a fraqueza da Simaquia do Peloponeso.

Depois a política de Esparta com os aliados alterou-se e passou a ter um comportamento mais dominador. Dar às forças aliadas generais espartanos (os *xenagoi*) marca o início dessa mudança. Apesar disso, só talvez no decurso do século V a. C., foram substituídas as alianças bilaterais por um pacto colectivo que ligava cada cidade a Esparta, com a promessa de mútuo apoio. E surge a fórmula: ter os mesmos aliados e os mesmos inimigos de Esparta. E ela traduz um sinal de um domínio que se cimenta.

Tal domínio encontra-se materializado nos fins da Guerra do Peloponeso: Esparta reduz os novos aliados a súbditos do seu império; impõe-lhes guarnições e harmostas – governadores da Simaquia do Peloponeso que os Lacedemónios estabeleceram, durante a sua hegemonia, nas cidades estrangeiras que estavam sob o seu domínio (cf. Tucídides 8. 5; Xenofonte, *Helénicas* 2. 4. 28); sujeita-os a pagar tributos e estabelece um tesouro federal, constituído pelos fundos destinados à guerra, contributos de cada cidade em proporção com a força militar que possuía (cf. Lísias, *Contra Nicómaco* 22; Xenofonte, *Helénicas* 5. 1. 21-22; Aristóteles, *AP.* 39. 2). Além disso, obriga ainda os novos membros a adoptarem constituições oligárquicas; por exemplo, os Trinta Tiranos em Atenas depois da derrota na Guerra do Peloponeso em 404 a.C. E é muito provável – ou quase certo mesmo – que os Espartanos fossem chamados pelas facções locais que disputavam o poder a apoiá-los nas suas tentativas de imporem regimes oligárquicos. Quase se pode dizer que, após a vitória de Esparta em 404 a. C., a Simaquia do Peloponeso se estendeu à maioria das cidades gregas, inclusive a Atenas, embora por pouco tempo (Lísisas, *Contra Nocómaco* 22; Xonofonte, *Helénicas* 2. 2. 20; Arsitóteles, *AP.* 39. 2).

Lisandro depois de 404 procura renovar a Simaquia e dar-lhe como finalidade a guerra contra os Persas. Mas desde cedo também se manifesta em Esparta a política contrária: Pausânias, contra a opinião de Lisandro, faz triunfar na Simaquia o princípio da autonomia das cidades e aceita a restauração da democracia em Atenas.

Em conclusão, o respeito inicial pela autonomia dos aliados e a entrega sobejamente proclamada ao interesse federal explicam o papel que a Simaquia desempenhou no desencadear da Guerra do Peloponeso. Em sintonia, Esparta – que era potência hegemónica, mas não imperialista – podia apresentar-se como defensora da liberdade grega contra o imperialismo de Atenas.

Depois da sua vitória na Guerra do Peloponeso, a pólis lacedemónica transforma a sua situação hegemónica na Simaquia em imperialismo militar. A organização adquire carácter ideológico e são impostas ou apoiadas instituiçíes oligárquicas.

As simpolitias são alianças que se unem e conseguem estabelecer uma cidadania comum – a *sympolitia* – que se sobrepõe as cidadanias individuais. Os estados federais desenvolvem-se, de preferência, de unidades ou grupos tribais – o *ethnos* : Beócios, Acaios, Etólios, Tessálios. Nunca se chega à criação de um verdadeiro Estado unitário, mas a graus vários de uniões federais. A união não se fez, talvez por ser já demasiado tarde. Esses estados ou confederações apresentam soberania própria, cidadania comum e ultrapassam os quadros políticos dos Estados que formam a simpolitia. Vejamos agora rapidamente o exemplo da Simpolitia dos Beócios.

A Simpolitia dos Beócios aparece nas fontes designado por *koinon* dos Beócios ou simplesmente Beócios. Até 520 a. C., os Beócios não tinham qualquer unidade de acção nas questões externas: os Tebanos eram aliados de Clístenes de Sícion; Orcómeno tinha relações de amizade com a Tessália. Não constituíam um grupo organizado e por isso não tinham uma política coerente. Apenas um povo com o mesmo dialecto, as mesmas atitudes sociais, os mesmos cultos … e muito ódio uns pelos outros.

Pelos fins do século VI a. C., talvez por volta de 520, a Beócia começa a ver-se sob e ameaça crescente da Tessália que controlava a Fócida e tinha uma aliança com os tiranos de Atenas, os Pisístratos. A Beócia, no meio dessas duas regiões, tornou-se naturalmente alvo do apetite dos Tessálios. A pressão destes culminou numa invasão da Beócia que não deve ser anterior a 525 e deve rondar o ano de 520 a. C., talvez usando como pretexto amizade de Orcómeno. Então algumas cidades dessa região grega, organizadas em federação política e militar, enfrentam a ameaça dos Tessálios. Sob a liderança de Tebas opõe-se à invasão: os Tessálios são vencidos em Cereso e o seu chefe Latamias morre durante o combate.

Não temos dados que permitam afirmar se a federação se formou para fazer frente à invasão; ou se a sua constituição é anterior e a Tessália invadiu a Beócia para dissolver uma nova e perigosa aliança. É possível que tal formação seja, de facto, anterior à invasão. Talvez as cidades suspeitassem das intenções da Tessália, e uniram-se em nova federação militar. Baseada em associação religiosa preexistente, o núcleo inicial da federação era constituído por Tebas, Coroneia, Haliarto, Tanagra e Téspies. Foram várias as tentativas da federação em agrupar as restantes póleis da Beócia. Ao núcleo inicial juntaram-se depois Acréfia e Tetracómia. Orcómeno e Plateias, solicitadas a aderir nos primeiros tempos, conseguem resistir à pressão: a primeira com a ajuda dos Tessálios e a segunda graças ao conselho de Esparta e ao apoio de Atenas.

Em 510, os Tessálios sofrem um revés em Atenas com a queda dos Pisístratos e Orcómeno, isolado, foi obrigado a aderir à Confederação em 507 a. C.

E pela mesma época entram na Confederação Lebadia, Queroneia e Hieto. Em 506, Beócios, Calcídios, Espartanos formam uma frente unida na intenção de se oporem à democracia ateniense nascente e de anexarem Plateias à confederação. Por essa altura, o rio Asopo passou então a ser a fronteira da Confederação, e apenas o território de Tanagra o ultrapassava um pouco para o sul [11].

A federação, que cunhou moeda federal, tinha como instituições principais a Assembleia, o Conselho e os magistrados O Conselho era considerado como uma parte dos *koina patria* desde os começos, ou pelo menos desde a primeira reforma (cerca de 510?). Tinha função importante em matéria religiosa (mensagens de oráculos); estabelecia a política de negociações com Estados estrangeiros. O conselho constituía um mecanismo de controlo dos Beotarcos: no estabelecimento da política, na assinatura de tratados, no recebimento de documentos, na ratificação de acordos, na preservação da continuidade e domínio de Tebas que tinha papel hegemónico na Confederação[12].

Os Magistrados tinham o nome de Beotarcos que eram os representantes das póleis, espécie de distritos da Confederação. Eram oficiais militares da simpolitia, que acumulavam também a supervisão das relações externas. Se tinham de início funções religiosas ou anfictiónicas, abandonaram-nas na altura da formação da confederação por volta de 520 em favor de outros magistrados, talvez os Afedríates[13]. Nomeados pelas suas cidades, não se sabe se os Beotarcos eram reeleitos, embora e reeleição fosse possível[14].

A entrada tardia de Orcómeno e outras cidades beócias na Confederação coloca-nos perante a questão da selecção, número e poderes dos Beotarcos. De início o seu número teria sido de sete: Tebas, Tanagra, Coroneia, Téspies, Haliarto, Acréfia e Tetracómia. Depois, com a adesão dessas cidades, o seu número subiu para onze: aos das sete anteriores juntaram-se mais os de Orcómeno, Lebadia, Copas e Antédon ou Queroneia[15]. Mas, partir de certa altura – possivelmente desde muito cedo –, Tebas, Orcómeno e Téspies passaram a ter representação dupla.

A Simpolitia da Beócia faz uma aliança com Egina e entra em luta com Atenas em 505 a.C. É, porém, vencida e em 503 e vê-se obrigada a fazer um tratado com Atenas. Desde essa altura até às Guerras Pérsicas não existem muitos dados sobre o que aconteceu na Beócia. Parece que Tebas aumentou a sua influência na simpolitia.

A questão do medismo da federação, por ocasião da segunda invasão dos Persas, contém alguns aspectos com interrogações. Se é um facto que toda o

---

[11] Buck 1979: 153.
[12] Buck 1979: 125-126.
[13] Buck 1979: 124-125 e 157-158.
[14] Buck 1979: 123-124.
[15] Buck 1979: 124.

confederação, com excepção de Téspies – Plateias não pertencia e era aliada de Atenas – ajudou os Persas, no entanto, ao contrário do que pensam outros, é de opinião de que, de início, em 481, a simpolitia enviou Probulos ao Congresso dos Aliados e que, ao lado deles, tomou parte na expedição a Tempe e na ação das Termópilas[16]. Só depois a confederação se teria colocado ao lado dos Persas e desse modo evitou a destruição das suas cidades. De qualquer modo o seu papel durante as Guerras foi importante, se bem que pouco glorioso – um período em que alargou bastante o território. Todavia, no fim das Guerras, as suas fronteiras devem ter ficado reduzidas aos limites estabelecidos por volta de 506 a. C.

A Confederação passa por uma série de dificuldades, após as Guerras Pérsicas, e coloca-se mesmo a questão da sua dissolução após a derrota dos Persas no conflito, como era opinião geralmente aceite até há pouco de que tinha sido dissolvida. Hoje esta posição tem sido posta em causa e tende-se a aceitar que a Simpolitia continuou, embora sob a hegemonia de Tanagra e não de Tebas como até então (cf. Tucídides 1. 108-109)[17]. Apesar disso, a importância e influência de Tebas não deve ter dimunuído substancialmente[18].

Em 457 a.C., Esparta invade a Beócia, obtém uma vitória em Tanagra e procura criar aí uma potência suficientemente forte para pôr em cheque Atenas: uma confederação. Fez de Tebas a cabeça dessa federação beócia e obrigou todas as cidades beócias e entrar nela. Esparta deixa a Beócia e pouco depois Atenas invade a região. Vence as forças da confederação, em 457, na batalha decisiva de Enófila e ocupa toda a zona, com excepção de Tebas. A Confederação fica sob o seu controlo. A Confederação continuou a existir. Democracias incompetentes e oligarquias pro-Atenas pouco leais. Atenas começa a ter problemas em 447 e acaba por assinar um tratado com os Beócios em 446 (?). Plateias deve ter abandonado então de novo a confederação. Dela ainda não faz parte em 431, altura em que a federação tenta, sem sucesso, a conquista de Plateias[19].

Há quem defenda a adesão de Plateias à Confederação nesta altura, mas o mais natural é ter-se mantido afastada e só ter aderido, como defendem outros, na altura do domínio ateniense, após a batalha de Enófita em 457 a. C.[20].

Os governos continuaram a ser oligárquicos como anteriormente, embora seja controverso o caso de Tebas. Defendem uns o estabelecimento da democracia em Tebas depois da derrota dos Persas[21]. Outros colocam essa alteração na década de 450, na altura da domínio ateniense, após as intervenções de Esparta

---

[16] Buck 1979: 128-135.
[17] Buck 1979: 141-142.
[18] Buck 1979: 142.
[19] Buck 1979: 161-162.
[20] Buck 1979: 142-143 e 148-149.
[21] Cf. Pseudoxenofonte, *Rep. dos Atenienses* 3. 11; Platão, *Menéxeno* 242a. Vide Ehrenberg 1973: 212.

e de Atenas, com as batalhas de Tanagra e Enófita[22].

Diversos são, pois, os modelos e as materializações que cada polis foi criando e individualizando ao longo dos tempos. Mas quais eram os traços essenciais comuns a todas as póleis?

Traduzido o termo pólis, nas línguas modernas, por "cidade-estado" ou apenas "cidade", nenhuma dessas designações corresponde exactamente à pólis que não era, para os Gregos, o estado como entidade jurídica abstracta – noção ainda não plenamente formada – mas o concreto dos cidadãos, no seu conjunto ou, para me servir das palavras de Tucídides (7. 77. 7), «os cidadãos e não as muralhas nem os barcos viúvos de homens». Vendo nos cidadãos o cerne do Estado, o aglomerado urbano e o território, importantes sem dúvida, surgiam, em última análise, como o local em que os homens construíam uma comunidade, política e humana, com seus hábitos, normas e crenças[23]. Daí admitirem – o que para nós pode parecer um tanto estranho – que a pólis seja transferível para outro sítio, como nos mostra um episódio narrado por Heródoto (8. 62) em que o dirigente de Atenas Temístocles – face à proposta de Espartanos e outros Estados gregos de retirada para o Peloponeso e construção de uma muralha defensiva no Istmo de Corinto, abandonando desse modo às forças de Xerxes (480 a. C.) a Ática e as outras regiões gregas do continente – ameaça abandonar a causa grega e transferir a pólis ateniense para outro lugar: para Síris, na Itália.

Se a pólis são os cidadãos, neles residia a soberania, com a primazia a ser atribuída à lei, quer resulte de uma concessão de entidade superior, divindade ou legislador para isso nomeado (*thesmós*); quer nasça de uma espécie de contrato social dos cidadãos (*nómos*); quer se trate do conjunto de costumes, tradições e normas, que davam forma à vida da pólis, ou seja, a constituição (*politeia*)[24]. *Politeia* – que apresenta um sentido amplo, a oscilar entre 'constituição', 'cidadania', 'governo', e é o correspondente grego do latino *república*, que o superou – era usado para designar o conjunto de tradições e leis, ou seja a *constituição* que dava forma ao viver do Estado, mas também a *cidadania* que permitia tomar parte activa na condução dos destinos dessa pólis ou Estado. Podemos ver estes diversos aspectos especificados num passo de Demóstenes, *Contra Aristogíton* I. 15-16, que põe em realce a oposição entre a natureza e as leis – a *physis* e os *nomoi* – leis que, desejando o que é justo, belo e útil, o procuram e, ao encontrá-lo, «proclamam-no ordem

---

[22] Buck 1979: 143-148.

[23] Sobre os diversos traços que distinguem esta comunidade social, política e humana que era a pólis vide o meu trabalho Ferreira 2004: 13-35. Um desses aspectos me parece conveniente realçar, o religioso. Se hoje se aceita o princípio de que o Estado deve estar separado da religião, matéria que pertenceria ao foro íntimo e à consciência de cada um, tal ideia era impensável para os Gregos, que consideravam a religião parte integrante e nuclear da pólis, pelo que as cerimónias e os actos do culto não poderiam senão ser funções da alçada dos governantes.

[24] *Thesmós* e *nomos* são dois termos que significam lei, mas que designam realidades diferentes, pelo menos quanto à origem e autoridade. Vide Ferreira 1993:151 sqq.

comum, igual e a mesma para todos». Considera, além disso, que «toda a lei é uma criação e um dom dos deuses, uma decisão dos homens sábios, um correctivo para os erros, voluntários ou involuntários, um contrato comum da pólis, segundo o qual todos devem viver nessa sociedade». Assim as leis aparecem já como contrato social e simultaneamente como uma dádiva divina. Por essa razão, as determinações da cidade-estado não podiam contrariar os ditames dos deuses, sob pena de graves consequências, como acentua a *Antígona* de Sófocles[25].

Na aceitação absoluta da Lei e na vigência de uma administração despersonalizada se realizava a polis e se satisfazia o Grego, cioso de ter a Lei por único soberano. Péricles, na "Oração fúnebre" que pronuncia em honra dos que caíram em combate e que Tucídides lhe atribui, faz o elogio da Constituição ateniense e, em determinada altura, põe em realce a obediência das leis, especialmente as que protegiam o oprimido e as que, mesmo sem serem escritas, causam vergonha em quem as transgredir (2.37.3).

A obediência do grego às leis impressionava os Bárbaros, como o mostra um passo de Heródoto em que o historiador assenta a força da Grécia na pobreza em que foi criada, na aretê ou excelência, na obediência à lei (VII.102):

A Grécia foi sempre criada na pobreza, mas junta-se-lhe a virtude (*aretê*), amassada na sabedoria e numa lei rigorosa. Apoiando-se nelas a Grécia defende-se contra a pobreza e contra a sujeição[26].

Boa parte da força da pólis radicava, pois, no facto de os seus cidadãos, apesar de gozarem de grande liberdade, permanecerem observantes da lei, por terem a consciência de que a desordem ou anarquia favorecia os que detestavam o regime republicano, que era essencialmente o da pólis, e o queriam destruir. Vejamos o que diz Atena, em *As Euménides* de Esquilo, quando institui o Areópago para acabar com a vingança pessoal e familiar e para julgar e fazer justiça (vv. 696-699):

> Nem anarquia, nem despotismo eu quero
> que os meus cidadãos cultivem com devoção.
> E que não se lance o temor fora da cidade.
> Sem nada recear, qual dos mortais seria justo?[27]

É que a falta de temor à lei e à justiça, a anarquia são propícias aos ambiciosos e sedentos de poder que delas se servem para ascenderem à chefia da pólis e imporem regimes despóticos: aproveitam-se das lutas sociais por que passaram quase todos os Estados gregos nos séculos VII e VI a.C. e, por meios não constitucionais e pela força, instituem um regime autocrático, a que os Gregos deram o nome de tirania. Governo e vontade de um só, exercia poder

---

[25] Sobre o assunto vide Rocha Pereira 2008: 16-38.
[26] Tradução de Rocha Pereira 2009: 259.
[27] Tradução de Rocha Pereira 2009: 236.

absoluto sobre as pessoas e colidia ou opunha-se ao sistema republicano da pólis que tinha por único soberano a lei, exercida pelas instituições (discutiam, aprovavam, punham em prática as determinações tomadas), em que tinham assento os cidadãos.

Para o Grego, a liberdade significava assim o reinado da lei e a participação no processo de tomada de decisões; não residia na noção de um domínio privado intangível para o Estado nem na posse de direitos inalienáveis, de cuja existência, como observa Finley, não havia ainda o reconhecimento, pelo menos não muito nítido e geral[28]. A esse propósito são significativas as afirmações de Sócrates no *Críton* de Platão, no episódio da "Prosopopeia das Leis" (50a sqq.). Quando o protagonista do diálogo, na noite anterior à execução do mestre, lhe propõe fugir, Sócrates recusa com o argumento de que as Leis o acusariam de, com tal acção, deitar a perder a polis: se a constituem o conjunto dos cidadãos, ela é também senhora plena de cada um deles; além disso, nenhum Estado pode subsistir quando as sentenças proferidas não têm poder.

Mas será que a dependência da vontade da pólis aí defendida cabe, na perspectiva actual, dentro do conceito de liberdade?

Desde que nasce, o habitante habitua-se ao modo de vida da pólis, às suas leis e costumes, às normas que regulam os actos mais comezinhos, às cerimónias religiosas e crenças. Comunidade viva que, aos poucos, conformava o jovem à sua maneira de ser e de viver, a polis era, como afirma o fr. 90 West de Simónides, a «mestra do homem». Ou seja, uma entidade activa, formativa, que exercitava o espírito e formava o carácter dos cidadãos. Constituía uma preparação para a aretê – excelência ou virtude –, função de que o Estado moderno se desliga quase por completo.

Essa aretê ou excelência pode variar de pólis para pólis, de acordo com a evolução e a prática política e social de cada Estado ou pólis. Era, contudo, sempre o ideal que cada pólis ia instituindo, e criava.

Esse ideal de vida republicano que assentava no poder e obediência às leis, corporizado nas instituições da pólis espalhou-se pelo mundo conhecido de então, graças à colonização.

Ao percorrer um mapa das margens do mediterrâneo (mapa), deparamos com um conjunto de topónimos que nos são mais ou menos familiares, mas que a maioria não identifica como termos gregos e antigas colónias helénicas: Estambul, Sebastopol, Apolónia (cidades da Palestina, Ilíria, Líbia, Trácia), Nápoles (de *nea +polis* "nova pólis"), Mónaco (de Herakles Monoikos), Marselha, Nice (de *nike* "vitória"), Antibes (de Antipolis "a cidade em frente"), Agde (de *agathê*, fem. de *agathos*, "a boa terra"), Ampúrias, Cirene e tantas outras. Permita-se-me uma observação sobre Estambul que é um caso particular por ter tido três nomes e todos eles de origem grega: começou por ser a colónia grega de Bizâncio (séc.

---

[28] Finley 1973: 78.

VII a.C .), depois passou a Constantinopla (de Constantino + pólis), para tomar por fim o nome de Estambul – "na cidade" ou "para a cidade" *eis ten pólin*.

E as cidades que ostentam tais nomes são fruto do fenómeno da colonização que convém distinguir de migrações. Enquanto estas, como vimos, constituíam uma movimentação de populações não organizada – devida ora ao nomadismo, ora a desalojamento por outros povos, ora a fuga de locais de guerra – a colonização usa de planeamento, com a escolha do sítio a colonizar, com a nomeação do comandante (o *oicista*), com a definição dos integrantes da expedição. Fenómeno característico da época arcaica grega, inicia-se em meados do século VIII a.C., quase em paralelo temporal com os começos da pólis, e prolonga-se até ao período helenístico, espalhando os Gregos pelas margens do Mediterrâneo.

Com frequência, por circunstâncias climáticas ou políticas, a pólis via-se em dificuldades para alimentar a população e optava por enviar uma parte dos seus habitantes para outro lugar com a missão de fundar uma colónia – a que os Gregos chamavam *apoikia* "residência distante". Tomada a decisão, definiam-se os objectivos da expedição e os princípios que presidiriam à selecção dos seus componentes, procedia-se à escolha do local – de modo geral zonas de terras férteis e boas para o cultivo dos cereais, pelo menos nos primeiros tempos: as colónias de povoamento, em locais com sítio adequado para instalar a parte urbana e com amplos espaços de terras necessárias ao auto-abastecimento.

Antes da escolha do local, consultava-se o oráculo de Apolo em Delfos que superintendia em tal matéria e aprovava a escolha feita ou indicava outro local. E o caso de Cirene é elucidativo quanto à influência de Delfos, em tal domínio (cf. Heródoto 4. 151-159). Só com esse assentimento a expedição colonizadora podia partir, comandada pelo *oikistes* que, uma vez chegados ao local de destino, procede à instalação e à distribuição de terras, recebendo depois honras e culto de fundador.

Da cidade de origem – a metrópole ou "cidade mãe" – os colonizadores transportam o fogo sagrado, os cultos, o alfabeto, o dialecto, o calendário; naturalmente também o regime político e as instituições. As colónias fundadas na Sicília e em Itália – a Magna Grécia –, no Ponto, em África reproduzem nessas terras distantes as estruturas e as formas políticas e económicas da metrópole ou 'cidade mãe', mas as ligações tornam-se pouco mais do que formais. Entre a metrópole e a colónia não havia qualquer grau de dependência política e económica: os membros da expedição colonizadora perdiam geralmente a cidadania anterior no momento da partida e tornavam-se cidadãos de outra pólis – a colónia. Nasciam para um novo sistema de vida que construiriam de acordo com os novos condicionalismos locais que vão encontrar, com os seus gostos e possibilidades, hábitos e normas, com evolução própria[29]. Daí que este fenómeno grego se não enquadre no nosso conceito actual de colonização que implica a colónia como uma extensão territorial da metrópole e a sua dependência política e económica.

---

[29] Vide Littmann 1974: 59-60.

Entre colónia e metrópole apenas existiam laços de ordem moral – pelo que era aberrante uma declarar guerra à outra. Não esqueçamos, contudo, que no século V a. C. começam a aparecer as cleruquias que já correspondiam à nossa colonização: os seus habitantes, os clerucos, continuavam cidadãos da metrópole, ao contrário do ápoikos que perdia a cidadania da pólis de origem.

Nestas colónias de povoamento, sempre ou quase sempre a ocupação do lugar provoca, como é natural, conflitos com os nativos, em regra violentos, como mostra a arqueologia, ainda que por vezes de início os contactos possam ter sido pacíficos. E de novo recorro a Cirene, na Líbia, como exemplo desse processo de primeiros contactos pacíficos que depois resvalam para a violência (cf. Heródoto 4. 158-159). De modo geral, como a delegação de colonos era constituída apenas por elementos masculinos, na ocupação violenta do local escolhido, os Gregos tomavam as mulheres indígenas, para proverem ao crescimento demográfico, e escravizavam os homens para trabalharem nos campos ou nos serviços domésticos da cidade.

De qualquer modo, como o mostrou J. Boardman, desde o início da colonização (séc. VIII a.C.), há também intercâmbio de bens físicos, como cerâmica, vinho e azeite, perfumes (1986). Os vasos gregos, que se encontram a bem dizer espalhados por todas as margens do Mediterrâneo – e vão também aparecendo em diversos locais da orla do Atlântico europeu –, são precisamente os recipientes que transportavam os líquidos – azeite, vinho, perfumes. Os primeiros a empreenderem viagens com intuitos comerciais foram os habitantes de Cálcide e de Erétria, na Eubeia, que se deslocaram primeiro para Oriente (Chipre, Síria, Fenícia), depois para Ocidente, até ao golfo de Nápoles e à Etrúria – locais onde, como provam os dados arqueológicos, começaram por estabelecer núcleos destinados ao comércio, os *emporia*, alguns já existentes no século VIII a.C. (caso de Al-Mina, na foz do Rio Orontes), como a arqueologia tem mostrado. São, porém, feitorias comerciais sem estatuto político, não verdadeiras colónias ainda.

A penúria do solo helénico em contraste com a abundância em muitas das colónias, por um lado, e a ocupação violenta das terras que impedia as trocas com os nativos, por outro, provocam movimentos dinâmicos e criam uma predisposição a trocas, originando relações comerciais entre as colónias e o continente grego – não necessariamente com a metrópole. Gera-se assim um sistema de trocas cada vez mais activo entre a bacia oriental do Mediterrâneo e a ocidental. Em meados do século VII a. C., o comércio estava espalhado. Então, ao lado das agrícolas, assistimos à fundação de colónias comerciais – os *emporia* –, de modo geral estabelecimentos de reduzida dimensão, situados na foz de rios ou em baías costeiras que possibilitam a comunicação com o interior do território[30].

Tal incremento vai, por sua vez, estimular a indústria, sobretudo a produção de cerâmica. São famosos, desde a época arcaica, os vasos de Corinto

---

[30] Vide Mossé 1970 : 31-35 e 64-69.

e de Atenas. As escavações arqueológicas mostram que nessas duas cidades se verificou um grande surto de oficinas nos séculos VII e VI a. C.

Nos estabelecimentos ou colónias comerciais o procedimento era diferente do adoptado nas *apoikiai*: não se recorre à ocupação violenta de terras, mas procura-se que as relações com os nativos assentem na confiança recíproca, nas ligações matrimoniais e nos presentes que revelam interesses comerciais recíprocos. Estão neste caso o comportamento do coríntio Demarato nos confrontos com os Etruscos; a usual actuação dos Iónios de Foceia que chegaram às costas meridionais da França, onde, graças à amizade ou *philia* com o rei dos Segóbrigos, conseguem fundar uma colónia em Marselha; percorreram a costa mediterrânica da Península Ibérica, ultrapassaram mesmo o Estreito de Gibraltar – as Colunas de Héracles de então – e atingiram Tartessos (Heródoto 1. 163)[31].

Em Massalia ou Marselha aparecem, além de exemplares de cerâmica coríntia e ática, também vasos lacónios, calcídicos, greco-orientais (ródios, quiotas). A helenização do sul da França no séc. VI a.C. era considerável. Os gregos aí introduziram a cultura da vinha e da oliveira. Penetraram no interior e foi encontrada cerâmica dos sécs. VII e VI a.C. na Germânia e na Suíça (Boardman 1986: 237-245).

A fundação de Marselha mostra a vocação *empórica* da colonização de Foceia, empenhada em estender sucessivamente as subcolónias para sul: Agde na Languedoc, Ampúrias e Rosas na Catalunha. Massalia fundou no norte de Espanha Emporion (a actual Ampúrias) onde se descobriu cerâmica coríntia já dos inícios do séc. VI a.C. E também vasos áticos, é evidente (Boardman 1986: 239). Esse caminhar para sul e ocidente visava o comércio de metais – tão necessários à Hélade e vindos do interior – que era realizado em locais que não chegavam ao estatuto de *empórion*.

Os Foceenses privilegiaram o ocidente e continuaram a sua rota até ao Atlântico. Por exemplo, no território português já apareceram, na foz de quase todos os grandes rios, com excepção de um deles, vasos ou fragmentos de cerâmica, alguns dos sécs. VII-VI a.C. – caso de fragmentos cerâmicos coríntios e áticos encontrados no Algarve (Castro Marim, Tavira, Lagos, Faro); na Quinta de Almaraz, nos arredores de Lisboa; foz do Sado, Tejo, Mondego[32].

Se seguíssemos outros povos gregos que preferiram a via oriental e entraram pelo Mar Negro, encontraríamos passos e atitudes idênticos.

São assim os caminhos da colonização.

---

[31] Vide Boardman 1986: 297 nota 12.

[32] Vide Arruda 2005: 23, 59-74 (frg. de Castro Marim, Tavira, Lagos, Faro), 31 (frg. da Quinta de Almaraz), 82-83 (foz do Sado, Tejo e Mondego).

El culto imperial como punto de encuentro entre culturas. Una aproximación sucinta.
(The Imperial Cult as an Element of Integration between Cultures: a Succinct Outline)

Marc Mayer i Olivé (mayerolive@yahoo.es)
Institut d'Estudis Catalans - Universitat de Barcelona

Abstract – The aim of this paper is to examine in a brief and summarized manner what imperial honors and the worship of the *domus divina* meant as an element of integration between cultures in the Roman World.

Keywords: Roman Cult, Roman Empire, Imperial Cult, Emperors, Rome, Roman Religion.

El culto imperial, o quizás mejor los honores y la presencia de la familia imperial, en las ciudades y comunidades, resulta ser, sin duda, un punto de encuentro común, y a pesar de la diversidad étnica y cultural, de los pueblos que agrupa y rige el imperio romano. Desde este punto de vista queremos tratar nuestro tema, insistiendo sobre el papel, que nos atreveríamos a llamar nivelador, de estas formas de honores que derivan, primero en Oriente y después en Occidente, en un culto verdadero y propio. La *domus Augusta* se transformará en *domus divina* y se podrá identificar una clara evolución, de reinado en reinado y de dinastía en dinastía, hasta llegar a las formas cristianas[1].

El primer elemento que llama la atención, cuando nos enfrentamos a un tema de tal complejidad, es la aparente uniformidad, sin menoscabo de la amplia dispersión de los resultados. De aquí la importancia del análisis de este fenómeno que presentará particularidades locales y formas de expresión, propias y personales, por zonas o grupos sociales, pero que a la postre pueden ser interpretadas a partir de los mismos parámetros, con relativamente pocas variaciones en las pautas de conducta.

La epigrafía y la escultura son en este campo, como en muchos otros, la vía de penetración privilegiada, ya que es aquella que nos proporciona datos sobre la presencia, evolución y dispersión geográfica del fenómeno. Menos explícitos en cambio pueden resultar los espacios reservados a la exhibición de las estatuas e inscripciones que en muchas ocasiones son concebidos, delimitados y construidos precisamente con esta finalidad, aunque no parecen responder a criterios que

---

[1] Insiste por ejemplo en la influencia oriental el famoso libro de Gagé 1968. Un ejemplo sintético de evolución para una zona en Mayer 2007a. En general Clauss 1979.

https://doi.org/10.14195/978-989-26-1280-5_17

podríamos llamar normalizados[2]. Los principios generales, alusivos y teóricos deducibles de los textos literarios hallan su plasmación concreta y explícita en la realidad material de las inscripciones y en los monumentos que éstas ilustran y acompañan. No entraremos en esta ocasión en el tratamiento de otra forma generalizada de propagación de la imagen y las consignas imperiales como es el caso de las monedas, ya que constituyen por sí mismas un campo de investigación que iría mucho más allá de nuestra intención en esta breve introducción a un fenómeno complejo, y que por otra parte tiene criterios de comportamiento complementarios que se mueven, sin embargo, con parámetros relativamente distintos[3].

La existencia de formularios específicos y de formas de expresión escrita y plástica precisas ayuda de forma muy clara a establecer un panorama coherente y diacrónico en el campo epigráfico y a detectar modelos oficiales y adaptaciones locales. El hecho no se produce sin embargo tan sólo en el campo epigráfico, sino que debe ser entendido como una característica fundamental que afecta a todos los conjuntos monumentales y a todos los documentos de presencia y memoria de estos elementos de honor y eventualmente de culto. Las particularidades no hacen más que comprobar la extensión del fenómeno confirmándolo y no limitándolo o delimitándolo. El modelo de la *Vrbs* juega un papel innegable en la circulación de todo tipo de ideas y procedimientos que se extenderá a las provincias[4].

El mismo hecho de la existencia de una retratística imperial de carácter provincial aboga a favor de la generalización de honores y de su derivación en una forma de culto de la *domus* reinante. Paul Zanker ha dedicado a este tipo de imágenes un estudio que sigue siendo substancialmente válido en el momento actual[5] y que puede integrarse en el cuadro más amplio y complejo de la representación escultórica del emperador, su familia y del poder imperial[6].

Otro elemento importante, "a contrario", vendría dado por la importancia que reviste la *damnatio memoriae* y la ejecución material y real de la misma sobre la epigrafía y la escultura[7], que son en último término los elementos esenciales para la comprensión del fenómeno que estudiamos.

---

[2] Cf. ahora de modo general el reciente volumen de Ewald y Norena, eds. 2010. De forma muy general Mayer 1998. Recordemos el trabajo pionero de Gasperini 1977.

[3] Véase por ejemplo Manconi y Catalli (eds.) 2005, dedicado al retrato numismático.

[4] Sobre esta circulación, Eck 2006. Cf. para esta difusión Fishwick 2005. Además Scheid 2015 para los rituales.

[5] Zanker 1983, para algunas de las características generales simbólicas de la representación divina del emperador, cf. Bergmann 1998.

[6] Cf. por ejemplo, Boschung 2002. Además Rose, 1997; Boschung, 1993b; Kiss 1975; más especializado todavía Boschung 1993a; Vierneisel y Zanker, 1979, con incidencia importante sobre el valor ideológico. Para los emplazamientos y la significación de este tipo de esculturas cf. Stemmer (ed.) 1995, y Witschel 1995a , y Witschel 1995b; véase además Witschel 2002. Sobre una de sus formas, Hallet 2005, para los miembros de la familia imperial.

[7] Cf. para esta última Varner 2004; especialmente Varner 2004: 1-20 (para los aspectos teóricos) y 289-305 (para la excelente bibliografía selecta).

Un aspecto de carácter decisivo es el que viene dado por lo que podríamos denominar como "augusteización", es decir la aplicación del epíteto *Augustus, -a* a una divinidad, una forma de integración de los propios dioses en un panteón imperial, en el que se incluirán además la propia casa imperial y el culto de Roma, junto con un gran número de abstracciones de hechos y virtudes imperiales. En el caso de Hispania el proceso fue muy bien estudiado por Robert Étienne, tanto en lo que concierne a las divinidades, cuanto a los sacerdocios y cuasi-sacerdocios a este culto vinculados[8]. El trabajo de R. Étienne ha sido el modelo de este tipo de estudios y marca un paso muy importante para la evolución de las investigaciones centradas en la zona occidental del imperio romano, los cuales nos muestran un panorama que, si bien no parece homogeneo, resulta de una gran coherencia, de una considerable aparente reglamentación y una indudable extensión por todo el territorio, con algunas particularidades provinciales que dependen de la propia evolución local de los modelos y pautas[9].

Los trabajos sobre el culto imperial, como hemos ya dicho, han sido muy numerosos[10], e incluso en los últimos años se ha incrementado la intensidad de la atención hacia este tipo de temas[11].

La evolución por zonas puede resultar sorprendentemente semejante, especialmente en los momentos mejor atestiguados y documentados, como es el caso del período julio-claudio y el antonino[12], sea en Oriente o en Occidente[13].

La capacidad de absorción por parte de la sociedad romana del culto imperial, y al mismo tiempo la capacidad de asimilación del mismo, tiene un claro antecedente en lo que técnicamente en los estudios que versan sobre religión romana se ha dado en llamar, utilizando una expresión latina de Tácito

---

[8] Étienne, 1974. Véanse también algunos de los trabajos reunidos por Wlosok (ed.) 1978.

[9] Castillo 1998; Bassignano 1974; Arnaldi 2010; Alföldy 1973; de forma general Fishwick 1970; Fishwick 2002; Szabó 2008; Szabó 2007. Un elenco con biografías de los integrantes de estos sacerdocios en Rüpke 2005. Es importante considerar la lex *de flamonio provinciae Narbonensis* (*CIL* XII 6038 = *ILS* 6964 = *FIRA* I. 199–202, núm. 22).

[10] Así el trabajo de síntesis de Hänlein-Schäfer 1985, con un inventario. Para Oriente resulta especialmente útil Price 1984: 249-274, con un catálogo de templos y altares de culto imperial que incluye 156 ejemplos; además Camia 2011. Cf. en general la bibliografía recogida en Herta 1978, y además Tuchelt 1981.

[11] Gasperini y Paci (eds.) 2008, con especial atención a Gasperini 2008. Para la evolución cf. por ejemplo el reciente volumen de Hekster, Schmidt-Hofner y Witschel (eds.) 2009, esp. Chaniotis, 2009.

[12] Cf. Kantiréa 2007. Un ejemplo en ámbito oriental especialmente bien estudiado en Quadrino 2007. Para el caso de Grecia puede verse también el libro reciente de Lorenzo Gómez 2010.

[13] Para el momento inicial es importante Forni 1973 (ahora en Forni 1994), muy notable por la comparación entre conceptos griegos y latinos al respecto. Para un momento posterior, Mayer 2009 y Mayer 2010.

no exactamente equivalente, "*interpretatio Romana*"[14]. La *interpretatio* depende precisamente de la capacidad de asimilación y de sincretismo muy notable que está presente en las actuaciones de los romanos y especialmente en su expansión conquistadora. De nuevo la Península Ibérica ha dado pie a algunos de los estudios más iluminadores sobre este fenómeno[15]. Los términos *deus*, *dea* mismos son ya indicios de romanización activa[16]; la *domus divina* y los honores y culto que recibe representarán el cierre de este proceso[17], antes de que se produzcan las nuevas formas que impondrá el dominado y más tarde el cristianismo.

Pero más allá del procedimiento resultan sintomáticos los resultados de la transformación de Marte en *Mars Augustus*, o bien de Mercurio en *Mercurius Augustus*, o incluso de Apolo, la divinidad protectora y favorita de Augusto[18], que pueden representar un procedimiento singular, pero hasta cierto punto no sorprendente; lo resultan en cambio casos como los de *Nemedus Augustus* en la Cueva de La Griega (Pedraza, Segovia)[19] o bien el de *Bacax Augustus* en la gruta de Taya en Ghar el-Djema (Algeria), en el flanco norte del Djebel Taya[20].

Los pasos de evolución de estos honores y culto son bien conocidos en sus líneas generales pero no estará de más matizarlos sintéticamente:

Los precedentes responden, sin duda alguna, a formas orientales de culto al gobernante importadas a Italia a partir de la influencia seléucida ejercida desde el siglo II a.C. sobre los magistrados romanos. La situación se consolidará en Italia fundamentalmente durante el período silano y se configurará definitivamente con los honores y la divinización de Julio César[21].

Un período incipiente se desarrolla en el reinado de Augusto[22], al menos muy claramente en Oriente, pero no hallará su plasmación definitiva hasta el reinado de Tiberio, que, una vez más, aparece como organizador y factor de consolidación de la obra de su predecesor. Un culto que se formalizará, en buena parte de los casos, a través de edificios o recintos, con una función entre representación y culto, que contienen galerías de retratos de los miembros de la familia imperial[23].

---

[14] Cf. al respecto por ejemplo, Marco 1996. Un buen estado de la cuestión con nuevas aportaciones en Baratta 2005; Ando 2006.

[15] Véase, en primer lugar, la apretada y precisa síntesis de Étienne, Fabre, Le Roux, Tranoy 1976, especialmente: 101-104. También Étienne 1973. Sobre el inicio del culto imperial, Edmonson 1997; Fishwick 1982; además Garriguet 2004.

[16] Mayer 1980.

[17] Cf. para los aspectos formales, Raepsaet-Charlier 1975.

[18] Gagé 1955.

[19] Abásolo y Mayer 1997. Cf. Marco 1993.

[20] Cf. Pflaum 1976, núms. 4502-4585, a excepción de 4580.

[21] Una aproximación en Mayer 2008; Weinstock 1971. Cf. para el proceso posterior, Panciera 2003.

[22] Véase por ejemplo, Wallace-Hadrill 2005.

[23] Mayer 2007b y 2015. Para Italia cf. Cogitore 1992, y para el mundo romano Hurlet

Los cambios producidos ya en el reinado de Nerón anunciarán las nuevas formas de la dinastía flavia[24].

El advenimiento de los flavios, sin producir formas nuevas, cancela en parte el concepto de *domus* julio-claudia, limitando el antecedente, del que se consideran sucesores, a la figura de Augusto, que será en los siguientes reinados puesta en paralelo con la figura de Vespasiano divinizado[25], como es evidente, por ejemplo, en un caso de *Tarraco*[26]. El uso literario, de carácter excepcional, en época de Domiciano del apelativo *dominus et deus* para el emperador no tendrá continuidad oficial hasta más tarde[27].

El reinado de Trajano comportará novedades en los que concierne al culto familiar, el *divus Traianus pater* y las mujeres de la casa imperial, que tendrán no sólo trascendencia pública sino incluso gran importancia y trascendencia política[28].

El reinado de Adriano comporta la introducción renovada de la figura de Roma[29], y de la ciudad que la representa, con un mayor relieve: la celebración del

---

1996, que hace un inventario de las series conocidas en todo el Imperio romano, sea de inscripciones, sea de estatuas, cf. Hurlet 1996: 573-600 y 601-612; además Cesarano 2015. El conjunto de *Roselle*, junto a Grossetto, es quizás el más notable, cf. Conti 1997, cf. ahora Conti 1998: 111-123, núms. 5-26; además para la escultura Melani y Vergari 1985: 83-86; Nicosia (ed.) 1990: 66-70, con un estudio de la epigrafía por parte de Panciera. Este conjunto resulta en todo caso de gran trascendencia en especial para analizar la evolución final de estas galerías de retratos imperiales julio-claudios, cf. Liverani 1994. Para el final de otro conjunto de este tipo como es el caso de *Narona* cf. Mayer 2004. Zecchini (ed.) 2015; Gros, Marim, Zink (eds.) 2015.

[24] Cf. las notas anterior y siguiente. Además, Scott 1936. Un ejemplo incipiente en época neroniana de este cambio puede ser *CIL* VI 40334, con sucesivos estados, y *CIL* XI 6955 =*ILS* 8902, que presenta ya una situación semejante a la de las dedicatorias a los flavios, limitada a Nerón, Popea y su hija ya muerta Claudia, cf. Mayer 2007b: 196.

[25] Cf. ahora sobre estos aspectos, Kramer y Reitz (eds.) 2010, especialmente los trabajos contenidos en la segunda parte, "Mediale Strategien der neuen Ordnung", en sus apartados "I. Die Selbtsdartellung der Dynastie", pp. 167-307, y "II. Symbolische Kommunikation im Imperium Romanum", pp. 311-427; Ando 2003. Además McCrum y Woodhead 1961: 44-59, para los documentos sobre la familia reinante y el culto imperial.

[26] *CIL* II² 14, 881 y 894 = *RIT* 67 y 68 de *Tarraco*, que son dos pedestales iguales dedicados a los *divi Augustus* y *Vespasianus* respectivamente a cargo del mismo dedicante, sin embargo *CIL* VI 692, de Roma, presenta conjuntamente a Vespasiano, Tito y Domiciano. Cf. sobre este tema Mayer 1993 y Mayer 1999.

[27] SVET. *Dom.* 13, 4: *Pari arrogantia, cum procuratorum suorum nomine formalem dictaret epistulam, sic coepit: Dominus et deus noster hoc fieri iubet.*

[28] Kolb (ed.) 2010; además Temporini 1978, esp. pp. 167-175, para Plotina, pp. 194-259, para Marciana y Matidia. Sobre la iconografía de las emperatrices en general cf. Alexandridis 2004.

[29] Cf. al respecto, Beard, North y Price 1998, especialmente: 174-176; mantienen, p. 176, que el tema romuleo de la celebración se transforma en principal a partir del 121 d.C. cuando Adriano construye el templo de Venus y Roma y se celebran los *Romaea*, el festival de Roma; cf. también Beard, North y Price 1998: 116-119, para la intervención personal de Adriano. Sobre este culto cf. Fayer 1976, con una gran labor de identificación del culto imperial y sus

natalis Vrbis es un buen ejemplo[30]. Su reinado será, por otra parte, herencia de la situación anterior en lo que concierne a los honores familiares[31].

Con Antonino Pío se producen nuevas circunstancias: la adopción de Marco Aurelio y Lucio Vero, y la consideración oficial de Faustina, hija de Antonino Pío y esposa de Marco Aurelio, como Augusta así como la excepcional fertilidad de la misma. Todo ello dará origen a un nuevo concepto dinástico mucho más cercano a la sociedad, por lo que parece que cristalizará, e incluso seguramente se teorizará ideológica y políticamente, por obra de la segunda sofística durante el reinado de Marco Aurelio[32]. Hay que señalar, según se desprende de la correspondencia intercambiada entre Marco Cornelio Frontón, preceptor y maestro de Marco Aurelio y Lucio Vero, con su pupilo Marco Aurelio antes y después de alcanzar este último la púrpura imperial, que la integración de los miembros de la casa imperial en esta presencia pública del poder parece responder a las características personales de gran vinculación y atención a la propia familia por parte del propio emperador, que propiciaría iniciativas privadas y oficiales de este tipo[33].

Septimio Severo representa un afán de continuidad dinástica respecto a los antoninos, reflejado claramente en su titulatura[34], aunque el intermedio de Pértinax sea también para él importante, al menos al inicio del reinado. La falsa filiación de Septimio Severo que se remonta Nerva y convierte a Marco Aurelio en su padre y a sus hijas en hermanas, así como incluso la rehabilitación de la figura condenada de Cómodo como hermano del emperador reinante, comporta,

---

sacerdocios, resulta muy intersante el índice de divinidades veneradas junto a la *dea Roma*, p. 317. Para el mundo griego, cf. Mellor 1975; además Mellor 1981 especialmente: 966-968, para los *Romaia*; Mellor 1981: 997 para la intervención de Adriano. Véase también Gagé 1936; Gagé 1974, la celebración continua viva en 289 d.C.

[30] Cf. Johnson 1960.

[31] Cf. Para sus representaciones escultóricas Evers 1994.

[32] Herodes Ático en la *exedra* del ninfeo que hizo erigir en Olimpia (*ILS* 8803a-c) situó las de la familia imperial de su discípulo el emperador Marco Aurelio, junto a las de toda su propia familia con una presentación casi de igual rango que las de la casa imperial (*ILS* 8824a-b, y *Syll.*3 853-865, para las inscripciones de la familia de Herodes). Cf. Bol 1984, para el material epigráfico pp.108-141; y además Dittenberger y Purgold 1896 (=*IvO*), núms. 610-632; en *SEG* XXXIII, 331-349, se hace una colación entre el trabajo de Bol e *IvO*. Cf. también, Bowersock 1969: 78-82 y 92-100. Para otros casos particulares de la aplicación de estos principios, véase Slavazzi 2006; sobre las inscripciones en honor de la familia de este personaje cf. ahora, Kalinowski 2007; pueden también ser útiles para este tema algunos de los trabajos recogidos en Cordovana y Galli (eds.) 2007, en especial Barresi 2007: 140-143; además Schmidt y Fleury 2011. Para el papel posiblemente representado por Elio Aristides cf. Boulanger 1923; recientemente se han publicado las obras apócrifas que le son atribuídas cf. Patillon 2002, cf. además la excelente introducción de Behr 1973, especialmente: VII-XXI.

[33] Cf. Mayer 2009. La divinización *de Faustina minor* después de su prematura muerte será un elemento consolidador de un proceso que había empezado bajo Antonino Pío.

[34] De forma general un buen compendio sobre el tema en Magioncalda 1991; concretamente sobre la familia de Septimio Severo, Mastino 1981.

sin duda, la conciencia marcada de la importancia, nos atreveríamos a decir que popular, del *nomen Antoninorum*.

La situación particular bajo el reinado de los demás Severos comporta novedades muy importantes como es el caso de la consideración de las damas dominantes de la casa no sólo como *Augustae* sino también en la insistencia de denominarlas *mater castrorum* o incluso *mater senatus*[35]. Hay que prestar una especial atención a las innovaciones efímeras de Heliogábalo[36].

La evolución posterior hasta el dominado se moverá en una continuidad, paradójicamente, discontinua de algunos de los rasgos señalados a partir de los antoninos. Momentos como el reinado de Decio merecen, sin embargo, especial atención por algunos rasgos originales. El emperador calificado como *dominus*, conocido ya de forma oficial, esporádicamente desde época de Trajano, irá cobrando fuerza paulatina hasta convertirse esta denominación en la justificación del poder.

La teorización política que caracteriza el reinado de Diocleciano es una muestra clara de cómo la concepción de familia imperial se debe adaptar a las nuevas situaciones políticas, que son revestidas también de connotaciones religiosas: dos *Augusti*, uno *Iovius* y uno *Herculeus*, así como dos Césares con las mismas características, combinadas con el establecimiento de lazos familiares en paralelo a la promoción de los descendientes[37], son un camino interesante y efímero que, no obstante, no llegará a funcionar en su integridad y se disolverá en función de sus mismas contradictorias características[38].

El reinado de Constantino supondrá el inicio de un camino intrincado de progresiva cristianización del poder público y por tanto de constitución de una "religión de estado"[39], dando lugar a los que los historiadores franceses han llamado "l'Empire chrétien", que se irá consolidando paulatinamente hasta el reinado de Teodosio, con episodios de gran importancia para comprender la cultura del momento como es el caso de la denominada "réaction païenne"[40].

A grandes rasgos lo que acabamos de exponer caracteriza al menos sumariamente el cuadro en el que se produjo la integración social y, hasta cierto punto, religiosa del imperio romano, y naturalmente el crisol en el que se fundieron las más diversas identidades.

---

[35] Sobre la evolución del papel representativo de las mujeres de la casa imperial, véanse los trabajos citados en nota 28.

[36] Por ejemplo, Icks 2001.

[37] Así Stefan 2005.

[38] Para la Tetrarquía puede encontrarse una abundante y documentada información en trabajos como el de Kuhoff 2001.

[39] Cf. de manera general el reciente manual de Brandt 1998; y también la ya clásica exposición de Sordi 1965; Sordi 1984, además Siniscalco 2004. Para Constantino y su época, un resumen de los problemas, con abundante bibliografía, en Mayer 2005. Un estudio ya clásico, Alföldi 1948.

[40] Por ejemplo: Piganiol 1972; De Labriolle 1934, una monografía clásica sobre el tema.

El culto imperial en sus diversas formas y manifestaciones constituyó un medio seguro de promoción social, que incluso llegó a especializarse por clases y marco la evolución social de las familias. Desde el sevirato augustal, reservado principalmente a los libertos, a los flaminatos y pontificados coloniales y municipales, reservados a los magistrados locales, que podían tener su culminación en los correspondientes flaminatos provinciales. Hay, además, sacerdocios reservados también a mujeres[41], que siguen así la promoción social de maridos e hijos y que culminan junto al marido en el flaminato provincial[42].

Los mismos sacerdocios tradicionales de la propia Urbe, Roma, se teñirán de culto imperial de modo progresivo, y, seguramente, comportarán las nuevas formas de presencia pública.

Una última observación final bastará para evaluar hasta que punto hundió sus raíces profundamente este culto en el tejido social. Cuando algunos de los cánones del llamado "concilio de *Iliberris*", en el siglo IV[43], se preocupan de los *flamines* del culto imperial y de su papel en una sociedad, seguramente ya mayoritariamente cristiana, no hacen más que reflejar una situación importante: la indispensabilidad de estos sacerdocios para asegurar la promoción y el *status* social a pesar de los avances del cristianismo, en puertas de vencer la batalla. Victoria que a continuación comportará, como contrapartida, el progresivo e interesado ascenso y consecución de los episcopados por parte de los notables, como una forma de adaptación a la nueva realidad religiosa y social.

Si nos queremos acercar por último a un ejemplo cercano a Coimbra y consideramos el caso de *Conimbriga*, Condeixa-a-Velha, vemos como el único testimonio de este tipo de culto imperial hallado en la ciudad es una inscripción dedicada al *divus Augustus* por un personaje que lleva por nombre *Lucius Papirius* y es *flamen augustalis provinciae Lusitaniae*[44]; podemos añadir además la dedicatoria al emperador Tito erigida en Mérida, *Emerita Augusta*, por la *provincia Lusitania*, siendo legado del emperador *Gaius Arruntius Celer* y *flamen provinciae Lusitaniae* el *Conimbrige<n>sis Marcus Iunius Latro*[45]. Las noticias parecen ser pocas, pero si las complementamos con la presencia de *Apollo Augustus*[46], *Mars*

---

[41] El modelo lo dan los sacerdocios de la propia Roma reservados a las clases superiores de la sociedad; una puesta a punto reciente en Raepsaet-Charlier 2005.

[42] El caso de *Tarraco* es muy ilustrativo, cf. Alföldy 1973. Otros casos hispanos en Melchor Gil 2010; Navarro Caballero 2003.

[43] Cf. Vives, Marín y Martínez 1963, para el texto; Suberbiola Martínez 1987, para los diversos estratos que se acumulan en la colección de cánones; puede verse además el ya clásico artículo de Duchesne 1886.

[44] *CIL* II 41*, que fue considerada falsa por E. Hübner, aunque estudios posteriores han mostrado su naturaleza genuina: cf. Etienne, Fabre, P. y M. Lévêque 1976: 51-52 (a cargo de R. Etienne y G. Fabre).

[45] *CIL* II 5264 = *ILS* 261, Etienne, Fabre, P. y M. Lévêque 1976: 49-51.

[46] *AE* 1924, 12, Etienne, Fabre, P. et M. Lévêque 1976: 20-21.

Augustus[47], la *Pietas Augusta*[48], y los menos claros, y seguramente de origen prerromano, *Remetes Augusti*[49], el panorama parece hacerse, evidentemente, más rico. Sin duda alguna la plegaria ritual que se realizaba en un recinto, *ariae* (sic), verosímilmente dedicado a *Mars Augustus*, presente en otro epígrafe muy fragmentario, resulta una pieza clave sobre la que habrá que volver[50]. Los miliarios de la zona aseguran la memoria de Tácito, Constancio Cloro, Maximiano y Constancio II[51], y no faltan tampoco las inscripciones cristianas, que documentan el fin del proceso expuesto[52]. Vemos, en consecuencia, como una simple realización local, a pesar de los pocos elementos conservados, muestra una evolución que debió de estar, evidentemente, completamente documentada en su momento. Una prueba más de la realidad del fenómeno que aglutinó de forma muy sólida al conjunto del imperio romano de uno a otro extremo.

Sin duda el esfuerzo de claridad y de indicar solamente, en razón del espacio reservado, los rasgos esenciales del proceso que estudiamos, habrá conllevado a cierta simplificación y reducción de algunos fenómenos muy complejos, pero creemos con ello haber conseguido nuestro objetivo de presentar el culto imperial como punto de encuentro para la sociedad multiétnica y plural romana. Se trata, pues, de un factor esencial de vertebración y de evolución de la misma, a partir de unos parámetros que superan y al mismo tiempo abarcan y transforman las realidades locales, para conseguir un panorama social aparentemente uniforme, a pesar de una lógica diversidad, la cual aflorará, no obstante, en numerosas ocasiones, como resulta inevitable todavía hoy en situaciones y circunstancias de este tipo.

---

[47] Etienne, Fabre, P. y M. Lévêque 1976: 34-35.

[48] Etienne, Fabre, P. y M. Lévêque 1976: 37-38.

[49] *AE* 1946, 7, Etienne, Fabre, P. y M. Lévêque 1976: 38-40., divinidades que se han querido poner en relación con los *Lares Aquites*, presentes también en *Conimbriga*, cf. Etienne, Fabre, P. y M. Lévêque 1976: 28; *HEp.* 2, 799.

[50] Etienne, Fabre, P. y M. Lévêque, 1976: 40-42.

[51] Etienne, Fabre, P. y M. Lévêque 1976: 117-119.

[52] Etienne, Fabre, P. y M. Lévêque 1976: 106-11 y 121-124.

I mercati: merci e culture
(The Markets: Goods and Culture)

Giulia Baratta (giulia.baratta@unimc.it)[1]
Università degli Studi di Macerata

Riassunto – Nel contributo si vuole mostrare come alcuni aspetti dell'economia, legati in particolare alla circolazione delle merci, possano costituire degli elementi culturalmente molto significativi tali da modificare abitudini ed usanze pregresse. Nel caso del vino, ad esempio, i cambiamenti non riguardano solo l'alimentazione e le produzioni connesse al consumo del cibo ma anche l'ambito religioso ed addirittura il paesaggio.

Parole chiave: merci, mercati, vino, religione, Gallia, Germania, *torcularia*, *cupae*, *Sucellus*, paesaggio, arqueologia, storia romana

Abstract – This contribution intends to show how certain aspects of the economy, in particular those linked to the circulation of goods, were able to evolve from elements that were culturally significant so as to modify prevailing habits and practices. In the case of wine, for example, the exchanges do not involve merely subsistence and production connected with the consumption of food but also encompass the realm of religion and, in truth, the landscape.

Keywords: Goods, markets, wine, religion, Gaul, Germania, *torcularia*, *cupae*, *Sucellus*, landscape, archaeology, roman history.

Gli scontri incontri tra culture e popoli influiscono sulla realtà di tutte le entità coinvolte modificandola in molti aspetti della vita pubblica e privata, della politica, dell'economia e dell'arte. Naturalmente in alcuni ambiti l'effetto è più evidente se non adddirttura eclatante come può essere il caso della scomparsa di numerose lingue soppiantate da una, nel caso di Roma il latino, soprattutto nella parte occidentale dell'impero, che diviene maggioritaria e che a sua volta attinge, necessariamente, vocaboli e forme indispensabili alla sua stessa sopravvivenza da quelle che ha soppresso. Anche in campo artistico i vicendevoli influssi sono evidenti nell'adozione di tecniche, formule, modelli e modi espressivi tipici di altri contesti e che finiscono per diffondersi in buona parte dei territori dell'impero.

Nei complessi meccanismi della formazione dell'impero romano e dei conseguenti fenomeni così detti di romanizzazione e di *interpretatio*[2] hanno giocato

---

[1] Università degli Studi di Macerata, Dipartimento di Scienze Archeologiche e Storiche dell'Antichità. Nelle more della pubblicazione questo dipartimento è stato assorbito da quello di Studi Umanistici. Il testo è quello consegnato nel 2011 per cui la bibliografia citata non risulta aggiornata all'anno di edizione.

[2] Sull'*interpretatio* vedi più di recente Ferri 1976: 125-133; Marco 1996: 217-238; Spickermann 1997: 145-167; Radnoti Alföldi, Rasbach 1999: 597-605; Saddington 1999:

https://doi.org/10.14195/978-989-26-1280-5_18

un rolo determinante l'imposizione da parte dei Romani di costanti politiche, linguistiche e culturali loro proprie, ma anche la recezione e l'assimilazione degli elementi culturali locali. Nella formazione della nuova cultura sempre in continua modificazione e varia, naturalmente, per cronologia e località, un aspetto estremamente importante è quello legato alle merci e ai mercati in generale, tra i quali giocano un ruolo affatto secondario i generi alimentari.

Nel mondo romano, a dispetto dei condizionamenti climatici e delle grandi distanze da percorrere, proprio nel campo alimentare si è data vita ad una sorta di globalizzazione *ante litteram*. Alcuni prodotti, per necessità e gusto, sono stati diffusi ovunque nel vasto territorio dell'impero incidendo sugli abiti locali e modificando le culture, non solo alimentari, preesistenti all'arrivo dei Romani.

In questo senso ha avuto un ruolo estremamente importante il vino[3], la bevanda alcolica per eccellenza del mondo romano, anche se non l'unica[4]. Il vino non è stato solo uno degli elementi portanti della cultura alimentare romana, un prodotto fortemente apprezzato per le sue qualità organolettiche, ma era strettamente legato anche alla cultura religiosa, sicuramente in virtù dei suoi effetti "secondari", e fonte di ispirazione e soggetto frequente in quella artistica, sia letteraria che figurata. Il vino è stato uno dei grandi motori dell'economia antica: prodotto in grandi quantità, si potrebbe dire "industriali", se il termine applicato all'antichità fosse legittimo, e commercializzato per tutto l'impero lungo le vie d'acqua e quelle di terra.

Le fonti scritte e quelle archeologiche sono particolarmente interesanti per quanto riguarda le province dell'Europa continentale, soprattutto le *Galliae* e le *Germaniae*. Queste, infatti, attestano non solo la capillare diffusione ma soprattutto i tentativi fatti per produrre il vino e, dunque, far attecchire la vite anche a latitudini poco favorevoli alla sua crescita allo scopo di ridurre le difficoltà dei lunghi e complessi trasporti e non rinunciare al nettare di Bacco[5]. I Romani hanno potuto esportare la vite e sono riusciti a coltivarla con successo sino alla valle della Mosella, limite ultimo oltre il quale il clima ha loro impedito un ulteriore sviluppo della coltura.

Per la produzione su larga scala del vino si sono create grandi installazioni nelle quali si manovravano uno o più torchi e che, come si può calcolare sulla base dei *dolia* in cui si invasava il mosto per la fermentazione, disposti in file

---

155-169; Wojciechowski 2002: 29-35; Battaglia 2003: 373-401; Baratta 2005c: 123-134; Cardim Ribeiro 2005: 721-766; Muñoz 2005: 145-152; Cadotte 2007; De Bernardo Stempel 2008: 65-73; Olteanu 2008: 197-224.

[3] Sul vino nell'antichità, in particolare nelle province europee, vedi tra l'estremamente ampia letteratura in materia più di recente Tchernia 1986; AA.VV. 1990 : 1-259 ; Amouretti, Brun 1993; AA.VV. 1998; Katz; Fleming; McGovern 1996; AA.VV. 1999; Etienne, Mayet 2000; Brun 2003; AA.VV. 2004; Brun 2004; Brun 2005.

[4] Oltre al vino prodotto con uva si consumavano anche bevande alcoliche ricavate dalla fermentazione di altra frutta e soprattutto birra, cfr. Hoffmann 1956; Helck 1971; Valiño 1999 : 60-71; AA.VV. 2001.

[5] Vedi ad esempio il XXX libro della Naturalis Historia di Plinio dedicato alla viticoltura.

regolari in ampi magazzini, poteva anche arrivare a superare diverse centinaia di migliaia di ettolitri[6]. I *torcularia*[7], riconducibili nelle province occidentali perlopiù ai tipi descritti da Catone[8], Vitruvio[9] e Plinio[10] con *prelum* azionato da una *sucula* o con contrappeso (fig. 1-2), o a vite diretta (fig. 3), a prescindere da differenze tecniche che riguardano singole parti della struttura e che sono spesso legate anche alla loro cronologia, sono sostanzialmente simili, frutto di una sorta di koiné tecnica che ha unito tutte le province caratterizzate da questa produzione e che ha lasciato poco margine all'inventiva o a eventuali tradizioni locali.

Anche il trasporto del vino nelle province dell'Europa continentale segue le stesse modalità già note per altri territori. Come rivelano le testimonianze figurate e i dati archeologici si prediligevano le vie d'acqua, lungo le quali i pesanti carichi viaggiavano con maggiore facilità anche quando si doveva fare ricorso all'alaggio (fig. 4), e si tentava di ridurre al minimo i tragitti via terra con carri cisterna certamente più scomodi e lenti rispetto alle imbarcazioni e che consentivano solo il trasporto di piccole quantità di merce (fig. 5). La cultura delle popolazioni centroeuropee ha apportato però una novità in questo campo: un nuovo contenitore per lo stoccaggio e il trasporto del vino, e non solo, la vera alternativa all'anfora, la botte, che i Romani hanno chiamato *cupa*[11] (fig. 6). La botte entra a far parte a pieno titolo dei contenitori commerciali usati dai Romani anche se la documentazione archeologica di cui disponiamo è certamente più scarsa di quella lasciataci della anfore perché il legno, a differenza della ceramica, non si è conservato se non in particolari condizioni. La diffusione e l'importanza di questo nuovo contenitore anche fuori dai confini delle *Galliae* e delle *Germaniae* sono evidenti dal fatto che da mero oggetto di uso pratico esso diviene addirittura simbolo, legato in virtù del suo contenuto, al mondo dei morti e dell'oltretomba, presente su sarcofagi (fig. 7) e lastre di loculo (fig. 8)[12] e modello di una particolare tipologia di sepolture dette appunto *cupae* (fig.

---

[6] Vedi ad esempio l'installazione per la produzione di vino scoperta sul sito di Molard a Donzère, Odiot 2004: 202-203.

[7] Sui *torcularia* e le loro caratteristiche tecniche vedi tra i lavori più recenti Rossiter 1978, pp. 49 ss.; Brun 1986; Baratta 2005b; Gilles, König, Schumann 1995; Peña Cervantes 2010.

[8] Cato, Agr. 18, 1-9.

[9] Vitruvius, Arch., VI, 6, 2-3.

[10] Plinius, nat.hist. 18, 317.

[11] Per le attestazioni archeologiche, iconografiche e letterarie delle botti vedi Ulbert, 1959: 6-29; Tchernià 1986: 285-292; Desbat 1991: 319-336: Baratta 1994: 232-260; Baratta 1997 : 109-112; Marlière 2001: 181-201; Marlière 2002. Vedi anche il lavoro ancora non pubblicato di I. Tamerl, *Das Holzfass in der römischen Antike mit einer Studie zu Fassfunden in Raetien* (Diplomarbeit presso l'Università di Innsbruck 2008) consultabile presso la Universitäts- und Landesbibliothek Innsbruck DG43696.

[12] Per l'uso simbolico delle botti vedi Baratta 2005a: 95-108; Baratta 2007: 191-215; Baratta 2006 (2008): 65-120.

9)[13]. La botte è un oggetto evidentemente tanto quotidiano e diffuso, presente nell'immaginario collettivo dei Romani, che le fonti scritte non lo registrano come particolarità e lo documentano solo marginalmente cosiché oggi la sua memoria è affidata, oltre che ai ritrovamenti archeologici, soprattutto alle testimonianze iconografiche ben più ricche e significative di quanto sino ad ora supposto. La *cupa* è stata ed è un recipiente di successo. Ha vissuto in parallelo con le anfore e ben oltre ad esse giungendo, come contenitore privilegiato per la fermentazione e la conservazione dei vini e di altri eccellenti prodotti alimentari, sino ai nostri giorni.

Anche lo spaccio dei generi alimentari, e naturalmente del vino, ricalca in queste province forme tipiche della cultura romana. Gli spazi adibiti alla vendita, i *macella*[14], ovvero i mercati realizzati in strutture fisse ripetono ovunque nell'impero uno stesso schema che prevede una, o più raramente, due *tholoi* centrali e bottege lungo il perimetro dell'area, con varianti legate allo spazio a disposizione ed alle effettive necessità dei singoli luoghi. Soprattutto per la vendita al dettaglio e per il consumo diretto si esporta il modello della *taberna*, della *popina* o della *caupona* che, come dimostrano i dati di scavo e le numerose testimonianze iconografiche ha goduto di grande successo. Se i banconi delle *tabernae* delle città italiane presentano dei recipienti di terracotta inseriti nel cementizio, quelli gallici e germanici sono corredati di un imbuto passante attraverso cui versare il vino direttamente nel recipiente dell'acquirente (fig. 10); se gli avventori delle *popinae* di Pompei sono seduti a bere e mangiare anche quelli delle analoghe *cauponae* germaniche siedono ad un tavolo per la consumazione di vino e cibo (figg. 11-12) con la differenza che oltralpe la *cupa* è un elemento costante e distintivo di questi luoghi e ricorre frequentemente nelle fonti iconografiche.

L'introduzione della cultura del vino incide profondamente sulle realtà preesistenti. La bevanda alcolica ottenuta dalla fermentazione delle uve, infatti, entra in diretta concorrenza con altre bevande di tradizione locale, realizzate sulla base della fermentazione di altri frutti o di cereali, prima tra tutte la birra[15], e finisce con l'imporsi quasi prepotentemente sul mercato a scapito di queste ultime. Cambiano dunque le mode alimentari e con esse le usanze legate al consumo del cibo e delle bevande. Di conseguenza nasce l'esigenza di creare

---

[13] Per questi monumenti e la problematica loro legata vedi Leite de Vasconcelos 1913: 401-406 ("bahus" o *cupae*); i numerosi volumi di Ésperandieu 1916- alla definizione "bloc de forme arrondie"; Julia 1962: 29-54; Berciu, Wolski 1970: 919-965; Tortorici 1975: 135-157; Caldera de Castro 1978: 455-463; Bonneville 1981: 5-38; Khanoussi 1983: 93-106; Balil 1984-88: 111-115; Bacchielli 1986: 303-319; Stefani 1986: 115-160; Stefani 1988: 167-175; Bejarano Osorio 1996: 37-58; Baldassarre et alii 1996; López Vilar 1999-2000: 65-103; Chelotti 2003; Baratta 2006: 355-368; Romano (2006) 2009: 149-219.

[14] Per i *macella* vedi de Ruyt 1983.

[15] Vedi *supra* nota nr. 4.

nuove forme di recipienti per conservare, servire e bere il vino nel rispetto delle molteplici e varie ricette legate alle più diverse occasioni. Si sviluppano, dunque, nuove forme di contenitori e vasi potori in ceramica, vetro e metallo in parte direttamente derivate, quanto a tipologia e a decorazione, dalla tradizione romana ed in parte, invece, del tutto originali perché ispirate ad elementi culturali locali. Questo è il caso, solo per citare due esempi, dei c.d. bariletti frontiniani, brocche in vetro dalla forma di una botticella (fig. 13), prodotte a partire dal II secolo d.C. in *Gallia*[16] o della più tarda "trierer Weinkeramik" o "Moselwein-Keramik" o "Spruchkeramik"[17], una produzione ceramica del III secolo d.C., caratterizzata da varie forme tutte con una ingubbiatura nera ed una decorazione a barbotine con frasi benauguranti o volte ad invogliare il consumo di vino (fig. 14).

L'introduzione della coltivazione della vite e, dunque, della cultura del vino non più solo prodotto di importazione, non ha comunque influito solo sugli abiti alimentari ma ha modificato anche altri atteggiamenti culturali tra cui quelli religiosi. Se, infatti, con l'arrivo dei Romani nei territori della *Galliae* e delle *Germaniae* si introducono divinità del pantheon greco-romano, come ad esempio Bacco, per rimanere in tema vitivinicolo, che diviene parte integrante anche dell'immaginario artistico delle province in questione, non per questo vengono meno le divinità locali con le quali possono esistere delle contaminazioni nell'ambito del più generale fenomeno dell'*interpretatio* o che possono subire degli adattamenti alle nuove realtà culturali. Un caso emblematico, legato appunto all'introduzione della viticoltura, è quello del dio *Sucellus*[18], divinità gallica connessa al mondo della vegetazione e con elementi ctonii, che si presenta nelle vesti di una figura maschile con corta tunica, folta capigliatura e barba fluente ed un lungo martello come elemento costante tra i suoi attributi (fig. 15). E' interessante notare come esattamente lungo le vie di introduzione della viticoltura nelle *Galliae* e nelle *Germaniae* nei primi secoli dell'impero *Sucellus* subisca una modificazione (fig. 16). In queste zone, infatti, mantiene intatta la sua apparenza esteriore, peraltro simile a quella di *Silvanus*, ma aggiunge, come elemento caratterizzante tra i suoi attributi, una botte che lo lega inequivocabilmente alla nuova coltura indicando il suo ampliato raggio di azione (fig. 17). In queste zone, dunque, *Sucellus* diviene specificamente dio del vino mantenendo sicuramente i suoi caratteri ctonii ben conciliabili con il nettare di Bacco.

Infine, ultima ma non certo per ordine di importanza, tra le tante trasformazioni e modificazioni legate all'introduzione della vite va ricordata anche quella

---

[16] Per questa speciale categoria di recipienti vedi Chassaing 1961: 7-33, 89-106; Gilles 1987: 143-144 (a) con altri recipienti a forma di botticella di differente produzione.

[17] Oelmann 1914; Loeschcke 1932: 42-60; Loeschcke 1933: 38-58; Gose 1976: 15-19; Gilles 1987b: 132-133 Topál 1990: 177-184; Pirling 1993: 387-404; Künzl 1997.

[18] Per il dio *Sucellus* vedi Binsfeld 1979: 263-269; Boucher 1987: 77-85; Baratta 1993: 233-247; Baratta 1997: 482; García Bellido 1993: 161-170; Nemeti 1998: 95-121; Sergent 2006; Sterckx 2008: 223-229.

del territorio[19]. La valle attraversata dalla Mosella, ad esempio, costituisce un chiaro ed evidente caso di come la coltura estensiva della vite a partire dall'epoca romana abbia comportato profondi ed irreversibili cambiamenti nell'aspetto del paesaggio sin dall'epoca antica. La "nuova" vallata traboccante di vigneti e rilucente dei colori intensi delle viti, e pertanto radicalmente diversa da come appariva anteriormente all'arrivo dei Romani, è già descritta e ben documentata nel poema dedicato da Ausonio proprio a questo fiume. Nei suoi versi il corso d'acqua e le sue pendici sono descritte come *...culmina villarum pendentibus edita ripis / et virides baccho colles....* (vv. 20-22) e *...Quis color ille vadis, seras cum propulit umbras / Hesperus et viridi perfundit monte Mosellam! / Tota natant crispis iuga motibus et tremit absens /pampinus et vitreis vindemia turget in undis. / Adnumerat virides derisus navita vites...* (vv. 192-197). Un'immagine, dunque, non troppo diversa da come appare la vallata oggi, famosa ed apprezzata proprio per i suoi talvolta ripidissimi declivi coperti di viti e per i vivi colori che la caratterizzano in particolare in alcune stagioni dell'anno.

---

[19] Per quanto concerne la problematica su come risalire dal paesaggio attuale a quello antico e su quali discipline concorrono alla sua ricostruzione vedi, ad esempio, il caso specifico di Arles, Leveau 1992: 597-636. Sull'archeologia del paesaggio vedi anche Guilaine 1991; Kelso 1990; AA.VV. 1992; AA.VV 1997; Aston 1997; Dörfler, Evans, Löhr 1998: 119-152; AA.VV. 1999b; Colecchia, Bertolani, Marcante, et alii 2004; de Vos, Andreoli, Attoui et alii 2007: 13-39; David, Thomas 2008.

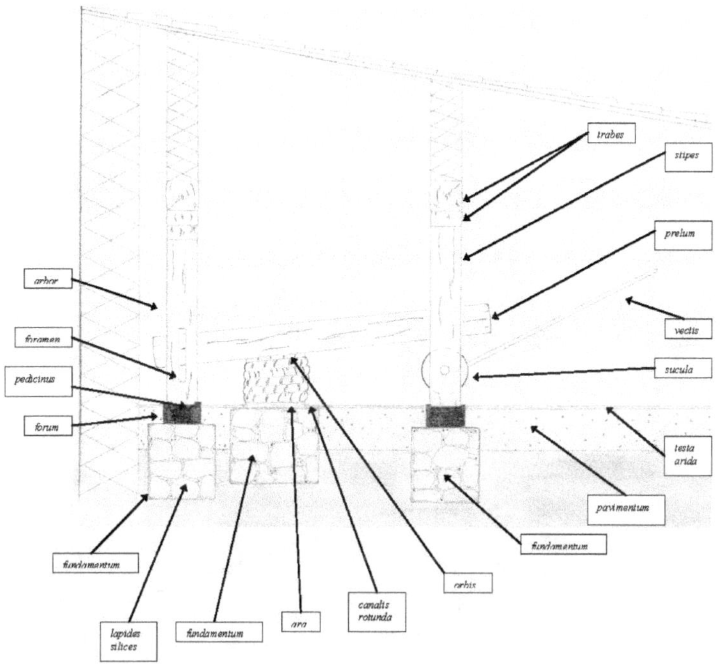

Fig. 1 Sezione del torchio catoniano (*Agr.*, XVIII, 1-9; XIX 1-2). Disegno G. Baratta

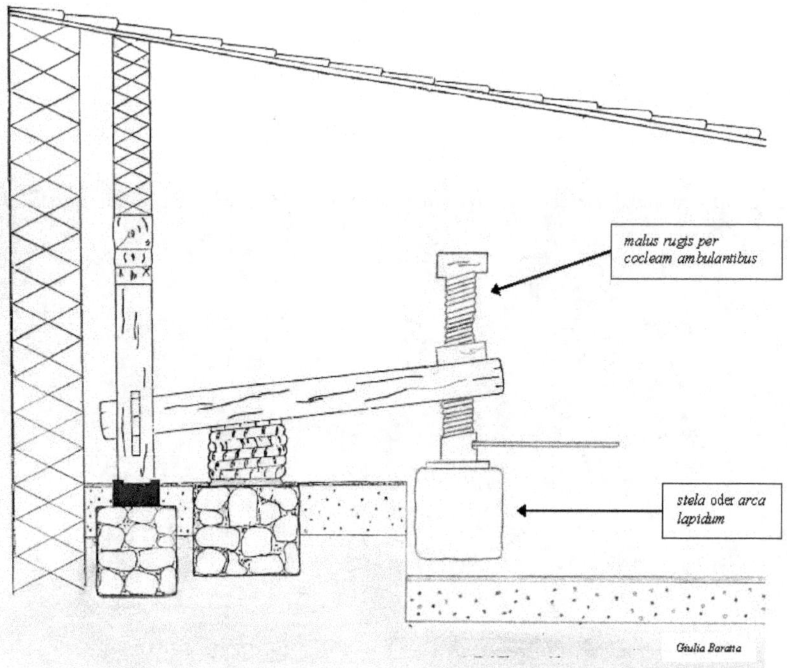

Fig. 2 Sezione del torchio pliniano (*N.H.*, XVIII, 317). Disegno G. Baratta

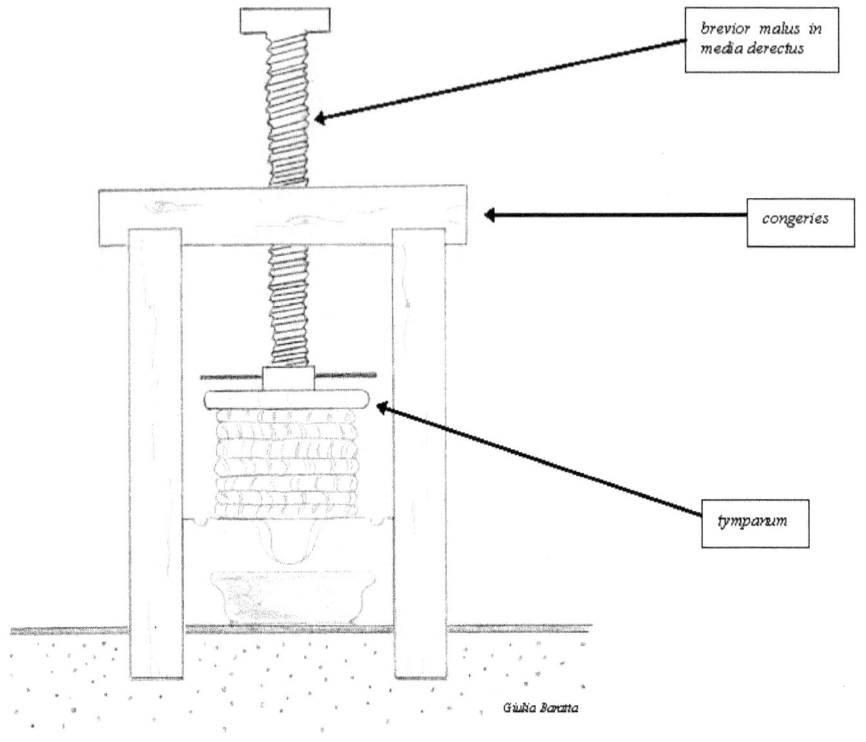

Fig. 3 Ricostruzione ideale del torchio a vite pliniano (*N.H.*, XVIII, 317). Disegno G. Baratta

Fig. 4 Rilievo con scena di alaggio da Cabrières-d'Aigues

Fig. 5 Rilievo con scena di trasporto di botti su carro da Augsburg

Fig. 6 Botte rinvenuta negli scavi di Regensburg

Fig. 7 Sarcofago di Palazzo Rondanini, Roma

Fig. 8 Lastra di loculo conservata a S. Maria in Trastevere, Roma

Fig. 9 Cupa di S. Lussurgiu (Sardegna), Italia

Fig. 10 Avventori al tavolo, caupona di Salvius, Pompei

Fig. 11 Rilievo sepolcrale da Augsburg

Fig. 12 Dettaglio di un rilievo di Treviri con scena di *taberna*

Giulia Baratta

Fig. 13 Bariletto frontiniano, da 2000 Jahre Weinkultur an Mosel-Saar-Ruwer...cit., p. 144,
    fig. 98-

Fig. 14 „Trierer Weinkeramik", da Loeschcke, 1933 tav. IX

Fig. 15 Sucellus da Bergen op Zoom

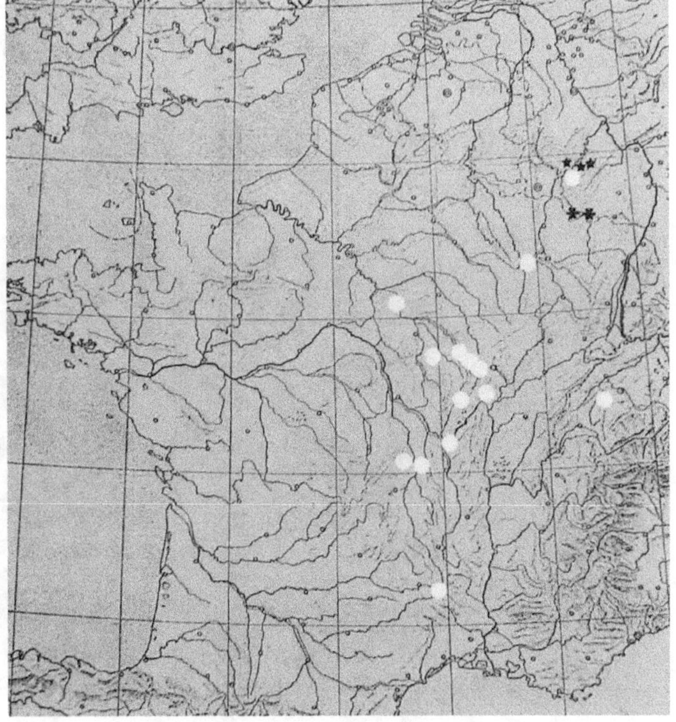

Fig. 16 Carta di distribuzione delle raffigurazioni di Sucellus con la botte, G. Baratta

Fig. 18 Sucellus da Mâlain d'Anely

Vrbes and *Oppida* in Dimitrie Cantemir's *Descriptio Moldaviae*

Ioana Costa (ioana.costa@lls.unibuc.ro)
University of Bucharest

Abstract – Dimitrie Cantemir, who reigned for less than one year, as a member of the Moldavian dynasty founded by his father, Constantin Cantemir, was far more important as a scholar and savant. Indeed, he influenced the culture of his time (but only slightly its history). He became, in 1714, a member of the institution that would later be known as the Academy of Berlin. In this specific intellectual context he wrote *Descriptio Moldaviae*, a geographical, political, and historical presentation of the Moldavian state, and *Historia moldo-vlahica*, a learned work on the origins of the Romanians from Moldavia, Muntenia (*i.e.*, Wallachia) and Transylvania. Interpreting this project as single endeavour with two inseparable facets, these writings put forward a horizontal, synchronic description of Moldavia as well as a vertical, diachronic one. The first of them, with an adventurous narrative, includes an extensive chapter devoted to the geography of the three regions of Moldavia (*Inferior Moldavia, Superior Moldavia,* and *Bassarabia*). That description includes 45 distinctive settlements, most of them towns and villages (*urbes* and *oppida*); these reports are both written to scientific standards and literarily appealing.

Keywords: Cantemir, Moldavian history, Latin literature, geography, cartography.

The Cantemir dynasty is both slight and significant, in two different dimensions, of political and literary coordinates. The destiny of the Cantemir family was impressed with the seal of volatility, which seemed to be the only constancy throughout the life of its members. Different countries, different political scenes, different cultural environments favoured a never-ceasing change of fate on a span of three generations, that equalled the founding and perish of this political and literary dynasty. Dimitrie Cantemir is the nodal point of this rare human configuration.

His father, Constantin Cantemir, was preceded by generations that meant nothing in the history and are therefore absent in the documents that survived and, most probably, in the documents ever written. He presumably was a peasant, in the prestigious alternative of *razes*; the *razesi* of Moldavia were those who participated in the war without being supported or trained on public charge, nor were they paid by the ruling prince. They were driven by faith, and their loyalty was based on the certainty that, fighting against the pagans (Turks, actually), would preserve their immortal souls. As a reward for trustworthiness, the prince used to give them rights of land property or some public tasks. Subsequently, the *razesi* families had the benefit of social prestige and relative prosperity. Bearing on his face and body the scars of many battles, Constantin Cantemir grew to be *boyar* and entered the highest families of the country; in 1685, at the age of 73, after participating in many campaigns of the Great Turkish War, assisting the Ottomans in their campaigns against the Polish-Lithuanian Commonwealth and the Habsburg Monarchy, he was invested *voivode* (*id est*, Prince) by the *Aula Ottomanica*. The step was immense and changed for ever (that means the succeeding two generations) the fate of his family. The fact that Constantin himself was illiterate and could only write his own signature (though remarkably competent in speaking foreign languages), as a trustful chronicler of his time acknowledged, is most likely to be the *punctum mouens* of the brilliant education he offered his two sons. He never thought of himself as the supreme accomplishment of the Cantemir family, but much more, as the foundation of a dynasty. The political treatises he secretly signed included this stipulation. The dynastic dream was the forceful legacy he left to his descendants. Dimitrie, his younger son, reigned twice, for less than one year (in 1693, for five weeks, and in 1710-1711, being succeeded/preceded by his elder brother, in 1695-1700 and 1705-1707). Nevertheless, he got far more recognition than his father, who reigned about ten times longer. While still a teen (15 or, maybe, 12 years old), in 1688, he was sent to Istanbul, as a guaranty of his father's loyalty toward *Aula*: this was the convention and the long established practice. He had already benefited from the lessons of an outstanding Greek teacher, Ieremia Cacavela, both cautiously and astutely chosen by Constantin Cantemir. In Istanbul, the fruits of these first lessons are enormously multiplied by his thirst for knowledge and the motivating cultural challenge. The ample and intricate netting of his personality is set out here: modern sources now briefly describe him as a philosopher, historian, composer, musicologist, linguist, ethnographer and geographer. He became in 1714 member of the *Societas Scientiarum Branderburgica*, afterwards known as Academy of Berlin. This institution played a decisive role in the genesis of two major works Cantemir wrote in his mature age (that was surprisingly fertile, given the length of his life: only five decades): *Descriptio Moldaviae*, a geographical, political and historical presentation of the Moldavian state, and *Historia moldo-vlahica*, an erudite work on the origins of the Romanians from Moldavia, Muntenia (*id est* Wallachia) and Transylvania. Considered as a unit with two inseparable facets, these writings put forward a horizontal, synchronic description of Moldavia and a vertical, diachronic one. After the death of Prince Cantemir, in Rusia, the Academy of Berlin vainly tried to regain possession of the works written on its own request. A manuscript of *Descriptio* was taken by his son Antioh Cantemir (better known as Antiokh Dmitrievich Kantemir, Russian Enlightenment man of letters and diplomat) in his European voyages, as envoy of Russia in London and minister plenipotentiary in Paris. In 1737, Antioh succeeded in publishing the map of Moldavia, in Amsterdam. The text of *Descriptio* finally appeared in German translation (*Beschreibung der Moldau*), in 1769-1770, as recognition of the role Academy of Berlin played in its genesis.

The oldest manuscripts (copies) of this work (A and B) are to be found in the Russian archives that inherited the Asiatic Museum of the Imperial Academy of Science in Sankt Petersburg; at present, they are included among the documents of the Oriental Institute of the Academy of Science in Petersburg (Fond 25, D. 7 and D. 8). These manuscripts got to be known to Romanian scholars by the end of the XIXth century, throughout a copy made *manu propria* by I. C. Massim and, later, by Al. Papiu-Ilarian, that produced the first Romanian edition, bearing the marks of its epoch and particular circumstances. Another Latin manuscript is a copy dated around 1760 and, being the probable source of the German translation of Joh. Ludwig Redslob, 1769, corrected by D. Büsching, is to be considered a valuable witness-codex. By the XVIIIth century dates a different copy (C, known under the name *Sturzanus*), work of a scholar, who intimately knew Latin language, that emended A and B. It has recently been published the first critical edition of *Descriptio Moldaviae*, accomplished by late professor Dan Slusanschi.

One extensive chapter (IV) of the first part, on Geography of Moldavia, is devoted to the three regions: *Inferior Moldavia* (*incolis Czara de dzios dicta*), *Superior Moldavia* (*incolis Czara de sus dicta*) and *Bassarabia*. Each of them is described according to an administrative division in *agri* and, for each *ager*, are mentioned the settlements – *urbes, oppida, munimenta/ fortalia*.

This chapter (I.IV) includes 45 distinctive settlements, most of them towns and villages. The description format is surprisingly constant, so that these pages of *Descriptio* might be transformed into a collection of modern cards (the *fiche* type), with twelve segments:

1-2. geographical information, either placing the settlement inside the *ager*, or related to another settlement, frequently using precise data (distance units, compass reading); proximity to water;

3. etymology, whenever something interesting and/or plausible is to be said;

4. the protection facilities and/or, rarely, naturally protected settlements;

5-7. the status of the settlement: generic (including the commercial potential), political and religious;

8. historical events related to the settlement;

9-10. buildings and inhabitants;

11. decay from an illustrious status;

12. Cantemir's personal inquiries on the specific settlement.

Not all the data are to be found in every of the 45 descriptions, which, therefore, might seem irregularly accomplished. What is a loss in rigid information becomes a quality of a literary text that, covering the needs of a precise description, is to be read with constant interest and delight.

The driest and, not surprisingly, most recurrent information regards the proximity to water of each and every settlement. Though some of the "cards" lack the general geographical coordinates (considered somehow obvious), none of them lacks the aquatic element, except for those few that do not have a certain water source, with a known name, defined as variety (*flumen, rivus, rivulus* etc.). So: *Iassi* is *ad fluvium Bahluy, Tyrgul Frumos* is *ad eundem Bahluy fluvium, Roman* is *in confluente Moldavae et Sireti fluminum, Wasluy* is *ad hostium rivuli Wasluy, ubi se in Barlad conicit, Tecuczio* is *ad fluvium Barlad, Czetate de Pamint* is *ad eandem ripam* (*id est*, Barlad) *Foczanii* is *ad amnem Milcow, Adziud* is *ad fluvium Sireth, Giergina* is *in orientali Sireti ostio, Falczii* is *ad Hierasum, Tigine* is *ad Tyratem, Kissnou* is *ad flumen Bicul, Orhei* is *ad fluvium Reut, Soroca* is *ad Tyratem,* Hotin is equally *ad Tyratem, Dorohoi* is *haud procul a Ziziae fluminis fontibus, Stephanestii* is *ad Hierasum* (with the historically relevant detail that the Turks, *expurgato amne*, established a *navale*, "dock", and a *promptuarium*, "storehouse"), *Czernaucii* is *in boreali Hierasi ripa situm, Cozmin* is *ad amnem Cuczur, Radauz* is *ad eundem* (id est, *Suczava*) *amnem, Piatra* is *ad flumen Bistriciam, Bacovium* is *in insula Bistriziae fluvii, Causzenii* is *ad fluvium Botna* (with the supplementary remark that [*Botna*] *exiguum spatio eam regionem tangit*), *Tartarpunar* is *ad ripam Tyratis* (with another aquatic detail: [*rupi*] *e cuius radicibus fons limpidissimus emanat*), *Tint* is *ad flumen Ialpuh, Tobak - Pontum tangit, Akkierman* is *in ipso Ponti Euxini littore sita, Kilia* is *ad septentrionale Danubii ostium, Ismail* (the region, *ager*, and its fortress, identically named) – *interiores Danubii ripas legit, Cartal* (and *Isakcze*, jointly presented) is *ad Danubium, ubi Ialpuh flumen recipit, Renii* is *ad Danubium situm.*

Some of the settlements are named in direct connection to the water in the vicinity: *Barlad* is defined as *urbs ad fluvium cognominem, Niamcz* is *ad amnem cognominem, Lapussna* is *ad rivum sunovnumon situm*; in few cases, there is no special remark, except for the obvious name overlapping: *Siret* is *ad* [...] *angulum Sireti fluminis sita, Trotusz* is *ad amnem Trotusz.*

Only five descriptions lack any information regarding water: *Kracsuna, Husz, Harlev, Cotnar, Pharaoni.*

By contrary, some towns are flourishing as a direct result of a water presence: *Galacz* is *emporium totius Danubii celeberrimum*, nevertheless *Stephanestii, vide supra*, with *navale* and *promptuarium.*

Explicitly or implicitly, the homonymy settlement/water works as an etymological explanation; *Suczava* is *ad amnem Suczava, qui ipsi et nomen dedisse videtur.*

Regarding etymologies themselves, there is a constant care toward a scientific approach and a neat marking of popular beliefs. Relevant or not, the second section, devoted to *Superior Moldavia*, except for the obvious one just mentioned, on Suczava, includes no etymological explanation. Cantemir briefly – and rather confidently – tells the legend of *Iassi*, as place originally inhabited by some old mill man (*seniculus quidam molitor*), named *Ioannes* and hypocoristi-cally addressed as *Iassi*. Some etymologies are simple translations from or into Latin: *Tyrgul Frumos* is explained: *secundum etymon forum pulchrum*; *Czetate de Pamint, i.e. civitas terrea appelata*; reversely, *Roman* is *Forum Romanum*, *Tartarpunar – id est puteus Tartarorum*. *Kilia* is etymologically interesting only in a previous stage: *olim Lycostomon, eodem nomine a Graecis nautis appellare solitum, quod lupinarum faucium instar undas eructare videretur.*

Some of the place names (mostly the perceptible ones, meaningful) are explained in several languages: *Akkierman – incolis Cetatea alba, Romanis olim Alba Iulia, Graecis Monkastron, Polonis Bielograd*;

For some of the settlements there are only registered the linguistic variants, such as: *Tigine – Turcis Bender*; *Soroca – olim Alchionia*; *Ismail, Moldavis olim Smil dictus*; *Renii olim Moldavis dictum, nunc Turcis Timarova*; *Kissnou* (on the Bicul river) – *vernacula lingua kieile Bykului vocant, id est* the "Canyon of Bykul". Surprisingly, a place name like *Piatra* (*id est*, "Rock"), does not interest Cantemir etymologically, probably due to its obvious meaning (or, on the same basis, an unintentional error, a *lapsus*).

Falczii is of special interest to Cantemir, as he (*vide infra*) personally tried to establish the history of the place; the name is seen as a confirmation of his own opinion: *Falczii a Taiphalia corrumptum esse*. His inquiry (*nostris curis*) implied an expedition: intrigued by a passage in Herodotus that somewhere in this region (*ad Hierasum tribus diebus ab Istro*) lived the Taiphali warriors and built a massive town, he sent (*misi exploraturos*) some individuals to search for ruins or any other sign of historical testimonies; they found there deserted walls, ruined towers, fundaments of fired bricks, arranged in an elliptical shape.

A similar field investigation is suggested by the end of *Cozmin* description: looking for some ruins eloquent about the founders, although he thoroughly researched, could not find any (*nulla ullibi potuimus reperire indicia*).

Kissnou is another place that interested Cantemir, mostly to contradict the common belief: in the vicinity there are some rocks thought to be human work (*humana industria*); his judgement could not accept that, given the dimensions of the rocks and the distance they cover. He prefers to mention a local legend, claiming that it was the work of Devil, meant to stop the flow of river *Bykul* (just as many voivodes tried to do, for a long time).

A different approach in Cantemir's explicit inquiry is a reference to a chronicler's work, maintained at a *livresque* level (unlike the Herodotus passage mentioned above): Nicolaus Costin, *scriptor Moldavus*, mentioned the old name *Olchionia* for *Soroca*, but Cantemir only found *Alchionia* and had no hint about Costin's source (*unde acceperit indagare non potui*).

The status of the described settlements is regularly (though not always) mentioned, in various degrees. *Iassi* is *totius metropolis Moldaviae*, is *sedes principatus* and there is *archiepiscopus Moldaviae*, though he is officially called *non Iassiensis*, *sed Suczaviensis*. Suczava itself is described as *olim metropolis, olim principis sedes, olim archiepiscopi sedes*, now ruled by *Hatmanus, sive supremus exercitus dux*.

Hotin is one of the greatest cities, *inter amplissimas Moldaviae civitates, non inmerito elegantissima munitissimaque Moldaviae civitatum appellari posit*; it used to be ruled by a prefect and, when Turks conquered it, by *pasza turcico*.

Barlad is *sedes Vornicii de Czara de dzios (procuratoris inferioris Moldaviae)*. In *Ager Czernauciorum*, the most important *oppidum (praecipuum)* is *Czernaucii*, ruled by *magnus Spatharus*.

Wasluy is *urbs, aliquando principum sedes*; is ruled by a *parcalabius*. *Tigine* is also *urbs*, and so is *Niamcz*; *Akkierman* is *urbs satis ampla*, ruled in Cantemir's time by a *Ianiczar Aga*. *Vrbs praecipua* is *Kilia*, not large, but famous for its commercial qualities (*emporium celeberrimum*, visited not only by neighbours, but also by traders from Egypt, Venice and Ragusa, *inde ceram et cruda boum coria solent abducere*), ruled by a *Nasir (quem inspectorem vulgari nomine diceres)*

Orhei is an *urbs non adeo magna, sed elegans*. *Soroca* is *urbs praecipua* in its region (*Ager Soroccensis*), *parva quidem*.

Kissnou is *non magni momenti urbecula*.

Roman is *oppidum, sedes episcopalis*; is ruled by two *parcalabii*, named by the Prince. *Husz* is *oppidum exiguum, episcopi sedes*. *Tyrgul Frumos* is *oppidum haud contemnendum*, ruled by a *parcalabium, h.e. commendans*. *Lapussna* is *praecipuum oppidum*, ruled by two *parcalabii*. Are also *oppida*: *Galacz, Falczii, Stephanestii, Botoszany* (that pays tribute to the wife of the Prince and is ruled by *camerarius dominae principis*), *Radauz* (also *sedes episcopalis*), *Piatra, Bacovium* (*sedes agri Bacoviensis*, praised for its fruits: *pomorum fructuumque ubertate celebratum*), *Ocna* and *Trotusz* (of no significance except the salt mines in the vicinity: *nulla re magis memoranda oppida quam egregiis salis meatibus, quae ibi in viciniis reperiuntur*), *Tobak*,

Tecuczio is *oppidum parvum*, ruled by two *parcalabii*. *Dorohoi* is *oppidum non adeo nobile*, being *sedes* for the *vornicus de czara de sus*, id est *procurator Superioris Moldaviae*.

Foczanii is *oppidulum*, ruled by *starosta* (explained in a note *eiusdem cum commendante ex lingua Polona significationis*).

Adziud is *non magni momenti oppidum*; *Harlev* is *non magni nominis oppidum*, ruled by a *parcalabius*; *Cotnar* is *oppidum* of no significance but its vineyards: consequently, it is ruled by *magnus Paharnicus, id est Pincernar*.

Ismail is a *munimentum*, ruled by a *Muteweli*; *Cartal* is a *fortalitium*, ruled by a *Dizar, h..e. commendans*; *Isakcze* is a *fortalitium non magni nominis*; a similar status has *Renii*, ruled by a *praefectus* whose title is register in various languages: *vulgo Beszliagasi vocatus, silistrensi Bassae, qui semper Seraskier esse solet*.

Only one *pagus* is mentioned, for a good reason, being a family property: *Pharaoni* is *praecipuus Cantemiriorum pagus*.

Czetatea de Pamint is defined by its own name: *civitas (terrea)*.

Nothing about: *Kracsuna, Giergina, Kozmin, Siret, Causzenii, Tartarpunar* (except for some ancient ruins: *rudera antiquissimae civitatis*), *Tint,*

Special mentions regarding the inhabitants are mostly on massive displacements and/or ethnic or religious minorities. In *Roman* were located inhabitants coming from *Smedorova*; in *Cotnar* are people *catholicae religionis*. In *Bacovium* is a catholic bishop, *Bacoviensis nominator*, given the numerous catholic people brought here by Stephan the Great, after defeating Mathia, king of Hungary; similarly, in the vicinity, *Pharaoni*, are more than 200 catholic families. *Kilia*, famous trade centre, is home for Turks, Jews, Christians, Armenians and other populations.

The 45 description cards we can extract from Cantemir's chapter on towns and villages of Moldova are both scientifically uniform and literarily appealing. They gain their full meaning when strictly related to the map designed by Cantemir: this map accompanied the text of *Descriptio Moldaviae* – as much as the copying and printing means were available – and, nevertheless, circulated independently, as the first real map of the country, contributing to the fame of its author as praised cartographer. Chapter IV (pars I) is to be seen basically as a corpus of information for labelling the map.

LE CARACTÈRE COSMOPOLITE ET MULTICULTUREL DES COLONIES GRECQUES OUEST-PONTIQUE
(The Cosmopolitan and Multicultural Character of the West-Pontic Greek Colonies)

Florica Bechet (floribecus@yahoo.com)
Université de Bucarest

Résumé – L'intention de notre article est de mettre en évidence les particularités cosmopolites et les principales directions culturelles qui distinguaient les colonies grecques, fondées par l'antique Milet et par Mégare ou par d'autres de ses colonies sur la rive ouest du Pont Euxin, sites archéologiques qui se trouvent de nos jours en Roumanie. Dans l'Antiquité, cette région était considérée, à la fois, un vrai Eldorado, grâce à ses richesses, mais aussi un paradigme de la sauvagerie, en comparaison avec la civilisation du monde grec. Dans notre démarche l'accent tombe sur deux éléments: d'un côté, les cultes religieux de la zone, de l'autre côté, les multiples aspects culturels manifestés dans ces colonies. On y trouve présentées les principales divinités cultivées dans cette région, qui sont, en premier lieu, les divinités des métropoles, identifiées par les épiclèses, mais aussi des dieux inconnues dans les métropoles, mais retrouvés dans d'autres colonies du basin de la Mer Noire; en deuxième lieu, il s'agit des divinités locales et des cultes qui leur sont attribués. Dans la partie dédiée à la culture nous présentons la situation de l'école et le niveau d'éducation des habitants, qui ont donné de personnalités importantes, y compris des écrivains, affirmés aux grandes cours grecques ou égyptiennes et dont les noms se sont transmis à la postérité. Nous mettons en évidence les connaissances en architecture et les tendances artistiques et sportives des habitants, la vie dans les gymnases et les théâtres, la vie des livres, qui étaient commercialisés dans la zone en quantités impressionnantes et qui bénéficiaient d'une telle importance qu'ils accompagnaient les bibliophiles même dans la tombe, la pratique de la médicine et de la philosophie. Les habitants des colonies semblent être toujours au courant avec les événements culturels des métropoles et de tout le monde grec, mais aussi avec les grandes découvertes scientifiques, comme le calcul du temps et de l'heure exacte. L'étude des inscriptions, surtout celles en vers, font preuve d'une bonne langue correctement utilisée, avec talent et imagination. Rien ne confirme la sauvagerie que la culte mais la hautaine Grèce attribuait à ce pays.

Mots-clé: Mer Noire, colonie, religion, culture, cosmopolite

Abstract – This paper sets out to highlight the cosmopolitan features and the main cultural trends which characterize these Greek colonies. They had been founded by ancient Miletos and Megara or by colonies of the latter on the western shore of the Pontos Euxeinos, and are now archaeological sites in Romania. In antiquity, this region was considered for its time a veritable Eldorado on account of its riches, but also a paradigm of wilderness, as compared to the civilization of the Hellenic world. The emphasis

https://doi.org/10.14195/978-989-26-1280-5_20

of my endeavour falls upon two elements: on the one hand, the local religious cults, on the other, various cultural aspects manifested in these colonies. I present the main deities worshiped in this area, which are, in the first place, the deities of the *metropoleis*, identified by their *epikleseis*, but also some deities that do not appear in the *metropoleis*, which the West Pontic settlements share with other colonies in the Black Sea basin. Secondly, there are the local deities and the cults that are attached to them. The part of the study that is reserved for culture focuses upon schooling and the educational level of the natives, among whom many notable people arose, including writers who became prominent at the great Greek or Egyptian courts and whose names have been handed down to posterity. The architectural knowledge and the artistic and athletic inclinations of the natives are highlighted, as well as life in gymnasia and in theatres; also the life of books, which used to be traded in impressive numbers in the region and were held in such esteem that they accompanied bibliophiles in their tombs; and finally the practice of medicine and philosophy. Nor only do the inhabitants of the colonies seem always to have been acquainted with the cultural events of the metropoleis and of the entire Greek world, but also with the great scientific discoveries, like those in calculating time. The study of inscriptions, especially of the ones in verse, reveals a correct usage of language, handled with knowledge, talent, and imagination. None of these characteristics confirms the savagery with which cultivated, but haughty, Greece labelled these lands.

KEYWORDS: Black Sea, colony, gods, culture, cosmopolite

Dès avant le VIIIème s. a. J.-C., quand dans la littérature grecque apparaissent pour la première fois certaines mentions sur la zone[1] pontique, le mental collectif grec percevait le nord traco-scythique, depuis les Carpates et la Mer Noire jusqu'à la Mer Caspienne, comme un vrais Eldorado. Une partie de cette zone, le littoral ouest-pontique, présentait d'incontestables avantages pour les étrangers venus de loin. Il s'agit, en premier lieu, d'excellentes conditions d'emplacement pour des installations portuaires, offerte à l'heure par les golfes. Ensuite, par une zone favorable pour l'agriculture et, vers l'intérieur du pays, par des collines couvertes de forêts et des prés fertiles, au moins une excellente source d'eau (celle de Fântânele), ainsi que des carrières de calcaire (les collines de Babadag) ou de cuivre (la mine d'Altân-Tepe). Evidement, ces étrangers se sont rendu compte du rôle que pourraient jouer leurs fondations pour le transport vers le monde égéo-méditerranéen des fruits de l'immense réservoir céréalier nord-danubien. Mais, malgré tous ces avantages et richesses, les habitants de ce pays représentaient un constant paradigme de la sauvagerie par rapport à l'humanisme civilisé du monde grec.

En même temps, les bords de la Mer Noire sont devenus, surtout après «la grande colonisation grecque» des VIIe-VIe siècles av. J.-C., un vrai empire milésien. Deux des ces colonies fondées par la ville de Milet, Histria/Histros (Constanța) et Tomi, se trouvent en Roumanie. On leur ajoute une localité située vers l'intérieur, peut-être dans la *chora* histriote, Orgamê, à une étroite relation avec Histros, et la dorienne Kallatis (Mangalia), colonie de la mégarienne Héraclée du Pont.

Notre intention est d'examiner les cultes et la culture attestés dans ces colonies et les conclusions qui en dérivent du point de vue du caractère cosmopolite et multiculturelle de cette région.

I. LES CULTES LOCAUX

Les riches données fournies notamment par les inscriptions provenant de ces colonies, mais également par les monnaies et par certains documents iconographiques permettent de classer les divinités attestées dans le panthéon de cette zone selon un schéma composé de divinités appartenant sûrement à la couche initiale des cultes célébrés par les colons arrivés, directement et pindirectement, de leurs métropoles grecques (Milet et Mégare, en passant par une première fondation de celle-ci, l'Héraclée du Pont),.

Tout comme pour les institutions, la configuration originaire du panthéon de ces colonies a été déterminée par le «bagage initial» des colons.

Apollon

À Istros le culte fondamental était consacré à Apollon *Ìètros* («Médecin»), un dieu à vocation de sauveur connu uniquement grâce à des documents milésiennes de la mer Noire: (Apollonia du Pont, Istros, Tyras, Olbia, Panticapéé, Hermonassa, Phanagoreia), mais pas à Milet. Il est bien possible qu'il s'agisse d'un ancien dieu ionien qui aurait disparu sans trop laisser de traces en Asie Mineure[1]; il s'agit d'un culte typique de *génos* aristocratique, dont le sacerdoce était monopolisé[2] par les descendants de *l'oeciste*.

À Istros le culte du «Médecin» est attesté indirectement à une époque très haute (première moitié du VIe s. av. J.-C.) grâce à la base de sa statue de culte, portant une dédicace datée du début du IVe s. av. J.-C. (*ISM* I 169)[3] et à un graffite mentionnant le nom théophore *Ìètrodôros*. L'éponyme de la cité était le prêtre d'Apollon *Ìètros* (*ISM* I 7, 54, 63), et longtemps on a affaire à une vraie dynastie sacerdotale composée des successeurs du fondateur de la cité[4] (*ISM* I 144, 169, 170)[5]. Distinctement d'Olbia, à Istros il n'y a jusqu'à l'heure aucun témoignage d'Apollon *Delphinios*. À l'époque romaine a pénétré à Istros le culte d'Apollon *Phôleutèrios* (*ISM* I 105: IIIe s. av. J.-C.)[6], en directe relation avec la célèbre école de médicine fondé par Parménide.

---

[1] Ehrhardt 1989.

[2] Alexandrescu-Vianu 1988.

[3] Alexandrescu-Vianu 1990: 185-187 et fig. 3; Alexandrescu-Vianu 2000: cat. No 101 et pl. 43.

[4] Voir aussi les dédicaces *ISM* I 104 et 314 A.

[5] Lambrino 1937; Alexandrescu-Vianu 1988.

[6] Cette épiclèse est un *hapax*. On a proposé d'en voir un adjectif tiré de *pholeos* (la célèbre école médicale fondé par Parménide) et d'expliquer l'introduction de ce culte par certains Éléates comme celui attesté à Callatis: Vinogradov 2000.

De l'autre coté, le plus important des dieux mégariens est aussi Apollon, dont le culte est attesté également dans les colonies[7]. Mais il n'y ait jusqu'à l'heure aucune inscription qui révèle l'épiclèse *Pytios*: car Apollon célébré à Mégare est par excellence celui de Delphes. Pourtant les monnaies l'attestent pleinement. De plus, les relations de cette ville avec l'oracle de Delphes sont illustrées par nombre de documents. En revanche, c'est une épiclèse plus rare, universellement dorienne plutôt que typiquement mégarienne, qui est attestée à Kallatis: *Agyeus* (*ISM* III 30); attestée aussi à Tomi (*ISM* I 116 I, contamination avec le panthéon kallatien). À leur tour, les inscriptions oraculaires kallatiennes du IIe s. av. J.-C. font connaître des épithètes plus banales d'Apollon, comme *Nomios* (*ISM* III 48 B et 49; Tropaeum Traiani d'Adamclisi).

Artémis

Les cultes consacrés à Artémis à Istros, dont on ne dispose de témoignages épigraphiques qu'à l'époque hellénistique (*ISM* I 172, 243, 256, 266) et de Léto (*ISM* I 170, du IVe s. av. J.-C.) se situent dans un rapport étroit avec le culte d'Apollon. À Kallatis Artémis est attesté par une épigramme funéraire du IIIe s. av. J.-C. pour une de ses prêtresses (*ISM* III 132) et par une *hiera trapéza* que lui consacre au IIIe s. av. J.-C. une autre prêtresse (ISM III 32). Son culte est largement illustré par des documents divers à Mégare et dans ses colonies; à Kallatis il appartenait donc sans l'ombre d'un doute au bagage initial des colons ayant fondé la ville[8].

Zeus

La couche originaire du panthéon mis en place par les colons milésiens peut être complétée par le culte de Zeus, dont le temple (avec son *bothros*) et l'autel ont pu être identifiés grâce aux fouilles archéologiques dans la zone sacrée de la ville, mais aussi par un décret du IIIe s. av. J.-C.. L'épithète *Polieus* qui accompagne Zeus dans les inscriptions hellénistiques (*ISM* I 8, 54) et impériales (*ISM* I 222) témoignent du caractère civique plus tardif du culte. Cela dit, on serait assez proche de l'époque de l'apogée de l'influence d'Athènes, la patrie par excellence de Zeus *Polieus*, et éventuellement de la chute du régime oligarchique à Istros dont parle Aristote.

La relation entre Zeus et la famille d'Apollon est magistralement exprimée dans un beau relief daté du IIe s. av. J.-C. et représentant Apollon Citharède, Zeus et Artémis[9], ce qui a contribué à l'hypothèse d'une «famille de culte» du

---

[7] Hanell 1934: 134; Antonietti 1999.

[8] Sur le droit de certaines monnaies de bronze hellénistiques est figurée la tête d'Artémis: Pick 1898: no 248-253; cf. la contremarque au buste de la déesse avec arc et carquois, no 224a. À l'époque impériale, Artémis est représenté comme chasseresse sur le revers des monnaies de Septime Sévère (no 303), Iulia Mamaeaa (no 336), Philippe l'Arabe (no 351), Otacilia (no 363). Un beau relief d'époque hellénistique représente Artémis à la chasse: Preda, Popescu et Diaconu 1962: 450, fig. 10c; Bordenache 1960: 498 et fig. 10-11.

[9] S. Lambrino 1937 (qui date le relief du IVe s. av. J.-C.). Bordenache 1961: 201, fig. 16

type attesté à Didymes, le sanctuaire proche de Milet (Apollon-Zeus-Léto)[10].

À Kallatis aussi Zeus fait partie des dieux de la communauté civique et des magistrats (cf. le graffite *ISM* III 254, du début du IVe s. av. J.-C., qui est une dédicace à Zeus *Sôtér*). De l'époque hellénistique date un minuscule fragment d'inscription avec l'épiclèse *Polieus* (*ISM* III 22), et dans les inscriptions oraculaires du IIe s. av. J.-C. Zeus est attesté comme *Hypatos* (*ISM* III 48 B), *Agoraios* (?) et *Hyperdexios* (ISM III 49). Une épiclèse locale de Zeus,– *Ombrimos* («le pluvieux»), épiclèse homérique, utilisée seulement dans les sources littéraires, qui mélange de culte religieux et de culture littéraire, – pourrait être suggérée par les fêtes des *Diombries* (*ISM* III 31).

Athéna

La présence d'Athéna du panthéon milésien, avec sa «famille de culte» Apollon *Delphinios*-Zeus-Athéna, est discrète dans les documents épigraphiques d'Istros.

Par contre, son culte appartenant à la couche originaire du panthéon kallatien. À suivre Pausanias (I, 42, 4), la déesse était adorée à Mégare dans trois sanctuaires, consacrés respectivement à Athèna *Aiantis*, à Athéna *Nikê* et à une Athéna sans épithète, mais qui était sans aucun doute la *Polias*. Une Athéna *Polias* est connue à Kallatis dès le IVe s. av. J.-C. (*ISM* III 76). Elle est aussi *Hypata* et *Hyperdexia* dans les inscriptions oraculaires évoquées pour Zeus. À tout cela il convient d'ajouter les types iconographiques d'Athéna sur les monnaies kallatiennes[11].

Aphrodite

Un autre culte important introduit par les premiers colons milésiens était consacré à Aphrodite. Les recherches archéologiques effectuées à Istros en ont identifié le temple. C'est toujours de l'époque archaïque que datent la dédicace figurant sur un calyptère (premier quart du VIe s. av. J.-C.: *ISM* I 101) et quelques terres-cuites représentant «la déesse à la colombe»[12]. Les autres documents concernant Aphrodite sont plus tardifs, comme un superbe relief (fin du IIe ou début du Ier s. av. J.-C.) représentant les noces d'Aphrodite avec Arès ou Adonis[13]. L'iconographie de certaines terres-cuites d'époque archaïque renvoie au monde syrien: c'est peut-être la même Aphrodite syrienne que celle attestée par des graffites d'Olbia[14].

= Bordenache 1969: cat. no 293 et pl. CXXVII; Alexandrescu-Vianu 2000:, cat. No 127 et pl. 57.

[10] Ehrhardt 1988: 121-161, 190.

[11] Pick 1898: no 234-247 et pl. I 24, 25 (époque hellénistique); 267-274, 309, 340 (époque impériale).

[12] Pippidi 1971; fig. 10-11.

[13] Alexandrescu-Vianu 2000: cat. no 124 et pl. 51-54.

[14] Alexandrescu-Vianu 1994, Alexandrescu-Vianu 1997. La seule épithète d'Aphrodite révélée par les inscriptions d'Istros est *Pontia* (*ISM* I 173).

D'autre part, l'inscription oraculaire *ISM* III 49 et *ISM* III 48 B nous font part d'un groupe de divinités de l'agora kallatienne: Thémis *Agoraia*, Zeus, Aphrodite *Agoraia*[15,] Hermes *Agoraios*[16], Apollon *Apotropaios* et Poseidon *Asphaleus*.

Poséidon

Pour continuer avec les dieux d'origine milésienne d'Istros, il convient de mentionner aussi Poséidon, adoré à Istros et à Tomi comme *Hélikonios* (*ISM* I 143, IIIe s. av. J.-C.) et notamment, à Istros, comme *Taurios*: les documents attestent, au IIe s. av. J.-C., une association de Tauréstai; (*ISM* I 60 et 61)[17].

Divinités agraires

En ce qui concerne d'autres divinités, attestées à la fois à Istros, à Tomi et à Milet, sans pouvoir démontrer la filière milésienne, on peut citer Déméter *Chtonia* et Ga (*ISM* I 109, 115, 120, 125; *ISM* II 36 – la déesse tient l'éponymie divine de la cité: Ier s. av. J.-C.; *ISM* II 59, 118?, 150 – associée à Korè et à Plouton). Comme déesse agraire, Déméter semble avoir été très populaire dans le territoire, comme le preuve le sanctuaire extra-urbain de Nuntaşi, où Démeter est associée à Cybèle et à Nike[18]. À leur tour, Korê et Cybèle sont connues depuis d'époque archaïque tardive[19].

Pour Kallatis une inscription de la fin de l'époque hellénistique nous renseigne sur l'existence d'une association cultuelle de *thoinatai* consacrée à Déméter *Chtonia* (ISM III 40), alors qu'une dédicace fragmentaire d'une autre association (d'époque impériale) est consacrée à Déméter *Ploutodoteira* (*ISM* III 259). D'autre part, Déméter est représentée sur des monnaies de bronze d'époque hellénistique[20] de Tomi et de Kallatis.

C'est à Gé (Ga) de compléter la liste des divinités chtoniennes kallatiennes: un sanctuaire en est mentionné dans l'inscription oraculaire *ISM* III 48 B du IIe s. av. J.-C., mais les origines du culte remontent sûrement à la fondation de

---

[15] À Kallatis, Aphrodite est connu comme *Pandamos* dès le IVe s. av. J.-C. dont le caractère est également éminemment civique. On peut ajouter un torse d'Aphrodite et d'Éros du Ier s. av. J.-C. (Bordenache 1069: 30-31, no 38) et une statue d'Aphrodite consacré par une prêtresse au IIIe s. ap. J.-C. (*ISM* III 94).

[16] La tête de Hermès est représentée sur des monnaies kallatiennes de bronze d'époque hellénistique : Pick 1898: no 253.

[17] Il faut y ajouter une troisième inscription (fragmentaire) de la même époque, trouvé dans la zone sacrée et encore inédite, ainsi qu'un document plus tardif, du IIe s. ap. J.-C. (*ISM* I 57). Dans le calendrier de Histros on trouve le mois *Taureon* (*ISM* I 26) et une fête *Taures* est également connue (*ISM* I 60).

[18] Domăneanţu 1993.

[19] Alexandrescu-Vianu 1990; Alexandrescu-Vianu 1990. En Revanche, toutes les attestations épigraphiques de Cybèle (*Meter aeon*) datent de l'époque impériale :*ISM* I 57 (I, 16), 126-128.

[20] Pick 1898: nos 225-226 et pl I 22. Représentations de la tête de Déméter sur les monnaies de bronze d'époque impériale: nos 279-288.

la cité.

En ce qui concerne Kallatis, il convient tout d'abord de rattacher au groupe initial Dionysos *Patrôos* et *Dasyllios*, Aphrodite *Pandamos*, Peithô, Artémis, Déméter (Damater) *Chthonia* et Cronos. Le seul dieu qui n'appartient pas à cette catégorie d'anciennes divinités, bien qu'il figure dans la même liste, est Dionysos Bakkheus. Les épithètes *Patrôos* et *Dasyllios* de Dionysos sont exclusivement mégariennes, ce qui prouve que le culte a été introduit par les colons venus de Mégare à Héraclée du Pont et à partir dici à Kallatis. La plupart de ces divinités se retrouvent dans la description donnée par Pausanias (I 43, 5-6) du *téménos* de Mégare: il est donc à supposer que le *téménos* de Kallatis en fût une copie assez fidèle.

Dionysos

À Istros, les monnaies hellénistiques de bronze à la représentation de la tête de Dionysos[21] mises à part, le culte du dieu de la vigne n'est attesté, par des inscriptions et par des monuments figurés, qu'à l'époque impériale[22]. Tout cela suggère une pénétration plus tardive de Dionysos dans le panthéon d'Istros.

Les documents de Tomi attestent des cultes de date récente, comme, par exemple celui de Dionysos *Katêgémoneus* «le dirigent» ou *Pyribromos* «l'étincelant».

Au contraire, à Kallatis le dieu bénéficiait de la plus riche documentation est: 11 inscriptions s'échelonnant depuis le IVe s. av. J.-C. jusque vers la fin du Ier s. ap. J.-C. La place occupée par Dionysos dans le panthéon de la cité est, d'autre part, mise en évidence par les monnaies hellénistiques de bronze à la représentation de Dionysos sur le droit[23].

Les inscriptions révèlent trois épiclèses. La liste des divinités au IVe s. mentionne Dionysos *Patrôos*, Dionysos *Bakkheus* et (Dionysos) *Dasyllios*. Très importante s'avère la première des trois épiclèses; car il s'agit de la première attestation épigraphique de cette épiclèse adjointe à Dionysos, qui est confirmée par Pausanias (I 43, 5) à Mégare. Le reflet presque parfait des cultes du Dionysos mégarien à Kallatis est également illustré par la troisième des épiclèses mentionnées, supposée par un sanctuaire désigné comme *Dasyllieion*. Cette épiclèse est, elle aussi, uniquement mégarienne, comme le prouvent Pausanias et Nonnos (*Dionysiaques* XXX 188-190).

L'épiclèse *Bakkheus*, attestée dès le IVe s. av. J.-C., se retrouve dans les dédicaces *ISM* III 79 et 80. D'autre part, le thiase dont on connaît plusieurs décrets est une fois désigné (*ISM* III 45) comme *bakkhikos thiassos*, alors que dans le

---

[21] Pick 1898: no 469, 470.

[22] Les inscriptions (*ISM* I 100, 142, 1167, 198, 203-206; 221; cf. *SCIVA* 50, 1999, 1-2, p. 71-77) mentionnent pour la plupart Dionysos *Kepophoros*. Parmi les reliefs, il n'y en a qu'un seul à dater éventuellement de l'époque hellénistique tardive: Alexandrescu-Vianu 2000: cat. No 173 et pl. 71.

[23] Pick 1898: nos 217-224 a et pl. I 20-21.

règlement sacré (*ISM* III 47) figurent entre autres les *néobakkhoi*.

Quelques fêtes consacrées à Dionysos sont connues d'une manière plus ou moins satisfaisante. Il s'agit tout d'abord des fêtes triétériques (*ISM* III 35 et 44) célébrées au mois *Dionysios* et les *Dionysia ta xénika* (*ISM* III 3 et 44), célébrées au mois *Lykeios*, qui sont les «fêtes où l'ont accomplit le *xénismos* de Dionysos».

Les données des inscriptions sur les édifices de culte consacrés à Dionysos complètent le tableau. Il s'agit, d'une part, du *Dasyllieion*, le sanctuaire de Dionysos *Dasyllios*, situé selon toute évidence à l'extérieur de la ville (*ISM* III 47), d'autre part, d'un temple désigné comme *mykhos* (*ISM* III 44) qui semble imiter une grotte dionysiaque prête à abriter des cérémonies accompagnées du mystères[24].

Autres divinités

À côté des cultes d'origine milésienne ou transmises, plus ou moins probablement, par une filière milésienne, on découvre dans le panthéon d'Istros beaucoup d'autres divinités dont la pénétration peut être explicite par des influences venues d'ailleurs, notamment à l'époque hellénistique. Un culte qui n'est pas encore attesté à Milet mais qui était, selon toute évidence, très populaire sur la côte occidentale de la mer Noire est le culte consacré aux Dioscures, «chargés» de l'éponyme de la cité (*ISM* I 142) et vénérés comme «sauveurs» (*ISM* I 112). À Tomi, ils sont nommés *Dioskorous ktistas poléôs*, ce qui représente le seul cas de ce type attesté dans le monde grec, mais qui peut plaider pour la fondation ou du moins une deuxième fondation de Tomi par Istros.

Les Dieux de Samothrace

Parmi les cultes introduits à l'époque hellénistique, il convient de réserver une place spéciale aux Dieux de Samothrace (voir en particulier *ISM* I 19), d'ailleurs très populaires dans tout le bassin de la mer Noire. À Istros est mentionné un *Samothrakion* (*ISM* I 11, 19, 58). La prêtrise des Dieux de Samothrace était publique (*ISM* I 19, I, 21-22) et va de pair avec l'intérêt porté par la cité, tout aussi que par Tomi (*ISM* II 1), aux relations avec le sanctuaire de Samothrace. Les mêmes dieux sont très en vogue à Kallatis, où ils ont d'un *Samothrakion*.

Le Grand Dieu

Une divinité tout à fait énigmatique est le «Grand Dieu» (*Théos* mégas), auquel un citoyen de Thasos dédie vers le milieu du IIIe s. av. J.-C. un temple (*ISM* I 145). Ce dieu n'a rien à voir avec le «Grand Dieu» *Derzelas*, un dieu d'origine thrace (le nom en prête serment), attesté à Odessos et dans ses environs par des inscriptions et des monnaies plus tardives; il n'est donc pas question, à Istros, d'un syncrétisme gréco-thrace.

Divinités secondaires

Hèrmès

Quant à Hèrmès, son attestation comme *Agoraios* à Istros (*ISM* I 175 et

---

[24] Avram 1995 = 2002; Jaccottet 2003 II: 152-153.

176) ne fait qu'enrichir le dossier déjà volumineux des divinités protectrices des magistrats dans le monde hellénistique, alors que l'existence des fêtes *Hermaia* dans le gymnase (*ISM* I 59) est en état de confirmer le rôle du dieu dans ces lieux.

Dans le panthéon de Kallatis, c'est le héros Héraclès qui occupait une place de choix. Dans ce cas, le culte n'était pas mégarien, mais héracléote. Outre qu'il était le héros éponyme de la métropole, il n'est pas sans portée qu'Héraclès figurait à partir du IVe s. av. J.-C. sur les premières émissions monétaires d'argent de Kallatis. D'autre part, le premier sanctuaire attesté à Kallatis est celui de Héraclès (*ISM* III 3). Une éventuelle origine béotienne, filtrée par Mégare, pourrait être suggérée par l'épithète *Aléxikakos* porté par le héros dans une dédicace des *thoinâtai* du Ier s. ap. J.-C. (*ISM* III 68).

Asclépios et ses conjoints

L'époque hellénistique offre à Istros les premiers témoignages des cultes consacrés à Asclépios (*ISM* I 124: IIIe s. av. J.-C.).

À Kallatis plusieurs divinités sont documentées d'une manière indirecte: Asclépios (?)[25] et Hygie[26] (*ISM* III 48 B, mais aussi à Tomi *ISM* II 117), les Nymphes accompagnées de Pan (?), d'Hermès (?) et de Dionysos (?) dans un ensemble de divinités pastorales dans la même inscription.

Cronos appartient à un groupe d'anciennes divinités chtoniennes, qui comprend également Déméter *Chthonia*.

Divinités marines

Comme il est naturel dans un pays de marins et de commerçants, les épigraphes et les représentations figurées prouvent l'existence d'un culte de plusieurs divinités marines mineures, comme Phorkys. On ne peut pas négliger le dieu Pontos, représenté aux cotés de la déesse Fortuna dans une fameuse sculpture.

Divinités étrangères

On constate une pénétration des cultes orientaux, avec Cybèle en tête de file, représentée à Kallatis par quelques reliefs de marbre ou de terre cuite et par des représentations monétaires. Elle figure parfois associée au Cavalier Thrace. Attis est, à son tour, documenté par des terres cuites d'époque hellénistique.

C'est toujours vers le début de l'époque hellénistique que l'on voit les cultes égyptiens pénétrer en mer Noire. Il est peut-être utile de rappeler qu'un Alexandrin est attesté à Kallatis au IIIe s. av. J.-C. (*ISM* III 155), qu'un Kallatien figure comme mercenaire dans l'armée d'Alexandre le Grand et que des intellectuels d'origine kallatienne fréquentent les milieux alexandrins et s'établissent même à Alexandrie. C'est, non pas en dernière ligne, grâce à de tels personnages que les cultes égyptiens (Sarapis, Isis et Anoubis) se propagèrent dans les villes

---

[25] Représentation sur des bronzes d'époque impériale : Pick 1898; no 352.

[26] Représentations sur des bronzes d'époque impériale: Pick 1898: nos 330 et 353.

pontiques.

Le Cavalier Thrace est en vogue, comme à peu près partout dans la région balkanique, à partir de la basse époque hellénistique, mais surtout à l'époque impériale.

Les abstractions

Il y a enfin un groupe de cultes dont il est permis de supposer, au moins dans l'état actuel de nos connaissances, qu'ils aient été introduits à l'époque impériale plutôt qu'à une date plus ancienne.

Un exemple en est Némésis, dont la statue consacrée par les magistrats («archontes») après le milieu du IIIe s. ap. J.-C. (*ISM* III 75) est l'un des documents épigraphiques à témoigner de son culte.. À part les dieux et les déesses, le répertoire kallatien compte ensuite quelques abstractions divinisées. Il s'agit de *Peithô* (la *Persuasion*), attestés dès le IVe s. (*ISM* III 48 A). Il convient d'ajouter *Agatos Daimôn*, qui tient l'éponymie à la date du décret *ISM* III 38 du Ier s. av. J.-C., *Agatê Tyykhê* et la *Concorde – Omonoïa* (*ISM* III 1 et 41).

C'est toujours à une époque plus tardive, plus exactement à partir de la fin du IIIe s. ap. J.-C., que sur certaines monnaies locales de bronze figure une personnification de la ville de Kallatis.

À Istros, la communauté civique entretenait un culte du «Peuple» personnifié (*Dêmos*) dont une statue était exposée dans l'*agora* (*ISM* I 19). Dans le temple d'Aphrodite était déposée la triade des *Moïraï*.

La culture locale

L'impression générale qui résulte de l'analyse des documents est celle d'une culture provinciale, évidemment plus modeste par rapport aux grands centres de l'époque, mais pas moins hellène dans son ensemble.

Les plus riches informations se réfèrent aux divers aspects de la vie du gymnase. Le gymnase d'Istros, avec ses gymnasiarches, est bien connu depuis le IIIe s. av. J.-C. (*ISM* I 44, 59, etc.). Nous trouvons des informations sur les fêtes célébrées ici, surtout pour Hermès et Héraclès, divinités par excellence protectrices du gymnase. Une inscription de l'époque impériale montre les nombreuses bienfaits d'une dame Aba, la fille du notable Hekataios, adressées aux diverses associations, entre autre celle de professeurs, *paideutai*. Nous avons aussi des renseignements sur le gymnase et les gymnasiarches de Tomi et de Kallatis,. Les inscriptions parlent d'un *paidotribas* (*ISM* III 16) et d'un *didaskalos* doté de la qualité de proxène de Messambria pour ses mérites didactiques (*ISB* I2 307bis).

Les inscriptions parlent d'un théâtre à Istros et à Kallatis, mais en existait-il peut-être aussi à Tomi.

Au plaisir d'une élite istrienne de cultiver les lettres et les arts a répondu, au IIIe s. av. J.-C., un bienfaiteur local, Diogène, fils de Glaukias, qui a consacré un lieu de culte aux Muses (*Mouseion*), dont la prêtrise lui a été accordée de façon héréditaire, toute la famille ayant la grâce de grades honneurs publiques.

Il faut tenir compte du fait que le commerce a favorisé non seulement la circulation des marchandises, mais aussi celle des idées. On est certain que les écritures les plus importantes pénétraient dans les milieux grecs pontiques (voir une mention de Xénophon, *Anabasis* VII, 5, 14, qui avait vu à Salmydessos «beaucoup de rouleaux de papyrus écrits» parmi les débris des épaves de navires venues du Pont Euxin). Nous avons la première preuve du commerce des livres dans l'Antiquité, preuve confirmé par une découverte d'importance exceptionnelle à Kallatis: «la tombe à papyrus» (IVe s. av. J.-C.) – tombe tumulaire à ciste de pierre, où se trouve le squelette d'un personnage qui tient dans sa main droite un papyrus. Il y a aussi beaucoup de reliefs funéraires des maîtres d'école représentés avec leurs élèves qui, eux aussi ont un rouleau de papyrus.

Comme l'enseignement local ne suffisait pas, beaucoup de jeunes gens partaient à l'étranger, pour continuer leurs études dans les grands centres du monde hellénistique.

D'autre part, les villes de Doubroudja profitaient des séjours, plus ou moins longs, des professionnels qui donnaient des conférences (*akroaseis*), comme un médecin de Cyzique, honoré par un décret d'Istros (*ISM* I 26). Le culte d'Apollon *Pholeutrios* dans la même cité (*ISM* I 105) fait probable la présence dans la zone des médecins éléates (comme un citoyen d'Élée mentionné à Kallatis (*ISM* III 8) ou celle des citoyens du Pont qui effectuaient des stages à la célèbre école fondée par Parménide (*phôléos*). C'est entre autres grâce à la qualité de son enseignement que la ville de Kallatis a pu produire quelques historiens; écrivains et philosophes qui allaient acquérir une certaine renommée parmi leur contemporains et dont les activités ont parfois été retenues même par la postérité.

Le niveau de culture dans les colonies ouest-pontiques peut être apprécié satisfaisant, même remarquable, grâce aux textes conservés par les inscriptions. Bien qu'ils gardent des éléments dialectaux ioniques (jusque vers le milieu du IVe s. av. J. C.), respectivement, à Kallatis, des éléments du dialecte dorique, jusque vers les premières années de l'ère chrétienne, passant ensuite à la κοινή, les inscriptions offrent des textes non seulement corrects, mais parfois même d'une rédaction élégante. Par exemple, les décrets d'Istros (*ISM* I 15 ou 64) présentent une narration comparable, du point de vue stylistique, aux œuvres historiques de l'époque hellénistique. Les épigrammes funéraires sont des productions littéraires remarquables, qui usent avec grand ingénuité des thèmes communs dans le domaine; elles sont très correctes – à l'exception de très peu d'exemples tardifs – du point de vue métrique. La présence même de ces thèmes dans ce coin «sauvage» du monde antique est une preuve de plus de la circulation des idées et de l'intégration de la zone en question dans cette circulation.

La ville de Kallatis a donné même des gens de lettres. La postérité a gardé la mémoire de quelques lettrés dont les œuvres se sont perdues. Il s'agit de Démétrios, originaire d'Odessos, mais connu comme Démétrios de Kallatis, grâce au fait qu'il était devenu citoyen de cette ville (dans la deuxième moitié du IIIe s.). Son œuvre en 20 livres, *Sur l'Europe et sur l'Asie*, mentionnée par Diogène Laërce dans les *Vitae* (V 83) a été utilisée par Pseudo-Skymnos et louée *expressis uerbis* (v. 718-720) comme une autorité incontestable en questions d'histoire locale.

Il y a aussi Hérakléidès, le fils de Sarapion (surnommé *Lembos*), un Kallatien du IIe s. av. J. C., qui a fait une carrière notable en Egypte dans la suite du roi Ptolémée le VIe Philométor (Diogène Laërce, *Vitae* V 94; cf. VIII 7; 44; 58), l'auteur d'un impressionnant nombre de biographies et de compilations de philosophie.

En troisième lieu, il y a Istros de Kallatis qui, d'après Stéphane de Byzance (*Kallatis* s. v.) avait écrit «un beau livre sur la tragédie». Diogène Laërce (*Vitae* I 38) mentionne aussi un rhéteur Thalès.

Il paraît que même les sciences exactes n'étaient pas négligées dans ces colonies. Les Grecs des colonies mesuraient le temps de la même façon que ceux de la métropole. Nous savons qu'ils avaient gardé, par exemple, les mêmes mois de l'année qu'à Milet ou à Mégare. Donc l'année était coupée de la même façon et marquée par les mêmes fêtes. Pour mesurer le temps d'un jour on utilisait, tout comme les gens de la métropole, les cadrans solaires. À Istros et dans un village de la *chôra* tomitaine les archéologues ont découvert deux cadrans solaires de facture milésienne. Mais, chose d'une importance exceptionnelle, ces objets n'étaient pas importés de Milet. Les istriens s'étaient rendu compte qu'un cadran solaire de Milet n'étant d'aucune utilité à Istros. Alors ils se sont procuré un instrument très précis, parfaitement adapté aux coordonnés de leur villes. C'est le savant Constantin Popescu Cârligel qui, par des impressionnants calcules, a démontré les particularités du cadran d'Istros. Les historiens avaient peut-être envoyé à Milet des compatriotes qui apprennent l'art du calcul et de la construction des cadrans solaires ou, chose moins probable, ils ont fait venir un spécialiste de Milet (il y a quand même deux cadrans).

Donc, comme on peut voire, même s'ils gardaient leur ancien bagage religieux, ces «sauvages» des colonies ouest-pontiques accordaient leurs montres à toutes les clepsydres de leur temps.

Iter Populo Debetur:
REDE VIÁRIA E LEGISLAÇÃO NO IMPÉRIO ROMANO
(*Iter Populo Debetur*: Road Network and Legislation in the Roman Empire)

Vasco Mantas (vgmantas@yahoo.com)
Universidade de Coimbra

Resumo – A rede viária romana, impressionante tanto pela extensão e volume de trabalhos que exigiu, como pelas funções que lhe foram atribuídas, conta com raros testemunhos escritos de tipo técnico, obrigando a recorrer largamente à arqueologia para suprir esta surpreendente lacuna. Situação totalmente diferente é a que se refere às fontes disponíveis, jurídicas, literárias e epigráficas, para o estudo da legislação viária nas suas mais diversas vertentes, estatais, públicas e privadas, realçando claramente uma das características essenciais da civilização romana, o uso da Lei ao serviço da comunidade.

Palavras-chave : Roma, Vias, Legislação, Mobilidade, Ideologia

Abstract – The Roman road network, quite impressive in its size and the magnitude of the maintenance that it required, is rarely associated with written technical evidence. This obliges us to call on archaeology to remedy this striking information gap.

A different situation characterizes the study of road legislation from the available juridical, literary, and epigraphic sources. These attestations elucidate the road network, including its public and private facets, clearly exemplifying an essential trait of Roman civilization, the use of law on behalf of the community.

Keywords: Rome, Roads, Legislation, Travelling, Ideology

O reconhecimento da importância da rede viária construída pelos Romanos e da sua função unificadora do Império é consensual, ainda que a sua expressão varie significativamente, quer a encontremos num texto literário, num texto de teor rigidamente científico ou numa despretensiosa obra de divulgação[1]. Não faltam vestígios dispersos pelos quatro cantos da Româniapara suscitar e sustentar esta admiração colectiva, imponentes, uns, mais modestos na maioria dos casos, mas sempre testemunhos de uma vontade forte, capaz de vencer a oposição dos homens e da natureza[2]. Não devemos, portanto, estranhar que o assunto tenha motivado enorme bibliografia, sempre crescente, contemplando aspectos gerais ou estudos específicos, estes mais numerosos. Se considerarmos que o *Itinerarium Antonini Augusti*, famoso roteiro viário romano elaborado no século III a partir de

---

[1] Abreviaturas no texto: *Corpus Inscriptionum Latinarum*, Berlim (=*CIL*); *Ephemeris Epigraphica*, Berlim (=*EE*); *Année Épigraphique*, Paris (=*AE*); *United States Air Force* (=*USAF*). Agradecemos cordialmente a preparação das figuras desta comunicação ao Dr. Luís Madeira.

[2] Kleiner 1991: 182-192.

https://doi.org/10.14195/978-989-26-1280-5_21

documentos que ainda se discutem[3], enumera 372 grandes itinerários cuja extensão, segundo este fundamental documento, atinge 53638 milhas, ou seja, cerca de 80000 quilómetros, teremos uma noção clara da envergadura do trabalho executado, sublinhando que o roteiro está longe de incluir todas as estradas do Império, nomeadamente aquela que conserva um dos mais impressionantes monumentos viários romanos, a lusitana Ponte de Alcântara, sobre o Tejo[4].

Deixemos que os Antigos se pronunciem, ainda que de forma retórica, como no texto de Élio Aristides que transcrevemos[5], sobre o que realmente significou a mobilidade existente no mundo romano: *Fostes ainda vós quem melhor estabeleceu a geral asserção que a Terra é mãe de todos e pátria comum. De facto, agora é possível para Helenos e não Helenos, com ou sem a sua propriedade, viajar por onde queiram, à vontade, como se fossem de pátria em pátria. Nem as Portas Cilicianas, nem os estreitos e arenosos caminhos para o Egipto, através da região árabe, nem as inacessíveis montanhas, nem os caudalosos cursos de água, nem as tribos inóspitas de bárbaros causam terror, pois para segurança basta ser cidadão romano, ou antes, ser um dos que se uniram sob a vossa hegemonia. Homero disse: "Terra comum para todos", e vós tendes feito com que isso seja verdade. Percorrestes e registastes a terra de todo o mundo civilizado; estendestes sobre os rios todas as espécies de pontes e cortastes estradas das montanhas e enchestes as estéreis áreas com postos de correios, habituastes todas as regiões a um determinado e ordeiro modo de vida* (Élio Aristides, *Or. Rom.*, 26).

A rede viária romana, nascida de necessidades militares, desde logo na Itália e depois ao acompanhar o desenvolvimento territorial do Império, constituiu não apenas um formidável instrumento de domínio, mas sobretudo um fundamental factor de unificação. As comunicações, terrestres e marítimas, permitiram desenvolver contactos regulares entre as várias províncias e destas com a Itália, constituindo-se fluxos económicos e culturais que gradualmente moldaram o Império[6]. Não nos interessa, neste momento, questionar o sentido do imperialismo romano. Limitar-nos-emos a sublinhar os seus múltiplos aspectos positivos, um dos quais consistiu na existência de um fenómeno novo, ou pelo menos com uma envergadura até então desconhecida, o de uma mobilidade à escala do mundo, como o cordovês Lúcio Seneca tão claramente o exprimiu: *Nil qua fuerat sede reliquit pervius orbis: Indus gelidum potat Araxen, Albin Persae Renhumque bibunt* (Séneca, *Medea*, 371-374).

A sociedade romana, desde os tempos mais recuados até aos dias finais do Império do Ocidente, atribuiu sempre valor simbólico à construção de estradas e das necessárias obras-de-arte, com particular destaque para as pontes. Recordamos o dito de Tito Lívio, classificando como bárbaro um povo sem estrada (Lívio, 34, 20, 2), e a epístola de Plínio-o-Moço ao poeta Canínio, que lhe anunciara o

---

[3] Roldán Hervás 1975: 19-37; Salway 2001: 22-28, 39-43; Mantas 2012: 76-82.
[4] Blanco Freijeiro 1977; Durán Fuentes 2005: 264-272; Mantas 2012: 237-241.
[5] Fontanella 2008: 203-216.
[6] Chevallier 1988; Laurence 2001: 167-176.

intento de escrever um poema sobre a conquista da Dácia, felicitando-o por cantar novas pontes lançadas sobre os rios (Plínio-o-Moço, *Epist.*, 8, 4).

Não faltam, naturalmente, testemunhos do valor político dos empreendimentos viários, testemunhos que se repartem por fontes literárias, epigráficas e numismáticas. Muitas grandes carreiras começaram, como a de *C. Iulius Celsus*, personalidade equestre conhecida por uma epígrafe proveniente do santuário do Sol e da Lua que existiu no Alto da Vigia, perto da Praia das Maçãs (Sintra), pela curadoria das grandes vias, neste caso a Via Emília e a Via Triunfal, na Itália[7].

Os imperadores, desde logo Augusto, utilizaram os trabalhos viários como elemento de propaganda, associando à imagem nova do evergetismo imperial, de forma feliz, uma tradição cara aos magistrados republicanos (Fig.1). São particularmente significativos os testemunhos numismáticos que comemoram trabalhos viários empreendidos por iniciativa imperial, sobretudo na Itália, parte de um sistemático discurso ideológico repetido em milhares de miliários dispersos por todo o Império e nas inscrições monumentais dos arcos que ornavam, aqui e ali, as grandes pontes do mundo romano[8], sob muitas das quais continua a passar a água e o tempo. Imagem quotidiana da *Utilitas* ao serviço da *Res Publica*, tornam-se estes trabalhos uma afirmação da grandeza pragmática de Roma e da sua missão civilizadora universal, a que outros chamarão imperialismo, sem que em nada possam ser diminuidos enquanto reflexo de progresso numa concepção linear do tempo histórico, aliás tão ao gosto contemporâneo. A importância simbólica dos trabalhos viários no Império foi tal que, cremos, se projectou nas alterações sofridas pelo culto imperial a partir do século III, gradualmente menos visível em ambientes urbanos à medida que os miliários honoríficos se multiplicam em consequência de uma autêntica liturgia através da qual as cidades celebram o imperador custeando trabalhos viários como anteriormente lhe dedicavam termas ou teatros.

Fig.1 - Denário de Augusto comemorativo da reconstrução da Via Flaminia.

---

⁷ Lambrino 1952: 142-150; Ribeiro 2002: 235-239.
⁸ Pensa 1979. 19-27; Arzone 2011: 77-92.

Este valor simbólico da via romana sobreviveu à queda do Império, ganhando aspectos novos, alimentadores de lendas ou, posteriormente, inspiradores da busca de uma unidade para sempre perdida com o ocaso imperial. Por isso, não é difícil compreender o extraordinário desenvolvimento do mito da perenidade e ubiquidade das vias e pontes romanas. Com feito, basta atentar no que dizem os textos antigos sobre a condição de muitas estradas ou considerar as inúmeras referências a trabalhos de reconstrução que os miliários ostentam, para que esta perniciosa mania erudita se reduza às dimensões da realidade. Uma obra recente de Manuel Durán Fuentes sobre as pontes romanas da Hispânia limita a trinta e cinco o seu número[9], o que, mesmo considerando a possibilidade de incluir mais algumas, mostra como a raridade prevalece sobre a vulgaridade, conclusão que se pode alargar aos troços de vias romanas conservados.

Espalhou-se também a ideia de que na Idade Média pouca atenção se prestou às estradas e às pontes, o que é, no mínimo, um exagero evidente. Eis o que, no século XVI, o Doutor João de Barros escreveu sobre pontes e calçadas: *São muitas as pontes de Entre Douro e Minho que alguns estimarão em duzentas, o que me parece que pode ser antre as quais ham muitos caminhos, Calçadas de pedra onde se requerem, em tal maneira que os que vem a Lisboa daquella terra não tem paciência quando passam pela Serra de Ancião, que com falta de deligência não se pode andar no inverno e quasi assim no verão*[10]. Este texto é particularmente elucidativo quanto à existência de estradas no início da Idade Moderna, em parte herdadas do período anterior, assim como quanto ao estado de degradação da rede viária romana, pois nas proximidades de Ansião passavam duas importantes vias romanas unindo *Seilium* (Tomar) a *Conimbriga* (Condeixa-a-Velha).

Não se pense, todavia, que a má qualidade de muitas estradas romanas se limitava a zonas periféricas do Império ou a áreas de menor interesse e fraca população. O que Horácio escreveu no conhecido texto em que descreve a viagem a Brindisi, envolvido nos meandros negociais do Segundo Triunvirato, é muito significativo, tanto mais que se trata da *Via Appia*. Vejamos apenas uma passagem: *Em seguida chegámos a Rubi, muito fatigados, porque tinhamos desfiado uma longa estrada que, ainda por cima, a chuva tinha danificado. No dia seguinte o tempo melhorou, o caminho piorou, até aos muros da piscosa Barium* (Horácio, *Sat.*, 1, 5). A razão para este tipo de queixas tem muito que ver com a categoria e tipologia das estradas, que durante muito tempo, mesmo na Península Itálica, foram de construção mais ligeira do que

---

[9] Durán Fuentes 2005: 351-352.
[10] Barros 1919: 125.

normalmente se admite, pois muitas das obras que deram às grandes vias o aspecto de autênticas calçadas remontam apenas a trabalhos efectuados no século II. Não vamos, porém, desenvolver a análise dos processos construtivos das vias romanas, uma vez que o nosso objectivo consiste essencialmente em enumerar alguns aspectos jurídicos relacionados com a construção, manutenção e utilização das vias, ainda que referências às características técnicas não estejam ausentes da literatura jurídica.

Quais são, afinal, as fontes disponíveis para o conhecimento da rede viária romana, entendida *senso lato* e não apenas no que toca às grandes estradas? Em primeiro lugar, naturalmente, os testemunhos de tipo arqueológico, ou seja, os restos físicos da estrada e do seu equipamento. Embora menos vulgares do que geralmente se admite, como já referimos, como fonte primária que são possuem um valor muito especial. O seu estudo permite esclarecer dúvidas ou comprovar afirmações existentes noutro tipo de fontes. É de realçar a pobreza de textos técnicos referindo os métodos de construção viária, circunstância que parece anormal considerando o relevo atribuído à rede de estradas. Não tentaremos explicar a razão desta lacuna, devida tanto a um certo desinteresse por esta matéria, característico de uma sociedade que se interessava mais pelo objecto do que pela sua produção, como pelo alheamento dos copistas medievais em relação a qualquer possível códice que tenha sobrevivido.

Na verdade, não se conhece nenhum texto específico sobre as técnicas de construção de estradas, pois aquilo que se atribui a Vitrúvio e a Plínio-o-Antigo como descrevendo a infraestrutura de uma via nada tem que ver com estradas (Vitrúvio, *De Arch.*, 8, 1; Plínio, *N.H.*, 36, 25, 184-187). Curiosamente, o texto mais completo e elucidativo ocorre sob a forma de poema, um dos trinta e dois que fazem parte das *Silvae* de Públio Papínio Estácio, denominado *Via Domitiana* (Estácio, *Silv.*, 4, 3), no qual o poeta descreve minuciosamente a construção desta via na Campânia, estrada de que subsistem ainda hoje importantes vestígios visíveis, como o celebrado *Arco Felice* (Fig.2), perto de Pozzuoli, e outros submersos na baía de Nápoles, denunciados pela ondulação. As fontes escritas facultam informações de interesse, mas bastante dispersas, reflectindo a sua própria variedade. Os roteiros viários sobreviventes, como o *Itinerário de Antonino*, o *Burdigalense* e a *Cosmografia* do Anónimo de Ravena, embora fundamentais para o conhecimento geral das vias romanas, pouco ou nada oferecem do ponto de vista legal, ainda que o segundo destes especifique cuidadosamente a categoria das diferentes estações viárias: *civitates, mansiones, mutationes.*

Fig.2 - O *Arco Felice*, viaduto da *Via Domitiana* entre Pozzuoli e Cumas.

A *Tábua de Peutinger*, cópia medieval de um mapa viário romano conservada em Viena, transmite um dado interessante ao informar ser a légua (= 2222 metros) e não a milha romana normal a medida oficial de distância em determinadas regiões do Império, nomeadamente no norte da Gália e na Germânia[11]. Um dos

---

[11] Grenier 1934: 101.

relevos do monumento funerário dos *Secundini,* em Igel, perto de Trier, parece mostrar um miliário com a indicação L IIII, correspondente a quatro léguas (Fig.3). O problema do valor da milha, que continua a ser discutido sem razão e que, na Hispânia, foi particularmente complicado pela pretensa existência de uma milha ibérica, de valor variável, encontra fácil solução se aceitarmos o que Políbio escreveu a propósito da *Via Domitia,* estrada que conduzia à Hispânia através da Narbonense: *Os Romanos arranjaram esta estrada e marcaram-na cuidadosamente com marcos de oito em oito estádios, quer dizer, de milha em milha* (Políbio, 3, 3, 8). Esta referência, inserida num texto historiográfico, permite atribuir à milha romana o seu valor legal normal, equivalente a 1480 metros[12], valor plenamente confirmado pelos miliários *in situ.* Os exemplos que indicámos, envolvendo fontes cartográficas, epigráficas, literárias e iconográficas, demonstram que só através do cruzamento de dados é possível conhecer muitos dos aspectos directa ou indirectamente relacionados com a legislação viária, embora alguns dos mais triviais continuem desconhecidos, como sucede com o sentido de circulação, embora existam alguns indicativos de que, pelo menos no Ocidente, se fizesse pela esquerda.

Fig.3 - Relevo de Igel (Trier) mostrando um marco indicando a distância em léguas.

---

[12]Trata-se, seguramente, do estádio alexandrino, equivalente a 185 metros.

O estudo da rede viária romana não pode concretizar-se, portanto, através da análise exclusiva dos restos arqueológicos das estradas, como não pode limitar-se aos trajectos terrestres, considerando a importância que os percursos fluviais e as vias marítimas conheceram como parte de um sistema de comunicações integrado. As tarifas de transporte terrestre, fluvial e marítimo, incluídas no Édito do Máximo, sob a Tetrarquia[13], são mais do que elucidativas quanto a este aspecto fundamental da mobilidade no mundo romano. Não pode também, como tantas vezes sucede, limitar-se o estudo da rede viária à tentativa de estabelecer com maior ou menor rigor o traçado das estradas através do estudo arqueológico dos seus restos, relativamente fácil em estradas como a Via de la Plata, entre Mérida e Astorga, ou a *Via Nova*, entre Braga e Astorga, uma e outra balizadas ainda hoje por muitas dezenas de miliários[14], mas muito mais difícil quando se trata de estradas secundários ou caminhos vicinais. Assim, muito para além do aspecto arqueológico existe um imprescindível estudo histórico da rede viária, nitidamente atrasado em relação ao estudo dos traçados e no qual os aspectos legais assumem primordial importância.

As fontes epigráficas revelam-se, a par de algumas fontes literárias, particularmente valiosas para estabelecer a história de uma determinada estrada (Fig.4), ainda que as informações se refiram quase sempre a vias de primeira importância, como acontece com a maior parte dos cerca de 10000 miliários que sobreviveram até aos nossos dias. Muitas vezes a cronologia de um terminado traçado só pode estabelecer-se a partir das informações facultadas por estes monumentos, cujas fórmulas contidas nas epígrafes eram, em princípio, estabelecidas oficialmente pelo governador provincial a partir de instruções recebidas da secretaria imperial[15]. Os miliários contêm com alguma frequência informações sobre as circunstâncias da construção ou reconstrução da estrada, magistrados envolvidos e, muito raramente, o financiamento da obra, como se verifica, por exemplo, em certos troços da *Via Appia*, custeados pelo imperador Adriano e particulares, e que importaram em mais de 100000 sestércios por cada milha beneficiada[16].

---

[13] Giachero 1974; Crawford, Reynolds 1979: 163-210.

[14] Puerta Torres 1995: I, 19-30, 107-146; Rodríguez Colmenero, Ferrer Sierra, Álvarez Asorey 2004: 353-400.

[15] Pekary 1968: 8-6.

[16] Pekary 1968: 93-97, 167; Melchor Gil 1992:121-137.

Fig.4 - Inscrição honorífica a Caracala, dedicada pelos *mancipes* das vias *Appia, Traiana* e *Annia* (Museo della Civiltà Romana).

Particularmente interessantes são as inscrições honoríficas colocadas em monumentos comemorativos directamente associados à via, por vezes colocadas em arcos, como já vimos, ou de forma mais simples, gravadas junto ao leito da estrada, caso da *Tabula Traiana*, junto ao Danúbio, nas Portas de Ferro (Fig.5). Em Polla, na Lucânia, sobreviveu uma longa inscrição numa base de estátua levantada a um pretor desconhecido, provavelmente do último terço do século II a.C., cujo texto constitui um excelente exemplo deste tipo de fontes (*CIL* I 551 = *CIL* I[2] 638), valorizado, neste caso, pela evidente antiguidade. Reproduzimos aqui apenas a parte do texto relacionado com as estradas: *Viam fecei ab Regio ad Capuam et / in ea via ponteis omneis miliarios / tabelariosque poseiui hince sunt / Nouceriam meilia LI Capuam XXCIIII / Muranum LXXIIII Cosentiam CXXIII / Valentiam CLXXX [-] ad Fretum ad / statuam CCXXXI [-] Regium CCXXXV[II] / suma af Capua Regium meilia CCC/XXI[-].* De acordo com o teor do *elogium* não parece difícil situar o monumento no cenário político das reformas empreendidas pelos Gracos[17].

Fig.5 - A *Tabula Traiana*, nas Portas de Ferro (Kladovo), comemorando as obras viárias de Trajano no Danúbio.

---

[17] Bracco 1985: 93-97; Salway 2001: 48-49.

Por vezes o testemunho de trabalhos viários é mais lacónico, limitando-se a indicar simplesmente a unidade militar envolvida na obra, como a *Legio VI Victrix*, na Ponte de Martorell[18], perto de Barcelona ou, como no formidável corte de Prisco Montano, destinado a facilitar a passagem da *Via Appia* em Terracina, onde apenas subsistem os numerais gravados à medida que o trabalho avançava na encosta do Monte Santangelo, até quase ao nível do mar, 138 metros abaixo. Ainda que este tipo de testemunhos não possa situar-se entre os dados de tipo administrativo ou jurídico, como é evidente, não deixam de contribuir para a interpretação do que se conhece através de outras fontes, pelo que nos pareceu importante recordá-los aqui.

Passemos então às fontes jurídicas propriamente ditas. Estas, com toda a probalidade, reflectem na sua relativa abundância, contrastante com as fontes de natureza técnica, uma das características essenciais da mentalidade romana, o gosto pela organização e enquadramento legal das diversas actividades do quotidiano. As fontes jurídicas podem ser de duas qualidades principais: directas e indirectas. Fontes directas são aquelas que correspondem a textos legais que se referem estritamente a questões viárias, como sucede na *Lei das Doze Tábuas* quanto este código fundador do Direito Romano determina que uma *via* deve ter 8 pés de largura, um *actus* deve ter 4 pés e o *iter* metade desta medida, ou seja, 2 pés (*Digesta*, 8, 3, 1). É claro que se trata de um texto arcaico, que não pode ser invocado dogmaticamente para assegurar a classificação como romanos de caminhos muito posteriores, da mesma forma que não pode impedir a classificação de autênticas estradas romanas que não coincidam com as referidas medidas. Basta recordar os valores que o agrimensor Higino, distinto de outro Higino que terá vivido na época de Trajano[19], ao referir uma lei de Augusto, concede aos eixos das centuriações: *decumanus maximus*: 40 pés; *kardo maximus*: 20 pés; *decumani* e *kardines* secundários: 8 pés (Higino Gromático, *Constitutio Limitum*: Thulin 157). Veremos oportunamente como a terminologia viária também evoluiu desde então e até à época imperial, obrigando a considerar cautelosamente as indicações da *Lei das Doze Tábuas*, cujo contexto é o dos primórdios da República Romana, quando os limites da cidade eram exíguos e as necessidades do tráfico reduzidas. A legislação viária recolhida no *Código de Teodósio* permite aferir a amplitude das modificações verificadas ao longo de oito séculos[20].

As fontes jurídicas indirectas são bastante numerosas, sobretudo as de ordem historiográfica e as de ordem oratória e epistolar. No primeiro caso recordamos, apenas como exemplo, as numerosas informações contidas na obra

---

[18] Durán Fuentes 2005: 120-121.
[19] Clavel-Lévêque 1996: ix-xiv; Behrends 2000: vii-xxii.
[20] Pharr 2008.

de Tito Lívio[21]; no segundo caso não faltam referências a aspectos legais nos discursos de Cícero, como no *Pro Fonteio*, muito elucidativas sobre as práticas que envolviam a construção de estradas: *Acusa-se também Marco Fonteio de ter obtido benefícios da reparação de estradas, porque ou não as fazia reparar, dizem, ou não recusava a aprovação a nenhuma das reparações efectuadas. Se todos foram obrigados a colaborar nas reparações e são muitos os que viram as obras recusadas, é falso que se tenha dado o dinheiro para a dispensa, porque ninguém foi eximido, nem para a aprovação porque muitos trabalhos não foram aprovados [...]. Ocupado como estava Marco Fonteio em assuntos mais importantes para a República, e sendo do interesse público que fosse reparada a Via Domitia, encarregou do assunto homens de primeira fila, os seus legados Gaio Ânio Beliano e Gaio Fonteio. Por isso eles dirigiram as obras; dispuseram, conforme à sua dignidade, o que lhes parecia a propósito e aprovaram os trabalhos* (Cícero, *Pro Font.*, 8, 17)[22].

A epistolografia, uma arte humanista em vias de se perder definitivamente, permite identificar numerosas referências a actividades ou factos relacionados com aspectos administrativos ou jurídicos das estradas romanas. Lembramos apenas uma carta de Trajano a Plínio-o-Moço, na qual, mais uma vez deparamos com o problema da mão-de-obra forçada: *Àqueles que foram condenados durante estes últimos dez anos e que foram libertados sem ordem válida, é necessário fazer-lhes cumprir a pena. Se houver alguns julgados anteriormente, os velhos condenados há mais de dez anos, é preciso ocupá-los em trabalhos que se aproximem da sua pena. Em casos semelhantes é costume empregar as pessoas nas termas, na limpeza de esgotos, na reparação de vias e ruas* (Plínio-o-Moço, *Epist.*, 4, 10). Os aspectos relacionados com o recrutamento da mão-de-obra para os trabalhos são dos que mais ocorrem, como neste caso, nas fontes concernentes à rede viária. Como é evidente, a construção de estradas era, e é, um trabalho pesado e por vezes violento, pelo que o recurso a militares, prisioneiros e turmas obrigadas às corveias, determinadas legalmente, era habitual e deixou forte presença nas fontes escritas.

A reserva que é necessário ter quando se trata, como na definição dos tipos de caminhos na *Lei das Doze Tábuas*, de fontes particularmente antigas deve alargar-se à terminologia que ocorre na documentação, pois também ela evoluíu e não é apenas o significado inicial do termo *Pontifex* que continua a suscitar dúvidas e as consequentes interpretações divergentes[23]. Assim, na *Lei das Doze Tábuas*, uma *via* é um caminho que permite o cruzamento de dois carros, com uma largura média de 8 pés (cerca de 2,40 metros), acabando por designar de forma geral ruas e estradas, independentemente

---

[21] Chevallier 1972: 9-10.

[22] Sobre a *Via Domitia*: Moreno Gallo 2006: 27-31.

[23] Heurgon 1950-1951: 145-154; Van Haeperen 2002: 11-42.

da sua categoria. Pelo contrário, *iter*, que inicialmente aludia a um direito de passagem ganha novos significados, como via, vereda ou caminho percorrido ou a percorrer, como no *Itinerário de Antonino*. Quanto a *actus*, que como vimos também ocorre na *Lei das Doze Tábuas*, tinha inicialmente um sentido muito mais especializado, pois antes de referir um caminho modesto e de circulação limitada designava um direito de passagem ou de condução de gado. Resulta, portanto, necessário ter em atenção a cronologia e o contexto do documento que se utiliza, sobretudo quando se trata de fontes pertencentes aos primeiros séculos de Roma, quando as influências etruscas no que se relaciona a estradas foram, para além de todas as dúvidas que possam existir, relevantes.

Um aspecto que de alguma forma se relaciona com a terminologia das vias é o do nome oficial que se atribuía às estradas principais. Não existia nenhuma lei que regulasse a atribuição dos nomes às vias, assim como também não eram, como uma má interpretação da ordem pela qual os grandes itinerários são referidos no *Itinerário de Antonino* pode sugerir, designadas por um numeral[24]. Normalmente recebiam, na época republicana, o nome do magistrado que as mandava construir, passando depois a receber o nome do imperador: *Via Appia, Via Flaminia, Via Domitia* ou *Via Augusta, Via Traiana, Strata Diocletiana*. Na maior parte dos casos, todavia, na época imperial as vias não receberam nomes honoríficos, ainda que algumas contassem com denominações distintivas, como a *Via Nova* entre Braga e Astorga.

Bastante mais precisa era a classificação das estradas de acordo com a sua condição jurídica. Os textos de Sículo Flaco[25], um *gromaticus* que viveu na segunda metade do século I, e de Ulpiano, famoso jurista do século III, revelam-se particularmente importantes neste aspecto da condição das vias, semelhante ao enorme esforço de sistematização efectuado para estabelecer a condição jurídica das terras públicas e privadas. Não será descabido recordar neste momento a diferença que existe entre as fontes técnicas, praticamente desconhecidas, e a precisão dos textos jurídicos que definem a qualidade e o estatuto das vias de comunicação terrestres (Fig.6), reflexo indiscutível de uma mentalidade legalista e pragmática.

---

[24] Esta prática, muito divulgada em Espanha e em Portugal, foi introduzida nos estudos viários peninsulares pelo investigador espanhol Eduardo Saavedra, em 1862, a partir da ordem presente na edição Wesseling do *Itinerário de Antonino* (1735). A chamada Via XVI, de *Olisipo* a *Bracara*, por exemplo, é um itinerário constituído pelo menos por três estradas diferentes.

[25] Clavel-Lévêque 1993: ix-xi.

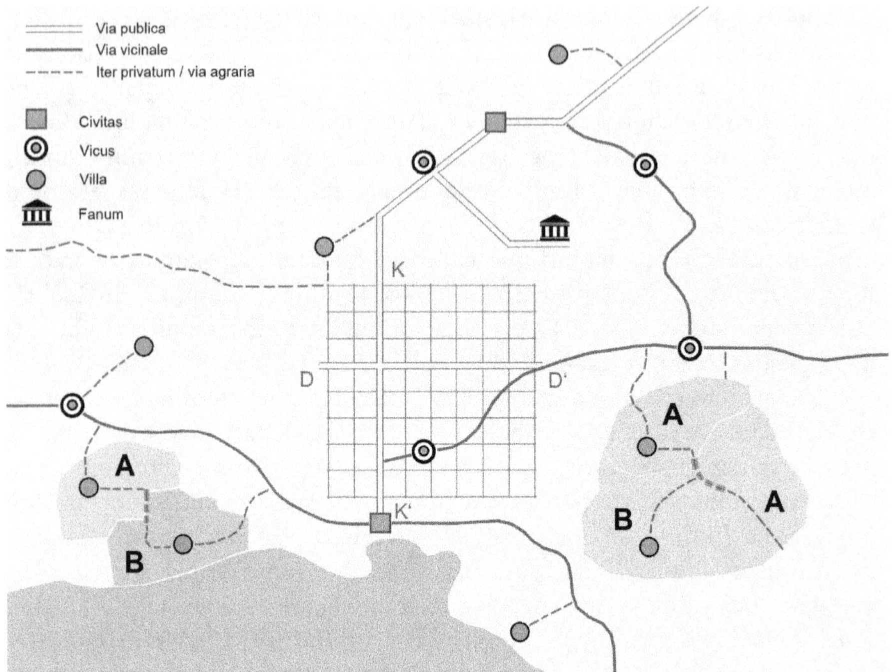

Fig.6 - Exemplo de estradas romanas de acordo com o seu estatuto jurídico.

Vejamos o texto de Sículo Flaco: *Há as vias públicas construídas à custa do Estado e que ostentam os nomes daqueles que as traçaram. Estas estradas estão sob a vigilâncias dos curadores que as fazem construir por empreiteiros. Para algumas delas exige-se também, periodicamente, uma soma fixa aos proprietários da região. Além disso há as vias vicinais que, entroncando na estrada principal, conduzem através dos campos e por vezes atingem elas póprias outras vias públicas. São construídas e mantidas por pagi, quer dizer, pelos magistrados dos pagi que, normalmente, exigem dos proprietários as corveias necessárias ou de preferência atribuem a cada proprietário o cuidado de conservar a porção da via que atravessa o seu domínio. Nos limites destes percursos vêem-se mesmo inscrições indicando qual é o território, qual é o proprietário e qual é o percurso que ele deve conservar. O acesso de todos estes caminhos é livre.*

Há enfim caminhos atravessando os domínios privados que não devem dar passagem a toda a gente mas apenas àqueles que têm necessidade disso para atingir os seus campos. Estes caminhos partem das vias vicinais. Também por vezes entroncam em vias pertencendo em comum a dois proprietários que se entenderam para os fazerem seguir pela extremidade dos seus domínios e para os conservarem em comum.

Em conclusão, as vias públicas ou caminhos vicinais e entre os caminhos privados aqueles que pertencem em comum a dois proprietários, coincidem com limites. Estes caminhos, todavia, não foram traçados para servir de limites mas para abrir comunicações (Sículo Flaco, *De Conditionibus Agrorum*: Thulin, 110-111).

Este longo excerto, bom exemplo da literatura gromática e da preocupação romana com a definição de situações sancionadas pela lei e pela prática, característica de uma mundividência condicionada pelos valores da ordem e do interesse público, refere não só a classificação dos caminhos quanto ao seu estatuto público ou privado, como alude a diversos aspectos do maior interesse, como o direito de passagem, as serventias, o financiamento da construção e manutenção das estradas e os seus procedimentos, o recurso a corveias e a existência de informação escrita, parecida com a que consta na epígrafe de Santiago da Guarda (Ansião), onde se estipula que os *vicani* devem pagar os impostos no município vizinho[26]. Resumindo o que Sículo Flaco escreveu podemos dividir os caminhos em vias públicas, vias vicinais e vias privadas. Há ainda que ter em conta o caso especial das centuriações em que os *decumani* e os *kardines* podem ter características de vias públicas ou privadas, conforme esses caminhos, ditos *iter populo debetur* ou *non debetur*, eram de serventia pública ou privada[27].

A lição de Ulpiano corrobora a classificação de Sículo Flaco. O jurista distingue *viae publicae, viae vicinales* e *viae privatae*. As *viae publicae*, estabelecidas em terreno pertencente ao domínio público do Estado ou das *civitates*, originariamente ou por expropriação, estavam abertas a todos os que as quisessem utilizar. As *viae vicinales*, cuja denominação deriva de *vicus*, com o sentido de povoação rural, aldeia, constituiam a parte mais numerosa da rede viária. Na prática, *viae publicae* e *viae vicinales* confundem-se enquanto caminhos de circulação livre. Ulpiano considera, todavia, a possibilidade das *viae vicinales* serem incluídas entre as *viae privatae* quando construídas e não apenas conservadas pelos particulares proprietários do solo, aproximando-se assim do estatuto dos caminhos privativos dos domínios particulares rurais, as *viae agrariae* (*Digesta*, 43, 8, 2, 21-24). Conservaram-se algumas epígrafes testemunhando a existência de *viae privatae*[28], de que damos dois exemplos, uma placa dos arredores de Córdova e uma inscrição rupestre de Belley, França: *Viator. Viam / publicam dex/tra pete* (*AE*, 1969-70, 254); *Iter via priv/at/a* (*CIL* II 2527).

Uma categoria especial das *viae publicae*, causadora de muitas discussões entre especialista, era a das *viae militares*, largamente referidas nas fontes antigas. As opiniões em causa tanto as consideram simples estradões, abertos por razões puramente militares, como antigas estradas estratégicas que passaram à categoria das *viae publicae*. Sucede, porém, que Suetónio afirma claramente que Augusto organizou o *cursus publicus*, o serviço oficial de correios da administração imperial[29], *per militares vias* (Suetónio, *Aug.*, 49), relação que foi há alguns anos

---

[26] Monteiro, Encarnação: 1993-199: 303-311.
[27] Saumagne 1928: 320-353.
[28] Beltrán, Arasa 1979-1980: 7-29.
[29] Chevallier 1972: 207-211; Kolb 2001: 95-105.

reforçada pelo achado de um miliário de Domiciano perto de Córdova (Fig.7), miliário cujas linhas finais da inscrição parecem sugerir para as *viae militares* fins essencialmente administrativos, como suportes do exercício do *Imperium*, funções de que eram excluídas a maioria das *viae publicae*, como Camile Jullian suspeitou há muitos anos[30]. Eis as linhas que nos interessam: *Ab. arcu. unde. / incipit Baetica / Viam. Augustam. / militarem. vetus[t]ate. / corruptam restituit. LXVIII.* Cuidadosamente construídas, de forma a garantir durante todo o ano o trânsito aos veículos do *cursus publicus*, é sobre estas estradas que se concentram alguns dos mais significativos vestígios arqueológicos viários existentes, entre os quais as pontes que as serviam. No início da Idade Média ainda se relacionava o *cursus publicus* com as calçadas de cuidada construção, identificadas como *viae militares* por Isidoro de Sevilha: *Agger est media stratae eminentia coggeratis lapidibus strata, ab aggere, id est coacervatione dicta; quam historici viam militarem dicunt* (Isidoro, *Orig.*, 15, 16, 7). Os miliários também se concentram de forma muito significativa no traçado destas estradas, como se verifica facilmente na Via de la Plata, com um total de 189 miliários ou na *Via Augusta*, que possui mais de metade dos 106 miliários recolhidos por Pierre Sillières para toda a Espanha meridional[31].

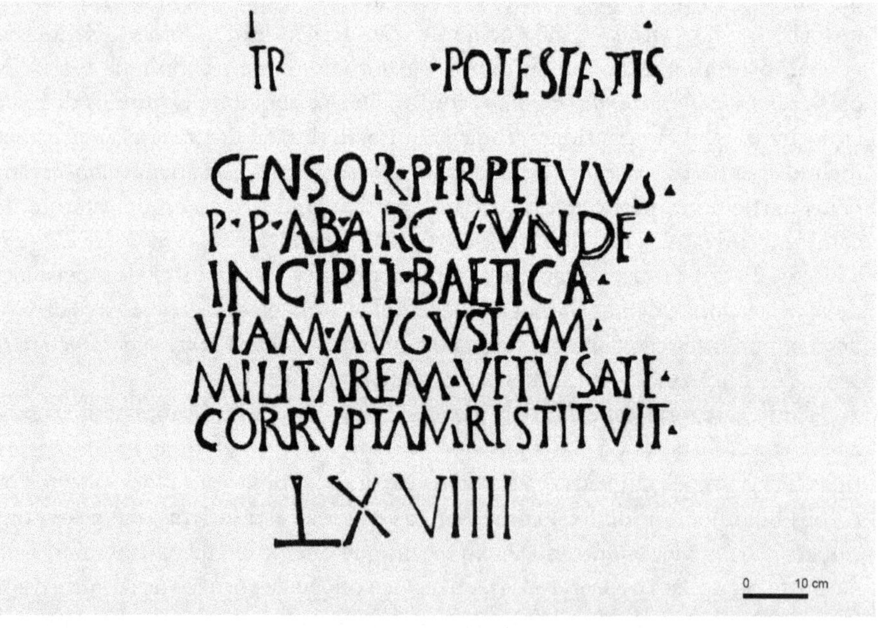

Fig.7 - Inscrição de um miliário de Córdova referindo a *Via Augusta* como via militar (segundo Pierre Sillières).

---

[30] Sillières 1990 783-790; Jullian 1926: 147.
[31] Puerta Torres 1995: II, 281-519; Sillières 1990: 68-115.

Embora sem desenvolver pormenores técnicos construtivos, as fontes de tipo jurídico, *senso lato*, também classificam as vias segundo a tipologia. Assim Tito Lívio, referindo os censores em funções em 170 a.C., divide as vias, segundo o tipo de revestimento em dois grupos, vias lajeadas, em Roma, e vias simplesmente revestidas de gravilha ou saibro no exterior da cidade: *Censores vias sternendas silice in urbe, glarea extra urbem substruendas marginandosque primi ominium locaverunt pontesque multis locis faciendos* (Lívio, 41, 32). Como bom jurista, Ulpiano é muito mais preciso quando classifica as vias, e agora não apenas em relação a Roma e à Itália, mas de forma generalizada, referindo-se, evidentemente, às características da superfície de rolamento: *Propter quod neque latiorem neque longiorem neque altiorem neque humiliorem viam sub nomine refectionis is qui interdicit potest facere, vel in viam terrenam glaream inficere aut sternere viam lapide quae terrena si vel contra lapide stratam terrenam facere* (Digesta, 43, 11). Temos assim vias de terra, vias pavimentadas com gravilha e pequenas pedras e vias empedradas ou lajeadas (Fig.8). O termo *strata* (revestida), embora já utilizado nos finais da República apenas volta a surgir de forma regular nos miliários do século III, vulgarizando-se no século IV. Permaneceu na maioria das línguas românicas (*estrada*; *strada*; *stradă*), na língua germânica (*straße*) e também no árabe (*al-shirat*).

Fig.8 - Troço lajeado da *Via Appia* nos arredores de Roma.

A classificação de Ulpiano aplica-se à totalidade das estradas romanas, das quais a maior parte pertencia ao primeiro e ao segundo tipo, sendo pouco vulgares as estradas cujo traçado correspondia totalmente à categoria das *viae silice stratae*, sobretudo nas províncias. As *viae terrenae* eram as mais numerosas, embora apresentassem incómodos problemas, sobretudo de pó ou lama, consoante a época do ano, mas também tinham algumas vantagens, desde que não se utilizassem veículos de rodas. Plínio-o-Moço refere-se a uma estrada deste tipo, neste caso um *iter privatum* arenoso que ligava a sua *villa* à *Via Laurentina* ou à *Via Ostiensis*, escrevendo: *As atrelagens avançam nela com alguma dificuldade e lentidão, mas o caminho é curto e bom para um cavaleiro* (Plínio-o-Moço, *Epist.*, 2, 17). Outra figura literária de nomeada, o bordelês Ausónio, referiu-se, no século IV, às vias revestidas com gravilha e cascalho existentes na Aquitânia: *Aut iteratum qua glarea trita viarum / Fert militarem ad Blaviam* (Ausónio, *Epist.*, 10, 12).

Os textos que aqui incluímos mostram que existia uma preocupação com a classificação técnica das vias, confirmando a uniformidade da sua construção em cada uma das categorias consideradas, ainda que a dependência da administração local, nomeadamente das *civitates*, tenha ocasionado uma série de diferenças construtivas que os arqueólogos identificam sem dificuldade desde que não se deixem distrair pela famigerada teoria das quatro camadas difundida por Nicolas Bergier[32]. É exactamente este factor, da maior importância para o estudo da rede viária, que se destaca no trecho de uma carta do imperador Juliano, contrastando a má construção das estradas na região de *Chalcis* com outras utilizando a mesma técnica: *Fui até Litarba (este povoado pertence a Chalcis) e encontrei uma estrada que tinha no seu traçado as ruínas de um campo de inverno antioquiano. Deste caminho uma parte era pântano, outra parte montanha, se me é permitida a expressão; mas todo ele era rude e as pedras jaziam no pântano com ar de terem sido lançadas intencionalmente, mas reunidas sem arte alguma e contrariamente ao uso das outras cidades, onde, para as calçadas da mesma forma que para as alvenarias, sobre um leito de terra aglomerada a modo de argamasa se apertam as pedras umas contra as outras, como num muro* (Juliano, *Epist.*, 98).

No período republicano conhecem-se algumas leis viárias, embora de forma bastante vaga, como a *Lex Sempronia Viaria*, de Gaio Graco e uma lei agrária do ano 111 a.C., onde se refere pela primeira vez que os cidadãos estabelecidos em terras do *agger publicus* junto às vias (*viasii vicani*) devem proceder à sua conservação[33]; no ano da derrota de Espártaco, em 71 a.C., estava em funções um *Curator viarum e lege Visellia* (*CIL* I 593). Alguns anos depois, uma das cartas de Cícero alude a uma proposta de Escribónio Cúrio,

---

[32] Chevallier 1972: 93-95.
[33] Lintott 1992: 179-180.

não aprovada, segundo a qual este ficaria encarregado durante cinco anos de construir estradas com o produto de uma taxa sobre carros (Cícero, *Ad Att.*, 6, 1, 22). De uma maneira geral as vias competiam, como já vimos, aos magistrados principais, podendo o Senado delegar em edis ou questores a gestão dos assuntos viários. Ocasionalmente surgem referências a *curatores* (Fig.9), a mais antiga das quais remonta a 92 a.C: *Curator viis sternundis* (*CIL* I², p.200, XXXIII); as fontes epigráficas referem outros no mesmo século (*CIL* I 593; *CIL* VI 1283, 1299, 3824, 31590, 31603).

Fig.9 - Inscrição da *villa* de Nossa Senhora da Tourega (*CIL* II 112), referindo dois irmãos *curatores viarum* (foto Delfim Ferreira).

Com o advento do Principado o Senado encarregou Augusto, em 20 a.C., da manutenção das grandes vias itálicas, substituindo os censores, abolidos. O imperador delegou essas funções em *curatores viarum*, inicialmente responsáveis pela totalidade das vias mas que a partir de Cláudio ou Nero passaram a responder apenas por vias específicas[34], auxiliados por *subcuratores* e por *tabularii*. Adjudicavam os trabalhos aos arrendatários dos mesmos (*mancipes*) e vigiavam para que a sua execução decorresse de acordo com o estabelecido, assim como autorizavam novos trabalhos e ordenavam, quando necessário, a demolição dos não permitidos (Fig.10). No século II passaram a controlar os magistrados municipais responsáveis pelos *alimenta* e pelas estradas (*CIL* XIV 2345). O cargo de *curator viarum*, que existia ainda na época de Constantino (*CIL* X 3732), já não ocorre na *Notitia Dignitatum*.

---

[34] Besnier 1913: 787-790; Pekary 1968: 7-10.

Fig.10 - Inscrição da Ponte Fabrícia (62 a. C.), em Roma, nomeando o curador *L. Fabricius* e os autores de uma reparação no ano 21 a.C. (foto Vasco Mantas).

Nas províncias os grandes trabalhos viários dependiam do governador, ainda que o seu financiamento incluisse diversas possibilidades, como aliás também sucedia na Itália. A construção e manutenção das vias secundárias competia aos magistrados das cidades (*CIL* V 3341; *CIL* IX 2345), podendo os decuriões nomear curadores para se ocuparem das estradas. A epigrafia, mais uma vez, dá-nos notícia de magistrados directamente empenhados em trabalhos viários (*CIL* X 372; *EE* II 20). As verbas necessárias provinham, como já vimos, das contribuições impostas (*vectigalia*), da munificência de algum patrono ou notável local, da colaboração entre a *ordo* e os *possessores* (*CIL* XI 6658) e das portagens (*CIL* XI 5694), bastante vulgares mas que normalmente isentavam os chamados *instrumenta itineris*, animais e carros.

Nalguns casos especiais, devido ao interesse evidente dos trabalhos e ao seu elevado custo, a intervenção estatal, técnica e administrativa, parece evidente. Assim sucedeu seguramente com a construção da Ponte de Alcântara (*CIL* II 760), subsidiada por onze *municipia* lusitanos, e com a Ponte de Chaves (*Aquae Flaviae*), edificada com o contributo de dez *civitates* e na qual a intervenção estatal se encontra identificada de forma muito clara[35]. Parece evidente, em

---

[35] García Iglésias 1976: 263-276; Tranoy 1981: 60-61, 164.

qualquer dos casos, a insuficiente capacidade das cidades para empreenderem, isoladamente, obras desta envergadura, de significativa importância para a boa administração provincial. Como as estradas eram muito caras, as cidades foram chamadas a participar em primeiro lugar na construção e manutenção de vias de especial interesse administrativo e económico, pelo que o mesmo itinerário acusa com frequência, como no caso da via *Ebora-Pax Iulia*, diferenças marcadas consoante o território atravessado pela via pertence a uma ou outra cidade.

Ainda assim, pelo menos durante o Alto Império, o imperador procurou não sobrecarregar as cidades com taxas excessivas, intentando limitar despesas desnecessárias, como se depreende do texto da célebre tábua achada em *Sabora* (*CIL* II 1423) ou do teor de algumas das epístolas trocadas entre Trajano e Plínio-o-Moço, enquanto este era governador da Bitínia, visando contenção nos gastos públicos. O facto da construção de estradas competir em parte às cidades conduziu a grande variedade, o mesmo acontecendo também em épocas bastante recentes, como se verifica, por exemplo, através do que se pode ler num opúsculo alemão dedicado ao programa de auto-estradas iniciado em 1933: *Centenas de repartições diferentes nos diversos estados e províncias disputavam sobre a sua competência na construção de estradas e na sua conservação. E tais circunstâncias motivaram, antes de tudo, o estado variado das estradas de rodagem. Aqui, rodava-se sobre asfalto, ali, sob pedregulho, acolá, estavam os caminhos sem conserto, e noutros lugares, enfim, a estrada consistia apenas num caminho de areia*[36]. Este trecho evoca, sem dificuldade, as queixas do imperador Juliano e a de muitos outros viajantes ao longo dos séculos.

Por vezes o imperador procurava motivar as cidades para aplicarem determinados legados testamentários em obras viárias, quando atribuídos a outros fins menos úteis, ou assim considerados. Uma referência de Suetónio mostra claramente que assim era: *Outra vez* (Tibério) *pediu que os habitantes de Trébia fossem autorizados a consagrar à abertura de uma estrada a importância que lhe tinham legado para construir um novo teatro, mas não o conseguiu e a vontade do testador foi ratificada* (Suetónio, *Tib.*, 31). É claro que neste momento estamos ainda muito longe do totalitarismo do Baixo-Império, quando o Estado põe de lado o princípio da cooperação para fazer incidir impiedosamente sobre as cidades e sobre os particulares, sem distinção, os custos, sempre renovados, da manutenção da rede viária, como os éditos e constituições do *Código de Teodósio* ilustram dramaticamente.

No território português a maior parte dos muitos miliários que se conservaram reflectem a iniciativa das cidades na construção da rede viária, em especial no território outrora pertencente à Lusitânia. Uma interessante inscrição rupestre em Numão testemunha a construção de uma estrada (Fig.11), provavelmente

---

[36] Pflug 1941: 15.

uma *via terrena*, por iniciativa de uma comunidade local, estrada destinada a ligar o *vicus* a uma via principal, constituindo um excelente exemplo deste tipo de trabalhos ao nível das *viae vicinales*, absolutamente de acordo com o que nos diz Sículo Flaco e também Ulpiano quando explica a origem destes caminhos e remete a responsabilidade sobre eles para os magistrados dos *vici* (*Digesta*, 43, 7, 3): *As(s)anianc(enses). Via(m) / Fecerunt*[37]. Este tipo de fontes ajuda a compreender a dificuldade em identificar no terreno caminhos que tiveram na maior parte dos casos construção muito ligeira ao mesmo tempo que comprovam o alheamento do Estado em relação à maior parte da rede viária secundária ou de características locais, limitando-se a estabelecer as regras a que deveria obedecer a sua construção e manutenção.

Fig.11 - Inscrição rupestre de Numão, informando da construção de uma estrada vicinal (foto Patrício Curado).

Este aspecto é particularmente importante e vamos encontrá-lo sistematicamente presente nas leis coloniais e municipais, de que existem diversos testemunhos na Hispânia. Limitar-nos-emos a invocar a *Lex Colonia Genitivae Iuliae*, ou *Lex Ursonensis* (*CIL* II 5439), da cidade de *Urso* (Osuna) na Bética[38]. O artigo LXXVIII determina que os caminhos públicos existentes à data da fundação da colónia, em 44 a.C., mantenham a mesma condição, reproduzindo uma regra constantemente recordada na legislação e pelos *gromatici*. O artigo XCVIII estipula que a contribuição pessoal, directa ou através de escravos ou de animais, para obras públicas, nomeadamente construção e reparação de estradas deve ser

---

[37] Curado 1985: nº48.
[38] Ors 1953: 167-280; Manuel Abascal / Espinosa 1989: 91-110.

determinada em reunião dos decuriões, por maioria. Ficavam isentos apenas os jovens de menos de catorze anos e os homens com mais de sessenta anos, cabendo cinco dias de trabalho anual aos restantes, mesmo que não residissem na colónia.

Por nos parecer particularmente importante transcrevemos este artigo na íntegra: *Quamcumque munitionem decuriones huiusce coloniae decreverint, si maior pars decurionum atfuerit, cum ea res consuletur, eam munitionem fieri liceto, dum ne amplius in annos singulos in que homines singulos puberes operas quinas et in iumenta plaustraria iuga singula operas ternas decernant. Eique munitioni aediles qui tum, erunt ex decurionum decreto praesunto. Uti decuriones censuerint, ita muniendum curanto, dum ne invito eius opera exigatur, qui minor annorum XIIII aut maior annorum LX natus erit. Qui in ea colonia intrave eius coloniae fines domicilium praediumve habebit neque eius coloniae colonus erit, is eidem munitioni uti colonus parento.*

O artigo CIV determina que se respeitem os novos caminhos abertos na área da colónia, assim como as *fossae limitales*, proibindo que se obstrua a passagem, se construa neles ou se intercepte a livre circulação, assim como se tapem ou obstruam as *fossae*. Este artigo, nitidamente inspirado pelo capítulo LIIII da *Lex Roscia Peducaea Alliena Fabia*[39], não permite dúvidas quanto à existência de uma centuriação no território ursonense, ainda visível nas fotografias aéreas do século passado (*USAF* 1956 19096-19097, 19104-19106): *Qui limites decumanique intra fines coloniae Genetivae deducti facti que erunt, quaecumque fossae limitales in eo agro erunt.* Ao longo de todo este articulado prevalece o cuidado em respeitar e fazer respeitar o princípio de livre circulação definido como *iter populo debetur* (Higino Gromático: Thulin 134-135; Higino: Thulin 91, 97). Determinações semelhantes ocorrem noutros textos do mesmo tipo encontrados na Península Ibérica, ligeiramente posteriores.

A liberdade de circulação tinha, todavia, algumas limitações, naturalmente estabelecidas de forma regulamentada e totalmente alheia às arbitrárias e extremas medidas contra o seu exercício normal de que se queixa Apuleio: *Os cultivadores de um domínio rural junto do qual passámos, vendo-nos tão numerosos tomaram-nos por bandoleiros [...]. Eles açularam contra nós enormes cães* (Apuleio, *Met.*, 8, 17). As restrições levantadas à utilização das *viae publicae* e de outros caminhos não privados, independentemente da existência de portagens, que não consistem numa prática restritiva do uso da estrada, resultam apenas de determinadas condições que obrigam ou aconselham um melhor controlo da circulação. Delas nos ficaram também diversos testemunhos. Um dos mais interessantes registou-se no regulamento da grande mina de *Vipasca* (Aljustrel), documento datado do século II, onde no artigo nono se proibia o transporte de minério entre o ocaso e o amanhecer, naturalmente com o intuito de evitar fraudes: *No respeitante ao minério que estiver amontoado junto dos poços, os respectivos proprietários deverão transportá-lo para os fornos desde o nascer ao pôr-do-sol. Aquele*

---

[39] Hardy 1925: 185-191.

que depois de pôr-do-sol ou de noite retirar minério de junto dos poços, deverá, depois de provado o crime, pagar ao fisco mil sestércios[40].

Outras determinações tinham características mais gerais, como o édito de Cláudio que limitava a circulação de carros nas cidades italianas, alargando uma anterior determinação de Júlio César relativa a Roma, como informa Suetónio: *Por édito expresso recomendou aos viajantes que não atravessassem as cidades de Itália senão a pé, de cadeirinha ou de liteira* (Suetónio, *Claud.*, 25). Esta proibição será alargada a todas as cidades do Império por Marco Aurélio. Note-se que o direito de usar uma liteira como meio de transporte estava longe de ser comum, estando vedado a largas franjas da sociedade romana. Quanto aos carros transportando os imprescindíveis abastecimentos e materiais necessários à Urbe, só podiam circular de noite, com excepção daqueles ao serviço de empreiteiros, com os inevitáveis inconvenientes daí resultantes, bem evidenciados nas sátiras de Marcial e de Juvenal. Escreveu o segundo: *Em que apartamento alugado é possível o sono? A passagem dos carros nas esquinas das ruelas, as pragas dos arrieiros que não avançam, tirá-lo-iam ao próprio imperador Cláudio e às suas focas* (Juvenal, *Sat.*, 3, 245). Com efeito, abastecer, com os meios técnicos da época, uma cidade com cerca de um milhão de habitantes representou um enorme, permanente e barulhento desafio[41].

Em determinadas estradas com funções mais vincadamente militares, de forma a condicionar a circulação não necessária ou considerada dispensável era normal a introdução de tarifas de utilização, que não podem considerar-se como simples portagens, pois a importância cobrada dependia de factores circunstanciais. Assim aconteceu no Egipto na grande estrada militar através do deserto unindo o Mar Vermelho a Coptos, no Nilo. Reproduzimos a tarifa aí em vigor no ano 90, que deve ser considerada como taxa mista entre a portagem e os direitos alfandegários aplicada numa área de circulação restrita directamente relacionada com os importantes portos de *Berenike* e *Myos Hormos*, centros do comércio marítimo com a Arábia e o Índico. O documento (Fig.12), gravado em língua grega numa estela por ordem do prefeito de Monte Berenice, Lúcio Antístio Asiático, cumprindo uma determinação do prefeito do Egipto, estipula os valores a pagar, muito distintos entre si[42], que se indicam seguidamente:

Por um capitão de navio do Mar Vermelho	8 dracmas
Por um piloto	10 dracmas
Por um guarda	10 dracmas
Por um marinheiro	5 dracmas
Por um carpinteiro naval	5 dracmas

---

[40] Encarnação 1984: 212-214; Magueijo 1970: 125-163.
[41] Carcopino s/d: 23-35; Homo 1972: 93-126, 205-217.
[42] Charles-Picard, Rougé 1969: 224-1227; Burkhalter-Arce 2002: 199-233.

Por um artesão	8 dracmas
Pelas mulheres fazendo ofício de cortesãs	108 dracmas
Pelas mulheres dos que chegam por mar	20 dracmas
Pelas mulheres dos soldados	20 dracmas
Por uma autorização para camelos	1 óbolo
Pelo carimbo num passaporte	2 óbolos
Pelo visto para um homem regressado de uma viagem longa	1 dracma
Por todas as mulheres no regresso	4 dracmas
Por um burro	2 óbolos
Por um carro pequeno com toldo	4 dracmas
Por um mastro	20 dracmas
Por uma verga	4 dracmas
Por um funeral, ida e volta	1 dracma e 4 óbolos

Fig.12 - Inscrição de Coptos com as tarifas devidas pela utilização da estrada para o Mar Vermelho (foto J. G. Milne).

Recordamos que a área atravessada pela estrada era relativamente perigosa, o que justificava o controlo militar, tanto mais que se tratava de uma via por onde entravam no Império artigos de elevado preço ou materiais muito procurados, como a madeira de construção naval, inclusive teca indiana. O Egipto, graças às condições naturais muito favoráveis facultou numerosa documentação em papiro relacionada com o funcionamento e a contabilidade das *mansiones*, extremanente rara noutras regiões do Império[43]. Situação relativamente semelhante parece ter sucedido no Norte de África, onde as fortificações associadas ao *Limes* correspondentes a diversas *clausurae* teriam como função controlar o fluxo do comércio saariano e o acesso dos nómadas, através das vias militares da região, às áreas que constituiam uma zona tampão, militarizada, entre o deserto e os territórios cultivados e urbanizados do litoral (Fig.13). Cremos que o complexo de *clausurae* servia, para além das funções fiscais que alguns investigadores lhe atribuem, como regulador dos movimentos de populações nómadas, nomeadamente o acesso a áreas de pastagem, como sistema de vigilância de zonas tradicionalmente inseguras[44]

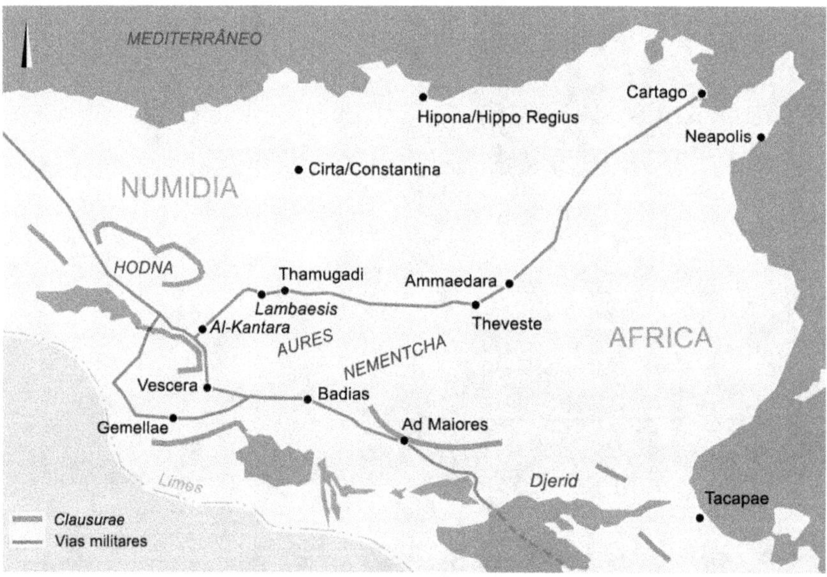

Fig.13 - Localização das principais *clausurae* norte-africanas.

Uma das fontes mais interessantes para conhecimento da legislação relacionada com as estradas e a sua utilização é, como referimos, o *Código de*

---

[43] Adams 2001: 142-144.
[44] Cherry 1998: 74-94; Mantas 2011: 31-33.

Teodósio, elaborado entre 429 e 439 por iniciativa de Teodósio II, e aplicado no Ocidente e no Oriente. A legislação recolhida no *Código* permite abordar muitos aspectos da actividade viária do Baixo-Império, verificando-se que parte das determinações reproduz os grandes princípios do direito romano anterior que especificamente lhe interessava. Porém, no conjunto dos documentos que nos foram transmitidos sobressai uma nota dissonante, premonitória, reflectindo as dificuldades crescentes sentidas pelo Estado para fazer respeitar a lei, a penúria financeira, a ascensão do poder eclesiástico e o desinteresse geral pela manutenção das vias num mundo em que se desenvolvem os particularismos e a anarquia, depois do rigorismo estabelecido pela Tetrarquia, preludiando a Idade Média.

São particularmente importantes os capítulos VIII (*De Cursus Publico, Angaris et Parangaris*) e XV (*De Itinere Muniendo*). No primeiro caso, além de uma série de determinações relacionadas com o funcionamento do *cursus publicus* e do equipamento das *mansiones* e *mutationes* ao serviço do mesmo, encontramos normas referentes à capacidade de carga de carros e animais, como nesta constituição de Constâncio II datada de 357: *O mesmo Augusto e Juliano César a Tauro, prefeito do pretório. Ordenamos que apenas 1000 libras de peso possam ser carregadas numa carroça (rheda), 200 libras num veículo de duas rodas (birota) e 30 libras num ginete, pois parece não poderem suportar cargas maiores. A uma carroça devem ser atreladas oito mulas, no Verão, naturalmente, mas dez no Inverno. Julgamos que três mulas são suficientes para uma viatura de duas rodas* (*Cod. Theod.*, 8, 5, 8).

Vejamos agora um rescrito de Honório e Teodósio II, datado de 423, relacionado com a construção e manutenção das estradas: *Os mesmos Augustos a Asclepiódotos, prefeito do pretório. Está longe de nós considerarmos a construção de vias públicas e de pontes e o trabalho nas calçadas consagradas pelos títulos de grandes imperadores como serviços públicos compulsivos de natureza servil. Por isso, nenhuma classe de homens, por mérito de qualquer elevada dignidade ou veneração, deve ser isenta da construção e reparação de estradas e pontes. Também nós alegremente aplicamos os haveres da divina casa imperial e as veneráveis igrejas a um tão louvável fim. Os juízes de todas as províncias devem ser notificados desta lei de forma a saberem que o que a antiguidade decretou dever ser consignado às vias públicas tem que ser cumprido sem exceptuar ninguém por razões de reverência ou elevada dignidade* (*Cod. Theod.*, 15, 3, 1).

Este tipo de documentos ajuda a compreender as dificuldades reais sentidas pelo Império, em fase de desagregação no Ocidente, assim como a anterior proliferação de miliários honoríficos como reflexo de obras impostas. A referência no *Código de Teodósio* ao pessoal e equipamento das estações viárias permite também ter uma ideia da dimensão destes estabelecimentos, mal conhecidos através da arqueologia, muitos dos quais deram origem a pequenos povoados, particularmente em zonas de fraca urbanização. As *mansiones* contavam com ferreiros, carpinteiros, palafreneiros, veterinário (*mulomedicus*) e outro pesoal, dirigido pelo *manceps* ou *stationarius*. A partir da informação do *Código de Teodósio* quanto ao número de cavalos e mulas atribuídos a cada vicário em viagem, o qual podia requisitar um máximo de 10 cavalos e 30 mulas, correspondendo um palafreneiro (*mulio*) a cada três animais, teremos uma ideia aproximada destes aglomerados.

Mantendo a proporção indicada e tendo em conta a informação de Procópio acerca do número mínimo de 40 cavalos por cada estação, teremos 120 mulas, 40 cavalos e pelo menos meia centena de *muliones*, normalmente de condição servil (*Cod. Theod.*, 8, 5, 38; Procópio, *Hist.*, 30, 4). Acrescentando a este grupo outros trabalhadores ocupados na cozinha, no balneário, na recolha de lenha e de forragens e noutros trabalhos, atingiremos um agrupamento muito significativo para a época, constituindo uma comunidade permanente cujo poder de atracção não pode ter deixado de influenciar a população circundante. Cremos que assim sucedeu na Lusitânia com o estabelecimento romano de Centum Celas (Belmonte), no grande itinerário entre *Emerita* e *Bracara*[45], onde a *mansio* parece ter dado origem a um *vicus* (Fig.14), aliás atestado epigraficamente[46]. Sem descurar

Fig.14 - Ruínas da estação romana de Centum Celas, perto de Belmonte (foto Vasco Mantas).

---

[45] Mantas 2008-2009: 254-255.
[46] Ferraz 2002: 467-469.

a possibilidade de Centum Celas, cujo nome antigo se ignora, ter conhecido funções administrativas, confirmadas noutras situações semelhantes[47], não cremos que a recente proposta interpretando as ruínas como forum seja sustentável[48]. A estrada exerceu, mais uma vez, a sua especial capacidade para influenciar o povoamento e, consequentemente, para difundir novos hábitos e alargar horizontes, sob todos os aspectos, como reconheceu sem hesitações Plínio-o-Antigo: *O poder de Roma conferiu unidade ao mundo. Todos devem reconhecer os serviços que ela prestou aos homens, facilitando as suas relações e permitindo-lhes fruir em comum os benefícios da paz* (Plínio, *N.H.* 14. 2).

Elemento fundamental da romanização, que podemos interpretar como o *determinado e ordeiro modo de vida* referido por Élio Aristides, a rede viária e a vida da estrada não podiam ficar à margem da mentalidade legalista que caracterizou a cultura romana. A estrada não se limitou a quebrar isolamentos regionais, contribuindo para a unificação do Império ao colocar em contacto tradição e inovação, através de uma dinâmica apoiada no exercício da autoridade. Não há império sem comunicações, como os Romanos e outros depois deles muito bem compreenderam, assim como não há estrada sem lei. O que Roma realizou neste aspecto bastaria para a colocar entre as grandes civilizações, mau grado as críticas de moda. Terminaremos com a apreciação realista que, na época de Augusto, Dionísio de Halicarnasso exprimiu e que, dois mil anos depois e apesar do ocaso da cultura clássica, não escapou aos Monty Phyton: *A extraordinária grandeza do Império Romano manifesta-se, acima de tudo, em três coisas: os aquedutos, as estradas pavimentadas e a construção de canalizações* (Dionísio, *Ant. Rom.* 3. 67. 5).

---

[47] Hanley 2000: 36-39.
[48] Guerra, Schatner 2010: 333-342.

Os Humanistas e o poder. Direito e Cência Política no Contexto do Renascimento
(Humanists and Power. Law and Political Science in the Context of the Renaissance)

Nair de Nazaré Castro Soares (ncastrosoares@gmail.com)
Universidade de Coimbra

Homenagem a meu saudoso Irmão
Hélio Mário de Castro Pereira
Jurista ilustre e "Advogado dos pobres".
Exemplo de Sabedoria e Generosidade*

Resumo – O interesse que o direito romano suscitava na Europa, de que foram intérpretes os primeiros humanistas – praticamente todos foram juristas – foi um dos aspectos essenciais na evolução do processo histórico. Desde o tempo de D. João II, a cultura jurídica de formação italiana conhece grande prestígio. Cataldo Parísio Sículo, considerado o introdutor do Humanismo em Portugal, é Doutor em Direito pela Universidade de Ferrara e mestre na de Bolonha. D. João III regulamenta, em termos modernos, o ensino das Leis na sua Academia e ordena a leitura de S. Tomás na primeira cátedra de Teologia, regida por Martin de Ledesma, um dos discípulos mais famosos de Francisco Vitória, na conhecida Escola Jurídica de Salamanca. Apesar do romanismo nascente e da publicação de *Il principe* de Maquiavel, o modelo do príncipe, elaborado de acordo com o idealismo político-social e religioso, imbuído de neoplatonismo, divulgado por Erasmo, impôs-se na literatura europeia, e de forma particular na Península Ibérica. No contexto do Renascimento, as relações dos humanistas com o poder, assentes na ciência política e no direito – ancorados na mensagem da Antiguidade clássica, assimilada aos valores do Cristianismo – reflectem uma nova dimensão do humano, presente na ideologia e na doutrina que caracterizam a literatura do século de ouro português e europeu.

Palavras-chave: Humanismo do Renascimento; ciência jurídica; pedagogia política; o modelo do príncipe "umanizzato"; literatura e parénese; os humanistas e sua relação com o poder.

Abstract: The interest of Renaissance Europe in Roman law exemplifies one of the main aspects of European historical evolution. The early humanists were nearly all

---

* Hélio Mário de Castro Pereira (Alvarenga, 18 de Maio de 1947 -Portalegre, 19 de Abril de 2015) distinguiu-se, desde muito cedo, pela grandeza de carácter, inteligência, natural bondade e desprendimento. Serviu, como Alferes Miliciano, "Oficial de transmissões", na Guerra Colonial, em Moçambique, sob a divisa horaciana (*Ode* 3. 2. 13), *Dulce et decorum est pro patria mori*. O seu saber jurídico, adquirido na *Alma Mater Conimbrigensis*, e um inexcedível sentido dos outros deram brilho à sua abnegada vida de advogado. Autor da famosa "Sentença de Portalegre", defendia empenhada e graciosamente os mais desfavorecidos, tendo merecido ser homenageado, na Assembleia da República, a 24 de Abril de 2015, como "O Advogado dos Pobres".

https://doi.org/10.14195/978-989-26-1280-5_22

jurists who applied themselves to the interpretation of Roman law. From the time of King João (John) II, legal culture under Italian inspiration had attained great prestige. Cataldo Parísio Sículo, who is considered the introducer of humanism into Portugal, had been made a Doctor in Jurisprudence by the University of Ferrara and had been a Master at the University of Bologna. King João III regulated, in modern terms, the teaching of law in his Academy and orders lecturing on Thomas Aquinas for the first chair of Theology, held by Martin de Ledesma, one of the most famous students of Francisco de Victoria at the renowned School of Law at Salamanca. Despite the success of Machiavelli's *Il Principe*, the ideal of the 'prince', conceived in accordance with sociopolitical and religious idealism, and deeply influenced by a Neoplatonism disseminated by Erasmus, impressed itself on European literature and, particularly, on Iberian literature. In the context of the Renaissance, the relations of Humanists with state power, based on a conception of jurisprudence – one anchored in the heritage of Classical Antiquity as assimilated to the values of Christianity – reflect a new dimension of human values present in the ideology and learning that characterize Portuguese and European literature of the Golden Century.

Key words: Renaissance Humanism, jurisprudence, political pedagogy, humanist prince ideology, literature and *paraenesis*, humanists and state power.

O ideal de perfeição humana, ligado ao conceito da formação integral da personalidade, vai ser a tónica do Humanismo Renascentista, cívico e pedagógico, herdeiro do ideal de *aretê politikê* e de *paideia*, transmitido sobretudo pelos autores gregos do século IV a. C.

Já Isócrates definira os princípios éticos que deveriam orientar a conduta do governante, factor único da sua missão, num tratado *A Nícocles*, que pode considerar-se o primeiro deste género literário e é apontado por Erasmo como fonte da sua *Institutio principis christiani*, modelo privilegiado no quinhentismo europeu.

A literatura da época helenística e os sistemas filosóficos então em vigor fomentaram a perspectiva moralizante da problemática política. A interdependência ou aliança da moral e da política vigora também no período imperial romano e consolida-se sobretudo a partir dele.

A Idade Média cristã vai delinear com contornos mais definidos os parâmetros ético-religiosos em que a política se desenrola. Muitos são os tratados que então se escrevem para a educação de príncipes ou para a orientação de reis ou de personalidades no uso de funções governativas. Poderá mesmo dizer-se que, a par dos *Livros de Horas*, foram os primeiros livros de reflexão moral e de formação de leigos.

O carácter formativo destes textos presidia à intenção primeira da sua elaboração e do seu uso. A sua mensagem dirigia-se ao enaltecimento das virtudes cardeais – e entre elas a justiça, como a primeira entre todas – , e ao encorajamento do vigor militar e guerreiro. O ideal cavaleiresco encontra nestas obras o seu guia, a expressão acabada do seu código de virtudes.

Nos séculos XII e XIII, esta literatura começa a seguir uma nova trajectória, caracterizada pela união dos ideais ético-políticos dos autores da Antiguidade clássica com os ideais, por assim dizer monásticos e guerreiros, que prevalecem na Idade Média. No entanto, a inspiração clássica já se afirmara, séculos antes, na época carolíngia. Aliás, foi com Carlos Magno que surgiram os tratados de educação de príncipes cristãos como género definido e independente.

As invasões bárbaras e os designados "séculos de trevas", que se contaram entre as duas Renascenças medievais, a carolíngia e a dos séculos XII-XIII, não podem contudo ser ignorados. É no século XIII, marco importante para a história das ideias políticas, que surge S. Tomás de Aquino, intérprete fiel da mensagem aristotélico-ciceroniana e do direito romano. A importância e originalidade de que se reveste a doutrina política de S. Tomás devem-se aos seus fundamentos jurídico e moral e à arte de utilizar conceitos da tradição patrística e de os elaborar, hamonizando-os com as novas orientações e directrizes do seu pensamento. O *De regno* ou *De regimine principum ad regem Cypri* (ca. 1265-1266) de S. Tomás e o tratado do mesmo nome de Egídio Romano vão ser cartilha a seguir por todo o governante e modelo literário de toda a tratadística futura até aos tempos modernos[2].

Na obra de S. Tomás se encontra a formulação dos princípios gerais que definem uma democracia coroada pela teocracia: preferência pela monarquia electiva, onde o povo tem o direito de eleger o seu representante, o rei, cujas qualidades são fiança de o regime não degenerar em tirania, pelo que compete à colectividade, à autoridade pública, e em última análise ao poder da Igreja, e jamais a alguém individualmente, depor o tirano, sem praticar o tiranicídio[3]. Um aspecto moderno desta teorização sobre os deveres do poder real, que não aparece em Platão, Aristóteles ou Cícero e reflecte a orientação cristã da sua política, diz respeito à assistência aos desfavorecidos, à caridade pública[4].

Apesar de as suas ideias se apresentarem pouco sistemáticas, ao longo das diversas obras, não se pode negar o pendor democrático dos preceitos enunciados que irá reflectir-se nos autores da chamada segunda escolástica, nos finais do séc. XVI, e é bem notório, entre nós, no tratado de D. Jerónimo Osório, Bispo de Silves, *De regis institutione et disciplina* (1572), escrito para a educação do jovem rei D. Sebastião[5].

---

[2] Gilson 1983, 6ª ed., IIIe partie: 313-435.

[3] *De reg. princ.* 1. 6-7.

[4] Ibidem, lib. 2.

[5] As reflexões políticas do Doutor Angélico encontram-se essencialmente na *Summa Theologica*, nos *Comentários às Sentenças*, no comentário que dedica à obra de Aristóteles e no *De regimine principum*. O seu *Tratado das Leis*, que se integra na *Summa Theologica* (I a–II ae –108), é um dos monumentos do pensamento da Idade Média, que esteve na base de tudo o que se escreveu sobre o assunto até ao séc. XVI – de recordar F. Suárez que o parafraseia, a cada passo – e mesmo ao longo do séc. XVII. Conhecida é a sua importância na obra de famosos teólogos e juristas como D. Soto, O. P. (1494-1560), *De iustitia et iure* (Lugduni 1582), e.g. l.

A Idade Média não tinha conhecido a *República* de Platão: o pensamento do filósofo era divulgado apenas através de *Compendia*. A descoberta da *Política* de Aristóteles dá-se no séc. XIII. A obra de Diógenes Laércio, *De uita et moribus philosophorum libri X*, que ilustra todas as escolas filosóficas antigas, é encontrada nos primeiros anos de Quatrocentos[6].

Os humanistas do primeiro Renascimento abandonam o Aristóteles lógico e físico, símbolo da barbárie estilística medieval[7], e procuram na filosofia uma finalidade profundamente humana e um conteúdo mais vasto, que abarcasse motivos político-morais e os problemas da vida concreta da sociedade do tempo.

Este distanciamento do formalismo escolástico coincide com a reabilitação do neoplatonismo. É sem dúvida através do platonismo, configurado com o cristianismo, a ética aristotélica, ou mesmo com a tradição hermética e cabalística que os conceitos do saber medieval vão ser alvo de renovação.

Percebe-se a influência do platonismo em personalidades como Petrarca, o primeiro humanista, ou Pier Paolo Vergerio que se entrega ao estudo de Platão, com intuitos ético-pedagógicos[8]. Marsílio Ficino traduz a obra deste filósofo.

Concede-se então o maior relevo ao pensamento moral e político do Estagirita, conciliado com a doutrina platónica. Platão e Aristóteles lançam as bases teóricas e filosóficas de uma problemática política intemporal.

Aristóteles, apesar de considerações feitas em obras representativas como a *Retórica*, dedica especialmente à formação civil e política do homem de estado e do cidadão comum a *Política*, a *Ética a Nicómaco* e a *Ética a Eudemo*. Este filósofo da vida activa e educador de Alexandre, vai, segundo a tradição, servir de modelo no que se refere à origem da sociedade, às diferentes formas de constituição – com manifesta superioridade da monarquia –, aos processos de evitar as mutações, à caracterização do bom rei e do tirano, à organização dos poderes legislativo, executivo e judicial, à finalidade última do estado, o bem comum, traduzido no plano individual, social e público.

Por seu lado, Platão, na *República*, no *Político* e nas *Leis*, com um carácter político acentuado, para além das preocupações deste teor, mais ou menos conscientes, que perpassam em todas as outras, é reconhecido pelos humanistas como mais religioso e mais profundo do que Aristóteles: a organização social que preconiza a aquisição das virtudes cívicas, em que sobressai a justiça resultante

---

I, qu. 3, a.1; l. II, qu. 3, a. 8; l. III, qu. 3, a. 3; B. Medina (1528-1580), *Expositio in Primam Secundae Angelici Doctoris D. Thomae Aquinatis*, Salmanticae, 1578; F. Suárez (1548-1619), *De legibus ac Deo legislatore* (Lugduni, 1613). Vide Soares 1994: 380-410.

[6] Vide e. g. a edição de Lugduni, Apud Antonium Vincentium, 1561. Sobre a vulgarização da obra de Diógenes Laércio, em Portugal, vide Carvalho 1949: 17-18

[7] Petrarca, principalmente no *De sui ipsius et multorum ignorantia* (1367), exprime a sua aversão ao formalismo escolástico dominado por Aristóteles e Averróis e invoca o pensamento de Platão, Cícero e Santo Agostinho.

[8] Vide Garin 1955: 339-374, maxime, p. 345-346; Idem 1966: I, II parte, caps. II e III.

da harmonia entre todas elas são aspectos relevantes da sua filosofia política, recolhidas pelo Humanismo Renascentista[9].

Notória é a complementaridade destes dois filósofos na forma como foram assimilados pelo pensamento moderno[10]. A importância conferida aos ensinamentos de Platão e Aristóteles, em matéria de pedagogia régia, é explicitamente revelada pelo humanista eborense André de Resende, no seu poema *De uita aulica*, dedicado a Damião de Góis, em 1535: *Ille suo ingenio in sophiam propensus honestam/ quicquid Aristoteles argutus, quicquid amoenus/ dixerat ante Plato, mire cognoscere auebat,/ ut melius quonam pacto foret ipsa gerenda/ publica res sciret, consultis utpote libris,/ Fallere quid nequeant, quod non adfectibus ullis/ subcumbant, quod nil sperent metuantue nec aequum/ calliditate mala faciant uideatur iniquum.*[11].

Os dois mestres da Antiguidade – em torno dos quais se gerou a polémica da sua superioridade relativa[12] – vão ser lidos no original e compreendidos na profunda substância do seu pensamento: Leonardo Bruni Aretino traduz a Ética, a *Política* e o *Económico* de Aristóteles. Sucedem-se os comentários à obra do Estagirita, da maior importância na difusão do seu pensamento político-moral, por parte de humanistas, dos séculos XV e XVI, como Francesco Filelfo, Donaldo Acciaioli, Ermolao Barbaro, Francesco Piccolomini, Alessandro Piccolomini, Jacques Lefèvre d'Étaples, Melanchthon, John Case, Sebastian Fox Morcillo[13].

A descoberta de obra de Cícero, as *Epistulae ad Atticum*, por Petrarca, em 1345, e as *Epistulae familiares* por Coluccio Salutati, além de provocar a controvérsia humanística sobre *imperium* e *respublica* – a glorificação de César ou de Bruto – , leva à discussão da figura histórica de Cícero, pensador e cidadão romano[14]. O próprio Petrarca, que viu em Cícero um modelo de renúncia às

---

[9] Vide Touchard 1959: 29. e Pérez Ruiz 1984: 257-295. Sobre o carácter "eudemónico" da filosofia moral da Antiguidade e a importância da mensagem espiritual de Platão, vide Sigeia 1970: 40.

[10] Vide e. g. Alessandro Piccolomini, na sua obra *Della institutione morale libri XII* (Venezia, 1583), considerada como síntese completa das ideias político-pedagógicas do século XVI; e Louys le Roy, comentador de Platão e Aristóteles, não com a intenção de esclarecer o seu pensamento, mas com o propósito de colher nos dois autores ensinamentos para a vida política.Vide Soares 1994: 215-216.

[11] 'O Rei [D. João III], por sua inclinação, propenso à honesta sabedoria, tinha um grande desejo de conhecer o que haviam dito outrora o subtil Aristóteles, o agradável Platão, para melhor saber como gerir a república, pela consulta de livros que não podem enganar, visto como não sucumbem a parcialidades, nada ambicionam nem receiam, e não fazem, com má astúcia, que o justo pareça injusto...'. Cf. Ramalho 1985: 197.

[12] A violenta disputa que, em meados do século XV envolveu vários humanistas, entre eles Giorgio Gemisto Pletone e Giorgio de Trebisonda, encontrou vitalidade ainda no séc. XVI, aquando da polémica que opôs Pierre de la Ramée, no seu ataque aos esquemas da lógica aristotélica, ao famoso jurista português António de Gouveia (Cf. deste autor o seu *Pro Aristotele responsio adversus Petri Rami calumnias* Paris, 1545).

[13] Vide Kristeller 1961 3ª ed.: 302 e 308-309.

[14] Vide Baron 1938: 84-89; Idem 1970: cap. VI, maxime, p. 135-143; Bentley 1987: 196-197; Burke 1987, 3º ed.: 38.

paixões que dominam na vida pública, escreveu a famosa carta de acusação à sua sombra no Hades[15]. Esta carta, que suscitou a defesa de Cícero por Coluccio Salutati em 1392, teve uma réplica em 1394 de Pier Paolo Vergerio que, em nome do próprio Cícero, defende o seu espírito cívico e empenhamento político[16].

O sábio estóico das *Tusculanae disputationes*, que prendera a atenção da Idade Média, dá lugar ao homem político e ao enaltecimento da *uita actiua ciuilis*.

Coluccio Salutati, no *De nobilitate legum et medicinae* vai reflectir sobre o papel das leis na sociedade17. Para Salutati, a jurisprudência tinha como objecto a perfectibilidade do homem na comunidade social[18]. O estado era o quadro normal e necessário à actividade humana. As leis traduziam os valores supremos que deviam orientar essa mesma actividade. Assim, o universo moral confundia--se, na sua própria fonte, com o universo legal. A superioridade da vida activa sobre a contemplativa, defendida nesta obra, aparecia ligada a uma visão verdadeiramente política da vida humana.

A exaltação da vida da *ciuitas*, que as leis ordenavam ao bem comum, pertence à tradição aristotélico-tomista que dominou a política de inspiração cristã, característica deste período. Além disso, a convergência do pensamento moral de Aristóteles com a doutrina platónica, defendida já por Giovanni Pico della Mirandola, é bem manifesta na obra de Salutati, significativa na orientação ideológica humanista.

Sob o signo do franciscanismo e do scotismo, Salutati será o pregoeiro do ideal de vida activa e integrará com Leonardo Bruni, seu discípulo, e Leon Battista Alberti a primeira geração do humanismo civil italiano. Na verdade, grande é o alcance do movimento cultural florentino[19]. A obra de Pier Paolo Vergerio e a modernidade do seu pensamento no *De monarchia* revelam bem a renovação ideológica então operada[20].

---

[15] Petrarca 1942 3ª ed.: vol IV: 226 sqq. (Ep. XXIV).

[16] Vide Vergerio 1934: 436-445.

[17] Coluccio Salutati é também autor de um tratado *De tyranno*, onde dá uma definição objectiva de tirania, tal como Bártolo, na linha do *Defensor pacis* (1324) de Marsílio de Pádua, um dos jurisconsultos mais célebres da sua época. O*Defensor pacis* , apoiado nas doutrinas de Aristóteles e de S. Tomás, contribui para a vitória das doutrinas democráticas, ao afirmar que o povo, a *universitas civium*, é a fonte de autoridade, a *pars valentior*. Marco importante no desenvolvimento da controvérsia ideológica, que opôs partidários e adversários do papado e do império, esta obra corresponde a uma tomada de consciência progressiva por parte dos pensadores medievais dos problemas da soberania e do estado. O crescimento da força e do papel dos estados, cuja ascensão é paralela ao declínio do papado e do império, é notório até ao século XVI, altura em que aparecem firmemente estabelecidos. Sobre o fervilhar das novas ideias no século XIV e os teorizadores dos novos estados, vide N. Soares 1994: 75-79.

[18] Cf. Ullman 1980: 209 e sqq.

[19] Baron 1970: 485.

[20] Baron 1970:140 e sqq. Embora com o mesmo nome, a obra de Dante, *De monarchia* (1311), mantém o princípio da superioridade espiritual do papa sobre o imperador, na linha dos pensadores teocráticos contemporâneos, e parte da universalidade do género humano para expor de forma leve e agradável as razões em favor da monarquia universal. Estas razões

A par deste humanismo florentino de cunho cívico, florescia o humanismo paduano como exemplo de uma cultura civil fundida com o classicismo, desde os tempos de Albertino Mussato, nos inícios do séc. XIV. Isto, apesar de Pádua e Bolonha se tornarem conhecidos centros de irradiação do aristotelismo averroísta, defensor de um saber apoiado nas categorias lógicas, de carácter puramente especulativo, sucedâneo do medieval.

O desabrochar para uma nova era vem acompanhado de um enorme interesse pela educação e pela formação de uma sociedade renovada. É neste contexto que o ideal do príncipe perfeito do Renascimento vai ter origem. Ao próprio Petrarca cabe a formulação deste ideal no seu *De republica optime administranda liber*, seguido de um *De officio et uirtutibus imperatoriis liber*[21]. Petrarca, na verdade, "aveva stabilito un modelo umanistico con uno *spechio per i principi*, dedicado a Francesco il Vecchio Da Carrara nel 1373"[22].

Em Portugal, na dinastia de Avis, a leitura de *Regimentos de príncipes* era considerada essencial à formação do governante, como dá a entender o passo da carta dirigida pelo infante D. Pedro a D. Duarte, por ocasião da sua subida ao trono[23].

Era o hábito da leitura de obras adequadas ao ofício real uma das preocupações básicas da formação do príncipe da Idade Média, como prova já, no séc. XII, a teorização do *Policraticus* (VI) que chega a afirmar *Rex illiteratus quasi asinus coronatus*, expressão esta que, no séc. XV, Cristina de Pisano, em *Songe du Vergier* (I, 132) vai adaptar ao seu estilo, cheio de frescura e graciosidade: "Un roy sans letture est comme un nef sans aviron et comme ung oiseau sans ales".

A expressão usada pelos escritores medievais vai ter enorme fortuna entre os humanistas, a ponto de Gioacchino Paparelli afirmar: "E diverrà popolarissimo fra gli umanisti il motto caro a colui che resterà un tipico esempio di principe umanizzato, Alfonso il Magnanimo: Un re non letterato è un asino coronato"[24].

Entre nós, Frei Heitor Pinto, no *Diálogo da justiça*, referindo-se ao prelado – que identifica, pela sua função, com o príncipe –, vai traduzir e adaptar da forma seguinte a expressão do *Songe du Vergier*: "Prelado sem letras é ave sem penas, e navio sem leme, e relógio sem pesos"[25].

A diferença de sentido destas expressões, usadas em épocas distintas, residia apenas no programa educativo que lhes era subjacente e a que implicitamente se reportavam.

---

tocaram Maquiavel que, com os ensinamentos ministrados no seu *Il principe*, acredita poder instaurar essa poderosa monarquia, sob a chefia de um príncipe italiano.

[21] Vide Petrarca (1581): 372 sqq. e 386 sqq.

[22] Cf. Baron 1970: 146.

[23] Cf. Carta inserta por Rui de Pina, na *Chronica do Senhor Rey D. Duarte*, cap. IV. Cf Pina 1970: 496.

[24] Paparelli 1973:100.

[25] Pinto 1952: 166.

Jacques Krynen, na sua obra sobre os tratados de educação de príncipes na Idade Média tardia, refere a importância que se dá, a partir da renascença das letras, no século XII, à cultura do príncipe[26].

As leituras recomendadas pelos diversos autores desta época, quer de obras religiosas, morais, históricas, políticas ou militares visavam sempre a aquisição de uma sabedoria política[27]. Assim se compreende a grande importância que os *Regimentos de príncipes*, compostos com esse fim, teriam na formação do jovem rei.

Gomes Eanes de Azurara, na *Chronica do Conde D. Pedro de Menezes*[28], dá--nos notícia, através da alocução proferida por D. João I em Ceuta aos membros que iriam permanecer na praça, que o *Regimento de príncipes* de Egídio Romano era lido na câmara real perante os fidalgos. Vários destes *Regimentos de príncipes* se encontravam na relação dos livros pertencentes à biblioteca do rei D. Duarte[29]. Isto, se para tanto não bastasse a obra que nos legou, o *Leal Conselheiro*, repassado de afinidades ideológicas com este género de literatura[30]. Se acreditarmos em Rui de Pina, o infante D. Pedro "tirou de latym em linguajem o Regimento de Pryncipes, que Frey Gil Correado compos, e assy tirou o livro dos Offycios de Tullio, e Vegecio de Re Militari, e compos o livro que se diz da Virtuosa Benfeytorya."[31].

Na verdade, a produção literária dos príncipes de Avis, mesclada de citações da Sagrada Escritura e de autoridades do mundo antigo ou medieval, apresenta-nos os próprios príncipes e reis a reflectirem nos valores humanos, requeridos a todo o cidadão, e na própria condição da realeza, como outrora fizera Marco Aurélio.

D. Afonso V vai ser educado por mestres italianos, Estêvão de Nápoles e Mateus Pisano, o famoso autor do *De belli Septensi*[32], que Zurara qualifica de "poeta laureado, e hum dos suficientes Filosofos e Oradores que em seus dias concorreram na christandade"[33]. Este monarca chama à corte Fr. Justo Baldino, doutor *in utroque iure* para narrar em latim os feitos dos Portugueses[34]. Faleceu antes de realizar a sua empresa.

---

[26] Krynen 1981: 97 e sqq.

[27] Ibidem, p. 100.

[28] Serra 1972: 237-249..

[29] Sousa 1946-1954: 257-259.

[30] Vide sobretudo os capítulos L e LIII, que dizem respeito à educação do príncipe. A par da edição latina, a versão castelhana de Frei Juan García de Castrojeriz (Sevilha, 1494) do *De regimine principum* de Egídio Romano poderia ter sido usada por D. Duarte, ao compor o seu *Leal conselheiro*, em especial os capítulos L e LI, no que toca à virtude da prudência. Aliás a obra de D. Duarte abunda toda ela em citações daquele tratado. Sobre os muitos autores que chamaram a atenção para este facto, vide. Rebelo 1983: 96 e sqq.

[31] Pina 1977: 754.

[32] Zurara 1972: 215.

[33] Cf. Gomes 2006

[34] Cf. a carta de Ângelo Policiano a D. João II em tradução de Epifânio da Silva Dias in Carvalho 1947-1948: 25-27.

Assim, quando o movimento humanista se inicia em Itália, ali se encontrava um escol português de eclesiásticos e embaixadores, junto da cúria, ou de estudantes que cursavam as universidades de Siena, Pádua, Pavia e Bolonha, famosas pelo estudo do Direito.

A sociedade portuguesa, estruturada até então segundo o modelo da hierarquia eclesiástica[35], inicia uma *renovatio*, nos vários domínios da cultura, que pretendia garantir a consolidação da consciência nacional, de acordo com as solicitações do mundo civilizado de então, de que a corte de Borgonha dava o exemplo[36].

A intensificação das relações comerciais com a França, a Flandres, a Itália e os contactos mais estreitos com a Inglaterra, país de origem de D. Filipa de Lencastre, e com Castela, centro de unidade cultural peninsular, favoreceram a abertura de um país que o feudalismo mantivera sobretudo voltado sobre si mesmo.

Um novo conceito de estado e da função do governante se começava já a esboçar: "conviviam, pois, ainda na geração de Avis, o antigo e o moderno. Mas a marcha do futuro estava encetada"[37].

Caberá ao Renascimento sintetizar e desenvolver muitos dos princípios, latentes já no final da Idade Média.

O interesse que o direito romano suscitava na Europa, a partir da primeira metade do séc. XII[38], de que foram intérpretes os primeiros humanistas[39], foi um dos aspectos essenciais na evolução do processo histórico[40]. Segundo Nuno J. Espinosa Gomes da Silva, a Idade Média aparecia concretizada aos olhos da Renascença como época que vivera o direito romano justinianeu, na sua interpretação lentamente destilada por glosadores e comentadores"[41]. Caberá aos humanistas iniciar a *restitutio* do *Corpus Iuris*[42].

A *communis opinio,* que se impunha aos juristas medievais como critério de verdade, é substituída pela perícia interpretativa dos humanistas, com base no conhecimento das *bonae litterae* e no uso da ciência dialéctica. Em Itália, Lorenzo Valla, e a seguir Angelo Poliziano são os primeiros a aplicar o método filológico na interpretação do direito justinianeu, cheio de incoerências e aspectos nebulosos.

---

[35] Vide o ordenamento social das classes, estabelecido nas *Ordenações Afonsinas* in Peres 1952. 271. Sobre o conceito da nossa realeza medieval, o artigo de P. Merêa "Organização social e administração pública" in 1929. (vol. II, terceira parte, p. 461, col.2); Huizinga 1948 (cap. III) sintetiza de forma bem elucidativa a concepção teológica e política da hierarquizada sociedade medieval.

[36] Vide Monfrin 1964.

[37] Vide Albuquerque 1983: 153.

[38] Vide Ullmann 1980: cap. II: "La secolarizzazione del governo", maxime, p. 52-72; N. J. E. G. da Silva 1964: 31 e sqq.

[39] Ullmann 1980: 71; 136 e 222-225; F. Colasso 1951: 57-58.

[40] Ullmann 1980: 208-209.

[41] Ibidem: 31.

[42] Ibidem: 35.

Também em Portugal se verificou o incentivo do estudo do Direito, nos alvores do nosso humanismo, com preferência pelas Universidades de Itália, onde a ciência jurídica concorria com a cultura das letras[43].

Foi o direito romano o primeiro factor a favorecer a secularização, de importância capital na evolução do conceito de estado e da função do governante[44]. Contudo, várias linhas de força convergiram no sentido desta evolução: o direito romano, o bartolismo, o aristotelismo político, o laicismo[45].

À concepção teocrática medieval, Walter Ullman opõe o modelo do principe "umanizzato" do Renascimento, que não se cinge à simples imitação do passado, mas desenvolve e adapta as funções do imperador tardo-romano às exigências do seu reino[46].

Na verdade, enquanto na Idade Média se considerava o direito como emanação de uma lei natural, identificada com a vontade divina, e se sujeitava o estado aos ditames universalísticos dessa lei, no Renascimento é a vida, são as exigências do estado que vão levar à sua formulação[47]. Diz J. A. Maravall: "Lo cierto es que desde los siglos bajomedievales, siglos de preparación de las nuevas formas políticas, hasta la época del Renascimiento, uno de los factores que participan eficazmente en la evolución del Estado moderno es del derecho particular o estatalizado"[48]. A *lex omnium generalis* em que se apoiava a jurisdição do estado medieval vai dar lugar ao *ius proprium,* que implica "la voluntad del príncipe proprio"[49].

Entre nós, comprovam este facto de forma bem evidente as *Ordenações régias,* pela primeira vez publicadas em meados do séc. XV (1446-1448), no reinado de D. Afonso V, que, a partir de então, assumem um papel de relevo na estrutura governativa portuguesa. Além disso, as cortes começaram a ser convocadas cada vez menos frequentemente, sobretudo a partir de D. João II, o que comprova a progressiva centralização de poderes e entre eles o poder legislativo na pessoa do rei[50]. O florescimento das *humaniores litterae* fundou-se na ânsia de conhecer a conduta do homem no mundo antigo, para dela extrair paradigmas. Assim se desenvolveu o estudo da ciência política.

Como observa Walter Ullman, um aspecto deve ser evidenciado: praticamente todos os primeiros humanistas foram juristas[51]. É que "L'umanesimo trovò

---

[43] Ibidem: 112 e sqq.; V. Rau 1969: 185-201.

[44] Ullmann 1980: 70-71.

[45] Vide Albuquerque 1983: 151-152 e os passos da obra de Walter Ullmann em que se apoia.

[46] Ullmann 1980: p. 70-71.

[47] Vide Moncada 1974: 89-92.

[48] Maravall 1972: II, 412.

[49] Maravall 1972: 414-415.

[50] D. João I, eleito por vontade popular, convocou as cortes vinte e cinco vezes; D. Duarte, no seu breve reinado de seis anos, quatro; D. Afonso V, vinte e duas; D. João II, quatro. D. Manuel, durante um reinado de vinte e seis anos, convocou-as quatro vezes; e D. João III, que reinou durante trinta e um anos, apenas três vezes.

[51] Ullmann 1980: 225.

la sua primitiva espressione in connessione con il rinascimento del cittadino in quanto membro integrante della (nuova) idea dello stato"[52].

É sobretudo no tempo de D. João II que a cultura jurídica de formação italiana conhece grande prestígio, em Portugal. No seu fascínio pela Itália, o nossa monarca, além das relações estabelecidas com a corte de Médicis e com Poliziano, convida para desempenhar os cargos de *orator regius* e de preceptor de D. Jorge, seu filho bastardo, o italiano Cataldo Parísio Sículo – Doutor em Direito pela Universidade de Ferrara e mestre na de Bolonha –, considerado o introdutor do Humanismo em Portugal.

Manda os primeiros bolseiros portugueses estudar às universidades italianas, onde floresciam as *humaniores litterae*: os filhos de João Teixeira, Aires Barbosa, Henrique Caiado, Martinho de Figueiredo, Gaspar Vaz, entre os principais. Eles abririam caminho a muitos outros que, ajudados por D. Manuel e D. João III se viriam a formar nas escolas mais famosas de então. São estes juristas, entusiastas decididos da renovação humanista em Portugal, seguidores dos métodos interpretativos de Valla e Poliziano e do espírito cívico que impregnou a sensibilidade dos homens do *Quattrocento*.

Curioso é que, entre os bolseiros do rei , o poeta elogiado por Erasmo, Henrique Caiado – que troca o estudo das Leis pelas Letras e ataca, nas suas *Eclogae*, a *seditiosa cohors* de causídicos que superam em riqueza os próprios reis, *Reges diuitiis superent*[53] – é autor de uma oração em louvor da jurisprudência.

Esta obra tem para nós o interesse de revelar Caiado como um fiel discípulo do ideal cívico do humanismo italiano. Como Petrarca e Salutati faz a exaltação da vida activa, do *facere* subordinado à *ratio* e ao *consilium*, a apologia da interpenetração do *ius* e da *ciuitas*, da indispensabilidade do direito à *rei publicae gubernatio*.

Se Bártolo, Baldo e Acúrsio continuam a ser autoridades entre nós, como diria André de Resende com verdade, o certo é que o método jurídico medieval tinha sido ultrapassado[54]. Neste particular, é já claro o *Regimento da Instituta* de 17 de Setembro de 1539[55], em que D. João III impõe ao ensino das Leis, na sua Academia, a razão acima das autoridades, a opinião reflectida e avisada do jurista acima da *communis opinio*, escamoteada por glosadores e comentadores da época precedente.

Além disso, por alvará 26 de Outubro de 1541, ordena este monarca a leitura de S. Tomás, em vez de Durando, na Universidade de Coimbra, cabendo

---

[52] Ullmann 1980: 137.

[53] Vide Caiado 1745: 217 (*Epigramma XLII, Ad Bart. Blanchinum*); 154 (*Epigramma XXIII, Ad Benedictum Barbatiam*). Sobre a crítica à prática jurídica na pena de Henrique Caiado, vide também N. J. Silva 1964: 149 e sqq. Tema recorrente no século XVI é a crítica à ambição dos causídicos, designados ironicamente por "causíficos".

[54] Vide André de Resende, *De uita aulica*, composta em 1535 e publicado em Lovaina em 1544 com dedicatória a Damião de Góis. Cf. Freire (ed.) 1916: 142.

[55] Brandão 1937: 188 (doc. CXIII); cf. também, neste particular, Leite (ed.) 1963: 99 (cap. 31, *Do modo que lerão os lentes de cadeiras piquenas de Canones e Leis e Instituta*).

o magistério desta primeira cátedra de Teologia a Martin de Ledesma, um dos discípulos mais famosos de Francisco Vitória, na conhecida Escola jurídica de Salamanca.

O humanismo não irrompeu abruptamente, como movimento novo e antagónico às concepções tradicionais do mundo medieval. Não houve de forma alguma solução de continuidade, nem antítese entre as duas mentalidades: foi antes a humanística a "sublimação última da intuição medieval"[56].

É assim que, no que se refere à fundamentação do poder político, o tomismo e o bartolismo dominaram o pensamento dos nossos humanistas, cuja nova intuição da vida se afirmava em diversos campos, onde era grande a força da tradição[57]. Importa referir, todavia, que a doutrina tomista era válida apenas nos aspectos em que, por assim dizer, traduzia em termos teológicos a concepção clássica da política e da moral.

A fórmula do direito romano que liberta o governante de obedecer à lei que promulga, *quod principi placuit, legibus habeat uigorem*[58], ou *princeps legibus solutus est* [59], que se encontra em S. Tomás[60] – salvaguardada embora pelo princípio de que só é verdadeiro príncipe aquele que se conforma à lei da razão (o que justificava o direito de resistência) – não figura, em regra, na obra dos humanistas. Defendida a *lex regia* no século XIV por Cola de Rienzo, é posta em causa desde o *Quattrocento* italiano[61]. De interesse é a observação de Salutati, que vê nela a base do arbítrio do legislador e do governante e o reconhecimento da relatividade do direito positivo[62].

Nesta linha, o princípio ulpiano é discutido pelos nossos tratadistas que, seguindo uma tradição que entronca nos autores da época helenística[63], afirmam – à semelhança de Erasmo: *Nec protinus lex est, quod principi placuit* [64] – a subordinação do príncipe à lei.

Mesmo quando o conhecimento da posição dos romanistas condiciona a

---

[56] Vide Colasso 1951: 59.

[57] Sobre a dívida do Renascimento para com a obra de S. Tomás e Bártolo de Sassoferrato, vide Ullmann 1980: 157-158 e 180 e sqq.; Sforza 1951: 71. Sobre a sua influência entre nós, vide Andrade 1959: 5-8 e sqq.; Albuquerque 1981: 41-61.

[58] Cf. *Digesto*, I, 4, *De Const. Princ.*, 1 (Ulpiano).

[59] *Dig.* I. 3.31.

[60] *Summa Theologica*, Ia - IIae, qu. 90, a.1.3. Ibidem, Ia-IIae, qu. 96, a.5.3. Vide a análise de J. de la Croix Kaelin O. P., in S. Tomás de Aquino 1946: 25-29. Sobre a obrigatoriedade de o príncipe estar sujeito à lei no que diz respeito à *uis directiva*, embora não dependente dela no que toca unicamente à *uis coactiva*, vide J.-M. Aubert 1955: 83-84.

[61] Vide e.g. o primeiro grande tratadista do *Quattrocento* italiano, Francesco Patrizi (Senense). No seu *De regno et regis institutione* (II, 1) afirma que o príncipe é *ius animatum* e por isso seria iníquo se não obedecesse às leis que ele próprio prescreve aos outros (VIII, 6). Sobre esta obra, vide G. Chiarelli 1932: 716-738.

[62] Vide Sforza 1951: 72.

[63] Vide e. g. Platão, *Lg.* IV, 715b; VI, 775a-c, 762d, etc.

[64] Erasmo, *Institutio principis christiani, L. B.*, IV, 595 F.

expressão de autores como Lourenço de Cáceres, em que é evidente uma situação de compromisso, a fidelidade do príncipe a lei não é abalada[65].

João de Barros, no seu *Panegírico de D. João III*, afirma: "[...]por isso quer Platão que o príncipe obedeça em tudo às leis; e diz que onde a lei é sujeita ao rei e não o rei à lei, se deve recear que aquele reino se perca mui asinha; porque, quando governa a lei, governa Deus – o que não pode ser quando se tudo manda pelos apetites de um homem"[66].

Diogo de Teive na *Institutio Sebastiani Primi*, ou *Regras para a educação de El-Rei D. Sebastião*, exprime mesmo a sua oposição ao princípio do direito romano[67]: "Obedece o Rei às leis santissimas, / Obedece à razão e à justiça / O Tyranno à vontade, e appetite"// "Nem queira fazer tudo quanto póde, / Mas só quanto convém, quanto for justo, / E aqui de seu poder ponha os limites, / E entenda que também fica subjeito /Às leis que ele mandou que se guardassem, / Bem ao contrário do que n'outro tempo/.../ Aquella lisongeira lei mandava, / Que os Reis das suas leis isentos fossem".

Bem expressivos a este respeito são Diogo de Sá, em *Tractado dos Estádos Ecclesiasticos e seculares*[68], D. Jerónimo Osório, em *De regis institutione et disciplina*, ou os juristas Manuel Soares da Ribeira, Gonçalo Mendes de Vasconcelos e Jorge de Cabedo, entre outros[69].

Dirá Martim de Albuquerque: "o modo como em Portugal no século XVI foi encarada a temática das relações entre o rei e a lei, permite-nos concluir que – para lá de todos os debates e subtilezas doutrinais –, permanece, como princípio fundamental, a ideia de que o monarca deve também cumprir as próprias normas"[70].

Apenas Diogo Lopes Rebelo, defensor do absolutismo do monarca – exemplo de virtudes – vai ter em mente este postulado, tal como Guillaume Budé na sua *Institution du prince*, dedicada a Francisco I[71]. Com efeito, no *De republica gubernanda per regem*, Lopes Rebelo afirma que o rei é, no seu reino, por direito divino e humano, senhor da vida e da morte dos seus concidadãos: *Rex enim in suo regno iure diuino et humano, uitae et necis hominum dominus est*[72]. Apesar disso, não deixa de explicitar que os reis não podem promulgar leis contra o direito divino e que a lei iníqua não merece o nome de lei[73].

---

[65] Vide *Sobre os trabalhos do rei* de Lourenço de Cáceres, in Andrade 1965: 65.

[66] Barros 1937: 7.

[67] Teive 1756: 74-75 e 150-151.

[68] Sá, *Tractado dos Estados Ecclesiásticos e Seculares. Em que por muy breue e claro stillo se mostra como em cada hum deles se pode o Christão salvar. Author Diogo de Saa. Nelle se impugnão muitas heresias que muitos hereges teverão em cada hum dos estados*, Ms. da B. N. L., F. G.2725, p. 234-235.

[69] Albuquerque 1968: 280 e sqq.

[70] Ibidem: 271.

[71] Vide *Institutione du Prince*, fos. 7vº - 8rº, edição de Bontems 1965: 80. Sobre a defesa da monarquia absoluta por Budé, nesta obra e no *De asse*, Ibidem: 24-34.

[72] Cf. Rebelo 1951: 66-67.

[73] Vide a este propósito, Albuquerque 1968: 298-299.

A posição assumida por este tratadista, e mais veementemente por Guillaume Budé, difere, contudo, da perspectiva de S. Tomás e reflecte bem a tendência para o reforço do poder real[74], que começa a desenvolver-se no Renascimento e ganha vulto com a obra de Jean Bodin, *Les six livres de la Republique*, de 1576[75].

O século XV, em que crescera e se formara Maquiavel, nascido em 1469, assistira à tirania cheia de astúcia de um Luís XI, ao despotismo violento personificado em Carlos o Temerário, à posição política de um Gerson e de um Jean Petit, ou de um Philipe de Commines, historiador e conselheiro de Luís XI, à pregação, cheia de fanatismo do reformador religioso, Savonarola.[76]

Foi já observado que o idealismo e o arrebatamento político-religioso de Savonarola teria condicionado o tom realista e incrédulo de Maquiavel que, por ver os esforços vãos do seu compatriota, se teria decidido a trilhar o caminho oposto[77]. Na verdade, a obra *Il principe* (1513*)*, publicada apenas em 1532 e dedicada a Lourenço de Médicis, reflecte pelo menos a realidade da época conturbada em que viveu.

Bem diverso do príncipe "umanizzato" é o modelo de governante proposto por Maquiavel, confessado inovador neste domínio, ao apresentar em *Il principe* as condições técnicas necessárias à conquista do poder e à permanência nele[78]. No entanto, as doutrinas do Florentino não provocaram reacção apreciável até cerca de meados do séc. XVI, nem influenciaram a concepção humanista do modelo do príncipe, na literatura europeia e de forma particular na Península Ibérica – menos aberta a inovações que viessem pôr em causa o compromisso entre a moral e a política. O Florentino, como tem sido afirmado, abre a era dos filósofos políticos modernos, como Hobbes, Spinoza, Pufendorf e prefigura o estado racional que Hegel viria a definir[79].

Na mesma altura em que Maquiavel condensa em *Il principe* as suas conclusões políticas da Renascença italiana, Erasmo, nos países do Norte, exprime também, através de teorias ético-jurídicas, uma concepção bem diversa do

---

[74] Cf. Allen 1951: 281-282; Merêa 1941: 26; e introdução a Rebelo 1951: XXV.

[75] Esta obra de doutrina e teorização jurídico-política, que parte da reflexão crítica dos modelos da Antiguidade geco-latina e do direito romano, vai ser um marco importante para a produção política posterior. Vide Soares 1994:141-142.

[76] Curioso é que o futuro Chanceler de Florença fora, jovem ainda, um simpatizante da doutrina de Savonarola, cujos seguidores, os *piagnoni*, se opunham aos *arrabbiati*, defensores do governo dos Médicis.

[77] Vide Franck 1864: 337.

[78] Vide *Il principe*, cap. XII e sobretudo XV. Depois de investigar, no cap. XII, os meios pelos quais muitos adquiriram e conservaram o poder, conclui, no cap. XV, que um príncipe para se manter no governo deve aprender a nem sempre ser bom, para passar a ser conforme as circunstâncias e os interesses o exigirem. Mas é sobretudo nos capítulos XV-XIX, que se verifica uma ruptura definitiva com a ética aristotélica e os princípios apregoados pelo estoicismo, vivificado pelo cristianismo.

[79] Vide e. g. Maquiavel 1980: 108 e 155; Stegmann 1977: 498.

homem[80]. E Tomás Moro, o amigo dilecto de Erasmo, publica a sua *Utopia* (Lovaina, 1516), que apresenta o plano de uma república ideal, assente nos principios da moral tradicional e nos valores de uma renovada filosofia antropológica, neo-platónica, tão cara ao Humanismo Renascentista.

A *Institutio principis christiani* de Erasmo e a *Utopia* de Tomás Moro, editadas no mesmo ano, que representam as duas facetas neoplatónicas do idealismo político-social e religioso do humanismo europeu, estão na base de quantas se escreveram sobre o mesmo tema. Diríamos mesmo que a obra de Erasmo deu o tom a toda uma abundante literatura – os tratados de educação de príncipes – dentro da linha católica ortodoxa, que este século conheceu.

A atitude de oposição a Maquiavel ou aos autores reformistas, ou ainda a preocupação de orientar os príncipes dos diversos estados, salvaguarda dos interesses nacionais, postos acima dos interesses pessoais – que o absolutismo assente no regalismo romano favorecia – são os principais factores responsáveis pela enorme proliferação de tratados de educação de príncipes na Europa.

O importante papel que este tema assume na nossa literatura quinhentista implica que a sua ocorrência extravase em muito a tratadística tradicional. Está presente nas orações pronunciadas em cortes ou em juramentos de príncipes; em orações de entrada ou ainda em orações universtárias, em panegíricos; nos textos poéticos dos vários autores, desde o *Cancioneiro Geral* e Gil Vicente a Sá de Miranda, António Ferreira, Camões e tantos outros que, em língua portuguesa ou na latina, dedicaram os seus versos a reis, príncipes e figuras de relevo na governação; nas composicões dramáticas em verso e em prosa, nas tragédias plenas de teorização política e admoestação, nas comédias cheias de sátira social e denúncia de costumes depravados.

Apesar da leitura global da mentalidade colectiva da época, que esta produção apresenta, nela sobressai o eterno catálogo de virtudes, referência imutável que precede o olhar do pintor que traça o retrato do príncipe ideal e o condiciona[81]. As virtudes humanas, de cariz cínico-estóico, configuram-se com as virtudes cardeais do Cristianismo – justiça, fortaleza, temperança e prudência –, a que se ligam muitas outras que lhes são indissociáveis, lhes especificam o sentido e lhes conferem uma mais ampla dimensão humana e transcendental[82] – tal como no desenho preparatório do *Carro triunfal de Maximiliano I* de Dürer[83].

Imbuído de platonismo, este ideal do governante, modelo de virtudes, justo e bom administrador da justiça – simbolicamente, representante de Deus na

---

[80] Vide e.g. Mesnard 1977: 86-140.

[81] Vide Krynen 1981: 54 e sqq.

[82] O chamado cânone das virtudes cardeais foi enunciado pela primeira vez em Píndaro, *I.* 8. 50-56. Cf. também Platão, *R.*, 504a sqq.

[83] Vide Soares 1994: 190-197.

terra, qual sol que a todos ilumina. no dizer de Frei Heitor Pinto[84] –, que na sua *majestas* encarna o poder como lei animada, *nómos émpsychos*, e, na sua *magnificentia/ magnanimitas*, se impõe como norma de conduta e acção moral, é o ideal do homem do Renascimento e de todos os tempos, que Giovanni Pico della Mirandola exalta em *De hominis dignitate*.

No que se refere à justiça que, segundo Platão, inclui e resume todas as outras, a ela se ligam a clemência e a verdade – a misericórdia. Essa misericórdia de que nos fala Shakespeare, em cena de tribunal, no *Mercador de Veneza* (acto IV, cena I, v. 180-183)[85]: 'A misericórdia não é uma obrigação,/ cai do céu como um frescor de chuva/ sobre a terra. É uma bênção dupla:/ abençoa quem a dá e quem a recebe'[86].

Numa palavra, ao considerarmos as relações dos humanistas com o poder, no contexto do Renascimento, assentes no direito e na ciência política – ancorados na mensagem da Antiguidade clássica, assimilada aos valores do Cristianismo –, poderemos com toda a razão observar que elas reflectem uma nova dimensão do humano, presente na ideologia e na doutrina que caracterizam a literatura do século de ouro português e europeu.

---

[84] Vide Soares 1994: 287.

[85] The *Merchant Of Venice*: «PORTIA The quality of mercy is not strain'd,/ It droppeth as the gentle rain from heaven/ Upon the place beneath: it is twice blest;/ It blesseth him that gives and him that takes».

[86] Este passo shakespeariano foi citado pelo Papa Francisco – neste ano Jubilar da Misericórdia –, ao afirmar, na sua mensagem para a 50ª Jornada Mundial das Comunicações Sociais, que a linguagem da misericórdia deveria permear também a política e a diplomacia e ser praticada por todos aqueles que têm responsabilidades institucionais.

Los universitarios portugueses graduados en Bolonia, Alfonso de Cartagena y Poggio Bracciolini[*]
(Portuguese University Students who Graduated in Bologna, Alfonso de Cartagena, and Poggio Bracciolini)

Tomás González Rolán (tgrolan@filol.ucm.es)
Universidad Complutense de Madrid

Para Vítor Morgado,
Un hombre bueno, un gran amigo,
Que permanecerá para siempre en nuestro recuerdo.

Resumen – En este estudio tratamos de probar que el letrado que mostró algunas traducciones latinas de textos griegos escritas por el humanista Leonardo Bruni a Alfonso de Cartagena cuando estaba en Portugal, ha debido ser la misma persona que describió Vespasiano da Bistici y mencionó Poggio Bracciolini en una carta de 1441. Esta carta probablemente fue enviada a Alfonso de Cartagena: le pedía que le enviara la transcripción exacta de un manuscrito depositado en el monasterio de Alcobaça; sin embargo, se supone que este manuscrito contenía el texto completo de *Las Noches Áticas* de Aulo Gelio.

Palabras clave: Alfonso de Cartagena, Poggio Bracciolini, Portugal, Castilla, Bolonia.

Abstract – This paper has tried to prove that the lawyer who showed several Latin translations of Greek texts written by the humanist Leonardo Bruni to Alfonso de Cartagena when he was in Portugal has to be the same person who described Vespasiano da Bisticci, and referred to Poggio Bracciolini in a letter in 1441. This letter probably was sent to Alfonso de Cartagena: he was asked to send an exact transcription of a manuscript deposited in the monastery of Alcobaça; moreover, it is assumed that this manuscript contained the full text of *The Attic Nights* of Aulus Gellius.

Keywords: Alfonso de Cartagena, Poggio Bracciolini, Portugal, Castile, Bologna

1. Introducción

Es bien sabido que con el triunfo de las tropas portuguesas lideradas por João I sobre las castellanas en la célebre batalla de Aljubarrota (1385) comenzaba una historia de distanciamientos y desencuentros entre Portugal y Castilla, que muy pronto la diplomacia de ambos reinos trataría de remediar y superar con el establecimiento de treguas (1393) y sobre todo con la firma de la paz en 1411.

El monarca castellano, Juan II, hijo de Enrique III y Catalina de Lancaster, y por lo tanto sobrino del rey portugués, quien se había casado con Filipa de

https://doi.org/10.14195/978-989-26-1280-5_23

Lancaster, hermana de Catalina por parte de padre, en respuesta a las embajadas portuguesas de 1418 y 1419, y con el fin de ultimar el tratado de paz perpetua estipulado, como dijimos, en 1411, envió a la corte portuguesa a finales de 1421 una primera misión[1] presidida por Alfonso de Cartagena (1385-1456), que se prolongaría durante un año entero (diciembre de 1421-diciembre de 1422), y a la que seguirían otras tres (enero-abril de 1423; diciembre 1424-abril de 1425; enero[2] de 1426 - diciembre de 1427), misiones que culminarían con un rotundo éxito, ya que el 30 de octubre de 1431 se firmaba el tratado de paz entre Portugal y Castilla.

No hay duda alguna de que Alfonso de Cartagena contribuyó como el que más al anhelado y necesario encuentro político en las relaciones entre los dos reinos, sobre todo para la monarquía castellana, acosada cada vez más por el reino de Aragón en apoyo de los infantes de Aragón, pero su labor en Portugal no se limitó a esta vertiente política sino que logró impulsar una interrelación y vinculación cultural castellano-portuguesa que permanecería por encima de cualquier discusión o discrepancia política.

Se podría pensar que esta relación cultural entre Alfonso de Cartagena y los hombres cultos de la Corte portuguesa, entre los que se encontraban el Infante D. Pedro y su hermano, el heredero D. Duarte, a quien el embajador español dedicaría su primera obra original, el *Memoriale virtutum* y la traducción del *De inventione* ciceroniano, se estableció en un plano de desigualdad a favor del castellano que ejercería las veces de maestro en un país rezagado culturalmente. Esta es la opinión de Abdon M. Salazar (1976: 217) quien compara la influencia de Alfonso de Cartagena en la cultura portuguesa con la que ejerció el humanista bizantino, Manuel Crisoloras, en la Italia del Renacimiento: «Y en cierto sentido, Cartagena, difundiendo el entusiasmo por la cultura clásica en Lusitania, semeja al dicho Crisoloras diseminando el ideal de la paideia griega entre los italianos».

Más aceptable nos parece la opinión de Adeline Rucquoi (2003: 43) de que en esa relación hubo "une sorte d'égalité dans l' echange", pues por una parte «une image ressort qui montre les castillans comme les maîtres - és vertus ou és poésie - de jeunes princes portugais dont les talents dans ces domaines ont frappé leurs interlocuteurs», pero por otra parte no es menos cierto que estos "maestros" castellanos a su vez han aprendido a menudo de Portugal y de los portugueses: «Alfonso de Cartagena peut avoir connu les traductions de

---

[1] Cf. Abdón M. Salazar 1976:215-226 [especialmente p.216]

[2] Aunque Abdón M. Salazar 1976: 216 supone que la cuarta misión tuvo lugar en los meses de septiembre a diciembre de 1427, Luis Fernández Gallardo, en la biografía más completa hecha hasta el momento sobre Alonso de Cartagena (Fernández Gallardo 2002: 123) afirma que consta documentalmente que ya el 14 de enero de 1426 estaba Alfonso de Cartagena en Portugal, en Vila de Montemôr, lugar del obispado de Évora, en calidad de embajador

Leonardo Bruni et une serie de textes alors en vogue en Italie lors de son séjour au Portugal en 1427».

2. Alfonso de Cartagena y los estudiantes portugueses de Bolonia

En efecto, se puede afirmar que en el ambiente de admirable inquietud cultural de la Corte portuguesa Alfonso de Cartagena no sólo comenzó su andadura como escritor y traductor de autores clásicos, sino que con ocasión de las largas conversaciones mantenidas con intelectuales portugueses que habían realizado estudios en la prestigiosa universidad de Bolonia pudo ampliar su propio horizonte cultural y conocer algunas de las obras traducidas del griego al latín por uno de los humanistas italianos más relevantes de ese momento, Leonardo Bruni de Arezzo.

Con la sencillez y precisión que le caracterizan, Alfonso de Cartagena en sus *Declamationes*, escrito que forma parte del debate[3] que años más tarde sostuvo con el mismo Leonardo Bruni sobre la traducción del griego al latín de las *Éticas* de Aristóteles, nos relata sus largas charlas con titulados portugueses por la Universidad de Bolonia, quienes a él, que había estudiado en Salamanca, le recuerdan los nombres de sus muy célebres maestros en derecho civil y canónico, que consiguieron hacer de ese centro universitario la escuela de derecho por excelencia. Y en medio de estos asuntos relacionados con las actividades académicas, uno de esos (*ex illis quidam*) hombres instruidos (*studiosi*) graduados en Bolonia, que además se dedicaban al estudio de la elocuencia (*qui eloquentiae operam dederant*) ensalzó en este arte a un tal Leonardo Aretino, asegurando que estaba profundamente instruido tanto en la lengua griega como en la latina (*quendam Leonardum Aretinum in eloquentia extollebat, Graecae linguae pariter et Latinae doctissimum asserens*) . Y este letrado portugués, al advertir que Cartagena mostraba vivo interés por la actividad del humanista italiano, se ausentó de la conversación y se dirigió a su casa, de donde trajo varios opúsculos traducidos del griego al latín por L. Bruni entre los que se encontraban los discursos *Contra Ctesifontem* de Esquines y el *Pro Ctesifonte* de Demóstenes además de la *Oratio ad adolescentes* de Basilio de Cesarea (*Et cum me libenter haec audire cerneret, nonnulla opuscula e graeco per eum in Latinum conuersa apud se habere dixit et a communi colloquio festine abiens e domo confestim adduxit illas famosissimas orationes, quas Aeschines in Ctesiphontem et Demosthenes in Aeschinem pro Ctesiphonte...Addidit etiam libellum quendam Basilii, quem e Graeco in Latinum pro Colucio amico suo idem Leonardus conuerterat*).

Se supone que el contertulio portugués le prestó dichos opúsculos, pues Cartagena nos dice que los ha leído y ha quedado admirado de la elocuencia

---

[3] El texto latino y la traducción se toman del libro de González Rolán, Moreno Hernández, Saquero Suárez-Somonte 2000:194-199.

griega y de la elegancia de la traducción, hasta tal punto que por la riqueza y finura de la expresión latina así como por el primor de las palabras utilizadas compara a un hasta el momento desconocido como Leonardo Bruni con un nuevo Cicerón redivivo (*Quae cum legissem, illius saeculi eloquentiam, in quo illi elegantissimi oratores certarunt, cum quadam admiratione conspexi ac modernae translationis suauitas Leonardum eum ignotum carum mihi reddiderat: tanta enim cultura uerborum copiose ac polite cuncta Latine explicauit, ut ne in laudem eius sermonem longius traham, quendam nouellum dixerim Ciceronem*).

Así pues, el encuentro[4] de Alfonso de Cartagena con el Humanismo renacentista italiano y, más concretamente, con la obra de Leonardo Bruni, se debió a ese letrado portugués que había estudiado derecho en la universidad de Bolonia y que estaba entregado a la tarea de la elocuencia, del que el escritor castellano no nos da el nombre, si bien hace algunos años el excelente filólogo inglés Jeremy N. H. Lawrance (1990: 223, n. 8), ha apuntado la posibilidad de que se trate de "messer Valasco Roderighi, chantore Bragarensi di Portogallo" quien compró el 11 de marzo de 1425 en la librería florentina de Piero Betucci dos traduccciones del griego realizadas por Leonardo Bruni y un Terencio[5], lo que establecería la fecha del primer conocimiento por Cartagena de la obra de Bruni en la cuarta y última legación a Portugal (septiembre-diciembre de 1427). El que ese "messer Valasco Roderighi", chantre de Braga haya comprado en Florencia unas traducciones de Bruni, puede ser ciertamente un indicio favorable a la identificación de ese personaje con el que le prestó a Cartagena las referidas traducciones del humanista italiano, identificación que podrá realizarse siempre y cuando se pueda demostrar que dicho personaje había estudiado en Bolonia y se dedicaba a la elocuencia.

Como muy bien ha demostrado la Profesora Nair de Nazaré Castro Soares (2002: 112), «de grande significado na definição dos nossos ideais culturais é a influência directa da Itália em Portugal, pelo menos a partir do início do século XIV. Conhecida é a presença de letrados portugueses em Itália entre 1350 e 1450».

Los estudios, entre otros, de Virgínia Rau[6], Antonio Domínguez de Sousa Costa[7] y M. Augusto Rodrigues[8], además de los trabajos de Antonio Pérez Martín sobre el Colegio de España en Bolonia[9] nos permiten comprobar la presencia de alumnos portugueses en la mayor parte de las universidades europeas, si bien, como acertadamente señala Virgínia Rau[10], «l'Italia rappresentò realmente, durante tutto il secolo XV, un grande centro di attrazione per i nostri letterati.

---

[4] Cf. el reciente y minucioso estudio de Fernández Gallardo 2008:175-215.

[5] Cf. Florencia , Archivio di Stato, Conv. Sopp. 78 (Badia), vol. 261 I fol.31.

[6] Rau 1969: 185-206; 1973: 7- 28,

[7] Costa 1969.

[8] Rodrigues 1993: 345-362.

[9] Pérez Martín 1979 e 1999.

[10] Rau 1973: 8.

Da Bologna, Siena, Padova a Pavia, Perugia, Firenze, Pisa e Ferrara si mossero gli studiosi portughesi, alcuni dei quali ottenero perfino incarichi universitari».

Por lo que se refiere a la Universidad de Bolonia, se constatan por los referidos historiadores entre comienzos del siglo XV y 1430, una serie de nombres, entre los que figuran Brasio Alfonso, Estêvão Alfonso, Gomes Pais, Lourenço de Portugal, y de modo particular Alfonso Rodrigues Garcia, estudiante de derecho canónico en la universidad de Bolonia y doctor en 1417 por la de Padua, futuro arcediano de Lisboa y profesor de su Universidad, y su hermano Vasco (Valasco o Velasco) Rodrigues[11], doctor en derecho por Bolonia a partir de 1421, elegido por dicha Universidad para impartir la lectura extraordinaria del *Inforciato*, es decir, la segunda parte del *Digesto*, en el curso 1418- 19. Es este curioso y atractivo personaje al que de acuerdo con las investigaciones de Virginia Rau[12], Antonio Domingues de Sousa Costa[13] y las muy recientes de Clelia Bettini[14] se le ha de identificar con el que aparece descrito bajo el nombre de "Velasco di Portogallo" en la famosa obra de Vespasiano da Bisticci[15], *Vite di uomini illustri del secolo XV*. Según Bisticci "messer Velasco" era originario de Portugal , de noble y muy rica familia, que le había enviado a Italia para estudiar derecho canónico y civil. Al principio llevó una vida de estudiante bastante desordenada y jaranera, y porque confiaba mucho en su inteligencia, se dedicaba más a la lectura de obras literarias, como los sonetos de Petrarca, que a los textos jurídicos. Pero una vez que su padre cayó en desgracia ante el rey de Portugal y sus posibilidades económicas disminuyeron, se puso, nos dice Bisticci, a estudiar con gran diligencia y en muy poco tiempo se licenció y doctoró:

«Istato più tempo a questo modo, e vedendo il padre avere perduta la grazia del re e buona somma di danari, essendo fuori del regno, per lo sdegno fece pensiero di non vi tornare più, e misesi giù con grandissima diligenza a istudiare in iure civile e canonico, e per la prestanza dello igegno suo, in brevissimo tempo diventò singularissimo nell'una facultá e nell'áltra, e dottorosi con grandissima fama e riputazione, di natura che se n'érano dottorati pochi in Bologna di quella qualitá.».

Otras virtudes o cualidades que encuentra Bisticci en él es el de ser "eloquentissimo in iscrivere, perchè s'era dilettato di leggere più opere de'gentili", y sobre todo un gran amante de los libros, un bibliófilo que «aveva libri per parecchi migliaja di fiorini, perchè voleva tutti i più belli che trovava».

---

[11] Pérez Martín 1999: 46 en la entrada que dedica a este personaje señala que seguramente hay que identificarlo con el estudiante de Derecho Civil, ciudadano de Lisboa e hijo del noble Rodrigo García de Portugal, cuya estancia en Bolonia consta en 1418-19; cf. además G. Zaoli 1912:146; C. Piana, 1976.

[12] Rau 1969: 188-189.

[13] Costa 1990: 585-586.

[14] Bettini 2008: 207-216.

[15] Cf. edición de P. D'Ancona-E. Heschilimann, Milán, 1951:356-368; cf. también *Spicilegium romanum. Tomus I. Virorum illustrium-CII qui saeculo XV extiterunt, vitae*, pp. 677-682.

Terminados sus estudios, solicitó distintos beneficios eclesiásticos en Portugal, entre ellos el del arcedianato de Braga, entrando a formar parte del séquito de la Corte papal, donde consiguió ejercer como abogado consistorial. Un año antes de su muerte ocurrida en junio de 1457, ingresó en el monasterio de Santa Brígida del Paraíso de Florencia, donde escribió un *Parecer*[16], es decir, un dictamen sobre la aprobación que el Estado concede a las leyes de la Iglesia y demás actos de la autoridad eclesiástica para que puedan tener fuerza obligatoria en el respectivo país.

Así pues, no cabe ninguna duda de que Vasco (Velasco o Valasco) Rodrigues, hijo de una familia noble y adinerada, estudiante en la universidad de Bolonia, doctor en derecho civil en 1421 y en derecho canónico en 1442, solicitante de beneficios eclesiásticos en Portugal, entre ellos el arcedianato de Braga, amante y coleccionista compulsivo de libros en distintas ciudades de Italia (Padua, Florencia, Bolonia, Siena), aficionado a la lectura de los autores clásicos y humanísticos, dedicado a la elocuencia, es el "messer Valasco Roderighi" que compró en 1425, en Florencia, las traducciones del griego realizadas por Leonardo Bruni y el que se las prestó en Portugal a Alfonso de Cartagena aproximadamente dos años después.

Aunque según Vespasiano da Bisticci Vasco Rodrigues tenía un temperamento poco paciente que le impulsaba a resolver por la tremenda aquellas situaciones que le incomodaban, lo cierto es que tenía grandes cualidades, como el de ser generoso y desprendido, como vemos en el caso del préstamo de libros a Cartagena, o el de ser realmente 'moderno' por su bibliofilia, por su admiración de Petrarca y su afición a la lectura de autores de la Antigüedad clásica. Todo ello le debió de granjear amistades y relaciones entre los humanistas italianos y hombres de letras en general, como es el caso de Bisticci. Por lo que se refiere a las relaciones posteriores a 1427 entre Alfonso de Cartagena y Vasco Rodrigues no nos queda ningún documento, pero es muy posible que la amistad y agradecimiento forjados en Portugal perviviesen bien a través de una correspondencia que no nos ha llegado, bien por medio de posibles nuevos encuentros, ahora en el Concilio de Basilea, a donde llegó Cartagena formando parte de la embajada enviada por el rey de Castilla, Juan II, y donde pudo haber estado el letrado portugués, ya que desde 1427 entró a formar parte de la Corte papal, llegando, como dijimos, a convertirse en abogado consistorial.

Sí se conservan testimonios de las excelentes relaciones mantenidas por Vasco Rodrigues y por su hermano Alfonso con destacados humanistas italianos como Guarino de Verona o Gasparino Barzizza de Bérgamo[17].

---

[16] Cf. edición y amplio estudio preliminar de Nunes e Albuquerque 1968:97-139.

[17] Las cartas enviadas por estos humanistas han sido reproducidas y comentadas por Costa 1990: 579-588.

3. El destinatario de una carta de Poggio Bracciolini sobre un manuscrito de A. Gelio en el Monasterio de Alcobaça.

Otro muy ilustre humanista, Poggio Bracciolini, ha incluido en su epistolario[18] tres cartas dirigidas a un *Valascus Portugallensis*, fechadas en Bolonia, la primera[19] en otoño de 1436, la segunda[20] en invierno de los años 1436 y 1437, y la tercera[21] del 5 de julio de 1437; una cuarta[22], datada en Florencia el 20 de septiembre de 1441 va dirigida a un tal Alfonso (*Poggius plurimam salutem dicit Alfonso suo*), pero comienza diciendo que "Vasco, muy preclaro amigo tuyo, o más bien nuestro, me ha informado hace poco que habías encontrado en el monasterio de Alcobaça un Aulo Gelio de las Noches Áticas completo y no amputado como el que poseemos" (*Vir clarissimus Valascus tuus, vel noster potius, retulit dudum mihi te reperisse in monasterio Altobassi A.Gellium Noctium Acticarum integrum neque lacerum ut noster est*).

El *Valascus Portugallensis*, destinatario de las tres primeras cartas de Poggio Bracciolini debe sin duda alguna identificarse, como muy bien ha hecho Helene Harth, con Vasco Fernández de Lucena[23], español (cordobés) de origen converso que pasó su larga vida (casi cien años) en Portugal ejerciendo importantes funciones como diplomático (*orator regis Portugaliae*), y sobre todo como traductor a la lengua portuguesa de textos de autores clásicos (Cicerón, Plinio) o

---

[18] Seguimos la edición de Helene Harth, *Poggio Bracciolini, Lettere*, 3 vols., Florencia, 1984.

[19] Cf. H. Harth, op. cit. II, pp. 213-214.

[20] Cf. H. Harth, op. cit. II, p.220.

[21] Cf. H. Harth, op.cit., II, pp.245-246.

[22] Cf. H. Harth, op.cit.,II, pp.373-374. La carta dice así:Poggius plurimam salutem dicit Alfonso suo. Vir clarissimus Valascus tuus, uel noster potius, retulit dudum mihi te reperisse in monasterio Alcobassi Aulum Gellium Noctium Acticarum integrum, neque lacerum,ut noster est. Gauisus sum tum propter communem utilitatem doctorum uirorum, tum propter honorem tuum. Non enim parum glorie accedet tuo nomini ex hoc tam uberrimo lucro, quod multo pluris, quam auri thesaurus, extimandum est. Est quidem immortalis sola gloria litterarum, que ceteris rebus prestat, ne sint mortales. Equidem me profiteor fore bucinatorem tui nominis, si tua opera hic egregious auctor, quem negligentia hominum lacerauit, et pene discerpsit, sanus atque integer restituetur nobis. Date igitur huic operi potissime, ut liber transcribatur uel pingatur potius ad alterius similitudiem, et id cura, ne quid desit litterarum grecarum. Tu autem incumbe et id effice, ut liber quam primum ad nos mittatur, et eo modo, ut saluus adueniat. Preterea te rogo maiorem in modum, ut rursus peruestiges diligenter, qui libri sint gentiles in eo monasterio, in quo plurimi esse dicuntur, precipue uero Ciceronis nostri librorum curam habe, an ibi essent libri achademici, de consolatione, de gloria, de legibus, qui est omnibus membris intercisus. De Liuio insuper et ceteris historicis perquire. Plura insuper uolumina epistularum Ciceronis, et orationes quoque multe desunt nobis. Fac, te oro, inuentarium librorum omnium, qui gentiles appellantur, et ad nos mitte. Non enim dubito, quin aliquid lucremur ex hac tua industria, si solitam diligentiam adhibueris: hoc nihil preclarius, nihil laudabilius, nihil tibi honorificentius potes agere, quod ut facias te docti omnes et litterarum studiosi summopere deprecantur. Vale et ne obliuiscaris antique consuetudinis nostre. Florentie, die XX Septembris 1441.

[23] Sobre Vasco Fernández de Lucena, *cf.* Pinho 1999: 125-133.

humanísticos (Pier Paolo Vergerio, Jean Jouffroy, etc.). Y si en la primera de las cartas Poggio lo trata con consideración y le da algunos consejos sobre retórica latina, en las otras dos le recrimina duramente el haberle engañado y no haberle pagado lo estipulado, echándole en cara su origen judío, pues si hubiese sabido antes su ascendencia no hubiese confiado de ninguna manera en él.

Respecto a la carta fechada el 20 de septiembre de 1441, en la que Poggio se dirige a un tal Alfonso, que según le comunicó el amigo común llamado Vasco (*Valascus*) había descubierto un manuscrito completo de las Noches Áticas de Aulo Gelio, con el fin de hacerle llegar su enorme alegría por tal noticia y el gran renombre que le espera, así como solicitarle que proceda a su transcripción o exacta reproducción o calco de forma que no falte ni una sola de las letras griegas y que una vez terminada la envíe completa y clara (*Da te igitur huic operi potissime, ut liber transcribatur, vel pingatur potius ad alterius similitudinem, et id cura, ut quid desit litterarum grecarum. Tum autem incumbe et id effice, ut liber quamprimum ad nos mittatur et eo modo, ut salvus adveniat*). Le pide además que investigue otros libros de la Antigüedad Clásica, que se puedan encontrar en la biblioteca del monasterio, como algunos de Cicerón, Tito Livio y de otros historiadores. Termina solicitándole la confección y el envío de un inventario de todos los libros de autores paganos (*Fac, te oro, inventarium librorum omnium qui gentiles appellantur et ad nos mitte*).

Puesto que Poggio Bracciolini se refiere al destinatario y a su informador o intermediario con los escuetos nombres de Alfonso y *Valascus*, respectivamente, se han emitido distintas propuestas sobre su identificación.

Respecto al segundo de los nombres citados, Helene Harth[24] no incluye nota alguna que lo diferencie del *Valascus* de las tres cartas anteriores, lo que supone que para ella es el mismo personaje, pero ya Angelo Mai[25], a mediados del siglo XIX, había señalado que este Valascus era el doctor en derecho y abogado consistorial Vasco Rodrigues, descrito por Vespasiano da Bisticci: «*Est hic Valascus Lusitanus, cuius vitam habes apud Vespasianum*»; si bien se confunde al atribuir falsamente las otras cartas de Poggio a este mismo personaje, debido a un supuesto enfriamieno de su amistad: «*Huic fuit primum amicus Poggius, postea inimicus, ut ostendunt duae Poggi ad Valascum epistolae in editione parisina*».

El hecho de que Vasco Rodrigues y Poggio Bracciolini trabajasen en la Curia romana puede apoyar la suposición de un cierto conocimiento y amistad entre ambos, de modo que la identificación del Valascus de la carta con Vasco Rodrigues se ha ido imponiendo a través de las propuestas de N. Espinosa Gomes

---

[24] Pinho 1999: 373.

[25] Cf. Spicilegium Romanum, T. X, Roma, 1844, p. 339, n.1.

da Silva[26], Antonio Domingues de Sousa Costa[27] y Aires A. Nascimento[28].

Mucho más dificil se presenta saber a quién se refiere Poggio con el nombre de Alfonso. R. Sabbadini[29] en sus dos magníficos libros sobre los descubrimientos de manuscritos en los siglos XIV y XV sostuvo que el destinatario de la carta de Poggio era Alfonso de Cartagena, propuesta apoyada entre otros por Joaquim de Carvalho[30] y Helene Harth[31] pero rechazada por Antonio Domingues de Sousa Costa[32], quien sugiere, aunque de forma no indubitable, el nombre de Alonso Rodrigues Garcia, hermano de Vasco Rodrigues, y por Jeremy N. H. Lawrance[33] que presenta como alternativa el nombre de Álvaro Alfonso, obispo de Évora y previamente de Silves y del Algarbe, personaje ya sugerido como el destinatario de la carta de Poggio por Angelo Mai[34] y cuya biografía es trazada escuetamente por Vespasiano da Bisticci bajo el título "Alfonso di Portogallo, Vescovo".

Sousa Costa apoya su rechazo a Alfonso de Cartagena, en primer lugar en el hecho de que en 1441, fecha de la carta, Alfonso era obispo desde hacía seis años, y en este caso se esperaría un encabezamiento distinto del que se nos ha transmitido (*Poggius plurimam salutem dicit Alfonso suo*), ya que siempre que Poggio se dirige en sus cartas a obispos o cardenales, por muy amigos y familiares que sean, se sirve de las expresiones *Reverendo patri* y *Reverendissimo patri*, respectivamente.

Menor peso, a nuestro entender, tiene la segunda consideración, a saber, que durante el período en el que estuvo de embajador en el Concilio de Basilea (1434-1439) no consta que Alfonso de Cartagena se pasase por la Curia, es decir, se trasladase a Italia y así pudiese haberse encontrado con Poggio Bracciolini.

Si estas dos razones excluyen a Cartagena como el destinatario de la referida carta, también hay motivos, según Sousa Costa[35], para no aceptar la propuesta de Álvaro Alfonso, obispo de Évora, pues es evidente que Alfonso no era su nombre sino su apellido por lo que «embora de per si a sua carreira se não oponha à identificação e até alguns elementos a pudessem tornar plausível, parece que o facto de se tratar de pessoa só com o apelido de Afonso e não com tal nome, leve a excluir essa identificação».

---

26 Silva 164: 114-116.

27 Costa 1990: 590- 605.

28 Nascimento 1990: 38- 39; 1993: 270, n. 15.

29 Sabbadini 1905: 92, n. 29; 1994: 157 y 225.

30 Carvalho 1949: 39, n.1.

31 Harth 1984: 373.

32 Costa 1990: 594-598.

33 Lawrance 1990: 236, n. 41.

34 Mai 1844: 339, n. 1.

35 Costa: 1990: 594.

El argumento utilizado por Jeremy N.H. Lawrance[36] para no aceptar a Alfonso de Cartagena es que la primera carta que le envió Poggio está fechada dos años después, en 1443 :«Poggio's first letter to Cartagena is dated 1443».

Es en este último aspecto en el que insiste Aires A. Nascimento[37], pues, dice él: «Não faria sentido que ele tratasse na carta de 1443 formalmente o seu correspondente por *episcopo Burgensi* ou *praestantissime pater* se houvesse tido com ele a familiaridade que logo a própria saudação da carta anterior pressupõe; mais do que isso, na carta de 1443, Poggio deixa entender que as informacões que tem acerca do prelado procedem de interposta pessoa...e procura asegurar-se de uma amizade que parece estar nos começos...Deste modo, será de arredar a hipótese do bispo de Burgos».

Tenemos, pues, encima de la mesa tres nombres, Alfonso Rodrigues Garcia de Lisboa, hermano de Vasco Rodrigues, Álvaro Alfonso, obispo de Évora, y Alfonso de Cartagena, obispo de Burgos.

Aunque en su época de estudiante en Italia mantuvo relaciones de amistad con algunos humanistas italianos, no hay constancia alguna de familiaridad entre Alfonso Rodrigues y Poggio Bracciolini, argumento que podría aplicarse también a Álvaro Alfonso. Por otra parte, el comienzo de la carta de 1441, *Vir clarissimus Valascus tuus*, en el que al destinatario Alfonso le habla de "Vasco, muy preclaro amigo tuyo", nos lleva a suponer que el tal Vasco no es, como dijimos, Vasco Rodrigues, o bien que el destinatario Alfonso no es su hermano, opción esta última que nos parece más razonable y justificada, ya que es muy poco probable que Poggio se refiera a un hermano de su destinatario como "amigo suyo".

Respecto a Álvaro Alfonso, obispo desde 1453, ya hemos dicho que no hay constancia de amistad o familiaridad con Poggio, y por lo demás su residencia en Roma es posterior[38] a 1449, año en que participó en la batalla de Alfarrobeira, donde perdió la vida el Infante D. Pedro, pues es sabido que un hijo de éste último llamado Jaime, futuro cardenal de San Eustaquio, se trasladó a Roma en 1451 y con él se fue el referido Álvaro Alfonso.

Respecto a Alfonso de Cartagena, no podemos asegurar que conociese personalmente a Poggio Bracciolini, pero sí que éste alabó ya en 1437 la moderación y buen saber de Alfonso en la disputa que sostuvo con Leonardo Bruni , a quien le envió un escrito[39], fechado en Bolonia en el indicado año, para darle cuenta de que le han llegado dos cartas, una de Pier Candido Decembrio y otra de Alfonso dirigida al arzobipo de Mián (*altera Alphonsi Hispani*), quien a su entender a diferencia del primero habla con mucha más mesura (*Loquitur tamen Hispanus, ut mihi quidem uidetur, admodum moderate*). Debemos notar que

---

[36] Lawrance 1990: 236, n. 41.

[37] Nascimento 1990: 39.

[38] Cf. Fonseca 1982:323.

[39] Cf. González Rolán et alii 2002:286-287 y también Soria 1956:233.

se refiere a Alfonso de Cartagena, elevado al obispado dos años antes, en 1435, como *Alphonsus Hispanus,* mientras que designa a F. Pizzolpaso, arzobispo de Milán, como *archiepiscopus Mediolanensis.*

Como hemos visto, el encabezamiento de la carta remitida a Alfonso de Cartagena en 1443 es tan escueto que solo dice *Episcopo Burgensi*, sin especificar el nombre del destinatario, como en muchas otras ocasiones (por ejemplo: *Poggius plurimam salutem dicit Scipioni episcopo Mutinensi*). Cabe, pues, la posibilidad de que Poggio en la carta de 1441 se olvidase o, sencillamente, prescindiese conscientemente de la dignidad del destinatario y solo reparase en la dimensión humanística y cultural de Alfonso de Cartagena, que desde luego era bien conocida para él. Nadie, español o portugués, después de su debate con Leonardo Bruni y su estelar actuación en el Concilio de Basilea tenía tanta fama en Italia como Alfonso de Cartagena, hasta el punto de poder ser reconocido meramente por su nombre de pila, Alfonso o bajo la denominación de Alfonso Hispano.

Si se acepta la propuesta de Alfonso de Cartagena, aun reconociendo los obstáculos señalados, se puede explicar muy bien el nombre de *Valascus* como el joven que en Portugal le facilitó el primer acceso a la cultura humanística, es decir, Vasco Rodrigues, licenciado y doctorado en Bolonia.

En relación con el códice completo de las *Noches Áticas* de Aulo Gelio, nada se volvió a saber y lo más seguro es que se tratase de una información equivocada referida a que dicho códice tenía reunidas[40] las dos partes en que se había segmentado la tradición manuscrita, no que conservase los veinte libros completos.

---

[40] Como escribe Sabbadini 1905:92, los códices de Aulo Gelio anteriores al siglo XV se dividen en dos familias, la primera comprende los libros I-VII y la segunda los libros IX-XX. Estas dos familias fueron unidas en un solo volumen en el siglo XV, pero siempre con la ausencia del libro VIII, que se ha perdido irremediablemente. Por esto, cuando los humanistas hablan de hallazgo de un Gelio íntegro, o se trata de falsas noticias o, como mucho, de códices que tenían unidas las dos partes. Clelia Bettini (2008:218, n.38) sugiere que el códice alcobacense puede identificarse con el manuscrito de El Escorial e.III.6, biblioteca a donde fueron transferidos los manuscritos de Alcobaça en la época de Felipe II. Sobre la tradición manuscrita de Aulo Gelio puede consultarse el estudio de Marshall 1983: 176-180 y las introducciones de las recientes traducciones al español de M. A. Marcos Casquero-A. Domínguez García 2006:35-36, F. García Jurado 2007: 34-39 y S. López Moreda 2009:70-72.

Bibliografia Final

AA.VV. (1990), *Archéologie de la vigne et du vin. Actes du colloque 28-29 mai 1988*, Paris.

AA.VV. (1992), *Archeologia del paesaggio. IV Ciclo di lezioni sulla ricerca applicata in archeologia, Certosa di Pontignano (Siena) 14 - 26 gennaio 1991*, Firenze.

AA.VV. (1997), *Uomo, acqua e paesaggio. Atti dell'incontro di studio sul tema irreggimentazione delle acque e trasformazione del paesaggio antico*, S. Maria Capua Vetere 22 - 23 novembre 1996, Roma.

AA.VV. (1998), *El vi a l'antiguitat. Economia, producció i comerç al Mediterrani occidental. II Colloqui internacional d'arqueologia romana. Actes. Badalona, 6 - 9 de maig de 1998*, Badalona.

AA.VV. (1999), *El vino en la antigüedad romana. Simposio arqueología del vino, Jérez 2, 3 y 4 de octubre 1996*, Madrid.

AA.VV. (1999b), *Environmental reconstruction in Mediterranean landscape archaeology*, Oxford.

AA.VV. (2001), *La cerveza en la antigüedad*, Sevilla.

AA.VV. (2004), *Le vin. Nectar des dieux, génie des hommes*, Gollion.

Abascal, J. Manuel , Espinosa, Urbano (1989), *La ciudad hispano-romana. Privilegio y poder*, Logronho.

Abásolo, J. A., Mayer, M. (1997), "Inscripciones latinas", in S. Corchón (coord.), *La Cueva de la Griega de Pedraza (Segovia)*, Zamora, 183-259.

Abbondanza, L. (ed.) (2008), *Filostrato Maggiore*, Milano.

Acosta-Hughes, B. (2002), *Polyeideia. The Iambi of Callimachus and the Archaic Iambic Tradition*, Berkeley and Los Angeles.

Adams, C. (2001), "There and back again. Getting around in Roman Egypt", in Adams, C. and R. Laurence (eds.), *Travel and Geography in the Roman Empire*, Londres and Nova Iorque, 138-166.

Adams, J. N. (2003), *Bilingualism and the Latin language*, Cambridge.

Adams, J. N. (2003a), "*Romanitas* and the Latin language", *CQ* 53: 184-205.

Affatato, R. (2010), "Nueva York: recepción del mito de la ciudad en Federico García Lorca e Italo Calvino", in J. M. Losada Goya (ed.), *Mito y mundo contemporáneo. La recepción de los mitos antiguos, medievales y modernos en la literatura contemporánea*, Bari, 627-640.

Albuquerque, M. de (1968), *O poder político no Renascimento português*, Lisboa.

Albuquerque, M. de (1981), "Bártolo e bartolismo na história do direito português", *Boletim do Ministério da Justiça* 304: 41-61.

Albuquerque, M. de (1983), *Estudos de cultura portuguesa*, I, Lisboa.

Alexandrescu-Vianu, M. (1988), "O nouă posibilă genealogie a familiei lui Hippolochos, fiul lui Theodotod, de la Histria", *SCIVA* 39.3: 275-280.

Alexandrescu-Vianu, M. (1989), "Apollon Ietros. Ein verschollener Gott Ioniens?", *IstMitt* 39: 115-122.

Alexandrescu-Vianu, M. (1990), "Die Steinskulptur von Histria", in P. Alexandrescu, W. Schuller (eds.) *Histria. Eine Griechenstadt an der rumänischen Schwarzmeerkünste*, Xenia. Konstanzer Althistorische Vorträge und Forschungen 25, Konstanz, 179-232.

Alexandrescu-Vianu, M. (2000), "Une alternative d'identification de la statue colossale d'Istros", in A. Avram, M. Babeş (eds.) *Civilsation grecque et cultures antiques périphériques. Hommages à P. Alexandrescu à son 70ᵉ anniversaire*, Bucarest, 274-281.

Alexandridis, A. (2004), *Die Frauen des römischen Kaiserhauses. Eine Untersuchung ihrer bildlichen Darstellung von Livia bis Iulia Domna*, Mainz.

Alfayé, S., Marco, F. (2008), "Religion, language and identity in Hispania: Celtiberian and Lusitanian rock inscriptions", in R. Häußler (ed.), *Romanisation et épigraphie. Etudes interdisciplinaires sur l'acculturation et l'identité dans l'Empire romain*, Montagne.

Alföldi, A. (1948), *The conversion of Constantine and Pagan Rome*, Oxford.

Alföldy, G. (1969), *Fasti Hispanienses*, Wiesbaden.

Alföldy, G. (1973), *Flamines provinciae Hispaniae citerioris*, Madrid.

Alföldy, G. (1991), "Augustus und die Inschriften: Tradition und Innovation. Die Geburt der imperialen Epigraphik", *Gymnasium* 98: 289-324.

Allen, A. (1951), *History of political thought in the sixteenth century*. London

Altaner, B., Stuiber, A. (2ª ed. 1972), *Patrologia*, São Paulo.

Amouretti, M.C., Brun J.-P. (eds.) (1993), *La production du vin et de l'huile en Méditerranée. Actes du symposium international organisé par le Centre Camille Jullian et le Centre archéologique du Var, Aix-en-Provence et Toulon 20-22 novembre 1991* (BCH suppl. 26), Athènes.

Ando, C. (2003), "A Religion for the Empire", in A. J. Boyle, W. J. Dominik (eds.), *Flavian Rome. Culture, Image, Text*, Leiden, Boston 323-344.

Ando, C. (2006), "Interpretatio Romana", in L. de Blois, P. Funke, J. Hahn, (eds.), *The Impact of Imperial Rome on Religions, Ritual and Religious Life in the Roman Empire, Proceedings of the Fifth Workshop of the International Network Impact of Empire (Roman Empire 200 B.C. - A.D. 476.)*, Leiden, Boston 51-65.

Andrade, A. A. (1959), *S. Tomás de Aquino no período áureo da filosofia portuguesa*, Lisboa.

Andrade, A. A. de (1965), *Antologia do pensamento político português* (séc. XVI), vol. I. Lisboa.

Andrade, M. (1974), "Lira Paulistana", in *Poesias completas*, São Paulo.

Andreu, J. (2004), *Edictum, Municipium y Lex: Hispania en época flavia (69-96 d. C.)*, BAR Int. Ser. 1293, Oxford.

Antonietti, C. (1999), "Megara e le sue colonie: unità storico-culturale?", in C. Antonetti, P. Lévêque (eds.) *Il dinamismo della colonizzazione greca, Atti della tavola rotonda "Espansione e colonizzazione greca di età arcaica: metodologie e problemi a confront"*, *Venezia, 10-11/11*, Besançon-Paris, 17-24.

Aquino, T. de (1946), *Des lois de Saint Thomas d'Aquin*. Texte traduit et présenté par J. de la Croix Kaelin O. P., Paris.

Arnaldi, A. (2010), "Osservazioni sul flaminato dei *Divi* nelle provincie africane", in M. Milanese, P. Ruggeri, C. Vismara, (eds.), *L'Africa romana. Luoghi e le forme dei mestieri e della produzione nelle provincie africane. Atti del XVIII convegno di studio. Olbia 11-14 dicembre 2008*, vol. III, Roma, 1645-1665.

Arruda, A. M. (2005), "O 1º milénio a.n.e. no Centro e no Sul de Portugal: leituras possíveis no início de um novo século", *O Arqueólogo Português* Série IV: 23: 59-74.

Arzone, A. (2011), "Alcune considerazioni sulle immagini di pietre miliari e sui riferimenti alle strade nel documento monetale", in *I miliari lungo le strade dell'Impero*. Caselle di Somma campagna Verona, 77-92.

Asensi, R. M., Musso, O. (1990), "Un documento etrusco di Tarragona", *Quaderni della sezione di Studi Storici Alberto Boscolo* 1: 5-11.

Aston, M. (1997), *Interpreting the landscape. Landscape archaeology and local history*, London.

ATL = B.D. Meritt, WadeGery, H.T., McGregor, M.F., *The Athenian Tribute Lists*, 4 vs, Princeton.

Aubert, J.-M. (1955), *Le droit romain dans l'oeuvre de Saint Thomas*, Paris.

Avery, H. C. (1971), "Euripides' *Heraclidae*", *AJPh* 92: 539-565.

Avram, A., Lefèvre, F. (1995), "Les cultes de Callatis et l'oracle de Delphes", *REG* 108: 7-23.

Bacchielli, L. (1986), "Monumenti funerari a forma di *cupula*: origine e diffusione in Italia meridionale", in A. Mastino (ed.), *L' Africa Romana: atti del 3. convegno di studio Sassari 13-15 dicembre 1985*, Sassari, 303-319.

Bailly, A. (1963), *Dictionnaire grec-français*, Paris.

Balass, G. (s.d.), "The Female Breast as a Source of Charity: Artistic Depictions of *Caritas Romana*", www.*Academia.edu*/4006836.

Baldassarre, I. (1979), "Zetema (Ζήτημα)" (a. 1973), *Enciclopedia dell'Arte Antica*, Suppl. 1979: 944-945.

Baldassarre, I., Bragantini, I., Morselli, C. and Taglietti, F. (1996), *Necropoli di Porto. Isola Sacra*, Roma.

Balil, A. (1984-88), "Las *cupae* de *Barcino*. Contribución al estudio de un tipo de monumento funerario romano", *Arqueologia e Historia*: 111-115.

Baratta, G. (1993), "Una divinità gallo-romana. *Sucellus*. Un'ipotesi interpretativa", *ArchCl* 45: 233-247.

Baratta, G. (1994), "*Circa Alpes ligneis vasis condunt circulisque cingunt*", *ArchClass* 46: 232-260.

Baratta, G. (1997), "Le botti: dati e questioni", in *Techniques et économie antique et médiévale. Le temps de l'innovation. Colloque international, Aix-en-Provence 21-23 Mai 1997*, Paris, 109-112.

Baratta, G. (1997), "*Sucellus*", in *Enciclopedia dell'Arte Antica classica e orientale*, Supplemento 1991-1994, V, Roma, 482.

Baratta, G. (2005a), "La *cupa* nell'ambito femminile: dalla *caupona* al *loculus*?", in, F. Cenerini, A. Buonopane (eds.), *Donna e vita cittadina nella documentazione epigrafica*, 95-108.

Baratta, G. (2005b), *Römische Kelteranlagen auf der italienischen Halbinsel. Ein Überblick über die schriftlichen, bildlichen und archäologischen Quellen (200 v.Chr. - 400. n.Chr.)* (Cornucopia, 11), Murcia.

Baratta, G. (2005c), "Appunti sulle variabili e costanti dell'*interpretatio* religiosa nell'occidente romano, in F. de Oliveira, (ed.), *Génese e consolidação da Ideia de Europa*, vol.III, *O Mundo Romano*, Coimbra, 123-134

Baratta, G. (2006a), "Alcune osservazioni sulla genesi e la diffusione delle *cupae*", in *Atti del XVI Convegno internazionale de L'Africa Romana* (Rabat, 15-19 dicembre 2004), Roma, 355-368.

Baratta, G. (2006b), "Nuovi dati sull'iconografia delle mandorle nei sarcofagi strigilati. Un primo approccio ad un corpus", *Annali della Facoltà di Lettere e Filosofia dell'Università di Macerata 26*: 65-120.

Baratta, G. (2007), "La mandorla centrale dei sarcofagi strigilati. Un campo iconografico ed i suoi simboli", in F. Hoelscher, T. Hoelscher (eds.), *Römische Bilderwelten. Von der Wirklichkeit zum Bild und zurück. Kolloquium der Gerda Henkel Stiftung am Deutschen Archäologischen Institut Rom*, Heidelberg, 191-215.

Baron, H. (1938), "Cicero and the Roman civic spirit in the Middle Ages and the Early Renaissance", *Bulletin of the John Rylands Library* 22: 84-89.

Baron, H. (1970), *La crisi del primo Rinascimento italiano*, Firenze.

Barresi, P. (2007), "Il sofista Flavio Damiano di Efeso e la costruzione di terme-ginnasi nell'Asia Minore romana di età imperiale", in O. D. Cordovana, M. Galli, (eds.), *Arte e memoria culturale nell'età della Seconda Sofistica*, Catania, 137-151.

Barros, J. de (1919), *Geografia d'Entre Douro e Minho e Trás-os-Montes*, Porto.

Barros, J. de (1937), *Panegíricos – Panegírico de D. João III e da Infanta D. Maria*, Texto restituído, prefácio e notas por M. Rodrigues Lapa, Lisboa.

Bassignano, M.S. (1974), *l flaminato nelle provincie romane dell'Africa*, Roma.

Bastos, E. (1991), *Entre o escândalo e o sucesso. A semana de 22 e o Armory show*, Campinas.

Battaglia, M. (2003), "Il Vulcano dei Germani in Giulio Cesare (B.G. VI, 21, 1). Un caso di *interpretatio*?", *Athenaeum* 91: 373-401.

Beagon, M. (2005), *The Elder Pliny on the Human Animal:* Natural History *Book* 7, Oxford.

Beard, M., North, J., Price, S. (1998), *Religions of Rome*, vol. I, *A History*, Cambridge.

Behr, C.A. (ed.) (1973), *Aristides*, vol. I, *Panathenaic Oration in Defence of Oratory*, London.

Behrends, M. et alii (eds.) (2000), *Hygin. L'oeuvre gromatique*, Luxemburg.

Bejarano Osorio, A. M. (1996), "Sepulturas de incineración en la necrópolis oriental de Mérida: las variantes de *cupae* monolíticas", *Anas* 9: 37-58.

Belmonte, J. A. (2010), "Documentación fenicio-púnica en la Península Ibérica: estado de la cuestión", in G. Carrasco y J. C. Oliva (eds.), *El Mediterráneo antiguo: lenguas y escrituras*, Cuenca, 159-220.

Beltrán, F. ed. (1995), *Roma y el nacimiento de la cultura epigráfica en occidente*, Zaragoza.

Beltrán, F. (2000), "La vida en la frontera", in F. Beltrán, M. Martín-Bueno y F. Pina, *Roma en la Cuenca Media del Ebro. La romanización en Aragón*, Zaragoza.

Beltrán, F. (2002), "Identidad cívica y adhesión al príncipe en las emisiones municipales hispanas", in F. Marco, F. Pina y J. Remesal (eds.), *Religión y propaganda política en el mundo romano*, Barcelona, 159-187.

Beltrán, F. (2004), "El latín en la Hispania romana: una perspectiva histórica", in R. Cano (ed.), *Historia de la lengua española*, Barcelona, 83-106.

Beltrán, F. (2004a), "*Nos Celtis genitos et ex Hiberis.* Apuntes sobre las identidades colectivas en Celtiberia", in G. Cruz Andreotti y B. Mora Serrano (eds.), *Identidades étnicas - Identidades políticas en el mundo prerromano hispano*, *Kronion* 1, Málaga, 87-145.

Beltrán, F. (2004b), "De nuevo sobre la tésera Froehner", *Palaeohispanica* 4: 45-65.

Beltrán, F. (2004c), "Imagen y escritura en la moneda hispánica", in F. Chaves y F. J. García (eds.), *Moneta qua scripta. La moneda como soporte de la escritura. Actas del III Encuentro Peninsular de Numismática Antigua*, Anejos de *AEspA* 33: 125-139.

Beltrán, F. (2004d), "Libertos y cultura epigráfica en la Hispania republicana", in F. Marco, F. Pina y J. Remesal (eds.), *Vivir en tierra extraña: emigración e integración cultural en el mundo antiguo*, Barcelona, 151-175.

Beltrán, F. (2005), "Cultura escrita, epigrafía y ciudad en el ámbito paleohispánico", *Palaeohispanica* 5: 21-56.

Beltrán, F. (2006), "Hispania y el Mediterráneo en los siglos II y I a. E.: diversidad cultural y movilidad social", in F. de Oliveira, P. Thiercy, R. Vilaça (eds.), *O mar greco-latino*, Coimbra, 223-240.

Beltrán, F. (2009), "Vltra eos palos. Una nueva lectura de la línea 7 de la *Tabula Contrebiensis*", in *Espacios, usos y formas de la epigrafía hispana en épocas antigua y tardoantigua. Homenaje al Dr. Armin U. Stylow*, Anejos de *AEspA* 48: 33-42.

Beltrán, F. (2011), "Lengua e identidad en la Hispania romana", *Palaeohispanica* 11:19-59.

Beltrán, F. (2011a), "¿Firmas de artesano o sedes de asociaciones comerciales? A propósito de los epígrafes musivos de Caminreal (E.7.1), Andelo (K.28.1) y El Burgo de Ebro (*HEp* 11, 2001, 621 = *AE* 2001, 1237)", in E. Luján y J. M. García Alonso (eds.), *A Greek man in the Iberian street. Papers in Linguistics and Epigraphy in honour of Javier de Hoz. Innsbrucker Beiträge zur Sprachwissenschaft* 140, Innsbruck, 139-147.

Beltrán, F. (2011b), "Les colonies latines d'Hispanie (IIe siècle av. E.): émigration italique et intégration politique", in N. Barrandon y F. Kirbihler (eds.), *Les gouverneurs et les provinciaux sous la République romaine*, Rennes, 131-144.

Beltrán, F. (2012), "Roma y la epigrafía ibérica sobre piedra del nordeste peninsular", *Palaeohispanica* 12: 9-30.

Beltrán, F. (inédito), "Diversidad cultural y epigrafía: el ejemplo de Hispania", *XII Congressus Internationalis epigraphiae Graecae et Latinae*, Barcelona septiembre de 2002.

Beltrán, F., Estarán, M. J. (2011), "Comunicación epigráfica e inscripciones bilingües en la Península Ibérica", in C. Ruiz Darasse y E. Luján (eds.), *Contacts linguistiques dans l'Occident méditerranéen antique. Collection de la Casa de Velázquez* (126), Madrid, 9-25.

Beltrán, F., Velaza, J. (2009), "De etnias y monedas: las "cecas vasconas", una revisión crítica", in J. Andreu (ed.), *Los vascones de las fuentes antiguas: en torno a una etnia de la antigüedad peninsular*, Barcelona, 99-126.

Beltrán, F., Arasa, F. (1979-1980), "Los itineraria privata en la epigrafía latina", *Historia Antiqua*, 9-10: 7-29.

Beltrán, F., Jordán, C., Marco, F. (2005), "Novedades epigráficas en Peñalba de Villastar (Teruel)", *Palaeohispanica* 5: 911-956.

Bentley, J. H. (1978), *Politics and culture in Renaissance Naples*, Princeton.

Berciu, I.,Wolski, W. (1970), "Un nouveau type de tombe mise au jour à *Apulum* et le problème des sarcophages à voûte de l'Empire romain", *Latomus* 29: 919-965.

Bergmann, M. (1998), *Die Strahlen der Herrscher. Theomorphes und politische Symbolik im Hellenismus und in der römischen Kaiserzeit*, Mainz.

Berruti, V., Magistà, A. (eds.) (2009), *L'automobile. Marche e modelli dalle origini a oggi*, vol. 6, *Lancia*, Roma.

Besnier M., Chapot, V. (1913), "Via", *Dictionnaire des Antiquités Grecques et Romaines*, 5, Paris, 777-817.

Bettini, C. (2008), "Tre Valascos nell'Italia del quatrocento: Meser Valasco di Vespasiano da Bisticci, Petrus Vallascis di Cataldo Siculo e Vasco Fernandes de Lucena", *Humanitas* 60: 205-226.

Bettini, M., Boldrini, M., Calabrese, O., Piccinni, G. (eds.) (2010), *Miti di città*, Siena.

Binsfeld, W. (1979), "Zu treverischen Kultdenkmälern", in *Festschrift 100 Jahre Rheinisches Landesmuseum Trier. Beiträge zur Archäologie und Kunst des Trierer Landes*, Mainz, 263-269.

Blackman, D. (1969), "The Athenian Navy and Allied Naval Contributions in the Pentecontaetia", *GRBS* 10: 179-216.

Blanco Freijeiro, A. (1977), *El puente de Alcántara en su contexto historico*, Madrid.

Boardman, J. (1986), *I Greci sui Mari. Traffici e Colonie*, Trad. ital., Firenze, Giunti.

Boffo, L. (1975), "Cimone e gli alleatidi Atene", *RIL* 109: 442-50.

Bol, R. (1984). *Das Statuen programm des Herodes-Atticus-Nymphäums*, Berlin.

Bona, G. (ed.) (1988), *Pindaro. I peani*, Cuneo.

Bonfante, G., Bonfante, L. (2002), *The Etruscan language. An introduction. Revised edition*, Manchester and New York.

Bonneville, J.-N. (1981), "Les *cupae* de Barcelone: les origines du type monumental", *MCV* 17: 5-38.

Bontems, C. (1965), *Le prince dans la France des XVIe e XVIIe siècles*, Paris.

Bordenache, G. (1960), "Antichità greche e romane nel nuovo Museo di Mangalia", *Dacia* N. S. 4: 489-509.

Bordenache, G. (1961), "Histria alla luce del suo materiale scultureo", *Dacia* N. S., 185-211.fig. 16.

Bordenache, G. (1969), *Sculture greche e romane del Museo Nazionale di Antichità di Bucarest I. Statue e rilievi di culto, elementi architectonici e decorativi*, Bukarest.

Boschung, D. (1993a), *Die Bildnisse des Augustus*, Berlin.

Boschung, D. (1993b), "Die Bildungstypen der julisch-claudischen Kaiserfamilie: ein kritischer Forschungsbericht", *JRA* 6: 39-79

Boschung, D. (2002), *Gens Augusta. Untersuchungen zu Aufstellung, Wirkung und Bedeutung der Statuengruppen des julisch-claudischen Kaiserhauses*, Mainz.

Boucher, S. (1987), "L'image et les fonctions du dieu *Sucellus*", *Caesarodunum* 23: 77-85.

Boulanger, A. (1923), *Aelius Aristide et la sophistique dans la province d'Asie au IIe siècle de notre ère*, Paris.

Bowersock, G.W. (1969), *Greek Sophists in the Roman Empire*, Oxford.

Braancamp Freire A. (ed.) (1916), *Notícias da Vida de André de Resende pelo Beneficiado Francisco Leitão Ferreira*, Lisboa.

Bracco, V. (1985), "Il tabellarius di Polla", *Epigraphica* 47: 93-97.

Brandão, M. (1937), *Documentos de D. João III*, I, Coimbra.

Brandt, H. (1998), *Geschichte der römischer Kaiserzeit. Von Diokletian und Konstantin bis zum Ende der konstantinische Dynastie (264-363)*, Berlin.

Briant, P. (2002), *From Cyrus to Alexander. A History of the Persian Empire*, Winona Lake.

Brown, B.R. (1957), *Ptolemaic Paintings and Mosaics and the Alexandrian style*, Cambridge.

Brown, T. S. (1946), "Euhemerus and the Historians", *HThR* 39: 259-274.

Brun, J.-P. (1986), *L'oléiculture antique en Provence. Les huiliers du departement du Var* (RANArb suppl. 15), Paris.

Brun, J.-P. (2003), *Le vin et l'huile dans la Méditerranée antique. Viticulture, oléiculture et procédés de transformation*, Paris.

Brun, J.-P. (2004), *Archéologie du vin et de l'huile dans l'empire romain*, Paris.

Brun, J.-P. (2005), *Archéologie du vin et d'huile en Gaule romaine*, Paris.

Bruneau, P. (1985), "Deliaca. Iconographie. L'image de Delos personifiée e pyxides de Spina", *BCH* 109: 551-556.

Búa, C. (1997), "Dialectos indoeuropeos na franxa ocidental hispânica", in G. Pereira (ed.), *Galicia fai dous mil anos. O feito diferencial galego, volumen I. Historia*, Santiago de Compostela, 51-99.

Buck, R. J. (1979), *A History of Boeotia*, Edmonton.

Bulloch, A. W (1985), *Callimachus. The Fifth Hymn*, Cambridge.

Bulloch, A. W (2010), "Hymns and Encomia", in J. J Clauss and M. Cuypers (eds.), *A Companion to Hellenistic Literature*, Malden/Oxford, 166-180.

Burazacchini, G. (ed.) (2005), *Troia tra realtà e legenda*, Parma.

Burckhardt J. (1949), *The Age of Constantine the Great*, Berkeley.

Burke, P. (1987 3ª ed.), *The italian Renaissance culture and society in Italy*, Cambridge.

Burkert, W. (1991), *Mito e Mitologia*, Ed. 70, Lisboa.

Burkhalter-Arce, F. (2002), "Le tarif de Coptos". La douane de Coptos, les fermiers de l'apostolion et le préfet du desert de Bérénice", *Topoi* Supp. 3: 199-233.

Burnett, A. P. (2005), *Pindar's Songs for Young Athletes of Aigina*, Oxford.

Bury, J. B., Cook, S. A., Adcock ,F. E. (eds.), *The Cambridge Ancient History*, Vol. 4, Cambridge.

Butcher, K. (2003), *Roman Syria and the Near East*, London.

Buxton, R. (ed.) (1999), *From Myth to Reason? Studies in the Development of Greek Thought*, Oxford.

Caccamo Caltabiano, M. (2003), "Messana/Tyche sulle monete della città dello stretto", in *Archeologia del Mediterraneo. Studi in onore di Ernesto De Miro*, Roma, 139-149.

Cadotte, A. (2007), *La romanisation des dieux. L'interpretatio romana en Afrique du Nord sous le Haut-Empire* (Religions in the Graeco-Roman world 158), Leiden.

Caiado, H. (1745), *Eclogae et Sylvae et Epigrammata*, in Pe. A. dos Reis, *Corpus illustrium poetarum Lusitanorum, qui latine scripserunt*, Lisboa.

Cairns, D. L. (2010), *Bacchylides: five epinician odes (3, 5, 9, 11, 13)*, Cambridge.

Camia, F. (2011), Theoi sebastoi. *Il culto degli imperatori romani in Grecia (provincia Achaia) nel secondo secolo D.C.*, Athinai.

Caldera de Castro, M. D. P. (1978), "Una sepultura de cupa hallada en Mérida. (Consideraciones acerca de estos monumentos funerarios)", *Habis* 9: 455-463.

Calderón Dorda, E., De Lazzer, A., Pellizer, E., (eds.) (2003), *Corpus Plutarchi Moralium*, Naples.

Calvino, I. (1996), "Diario americano, 1959-1966", in *Eremita a Parigi. Pagine autobiografiche*, Milano, 20-124.

Calvino, I. (1996a), *Città invisibili*, Milano.

Camargos, M. (2001), *Villa Kyrial: crônica da Belle Époque paulistana*, São Paulo.

Cameron A. (1993), *The later Roman empire: AD 284–430*, Cambridge.

Cantemir, D. (2006), *The Salvation of the Wise Man and the Ruin of the Sinful World* [...], ed., trans., notes, indices Ioana Feodorov, Editura Academiei, Bucuresti.

Cantemirius, D. (1973), *Descriptio antiqui et hodierni status Moldaviae/* Dimitrie Cantemir, *Descrierea Moldovei*, trans. Gh. Gutu, introd. Maria Holban, hist. com. N. Stoicescu, cartographical study Vintilă Mihailescu, index Ioana Constantinescu, note D. M. Pippidi, Bucuresti.

Cantemirius, D. (2006), *Descriptio antiqui et hodierni status Moldaviae/* Dimitrie Cantemir, Principele Moldovei, *Descrierea stării de odinioară și de astăzi a Moldovei*, ed., trans. Dan Slusanschi, Bucuresti.

Cantineau, J. (1935), *Grammaire du palmyrénien épigraphique*, Le Caire.

Carcopino, J.(s/d), *A vida quotidiana em Roma no apogeu do Império* (trad A. J. Saraiva), Lisboa.

Cardim Ribeiro, J. (2002), "Soli Aeterno Lunae. O santuário", *Religiões da Lusitânia. Loquuntur Saxa*, Lisboa, 235-239.

Cardim Ribeiro, J. (2005), "O *deus sanctus Endovellicus* durante a romanidade. Uma interpretatio local de Faunus-Silvanus?", *Paleohispanica* 5: 721-766.

Carlier p. (1990), *Démosthène*, Paris.

Carneiro, A., d'Encarnação, J., de Oliveira, J., Teixeira, Cl. (2008), "Uma iscrição votiva em lengua lusitana", *Palaeohispanica* 8: 167-178.

Caro, A. (2009), "Una fase decisiva en la evolución de la publicidad: la transición del producto a la marca", *Pensar la publicidad*, III, 2: 109-114.

Caro, A. (2010), *Comprender la publicidad*, Barcelona.

Cartledge, P. (2009), *Ancient Greek Political Thought in Practice*, Cambridge.

Carvalho, J. de (1947-1948), *Estudos sobre a cultura portuguesa do século XVI*, 2 vols. Coimbra.

Carvalho, J. de (1949), *Estudos sobre a cultura portuguesa do século XV*, Coimbra.

Cascudo, L. C. (1974), *Prelúdio e fuga do real*, Natal.

Cascudo, L. C. (1983), *Civilização e Cultura, pesquisas e notas de etnografia geral*, Belo Horizonte.

Cascudo, L. C. (1983, 2ª ed.), *Anúbis e outros ensaios. Mitologia e folclore*, Rio de Janeiro, Natal.

Cascudo, L. C. (1987), *História dos nossos gestos*, Belo Horizonte, São Paulo.

Cascudo, L.C. (1966), "História de um livro perdido", *Arquivos do Instituto de Antropologia "Câmara Cascudo"* 2.1-2: 5-19.

Castelli, E. (1951) (ed.), *Umanesimo e Scienza politica. Atti del congresso Internazionale di Studi Umanistici, Roma-Firenze, 1949*, Milano.

Castillo, C. (1998), "Los *flamines* provinciales de la Bética", *REA* 100: 437-460

Cawkwell, G. (2005), *The Greek Wars. The Failure of Persia*, Oxford.

Cesarano, M. (2015), In honorem domus divinae. *Introduzione allo studio dei cicli statuari giulio-claudii a Roma e in Occident*e, Roma.

Clauss, M. (1979), *Kaiser und Gott: Herrscherkult im romischen Reich*, Berlin.

Chamie, M. (2009), *Paulicéia dilacerada*, Ribeirão Preto.

Chaniotis, A. (2009), "The Dynamics of Rituals in the Roman Empire", in O.

Hekster, S. Schmidt-Hofner, Chr. Witschel (eds.), *Ritual Dynamics and Religious Change in the Roman Empire. Proceedings of the Eight Workshop of International Network Impact of Empire*, Leiden, Boston, 3-29

Charles-Picard, G., Rougé, J. (1969), *Textes et documents relatifs à la vie economique et sociale dans l'Empire romain*, Paris.

Chassaing, M. (1961), "Les barillets frontiniens", *RAE* 12: 7-33, 89-106.

Chelotti, M. (2003), *Regio II, Apulia et Calabria, Venusia* (Supplementa Italica 20), Roma.

Cherry, D. (1998), *Frontier and Society in Roman North Africa*, Oxford.

Chevallier, R. (1972), *Les voies romaines*, Paris.

Chevallier, R. (1988), *Voyages et déplacements dans l'Empire romain*, Paris.

Chiarelli, G. (1932), "Il 'De regno' di Francesco Patrizi', *Rivista internazionale di filsosofia del diritto*, Anno XII. (Nov-Dec.): 716-738.

Cistercienses (Os). Documentos primitivos. Texto latino e tradução brasileira. (1997) Introdução e bibliografia Irmão François de Place, Tradução de Irineu Guimarães, Musa, S. Paulo; Lúmen Christi, Rio de Janeiro 1997.

Clauss, J., Cuypers, M. (eds.) (2010), *A Companion to Hellenistic Literature*, Chichester, West Sussex.

Clavel-Lévêque, M. et alii (eds.) (1993), *Siculus Flaccus. Les conditions des terres*, Nápoles.

Clavel-Lévêque, M. et alii (eds.) (1996), *Hygin l'arpenteur. L' établissement des limites*, Nápoles.

Clayton, P.A. (1989), *Le sette Meraviglie del mondo*, Torino. (*The Seven Wonders of the Ancient World*, London, 1988).

Cogitore, I. (1996), "Séries de dédicaces italiennes à la dynastie julio-claudienne", *MEFRA* 104 : 817-870.

Colasso, F. (1951), "Umanesimo giuridico", in E. Castelli (ed.), *Umanesimo e Scienza politica (Atti dei Congresso Internazionale di Studi Umanistici, Roma-Firenze, 1949)*, Milano, 57-58.

Colecchia, A., Bertolani, G. B., Marcante, A. et alii (2004), *L'Alto Garda occidentale dalla preistoria al postmedioevo. Archeologia, storia del popolamento e trasformazione del paesaggio* (Documenti di archeologia, 36), Mantova.

Colonna, G. (1980), "Virgilio, Cortona e la leggenda etrusca di Dardano", *Archeologia Classica* 32: 1-15.

Conger, G. P. (1952), "Did India influence Early Greek Philosophies?", *Philosophy East and West* 2.2: 102-128.

Conti, S. (1997), "Dinastia giulio-claudia a *Roselle*: una serie di dediche imperiali in Etruria", *Ann. Fac. Lett. e Filos. Univ. Siena* 18: 101-127.

Conti, S. (1998), *Rusellae, Suppl. It. n. s.* 16, Roma.

Cook, J. M. (1971), *Os Gregos na Iónia e no Oriente*, Lisboa.

Cooley, A. E. (ed.) (2002), *Becoming Roman, Writing Latin? Literacy and Epigraphy in the Roman West*. JRA Suppl. Ser. 48, Portsmouth.

Cooley, A. E. (2002), "The survival of Oscan in Roman Pompeii", in E. A. Cooley (ed.), *Becoming Roman, Writing Latin? : Literacy and Epigraphy in the Roman West, JRA Suppl. Ser.* 48: 77-86.

Cordovana, O. D., Galli, M. (eds.) (2007), *Arte e memoria culturale nell'età della Seconda Sofistica*, Catania.

Corell, J. (1989), "Notas sobre epigrafía romana del País Valenciano", *APL* 19: 271-281.

Costa, A. D. S. (1969), *Estudantes portugueses na reitoria do Colégio de S. Clemente de Bolonha na primeira metade do século XV*, Lisboa.

Costa, A. D. S. (1990), *Portugueses no Colégio de S. Clemente e Universidade de Bolonha durante o século XV*, vol. I, Bolonia.

Coulanges, F. de. (1971, 10ª ed.), *A cidade antiga*, Trad. e glossário de Fernando de Aguiar, Livraria Clássica Editora, Lisboa.

Crawford, M. H., Reynolds, J. M. (1979), "The Aezani copy of the Prices Edict", *Zeitschrift für Papyrologie und Epigraphik* 34: 163-210.

Crystal, D. (2000), *Language death,* Cambridge.

Curado, F. P. (1985), "Inscrição rupestre de Freixo de Numão", *Ficheiro Epigráfico* 11: nº48.

David, B., Thomas J. (eds.) (2008), *Handbook of landscape archaeology* (World archaeological congress research handbooks in archaeology, 1), Walnut Creek.

Davie, J. N. (1982), "Theseus the king in fifth-century Athens", *G&R* 29.1: 25-34.

DCPH = M. P. García-Bellido y C. Blázquez (2001), *Diccionario de cecas y pueblos hispánicos*, Madrid.

De Bernardo Stempel, P. (2008), "More names, fewer deities. Complex theonymic formulas and the three types of interpretation", in *Divindades indígenas em análise. Divinités pré-romaines. Bilan et perspectives d'une recherche. Actas do VII workshop FERCAN, Cascais, 25-27.5.2006*, Coimbra, 65-73.

De Hoz, J. (2001), "La lengua de los íberos y los documentos epigráficos en la comarca de Requena-Utiel", in A. J. Lorrio (ed.), *Los íberos en la comarca de Requena-Utiel (Valencia)*, Madrid, 49-62.

De Hoz, J. (2010), *Historia lingüística de la Península Ibérica en la Antigüedad. I. Preliminares y mundo meridional prerromano*, Madrid.

De Hoz, M. P. (1997), "Epigrafía griega en Hispania", *Epigraphica* 59: 29-93.

De Labriolle, P. (1934), *La reaction païenne*, Paris.

De Martino, D. (2010), "Spot, etica e letteratura", *La nuova ricerca. Pubblicazione annuale del Dipartimento di Linguistica, Letteratura e Filologia moderna dell'Università degli studi di Bari*, anno XIX. 19, 117-128.

De Martino, D. (2010bis), "Automobili da mito", in F. De Martino (ed.), *Antichità & pubblicità*, Bari, 443-522.

De Martino, D. (2011), *Io sono Giulietta. Letterature & miti nella pubblicità di auto*, Bari.

De Martino, D. (2012), "Una forma de subversión del mito literario: de la novela a la publicidad", in J. M. Losada Goya, M. Guirao Ochoa (eds.), *Myth and Subversion in the Contemporary Novel*, Cambridge, 421-436.

De Martino, D. (2013), *Dante & la pubblicità*, Bari.

De Martino, F., Vox, O. (1996) (eds.), *Lirica greca*, vol. 3, Bari.

De Ruyt, Cl. (1983), *Macellum. Marché alimentaire des romains*, Louvain-la-Neuve.

De Santerre, H. H. (1976), "Athènes, Délos et Delphes d'après une peinture de vase à figure rouges du V siècle avant J.-C.", *BCH* 100: 291-298.

De Vos, M., Andreoli, M., Attoui, R. et alii (2007), "Cilicia campestris orientale. L'economia rurale e la trasformazione del paesaggio intorno al Karasis", in *Geografia e viaggi nell'antichità. Atti del convegno internazionale di studi (Certosa di Pontognano, 9-10 ottobre 2005)*, Siena, 13-39.

Degl'Innocenti Pierini, R. (2012), "Le città personificate nella Roma repubblicana: fenomenologia di un motivo letterario tra retorica e poesia", in G. Moretti, A. Bonandini (eds.), *Persona ficta. La personificazione allegorica nella cultura antica, fra letteratura, retorica e iconografia*, Trento, 215-247.

Desbat, A. (1991), "Un bouchon de bois du Ier s. aprés J.-C. recueilli dans la Saône à Lyon et la question du tonneau à 1'époque romaine", *Gallia* 48: 319-336.

Dias, P. B. (2011 2ª ed.), "Notas introdutórias", in J. G Freire, *A versão latina por Pascásio de Dume dos Apophtegmata Patrum*, Coimbra, 1-34.

Dias, P. B. (2012), "Cristianismo e responsabilidade cristã na queda de Roma", in F. Oliveira et alli (coords.), *A queda de Roma e o alvorecer da Europa*, Coimbra, 43-67.

Dias P. B. (2013), "O legado de Constantino na identidade da Europa cristã: dois casos de estudo", in M. C. Pimentel e P. Farmhouse Alberto (orgs.), *Vir bonus peritissimus aeque. Estudos de homenagem a Arnaldo do Espírito Santo*, Lisboa, 455-463

Díaz, B. (2008), *Epigrafía latina republicana de Hispania*, Barcelona.

Dittenberger, W., Purgold, K. (1896), *Inschriften von Olympia*, Berlin.

Dixon, R. M. W. (1997), *The rise and fall of languages*, Cambridge.

Domăneanţu, C. (1993), "Un sanctuaire hellénistique du site de Nuntaşi II (comm. d'Istria, dep. De Constanţa)", *Dacia* 37: 59-78.

Dörfler, W., Evans, A., Löhr, H. (1998), "Trier, Walramsneustrasse. Untersuchungen zum römerzeitlichen Landschaftswandel im Hunsrück-Eifel-Raum an einem Beispiel aus der Trierer Talweite", in *Studien zur Archäologie der Kelten, Römer und Germanen in Mittel- und Westeuropa. Alfred Haffner zum 60. Geburtstag gewidmet*, Rahden, 119-152.

Dubuisson, M. (1981), "Utraque lengua", *L'Antiquité Classique* 50: 274-286.

Dubuisson, M. (1982), "Y a-t-il une politique linguistique romaine?", *Ktéma* 7: 197-210.

Duchesne, L. (1887), "Le concile d'Elvire et les flamines chrétiens", *Mélanges Renier*, Paris, 159-174.

Dunkle, J. R. (1969), "The Aegeus episode and the theme of Euripides' *Medea*", *TAPhA* 100: 97-107.

Durán Fuentes, M. (2005), *La construcción de puentes romanos en Hispania*, Santiago de Compostela.

Eck, W. (2006), "Herrschaft und Kommunikation in antiken Gesellschaften. Das Beispiel Rom", in U. Peter, S. J. Seidlmayer (eds.), *Mediengesellschaft Antike? Information und Kommunikation vom Alten Ägypten bis Byzanz*, Berlin, 11-33.

Eco, U. (2013), *Storia delle terre e dei luoghi leggendari*, Milano.

Eddy, S.K. (1968), "Four Hundred Sixty Talents Once More", *CP* 63: 184-95.

Edmonson, J. (1997), "Two dedications to Divus Augustus and Diva Augusta from Augusta Emerita and the early development of the imperial cult in Lusitania", *MM* 38: 89-105.

Edmondson, J. (2002), "Writing latin in the province of Lusitania", in A. E. Cooley (ed.), *Becoming Roman, Writing Latin? Literary and Epigraphy in the Roman West*, *JRA Suppl. Ser.* 48: 41-60.

Ehrenberg, V. (1973, 2ª ed.), *From Solon to Sócrates*, Londres.

Ehrenberg, V. (1976), *L'État grec*, Paris.

Ehrhardt, N. (1988*)*, *Milet und seine Koloniei. Vergleichende Untersuchung der kultischen und politischen Einrichtungen*, ed. a II-a, Frankfurt, Main-Bern, New York, Paris.

Elliger, W. (1975), *Die Darstellung der Landschaft in der griechischen Dichtung*, Berlin, New York.

Elliott, Th. (1990), "The Language of Constantinian Propaganda", *TAPhA* 120: 349-353.

Encarnação, J. d' (1984), *Inscrições romanas do Conventus Pacensis*, Coimbra.

Erasmo, D. (1703), *Opera omnia (in decem tomos distincta)*, Recognovit Joannes Clericus, Leiden.

Erodoto (1988), *Le Storie. Libro I. La Lidia e la Persia. A cura di David Astheri*, Milano.

Erskine, A. (ed.) (2003), *A Companion to the Hellenistic World*, Oxford.

Espérandieu, E. (1907-1981), *Recueil général des bas-reliefs, statues et bustes de la Gaule romaine*, Paris.

Estarán, M. J. (2012), "Las estampillas ibérico-latinas K.5.4", *Palaeohispanica* 12: 73-90

ET = Rix, H. (1991), *Etruskische Texte*, Tübingen.

Étienne, R. (1958), *Le culte impérial dans la Péninsule ibérique d'Auguste à Diocletien*, Paris.

Étienne, R. (1973), "Les syncrétismes dans la Péninsule Ibérique à l'époque impériale", in *Les syncrétismes dans les religions grecque et romaine*, Paris, 153-163.

Étienne, R., Fabre, G.; Lévêque, P. et M. (1976), *Fouilles de Conimbriga*, vol. II, *Épigraphie et Sculpture*, Paris.

Étienne, R., Fabre, G., Le Roux, P., Tranoy, A. (1976), "Les dimensions sociales de la romanisation dans la Péninsule Ibérique des origines à la fin de l'Empire", in D. M. Pippidi (ed.), *Assimilation et résistance à la culture gréco-romaine dans le monde ancien. Travaux du VIe Congrès International d'Études Classiques*, Bucureşti, Paris, 95-107.

Étienne, R., Mayet, F. (2000), *Le vin hispanique*, Paris.

Evans, J. A. S. (1981), "Notes on the debate of the Persian Grandees in Herodotus 3, 80-82", *QUCC* 36: 79-84.

Evers, C. (1994), *Les portraits d'Hadrien. Typologie et ateliers*, Bruxelles.

Ewald, C., Norena, C. F. (eds.) (2010), *The Emperor and Rome: Space, Representation, Ritual*, Cambridge.

Fabre, G., Mayer, M., Rodà, I. (1991), *Inscriptions romaines de Catalogne*, III, Paris.

Fayer, C. (1976), *Il culto della dea Roma. Origine e diffusione nell'Impero*, Pescara.

Fearn, D. (2007), *Bacchylides. Politics, performance, poetic tradition*, Oxford.

Fernandes, L., Carvalho, P., Figueira, N. (2009), "Divindades indígenas numa ara inédita de Viseu", *Palaeohispanica* 9: 143-155.

Fernández Gallardo, L. (2002), *Alonso de Cartagena. Una biografía política en la Castilla del siglo XV*, Valladolid.

Fernández Gallardo, L. (2008), "Alonso de Cartagena y el Humanismo", *La Corónica* 37.1: 175- 215.

Ferraz, C. (2002), "Conjunto de oito aras provenientes do *Lararium* de Centum Celas", in V. L. Raposo, J. R. Ferreira (Coords.), *Religiões da Lusitânia. Loquuntur Saxa*, Lisboa, 467-469.

Ferreira, J. R. (1988), "Grécia e Roma na Revolução Francesa", *Revista de História das Ideias* 10: 203-234.

Ferreira, J. R. (1990), *A democracia na Grécia Antiga*, Coimbra.

Ferreira, J. R. (1990a), *Participação e poder na democracia grega*, Coimbra.

Ferreira, J. R. (1993), *Hélade e Helenos I – Génese e Evolução de um Conceito*, Coimbra.

Ferreira, J. R. (2004 2ª ed.), *A Grécia Antiga. Sociedade e Política*, Lisboa.

Ferreira, J. R., (1991), "Presença da Grécia e de Roma na Revolução Francesa", in *Actas do colóquio A Recepção da Revolução Francesa em Portugal e no Brasil*, Porto, vol. I, 75-96.

Ferri, S. (1976), "Luci e ombre sulla interpretatio romana", in *Convegno internazionale "Renania romana" Roma 14-16 aprile 1975*, Roma, 125-133.

Ferrill, A. (1978), "Herodotus on tyranny", *Historia* 27.3: 385-398.

Figueira, T. J. (1998), *The Power of Money: Coinage and Politics in the Athenian Empire*, Philadelphia.

Figueira, T. J. (2003), "Economic Integration and Monetary Consolidation in the Athenian Arkhê", in G. Urso (ed.), *Moneta, Mercanti, Banchieri. I precedenti greci e romani dell'Euro*, Pisa, 71-92.

Figueira, T. J. (2005), "The Imperial Commercial Tax and the Finances of the Athenian Hegemony", *Incidenza dell'antico* 3: 83-133.

Figueira, T. J. (2006), "Reconsidering the Athenian Coinage Decree", *AIIN* 52: 9-44.

Figueira, T. J. (2011), "The Athenian Naukraroi and Archaic Naval Warfare", *Cadmo. Revista de História Antiga* 21: 183-210.

Figueira, T. J. (forthcoming[a]), "Archaic Naval Warfare", in N. Birgalias (ed.), *Great is the Power of the Sea: The Power of Sea and Sea Powers in the Greek world of the Archaic and Classical Periods*, Athens.

Figueira, T. J. (forthcoming[b]), "The Aristeidian Tribute on the Peace of Nikias", in S. Jensen, T. Figueira (eds.), *Athenian Hegemonic Finances*, Swansea.

Figueira, T. J. (forthcoming[c]), "Community Wealth and Military Might in Periclean Athens", in A.L. Pierris (ed.), *Mind, Might, Money: The Secular Triad in Classical Athens*, Patras.

Figueira, T. J. (forthcoming[d]), "Aigina: Island as Paradigm", in A. Powell and K. Meidani (eds.), *The Eyesore of Aigina: Anti-Athenian Attitudes in Greek, Hellenistic and Roman History*, Swansea.

Figueiredo, R., Lamounier, B. (1996), *As cidades que dão certo*, Brasília.

Finley, M.I. (1966), *The Ancient Greeks. An introduction to their life and thought*, Londres. Trad. port.: *Os Gregos Antigos* (Lisboa, 2ª ed. 1988).

Finley, M. I. (1973, 2ª ed.), *Democracy, ancient and modern*, London.

Finley, M.I. (1973a), *The ancient economy*, London.

Finley, M.I. (1982), *Authority and legitimacy in the classical city-state*, Kobenhavn.

Fishwick, D. (1970), "Flamen Augustorum", *HSCPh* 74: 299-312.

Fishwick, D. (1982), "The altar of Augustus and the municipal cult of Tarraco", *MM* 23: 222-233

Fishwick, D. (2002), *The Imperial Cult in the Latin West, 3/2, Provincial Cult / The Provincial Priesthood*, Leiden.

Fishwick, D. (2005), *The Imperial Cult in the Latin West. Studies in the Ruler Cult of the Western Provinces of the Roman Empire*, Leiden, Boston.

Fitton, J. W. (1961), "*The Suppliant Women* and the *Herakleidai* of Euripides", *Hermes* 89.4: 430-461.

Flower, M. F. (2007), "Appendix R: The Size of Xerxes Expeditionary Force," in Robert B. Strassler (ed.), *The Landmark Herodotus: The Histories*, New York, 819-23.

Fonseca, L. A. (1982), *O Condestável D. Pedro de Portugal*, Porto.

Fontanella, F. (2008), "The Encomium on Rome as a response to Polybius' doubts about the Roman Empire", *Columbia Studies in the Classical Tradition* 33: 203-216.

Forni, G. (1973), "El culto de Augusto en el compromiso oficial y en el sentimiento oriental", *BSAA* 39: 105-113.

Forni, G. (1994), *Scritti vari di Storia, Epigraphia e antichità romane*, Roma.

Franck, A. D. (1864), *Réformateurs et publicistes de l'Europe: Moyen Âge-Renaissance*, Paris.

French, A. (1972), "The Tribute of the Allies", *Historia* 21: 3-20.

Fuentes, M. J. (1986), *Corpus de las inscripciones fenicias, púnicas y neopúnicas de Hispania*, Barcelona.

Gabba, S., Drioton, É. (1954), *Peintures à fresques et scènes peintes a Ermoupolis - Ouvest (Touna el-Gevel)*, Le Caire.

Gaffiot, F. (s/d), *Dictionnaire latin-français*, Paris.

Gagé, J. (1936), "Le *templum Urbis* et les origines de l'idée de *Renovatio*", in *Mélanges Franz Cumont*, Bruxelles, 151-187.

Gagé, J. (1955), *Apollon romain. Éssai sur le culte d'Apollon et le développement du "ritus Graecus" à Rome des originrs à Auguste*, Paris.

Gagé, J. (1968), *"Basiléia". Les Césars, les rois d'Orient et les "mages"*, Paris.

Gagé, J. (1974), "Le *solemne Urbis* du 21 avril au IIIe siècle ap. J.-C.: Rites positives et speculations séculaires", *Mélanges d'histoire de religions offerts à Henri-Charles Puech*, Paris, 225-241.

García Bellido, M. P. (1993), "Sobre el culto de Volcanus y Sucellus en Hispania. Testimonios numismáticos", in F. Burkhater, J. Arce (eds.), *Bronces y religión romana. Actas del XI Congreso internacional de bronces antiguos, Madrid mayo - junio 1990*, Madrid, 161-170.

García Iglésias, L. (1976), "Autenticidad de la inscripción de municipios que sufragaron el puente de Alcántara", *Revista de Estudios Extremeños* 32.2: 263-276.

García Jurado, F. (2007), *Aulo Gelio, Noches Áticas. Antología*, Madrid.

García Romero, F. (2002), "Pervivencia de Penélope", in C. Morenilla Talens, F. De Martino (eds.), *El perfil de les ombres*, Bari, 187-204.

García Soler, M. J. (2010), "Gastronomia e pubblicità nella Grecia antica", in F. De Martino (ed.), *Antichità & pubblicità*, Bari, 345-366.

Garin, E. (1955), "Ricerche sulle traduzioni di Platone nella prima metà del XV secolo", *Medioevo e Rinascimento, Studi in onore di B. Nardi*, Firenze.

Garin, E. (1966), *Storia della filosofia italiana*, Torino.

Garriguet, J. A. (2004), "Grupos estatuarios imperiales de la Bética: la evidencia escultórica y epigráfica", in *Actas de la IV reunión sobre escultura romana en Hispania*, Madrid, 67-101.

Gasperini, L. (1977), "L'Augusteo di Firmo Piceno in un'epigrafe da rileggere", *AFML* 10: 57-87.

Gasperini, L. (2008), "L'Augusteo di Forum Clodii", en L. Gasperini, G. Paci, (eds.), *Nuove ricerche sul culto imperiale in Italia*, Tivoli, 91-134.

Gasperini, L., Paci, G. (eds.) (2008), *Nuove ricerche sul culto imperiale in Italia*, Tivoli.

Gaudemet J. (1947), "La législation religieuse de Constantin", *Révue d' Histoire de l'Église de France* 122: 25-61.

Genette, G. (1997), *Palinsesti. La letteratura di secondo grado*, Torino.

Gentili, B. (ed.) (1995), *Pindaro. Le pitiche*, Milano.

Ghedini, F. (2000), "Filostrato Maggiore come fonte per la conoscenza della pittura antica", *Ostraka* 9.1: 75-197.

Giachero, M. (ed.) (1974), *Edictum Diocletiani et Collegarum de pretiis rerum venalium in integrum restitutum e latinis gracisque fragmentis*, 1-2, Génova.

Gico, V. (1998), "Luís da Câmara Cascudo: perfil bibliográfico", in L. C. Cascudo, *Ontem. (Maginações e notas de um professor de província)*, Natal.

Gigli, D. (1985), *Metafora e poetica in Nonno di Panopoli*, Firenze.

Gilles, K. J. (1987), "Römische Glasgefäße", in AA.VV., *2000 Jahre Weinkultur an Mosel-Saar-Ruwer. Denkmäler und Zeugnisse zur Geschichte von Weinbau, Weinhandel, Weingenuß*, Trier, 143-145.

Gilles, K. J. (1987b), "Trierer Weinkeramik", in AA.VV., *2000 Jahre Weinkultur an Mosel-Saar-Ruwer. Denkmäler und Zeugnisse zur Geschichte von Weinbau, Weinhandel, Weingenuß*, Trier, 132-133.

Gilles, K. J., König, M., Schumann, F. (1995), *Neuere Forschungen zum römischen Weinbau an Mosel und Rhein* (Schriftenreihe des Rheinischen Landesmuseums Trier, 11), Trier.

Gilson, É. (1983, 6ª ed.), *Le thomisme*, Paris.

Gómara, M. (2007), "Una inscripción paleohispánica sobre cerámica altoimperial en Cascante (Navarra)", *Palaeohispanica* 7: 263-268.

Gomes, S.A. (1998), *Visitações a mosteiros cistercienses em Portugal. Séculos XV e XVI*, Ministério da Cultura – IPPAR, Lisboa.

Gomes, S. A. (2000), "Revisitação a um velho tema: a fundação do Mosteiro de Alcobaça", in *Cister: Espaços Território e Paisagens. Colóquio Internacional, 16-20 Junho de 1998, Mosteiro de Alcobaça. Actas*. I, Lisboa, 27-72.

Gomes, S. A. (2000), *O mosteiro de Alcobaça na transição dos séculos XIV e XV: o protagonismo de D. João Dornelas*, in *Cister. Espaços, Territórios, Paisagens. Colóquio Internacional. 16-20 Junho 1998. Mosteiro de Alcobaça*, Lisboa, 73-88.

Gomes, S. A. (2006), *D. Afonso V*, Círculo de Leitores-Colecção *Reis de Portugal*, Lisboa.

Gómez García, C. (2010), "La configuración de la ciudad de Berlin", in J. M. Losada Goya (ed.), *Mito y mundo contemporáneo. La recepción de los mitos antiguos, medievales y modernos en la literatura contemporánea*, Bari , 617-626.

González Rolán, T., P. Saquero Suárez-Somonte, P. (2001), "El Humanismo italiano en la Castilla del cuatrocientos: estudio y edición de la versión castellana y del original latino del *De infelicitate principum* de Poggio Bracciolini ", *Cuadernos de Filología Clásica. Estudios Latinos* 21: 115-150.

González Rolán, T., Moreno Hernández, A., Saquero Suárez-Somonte, P. (2000), *Humanismo y teoría de la traducción en España e Italia en la primera mitad del siglo XV. Edición y estudio de la Controversia Alphonsiana (Alfonso de Cartagena vs. L. Bruni y P. Candido Decembrio)*, Madrid.

Gorrochategui, J. (1987), "Situación lingüística de Navarra y aledaños en la antigüedad a partir de las fuentes epigráficas", *Primer Congreso General de Historia de Navarra* II, Pamplona, 435-445.

Gorrochategui, J. (2014), "Nueva inscripción funeraria celtibérica procedente de Clunia", *Palaeohispanica* 14: 229-236.

Gorrochategui, J. y Vallejo, J. M. (2010), "Lengua y onomástica. Las inscripciones lusitanas", *Iberografías* 6: 71-80.

Gose, E. (1976), *Gefäßtypen der römischen Keramik im Rheinland,* Köln.

Graham, A.J. (1964), *Colony and Mother City,* Manchester.

Grenier, A. (1934), *Manuel d'archéologie gallo-romaine 2, Les routes,* Paris.

Gros, P., Marin, M., Zink, M. (eds.) (2015), *Auguste, son époque et l'Augusteum de Narona. Actes du colloque organisé à l 'Académie des Inscriptions et Belles-letres /e 12 décembre 2014,* Paris.

Gualandi, M. L. (2001), *Le fonti per la storia dell'arte - I. L'antichità classica,* Roma.

Guarducci, M. (1974), *Epigrafia greca,* vol. III, Roma.

Guarducci, M. (1978), *Epigrafia greca,* vol. IV, Roma.

Guerra, A., Schatner, T. (2010), "El foro y el templo de Lancia Oppidana: nueva interpretación de Centum Celas (Belmonte)", in T. Mogale Basarrate (ed.) *Ciudad y Foro en Lusitania Romana,* Mérida, 333-342.

Guilaine, J. (cur.) (1991), *Pour une archéologie agraire: à la croisée des sciencies de l'homme et de la nature,* Paris.

Guilmartin, J. F. (2002), *Galleons and Galleys,* London.

Guilmartin, J. F. (2003), *Gunpowder and Galleys. Changing Technology and Mediterranean Warfare at Sea in the Sixteenth Century,* 2nd ed., Annapolis.

Hall, J. M. (1997), *Ethnic identity in Greek Antiquity,* Cambridge.

Hanell, K. (1934), *Megarische Studien,* Lund.

Hänlein-Schäfer, H. (1985), *Veneratio Augusti. Eine Studie zu den Tempeln der ersten römischen Kaisers,* München.

Hanley, R. (2000), *Villages in Roman Britain,* Princes Risborough.

Hansen, H. M. (1991), *The Athenian Democracy in the age of Demosthenes. Structure, Principles and Ideology,* Oxford.

Hardy, E. G. (1925), "The Lex Mamilia Roscia Peducaea Alliena Fabia", *The CQ* 19 (3/4): 185-191.

Harris, E. (1995), *Aeschines and Athenian Politics,* Oxford.

Harth, H. (1984), *Poggio Bracciolini, Lettere,* Leo S. Olschki Editore, Florencia.

Hekster, O., Schmidt-Hofner, S., Witschel, Chr. (eds.) (2009), *Ritual dynamics and Religious Change in the Roman Empire. Proceedings of the Eighth Workshop of the International Network Impact of Empire,* Leiden, Boston.

Helck, W. (1971), *Das Bier im alten Ägypten,* Berlin.

Hershowitz, A., (forthcoming), "Patterns in Variation in Tribute Assessment", in S. Jensen, T. Figueira (eds.), *Athenian Hegemonic Finances*, Classical Press of Wales, Swansea.

Herta, P. (1978), "Bibliographie zum römischer Kaiserkult (1955-1975)", *ANRW* II 18: 833-910.

Heubeck, A. (ed.) (1983), *Omero. Odissea*, Volume III (Libri IX-XII), Milano.

Heurgon, J. (1950-1951), "La syntaxe des routiers romains", *Bulletin de la Société des Antiquaires de France*: 145-154.

Heurgon, M. (1969), "Inscriptions étrusques de Tunisie", *CRAI*, 526-551.

Heurgon, M. (1969a), "Les Dardaniens en Afrique", *REL* 47: 284-294.

Higbie, C. (2007), "Hellenistic Mythographers", in R. Woodart (ed.), *The Cambridge Companion to Greek Mythology*, Cambridge, 237–54.

Hignett, C. (1963), *Xerxes' Invasion of Greece*, Oxford.

Hoffmann, C. (1991), *An introduction to bilingualism*, London, New York.

Hoffmann, M. (1956), *5000 Jahre Bier*, Berlin.

Holban, M., Bulgaru, M. M. A., Cernovodeanu, P. (eds.) (1980-83), *Calatori straini despre tarile române (Foreign Travellers about the Romanian Countries)*, Bucuresti, vol. VII: 1980; vol. VIII: 1983.

Homo, L. (1972), *Rome impériale et l'urbanisme dans l'antiquité*, Paris.

Hopkinson, N. (1984), "Callimachus' Hymn to Zeus", *CQ* 34: 139-148.

Hornblower, S. (2008), *A Commentary on Thucydides. Volume I: Books I-III*, Oxford - New York.

Houaiss, A. (2001), *Dicionário Houaiss da língua portuguesa*, Rio de Janeiro.

Howgego, Chr, Heuchert, V. Burnett, A. (eds.) (2004), *Coinage and identity in the Roman provinces*, Oxford.

Howgego, Chr. (2004), "Coinage and identity in the Roman provinces", in Chr. Howgego, A. Heuchert y Burnett (eds.), *Coinage and identity in the Roman provinces*, Oxford, 1-18.

Huizinga, J. (1948), *Le déclin du Moyen Âge*, Paris.

Hunter, R., Fuhrer, T. (2002), "Imaginary Gods? Poetic Theology in the *Hymns* of Callimachus", in F. Montanari, L. Lehnus (eds.), *Callimaque. Sept Exposés suivis de discussions*, Vandoeuvros-Gender, 143-175.

Hurlet, F. (1996), *Les collègues du prince au temps d'Auguste et de Tibére: de la légalité républicaine à la légitimité dynastique*, Roma.

Hutchinson, G. O. (1988), *Hellenistic Poetry*, Oxford.

HCT = Gomme, A. J., (1970), *A Historical Commentary on Thucydides. vs. 1-2*, Oxford.

Icks, M. (2001), "Priestohood and Imperial Power. The Religious Reforms of Heliogabalus 220-222", in L. de Blois (ed.), *Administration, Prosopography and Appointment Policies in the Roman Empire. Proceedings of the First Workshop of the International Network Impact of Empire (Roman Empire, 27 B.C. – A.D. 406)*, Amsterdam, 169-178.

IRT = Reynolds , J. M., Ward-Perkins, J. B. (1952), *Inscriptions of Roman Tripolitania*, Rome.

Jackson. K. (1953), *Language and history in Early Britain*, Edinburgh.

Jacoby, F. (1923), *Die Fragmente der griechischen Historiker,* Part I-III, Berlin.

Jaeger, W. (s.d), *Paideia,* Trad. de Artur M. Parreira, São Paulo.

Janko R. (1982), *Homer, Hesiod and the Hymns,* Cambridge.

Jiménez, A. J. (1995), "La imagen de Teseo en las *Suplicantes*", in J. A. López Férez (ed.), *De Homero a Libanio*, Madrid, 145-161.

Johnson, L. (1960), *"Natalis urbis* and *principium anni"*, *TPAPhA* 91: 109-120

Julia, D. (1962), "Les monuments funéraires en forme de demi-cylindre dans la province romaine de Tarragonaise", *MCV* I : 29-54.

Jullian, C. (1926), "Notes gallo-romaines", *Révue des Études Anciennes* 28. 2: 139-151.

Little, K. (2002), "Monasticism and Western Society: from marginality to the establishment and back", *Memoirs of the American Academy in Rome* 47: 83-94.

Kaimio, J. (1979), *The Romans and the Greek Language*, Helsinki.

Kalinowski, A. (2007), "A series of honorific statue bases for the Vedii in the market agora at Ephesos (*IvE* 725, 731, 3076-3078)", in M. Mayer, G. Baratta, A. Guzmán, (eds.), *Acta XII Congressus internationalis epigraphiae Graecae et Latinae. Provinciae imperii Romani inscriptionibus descriptae*, vol I, Barcelona, 757-762.

Kantiréa, M. (2007), *Les dieux et les dieux augustes. Le culte impérial en Grèce sous le Julio-claudiens et les Flaviens, Études épigraphiques et archéologiques,* Athènes.

Katz, S. H., Fleming, S. J., McGovern, P. E. (1996), *The origins and ancient history of wine. Food and nutrition in history and anthropology* 11, Amsterdam.

Kelso W.M. (ed.) (1990), *Earth patterns. Essays in landscape archaeology,* Charlottesville.

Kerkhecker, A. (1999), *Callimachus' Book of "Iambi"*, Oxford.

Khanoussi, M. (1983), "Nouvelles sépultures d'époque romaine", in Beschaouch A. et alii (eds.), *Recherches archéologiques franco-tunisiennes à Bulla-Regia,* I (CEFR 28/I), Roma, 93-106.

Kiss, Z. (1975), *L'iconographie des princes julio-claudiens au temps d'Auguste et de Tibère,* Varsovie.

Kleiner, F. S. (1991), "The trophy on the bridge and the Roman triumph over nature", *L'Antiquité Classique* 60: 182-192.

Koch, J. (2009), *Tartessian. Celtic in the South-west at the dawn of history*, Aberystwyth.

Koch, J. (2009a), "A case for Tartessian as a Celtic language", *Palaeohispanica* 9: 339-351.

Kolb, A. (2001), "Tansport and communication in Roman state: the cursus publicus", in C. Adams and R. Laurence (eds.), *Travel and Geography in the Roman Empire*, Londres - Nova Iorque, 95-105.

Kolb, A. (ed.) (2010), *Augustae. Machtbewusste Frauen am römischen Kaiserhof? Herrschaftsstrukturen und Herrschaftspraxis*, Berlin.

Kozakai, T. (2000), *L'étranger, l'identité. Essai sur l'integration culturelle*, Paris.

Kramer, N., Reitz, Chr. (eds.) (2010), *Tradition und Erneuerung. Mediale Strategien in der Zeit der Flavier*, Berlin, New York.

Kristeller, P. O. (1961, 3ª ed.), "The moral thought of Renaissance humanism", in *Chapters in Western civilization*, I, New York, 289-335.

Krynen, J. (1981), *Idéal du prince et pouvoir royal en France à la fin du Moyen Âge (1380-1440). Étude de la littérature politique du temps*, Paris.

Kuhoff, W. (2001), *Diokletian und die Epoche der Tetrarchie*, Frankfurt.

Künzl, S. (1997), *Die Trierer Spruchbecherkeramik. Dekorierte Schwarzfirniskeramik des 3. und 4. Jahrhunderts* (Beihefte Trierer Zeitschrift 21), Trier.

Lambert, P. Y. (1994), *La langue gauloise*, Clamecy.

Lambrino, S. (1937), "La famille d'Apollon à Histria", *Aephem* 100: 352-362.

Lambrino, S. (1952), "Les inscriptions de São Miguel de Odrinhas", *Bulletin des Études Portugaises* 16: 134-176.

Lasserre, F. (1976), "Hérodote et Protagoras: le débat sur les constitutions", *MH* 33: 65-84.

Lateiner, D. (1984), "Herodotean historiographical patterning: the constitutional debate", *QS* 20: 257-284.

Laurence, R. (2001), "Afterword: travel and empire", in C. Adams and R. Laurence (eds.), *Travel and Geography in the Roman Empire*, Londres / Nova Iorque, 167-176.

Lausberg, H. (1990, 3ª ed.), *Handbuch der literarischen Rhetorik. Eine Grundlegung der Literaturwissenschaft*, Stuttgart.

Lawrance, J. N. H. (1990), "Humanism in the Iberian Peninsula", in A. Goodman, A. Mackay (eds.), *The Impact of Humanism on Western Europe*, Londres, 220-258.

Lazenby, J. F. (1993), *The Defence of Greece, 490-479 B.C.*, Warminster.

Leão, D. F. (2012), *A Globalização no Mundo Antigo. Do* Polites *ao* Kosmopolites, Coimbra.

Lehmann, K. (1962), "Ignorance and search in the villa of the Mysteries", *JRS* 52: 62-68.

Leite de Vasconcelos, J. (1913), *Religiões de Lusitania*, III, Lisboa 1989.

Leite, S. (ed.) (1963), *Estatutos da Universidade de Coimbra (1559),* Coimbra.

Lekai, L. J. (1987), *Los Cistercienses. Ideales y realidad*, Barcelona.

Lemny, S. (2010), *Cantemirestii. Aventura europeana a unei familii princiare din secolul al XVIII-lea* (*Les Cantemir: l'aventure européenne d'une famille princière au XVIIIe siècle*, 2006), Iasi, Polirom.

Lesky, A. (1995), *História da Literatura Grega*, Lisboa.

Leveau, Ph. (1992), "Le territoire agricole d'Arles dans l'antiquité. Relecture de l'histoire économique d'une cité antique à la lumiere d'une histoire du milieu", in M. Bernardi (cur.), *Archeologia del Paesaggio*, Firenze, vol. II, 597-636.

Levy, A. M. (2010), *Sex Acts in Early Modern Italy: Practice, Performance, Perversion, Punishment*, Farnham.

Lewis, D. M, Boardman, J., Hornblower, S., Ostwald, M (eds.) (1994), *The Cambridge Ancient History, Volume 6: The Fourth Century BC*, Cambridge.

Lewis, D. M. (1994), "The Athenian Tribute Quota Lists, 453-450 BC", *BSA* 89: 285-301.

Lima, D. C. (1998, 3ª ed.), *Câmara Cascudo: um brasileiro feliz*. Rio de Janeiro.

Lintott, A. (1992), *Judicial reform and land reform in the Roman Republic*, Cambridge.

Little K. (2002), "Monasticism and Western Society: from marginality to the establishment and back", *Memoirs of the American Academy in Rome* 47: 83-94.

Littman, R. J. (1974), *The Greek experiment, Imperialism and social conflict 800-400 B. C.,* Londres.

Liverani, P. (1994), "Il ciclo di ritratti del edificio absidato a Roselle", in *Roselle: iconografia imperiale e glorificazione Familiare, MDAI, RA* 101: 161-163.

Loeschcke, S. (1932), "Römische Denkmäler vom Weinbau an Mosel, Saar und Ruwer", *TrZ* 7: 42-60.

Loeschcke, S. (1933), *Denkmäler vom Weinbau aus der Zeit der Römerherrschaft an Mosel, Saar und Ruwer,* Trier.

López Moreda, S. (2009), *Aulo Gelio, Noches Áticas*, Madrid.

López Vilar, J. (1999-2000), "Consideracions sobre les *cupae* i altres estructures funeràries afins", *Bulletti Arcqueològic* V. 21-22: 65-103.

Lorenzo Gómez, F. (2010), *Un dios entre los hombres. La adoración a los emperadores romanos en Grecia*, Barcelona.

Losada Goya, J. M. (ed.) (2010), *Mito y Mundo contemporáneo. La recepción de los mitos antiguos, medievales y modernos en la litetatura contemporânea*, Bari.

Lucet, B. (1977), *Les codifications cisterciennes de 1237 et de 1257*, Paris.

Macan, R.W. (1908), *Herodotus, The Seventh, Eighth, & Ninth Books*, London.

Machado de Assis, J. M. (1971), "Esaú e Jacó"., in Machado de Assis, *Obra Completa*, Rio de Janeiro, José Aguilar Editora.

Maehler, H. (1982), *Die Lieder des Bakchylides I* (2 vols.), Leiden.

Magioncalda, A. (1991), *Lo sviluppo della titolatura imperiale da Augusto a Giustiniano attraverso le testimonianze epigrafiche*, Torino.

Magueijo, C. (1970), "A Lex Metallis Dicta", *O Arqueólogo Português* série 3, 4: 125-163.

Maltese, V. E.-Cortassa, G. (eds.)(2000), *Roma parte del cielo. Confronto tra l'Antica e la Nuova Roma di Manuele Crisolora*, Torino.

Mamede, Z. (1970), *Luis da Câmara Cascudo: 50 anos de vida intelectual 1918/1968*, Natal.

Manconi, D., Catalli, F. (eds.) (2005), *Le immagini del potere. Il potere delle immagini. L'uso del ritratto ufficiale nel mondo romano da Cesare ai Severi*, Perugia.

Mann, C. (2001), *Athlet und Polis im archaischen und frühklassischen Griechenland*, Göttingen.

Mantas, V. G. (2008-2009), "A rede viária romana em Portugal. Estado da questão e perspectivas futuras", *Anas* 21-22: 245-272.

Mantas, V. G. (2011), "Linhas fortificadas e vida quotidiana: da Muralha da China à Muralha do Atlântico", in C. Guardado da Silva (coord.), *A Vida quotidiana nas Linhas de Torres Vedras*, Torres Vedras, 15-56.

Mantas, V. G. (2012), *As vias romanas da Lusitânia*, Mérida.

Maquiavel, N. (2010, 8ª ed), *O príncipe*, Trad. de Pietro Nassetti, Martin Claret, São Paulo.

Maquiavel, N. (1980), *Le Prince de Maquiavel*, Traduction et commentaire de C. Roux-Lehman, Paris.

Maravall, J. A. (1972), *Estado moderno y mentalidad social (siglos XV a XVII)*, 2 vols., Madrid.

Marco, F. (1993), "*Nemedus Augustus*", in I. J. Adiego, J. Siles, J. Velaza, (eds.), *Studia Palaeohispanica et Indogermanica J. Untermann ab amicis Hispanicis oblata*, Barcelona, 163-178.

Marco, F. (1996), "Integración, interpretatio y resistencia religiosa en el occidente del imperio", in J. M. Blásquez, J. Alvard (ed.) *La romanización en Occidente*, Madrid, 217-238.

Marcos Casquero, M. A., Domínguez García, A. (2006), *Aulo Gelio, Noches Áticas*, vol. I, Universidad de León.

Marcy, G. (1936), *Les inscriptions libyques bilingues de l'Afrique du nord*, Paris.

Moreno Gallo, I. (2006),*Vías romanas: ingenieria y técnica constructiva*. Madrid.

Marlière, É. (2001), *Le tonneau en Gaule Romaine»*, *Gallia* 58: 181-201.

Marlière, É. (2002), *L'outre et le tonneau dans l'Occident romain*, Montagnac.

Marques, M. A. F. (1998), "A introdução da Ordem de Cister em Portugal", in *Estudos sobre a Ordem de Cister em Portugal*, Lisboa.

Marrou, H.-I. (1963), "L'Église dans la première moitié du quatrième siècle", in *L'Église de l'Antiquité tardive 303-604*, Paris, 26-35.

Marrou, H.-I. (1965, 6ª ed.), *Histoire de l' éducation dans l' Antiquité*, Paris.

Marshall, P. K (1983), "Aulus Gellius", in L.D. Reynolds (ed.), *Texts and Transmission. A Survey of the Latin Classics*, Oxford.

Martínez, A. (1993), "Dos esgrafiados ibéricos sobre una estela romana de Requena (Valencia)", *Saguntum* 26: 247-251.

Martínez-Pinna, J. (2002), "Los arcadios", in *La prehistoria mítica de Roma*, *Gerión. Anejos* 6: 135-167.

Martini, W. (1990), *Die archäischen Plastik der Griechen*, Darmstadt.

Mastino, A. (1981), *Le titolature di Caracalla e Geta attraverso le iscrizioni (indici)*, Bolonia.

Mattoso, A., (1935 2ª ed.), *Compêndio de história antiga,* Sá da Costa, Lisboa.

Maurice, F. (1930), "The Size of the Army of Xerxes in the Invasion of Greece 480 B.C.", *JHS* 50: 210-35.

Mayer, M. (1980), "La plasmación lingüística de la pervivencia de los cultos prerromanos en Hispania a través de los formularios epigráficos", *Revista Española de Lingüística* 10: 230-231.

Mayer, M. (1993), "El paganismo cívico de los siglos II y III en la Hispania citerior. Su reflejo en la epigrafía", in *Ciudad y comunidad cívica en Hispania. Siglos II y III d. C. Cité et communauté civique en Hispania*, Madrid, 161-175.

Mayer, M. (1995), "El primer horizonte epigráfico en el litoral noreste de la *Hispania citerior*", in F. Beltrán (ed.), *Roma y el nacimiento de la cultura epigráfica en Occidente*, Zaragoza, 97-119.

Mayer, M. (1998), "¿Qué es un *Augusteum?*, *Historia Antiqua* 4: 63-70.

Mayer, M. (1999), "Aproximación a la religión cívica en Hispania bajo los flavios", *Ktema* 24: 341-345.

Mayer, M. (2004), "El *Augusteum* de Narona (Vid, Metković, Croacia) en época de los Severos", in *Orbis Antiquus. Studia in honorem Ioannis Pisonis*, Cluj-Napoca, 283-289.

Mayer, M. (2005), "Constantino el Grande: deconstrucción y construcción de un Imperio", in F. de Oliveira (coord.), *Génese e Consolidação da Ideia de Europa*, vol. III, *O Mundo Romano*, Coimbra, 203-230.

Mayer, M. (2007a), "La presenza imperiale nelle città del *Picenum* tra l'epoca augustea e il regno dei Severi : un primo aproccio", *Studi Maceratesi* 41: 27-40.

Mayer, M. (2007b), "Las dedicatorias a miembros de la *domus* Augusta julio-claudia y su soporte: una primera aproximación", in G. Paci (ed.), *Contributi all'epigrafia del'età augustea. Actes de la XIIIe Rencontre franco-italienne sur l'épigraphie du monde romain*, Tivoli, 171-199

Mayer, M. (2008), "Sila y el uso político de la epigrafía", in M. Caldelli, G. L. Gregori, S. Orlandi (eds.), *Epigrafia 2006. Atti della XIVe rencontre sur l'épigraphie in onore di Silvio Panciera con altri contributi di colleghi, allievi e collaboratori*, Roma, 121-135.

Mayer, M. (2009), *"Los honores recibidos por la familia de Marco Aurelio en la parte oriental del imperio romano: ¿cambio o continuidad en el culto dinástico?"*, in A. Martínez Fernández (ed.), *Estudios de Epigrafía Griega*, La Laguna, 277-294.

Mayer, M. (2010), "La presència de la dinastia antonina a *Tarraco*", in *Studia Celtica Classica et Romana Nicolae Szabó septuagesimo dicata*, Budapest, 159-167.

Mayer, M. (2015), "La epigrafia y el Augusteum de Narona", in G. Zecchini (ed.), *L'Augusteum di Narona. Atti della Giornata di Studi. Roma 31 maggio 2013*, (Centro ricerche e documentazione sull' antichità clàssica, monografie, 3 7), Roma, pp. 19-41.

McCrum, M., Woodhead, A.G. (1961), *Select Documents of the Principates of the Flavian Emperors Including the Year of Revolution, A.D. 68-96*, Cambridge.

Mednikarova, I. (2003), "The accusative of the name of the deceased in Latin and Greek epitaphs", *ZPE* 143: 117-134.

Meiggs, R. (1972), *The Athenian Empire*, Oxford.

Melani, V., Vergari, M. (1985), *Profilo di una città etrusca Roselle*, Pistoia.

Melchor Gil, E. (1992), "Sistemas de financiación y medios de construcción de la red viaria hispana", *Habis*, 23: 121-137.

Melchor Gil, E. (2010), "Homenajes estatutarios e integración de la mujer en la vida pública municipal de las ciudades de la Bética", in F. J. Navarro (ed.), *Pluralidad e integración en el Mundo Romano*, Pamplona, 221-245.

Mellor, R. (1975), ΘΕΑ ΡΩΜΗ *the Worship of the Goddess Roma in the Greek World*, Göttingen.

Mellor, R. (1981), "The Goddess Roma", in *ANRW* II 17. 2, Berlin, New York, 950-1030

Menegazzi, L. (1995), *Il manifesto italiano* (prima ed. 1974), Milano.

Merêa, P. (1929), *História de Portugal*, Vol. II. Coimbra.

Merêa, P. (1941), *Suárez, Grácio, Hobbes*, Coimbra.

Mesnard, P. (1977), *Essor de la philosophie politique au XVIe Siècle*, Paris.

Messerschmidt, W. (2003), *Prosopopoiia: Personifikationen politischen Charakters in spätklassischer und hellenistischer Kunst*, Köln.

Michelini, A. N. (1994), "Political themes in Euripides' *Suppliants*", *AJPh* 115. 2: 219-252.

Millar, F. (1968), "Local cultures in the Roman Empire: Libyan, Punic and Latin", *JRS* 58: 126-134.

Millar, F. (1993), *The Roman Near East 31 BC-337 AD*, London.

Millar, F. (2006), *A Greek Roman Empire, Power and belief under Theodosius II 408-450*, Berkeley.

Minerath, R. (1996), *Histoire des Conciles*, Paris.

MLH = J. Untermann, J. (1975-2000), *Monumenta linguarum Hispanicarum*, I-V, Wiesbaden.

Moggi, M. (1976), *I sinecismi interstatali greci*, Pisa.

Moncada, C. (1947), *Filosofia do direito e do estado*, I, Coimbra.

Monfrin, J. (1964), "Humanisme et traductions au Moyen Age", in *L'Humanisme médieval dans les littératures romanes du XIIe au XIVe siècle* (Actes du Colloque organisé par le Centre de Philologie et de Littératures romanes de l'Université de Strasbourg), Paris.

Monteiro, N., d'Encarnação, J. (1993-1994), "A propósito de uma inscrição latina em Santiago da Guarda (Ansião)", *Conimbriga* 32-33: 303-311.

Moretti, G. (2007), "Patriae trepidantis imago. La personificazione di Roma nella *Pharsalia* fra *ostentum* e disseminazione allegorica", *Camenae* 2: 1-17

Morrison, A. D. (2007), *The Narrator in Archaic Greek and Hellenistic Poetry*, Cambridge.

Mosley, D. J. (1965), "The Size of Embassies in Ancient Greek Diplomacy", *TPAPhA*: 255-266.

Mosley, D. J. (1972), "Envoys and diplomacy in Ancient Greece", *Historia* 22: 1-97.

Mossé, Cl. (1970), *La colonisation dans l'Antiquité*, Paris, 27-99.

Mullen, A. (2007), "Linguistic evidence for 'romanization': continuity and change in Romano-British onomastics: a study of the epigraphic record with particular reference to Bath", *Britannia* 38: 35-61.

Muñoz, V. (2005), "La *interpretatio romana* del dios prerromano Bandue", *Veleia* 22: 145-152.

Munro, J.A.R. (1926), "Xerxes' Invasion of Greece", in *The Persian Empire and the West, Cambridge Ancient History*, Vol. IV, Cambridge, 268-316.

Nascimento, A. A. (1990), "Poggio e o seu interesse por códices de Alcobaça", *Revista da Faculdade de Letras de Lisboa* 13-14: 37-40.

Nascimento, A. A. (1993), "As librarias dos príncipes de Avis", *Biblos. Revista da Faculdade de Letras* (Coimbra). *Actas do Congreso Comemorativo do 6° Centenário do Infante D. Pedro* (25 a 27 de Novembro de 1992) 69: 265-287.

Nascimento, A. A. (1995), "La réception des auteurs classiques dans l'éspace cultural portugais: une questione ouvert", in C. Leonardi, B. Munk Olsen (eds.), *The Classical Tradition in the Middle Ages and Renaissance*, Spoleto, 47-56.

Nascimento, A. A. (1997), "Traduzir, verbo de fronteira nos contornos da Idade Média", in C. Almeida Ribeiro, M. Madureira (eds.), *O género do texto medieval*, Lisboa, 113-138.

Nascimento, A. A. (1999), *Cister. Os documentos primitivos. No 9.º Centenário da fundação de Cister* (1999). Introdução, tradução e notas de Aires A. Nascimento, Lisboa.

Navarro Caballero, M. (2003), "Mujer de notable: representación y poder en las ciudades de la España imperial", in S. Armani, B. Martineau-Hurlet, A. U. Stylow, (eds.), *Acta antiqua Complutensia IV. Epigrafía y sociedad en Hispania durante el Alto Imperio: estructuras sociales*, Alcalá de Henares, 119-127.

Nemeti, S. (1998), "Cultul lui Sucellus-Dis Pater şi al Nantosueltei-Proserpina în Dacia romană", *EphemNapoc* 8: 95-121.

Neumann, G., Untermann, J. (eds.) (1980), *Die Sprachen im Römischen Reich der Kaiserzeit. Beihefte der Bonner Jahrbücher* 40, Bonn.

Nicosia, F. (ed.) (1990), *Un decennio di ricerche a Roselle. Statue e ritratti*, Firenze.

Nunes, E., Albuquerque, M. (1968), "Parecer do doutor 'Valasco di Portogallo' sobre o beneplácito régio (Florença, 1954)", in V. Rau (ed.), *Do tempo e da historia*, Lisboa, t. 2, 97-139.

Ober, J. (1989), *Mass and Elite in Democratic Athens. Rhetoric, Ideology, and the Power of the People*, Princeton.

Odiot, T. (2004), "Le site du Molard à Donzère", in Brun, J.-P., Poux, M., Tchernia, A. (eds.), *Le vin. Nectar des Dieux. Génies des Hommes*, Gollion, 202-203.

Oelmann, F. (1914), *Die Keramik des Kastells Niederbieber*, Frankfurt.

Ohly, D. (1976), *Die Aegineten: die Marmorskulpturen des Tempels der Aphaia auf Aegina*. (a) *I. Die Ostgiebelgruppe*. München. (b) *II. Die Westgiebelgruppe*. *III. Altarplatzgrupen, Akrotere, etc*, München.

Olteanu, T. (2008), "El culto a Victoria y la *interpretatio* indígena en el Occidente de Hispania, Gallia y el norte de Britania", *BVallad* 74: 197-224.

Ors, A. de (1953), *Epigrafia juridica de la España romana*, Madrid.

Pacaut, M. (1993), *Les moines blancs. Histoire de l'Ordre de Cîteaux*, Paris.

Pallottino, M. (1952), "El problema de las relaciones entre Cerdeña e Iberia en la antigüedad prerromana", *Ampurias* 14: 137-155.

Panciera, S. (2003), "Umano, sovraumano o divino? Le divinità augustee e l'imperatore a Roma", in L. de Blois, P. Erdkamp, O. Hekster, G. De Kleijn, S. Mols, (eds.), *The Representation and Perception of Roman Imperial Power. Proceedings of the Third Workshop of the International Network Impact of Empire (Roman Empire c. 200 B.C. – A.D. 476)*, Amsterdam, 219-239.

Paparelli, G. (1973), *Feritas, humanitas, diuinitas. L'essenza umanistica del Rinascimento*, Napoli.

Parker, V. (1988), "Τύραννος. The semantics of a political concept from Archilochus to Aristotle", *Hermes* 126. 2: 145-172.

Patillon, M. (ed.) (2002), *Pseudo-Aelius Aristide, Arts rhétoriques*, Paris.

Pekary, T. (1968), *Untersuchungen zu den römischen Reichsstraßen*, Bona.

Pellegrini, D. P. M. (2003), *Le Grandi Storie dell'Auto*, vol. 2, *Alfa Romeo*, 35-35.

Pelling, Ch. (2002), "Speech and action: Herodotus' Debate on the Constitutions", *PCPhS* 48: 123-158.

Peña Cervantes, Y. (2010), *Torcularia. La producción de vino y aceite en Hispania. Catálogo de yacimientos analizados en cedé* (Sèrie documenta 149), Tarragona.

Pensa, M. (1979), "Genesi e svilupo dell'arco onorario nella documentazione numismática", *Studi sull'Arco Onorario Romano*, Roma, 19-27.

Peres, D. (1952), *História de Portugal*, II, Porto.

Pérez Martin, A. (1979), *Proles Aegidiana. I. Introducción. Los Colegiales desde 1368 a 1500*, Bolonia.

Pérez Martin, A. (1999), *Españoles en el Alma Mater Studiorum. Profesores hispanos en Bolonia (de fines del siglo XII a 1799)*, Murcia.

Pérez Ruiz, F. (1984), "El justo es feliz y el injusto desgraciado, justicia y felicidad en la República de Platon", *Pensamiento* 40, 159: 257-295.

Petrarca, F. (1581), *Francisci Petrarchae Florentini Opera*. Basileae, per Sebastianum Henricpetri.

Petrarca, F. (1942), *Epistolae familiares*, in V. Rossi (ed.), *Le Familiari*, Firenze.

Petri, Ch. (1989), "La politique de Constance II: un premier 'césaropapisme' ou l'*imitatio Constantini*?", in A. Dihle (coord.), *L'église et l'empire au IV siècle*, Genève, 113-178.

Pfeiffer, R. (1949-1951), *Callimachus*, 2 vols., Oxford.

Pflaum, H.G. (1976), *Inscriptions latines de l'Algérie*, t. II, vol. II, *Inscriptions de la Confédération cirtéenne, de Cuicul et de la tribu des Suburbures*, Alger.

Pflug, H. (1941), *As auto-estradas do Reich*, Berlim.

Pharr, C. et alii (2008), *The Theodosian Code and Novels and the Sirmondian Constitution. Translation, commentary and bibliography*, Union (NJ).

Piana, C. (1976), *Nuovi documenti sull'Universitá di Bologna e sul Collegio di Spagna*,I-II, Bolonia, Zaragoza.

Pick, B. (1898), *Die antiken Münzen Nordgriechenlands I, 2. Die antiken Münzen von Dacien und Moesien*, Berlin.

Piganiol, A. (1972, 2ª ed.), *L'empire chrétien*, Paris.

Pina, R. de (1977), *Chronica do Senhor Rey D. Affonso V*, cap. CXXV "Das feiçoões custumes e virtudes do Yfante Don Pedro", in M. L. de Almeida (Intro. e Revisão), *Crónicas de Rui de Pina*, Porto.

Pinheiro Futre, M. P. (2006), "Do Mito à Utopia: viagem ao mundo do imaginário grego" in *Actas do V Congresso da APEC – Antiguidade Clássica e nós: Herança e Identidade Cultural*, Braga, 569-581.

Pinho, S. T. (1999), "Os Príncipes de Avis e o Pré- Humanismo Português", in *Raízes Greco-Latinas da Cultura Portuguesa. Actas do I Congresso da APEC*, Coimbra, 99-133.

Pinto, Frei H. (1952), "Diálogo da justiça", in *Imagem da vida cristã*, I, Lisboa.

Pippidi, D. M. (1971), *I Greci nel Basso Danubio dall'età arcaica alla conquista romana*, Mailand.

Pirling, R. (1993), "*Ein Trierer Spruchbecher mit ungewöhnlicher Inschrift aus Krefeld-Gellep*", *Germania* 71: 387-404.

Podlecki, A. J. (1976), "Athens and Aegina", *Historia* 25.4: 396-413.

Poenaru Bordea, G. (1979), "Les statères ouest-pontiques de type Alexandre le Grand et Lysimaque", *RBNS* 125: 37-51.

Prag, J. R. W. (2002), "Epigraphy by numbers: Latin and the epigraphic culture in Sicily", in A. E. Cooley (ed.), *Becoming Roman, Writing Latin? Literacy and Epigraphy in the Roman West. JRA Suppl. Ser.* 48: 15-31.

Preda, C., Popescu, E., Diaconu, P. (1962), "Săpăturile arheologice de la Mangalia (Callatis)", *Materiale* 8: 439-455.

Pressouyre, L. (1990), *Le rêve cistercien*, Paris.

Price, S. R. F. (1984), *Rituals and Power. The Roman Imperial Cult in Asia Minor*, Cambridge.

Privitera, G. A. (1988), "Pindaro, *Nem.* III 1-5 e l'acqua di Egina", *QUCC* 58: 63-70.

Puerta Torres, C. (1995), *Los miliarios de la Vía de la Plata*, 1-2, Madrid.

Quadrino, D. (2007), *Una nuova iscrizione onoraria di Adriano e il Sebasteion di Kestros in Cilicia Tracheia*, Tivoli.

Radnoti Alföldi, M., Rasbach, G. (1999), "Zur Frage der interpretatio Romana", in *Festschrift für Günter Smolla*, Wiesbaden, 597-605.

Raepsaet-Charlier, M. Th. (1975), "La datation des inscriptions latines dans les provinces occidentales de l'Empire Romain d'après les formules « In H(onorem) D(omus) D(ivinae) » et « Deo, Deae »", in *ANRW II* 3: 232-282.

Raepsaet-Charlier, M. Th. (2005), "Les sacerdoces des femmes sénatoriales sous le Haut-Empire", in M.-F. Baslez, F. Prévot (eds.), *Prosopographie et histoire religieuse. Actes du colloque tenu en l'Université Paris XII-Val de Marne le 27 & 28 octobre 2000*, Paris, 283-304.

Ramalho, A. C. (1985), *Latim Renascentista em Portugal (Antologia)*, Coimbra.

Rapp, Cl. (2005), *Holy Bishops in Late Antiquity, The nature of Christian Leadership in an age of transition*, Berkeley.

Rau, V. (1969), "Italianismo na cultura jurídica portuguesa do século XV", *Revista Portuguesa de História* 12.1: 185-206.

Rau, V. (1973), "Studenti ed eruditi portoghesi in Italia nel secolo XV", *Estudos Italianos em Portugal* 36: 7-73.

Rawlinson, H. G. (1916), *Intercourse between India and the Western World from the Earliest Times to the Fall of Rome*, Cambridge.

Rebelo, D. L. (1951), *Do governo da republica pelo rei (de republica gubernanda per regem)*, reprodução fac-similada da edição de 1496, Introdução e notas de A. M. de Sá, Lisboa.

Rebelo, L. de S. (1983), *A concepção do poder em Fernão Lopes*, Lisboa.

Rebuffat, R. (2007), "Pour un corpus des bilingues punico-libyques et latino-libyques", in M. H. Fantar (ed.), *Osmose etnho-culturelle en Méditerranée*, Tunis, 183-242.

Regra do Patriarca S. Bento (1992), Edições "Ora & Labora", Singeverga.

Rhodes, P. J. (1993), *A Commentary on the Aristotelian* ATHENAION POLITEIA, Oxford.

Rhodes, P. J. (2006), *A History of the Classical Greek World 478-323 BC*, Molden.

RIB = Collingwood, R. G. (1965), *The Roman inscriptions of Britain. I. Inscriptions on stone*, Oxford.

RIG = P.-M. Duval (ed.), *Recueil des inscriptions gauloises*, Paris 1985-. I: M. Lejeune, *Textes gallo-grecs*, 1985; II.1: M. Lejeune, *Textes gallo-étrusques. Textes gallo-latins sur pierre*, 1988; II.2: P.-Y. Lambert, *Textes gallo-latins sur instrumentum*, 2002; III: P.-M. Duval y G. Pinault, *Les calendriers (Coligny, Villards d'Héria)*, 1988; IV: J.-B. Colbert de Beaulieu y B. Fischer, *Les légendes monétaires*, 1998.

Ripollés, P. P. (2004), "Coinage and identity in the Roman provinces: Spain", in Ch. Howgego, V. Heuchert, A. Burnett (eds.), *Coinage and identity in the Roman provinces*, Oxford, 79-93.

Ripollés, P. P., Velaza, J. (2002), "Saguntum, colonia latina", *ZPE* 141: 285-294.

Rodgers, B. (1989), "The Metamorphosis of Constantine", *CQ* 39.1: 233-246.

Rodrigues, M. A. (1993), "O infante D. Pedro e a Universidade", *Biblos. Revista de Faculdade de Letras* (Coimbra). *Actas do Congreso Comemorativo do 6° Centenario do Infante D. Pedro* (25 a 7 de Novembro de 1992) 69: 345-362.

Rodrigues, N. S. (2007), "Entre Europa e Io: elementos orientais na arte grega arcaica e clássica", *in* J. A. Ramos, L. M. Araújo, A. Ramos dos Santos (eds.), *Arte Pré-Clássica. Colóquio Comemorativo dos Vinte Anos do Instituto Oriental da Faculdade de Letras da Universidade de Lisboa*, Lisboa, 323-346.

Rodríguez, P., Díez de Pinos, E. (2014), "Nueva inscripción celtibérica en piedra de El Pueyo de Belchite (Zaragoza)", *Palaeohispanica* 14: 245-262.

Rodríguez Colmenero, A., Ferrer Sierra, S., Álvarez Asorey, R. (2004), *Miliários e outras inscricións viarias romanas do noroeste hispánico*. Santiago de Compostela.

Rocha Pereira, M. H. (1981), "O mais antigo texto europeu de teoria política", *Nova Renascença* 1: 364-370.

Rocha Pereira, M. H. (1990), "O 'Diálogo dos Persas' em Heródoto", *Estudos Portugueses. Homenagem a António José Saraiva*, Lisboa, 351-362.

Rocha Pereira, M. H. (2003), *Hélade. Antologia da Cultura Grega*, Asa, Porto.

Rocha Pereira, M. H. (2008, 8ª ed.), *Sófocles: Antígona*, Coimbra.

Roha Pereira, M. H. (2009, 10ª ed.), *Hélade*, Lisboa, Guimarães.

Rocha Pereira, M. H. (2012), *Estudos de História da Cultura Clássica*, vol.1 – *Cultura Grega*, Lisboa.

Roldán Hervás, J. (1975), *Itineraria Hispana. Fuentes antiguas para el estudio de las vías romanas en la Península Ibérica*, Madrid.

Röllig, W. (1980), "Das Punische im Römischen Reich", in G. Neumann, J. Untermann (eds.), *Die Sprachen im Römischen Reich der Kaiserzeit. (Bonner Jahrbücher des Rheinischen Landesmuseums in Bonn im Landschaftsverband*

Rheinland und des Vereins von Altertumsfreunden im Rheinlande 40), Köln, 285-299.

Romano, E. (2006-2009), "Le tombe "a *cupa*" in Italia e nel Mediterraneo. Tipologia architettonica, committenza e rituale", *StClOr* 52: 149-219.

Romilly, J. de (1959), "Le classement des constitutions d'Hérodote à Aristote", *REG* 72: 81-99.

Rose, C. B. (1997), *Dynastic Commemoration and Imperial Portraiture in the Julio-Claudian Period*, Cambridge.

Rosenthal, F. (1936), *Die Sprache der palmyrenischen Inschriften und ihre Stellung innerhalb des Aramäischen*, Leipzig.

Rosivach, V. J. (1977), "Earthborns and Olympians: the *parodos* of the *Ion*", *CQ* 27. 2: 284-294.

Rosivach, V. J. (1988), "The Tyrant in Athenian Democracy", *QUCC* 59: 43-57.

Rossillon, Ph. (ed.) (1995), *Atlas de la langue française*, Paris.

Rossiter, J. J. (1978), *Roman Farm Buildings in Italy* (BAR int. Ser. 52), Oxford.

Rössler, O. (1980), "Libyen von der Cyrenaica bis zur Mauretania Tingitana", in G. Neumann, J. Untermann (eds.), *Die Sprachen im Römischen Reich der Kaiserzeit. (Bonner Jahrbücher des Rheinischen Landesmuseums in Bonn im Landschaftsverband Rheinland und des Vereins von Altertumsfreunden im Rheinlande 40).* Köln, 267-284.

Rubenstein, L. (2004), "Ionia", in M. H Hansen, T. H. Nielsen (eds.), *An Inventory of Archaic and Classical poleis*, Oxford, 1053-1107.

Rucquoi, A. (2003), "Rois et princes portugais chez les auteurs castillans du XVème siécle», *Península. Revista de Estudos Ibéricos. Entre Portugal e Espanha. Relações Culturais (sécolos XV- XVIII). In Honorem Jose Adriano de Freitas Carvalho*, 0: 39-51.

Ruggini, L. C. (1989), "Felix Temporum Reparatio", in A. Dihle (coord.), *Realtà socio-economiche in movimento durante un ventennio di regno (Costanzo II Augusto, 337-361 d.C.), L'église et l'empire au IV siècle*, Genève, 179-243.

Rüpke, J. (2005), *Fasti sacerdotum. Die Mitglieder der Priesterchaften und das sakrale Funktionspersonal römischer, griechischer, orientalischer und jüdisch-christlicher Kulte in der Stadt Rom von 300 v. Chr. bis 499 n. Chr.*, Wiesbaden.

Rusjaeva, A., Vinogradov, Ju. G., (2000), "Apollon Ietros. Herrscher von Istros", in A. Avram, M. Babeş (eds.), *Olbia, Civilisation grecque et cultures antiques périphériques. Hommages à P. Alexandrescu à son 70e anniversaire*, Bucarest, 229-234.

Rutishauer, B. (2012), *Athens and the Cyclades. Economic Strategies 540-314 BC*, Oxford.

Sabbadini, R. (1905), *Le scoperte dei codici latini e greci ne' secoli XIV e XV*, Florencia.

Sabbadini, R. (1914), *Le scoperte dei codici latini e greci ne' secoli XIV e XV*, Florencia.

Saddington, D.B. (1999), "Roman soldiers, local gods and interpretatio Romana in Roman Germany", *ActaCl* 42:155-169.

Salazar, A. M. (1976), "El impacto humanístico de las misiones diplomáticas de Alonso de Cartagena en la Corte de Portugal entre medievo y renacimiento (1421-31)", in A. D. Deyermond (ed.), *Medieval Hispanic Studies presented to Rita Hamilton*, Londres, 215-226.

Salinas, M. (1995), "Los inicios de la epigrafía en Lusitania oriental", in F. Beltrán (ed.), *Roma y el naámiento de la cultura epigráfica en Occidente*, Zaragoça, 281-291.

Salway, B. (2001), "Travel, Itineraria and Tabellaria", in C. Adams and R. Laurence (eds.), *Travel and Geography in the Roman Empire*, Londres, Nova Iorque, 22-66.

Santo Agostinho (2009 12ª ed.), *A cidade de Deus*, trad. de Oscar Paes Leme, 2 v., Vozes, Petrópolis, São Paulo.

Santos, M. J. A. (1998), *Vida e morte de um mosteiro cisterciense. S. Paulo de Almaziva – Séculos XIII-XV*, Lisboa.

Saumagne, C. (1928), "Iter populo debetur", *Révue d'Histoire, de Littérature et d'Histoire Anciennes* 54: 320-353.

Scheer, T. S. (2003), "The Past in na Hellenistic Present: Myth and Local Tradition", in A. Erskine (ed.), *A Companion to the Hellenistic World*, Oxford, 216-231.

Scheid, J. (2015), "Les Augustea et le culte des empereurs. Réflexions sur les rites célébrés dans ces lieux de culte", in P. Gros, E. Marin, M. Zink (eds.), *Auguste, son époque et l'Augusteum de Narona. Actes du colloque organisé à l'Académie des Inscriptions et Belles-Letres et l'Université Catholique de Croatie (Zagreb) 12 décembre 2014*, 17-30, Paris.

Schilardi, G. (ed.) (1997), *Filostrato. Immagini*, Lecce.

Schmidt, R. (1980), "Die Ostgrenze von Armenien über Mesopotamien, Syrien bis Arabien", in G. Neumann, J. Untermann (eds.), *Die Sprachen im Römischen Reich der Kaiserzeit. (Bonner Jahrbücher des Rheinischen Landesmuseums in Bonn im Landschaftsverband Rheinland und des Vereins von Altertumsfreunden im Rheinlande 40)*. Köln, 187-214.

Schmidt, Th., Fleury, P. (2011), *Perceptions of the Second Sophistic and its Times. Regards sur la seconde sophistique et son époque*, Toronto, Buffalo, London.

Schwartz, J. (1960), *Pseudo-Hesiodeia: recherches sur la composition, la diffusion et la disparition ancienne d'oeuvres attribuées à Hésiode*, Leiden.

Scott, K. (1936), *The Imperial Cult under the Flavians*, Stuttgart.

Sealey, R. (1976), *A history of Greek city-states 700 -338 B. C.* Berkeley.

Seignobos, Ch. (1969), *Histoire sincère de la nation française*, Paris.

Semerari, L. (2000), *Aula Magna Università degli Studi di Bari*, Bari.

Sergent, B. (2006), "Sucellus et le tonneau", in *Anthropology of the Indo-European World and Material Culture. Proceedings of the 5th International Colloquium of Anthropology of the Indo-European World and Comparative Mythology*, Budapest, 61-80.

Serra, J. C. da (1972), *Academia Real das Sciencias de Lisboa*, II, cap. VII, Lisboa.

Sforza, W. C. (1951), "Osservazioni sul 'De nobilitate legum' di Coluccio Salutati", in E. Castelli (ed.), *Umanesimo e Scienza politica* (*Atti del congresso Internazionale di Studi Umanistici*, Roma-Firenze, 1949), Milano.

Shapiro, H.A. (1993), *Personification in Greek art: the representation of abstract concepts 600-400 b.C.*, Zürich.

Shaw, M. H. (1982), "The ἦθος of Theseus in 'The Suppliant Women'", *Hermes* 110. 1: 3-19.

Shorrock, R. (2011), *The Myth of Paganism: Nonnus, Dionysus and the World of Late Antiquity*, Bristol.

Sigeia, L. (1970), *Dialogue de deux jeunes filles sur la vie de retraite (1552)*, Présenté, traduit et annoté par O. Sauvage (ed.), Paris.

Sillières, P. (1990), *Les voies de communication de l'Hispanie méridionale*, Paris.

Silva, N. J. E. G. (1964), *Humanismo e Direito em Portugal no século XVI*, Lisboa.

Simón, I. (2013), *Los soportes de la epigrafía paleohispánica. Inscripciones sobre piedra, bronce y cerámica*, Zaragoza, Sevilla.

Siniscalco, P. (2004, 5ª ed.), *Il cammino di Cristo nell'Impero romano*, Roma, Bari.

Slavazzi, F. (2006), "Il ciclo di relievi della Kaisersaal del ginnasio di Vedio a Efeso", in *Iconografía 2005. Immagini e immaginari dell'antichità classica al mondo moderno*, Roma, 235-243

Smyth, A. C. (2011), *Polis and Personification in Classical Athenian Art*, Leiden.

Snodgrass, A. M. (1977), *Archaeology and the rise of the Greek state*, Cambridge.

Snodgrass, A. M. (1980), *Archaic Greece. The age of experiment*, Londres.

Soares, C. (2008), *Platão. O Político*. Tradução do grego, introdução e notas, Lisboa.

Soares, C. (2014), "Theoria e práxis política em Heródoto", *Cuadernos de Filología Clássica: Estudios griegos e indoeuropeus* 24: 57-79.

Soares, N. C. (1994), *O príncipe ideal no século XVI e a obra de D. Jerónimo Osório*, Coimbra.

Soares, N. C. (2002), "O infante D. Pedro e a cultura portuguesa", *Biblos. Revista da Faculdade de Letras* 78:107-128.

Sodano, A. R. (1970), *Porphyrii Quaestionum Homericarum Liber I*, Napoli.

Solas, J. G. (2008), "Escrito sobre la ciudad", *Pensar la publicidad*, II, n. 2: 37-62.

Sordi, M. (1965), *Il cristianesino e Roma*, Bologna.

Sordi, M. (1984), *I cristiani e l'impero romano*, Milano.

Soria, A. (1956), *Los humanistas de la Corte de Alfonso el Magnánimo (según los epistolarios)*, Granada.

Sousa, D. A. C. de (1946-1954), *Memória dos livros do uso del Rey D. Duarte*, in *Provas da história genealógica da casa real portuguesa*, tomo I, liv. III, Coimbra.

Sousa, R., Fialho, M. C., Haggag, M., Rodrigues, N. S. (2013), *Alexandrea ad Aegyptum: The Legacy of Multiculturalism in Antiquity*, Lisboa.

Spickermann, W. (1997), "Aspekte einer neuen regionalen Religion und der Prozess der *"interpretatio"* im römischen Germanien, Rätien und Noricum", in *Römische Reichsreligion und Provinzialreligion*, Tübingen, 145-167.

Spyridakis, S. (1968), "Zeus is Dead: Euhemerus and Crete", *CJ* 63: 337-340.

Stafford, E., Herrin, J. (eds.) (2005), *Personification in the Greek World from Antiquity to Byzantium*, Burlington.

Statuta capitulorum generalium ordinis Cisterciensis ab anno 1116 ad annum 1786 edidit Josephus M.ia Canivez (1933-1941), 8 vols., Louvain.

Stefan, A. (2005), "Le titre de *filius Augustorum* de Maximin et Constantin et la théologie de la tétrarchie", in M.-F. Baslez, F. Prévot (eds.), *Prosopographie et histoire religieuse. Actes du colloque tenu en l'Université Paris XII-Val de Marne le 27 & 28 octobre 2000*, Paris, 329-349

Stefani, G. (1986), "I cippi a botte della provincia Sardinia", *Nuovo bullettino Archeologico Sardo* 3: 115-160.

Stefani, G. (1988), "Cippi a botte nella basilica di S. Saturnino a Cagliari", *Quaderni della Soprintendenza archeologica per le province di Cagliari e Oristano* 5: 167-175.

Stegmann, A. (1977), "La place de la praxis dans la notion de 'raison d' État' ", in *Théorie et pratique politiques à la Renaissance*, Paris.

Steinbrecher, M. (1985), *Der Delisch-Attischen Seebund und die Athenisch-Spartanischen Beziehungen in der Kimonischen Ära (478/77 – 462/1)*, Berlin.

Stemmer, K (ed.) (1995), *Standorte – Kontext und Funktion antiker Skulptur*, Berlin.

Sterckx, C. (2008), "Sucellos et le casque d'Hadès", in *Philomythia. Mélanges offerts à Alain Moreau*, Monts, 223-229.

Stern, J. (1996), *Palaephatus. Peri Apiston: On Unbelievable Tales*, Wauconda.

Stern, J. (1999), "Rationalizing Myth: Methods and Motives in Palaephatus" in R. Buxton, R. (ed.), *From Myth to Reason? Studies in the Development of Greek Thought*, Oxford, 215-222.

Stewart, A. (1990), *Greek Sculpture: an exploration*, New Haven, Yale.

Storey, I. C. (2003), *Eupolis poet of old comedy*, Oxford.

Stowe Mead, G. R. (1901), *Apollonius of Tyana, the Philosopher-Reformer of the First Century A.D.*, London.

Strassler, R. B. (ed.) (2007), *Landmark Herodotus: The Histories*, New York.

Strassler, R.B. (ed.) (2009), *Landmark Herodotus: The Histories*, New York.

Strootman, R. (2010), "Literature and the Kings", in Clauss, J., Cuypers, M. (eds.), *A Companion to Hellenistic Literature*, Malden, Oxford, 30-45.

Suberbiola Martínez, J. (1987), *Nuevos concilios hispano-romanos de los siglos III y IV. La colección de Elvira*, Málaga.

Szabó, Á. (2007), *Daciai papság*, Budapest.

Szabó, Á. (2008), "Sulla questione dello statuto giuridico dei sacerdoti provinciali durante il principato. Studio preliminare", *Iustum Aequum Salutare* 4: 71-81.

Tamerl, I. (2008), *Das Holzfass in der römischen Antike mit einer Studie zu Fassfunden in Raetien*, Diplomarbeit presso l'Università di Innsbruck, consultabile presso la Universitäts- und Landesbibliothek Innsbruck DG43696.

Tate, J. (1927), "The Beginnings of Greek Allegory", *CR* 41.6: 214-215.

Tchernia, A. (1986), *Le vin de l'Italie romaine. Essai d'histoire économique d'après les amphores* (BEFAR 261), Rome.

Teive, D. de (1786), *Epodos Que Cont'em Sentenças Uteis A todos os Homens, A's quaes se acrescentão Regras para a boa educação de hum príncipe*. Trad. no vulgar em verso solto por Francisco de Andrade (conforme à ed. de Lisboa, 1565), Lisboa, Na Of. Patr. de Francisco Luiz Ameno.

Temporini, H. (1978), *Die Frauen am Hofe Trajans. Ein Beitrag zur Stellung der Augustae im Principat*, Berlin, New York.

Thomson de Grummond, N. (2006), *Etruscan Myth. Sacred History, and Legend*, Philadelphia.

Tomlin, R. S. O. (1987), "Was ancient British Celtic ever a written language? Two texts from Roman Bath", *Bulletin of the Board of Celtic Studies* 34: 18–25.

Topál, J. (1990), "Der Import der sogenannten Moselweinkeramik in Pannonien", *ReiCretActa* 27-28: 177-184.

Tortorici, E. (1975), *Castra Albana. Forma Italia, Regio I*, Roma.

Touchard, J. (1959), *Histoire des idées politiques*, I. Paris [trad. port. Lisboa, 1970].

Tranoy, A. (1981), *La Galice romaine*, Paris.

Tuchelt, K. (1981), "Zum Problem Kaisareion-Sebasteion. Eine Frage zu den Anfängen des römischen Kaiserkultes", *MDAI*, 31 : 167-186.

Ulbert, G. (1959), "Römische Holzfässer aus Regensburg", *Bayerische Vorgeschichtsblätter* 24: 6-29.

Ullman, B. L. (1963), *The humanism of Coluccio Salutati*, Padova.

Ullmann, W. (1980), *Radici del Rinascimento* (tr. ital.), Roma, Bari.

Unz, R.K. (1985), "The Surplus of the Athenian *phoros*", *GRBS* 26: 21-42.

Ureña Prieto, M. H. (2001), *Dicionário de Literatura Grega*, Lisboa.

Valiño, A. (1999), "La cerveza en las fuentes romanas. Base textual y fijación de su importancia", *AncHistB* 13: 60-71.

Van Haeperen, F. (2002), "Le collège pontifical (3ème s. a.C.-4ème s. p.C.)", *Études de Philologie, d'Archéologie et d'Histoire Anciennes* 39: 11-42.

Varner, E.R. (2004), *Mutilation and transformation*. Damnatio memoriae *and Roman Imperial Portraiture*, Leiden, Boston.

Várzeas, M. I. O. (2013), "Callimachus and the New Paths of Myth", in R. Sousa et alii (coord.) *Alexandrea ad Aegyptvm: the legacy of multiculturalismo in antiquity*. Lisboa.

Velaza, J. (2003), "Epigrafía ibérica emporitana: bases para una reconsideración", *Palaeohispanica* 3: 179-192.

Velaza, J. (2003a), "Las inscripciones monetales", in P. P. Ripollés, M. del M. Llorens, *Arse-Saguntum. Historia monetaria de la ciudad y su territorio*, Sagunto, 121-148.

Velaza, J. (2009), "Epigrafía y literacy paleohispánica en territorio vascón", *Palaeohispanica* 9: 611-622.

Vergerio, P. P. (1934), "Epistolario di Pier Paolo Vergerio", in L. Smith (ed.), *Fonti per la storia d' Italia*, vol. 74, Roma, 436-445.

Vierneisel, K., Zanker, P. (1979), *Die Bildnisse des Augustus: Herrscherbild und Politik in kaiserlichen Rom*, München.

Villar, F., Pedrero, R. (2001), "Arroyo de la Luz III", *Palaeohispanica* 1: 235-274.

Vinogradov, J. G. (2000), "Heilkundige Eleaten in den Schwarzmeergründungen", in M. Dreher (ed.), *Bürgersinn und staatliche Macht. Festschrift für Wolfgang Schuller zum 65. Geburtstag*, Konstanz, 133-149.

Vittinghoff, F. (1951), *Römische Kolonisation und Bürgerrechtspolitik unter Caesar und Augustus*, Wiesbaden.

Vives, J., Marín, T., Martínez, G. (1963), *Concilios visigóticos e hispano-romanos*, Madrid, Barcelona.

Voragine, T. (2004), *Legenda Áurea*. Apresentação do Cardeal Dom José Saraiva Martins e introdução do Doutor Aníbal Pinto de Castro. Tomo Segundo, Porto.

Waern, I. (1951), ΓΗΣ ΟΣΤΕΑ. *The Kenning in Pre-Christian Poetry*, Uppsala.

Wallace, M. B., Figueira, T. J. (2010), "Notes on the Island *Phoros*", *ZPE* 172: 65-69.

Wallace-Hadrill, A. (2005), "*Mutatas formas*: The Augustan Transformation of Roman Knowledge", in K. Galinsky (ed.), *The Cambridge Companion to the Age of Augustus*, Cambridge, 55-84.

Wallinga, H. T. (2005), *Xerxes' Greek Adventure. The Naval Perspective*, Leiden.

Walter, H. (1993), *Ägina: die archäologische Geschichte einer griechischen Insel*, München.

Walters, K. R. (1981), "Four Hundred Athenian Ships at Salamis?", *RhM* 124: 199-203.

Wankel, H. (1983), "Thukydides 1,74,1 und die Schiffszahlen von Salamis," *ZPE* 52: 63-66.

Wells, J. (1923), *Studies in Herodotus*, Oxford.

Wesseling, P. (ed.) (1735), "Itinerarium Antonini Augusti", *Vetera Romanorum Itineraria*, Amesterdão.

West, M. L. (1985), *The Hesiodic Catalogue of Women: Its Nature, Structure, and Origins*, Oxford.

Westrem, S. D. (2001), *The Hereford Map. A Transcription and Translation of the Legend with Commentary*, Turnhout.

Williams, D. (1987), "Aegina, Aphaia-Tempel XI: the pottery from the second limestone temple and the later history of the sanctuary", *AA*: 629-680.

Williamson, G. (2004), "Aspects of identity", in C. Howgego, V. Heuchert, A. Burnett (eds.), *Coinage and Identity in the Roman Provinces*, Oxford, 19-27.

Winiarczyk, M. (2013), *The «Sacred History» of Euhemerus of Messene*, Berlin.

Witschel, Chr. (1995a), "*Römische Tempelkultbilder und Römische Kaiserstatuen als Tempelkultbilder*", in K. Stemmer, (ed.), *Standorte. Kontext und Funktion antiker Skulptur; Ausstellungskatalog Abgußsammlung*, Berlin, 250-265.

Witschel, Chr. (1995b), "Statuen auf römischen Platzanlagen unter besonderer Berücksichtigung von Timgad (Algerien)", in K. Stemmer (ed.), *Standorte. Kontext und Funktion antiker Skulptur; Ausstellungskatalog Abgußsammlung*, Berlin, 332-358.

Witschel, Chr. (2002), "Zum Problem der Identifizierung von munizipalen Kaiserkultstätten", *Klio* 84: 114-124.

Wlosok, A. (ed.) (1978), *Römischer Kaiserkult*, Darmstadt.

Wojciechowski, P. (2002), "Il culto di Beleno ad Aquileia romana. Origini, interpretatio Romana e la cosiddetta rinascita celtica", in *Gli echi della terra. Presenze celtiche in Friuli. Dati materiali e momenti dell'immaginario. Convegno di studi, Castello di Gorizia, 5 - 7 ottobre 2001*, Pisa, 29-35.

Woodard, R. (ed.) (2007), *The Cambridge Companion to Greek Mythology*, Cambridge.

Woodhead, A. G. (1962), *The Greeks in the West*. London. (Trad. port., *Os Gregos no Ocidente*).

Woolf, G. (1996), "Monumental writing and the expansion of the Roman society in the Early Empire", *JRS* 86: 22-39.

Woolf, G. (2002), "Afterword. How the Latin West was won", in A. Cookey (ed.), *Becoming Roman, writing Latin? Literacy and Epigraphy in the Roman West*, JRA Suppl. Ser. 48: 181-188.

Yatromanolakis, Y. (2005), "*Poleos erastes*. The Greek city as the beloved", in E. Stafford, J. Herrin (eds.), *Personification in the Greek World: From Antiquity to Byzantium*, London, 267-284.

Young, T. Cuyler (1980), "480/479 B.C. – A Persian Perspective", *Iranica Antiqua* 15: 213-39.

Zamora, J. A. (2005), "La práctica de escribir entre los primeros fenicios peninsulares y la introducción de la escritura entre los pueblos paleohispánicos", *Palaeohispanica* 5: 155-19.

Zanichelli, G. Z. (2005), "Il mito di Troia nell'immaginario medievale", in G. Burzacchini (coord.), *Troia tra realtà e leggenda*, Parma.

Zanker, P. (1983), *Provinzielle Kaiserporträts. Zur Rezeption der Selbstdarstellung der Princeps*, München.

Zaoli, G. (1912), "Lo Studio bolognese e papa Martino V", *Studi e Memorie per la storia dell'Università di Bologna* I – série v. III: 105-188.

Zecchini, G. (ed.) (2015), *L'Augusteum di Narona. Atti della Giornata di Studi. Roma 31 maggio 2013*, (Centro ricerche e documentazione sull'antichità clàssica, monografie, 37), Roma.

Zimmermann, K. (2000), "Ἀφροδίηι' ἀνεθήκε.....Zu einem Dachziegel mit Votivinschrift", in A. Avram, M. Babeş (eds), *Olbia, Civilisation grecque et cultures antiques périphériques. Hommages à P. Alexandrescu à son 70ᵉ anniversaire*, Bucarest, 239-251.

Zurara, G. E. de (1972), *Chronica do Conde Dom Pedro de Meneses*, II, Lisboa.

Damião de Góis

De vita aulica: 307

Dante

De monarchia: 308 n.20

Demétrio Cantemir

Descrição da Moldávia cap. IV: 255 *passim*

Demóstenes

8.238: 39
14.29: 39 bis
18.238: 39
19.1-2: 80 n.3
19.44: 83 n.13
19.159: 82 n.11
23.209: 29 n.25

Contra Aristogíton I.15-16: 221

Filípica 2.19-23: 84 n.14

2.30: 83 n.12

Pro Ctesifonte: 321

Diccionario de cecas y pueblos hispánicos (=DCPH)

I 39: 131 n.76
II 18: 121 n.4
II 18, 119, 154 : 129 n.55
117 ss.: 130 n.60
II 127 ss., 318 ss.: 129 n.59

Diogo de Sá

Tratado dos estados eclesiásticos e seculares 234-235: 315

Diogo de Teive

Institutio Sebastiani princeps 74-75, 150-151: 315

Diodoro Sículo

2.4 ss.: 172 n.27
4.61.6-7: 170 n.20
5.55: 171 n.22
5.76: 162 n.14
11.3.7: 25, 36 *passim*
11.43.3: 24 n.18
11.44.2: 40
11.47.1-3: 29 n.25
11.60.3: 27 n.22, 40 bis
11.60.6: 40
11.60.67: 37 bis

11.62.1: 37
11.71.5: 40
11.77.1: 37
12.3.1: 40 bis
12.3.2: 37
12.3.3-4: 37
12.28.3: 31 n.32
13 ss.: 172 n.27

Diógenes da Cunha Lima

Câmara Cascudo: um brasileiro feliz: 176 n.1

Dionísio de Halicarnasso

Antiguidades Romanas 3.67.5: 301

Dioniso Épico

Bassaridas fr. 4.1-2 Heitsch: 206

Domingo de Soto

De iustitia et iure: 305 n.5

D. Duarte

Leal conselheiro: 310

Doutor Angélico

Tratado das Leis: 305 n.5

Egídio Romano

De regimini principum ad regem Cypri: 305, 310, 310 n.30

Eliano

Natureza dos animais 4.27: 171 n.25

Varia Historia 5.10: 40 *passim*

11.9: 29, n.25

Élio Aristides

Elogio de Roma 26: 274

Énio

História Sagrada: 151 n.9

Erasmo

Institutio principis christiani: 304

(LB) IV, 595F: 314 n.64

Ésquilo

Euménides 696-699: 222

Persas 181-195: 206 n.24

338-40: 39

341-43: 36

Prometeu Agrilhoado 803: 171 n.25

7.89.1-90: 19
7.89.1: 36 bis
7.89.2: 36
7.90: 36 bis
7.90-93: 19
7.91: 36
7.92: 36
7.93: 36 bis
7.94: 36
7.95.1: 26, 36 *tria*
7.95.2: 26, 36
7.102: 222
7.139: 206
7.139.1-5: 21
7.144.2-3: 24
7.168.1-4: 23
7.184.1: 36
7.184.2: 29 n.28
7.188.1-190: 36
7.194.1-3: 38
8.1.1-2.1: 38
8.2.1: 38
8.7.12: 36
8.11.2: 36
8.14.1: 38 bis
8.14.2: 36
8.16.3: 36, 38
8.16.3: 20
8.17: 38
8.18: 20, 38 bis
8.43.1-47: 39
8.44.1: 24
8.46.2: 24
8.48: 39
8.62: 221
8. 84-93.2: 36
8.85.2: 39
8.86: 28, 36
8.89.2: 36
8.91-93.2: 28
8.94.1-4: 29
8.94.4: 29
8.113: 168 n.6
8.125.2: 204
8.131.1: 39
8.131.4.2: 36
8.144: 122 n.17
9.31: 168 n.6
9.106.1: 36

Hesíodo
  Catálogo das Mulheres: 159 n.5
    fr. 205 M-W: 159
    frs. 215, 216 M-W: 159 n.5
  Trabalhos e Dias: 683
    640: 201
    651-655: 201
Higino
  Fábulas
    43: 170 n.20
    170: 171 n.21
    254: 173 n.30
Higino Gromático
  Constitutio Limitum: 283, 295
Hinos Homéricos
  A Apolo 50-72: 202
    140-150: 203
    156-164: 203
    428: 201
    438: 200
  A Ceres 151: 206
Homero
  Ilíada: 171
    2. 117-118: 202 n.13
    2. 547-548: 55
    2.768: 159
    3.3 ss.: 172 n.26
    3. 200-201: 200
    5. 774: 198, 199
    9. 24-25: 202 n.13
    9. 286-298: 204
    15.415-746: 159
    16.1-111: 159
    16.100: 202 n.13
    16.114-123: 159
    17.160: 198
    21.187-189: 159
    21.357-360: 200
  Odisseia 1.247: 200
    4.174-177: 200, 204
    9.21: 200
    9. 21-28: 200
    13.97: 200
    14.329: 200

Plutarco

De Herodoti malignitate 870B-871C: 29

Vidas Paralelas

Alcibíades

1.2: 77
1.3: 70
1.3.3-7: 70
2.1: 70; 77
4.1: 75
4.2: 71-72, 77
4.3-4: 76
4.5: 74-75
4.5-6: 71
6.1: 76
7.5: 76
10.4: 72
16.1-2: 77
16.6: 76
23.3: 77
35.1: 77
35.2: 77

Alexandre

13.4: 168 n.7
13.47.11: 168 n.7
13.55.9: 168 n.7
13.57.1: 168 n.7
13.59.1: 168 n.7
13.62.1, 4: 168 n.7
13.66.3-4: 168 n.7

António

81.4: 168 n.7

Aristides

24.1-7: 29, n.25
26.3: 29, n.25

Címon

11.1-3: 29
12.2: 20 n.11, 40
12.4: 22, 37 bis
12.5: 37 bis
12.6. 37
13.3: 22, 37 bis
14.1: 28
14.2: 27
18.1:40

19.2: 28

Crasso

16.2: 168 n.7

Demóstenes

7.2: 168 n.7
32.7: 168 n.7

Emílio Paulo

12.11: 168 n.7

Êumenes

1.5: 168 n.7

Licurgo

4.8: 168 n.7

Péricles

10.4: 40
11.4: 30

Pompeu

70.4: 168 n.7

Sertório

3: 127 n.40
14 : 127 n.43

Temístocles

18.5: 204

Teseu

22: 170 n.20
25: 64 n.19

(Pseudo-)Plutarco

Acerca dos Rios

1.1: 170 n.18
4.1: 170 n.19
16.3: 169 n.11
25.1: 170 n.16
25.4: 169 n.13

Poggio Bracciolini

Cartas: 325 n.22 *passim*

Políbio

3.3.8: 279

Porfírio

Questões homéricas: 150 n.2

Procópio

História Secreta 30.4: 300

Volumes publicados na Coleção Humanitas Supplementum

1. Francisco de Oliveira, Cláudia Teixeira e Paula Barata Dias: *Espaços e Paisagens. Antiguidade Clássica e Heranças Contemporâneas. Vol. 1 – Línguas e Literaturas. Grécia e Roma* (Coimbra, Classica Digitalia/CECH, 2009).

2. Francisco de Oliveira, Cláudia Teixeira e Paula Barata Dias: *Espaços e Paisagens. Antiguidade Clássica e Heranças Contemporâneas. Vol. 2 – Línguas e Literaturas. Idade Média. Renascimento. Recepção* (Coimbra, Classica Digitalia/CECH, 2009).

3. Francisco de Oliveira, Jorge de Oliveira e Manuel Patrício: *Espaços e Paisagens. Antiguidade Clássica e Heranças Contemporâneas. Vol. 3 – História, Arqueologia e Arte* (Coimbra, Classica Digitalia/CECH, 2010).

4. Maria Helena da Rocha Pereira, José Ribeiro Ferreira e Francisco de Oliveira (Coords.): *Horácio e a sua perenidade* (Coimbra, Classica Digitalia/CECH, 2009).

5. José Luís Lopes Brandão: *Máscaras dos Césares. Teatro e moralidade nas Vidas suetonianas* (Coimbra, Classica Digitalia/CECH, 2009).

6. José Ribeiro Ferreira, Delfim Leão, Manuel Tröster and Paula Barata Dias (eds): *Symposion and Philanthropia in Plutarch* (Coimbra, Classica Digitalia/ CECH, 2009).

7. Gabriele Cornelli (Org.): *Representações da Cidade Antiga. Categorias históricas e discursos filosóficos* (Coimbra, Classica Digitalia/CECH/Grupo Archai, 2010).

8. Maria Cristina de Sousa Pimentel e Nuno Simões Rodrigues (Coords.): *Sociedade, poder e cultura no tempo de Ovídio* (Coimbra, Classica Digitalia/ CECH/CEC/CH, 2010).

9. Françoise Frazier et Delfim F. Leão (eds.): Tychè *et* pronoia. *La marche du monde selon Plutarque* (Coimbra, Classica Digitalia/CECH, École Doctorale 395, ArScAn-THEMAM, 2010).

10. Juan Carlos Iglesias-Zoido, *El legado de Tucídides en la cultura occidental* (Coimbra, Classica Digitalia/CECH, ARENGA, 2011).

11. Gabriele Cornelli, *O pitagorismo como categoria historiográfica* (Coimbra, Classica Digitalia/CECH, 2011).

12. Frederico Lourenço, *The Lyric Metres of Euripidean Drama* (Coimbra, Classica Digitalia/CECH, 2011).

13. José Augusto Ramos, Maria Cristina de Sousa Pimentel, Maria do Céu Fialho, Nuno Simões Rodrigues (coords.), *Paulo de Tarso: Grego e Romano, Judeu e Cristão* (Coimbra, Classica Digitalia/CECH, 2012).

14. Carmen Soares & Paula Barata Dias (coords.), *Contributos para a história da alimentação na antiguidade* (Coimbra, Classica Digitalia/CECH, 2012).

15. Carlos A. Martins de Jesus, Claudio Castro Filho & José Ribeiro Ferreira (coords.), *Hipólito e Fedra - nos caminhos de um mito* (Coimbra, Classica Digitalia/CECH, 2012).

16. José Ribeiro Ferreira, Delfim F. Leão, & Carlos A. Martins de Jesus (eds.): *Nomos, Kosmos & Dike in Plutarch* (Coimbra, Classica Digitalia/CECH, 2012).

17. José Augusto Ramos & Nuno Simões Rodrigues (coords.), *Mnemosyne kai Sophia* (Coimbra, Classica Digitalia/CECH, 2012).

18. Ana Maria Guedes Ferreira, *O homem de Estado ateniense em Plutarco: o caso dos Alcmeónidas* (Coimbra, Classica Digitalia/CECH, 2012).

19. Aurora López, Andrés Pociña & Maria de Fátima Silva, *De ayer a hoy: influencias clásicas en la literatura* (Coimbra, Classica Digitalia/CECH, 2012).

20. Cristina Pimentel, José Luís Brandão & Paolo Fedeli (coords.), *O poeta e a cidade no mundo romano* (Coimbra, Classica Digitalia/CECH, 2012).

21. Francisco de Oliveira, José Luís Brandão, Vasco Gil Mantas & Rosa Sanz Serrano (coords.), *A queda de Roma e o alvorecer da Europa* (Coimbra, Imprensa da Universidade de Coimbra, Classica Digitalia/CECH, 2012).

22. Luísa de Nazaré Ferreira, *Mobilidade poética na Grécia antiga: uma leitura da obra de Simónides* (Coimbra, Imprensa da Universidade de Coimbra, Classica Digitalia/CECH, 2013).

23. Fábio Cerqueira, Ana Teresa Gonçalves, Edalaura Medeiros & JoséLuís Brandão, *Saberes e poderes no mundo antigo. Vol. I – Dos saberes* (Coimbra, Imprensa da Universidade de Coimbra, Classica Digitalia,2013). 282 p.

24. Fábio Cerqueira, Ana Teresa Gonçalves, Edalaura Medeiros & Delfim Leão, *Saberes e poderes no mundo antigo. Vol. II – Dos poderes* (Coimbra, Imprensa da Universidade de Coimbra, Classica Digitalia, 2013). 336 p.

25. Joaquim J. S. Pinheiro, *Tempo e espaço da paideia nas* Vidas *de Plutarco* (Coimbra, Imprensa da Universidade de Coimbra, Classica Digitalia, 2013). 458 p.

26. Delfim Leão, Gabriele Cornelli & Miriam C. Peixoto (coords.), *Dos Homens e suas Ideias: Estudos sobre as* Vidas *de Diógenes Laércio* (Coimbra, Imprensa da Universidade de Coimbra, Classica Digitalia, 2013).

27. Italo Pantani, Margarida Miranda & Henrique Manso (coords.), *Aires Barbosa na Cosmópolis Renascentista* (Coimbra, Classica Digitalia/CECH, 2013).

28. Francisco de Oliveira, Maria de Fátima Silva, Tereza Virgínia Ribeiro Barbosa (coords.), *Violência e transgressão: uma trajetória da Humanidade* (Coimbra e São Paulo, IUC e Annablume, 2014).

29. Priscilla Gontijo Leite, *Ética e retórica forense: asebeia e hybris na caracterização dos adversários em Demóstenes* (Coimbra e São Paulo, Imprensa da Universidade de Coimbra e Annablume, 2014).

30. André Carneiro, *Lugares, tempos e pessoas. Povoamento rural romano no Alto Alentejo.* - Volume I (Coimbra, Imprensa da Universidade de Coimbra, Classica Digitalia, 2014).

31. André Carneiro, *Lugares, tempos e pessoas. Povoamento rural romano no Alto Alentejo.* - Volume II (Coimbra, Imprensa da Universidade de Coimbra, Classica Digitalia, 2014).

32. Pilar Gómez Cardó, Delfim F. Leão, Maria Aparecida de Oliveira Silva (coords.), *Plutarco entre mundos: visões de Esparta, Atenas e Roma* (Coimbra e São Paulo, Imprensa da Universidade de Coimbra e Annablume, 2014).

33. Carlos Alcalde Martín, Luísa de Nazaré Ferreira (coords.), *O sábio e a imagem. Estudos sobre Plutarco e a arte* (Coimbra e São Paulo, Imprensa da Universidade de Coimbra e Annablume, 2014).

34. Ana Iriarte, Luísa de Nazaré Ferreira (coords.), *Idades e género na literatura e na arte da Grécia antiga* (Coimbra e São Paulo, Imprensa da Universidade de Coimbra e Annablume, 2015).

35. Ana Maria César Pompeu, Francisco Edi de Oliveira Sousa (orgs.), *Grécia e Roma no Universo de Augusto* (Coimbra e São Paulo, Imprensa da Universidade de Coimbra e Annablume, 2015).

36. Carmen Soares, Francesc Casadesús Bordoy & Maria do Céu Fialho (coords.), *Redes Culturais nos Primórdios da Europa - 2400 Anos da Fundação da Academia de Platão* (Coimbra e São Paulo, Imprensa da Universidade de Coimbra e Annablume, 2016).

37. Claudio Castro Filho, *"Eu mesma matei meu filho": poéticas do trágico em Eurípides, Goethe e García Lorca* (Coimbra e São Paulo, Imprensa da Universidade de Coimbra e Annablume, 2016).

38. Carmen Soares, Maria do Céu Fialho & Thomas Figueira (coords.), *Pólis/ Cosmópolis: Identidades Globais & Locais* (Coimbra e São Paulo, Imprensa da Universidade de Coimbra e Annablume, 2016).